THE
SHAHNAMEH
VOLUME IV

THE SHAHNAMEH

VOLUME IV

Hakim Abul-Ghassem Ferdowsi

Translated by Josiane Cohanim

GIROUETTE BOOKS

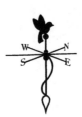

Girouette Books

New English translation copyright © 2023 Josiane Cohanim
Published in the United States of America
By Girouette Books
Santa Monica, California

Paperback ISBN 978-1-7349661-6-9
Ebook ISBN 978-1-7349661-7-6

girouettebooks.com

Cover art by ZariNaz Mottahedan
Cover design by Talia Cohanim
Typesetting and layout design by Sepehr Aziz

"Never take time to rest
When you have the chance to learn,
And never surrender your mind
To the illusion that you know everything."

CONTENTS
VOLUME FOUR

PART TWENTY-FOUR

I. The Thirty-Year-And-Two-Month Reign of Shahpoor, Son of Ardeshir

II. The One-Year-And-Two-Month Reign of Ormazd, Son of Shahpoor

III. The Three-Year-Three-Month-and-Three-Day Reign of Bahraam, Son of Ormazd

IV. The Nineteen-Year Reign of Bahraam, Son of Bahraam, His Rise to the Throne, His Advice to the Leaders, and His Death

V. The Four-Month Reign of Bahraam Bahraamian, His Rise to the Throne, and His Death

XII. The Thirty-Year Reign of Yazdegerd, the Wicked

XIII. The Sixty-Three-Year Reign of Bahraam the Hunter

PART TWENTY-FIVE

I. The Eighteen-Year Reign of Yazdegerd, Son of Bahraam the Hunter

II. The One-Year Reign of Hormoz, Son of Yazdegerd

III. The Eleven-Year Reign of Pirooz, Son of Yazdegerd

IV. The Five-Year-and-Two-Month Reign of Balaash, Son of Pirooz

V. The Forty-Year Reign of Ghobaad, Son of Pirooz

PART TWENTY-SIX

The Forty-Eight-Year Reign of Kesra Anushiravan

PART TWENTY-SEVEN

The Continuation of the Forty-Eight-Year Reign of Kesra Anushiravan

The Story of Gao and Talhand, and the Invention of Chess

Appendix:

PREFACE

"Wisdom is the conduit
To the discovery of worldly mysteries,
Inaccessible to the human eye." (Volume IV)

Volumes Four and Five shift to a different tone from Volumes One through Three. Gone are the kings and heroes of another age. Gone are Zaal and Rostam, Giv, Bijan, and Goodarz. Ferdowsi turns to a succession of kings from the Ashkanian (or Parthian) Dynasty (247 BCE to 224 CE) and Sassanian Dynasty (224-651 CE). We plunge into a semi-historical narrative less reliant on fact than on literary form and poetic license.

The relationships between the rulers and their leaders or advisors continue to be significant, but the historical kings are weaker and more fallible than their Kianian predecessors. They can be authoritarian, suspicious, intolerant, and incompetent. They can resort to detaining or killing their own sons or relatives to desperately hold on to the throne. In Volume Five, we find a prime example of this in Khosrow Parviz commanding the execution of his maternal uncles and the imprisonment of Shirooy, the son he had with the Caesar's daughter.

The most powerful kings of the Ashkanian and Sassanian periods are Ardeshir Babakan, the first Sassanian, and his descendants, Bahraam the Hunter, Kesra Anushiravan, Hormozd, and Khosrow Parviz. Interspersed in the narrative are romantic episodes, hunting scenes, and adventures that include the slaying of a supernatural giant worm, as well as confrontations with terrifying beasts and dragons. In addition, we listen in on Bozorgmehr, the loyal and sage vizier, as he enlightens the court on the importance of truth, learning, and wisdom, themes that are dear to Ferdowsi's heart. Here Bozorgmehr addresses King Anushiravan:

"If you wish for knowledge to bear fruit,

Release the jewels of wisdom in your speech.
If you wish to glorify your name,
Draw words out of your tongue
Just as you extract your sword from its sheath. ...
The union between your tongue and your heart
Tightly shutters and seals the door to perdition."

The concept of "word," or *sokhan,* is ever-present in *The Shahnameh*
and is a concept that functions on various levels. "Word" can refer to a
universal notion with resonance on a vibrational level, in the sense of
divine word or creation. This concept is mentioned very early on in the
Prelude:

"The highest path to follow is that of Seeker.
Toil in service to the Creator, forsaking idle chatter.
Delve deeply into divine order,
For sovereignty derives from this connection,
And knowing is attained through discovery.
Only thus will a wise man's heart
Become a powerhouse of his will.
There is no higher vibration than Word, for the mind
Is incapable of understanding source and life."

On another level, we have "word" as the poet's skillful integration
of rhythm and rhyme, alliteration, word play, repetition of sounds,
and metaphor to create a unified form of expression. For that reason,
The Shahnameh has always had a long tradition of oral recitation,
a tradition carried out to this day by modern-day troubadours, or
naghaals, who narrate their stories through a combination of verse
and prose in Iran's coffeehouses, tea-houses, and theaters. The poetic
language sounds like a chant or a song and brings magic to the minds
of Iranians who cherish the rhymes and delight in memorizing them.
The oral tradition, with its common improvisation by its entertainers,
can explain why Ferdowsi's account is replete with inconsistencies and
repetitions.

Finally, we have "word" as the language of conversation, where we are
advised to be cautious in our speech and to attempt to only "release
the jewels of wisdom."

"Words are more precious than royal jewels,
If one makes use of them wisely.
In order for the mind to evade grief,

Judgment must rule as king, and speech as warrior."

In this volume, under the rules of Yazdegerd the Wicked, Bahraam the Hunter, and Anushiravan, we see more interaction between Iran and its neighbors India and Mesopotamia and their respective cultures. In relation to India, we are further entertained by fascinating accounts detailing the inventions of the games of chess and backgammon, games derived from actual battle scenes. As regards Mesopotamia and the Arabs, we encounter the characters of Monzer and Noman, two compassionate Taazian rulers who safeguard the life of Bahraam, son of Yazdegerd, and help raise and educate him, protecting him from his father's corrupt and evil intentions.

Some elements in the poem have become commonplace in our world centuries later. One such example is the uncommon and extraordinary cesarean section performed on Rudaabeh to facilitate the birth of Rostam in Volume One. In the present volume, Ferdowsi toys with the idea of the prohibition of wine and the effects of alcohol on the mind. Ultimately, the king comes to the conclusion that consuming wine in moderate quantities is the wisest resolution and removes the restrictions.

Ferdowsi portrays various examples of societies and systems of government, such as socialism, as well as the application and allocation of taxes by governments. In one city, under the rule of Bahraam the Hunter, a village is destroyed when the royal vizier, Roozbeh, proclaims that any form of leadership and hierarchy must end:

"Great cries of joy surge over the village.
From here on, men and women have equal authority,
With servants and hired people
Rising to the same level as their masters."

The text shows this system of government was destined to fail from the outset, resulting in complete turmoil and anarchy.

"No longer restrained by fear, impure people
Cut the heads of their former masters and lords.
They attack each other, kill each other,
And spill each other's blood in faraway places."

In another instance, King Ghobaad allows himself to be influenced by the teachings of Mazdak whereby wealth is taken from the rich to be distributed to the poor:

"He treats the poor as equals, whether old or juvenile.
He takes from one and gives to another.
Wise men are distraught by his actions.
But the king, under the influence of Mazdak, adopts his faith,
Thinking that it will bring joy to the world...
The poor, those who earn their keep by their labor,
Gather around him ...
The wealthy, forced to relinquish their fortunes
To the poor, discard the path of virtue."

Furthermore, it is not surprising that gender equality has no place in a society deeply ingrained for centuries with the idea that women are the weaker sex. After all, Ferdowsi alludes to this:

"Women, however, may not gain fame in that arena,
For their domain is limited to food and sleep."

When asked to visit his sisters and stepmother in the harem, Siaavoosh says:

"What is there for me to learn in the women's chambers?
Are women meant to guide us down the path of wisdom?"

Still, we get a sense that the author doesn't believe that to be true. His female characters are crafted to be ingenious, virtuous, and daring. Faraanak, Sindokht, Rudaabeh, Gordaafareed, Manigeh, Faranguis, Queen Homay, Gordieh, and Shirin are just a few such examples of women whose ingenuity and actions are driven by a deep sense of wisdom, often surpassing that of their male counterparts. It is interesting to note that most of the women in the mythical section are non-Iranian foreigners, the majority being Tooranians, while Rudaabeh is from Kabul, a descendant of Zahaak, and Sudaabeh is from Haamaavaran, perhaps a reference to the land of Yemen. This is not the case in the historical portion. Though we see women from China, India, and Rum marry Iranian kings, Gordieh is Iranian born and Shirin appears to be Iranian born.

Past centuries of class division mark the Sassanian society, where a man was not eligible to function as a royal scribe without the gift of nobility. Kesra Anushiravan rejects such a man on the basis that:

"A merchant's son, no matter how skilled,
How learned, or how attentive he may be,
Could never rise to the status of a scribe. …
If this bootmaker had any talent,
The king would only see through his eyes,
And hear through his ears, while intelligent men
Of high birth would be left to sigh and grieve."

There are many lessons on kingship throughout the poem. *Farr,*
meaning "kingly glory and grace," is an essential quality. It is a gift
borrowed from a higher power allowing the king to be the keeper
of universal divine values. Other necessary attributes are lineage,
courage, wisdom, and a sense of justice:

"A king's throne can be weakened in three ways:
First, if the king acts toward his subjects with injustice.
Second, if he favors ill-mannered men
And raises them above skilled noblemen.
Lastly, if he hoards his wealth and thinks only
About his own gain and the accumulation of gold.
Put your passion into acts of generosity and charity,
Acts that spread justice and draw from wisdom
So that falsehood can never touch you.
Fib and fabrication tarnish a man's face,
And never does the evil man acquire glory."

The narrator repeatedly interrupts his long epic poem to comment
on the human condition, on fate and destiny, exposing the constant
paradox we face: The idea of choice and free will is juxtaposed with
the disquieting notion that man has no power over his destiny. The
author longs to understand a world so fickle that it gives us triumphs
on one hand but may at any moment plunge us into the depths of
despair. We must give up all attachment to this world to live a happy
and peaceful life. We must remember that no matter how wealthy
we are, the only thing we can take with us at the time of death is our
name and the way we have treated others. We must strive to acquire
wisdom, for wisdom is necessary not only for any king's or hero's
optimum evolution, but also for anyone's growth, regardless of status,
class, or gender.

About This Translation

This translation is based on two editions of *The Shahnameh*: the original Persian text edited by Dr. Seyed Mohammad Dabir Siaghi (2007), and a French edition, *Le livre des rois*, translated by Mr. Jules Mohl (1878).

Although Ferdowsi uses the past tense for his stories, it seemed more natural to narrate the English translation in the present tense. This provides a sense of continuity and permanence, as if the values he upholds cannot be constricted into a specific time frame.

Spelling and Pronunciation

In order to transfer text from Persian to English, we have used a simple form of transliteration. While it may vary from the more common methods, it makes sense to us and, we hope, will to the reader. In this approach, names of characters and places are spelled based on their pronunciation in Persian, rather than on their Romanized equivalent. For example, Zoroaster is *Zartosht*, Alexander is *Eskandar*, China is *Chin*, and Rome is *Rum*.

Most of the sounds for long syllables are pronounced as in English:
1. Aah sounds, as in "fall," are spelled *aa*, as in *Zaal* or *Rudaabeh*, except when a word ends in *ah*, as in *shah*, or *an*, as in *Iran*, *Tooran*, or *Nariman*. Some exceptions include *Baarmaan* and *Hoomaan*. One phonetic exception is in the second syllable of *Ghaaran* which has the *a* sound as in "fan."

2. Oo sounds as in "fool" are most often spelled *oo*, as in *Tooran* or *Fereydoon*. A few exceptions are *Zu* and *Tous*.

3. Ee sounds, as in "feel," are spelled *ee* as in *beed* and *deev*. At times we revert to -*i*- as in *Giv*.

Persian Words

The Persian language offers a unique perspective that requires careful consideration when translating into English. Finding an accurate English equivalent is often a daunting task. A number of words, such as *farr*, *kherrad*, and *ayeen*, are almost impossible to translate accurately. We have attempted to provide corresponding English words in footnotes and in the glossary; however, these may not completely capture the essence of the original words.

The absence of pronouns in Persian can lead to the use of vague terms such as "it", "this", or "that" to refer to a person or an object. This translation avoids pronouns when it comes to Yazdan, the divine Creator, and Sooroosh, the archangel. In the case of Simorgh, the mystical bird, we chose feminine pronouns to convey nurturing and maternal qualities.

VOLUME FOUR

From the Ashkanian Empire to the Reign
of Sassianian King Kesra Anushiravan

PART TWENTY–TWO

The Ashkanian Empire[1] – 200 years

◇◇◇◇◇◇◇◇◇◇◇◇◇◇◇
1 Ashkanian: Parthian or Arsacid. The Ashkanians overcame the Achaemenid Empire, (somehow omitted from *The Shahnameh*). Ferdowsi's account is far from accurate, as his sources were very limited. Historically, the Parthian Dynasty ruled from around 247 BCE to 224 CE and counts fifty monarchs.

1 | The Beginning of the Story of the Ashkanians: Small Tribal Rulers

Now, O aged poet, will you return
To the throne of the Ashkanians?
How did the ancient book preserve the history
And relate the true tales of men?
Which king was crowned after the reign of Eskandar?

The wise poet bard from Chaadj says
That the ivory throne remained vacant,
That brave noblemen, descendants of Aarash,
Seized provinces in every corner of the world.
Once happily secured on their seats,
They were given the names of Moolookeh Tavayef.[2]

Two hundred years pass, during which time
It was as if there were no king to rule the earth.

They did not remember the past;
They did not remember each other.
The earth enjoyed a time of peace.
This was in line with Eskandar's designs:
To secure the prosperity of Rum.

The first king was Ashk, a descendant of Ghobaad.
The second was the valiant Shahpoor, of royal birth.
Next came Goodarz the Ashkanian,
Bijan of Kianian race, Nersi and the powerful Ormazd,
And Aarash, the formidable prince.

When Bahraam the Ashkanian ascended the throne,
He distributed vast wealth to the needy and to dervishes.
Next came the illustrious Ardavan, a prudent man,
Intelligent and of serene heart,
Acclaimed as Ardavan the Great,
For he protected lambs against the claws of wolves.

◇◇◇◇◇◇◇◇◇◇◇◇◇◇
2 Moolookeh Tavayef: Tribal rulers.

He possessed Shiraz and Isfahan,
An area considered the borderland of noblemen.
He offered governance of Estakhr to Babak,
Whose bow sent shivers of fear through snakes.

Since the branches and roots of this family
Spanned a short period of time, the wise storyteller
Does not mention the duration of the reigns.
I have been apprised only of their names
Through *The Book of Kings*[3], where I found
No additional information on them.

2 | Babak Dreams of the Future of Sassan, Who Marries His Daughter

Once Dara meets death in battle,
The day dims for his family.

One son remains, intelligent and brave, named Sassan.
Seeing his father killed in such a troubling way,
Seeing the fortune of the Iranians overturned,
He flees before the Rumi host,
Avoiding being caught up in misfortune's nets.

Sassan travels to India, where he dies wistfully,
Leaving behind a young son.
For four generations, fathers name their sons Sassan.
They became either shepherds or camel drivers,
Struggling to keep poverty and exhaustion at bay.

One of these young men wearily departs, to seek work.
He arrives at the side of Babak's shepherds,
Enters the field, asks for their leader, and says,
"Do you have use for a man who values this sort of work
And who passes through these parts in utter misery?"

The head shepherd welcomes the wretched Sassan,
Who applies himself to the job, day and night,

◇◇◇◇◇◇◇◇◇◇◇◇◇◇
3 *The Book of Kings:* Must be a reference to *Khodaay Nameh,* or *Khvatay-Namak;* written
in prose and in the Pahlavi language, this book is one of Ferdowsi's sources for his
Shahnameh.

And is soon promoted to herd leader.

One night, the wise Babak has a dream where Sassan,
Seated on a war elephant, Indian sword in hand,
Receives visitors who pay homage to him.

Babak's kind words free afflicted hearts from grief.
The following night, at bedtime,
His mind reflects on his dream.
He conceives a new dream in which fire worshippers
Hold three blazes in their hands before Sassan,
Three blazes as dazzling as the flames
Of Aazargoshasp, Khorraad, and Mehr,[4]
Gleaming like the brilliant Sun, Saturn, or Venus,
And richly kindled with aloeswood.

Babak awakens, his mind and body troubled.
He assembles learned, wise men adept at reading dreams
And reveals to them his dream from beginning to end.

The wise men listen attentively.
Their leader reflects for a moment, then speaks:
"O noble ruler, beware of the interpretation of this dream.
The man in your vision will one day become king,
His head will rise above the sun.
Should this dream not be realized through him,
He will have a son who will possess the world."

Babak delights at these words.
He offers presents to each wise man according to rank.
Then he summons to his side the chief shepherd,
Who arrives at court on a frosty day,
Dressed in a coarse woolen coat sprinkled with snow,
Heart aquiver with fear.

Babak dismisses visitors, servants, and leaders,
Then receives Sassan amicably,
Offering him a seat next to him.
He addresses common questions to Sassan
About his lineage and his birth.

◇◇◇◇◇◇◇◇◇◇◇◇◇◇
4 Aazargoshasp, Khorraad, Mehr: Three ancient Iranian fire temples.

The shepherd is seized by fear and cannot reply.
Finally, he says to Babak, "O Prince,
If you wish to ensure your shepherd's life,
I shall reveal to you my origins
As soon as you place your hand in mine
And promise that you will not cause me harm,
Neither in public nor in private."

Babak invokes Yazdan, Giver of all that is good,
And says, "I shall not hurt you in any way.
I shall help you gain happiness
And assign you a place of honor."

The shepherd says to Babak,
"O noble hero, I am the son of Sassan
And a descendant of King Ardeshir, who lives
In the memory of men under the name of Bahman.
Bahman was the noble son of the hero Esfandiar,
Meant to be Goshtaasp's successor in the world."

At these words, Babak's keen eyes shed tears,
For he remembers the dream. He says to him,
"Go to the bathhouse and remain there
Until they bring you a fresh set of clothing."

Then he asks for a royal robe and a horse
With an armor worthy of a world warrior.
He prepares a magnificent palace for Sassan
And raises him above the rank of a chief shepherd.

Having settled him in the palace,
He assigns him slaves and servants,
Sees to his every need, and offers him vast wealth,
As well as his daughter's hand in marriage.
The daughter is gifted with beauty
And is the crown over the head of his family.

3 | The Birth of Ardeshir Babakan, and His Dealings With Ardavan

Nine months pass over the moon-faced beauty.
She gives birth to a child, as dazzling as the sun.
He resembles King Ardeshir and grows up
To prosper and delight the most somber hearts.

The sight of him fills the father with contentment,
And he gives him the name of Ardeshir.
He raises him tenderly in his arms,
And in this way much time passes.

Wise men call him Ardeshir Babakan.
He is taught everything a well-born man must learn.
His talents surpass the expectations of a child.
His skills, his stature, and his beauty are such
That it appears as if he illuminates the sky.

The reputation of the good manners of the youth
And his vast knowledge reach Ardavan's ears
As he is made aware
That in battle he resembles a fierce lion
And in feast he appears to be the planet Venus.

Ardavan writes a letter to Babak, illustrious hero:
"O wise man of good counsel,
Eloquent, learned, and powerful leader,
I have heard that your grandson Ardeshir
Is a skilled horseman of eloquent speech
As well as a keen observer. Send him to me in joy
As soon as you receive and read this letter.
I shall fulfill all his needs,
Assign him a place of honor among my heroes.
In the presence of my sons,
He will be treated like a member of our family."

Upon reading the king's letter,
Babak's lashes flood with tears.
He summons a scribe and calls the valiant youth,
To whom he says, "Read this letter from Ardavan.
Reflect on it in your serene mind.

I shall immediately write a letter to the king
And dispatch it with one of my loyal men.
I shall write:
> 'I am sending you my heart and my eyes.
> This brave young man whom I adore.
> I have advised him on how to conduct himself
> At your magnificent court.
> Treat him as dictates royal custom.
> Keep him safe and sound
> So that not even the air may affect him.'"

Swift as wind, Babak opens his treasury
And gives the young man various presents.
Nothing is too valuable for him when it comes to this child.
He asks for golden bridles, mace and sword,
Dinars, brocade, stallions and servants,
Bolts of Chini fabric, and lush golden cloths.
He places the lot before the youth, who is
To assume the position of Ardavan's attendant.

Ardeshir is to take gold, musk and amber,
And many more presents for the king.
The auspicious youth takes leave of his grandfather,
Marching in the direction of Rey and Ardavan's court.

4 | Ardeshir Babakan Visits Ardavan's Court

The arrival of Ardeshir is announced at court
Along with his request of an audience.
Ardavan calls him to his side in friendship
And speaks to him at length on the subject of Babak.
He seats him near the throne,
Asks for accommodations in the palace's outbuildings,
And sends him a variety of fare, attires, and carpets.

The young man, with his illustrious travel escort,
Marches to the site indicated by King Ardavan.

Once the sun places its throne above the vault of sky
And the earth glimmers like the face of a Rumi,
Ardeshir asks an envoy to carry the customary gifts
To King Ardavan, accompanied by a warrior.

Ardavan receives them and approves of them.
He cherishes the presence of the young man
And showers him with constant care and attention.
The king prefers to drink, eat, and hunt in his company,
Making no distinction between him and his own sons.

One day, King Ardavan, his escort, and
His four sons, each boasting the bearing of a king,
Scatter around the plain to engage in the hunt.

In the distance, they spot a herd of onager,
And a cry rises from this large group.
They launch their steeds of winded hooves,
And dust mixes with sweat on their bodies.

Ardeshir Babakan overtakes them all
And is the first to reach the animals.
He places an arrow on his bow
And strikes a male at the hip with his shot,
Tip and fletches sinking deep into the flesh.

In that moment, King Ardavan arrives,
Examines the huge fallen onager, and says,
"May the mind of the one able to overcome
Such a beast equal the strength of his hand!"

Ardeshir replies to the king,
"I brought the beast down with a shot of arrow!"

One of the king's sons says,
"I am the one who shot him down!
And I seek someone who is my equal."

Ardeshir replies, "The plain is vast.
Onager and arrows abound.
Go and kill one in the same manner.
Falsehood from a proud man is a liability."

Ardavan grows furious and hollers in rage at Ardeshir.
He speaks to him harshly: "In this matter, I am at fault.
For I am the one who wished to guide your education.
Why did I have to include you in my inner circle,
Welcome you to feast and to hunt with my troops?

Now you wish to compete with my son.
Now you present yourself as a powerful man.
Go to the stables and take care of my Taazian stallions
And find a dwelling in some ordinary residence.
I employ you as my stable manager, placing you,
In all matters, on equal footing with my servants."

Ardeshir walks away, eyes brimming with tears.
He reflects: "What misfortune
I must endure at the hands of Ardavan!
May his body fall ill and his mind suffer!"

Then he writes a letter to his grandfather,
Heart full of worry, head full of strategy.
He recounts to him all that occurred
And the reason why King Ardavan grew agitated.

Upon receipt of the letter, Babak keeps the affair secret,
Yet his heart burns with a sense of grief.
He retrieves dinars from his treasury, sending
Ten thousand pieces with an envoy on a race camel.
First he summons a scribe to write to Ardeshir:
"O foolish, unskilled young man,
When you attended King Ardavan in the hunt,
Why did you launch yourself ahead of his sons?
You are a servant to him and not a family member.
He is not to blame for the affront.
The culpability falls on you for lacking sense.
Now attempt to satisfy his desires, to please him,
And do not, for an instant, violate his orders.
I send you dinars and a letter full of advice.
Once you have exhausted this amount, ask for more,
Until these days of misfortune are behind you."

The speedy camel, mounted by a skilled old man,
Arrives in no time at the side of Ardeshir.
His heart constricts at the contents of the letter.
His soul surrenders to deceit and dishonesty.
He selects a home near the horses
And not a more suitable place.
He asks for all sorts of carpets to be spread,
All sorts of attires and provisions to be brought.

His sole preoccupation is to entertain himself,
Day and night, in the company of music and musicians.

5 | Golnaar Falls in Love With Ardeshir, and They Flee to Pars

Ardavan possesses a massive palace
Where a noble young woman serves him,
A moon-faced beauty named Golnaar,
Full of charm, color, and scent.
She assists Ardavan as an advisor
And as the treasurer of his wealth.
Cherishing her more than his own life,
He always smiles at the sight of her.

One day, from above, she catches a glimpse of Ardeshir,
Whose cheerful countenance delights her.
In fact, he makes quite an impression on her heart.

The beauty waits for the day to dim,
And at the advent of dusk, she attaches a rope
To the alcove, fastens a number of knots to it,
Tosses it over the wall, and boldly climbs down,
Invoking the name of the Creator, Giver of fortune.

She enters Ardeshir's home flirtingly, adorned
With jewels and exuding the scent of musk and amber.
She takes the young man's head in her hands,
Lifts it from the pillow of lush brocade,
And cradles it in her arms.

As he opens his eyes, Ardeshir contemplates
This beautiful young woman, her hair,
Her face, and her graceful attributes.
He asks the moon, "Where did you come from?
Are you here to charm my sorrowful heart?"

Golnaar replies, "I am here to be your slave.
My heart and soul lovingly yearn for you.
I am a source of peace to King Ardavan
And attend his needs as his treasurer.

He always delights in my presence.
If you wish, I can serve you and brighten your days.
I feel my very existence bound to the sight of you."

Ardeshir allows himself to be charmed
By the appearance of this ravishing beauty.

Some time passes in this manner.
Then misfortune descends on the protector of Sassan.
The prudent Babak, world master, dies
And leaves this ancient world to others.
At the news, Ardavan is deeply aggrieved.

Many princes ask for governance of the land of Pars,
But King Ardavan offers it to his eldest son
And commands him to beat the timpani
And drive his army from palace to plain.

The death of the ruler of serene heart, his protector,
Brings darkness to Ardeshir's heart.
He grows disenchanted by Ardavan's service.
As soon as he receives the news, he changes plans,
As grief stokes his sense of adventure.
On every side, he seeks a means of escape.

Later, it so happens that King Ardavan
Assembles at court a number of insightful astrologers
And asks them to interpret his horoscope.
He hopes they will identify the individual chosen
By the revolving dome to succeed him on the throne.

The king sends the mystics to Golnaar's pavilion
So that they may contemplate the stars
For the duration of three days.

Golnaar could hear their conversations
On the matter of stars and the mysteries within.
During these three days
And up to three-fourths of the night,
The young lady secretly spies on the astrologers
And listens to attentively to what they have to say,
Her heart burning with passion, her lips with sighs.

On the fourth day, the sages depart
To reveal their findings to Ardavan.
They descend from the young lady's pavilion
And march to the king's residence,
Holding before them their astrolabes.
They disclose the secrets of the sublime sky,
Why, when, and how the events will unfold.
They tell him that before long an incident
Will occur to send shivers of fear through him;
That one of his servants, the son of a prince
And a valiant man, would run away to become
A powerful, prosperous world master,
And a favorite of the stars.
Their words deeply trouble the noble king's heart.

As soon as the face of earth is black as pitch,
Golnaar pays a visit to Ardeshir.
The young man rages like the sea with anger:
"You are unable to stay away from the king!"

She recounts to him what the clear-sighted men
Revealed to the illustrious Ardavan.
Ardeshir's fury subsides, and he grows quiet.

The young man is concerned about what he hears
And eagerly seeks a means of escape.
He says to Golnaar, "If I depart for Iran,
The land of the brave, and take the direction of Rey,
Would you wish to come with me
Or would you prefer to stay here with the king?
Should you stay at my side, you will gain power
And will be the diadem on the head of my people."

She replies, "I am your slave, and no one
Can separate me from you for as long as I live."
She utters these words, lips full of sighs,
Eyes shedding tears of blood.

Ardeshir says to the moon-faced beauty,
"We must absolutely leave tomorrow."

She makes her way back to her pavilion,
Determined to risk her head and her life.

Once the surface of the world gradually brightens
And the dark night is captured in its noose,
Golnaar opens the doors to the treasury
And selects all the jewels made of garnet, and as many
Royal precious stones, and dinars as deemed necessary.

She enters her dwelling, jewels in hand,
Deeply troubled with thoughts:
"Even if he can escape King Ardavan,
How will he evade the royal sons?"

After night descends on the mountain,
She waits for Ardavan to fall asleep
And his assistants to vacate the palace.
Then, Golnaar exits like an arrow with the jewels
And takes the direction of the ambitious Ardeshir.
She finds him, cup in hand, standing by the horse keepers
Who are deep in a state of drunken slumber.
Keen on leaving in the middle of the night,
Ardeshir indulged them in drink
To the point of intoxication.

He had prepared two magnificent stallions,
Which he had kept saddled in the stables.
As soon as he spots Golnaar's face,
As soon as he sees the red gems and the gold coins,
He says, "We must leave this very instant.
We must shed any concern we may have.
I hope to extract myself from the dragon's clutches
With the aid of providence, champion of youth."

He puts down his cup, tosses the bridle
Over the heads of the Taazian stallions,
Dresses in a coat of mail, climbs on his horse,
Grabs a piercing, poison-coated sword,
And helps Golnaar saddle the other horse.

They ride out of the palace together
And take the direction of Pars,
Light-hearted and searching for the way.

6 | Ardavan Learns of the Flight Of Golnaar and Ardeshir

Day or night, Ardavan's only joy is the sight of Golnaar.
He never emerges from bed before having the chance
To glimpse into the young woman's charming face,
A sight, which for him, always represents a good omen.

The time to rise and to deck the throne arrives,
But the young lady does not appear at his bedside.
His fury mounts, and he rattles with rage.

His troops are positioned at the palace entrance.
The crown and throne have been decked,
And his administrator enters the king's chambers.
He says to him, "The land's noblemen and princes
Are at your door, sire, awaiting an audience."

The king says, "What is delaying Golnaar?
Why has she not appeared at my bedside as usual?
Does she have cause to blame me for anything?"

At this moment, the leader of the scribes
Enters and says, "Last night, Ardeshir departed,
Taking with him the white horse and the black horse,
Your majesty's two favorite mounts."

At the same time, the illustrious king finds out
That he has lost his valued and beautiful treasurer,
His beloved Golnaar, who has left with Ardeshir.
The valiant man's heart leaps in his chest.
He climbs on a bay horse and takes
A great number of cavaliers with him.
It is as if they are treading flames on the road.

On his way, he discerns a town full of men and horses.
He asks the townspeople whether they have heard,
After sunrise, the sound of horses' hooves,
Perhaps a sign that two young people
Might have passed through the region in haste,
One on a white horse, the other on a black one.

One of the inhabitants replies,
"Two people and two horses have indeed
Wandered through and taken the direction of the plain.
Behind them sprinted a beautiful, wild ram
Who stirred up the dust like a charger."

Ardavan asks his vizier, "Why do you think
A wild ram was running after them?"

The vizier replies, "It is a sign of royal dignity,
And good fortune has given him wings.
If this ram trails him, do not make haste.
This will be an affair that will take us far."

Ardavan dismounts in town,
Takes some nourishment, rests for a bit,
And resumes his race in pursuit of Ardeshir,
With the king and his vizier leading the escort.

Meanwhile, the two young people press on,
As fast as wind, without stopping for an instant.
The one befriended by the lofty dome of sky
Will not suffer any harm from the enemy.

Ardeshir ends up exhausted from the race and,
Discerning a reservoir of water high on a hill,
He says to Golnaar as he continues his gallop,
"Now that we and our chargers are exhausted,
We must dismount by this source of water.
Let us have a meal and depart once we are restored."

At the water's edge, his cheeks pale like the setting sun,
Ardeshir makes a motion to alight. But two young people
Standing by the water rush to him and exclaim,
"You must make use of bridle and stirrup!
You have escaped the dragon's jaws and breath.
Stopping now will not bring you good fortune.
You must not set foot on the ground to drink.
It would mean having to say goodbye to your life."

Ardeshir warns Golnaar, "Watch out! Do not dismount!"
He weighs down on the stirrups, releases the reins,
And raises his shiny spear to the sky.

Ardavan continues his chase, as swift as wind,
Growing weary, his heart dimming.
As half the day passes and the bright sun
Advances in the sky, he arrives at a beautiful city
Where many men come up to greet him.

The illustrious king asks the wise men,
"Have you seen two horsemen wander through?"

The leader replies, "O King of auspicious star
And pure intentions, at the time when the sun paled
And the dark night unfolded its cloak,
Two young people passed through this town
In haste, covered in dust, mouths parched,
Trailed by a ram more beautiful than anything.
It had wings like Simorgh, the tail of a peacock,
The head, ears, and hooves of the bold Rakhsh,
Purple fur, and the speed of a tornado.
No one has ever seen or heard of such a ram."

The vizier comes back to Ardavan and says,
"It is best for us to return to our land,
Prepare and gear up your army for war,
For a great struggle is upon us.
Good fortune rides behind Ardeshir, and
This chase will leave you holding nothing but wind.
Write a letter to your son, reveal this affair to him.
It is possible that he may receive news of Ardeshir.
We must not allow him to obtain the ram's milk."

Ardavan recognizes that his glory is on the decline.
He stops in this town and invokes the Creator.

7 | Ardavan Writes a Letter to Bahman, His Son

In the early morning hour, as night gives way to day,
Ardavan orders his escort to return.
His cheeks as pale as reeds, he arrives
In the town of Rey that evening.

He writes a letter to his son Bahman:

43

"Deceit rears its head to challenge my crown.
Ardeshir has left my side faster
Than an arrow slung from a bow.
He has traveled to the land of Pars.
Search to find the secret of his intentions,
And speak of this matter to no one."

8 | Ardeshir Mobilizes an Army

On his side, Ardeshir reaches the water's edge
And says, "O benevolent Creator,
You have rescued me from my wicked adversary.
May misfortune pursue him eternally!"

He rests for some time, then calls a boatman,
To whom he speaks at length of past actions.
The aging, intelligent boatman observes
Ardeshir's stature, his mien and his chest,
And concludes in joy that he must be of Kianian race,
For his expression shines with dignity, glory, and majesty.

The boatman rushes to the seaside, embarks,
And launches a boat to cross in every direction.
At the news of the arrival of Ardeshir,
An army assembles on the seashore.
All of Babak's powerful allies in Estakhr
Travel to pay their respects to Ardeshir.
Aging men from the lineage of the peaceful Dara
Find their hearts renewed at the mention of the youth.

Men, young and old, flock to the young prince,
Groups making their way from mountainside and seaside.
Intelligent, bold men from every city unite around him.
The young Ardeshir addresses them:
"O noble heroes of pure soul, there is no one
In this assembly of sensible, intelligent men
Who has not heard the tales of the wicked Eskandar
And the atrocious consequences of his deeds in the world.
He sentenced to death our ancestors, one by one,
And seized the world with terror and injustice.
Since I am a descendant of Esfandiar,

We cannot find Ardavan's rule in this land as rightful.
None of us remembers such an unjust emperor.
If you wish to join me, I shall allow no other
To enjoy glory and throne of power.
What do you say? What is your reply?
Tell me what is in your hearts."

Everyone present, whether swordsman or counselor,
Rises at the sound of this voice and kindly reveals
His soul's secret: "We are all descendants of Babak.
We are delighted to set our sights on your features.
Furthermore, as members of the Sassanian lineage,
We have cinched our waists to execute vengeance.
We are yours, body and soul.
Our worries, our joys, our losses and our prosperity,
Everything we have depends on you.
On both sides, your birth is a source of pride.
To you belong royalty and dominion.
Should you command us, we are willing
To convert mountain to plain with our swords,
Ready to change into blood the water's flows."

With this response, Ardeshir raises his head
Higher than Venus and Mercury.
He gives thanks to the noblemen
And nurtures in his heart thoughts of vengeance.
He casts at the water's edge the foundation of a city
That will become the siege of his activities.

A wise man says to him, "O King of auspicious star,
You enchant dim hearts, you renew the head of royalty,
But we must pluck out the weeds from the land of Pars
And then engage in war with Ardavan,
Since our star is young and young is our ruler.
Ardavan is the most wealthy king, the only one
Who has the power to cause you worry and grief.
Once you overthrow his throne, no one will oppose you."

The noble Ardeshir reflects on these agreeable words.
He leaves the water's edge as soon as the sun
Raises its head over the mountain crests
And marches toward the city of Estakhr.

Bahman, son of Ardavan, receives the news.
Heart troubled, soul dim, he climbs down the royal throne
And leads a well-equipped army to battle.

9 | Tabaak Joins Forces With Ardeshir, and They Vanquish Bahman

There lives an illustrious man named Tabaak,
A man of good counsel who possesses army and troops.
He rules over the city of Jahrom with skill and justice,
Is apt for command, and boasts seven blessed sons.

Once cognizant of the news, he leaves Bahman's side
And travels to the court of the noble Ardeshir
With army, timpani, and all the pomp of his rank.

At the sight of the leader, he dismounts as is customary
Before a superior, rushes to his side, kisses his feet,
And speaks to him at length of his ancestor Sassan.

The ambitious prince keeps him in his company graciously
For some time and expresses gratitude for his prompt arrival.
Nevertheless, he does not trust Tabaak.

On the road, a worried Ardeshir keeps his guard up
Toward the old man with a vast and powerful host.
Tabaak is an experience and prudent lord.
Sensing Ardeshir's concerns, he approaches him,
Zand Avesta in hand, and says,
"May the almighty Creator take away my hollow life
If my heart is impure and suppresses evil thoughts!
Once I heard that Ardeshir's host is on the seashore,
I was disgusted by the person of King Ardavan,
Just as a young man feels repelled by an old woman.
Know that I am a sincere and devoted servant,
That my mind is calm and able to hold a secret."

After these words, Ardeshir's perception shifts.
He treats Tabaak like a father, trustingly,
Placing him at the head of his troops.

The king relinquishes his misgivings and takes
The direction of the fire temple of Raam and Khorraad.
He prays there for divine guidance and happiness.
He prays for victory in all his ventures
And for the lofty, majestic tree to bear fruit.

Then he goes to his tent enclosure, where
The army inspector and the army chief appear.
They count the number of cavalry and infantrymen
Assessing their leaders and their soldiers.
They exceed fifty thousand dagger-wielding warriors.
The leader inquires after their names,
Deeply appreciating their numbers and their strength.

He pays dirhams to the troops, sees to their needs,
And invokes the just Creator, Giver of good.
Having thus formed an army akin to a bold leopard,
He marches against Bahman, son of Ardavan.

The fervent heroes advance toward each other.
Their troops form ranks on both sides,
Armed with spear, lance, and Indian sword.
They attack each other like warring lions,
The spilled blood swelling into flowing rivers.
They continue to battle until the sun fades,
The air fills with dust, the earth becomes covered in bodies.

The next morning, as the dark veil dissipates
To reveal the turquoise blue vault of sky,
Tabaak's army engages in a fierce battle.
A great storm surges, with dark clouds looming above.
Ardeshir advances from the army center.
Bahman, son of Ardavan, flees,
His body pierced by arrows, his soul afflicted.
Ardeshir pursues him with the blare of trumpets,
Sending a shower of shots over his head.
He chases him to the city of Estakhr,
The site of Bahman's fame and glorious crown.

At the sound of Ardeshir's voice,
A vast army clings to him, offering him
The great wealth Bahman painstakingly amassed.

Ardeshir distributes dirhams, his strength increasing.
He exits the land of Pars at the head of his host.

10 | The Battle of Ardeshir and Ardavan, and the Death of Ardavan

At the news regarding his son,
Ardavan's heart fills with fear.
His mind deeply troubled, he says,
"The secret of the firmament is revealed to me:
When a calamity beyond imagination occurs,
How can one avoid his fate?
I did not believe Ardeshir could be so ambitious
And turn into a national conqueror."

He opens the door to his treasury
And pays the balance to his troops.
He sends them away with loads and cargo.
Warriors arrive from Gilan[5] and Deylam.[6]
The dust stirred by the army rises to the moon.

On his side, Ardeshir leads a host so vast
That the wind could not carve a path through it.

The space between the two hosts measures two arrow staves.
So loud is the din of timpani and trumpet and the ringing
Of bells that snakes find themselves deprived of sleep.

Shouts echo, banners flash, purple blades sever
And sow heads. This battle lasts forty days,
And the world constricts for the king's subjects.
The surface of the plain is a mountain of corpses,
And the wounded find themselves weary of life.
Supplies and provisions are lacking
As the passage to accessible roads is blocked.

In the end, a black cloud appears,
Preventing this bitter struggle to continue.

◇◇◇◇◇◇◇◇◇◇◇◇◇
5 Gilan: A province in northwestern Iran bordering the Caspian Sea.
6 Deylam: A city in the Gilan Province of Iran, near the Caspian Sea.

A fierce and terrible storm swells,
Filling with dread the hearts of the combatants.
Mountains quiver, the ground splits open
With a crash that ascends beyond the sky.

Ardavan's army is seized by fear,
And common cries rise from it:
"The Creator is casting judgment on our king.
We are left to weep bitterly over our fate."

At the time the battle is at its most animated,
All the reasonable men ask for mercy.
Ardeshir advances to the army center.
The crackle of broken armor
And the plummeting rain of arrows echo,
And Ardavan sacrifices his sweet life and his crown.
He is taken prisoner in the brawl by a man
Named Khorraad who seizes his horse's bridle
And takes him bound up to the world seeker.

Ardeshir discerns him from afar.
Ardavan climbs down his horse in front of him,
Body wounded by shots and soul troubled.

Ardeshir says to the executioner,
"Take my adversary, cut him in half with your sword,
And strike with terror the hearts of the wicked."

The executioner accomplishes the deed.
This illustrious prince vanishes from the world.
Such is the conduct of the ancient dome of sky,
At times with Ardavan, at times with Ardeshir.
It raises one's fortune to the stars
Only to one day fling him into the dark dust.

Two sons of Ardavan are taken captive with him,
And the race of Aarash fades away because of him.
The powerful king sends the two princes
To the dungeon, feet bound with iron cuffs.

The two elder sons flee the battle, avoiding
Being caught in the noose of misfortune.
They abscond, shedding tears, to the land of India.

49

We would do well to recount their adventures.

The entire battlefield is covered with trappings,
Belts, armor, objects of gold and silver.
The king asks for the lot to be amassed
And distributed to the troops.

Tabaak emerges from the midst of noblemen
And washes the blood and dust off Ardavan's body.
He laments and has someone build a royal casket.
He covers the wounded body with golden silk,
Places a crown of camphor over his head,
But no one appears at the gravesite of Ardavan.

Then Tabaak presents himself before Ardeshir
And says, "O wisdom-seeking King,
Give your command and wed his daughter.
She is a beautiful and illustrious princess.
The crown and throne belong to her.
She will hand over the diadem, crown, and treasure
Amassed by Ardavan with great pain.

Ardeshir approves of his advice.
He instantly asks for her hand in marriage
And remains one or two months in the palace,
A powerful king with a powerful army.

Then the ambitious Ardeshir travels
From Rey to the land of Pars, where he rests
From his labors and from the noise that followed.
He founds a city full of palaces and gardens,
Full of fountains, plains, and boulders.
Today the old and illustrious poet bard
Calls this city Khorreh-yeh Ardeshir.[7]

There is an overflowing spring
From which a large number of gullies are diverted.
Next to this source he establishes
A fire temple in which he resurrects
The festivals of Mehregan and Saddeh.

◇◇◇◇◇◇◇◇◇◇◇◇◇
7 Khorreh-yeh Ardeshir: A city founded by Ardeshir in the province of Pars,
also referred to as Goor and as Firuzabad.

Gardens spread out all around, with a square
And a structure that form a huge establishment.
His majesty and power grow and expand.

The border governor names this city Goor.
Ardeshir builds villages around it for people to settle in.
On one side of the city, he finds deep waters,
But one had to tunnel through the mountain to reach them.
The workers excavate to open one hundred canals
With their blades, directing them to the king's city.

With water running through it, it flourishes
And fills with dwellings and animals.

11 | The Battle of Ardeshir With the Kurds and His Defeat

King Ardeshir exits Estakhr with countless troops,
Ready to engage in battle with the Kurds.
He asks the Creator to reward him for his good deeds
And to allow him to spill the blood of thieves.

At his approach, the Kurds march toward him
With their vast host, ready to fight him.
This is a simple affair rendered more challenging
By the fact that the people of the land
Align themselves with the Kurds.

A huge army forms.
For every Kurd, there are thirty Persian warriors.
They battle one full day until the descent of night, when
The king's troops have no other recourse but to abscond.
There are so many wounded men and so many
Dead bodies that the battlefield is restricted.

Besides the king and his small escort remaining
On the arena, all the noble warriors have fled.
The intense heat of the sun, mixed with the dust,
Creates a thirst that deepens their tongues' fissures.

As soon as night supplants day and raises its dark banner,

It puts an end to battle, commotion, and clamor.
At the notice of a blaze on the mountaintop, the world
Master takes its direction with his men, young and old.
Nearing the flames, he sees shepherds with sheep and goats.

The king and his men dismount,
Mouths full of the dust of battle.
Ardeshir asks the shepherds for water,
Which they bring along with curdled milk.
He rests, eats the fare before him, and once night is deep,
He removes his coat of mail, uses it as a bed worthy
Of a warrior, and rests his head on his royal helmet.

The Iranian king rises at dawn's first light
Reflecting on the water's surface.
The leader of the shepherds approaches him to say,
"May your days and nights be joyous!
What misfortune led you down this desert road?
Where did you find such a solid
And uncomfortable thing as a mattress?"

The king asks for directions to a place of rest.
The leader of the shepherds replies,
"Without a guide, you will not find a populated region.
But once you march away from here for four farsangs,
You will come across a place of rest."

Ardeshir organizes groups of ten, each led by a chief,
And takes with him a number of elders
From the herds to serve him as guide.
He crosses the mountain and arrives at a village
Whose ruler rushes to greet him.

From there, he dispatches riders
To Khorreh-yeh Ardeshir, with news of their king.
The army joyously takes the road.
He sends spies to the land of Kurds
To secretly scrutinize their activities.

These loyal men depart, and upon their return,
They dismount and say to the King of Iran,
"These illustrious and happy Kurds
Do not waste time worrying about your majesty.

They think that Ardeshir's glory has waned
And that his fortune has passed."

The words delight the king and snuff out
Thoughts of past deeds like a breath of wind.
From his glorious army,
He selects a cavalry of three thousand
Sword-wielding men and takes with him
One thousand more armed with bow, quiver, and arrow.

12 | Ardeshir Attacks the Kurds by Night

Ardeshir marches off with his troops at sundown,
Leaving behind those unfit for the expedition.

As half the night passes and darkness reigns supreme,
The king approaches the Kurds.
He finds the plain covered with slumbering men,
The entire army in a state of disarray.

Closing in on the sleeping men, he releases
The reins of his keen charger, draws his sword,
And strikes, placing a crown of blood
On the points of blades of grass.

The plain is covered with Kurdish heads and limbs,
Bodies recline, countless prisoners are captured.
Foolishness and frivolity rush them to their end.

Ardeshir plunders the land
And distributes dinars and crowns to his soldiers.
The king's justice and auspicious star are so powerful,
That an old man walking with a tray of dinars
On his head would go unnoticed.

The king does not remain to draw glory
From his courage but rushes back to Estakhr.
He gives the order to refurbish the horses
And repair the splintered armor of warriors
So that, once they are restored by feast,
They can reignite thoughts of battle.

The brave men enjoy life, and after some time,
Their waists no longer feel the weight of their belts.
Ardeshir contemplates new struggles and wars.

When you hear this story, do store it in your memory.

13 | The Story of Haftvaad's Worm

Listen to the poet bard's marvelous story
As he unveils the secrets of the city of Kojaran,
Situated on the Persian Gulf,
And he reports the dimensions of the land of Pars.

Many kind people reside there,
Working hard to make a living,
Among them are many poor maidens
Searching for ways to earn their keep.
On one end of the city is the mountainside,
Where young women meet, each carrying
Weighed cotton and poplar wood cattail.
They gather at the city gate and together
Walk to the mountain base, carrying their dinner,
A fare that does not much differ from one to the other.
The idea is not to waste time with eating or sleeping.
They place their honor and ambition in spinning cotton
And at night return home with embroidery thread.

In this town lives a poor man of cheerful countenance
Named Haftvaad, who draws his name and reputation
From the fact that he has seven sons.
In addition, he has one cherished daughter,
Though he deems the female gender of little value.

One day, at the hour of supper, these young girls
Set aside their cattails to season their food.
It so happens that the daughter of Haftvaad found,
On the road, an apple tossed off a branch by the wind.
She rushed to pick the fruit to enjoy at mealtime.
Now listen closely. My tale will astonish you:
She bites into the beautiful, juicy apple
To find a worm hiding within.

She removes it with her finger
And sets it down gently into the cattail bucket.
As she lifts the cotton, she says,
"In the name of the Creator, a Being without equal
Or mate, I shall show you today what one can spin
With the aid of an apple worm's star of fortune."

Her companions laugh at her,
Their faces full, their silver teeth exposed.
But the daughter of Haftvaad spins, on this day,
Twice as much as usual, marking her account on earth.

She rushes away like smoke to show her mother,
Who blesses her tenderly and says to her,
"The stars are showing you their favor,
O my beautiful sun-faced child!"

The next morning, after having counted
The threads from the previous day,
She takes twice as much cotton with her and,
Once in the company of the industrious group
Who apply heart, mind, and body to spinning,
She says, "O moon-faced friends favored by stars,
I shall, thanks to my propitious worm, spin so much
That I shall never again find myself in need."

She spins faster than the previous day.
Even if she had more, she would come to the end.
She returns home to witness
Her mother's heart bloom like a radiant paradise.

Every morning, the fairy-faced young lady
Offers the worm a tiny piece of apple,
And the more cotton she has, the more she spins.

One day, the father and mother say to the skilled girl,
"You spin so much that you must have made
A sister's pact with a fairy."

The young girl of silver stature reveals to them
The secret of the apple and the worm.
She shows them the tiny creature, her lucky charm.
The husband and wife are delighted.

Haftvaad takes this as a good omen.
He no longer concentrates on his trade
And ceaselessly speaks of the auspicious worm
And how his aging fortune has been renewed.

In this way, some time passes,
Every day more prosperous than the day before.
The worm is far from neglected and is provided
With abundant morsels that make it strong and plump.
Its head and back take on vibrant hues.
The bucket is soon far too narrow for it.
Its robe turns black as musk and,
On this dark background, a stripe of saffron
Runs from its back to the front.

Haftvaad builds a beautiful black box in which
He settles the worm. This man, once poor,
Finds himself honored, respected, and rich.
His seven sons become so powerful
So that no one in town dares speak,
Fairly or unfairly, without asking his advice.

There lives in town a proud Emir,
A noble personality who maintains troops.
He seeks a reason to extort money
From Haftvaad, a man of humble birth.
But Haftvaad gathers many illustrious warriors
Around him along with his seven valiant sons.

Trumpets blare through the town of Kojaran.
They file off, armed with lance, sword, and arrow,
Haftvaad marching at the lead.
They engage bravely in battle, take over the city,
Kill the Emir, and seize his vast treasure.

Men gather around Haftvaad in hordes.
He exits the city of Kojaran and takes the mountain road.
At the top he builds a fortress where residents gather.
He places an iron door at the entrance and makes it
At once a place of rest and a place of battle.

On the mountain, there is a spring that emerges
From the crest and flows to the castle's center.

He surrounds the area with a wall,
Its height imperceptible to the human eye.
Since the box is now too narrow for the worm,
They build a stone reservoir on the mountain.
Once the stone and mortar are sufficiently warm,
They gently and cautiously place the worm there.

Every morning, the worm's guardian exits
To prepare a ration for the worm's consumption
Consisting of a cauldron of rice.

Five years pass in this manner.
The worm grows as big as an elephant with horns.
After some time, Haftvaad names this place Kerman.

The daughter attends to the creature
While her father is the commander of the worm's host.
The worm is wrapped up in Chini silk,
Nourished with rice, honey, and milk.
It responds to acts of justice and injustice.

Haftvaad, the army chief, invades all the lands
From the Sea of Chin to Kerman with his host.
Each of his seven sons commands
Ten thousand sword-wielding warriors,
Each owner of vast wealth and artillery.

When a warring king wages war and advances
With troops toward the worm, they would soon
Be discouraged upon hearing this peculiar tale.
The gate of the illustrious Haftvaad and his treasure
Is guarded by troops and is the object of such terror
That the wind does not dare blow in its direction.

14 | The Battle of Ardeshir With Haftvaad and His Defeat

Tales of Haftvaad reach Ardeshir and displease him.
He dispatches an auspicious army avid for glory.

Haftvaad is not worried about the enemy's approach.

He organizes an ambush in the mountain fold
And advances with troops to engage in battle.

At the moment the troops fall upon each other,
Beating each other up with blows of mace and battleax,
The detachment comes out of the ambush,
And the world dims for Ardeshir's warriors.
The confusion is such that one could no longer
Distinguish between arms and feet.
It is as if their hands are fastened to the ground.
Valleys, plains, and mountains are so full of corpses
That the victors grow weary of killing.
Those able to escape rush back to the king.

They recount to Ardeshir the unfolding developments,
The losses of men and loads,
The blows administered and the blows received.
An afflicted Ardeshir gathers his troops.
He quickly distributes fresh weapons and coins,
And proceeds to march against Haftvaad.

Haftvaad, a man of low birth, raises his head to the sky,
Brings wealth and weapons from his castle,
Underplaying Ardeshir's host and the imminent battle.

Shahooy, his ambitious eldest son, separated from him,
Hears of the threats made against his father.
He abandons rest, feast, and sleep,
And takes a boat to the opposite waterfront.
His nature is malicious and evil.

Haftvaad's heart rejoices at the sight of his son.
He assigns him the command of the army's right wing.

The two hosts are in order of battle, full of ardor,
Each boasting a well-filled treasury.

Ardeshir observes them, and the heart
Of the young man ages quickly with worry.
The two hosts form two lines, the sun shines,
Swords flash, and timpani on elephant back
Resound to signal the start of battle.
For two miles, men are stunned by the racket.

The world fills with the blare of trumpets
And the blow of clarions.
The ground shakes with the pounding of horses' hooves.
The leaders' banners send sparks of ruby through the air,
And the sky takes leave of the earth
With the maddening sound of mace bashing on helmets.

Horses split the ground with their frantic race.
Valley and plain fill with headless corpses.
Haftvaad's troops resemble an undulating sea,
And the desert is so crowded with warriors
That ants and flies cannot find a path to cross.

This struggle continues until the day fades
And night spreads its shadowy veils.

Ardeshir gathers his scattered troops
And sets up camp on the water's edge.

Once the rust-colored brocade turns black,
The two armies rest with sentinels on the lookout.
The royal army lacks provisions and supplies
As the enemy is occupying and blocking the roads.

15 | Mehrak, Son of Nooshzaad, Pillages Ardeshir's Palace

There lives in Jahrom a man of Kianian lineage
Named Mehrak, son of Nooshzaad.
Once informed of Ardeshir's departure,
Of his waterside sojourn, and of his camp's distress,
Deprived of provisions and supplies,
He exits Jahrom and takes the road with a vast host.

They attack Ardeshir's palace,
Raiding and ransacking his treasury,
And distributing crowns and coins to troops.

This news fills the king with a sense of anguish.
Still at the waterside, he thinks,
"Why did I leave to fight with a foreigner

Without having first secured my own residence?"

He calls to his side his army leaders and speaks
To them at length on the subject of Mehrak:
"What are your thoughts on our vulnerable position?
I have tasted much bitterness from fate,
But I did not expect a grave insult from Mehrak."

They cry out in a common voice: "O King,
May your eye never witness bad fortune!
You must not despair at the thought
That Mehrak is secretly your enemy.
You are powerful, the world is yours,
We stand as your slaves, and command is yours."

The king asks for a spread, wine and cups,
Singers and musicians.
They prepare to feast upon a fare of lamb.

As Ardeshir is about to take a bite, a sharp arrow
Flies through the air to pierce and disappear into
The plump lamb sitting on a platter right before the king.

The noblemen, learned advisors, valiant warriors,
Remove their hands from the food
As trepidation drifts quickly into their hearts.

One of them extracts the arrow from the lamb and,
On it, finds writing in the language of Pahlavi.
The most learned man reads:
"O King full of knowledge, listen well:
This arrow was shot from the terrace
Of the palace secured by the fortune of a worm.
If I had cast the arrow to pierce Ardeshir,
It would have done so through and through.
A king of your stature must renounce to fight a worm,
For you would surely lose your life in the attempt."

After the reading, the hearts of noblemen constrict.
There is a distance of two farsangs to the castle.
They implore the almighty Creator for mercy.

16 | Ardeshir Learns the Worm's Secret

The king passes the night reflecting on the worm.
As the moon makes way for the sun,
He departs from the seaside with his troops
And marches quickly toward the land of Pars.

The enemy host follows Ardeshir,
Cuts the road short for him on all sides,
And kills all the illustrious men in his company.

The king flees as fast as he can with his closest allies.
A booming cry resounds behind them:
"May the fortune of the worm shine on the throne!"

Each person says, "What an astonishing thing!
Never will we understand this phenomenon."

Ardeshir continues his flight with a troubled heart,
Crossing mountains and valleys, the horses galloping
At twice the speed, rushing forth like wolves.
In the end, he comes across a vast city.

Approaching the city, the king pauses at a house.
Beneath its doorframe stand two young strangers
Who ask them, "Where are you coming from at this hour,
For you are in a state of disarray and covered in dust?"

The king replies, "Ardeshir passed through here,
And we remained behind in confusion.
He fled at the sight of Haftvaad's worm
And before the lowly creature's vile army."

The two youths tremble in fear.
Afflicted and saddened, they help Ardeshir
Dismount and shower him with blessings.
They set up a cheerful room, a banquet spread,
Place seats for the king and his men,
And proceed to serve them.

Then they say in a common voice,
"O noble man, neither grief endures nor joy.
Reflect on the fate of the unjust Zahaak,

What did he take of the royal throne?
Reflect on the malicious Afraasiyaab,
Who afflicted the hearts of kings.
Reflect on Eskandar, who came in our time
And killed all the kings of the earth.
They have all left. Only their infamous names remain.
None of them will gain admission into cheery paradise.
Similarly, the world will not remain for Haftvaad,
Who will soon subtract himself from the human race."

The king's heart blossoms like a spring rose.
This discourse full of grace brings him joy.
He reveals his secret: "I am Ardeshir, son of Sassan,
And I have need for counsel to relieve my heart.
What shall we do faced with Haftvaad and his worm?
May his name and race disappear from the world!"

As soon as the Iranian king discloses his identity,
The two youths pay proper homage to him
And exclaim, "May his majesty live eternally!
May misfortune keep at bay from him!
May we be his slaves, body and soul!
May his soul never bend!
We shall reply to your question
To help you design a way of salvation.
You will not overcome a struggle with the worm
Without resorting to scheme and strategy.
There is a place on the mountain crest where
Worm, treasure, and a crowd of men reside.
On one side is a city, on the other is a body of water.
Access to the castle on the mountaintop is undisclosed.
The worm whose essence derives from Ahriman
Is the enemy of the Creator.
We call it a worm, but beneath its skin
Is a bloodthirsty, wicked deev eager to fight."

Ardeshir feels a sense of friendship with the men.
He says, "Very well, I shall rely on you
For all good and bad that affect me."

The youths' response charms his sensible mind.
They say, "We stand before you as your slaves

And guides toward your goal of happiness.

The king departs in haste, eager for vengeance.
The youths accompany him on the road.
He travels thoughtfully and proudly
Until he arrives at Khorreh-yeh Ardeshir,
Where his troops and his wise noblemen
Of good advice gather around him.

After having rested for some time, he pays tribute,
Then marches against Mehrak, son of Nooshzaad.
Mehrak dares not fight with him.
The world turns black and narrow for him.

When Ardeshir nears Jahrom,
The traitor Mehrak hides from him.
But the king's heart is merciless,
And he remains there until Mehrak is seized.
He strikes him at the neck with his Indian sword
And flings his headless body into the fire.

Any member of Mehrak's family who falls into his hands
Instantly dies at the point of his sword.
Only one of his daughters evades him.
In vain they put the city in a stir to find her.

17 | Ardeshir Kills Haftvaad's Worm

From there, Ardeshir departs to battle the worm,
His entire army determined and eager.
He takes with him a corps of twelve thousand men,
Able cavaliers skilled in the art of war.

Once his scattered army is united,
He drives it to a location between two mountains.

There lives a man by the name of Shahrguir,
A commander of the king's army, full of wisdom.
Ardeshir warns him, "Be vigilant.
Dispatch rounds of skilled horsemen
To observe the roads, establish the lookouts,

And send guards and night sentinels
To watch over the army's safety day and night.
I shall attempt to strategize and execute a ruse
In the example of Esfandiar, my ancestor.
When your watchmen notice either daytime smoke
Or a nighttime fire blazing like the shining sun,
You will know that the worm is dead,
That its star, its days, and its schemes
Have decidedly reached their end."

He selects seven valiant warriors, battle lions.
He refrains from confiding in his closest friends
Or even confiding in the wind blowing through the air.
Without hesitation, he draws valuables from his treasury,
Precious stones, golden sheets, dinars, and more.
Then he crams two crates with lead and tin.
He adds a cauldron made of zinc to the loads,
An essential element to his strategy.

Having thus arranged the execution of his scheme,
He asks the head of the stables for ten donkeys.
He dresses in an outfit made of coarse wool,
In the manner of a donkey driver,
Though his load is rich with gold and silver.

His heart is agitated as he reflects
On the chances his plan may succeed.
But once the preparations are complete,
He is somewhat appeased and takes the direction
Of the castle with his friends and guides:
The two hospitable village youths.

Near the castle, they stop on the heights
To catch their breaths. They find sixty men
Serving the worm efficiently and faithfully.

One of them notices Ardeshir and asks,
"What are you transporting in your crates?"

The king replies, "I bring all sorts of merchandise,
Ornaments, clothing, objects in gold and silver,
Brocade, dinars, garments of silk, and fine jewels.
I am a merchant from Khorasan.

I work hard and rarely rest.
By the worm's grace, I possess fine things.
I am happy to appear before its throne.
I wish to testify to him my admiration,
For its auspicious influence helped me prosper."

The worm's servant shares the secret with the others.
They immediately open the castle doors.
Ardeshir enters with donkeys and loads.
He sets up a store, rushes to open one of the packages,
And distributes essential presents.

He places before the worm's servants
A cloth made of leather, such as used by donkey drivers.
He unties the ropes fastened to the crates,
Brings the keys, and fills the cups with wine.

The men who prepare the worm's dinner of milk and rice
Turn away from the cup of wine, saying that it is
Their turn to serve and they must not be inebriated.

At these words, Ardeshir rises abruptly and says,
"I have loads of milk and rice.
If the worm's chief servant allows me,
I shall be happy to feed it for three days.
I hope that such a deed will reward me with worldly fame
As I will profit from the worm's good fortune.
Drink wine with me for three days, and, on the fourth day,
As the world-illuminating sun rises,
I shall set up a magnificent store
With a roof more elevated than the palace walls.
I am a merchant and seek buyers.
I wish to gain honor in the eyes of the worm."

He attains the object of his desire. They reply,
"Very well, you may take charge of serving."

The alleged donkey driver ingratiates himself
In every way: He offers the men wine.
They drink, get properly intoxicated,
And, from being the servants of a worm,
They transform to servants of wine.

As their tongues slump into languor from
The effect of the spirits, the king and his host
Find the tin and the cauldron of zinc.
They light a fire in the middle of day,
And at the time of the worm's supper,
They prepare a meal of molten tin.

The worm sticks out its tongue to eat as usual,
A tongue round like a metal sphere.
The young man pours the tin down its throat,
And the worm quickly loses consciousness.
A deep sound rises from its throat,
Making the pit and the surrounding area shake.

Ardeshir and the two youths rush like wind,
Armed with sword, mace, and arrow.
None of the worm's drunken servants escapes alive.

The king produces a black smoke on the castle terrace
To signal the army leader of his victory.
A sentinel appears next to Shahrguir, crying,
"King Ardeshir has triumphed!"

The army commander departs right away,
Driving the troops to the king.

18 | Ardeshir Kills Haftvaad

Upon hearing the news of the events,
Haftvaad's heart fills with sorrow, his mouth with sighs.
He arrives to recapture the castle,
But Ardeshir climbs the walls in haste.
Haftvaad struggles for some time, but in vain,
For the lion's foot is firmly planted on the rampart.

On the other side is Ardeshir's army, like a mountain,
But Haftvaad's men are troubled and feel trapped.

Ardeshir cries out from the walls,
"Attack, O valiant Shahrguir!
If Haftvaad is able to escape,

We will gain only grief from this battle.
I have given the worm molten tin, thus shattering
The power of Haftvaad's impetuous nature."

At the king's words,
The Iranians cover their heads in iron helms,
Regain courage, and prepare to execute vengeance.
The wind blows on the worm's combatants,
And soon Haftvaad is captured, along with
His eldest son, Shahooy the bragger, his army chief.

Ardeshir swoops down the castle hurriedly
As Shahrguir advances toward him on foot.
The king climbs on a golden-harnessed charger.
He orders his men to place two high gallows
On the water's edge.
He attaches to them the two malicious men
And thus awakens his enemies' hearts.

Shahrguir emerges from the army center
And kills the two men with a shower of shots.

Ardeshir seizes Haftvaad's treasure
To distribute to his troops.
Servants bring valuables from every part of the castle,
And he selects highly prized objects
To carry back to Khorreh-yeh Ardeshir.

He establishes a fire temple in this land, where
He renews the festivals of Mehregan and Saddeh.
He offers province, throne, and crown
To his two blessed young hosts.
Then he departs victorious and happy,
And spreads justice throughout the land of Pars.

Once the men and horses are well rested,
He marches toward the city of Goor and sends troops
To Kerman with a man worthy of throne and crown.
From there, he leaves for Ctesiphon[8]

◇◇◇◇◇◇◇◇◇◇◇◇◇
8 Ctesiphon: An ancient city near the Tigris River and southeast of Baghdad; royal
capital of the Persian Empire during Parthian and Sassanian times over a period of
eight hundred years.

After having lowered the heads of his enemy's fortune.

Such is the custom of this unstable world:
It hides its secret from you and does not adapt to anyone.
You are the one who must adapt to the world
And to its ups and downs, as one day it will lower you
Only to elevate you the next day.

PART TWENTY-THREE

The Sassanian Dynasty

The Forty-Year-and-Two-Month Reign of Ardeshir Babakan

1 | The Ascent of Ardeshir Babakan to the Throne

Ardeshir sits on the ivory throne in Baghdad
And places on his head the heart-enlightening crown.
His belt fastened to his waist and mace in hand,
He decks his palace and assumes the title of King of Kings.
No one can set him apart from Shah Goshtaasp.

From atop his throne, the crown of power on his head,
He proclaims with joy and victory:
"My most valuable treasure is justice.
I renew the world with my fortune and my labors.
No one has the power to seize this treasure from me.
Misfortune only strikes men who commit evil deeds.
The pure World Master, content with my being,
Will not refuse me domination on this somber earth.
I am the shelter of the world.
It is in my nature to approve all that is just and fair.
We cannot allow a farmer or a righteous man
To fall asleep with a troubled heart,
Not with my governors, leaders, and valiant cavaliers.
This audience hall is open to all, friend or foe."

The assembly exalts him: "O King,
May the world prosper by your justice!"

He sends armies to every corner of the land and
To every hostile ruler so that he may either be led back
To the right path or be treated by way of the sword
Should he be keen on threatening his throne.

2 | The Story of Ardeshir's Adventure With Ardavan's Daughter

Once King Ardavan's blood spills to flow on the ground,
Ardeshir acquires the world
And seeks to wed Ardavan's daughter,
Hoping to discover the location of her father's treasury.

Two of Ardavan's sons are in India,
Inseparable in good and bad fortune;
Two more are held in King Ardeshir's prisons.
The father is dead while the sons live on,
Though nursing wounds inflicted by arrows' shots.

Bahman, the eldest son who lives in India,
Finding himself stripped of his empire,
Selects a messenger endowed with sense and reason
And entrusts him with a dose of poison, saying,
"Go to my sister and tell her,
        'You have two brothers in India,
        Allies in pain and misfortune.
        Never trust Ardeshir's expressions of affection.
        Two more brothers are bound in the king's prisons,
        Eyes brimming with tears, hearts bursting with blood.
        Would the Creator of the sky approve
        Of you breaking the bonds that connect us?
        If you wish to be queen of Iran, if you wish
        To be applauded by brave men everywhere,
        Take this deadly Indian poison
        And administer just one dose to Ardeshir.'"

The envoy arrives by night at the side of Ardavan's
Illustrious daughter and conveys the message.
Her heart on fire for her brothers' predicament,
She snatches the pricy poison presented to her,
Hoping to fulfill her brother's strategy.

One day, King Ardeshir returns from the hunt at midday
And marches to Ardavan's daughter's chambers.

The moon-faced beauty rushes to the king,
Brings him a cup of topaz filled with sugar, barley flour,

And fresh water to which she has mixed the poison,
Hoping to achieve Bahman's desired outcome.

King Ardeshir takes the cup, but before he can take a sip,
It slips out of his hand and shatters on the floor.
The king's daughter begins to tremble,
As if her heart is about to split in two.
At the sight of her shaking convulsively,
The world master suspects wrongdoing,
For he dreads the rotations of the skies.

He orders a servant to fetch four hens from the barn.
They release the fowls to roam around the flour.
Upon pecking the ground strewn with poisonous flour,
The four instantly die, circumstances that
Make it hard to believe the queen's innocence.

The prudent king calls for his wise minister
And asks him, "If you place your enemy on the throne,
And if it happens that your kind treatment intoxicates them
To the point where they foolishly attempt to take your life,
What is the just punishment for such an offense,
For such a person who has abused your trust?
How does one cure the harm one has done to oneself?"

The wise man replies, "A subject who extends
A hand to seize the life of the world master
Must surrender his or her guilty head.
You must not listen to anyone else's advice."

The king says, "Take the body of Ardavan's daughter,
And make it so that it can never meet her soul again."

The wise man departs with the princess walking before him,
Heart aquiver with the magnitude of her crime.
She says to him, "O wise man, my days and yours will pass.
If you must sentence me to death,
At least know that I carry Ardeshir's child.
If I deserve to have my blood spilled and to be hanged
At the gallows, then by no means disobey the king's orders,
But do so only after the child is born."

The wise man retraces his steps and says to Ardeshir

73

All that he has heard, but the king replies,
"Do not listen to her. Just follow my command."

3 | The Birth of Shahpoor, Ardeshir's Son

The wise man reflects, "Misfortune is ours
Because of the command of the king!
We all belong to death, young and old.
King Ardeshir does not have a son, and even if he still
Has countless years ahead, in the end, he will pass on,
And his throne will be abandoned to his adversaries.
I must then find a remedy to this sad state of affairs.
I must make an important resolution not to kill the moon,
In the hope that the king will regret his command.
I shall have a chance to exercise vengeance
Once the child is born from his mother's womb.
It is not a matter to be taken lightly.
Better be prudent than improvident."

He prepares a room in his chambers
Where he keeps her as if she were his body and soul.
He says to his heart, "It would be a calamity
For a breath of air to penetrate and to touch her."

He thinks that he has many enemies,
All full of suspicion and envy, and he says,
"I shall find a way to prevent these slanderers
To wickedly trouble the waters of my stream."

He shuts himself up and cuts off his testicles,
Cauterizes the area, and applies ointments
Before dressing the wound.
He quickly sprinkles salt over the cut pieces
And locks them up in a case, which he seals.

Then he exits, sighing deeply, cheeks pale,
And tells his servants to bring him a litter
To drive to the king at nightfall.

They raise him in this wretched state
And take him quickly on the litter to the palace.

King Ardeshir asks the wise man,
"What have you done?
Your face is the color of turmeric!"

The other replies, "This affair filled me with grief
And made my face a deep shade of yellow."

They place him before the lofty throne,
Corded, sealed case in his hand.
He says, "May the king kindly
Entrust custody of this box to his treasurer.
May he write the date, and may we note its provenance."

4 | Ardeshir Learns of Shahpoor's Existence After Seven Years

When Ardavan's daughter goes into labor,
The wise man does not confide his secret
To anyone, not even to the wind.
She gives birth to a son, an energetic child of royal mien.

The vizier dismisses everyone from his palace.
He gives the child the name of Shahpoor
And hides him for the duration of seven years.
During this time, the prince develops kingly features
And is full of grace, strength, and solemnity.

One day, the wise man visits the king
And finds his face drenched in tears.
He says to him, "O King, may you live forever!
What happened? Are you hiding a deep worry?
The world has given you all of your heart's desires.
You have flung down your enemies' heads,
Plucked them off their thrones.
Now is the time to revel, to drink wine,
And not to nurture worry in your heart.
The earth and the seven realms form your empire.
The army, the throne, and the true path are yours."

The king replies, "O wise man of pure heart,
You are the confidant of my deepest secrets.

My sword has indeed restored world order.
I have eased people's sorrows, pains, and vices.
But I am now more than fifty-one years old,
My black hair has turned to camphor white,
And the roses of my cheeks have faded.
I wish a son stood before me, a son to charm
Dim hearts, a victorious son and an insightful guide.
A father without a son is like a son without a father.
Never will a stranger hold him close to his heart.
After me, an enemy will inherit my throne and treasury,
And the gain that I will draw from grief will be my tomb."

The wise man thinks that it is time to speak:
"O benevolent King of serene and noble mind,
If you wish to secure my life,
I shall liberate you from further worry."

The king replies, "O sensible man,
Why would I want to take your life?
Tell me what you know, speak as long as you wish.
What is better than the words of a wise man?"

The minister replies, "O King of pure intentions,
A case was deposited with the royal treasurer.
It would be good for your majesty to request it."

The king addresses his treasurer:
"Bring me the case that he entrusted you with.
Return it to him so that we may assess its seal and contents.
And let us hope that I shall not have to live in grief."

The treasurer returns and hands the case to the vizier.
The king asks, "What does the case conceal?
Whose seal is that stamped upon it?"

The other replies, "This is my warm blood,
And it contains the shameful parts of my body.
You handed over to me the daughter of Ardavan,
Ordering me to separate her body from her soul.
I did not kill her because she carried your child,
And I feared the Creator.
I sacrificed my body and cut off my private parts,
So that no one can speak of me with evil words

76

And plunge me deep into the waters of disgrace.
Now your son, Shahpoor, has grown in the shelter
Of your vizier to be a boy of seven years of age.
No king has a son as magnificent as him.
He resembles the moon in the firmament.
Out of love, I assigned him the name of Shahpoor.
May the world rejoice through his good fortune!
His mother is still alive and raises her son,
Who holds ambitions to possess the world."

The king is confounded and reflects on the child.
In the end, he says to his minister,
"O man of serene heart and holy intentions,
You suffered greatly for this affair.
I shall not allow you to endure further suffering.
Take one hundred children of his age,
Resembling him in stature, mien, and limbs,
Have them all dress exactly like him.
Equip them with rackets, prepare a game of polo,
And ask them to convene at the castle.
Once the plain fills with beautiful children,
My soul will be moved
With tenderness at the sight of mine.
My heart will attest to the truth of your words
And will assist in recognizing my son."

5 | Shahpoor Plays Polo and Is Recognized by His Father

At dawn, the king's vizier gathers the children
On the castle square, all dressed alike
And equal in mien and stature, so that one
Could not be distinguished from the other.

It is as if there is a festival in the square.
In the midst of this crowd stands Shahpoor.
The children begin their game of striking the ball,
Each wishing to outdo the others.

The king arrives with his company of select men,
Young and old. He takes one look around,

Sighs deeply, and points a finger around, saying,
"I hope that one of them is Ardeshir's successor."

His advisor replies, "O King, your heart
Will reveal to you the presence of your son."

King Ardeshir turns to a servant and says,
"O ingenious man, smile at these children,
And throw a ball with your mallet toward me,
The child who rushes forth courageous as a lion
And who seizes the ball before my eyes,
Without fear or regard for anyone in the group,
That person is, without a doubt, my cherished son,
Derived from my lineage, my body, and my family."

The king's servant departs to obey the order.
He strikes the ball and sends it flying through the air.
The children sprint after it as fast as arrows.
They stop abruptly before Ardeshir,
Hesitating and disappointed.
But Shahpoor jumps on the ball, grabs it,
And throws it to the group of children.

The king's heart is delighted and renewed,
Like an old man who recovers his youth.
The riders raise the child from the ground
And pass him from hand to hand.
The King of Kings embraces him
And gives thanks to the Justice Giver.

He kisses the child on his head, face, and cheeks,
And says, "We must not conceal this marvel.
Never did I dare dream of such a thing,
For I was sure that he had been executed.
The Creator makes my empire prosper and
Wished to give me a successor to govern the world.
One cannot evade divine order,
Even if one's head is raised higher than the sun."

He selects jewels and dinars from his treasury,
A vast number of dazzling garnets.
Everyone at court sprinkles gold and gems,
Musk and amber over the child's head

Until he disappears beneath the weight
And his face is buried in the precious stones.

Next, the king scatters jewels over the vizier,
Places him on a seat inlaid in gold,
And offers him so much wealth that his palace
And his hall assume a dazzling glow.

He orders the return of Ardavan's daughter
To the palace, happily and in peace.
He forgives her past crimes and erases
From this moon any remaining trace of rust.

He summons scholars from the city,
Learned men knowledgeable in the sciences.
He asks them to teach the child writing in Pahlavi,
The ways of assuming a proud and royal stance,
The art of handling the reins and how to present,
While on horseback, the tip of his lance to the enemy.

He learns other skills:
The art of drinking, the art of charity and giving,
How to adhere to customs at banquets,
How to command an army,
And anything that has to do with battle and war.

Then the king orders gold and silver coins
To be produced, large and small,
Stamped on one side with Ardeshir's name
And on the other with the name of his blessed vizier.
The skilled old man and loyal guide is so illustrious
That his name is written on letterheads,
As he is rewarded with ring and seal.

The king offers generous gifts from his treasury
To the poor and destitute who earn their bread
From their hands' labors. He takes a barren,
Infertile region, cultivates it into a verdant
And lush place, and names it Gundeh Shahpoor.[9]

◇◇◇◇◇◇◇◇◇◇◇◇◇
9 Gundeh Shahpoor: Or Gundeh Shahpur, is a city in southwestern Iran and the literary center of the Sassanian Empire in the province of Khuzestan.

6 | Ardeshir Has His Fortune Read by the Indian Keid

Shahpoor grows as tall as a cypress tree.
His father, loyal as his son's vizier,
In fear of the evil eye, never leaves his side.
The wars afford Ardeshir no sense of peace.
The moment he gets rid of an enemy in one place,
A new foe threatens to raise his head in another place.

One day he says, "I ask the World Creator,
Openly and in private, to grant me peace,
To hold in my hand a world without adversary,
So that I may engage in the sole occupation
Of being a devout Yazdan worshipper."

His blessed vizier replies,
"O King of serene heart, you seek the true path!
Let us question the Indian Keid, a learned and helpful man
Able to calculate the motions of the sublime dome of sky.
He is familiar with the door to happiness
As well as the road to doom and defeat.
If you are meant to possess the earth's seven realms
Without rival, he will find out through divination."

Ardeshir hears him out, selects a noble, resourceful youth,
Hands over to him many golden stallions and bolts of silk,
And dispatches him to the wise Indian, saying,
"Go to him and tell him,
        'O fortunate man who seeks the true path,
        Gaze into the stars and determine whether
        I am destined to rest from the exertion of battle.
        When will I be the uncontested world ruler?
        Is such a thing even possible?
        If it is not, I shall stop laboring in war
        And no longer waste my wealth to that end.'"

The king's envoy rides toward Keid
With presents and offerings.
He repeats the words of the King of Kings
And reveals to the Indian all his secrets.

Keid asks him questions and grows concerned.

He applies himself to his skill and art.
He retrieves an astrolabe to look into the stars,
Opens before him an Indian astronomical table,
And observes to determine whether the actions
Of the sublime lofty sky promise rest
And recognition or rather grief and affliction.

He says to the envoy,
"I have made calculations for the king and Iran.
If he wishes to remain in power without having
To engage in war, he must unite his family
To the family of Mehrak, son of Nooshzaad.
His wealth will augment; his weariness will taper.
Cease to worry about the hostility between the two.
Once Ardeshir binds an alliance with the family,
The land of Iran will obey him,
And his heart's desires will be granted."

Keid offers the messenger some presents and adds,
"You must not conceal any of my words to the king.
If he does not stray, the magnificent dome of sky
Will satisfy all of his dreams as I have confirmed."

The messenger returns to the king and reiterates
All that he heard from the mouth of the wise man.

The communication fills Ardeshir's heart with grief,
And his cheeks grow a pale yellow shade.
He says to the envoy, "God forbid!
I shall never see someone from the family of Mehrak!
Such a thing would be like inviting an enemy
From the street into my palace,
Someone who conspires to snatch my land.
It would mean that I have spent my wealth,
Launched my hosts, and exerted myself in vain.
All that remains from Mehrak is a daughter,
Whose face no one has perceived.
I shall command now that they bring her to me,
Whether she is in Rum or Chin, India or Taraaz,
And, when I find her, I shall burn her alive,
I shall make her moan and weep
Over her misfortune and the dust of her tomb."

He sends some riders to Jahrom under the command
Of a hateful man expert at prying.

Mehrak's daughter, having been warned of the situation,
Rises, leaves her father's dwelling,
And settles in the home of a village chief,
Who treats her with utmost respect.
She grows up to be a tall cypress tree gifted with glory,
Grace, and beauty, and with no equal in the region.

7 | Shahpoor Weds Mehrak's Daughter

Listen now to the adventure of Mehrak's daughter
With the valiant, sword-wielding Shahpoor.

After some time, as the king's star shines brighter
Than ever, one early morning, Ardeshir marches
Off to hunt with the prudent Shahpoor.
The bold riders dart in every direction,
Stripping the plain of game.

In the distance, Shahpoor sees a town
Full of gardens, palaces, squares, and dwellings.
He sprints toward it and dismounts in front of
A lush garden at the home of the village chief.
There he spots a young lady, as dazzling as the moon,
Who lowers a bucket on a pulley into a well.

She sees Shahpoor, advances to pay her respects,
And says, "May the prince dwell in happiness!
May he smile and remain free from harm!
Your highness, your charger must be thirsty.
While the village water is salty,
This well offers fresh and tasty water.
Allow me to draw some for your mount."

Shahpoor replies, "O moon-faced beauty,
Why do you speak in this way?
I have servants who can accomplish the task."

The young woman covers her face before him

And sits further on the edge of the well.

The prince commands his servant to bring a vase
And to draw water from the well.

The servant obeys him and rushes back
With a rope, a bucket, and a turning wheel.
He plunges the bucket deep in the well,
Fills it with water, and attempts to haul it up.
Despite the effort, despite his face swelling with strain,
He is unable to extract the weighty liquid out of the abyss.

Shahpoor runs over and says to the servant,
"You are not even worth half a woman.
Have you not seen the way the young lady
Effortlessly handled the bucket, pulley, and rope,
Extracting as much water as she desired?
Meanwhile, here you are sweating from the effort
And asking others for help!"

He grabs the rope from his servant's hands,
But he similarly finds the task impossibly wearying.
In view of the challenges of the heavy bucket,
He praises the rosy-cheeked maiden and says,
"Someone able to handle such a heavy pail
Must indeed belong to the Kianian race!"

The young lady advances toward Shahpoor, saying,
"May you live in happiness for eternity!
May wisdom always serve you as guide!
By the power of Shahpoor, son of Ardeshir,
The water of this well will turn into milk."

The young man says to the eloquent maiden,
"How do you know that I am Shahpoor,
O soft-spoken beauty?"

She replies, "I have often heard from the mouth
Of honest people that Shahpoor is a warrior as strong
As an elephant and as generous as the River Nile.
His stature is as tall as a cypress tree, his body invincible.
He resembles Bahman in every way."

Shahpoor says to her, "Reply to me honestly.
Tell me what is your birth, for your face
Bears the imprint of the Kianian race."

She answers, "I am the daughter of the village chief.
That is why I am so beautiful and so brave."

Shahpoor says, "Never does falsehood
Succeed in the presence of kings.
A farmer will not have a moon-faced daughter
As strong and beautiful as you."

The young woman says, "O King, if you wish
To guaranty my life, I shall confide in you my origins.
But first reassure me against the king's grudge."

Shahpoor says, "Hostility toward friends
Does not grow in our garden.
Speak, and do not allow your heart to fear me
Or the illustrious king, giver of justice."

The young lady says, "In truth,
I am the daughter Mehrak, son of Nooshzaad.
A holy woman brought me here as a child
And entrusted me to the illustrious village chief.
It is for fear of the glorious king that I was forced
To learn to draw water from the well as a servant."

Shahpoor browses the place until
The village chief presents himself respectfully.
Shahpoor says, "Allow me to marry this beautiful
Maiden and take the firmament as my witness."

The chief grants him his wish, and they proceed
According to the rites of fire worshippers.

8 | Mehrak's Daughter Gives Birth to Ormazd, Son of Shahpoor

Not much time elapses until the cypress tree
Finds herself with child, a rose about to blossom.
Shahpoor takes his wife from the chief's residence
To his palace, where he keeps her like a fresh quince.

After nine months, the beauty gives birth
To a child who resembles his father.
It is as if Esfandiar had been reborn,
Or the glorious Ardeshir, the rider.

The prince gives him the name of Ormazd
As he looks like a cypress tree in the midst of fresh grass.
Seven years pass, and he becomes a child without equal.
He is kept hidden from sight, banned from playing outside.

One day Ardeshir goes on a seven-day
Hunting journey with Shahpoor.
Ormazd, tired of his lessons, secretly
Slips out of the palace and wanders to the square.
He holds a wooden bow in one hand
And two arrows in the other.

In Ardeshir's square, he joins a number
Of children holding mallets and balls.
At that moment, world master Ardeshir
Returns from the hunt with his retinue,
Accompanied by the wise grand master.

As the king emerges on the square,
One of the children tosses a ball that lands at his feet.
None of the other children dares pursue the ball.
They remain frozen in their position, discomfited,
With the exception of Ormazd, who springs
Out of the group and rushes to the king like wind.
He picks up the ball in front of his grandfather.

The escort murmurs about the courage of the child.
The boy shouts a triumphant cry that astonishes
The king on whom fortune shines:

"Mallet, square, and courage are mine.
I can fight and overcome any warrior!"

Ardeshir says to his wise man,
"O man of pure lineage, find out whose child this is."

The wise man asks around, but no one knows.
Everyone remains quiet, unable to answer.

The king commands the wise man to lift the child
And bring him to him.

The wise man obeys, raises the boy from the dust,
And presents him to the king of free men.

Ardeshir says to him, "O renowned child,
Which noble family do you belong to?"

Ormazd replies loudly, "I have no need to hide
My name and my birth. I am the son of Shahpoor,
Who is your son, and my mother is Mehrak's daughter.
And that is the truth!"

The world king is astonished and confounded.
He smiles and reflects: "This must be fate.
I must not nurture worry in my heart."

Then he summons Shahpoor and questions him.
Shahpoor fills with concern, and his cheeks pale.

The king smiles to see him in such a state
And says to him, "Reveal to me your secret.
We must have children, and they are welcome,
No matter where they come from.
They say that this one is the son of Shahpoor."

Shahpoor replies, "May you live in happiness!
May the world always boast a king of your stature!
This boy is mine; his name is Ormazd.
He shines like a tulip in the midst of grass.
I have hidden him for a long time,
Until the fruit from the tree is ripe.
This noble child belongs to me.

He is the son I share with Mehrak's daughter."

Then the son elaborates on the story of the water
And the well, and all that ensued.
The father listens, delighted with the account.
He returns to the palace with his vizier,
Holding in his arms the stunning child.
From the square, he decks the throne
And calls for a golden torque and a golden crown,
Which they place on the head of the little prince.

The king asks to draw dinars and gems
From his treasury to sprinkle over Ormazd
Until his head disappears beneath the load.
Then he pulls him out of the heap,
Distributes gold and jewels to the poor,
And gives the sensible child an even greater wealth.

They deck a fire temple with plush brocade,
The hall of Nowruz and the hall of Saddeh,
And prepare a festival for the noblemen,
Who engage in feast surrounded by musicians.

The king declares to the land's illustrious men,
"May no one ignore the words of the astrologers!
Keid the Indian announced that I would enjoy
Neither fortune nor royal crown,
Neither glory nor position, neither empire nor host
Unless someone from the family of Mehrak,
Son of Nooshzaad, blended their blood to mine.
For eight years now, the sky revolved to my wishes,
Since Ormazd has entered my residence
I have encountered in the world only obedience,
The seven realms are at my command,
And fortune has granted my heart's desires."

From this moment on, all the subordinates
Refer to Ardeshir with the title of King of Kings
On their letterheads and public documents.

9 | Ardeshir Forms the Administration of His Empire

Listen now as I elaborate on the subject
Of Ardeshir's sense of justice and wisdom,
Watch the rules he follows as he spreads
His affection and his kindness everywhere,
Making a show of his abilities in doing so.
Try to commit the events to memory.

He takes great pains to establish proper guidelines,
To fortify the army in siege of the empire.
He sends messengers in every direction to proclaim:
"Anyone who has a son must teach him certain skills,
Such as riding and learning how to compete
With mace, and bow and arrow of poplar wood."

When a young man acquires skills with exercise
And is deemed faultless in every area,
He travels from the province to the king's court
And presents himself before the illustrious seat.

The army inspector writes his name, assigns him
A role, a dwelling, and a place to exercise his drills.

Should a war break out, these skilled young men
Leave the court with a warrior who is
A noble wise man, able and eager to stand out.
Every group of one thousand young people
Is escorted by a supervising officer.
If someone makes a show weakness
And lacks proper valor or a strong constitution,
The supervisor would draft a report to the king,
To relate as much about the men of little value
As about those who flaunt their drive and prowess.

Upon reading the letter, the world master
Offers the messenger a seat before him,
Prepares presents for those who excel,
Selecting the most precious objects.
Then he takes note of those who behaved poorly,
To assure that they never appear in battle again.

He continues in this way until his host achieves a status
Beyond anything the stars have witnessed before.
If there is a man of good counsel,
The king elevates him above the crowd.
Heralds make the rounds of camp to proclaim:
"O illustrious warriors of the royal host,
Anyone who distinguishes himself with the king's favor,
Anyone who floods the earth with the blood of men,
Will receive a royal robe of honor, and his name
Will forever be etched in human memory."

In this way, Ardeshir maintains world order:
He is the shepherd guiding his herd of warriors.

Now pay attention to the settlements of the king
And how he organizes the work of writers.
He takes men, experts who have been tested,
Refusing to entrust his affairs to uneducated ones.
He expects the style and the writing of masters
To excel, and when a leader distinguishes himself,
The King of Kings rewards him with a pay increase.
Anyone with mediocre writing or below-average intellect
Is not allowed entrance into Ardeshir's hall.
He would be employed with the governor of provinces
While the expert writers would remain at court.

If he runs across a skilled writer,
Ardeshir would praise him and say,
"An accountant who earns money for the treasury
And spreads it around with acumen and effort
Helps the nation and the army prosper,
And eases the grief of subjects with need.
The writers are like the tendons of my soul:
They are the rulers of my secret sovereignty."

When a governor departs for a province,
The king would say, "Despise money.
Do not sell men to acquire wealth,
For this passing dwelling remains for no one.
Seek righteousness and awareness,
And may you fend off greed and foolishness.
Do not take your allies and relatives with you.

The escort I give you is support enough.
Give coins to the needy but not to evil men.
If you make our land prosper with justice,
You will thrive and live in a state of happiness.
But if the slumber of a poor man is troubled by fear,
It means you have sold your soul for gold and silver."

If a man arrives at the king's court
For a matter of importance or to demand justice,
The king's confidants would question him
On the governors to assess whether they act
In fairness or follow the path of greed
And to determine who strives to serve the king.

They inquire after the learned men of the land
Or the ones who remain in obscurity due to poverty.
They ask who is worthy of the king's favors,
Whether an old man from a noble family
Or a man of integrity, for the king would declare:
"No other needs to enjoy the fruits of my labors
And my treasures but learned men keen on observing.
What is more desirous than a wise old man?
I seek worldly men as well as elite young people.
It is a good thing to give to youth full of wisdom
And eager to learn the place assigned to older men."

If his army were to fight in some land,
The king would act with prudence and without haste.
He would take an intelligent and wise envoy,
A good observer, and charge him with a message
Always courteous and in line with custom,
So that no unjust war may threaten to erupt.

The messenger would reach the enemy
To gage their secret thoughts.
He would listen to their words, if sensible,
And would take for misfortune worries,
Weariness, and the calamities of war.
They would receive royal robes of honor,
A treaty, patented letters, and gifts.

But if their heads are enflamed with fury, their souls
With rancor, their bodies simmering with blood,

90

The king would pay tribute to the troops
So that no one remains in a state of discontent.
He would select a glory-seeking warrior,
Prudent, attentive and calm, and a skilled
Civil employee with knowledge of the rules to survey
Any misdeed the troops may have committed.

Then he would demand a man whose voice
Resonates for two miles to climb on an elephant
And to declare: "O illustrious warriors,
We have heart, fame, and honor.
No man, whether poor, or rich and illustrious,
Must have cause to complain from your deeds.
At every station, you will pay your fare
And respect the people you encounter.
Anyone who worships Yazdan will refrain
From seizing what belongs to another.
Anyone who turns his back on the enemy will meet
A tragic fate and dig up his grave with his own hands,
Or else chains will use up his chest and limbs,
His name will be crossed off, his nourishment
Will be dust, his bed will be the dim earth."

The king says to the army chief,
"Avoid a display of weakness.
Guard yourself from anger and a rush to action.
Always place the elephants at the lead,
Send scouts up to four miles.
Once the day of struggle and glory arrives,
Run your army and make your troops feel their dignity.
Explain the tasks they must fulfill on the battlefield.
Promise them robes of honor in my name.
They must know that one of our skillful riders
Is able to overcome one hundred of theirs.
But when the battle starts on both sides,
No matter how numerous your ardent warriors,
Do not allow them to fight and strip your center.
Have the left wing battle en masse
To choke the enemy's right wing.
Similarly, your army's right wing may crush their left.
May they engage in combat,
Their dim hearts beating in unison.

The army core will remain still.
Not a single soldier will move until
The enemy's center battalion begins to rattle.
Then you may advance with yours.

"Once you are victorious, make an effort
To stop bloodshed, since enemy troops will abscond.
Should one of them ask for mercy, you may
Grant it and renounce thoughts of vengeance.
At the sight of the enemy's back,
Do not rush; maintain your position.
You will have cause to suspect an ambush,
And the battlefield must remain occupied.
If you are assured of the contrary,
Then act without listening to anyone's advice.
Distribute the loot to the warriors,
To those who bravely risked their lives.
Bring to me the prisoners you have captured.
I shall build a great city for them in a thicket.
Do not deviate in any way from my counsel
If you wish to be spared pain and pity.
Once you are victorious, turn to the Creator,
Who, without a doubt, is your Guide."

When an ambassador arrives from some distant place,
Whether the land of the Turks or Rum,
Or a region of Persia, the border guard receives
The news and does not neglect the matter.

The envoy finds, everywhere on the road,
Prepared accommodations for him
With an abundance of clothing, food, and rugs.

Apprised of the reason the envoy travels to the king,
The administrator of the province sends
A servant riding a noble camel to Ardeshir's court
So that a procession may meet and greet the visitor.

The king then would prepare a turquoise throne,
Deck two rows of servants dressed in gold-trimmed garb,
And would call to his side the envoy,
Place him on the golden seat, and question
Him on secrets regarding good and bad fortune,

His name and fame, acts of justice and injustice,
Customs, his king and his host.
He would drive him to his palace
With the pomp and power befitting an ambassador.

Next he would invite him to feast with him,
Seated on a golden throne.
He would engage him in the hunt,
For which he would gather a vast escort.
Then he would dismiss him as required by his rank,
Giving him a gift of royal robes of honor.

He would send on all sides benevolent wise men,
Open-hearted and blessed with acumen.
He would spend vast wealth to have them build
Everywhere cities in order to give food and a home
To anyone deprived, anyone without resources,
Or anyone fortune contradicts.

In this way, the number of his subjects will grow.
His name will be blessed in the world,
In public and in secret. There is only one king
Who resembles him and who reminds us of him.

I sincerely wish to revive his name,
May he live happily until his ending days!
Look at all the marvels created by Ardeshir.
He makes the world prosper with his sense of justice.
He secretly speaks to countless people.
He has everywhere agents who report to him.
When the news reaches the king of a wealthy man
Losing his fortune, he would immediately arrange
To lift him out of the sad state of his affairs.
He would give him fertile land, a dwelling,
Servants and attendants, and arrange everything
Without the town having knowledge of his secrets.
He would place his children in the hands of teachers.
Should they have the gift of intelligence, he would create
A school and a site for the cult of fire on every street.

He would leave no one in the grips of need,
Unless it was a person keen on hiding his distress.
He would spread virtue equally without exception,

93

Whether a poor man or a friend's son.
The world prospers with his justice,
And the hearts of his subjects rejoice.

When the world master is the ally of justice,
Time has no means of erasing his impact.
Reflect on the rules followed by this noble man.
What solid foundation of glory he casts!
He sends throughout the world intelligent emissaries,
Clear-sighted men, to observe and evaluate.
When they would come across a place in ruins
Or a stream running out of water,
He would grant a tax rebate and would not
Consider it below his means to manage others' properties.

Should an impoverished landowner lack sustenance,
The king would offer him instruments and livestock,
And would not allow his mark to disappear.

Listen, O King,[10] to the words of a wise prince,
And make the world prosper in a similar way.
If you wish to liberate yourself from challenges
And vexations, fill your treasury carefully,
Without ever causing harm to others.
Guard yourself from oppressing your subjects,
And everyone will exalt your just ways.

10 | Ardeshir Speaks to His Noblemen

The empire, from Rum to Chin, and from the land
Of Turks to India, is under the rule of King Ardeshir,
Who dazzles the world like Rumi satin.

From every border, tributes and royalties flow in.
No one contests his crown and power.

Ardeshir summons all the noblemen of Iran,
Offers them golden seats according to rank,
Then he rises to pronounce truthful words:

◇◇◇◇◇◇◇◇◇◇◇◇◇◇
10 Reference to Sultan Mahmud, who lived during the time of Ferdowsi.

"O lords of the land, O sensible and wise men,
Know that the revolving dome of sky
Neither favors someone with justice
Nor will it extend its arms with affection.
It staunchly raises the favored one
To then brutally lower him into the dim dust.
All that remains is his name, as his rewards
And labors disappear along with him.
If you desire a happy end,
It is best to leave behind a good name.

"O Ormazd, your fate will unfold according
To divine will. Turn and open yourself to Yazdan,
Giver of our virtues and values.
Your happiness is in the hands of the Creator,
Your refuge in times of misfortune,
Who exercises power over good and evil,
Who will ease your moments of hardship,
Who is the source of your triumphant fortune,
Who gives you the ability to charm hearts.
Begin by taking me as an example.
Try to vividly remember my past, happy or sad.
As soon as I took shelter in the Creator,
My heart opened to possess the crown and throne,
My kingdom stretched over the earth's seven realms.

"I receive taxes from Rum and India,
And the world has softened in my hands
To be as pliable as Rumi satin.
I give thanks to Yazdan for giving me strength,
A powerful star, and the favor of Saturn and Sun.
Who can properly revere the Creator
And pray according to the greatness of the labor
In the hopes of accepting our submission?
Now let us speak of all the work to be done
In the spirit of justice, a justice that distributes joy.
As farmers and sages are my witness,
I have the right to one-tenth of the earnings of cities,
I shall distribute the sum to you, as well as
The earnings of the earth and the taxes from herds,
Hoping that my leaders will bring
The excess to my treasury.

"I have usefully applied the earnings I have obtained
And the other taxes more or less than the one-tenth;
I have maintained a considerable army;
I have worked for your happiness and serenity,
And the destruction of the cult of Ahriman.
Stretch your hands toward Yazdan;
Make every effort to fulfill your divine duty,
For the Creator gives and the Creator retains.
The Creator embroiders the stars into the sky
And liberates the oppressed.
Do not glorify yourself before others
In the face of divine glory.
Do not surrender your heart to deceit and greed.
Once you are positioned high,
Chances are you will sharply be brought down.

"Where are the ones whose thrones of yore
Grazed the clouds, those who seized lions as prey?
They now rest on a bed of dirt and brick.
Happy is the one who sows seeds of good.
To all of you who reside in my land
And pay heed to my advice,
I shall now attempt to indicate five paths
More valuable than crown and treasure."

11 | Ardeshir Shares His Last Wishes

Listen now, young and old,
To the words of the noble Ardeshir:
"Anyone assured of divine existence
Must venerate only the pure Creator.
Whether you are king or subject,
Avoid disparaging knowledge.
Remember that Word[11] is always renewed
In the memory of the wise man.
Know that fear of sin is far worse than being
Hanged, enchained, or falling into a well.
A malicious person's gossip
Is never honored by noblemen.

◇◇◇◇◇◇◇◇◇◇◇◇◇
11 Word: In the sense of divine word or creation; see Volume One page 30.

"I shall give you further advice, more valuable
Than what is observed by your eyes, soul, and mind.
Happy is the one who makes the world prosper
And whose behavior is the same in public and in private.
Next we turn to the soft-spoken,
Endowed with intelligence, humility, and warmth.
Do not waste your money in the interest of greed.
Do not imprudently spend on foolish things.
You will gain nothing, no one will be gratified,
And pious men will disapprove and denounce you.
If you opt for the middle course, you will support
Yourself, and sensible men will call you wise.
To pass through this world seamlessly,
You have before you five paths through which
Your faith and piety may guide you, and through
Which your health and your contentment will expand.
Your life's honey will not be followed by bane.

"In the first instance, try not to exceed, with greed
And ambition, what the Creator has accorded you.
The doe is satisfied with what it has
As the rosebush in spring bears flowers for it.
Secondly, forego lust and frivolity; abstain from
Revealing your secret in the company of women.
Thirdly, avoid reveling in war and battle,
For they will lead only to grief and sorrow.
In the fourth place, keep sadness at bay
And away from future ailments.
In the fifth place, do not meddle in other's affairs;
They are none of your business.
Keep an ear on my sound advice.
Always continue to learn and to enlighten your mind.
If you have a son, have him concentrate on his studies,
And reduce the time allotted to play.
All of you, pay attention to what I have to say
And the effort I exert on your account.
You are all just and endowed with serene minds,
Do not forsaken your intimacy for each other.

"Give your hearts some rest for four things
From which arise all that is good and useful:
First, fear, revere, and respect the Creator, your Guide.

Second, do not abuse your body, and guard
The hem of your faith's robe from being defiled.
Allow divine command to rule over your heart.
Admire me as you admire yourselves.
Thirdly, repel any inclination to fraud,
In order to allow righteousness to reign supreme.
Lastly, never turn your heart away from the wishes
Of the world king, neither in public nor in private.
Remain attached to him as if attached to your lives.
Obedience to his authority will renew you.
Take to heart all of his commands,
And maintain your minds on the path of loyalty.
You will love him like life itself
When you see that he watches over you with justice.

"The king burdens himself with his kingdom's troubles
And never worries about the losses he may incur.
If he does not intervene with justice upon finding out
That his governors or his warriors oppress the land,
He will never be worthy of the royal crown
And of the title of world ruler. His kingship would
Decline, and sovereign majesty would abandon him.
An unjust king is like a wild lion in a field.
Furthermore, a subject who does not conform
With zeal and heart to the king's commands
Will live a life of grief and sorrow and will not
Have a chance to age in this passing dwelling.
Joy and power cannot be obtained through arrogance.
May the hearts of my subjects dwell in happiness!
May the world prosper from our just ways!"

12 | Khorraad Praises Ardeshir

Once King Ardeshir takes his seat,
An old man walks toward the throne.
His name is Khorraad, and his mind and tongue are righteous.

He says, "O King, may you live as long as time itself!
May you dwell happily beneath a triumphant star!
The land, throne, and crown celebrate your reign.
You are so powerful that birds and wild beasts

Form ranks before your throne.
You are world master from one end to the other.
You raise your head above crown-bearing men.
Who has the ability to describe your uprightness?
Justice and power blend as your throne's bedrock.

"Let us renew our veneration for the world ruler!
Let us bless him for living in his era.
Eager to see your face, your words, and your affection,
We pray for your happiness in all things.
May you live in safety, for you keep us safe!
May we never fail you in devotion and loyalty!
You have blocked the road to our enemy, to the men
Of India and Chin, who could never be our equals.
Devastation, battle, and unrest came to an end.
We no longer hear the drumbeat of war.
May your mind remain eternally serene
And the weight of affairs be lifted by wise men!
No king is your equal in prudence;
Human thought cannot surpass your wisdom.
Thanks to you, your justice cast in Iran
A foundation that will benefit our children.
Your words have such vast influence
They have the power to restore youth to old men.

"Those present in this assembly of illustrious birth
Are beneficiaries of your fair customs.
Things have developed as a result of your words.
Your presence shines bright upon the world.
You are the robe of honor that dresses the Creator,
The army's headdress, belt, and throne.
Remain in this way happy, benevolent, and just.
Men will remember you more than any other king.
The world is safe in the shadow of your majesty.
Happy is the one in the shelter of your wings!
May the throne always be your seat!
May the earth remain subject to your will!"

O seeker of the Word's essence,
Pluck your heart from this ancient dwelling.
It has seen many men like you and me,
And it allows no one to linger here for long.

Whether you are a servant or a king,
You will depart when it is commanded.
Whether you live in grief or with crown and throne,
Ultimately you must pack up and leave.
Whether you are old or made out of steel,
The vault of sky will use you and not spare you.

When the enchanting cypress tree bends low,
When black eyes shed tears of sorrow,
When the visage of the rose turns the color of saffron,
When the head of the blissful man grows heavy,
When the mind surrenders to sleep
And the body assumes a reclining position,
Do not remain alone if your companions have left.
Whether king or subject, your dwelling will be dark dust.
Where are the powerful heads of crown and throne?
Where are the noble and able cavaliers?
Where are the leaders and the gallant warriors of yore?
They are asleep on a pillow of dust and brick.
Happy is the one who plants an honorable seed.

Such an outstanding example is King Ardeshir!
When you hear my story, commit it to memory.

13 | Ardeshir Surrenders Governance to Shahpoor

Once completing seventy-eight years of life,
The world master of awakened mind falls ill.
He feels death is closing in,
His life's verdant leaf turning a shade of yellow.

He summons Shahpoor to impart countless advice:
"Remember my recommendations.
Consider as wind the views of your detractors.
Now that you have heard my words, apply them.
I hope you will exhibit discernment:
The ability to distinguish
Between the meaningful and the trivial.
I restored world order with my sword of justice.
I have honored men of noble birth.
As sole ruler of the world's affairs,

I made the earth prosper in every way.
But now my life is on the decline.
I have taken great pains,
Sweated profusely to accumulate wealth.
You are now able to revel in riches and in festivities.
In every situation, there is a decline
Before there is a rise.

"The rotation of the revolving dome works in ways
That alternatively bring one pain and affection.
Your fortune can either be a capricious horse,
The source of your bad luck,
Or a launching charger full of good will.
Know, my dear son, that this treacherous world
Will not let you enjoy happiness without first
Having endured your share of frights.
Take care of your body and your mind
If you wish to spend your days free from harm.

"A king must give homage to religion:
Religion and royalty function as brothers.
Faith cannot sustain itself without the throne.
Conversely, the throne is worthless without faith.
They are two interlaced foundations of life,
Two structures welded together by wisdom.
They fall to ruins without each other.
The respect due kingship fails in the absence of faith.
Each is the guardian of the other.
It is as if they are enveloped in the same cloak.
They need each other for survival, and we see
Their union as a catalyst to the realization of good.
Anyone endowed with faith and wisdom
Will be prosper in both worlds.
If the king is the protector of the faith,
Then they are indeed brothers.
A man who utters vicious words about a just king
Is undoubtedly irreverent and faithless.
But if pious men show resentment toward a king,
Guard yourself from calling him a pure man.
A wise and eloquent sage once declared,
        'Reflect deeply, and you will conclude
        That faith is the very marrow of justice.'

"A king's throne can be weakened in three ways:
First, if the king acts toward his subjects with injustice.
Second, if he favors ill-mannered men
And raises them above skilled noblemen.
Lastly, if he hoards his wealth and thinks only
About his own gain and the accumulation of gold.
Put your passion into acts of generosity and charity,
Acts that spread justice and draw from wisdom
So that falsehood can never touch you.
Fib and fabrication tarnish a man's face,
And never does the evil man acquire glory.

"Avoid acting as the guardian of your treasury:
Men weary themselves with the acquisition of wealth.
A greedy king adds to his subjects' lassitude.
The king's wealth lies in his farmers' assets.
Whatever pain or effort it may cost him,
He must be the guardian of his subjects' capital
And make every effort for his labors to bear fruit.
Fight against the advances of anger.
Show the courage to close your eyes
When it comes to the faults committed against you.
If fury gets the better of you, you are sure to repent
When the transgressor pleads for pardon.
Every time a ruler allows himself to be riled,
The wise man calls him a worthless king.

"It is shameful for a king to wish poorly.
Compassion must fill his heart,
And if a sense of dread inserts itself,
His enemy's schemes will prevail.
Do not fear acts of generosity, O my dear son.
Appreciate, as much as you can, the value of things.
Know that kingship suits the one
Whose kindness embraces the world.
At times he will suffer, anxious for his empire's future.
He and his wise minister will hold counsel,
He will enquire after what is fair and unfair,
And keep in his kingly heart what he learns.
If you drink wine on the day of the hunt, you will weaken.
You cannot play two games at the same time:
You must choose between wine and feast,

Or hunting game and the outdoors.
An observation made long ago by noblemen states
That the body is weighed down by the effect of wine.

"Should an enemy approach, you must renounce
These activities, collect money, prepare swords,
Muster troops throughout the kingdom.
Do not adjourn for tomorrow today's affairs.
Do not offer a throne to a man of ill advice.
Do not seek to find righteousness in vulgar men,
An attempt sure to assail you with misfortune.
If a detractor speaks maliciously of someone,
Do not listen to him and do not let him vex you,
For he is neither devoted to the Creator nor to you.
If you wish to catch him by the foot,
You will find yourself holding his head.
Such is the measure of common people.
May wisdom be your share!
Fear men who secretly commit evil acts,
For they cause the world to constrict.
Do not trust and confide in an advisor,
For if he has friends and companions,
You might as well deem your affair lost
And divulged to the entire world.
Once your secret is exposed,
Your heart will grow restless.
Anger will set in, and you will long
For a wise man to appease your heart.

"Never draw attention to others' shortcomings.
The ones you seek to condemn will castigate you.
If your cravings surpass your wisdom, the sage
Will not count you as a member of the human race.
The king, world ruler, benevolent in all his endeavors,
Requires wisdom as his guide.
Heaven forbid for an irate, haughty man,
Who pursues quarrel and reprimand,
To stand by your side or to advise you as minister.
If you see pure men exhibit reverence and respect,
Keep anger and vengeance at bay.
A sensible man, a worshipper, does not place
Vanity above the splendor of the throne.

Avoid lengthy speeches, avoid bragging or boasting;
Listen carefully and commit to memory things of value.
Reflect before you attempt to capture someone.
Weigh the words you pronounce to wise men.
Always welcome others graciously
And with a good-humored and cheerful face.

"Do not treat with contempt a poor man who begs.
Do not offer a royal seat to a malevolent one.
Grant mercy and do not seek vengeance
With anyone who asks forgiveness for his crime.
Exercise justice for all; be their star of good fortune.
Happy is the generous and patient man!
When your enemy grows fearful,
He will attempt to deceive you with his words.
You must equip your troops, beat the timpani.
When the enemy is on the verge of yielding,
His hands growing weary, fling yourself into the scuffle.

"If he begs for peace and pledges to comply,
And if you do not detect falsehood in his heart,
Demand tribute from him, renounce vengeance,
And in this way you will spare his honor.
Embellish your mind with knowledge,
For the value of man lies in insight.
Since you know this for a fact,
Act according to this precept.

"Generosity will make you honored and loved,
Wisdom and justice will glorify you.
Keep in your soul your father's recommendations,
And pass them on to your son as a reminder of me.
When I leave my inheritance to my children,
I shall not harm anyone, and you will not
Ignore my injunctions or despise my words.
Do not forget your father's counsel.
Be inclined to do good and hold evil as wind.

"Five hundred years will pass; your power will wane.
Your descendants and members of your family
Will ignore my injunctions, abandon the path of wisdom
And knowledge, and refuse to listen to sage advice.

They will become infidels to the pact that binds them.
They will indulge in injustice, tyranny, and brutality.
They will unjustly torture their subjects
And treat Yazdan worshippers with scorn.
They will proudly put on the shirt of wickedness
And defile themselves with the cult of Ahriman.
At that time, all my work will be undone,
The faith that I have purified will be sullied,
My advice and last wishes will be null and void,
And the surface of my land will be an arid desert.

"I pray to the World Creator, the One apprised
Of the hidden and the visible, to keep you free from harm
So that you may leave a good name for yourself.
Yazdan and I will extol the one whose weft
Is wisdom and whose chain is justice,
The one who will not violate the agreement I made,
And will not convert to bitterness the honey I spread.

"Forty years and two months have passed
Since I placed the royal crown on my head.
I founded six great cities in the world,
Where the air exudes the fragrance of musk
And the water tastes pure and fresh.
I gave the name of Khorreh-yeh Ardeshir to one city:
Its air is healthy and its streams flow with milk;
Another city is Raameh-Ardeshir,
Which is on the way to Pars;
A third city is Ormazd-Ardeshir,
Where the winds renew the elderly:
It is the ornament of Khuzestan
And full of men, springs, wealth, and life;
Yet another is Barkeh-yeh Ardeshir,
Full of gardens, rose groves, and water basins;
Finally, two cities are in the land of Baghdad
And on the edge of the Euphrates River,
Full of fountains, animals, and plants.
You may call them Ardeshir's constructions.
When you hear talk of me, remember this.

"I have reached a point where I am ready for the grave.
Ask that my coffin be prepared, your throne be erected.

I have endured pain in the world, openly and privately.
Celebrate my manes with your just ways.
May you be victorious and happy on the throne!"

He speaks in this way and his fortune fades.
Alas, his head, his diadem, and his throne!
Such is the custom of the world,
To never reveal its mysteries.
Happy is the one who has no alliance to power.
He needs not descend from the throne.
We exhaust ourselves, we acquire wealth,
But neither man nor thing endures.
In the end, we are united with the dust
As we cover our cheeks with the shroud.
Let us all work for the common good, and let us not
Trample the earth nurturing wicked intentions.
Content is the one who, cup in hand,
Drinks to the memory of pious kings!
He will depart gradually like the wine in his cup
And fade away at the height of his happiness.

14 | In Praise of Yazdan and Sultan Mahmud

Praise to the Creator of the wonders of the world,
Giver of peace and happiness, a Being superior to all.
Source of every thing and end receiver of every thing.
Creator of sky, earth, time, and space, who brings
The world together in the most magnificent way;
The One whose existence is evident
In the tiniest, most insignificant thing and creature,
As well as in the highest realm of the firmament.
The sole Creator endowed with the ability
To identify every mystery, visible or invisible.

Praise to the prophet Muhammad and his disciples,
Pure and faithful men of effusive discourse!
Praise to the crown of the King of Kings,
Whose fortune shines upon the moon.
World master Mahmud, glorious and generous,
As he is the very essence of benevolence.
He spreads joy throughout the world

With his gifts of valor, grace, giving, and justice.
He is the owner of mace, sword, and hard work,
The owner of serenity, crown, and treasure.
Adored world master acquainted with virtue,
Beholden to Yazdan for possessing the crown.
He is wise, handsome, and eloquent,
Young in years but keeper of ancient wisdom.
Jupiter borrows its sheen from his glory.
Our greatest honor is to live in the shelter of his wing.
In times of war, the clatter of his troops rises to the sky.
In times of feast, he distributes jewels and gems all around.
His anger rattles a mountain to crumble into pieces
And the sky to tremble for the earth.

From father to father, he inherits kingship.
His being is the delight of heaven, Sun, and Moon.
May his name endure prominently in the world!
May his ending days be glorious!
I have extolled him at the start of my poem;
I have extolled his grandeur, his faith, and his path.
The crown borrows its sheen from him;
His good fortune shields him from harm.
Pure men respect and revere him
Since he ascended to the status of world king.

The sky's clarity is a result of his good fortune.
The earth is the foundation of his glorious throne.
In times of battle, he is a warring elephant;
In times of feast, he is as infinite as the sky in loyalty.
The thought of him brightens moments of revelry
As every wave rises from the sea of his existence.

In times of hunt, he chases princes and rulers.
Animals, wild and tame, bolt at the sight of him.
The sound of his mace on the day of battle
Tears to shreds the lion's heart and the leopard's skin.
May his head remain young and his heart just!
May the world never be deprived of his crown!

Now, let us turn to the kingdom of Shahpoor.
Let us speak of banquet, feast, and wine.

PART TWENTY–FOUR

From the Thirty-Year-and-Two-Month
Reign of Shahpoor, Son of Ardeshir
to the Sixty-Year Reign
of Bahraam the Hunter

I. The Thirty-Year-And-Two-Month Reign of Shahpoor, Son of Ardeshir

1 | Shahpoor Ascends the Throne and Advises the Army Leaders

Once Shahpoor takes his seat on the throne of justice
And places the world-illuminating crown on his head,
Wise, powerful, and learned men gather at his court.

King Shahpoor addresses them to say,
"O illustrious assembly, O wise advisors and noblemen,
I am the pure, legitimate son and heir of Ardeshir.
I am a seeker of knowledge, eager to learn.
Listen carefully to my commands,
And do not breach your loyalty to me.
Study everything I have to say, and do not hesitate
To call me out if you detect any falsehood.
When I observe the path that leads
To either prosperity or ruin, I see two options:
One is a king, world guardian,
Manager of the treasury, vast or small.
If a king is just and gifted with a fortunate path,
Wisdom will watch over him for sure;
Wisdom draws close to him as a well-wisher
And raises his head above dark, foreboding clouds.
His only desire will be for justice
And insight to calm his soul.

"The other is the man who makes use of his intellect
To prosper while maintaining himself on a just path.
His wisdom leads him to appreciate the Creator.
Happy is the wise and pious man!
The throne befits the insightful one,
For gold has no value next to wisdom.
A happy man is a wealthy man,

But a greedy heart, is a dwelling choked up by smoke.
The more we desire, the more we worry.
Better work hard and discard the fruits of desire.
Seek a life of honor and serenity.
Run away from pernicious men.
Those who lack wisdom will extend
Their hands to grab the possessions of others.
I feel for you an affection vaster than the starry sky.
Without fail, I shall maintain toward you the rules
That the powerful King Ardeshir established long ago.
I shall ask only one dirham out of thirty of farmers
So that I may give a portion to my army.

"As for me, I own cities and a full treasury;
I own courage, humanity, and established power.
I ask nothing of others, for a foe will gladly
Turn to friend for gifts offered.
You will always have access to me.
My heart is full of empathy for justice seekers.
I shall dispatch men with knowledge of world affairs
To every corner to instruct me on what is happening.
I shall ask only for blessings and nothing else
From the wise man of pure faith."

Noblemen, great and small, rise in unison,
Pronounce kind words, pay homage to Shahpoor,
And sprinkle chrysolite on his throne.
The customs of King Ardeshir blossom again,
And young and old alike rejoice.

2 | The War of Shahpoor With the Rumis

News spreads that the throne of the King of Kings
Is vacant, that the wise King Ardeshir is dead
And has abandoned his crown and throne to Shahpoor.
A great tumult rises on the borders, stirring
Territories from the land of Keydafeh[12] to Rum.

At the news, King Shahpoor prepares timpani,

◇◇◇◇◇◇◇◇◇◇◇◇◇
12 Keydafeh: Queen of Andalusia.

Gathers his army, and sends troops and banner
To the gates of Paloyeneh[13] without loaded camels.

An army advances from the land of Keydafeh
To obscure the sun with stirring dust.
Another exits Paloyeneh,
Led by a mighty chief named Bezanoosh,
A proud horseman, renowned and of brilliant mind,
Honored by the Caesar, skillful with noose.

As the drumming of timpani rises on both sides,
This glory-seeking warrior emerges from the army core.
At the same time, out of the Persian army,
Advances Garshaasp the lion, illustrious warrior,
Who in battle is a mighty elephant.
They fall upon each other, raising dust to the stars.
After much time and effort,
Neither one can overcome the other.

The two hosts charge like two mountains.
The sound of timpani and the shouts of men resound
On both sides, and the bold Shahpoor winces in his position.
The din of clarions and Indian bells shakes the sky.

Timpani are attached to the backs of elephants;
The racket of horses echoes for two miles.
The earth rattles, dust clouds form,
The spears of battle shimmer like flames,
And men retaining their senses are convinced
That the clouds drop showers of stars.
Any tongue that is united with wisdom
Can only utter the name of the Creator.

The valiant Bezanoosh is seized from the army center,
His heart swelling with blood.
Ten thousand Rumis are killed
In the line of battle in Paloyeneh;
One thousand six hundred are captured,
And the heart of the Rumi host fills with grief.

The Caesar sends an intelligent man to Shahpoor,

◇◇◇◇◇◇◇◇◇◇◇◇◇◇
13 Paloyeneh: Unclear location, but in the land of Rum.

Son of Ardeshir, to tell him, "How can you
Shed so much blood before our Supreme Judge?
Are your actions driven by the acquisition of gold?
What will you say on the day of judgment
When asked to give an account?
What excuse will you have before the Creator?
I shall send assigned tribute to ease human suffering.
Upon complying and paying due taxes,
I shall surrender numerous relatives as hostages.
It is only fair that you exit Paloyeneh,
At which time I shall send you anything you may desire."

Shahpoor remains until the Caesar sends tribute
And royalty fees in ten bags of buffalo skin,
Along with one thousand slaves and Rumi servants,
And an abundance of luxurious and plush brocade.

He is stationed in Paloyeneh for seven days,
Then withdraws from the Rumi territory
To advance toward Ahvaz.
He erects a great city named Shahpoor,
Working on it for the duration of one year,
Drawing on much effort and vast treasure.

At the gate of Khuzestan, he builds a beautiful town
For the Rumi prisoners, through which everyone passes.
In Pars, he founds another clean and beautiful city.
He erects the Kohan-Dej castle of Nishapur[14]
And completes it on the twenty-fifth day of the month.
Everywhere, he is accompanied by Bezanoosh,
Listening attentively to his words.

In Shushtar,[15] there is a river so vast
No fish can cross its width.
He says to Bezanoosh, "As a surveyor,
Could you build here a bridge similar to a rope?
We will one day return to the earth,
But the bridge will remain as testimony
To the technology given to us by the Creator.
You may draw from my treasury the necessary funds

◇◇◇◇◇◇◇◇◇◇◇◇◇◇
14 Kohan-Dej: A fort that houses the royal administrative offices.
15 Shushtar: A city in the province of Khuzestan.

To construct such a bridge one thousand cubits[16] long.
You may execute great works in this land,
Applying the science of Rumi learned men.
When you complete the bridge, return home,
Live in joy and security for the rest of your days,
And far from harm and from the hand of Ahriman."

The valiant Bezanoosh gets down to work
And in three years completes the bridge.
At that point, he leaves Shushtar and returns home.

3 | Shahpoor Communicates His Last Wishes to His Son Ormazd

King Shahpoor carries on,
His reign full of justice and wisdom,
His star and royal throne powerful.

After thirty years and two months,
His majesty and glory are on the decline.
He calls to his side Ormazd and says to him,
"The once verdant grass is now a dull yellow.
Maintain an awakened, alert mind,
And take governance of the world.
Always rule with a sense of justice.
Try not to place your trust in the kingdom.
Read the book of Jamsheed day and night.
Always act with virtue and integrity.
Be the shelter of the needy
And the glory of brave and noble men.
Renounce attaching yourself to dinars,
And always exercise generosity.
Dispense justice, and dwell in happiness.
If you wish good fortune to be on your side,
Do not aggrandize a small injury.
Pay close attention to my advice,
For it is the same advice handed to me by Ardeshir."

◊◊◊◊◊◊◊◊◊◊◊◊◊
16 Cubit: An ancient measure of length equivalent to the distance between the hand and elbow.

He utters these words, his cheeks blanch,
And the young man's heart fills with grief.
What do you expect from this passing dwelling?
Why should you take pride in your name?
Why should you expend yourselves to acquire wealth?
Ultimately, your part is a narrow casket, and that is that.
Another will come to enjoy the fruits of your labor.
Your son, your close friends, your allies will forget you.
You will inherit a share of curses and injuries.
Instead of an antidote, you will succumb to poison.
Turn to Yazdan, dispenser of good, and measure your words.
Furthermore, let us salute the prophet
And set a crown upon the pulpit of faith.

II. The One-Year-and-Two-Month Reign of Ormazd, Son of Shahpoor

1 | The Rule of Ormazd

Now I shall cast light on the throne of King Ormazd,
Bright as the inauguration of Ormazd day.[17]
Though he rules well and with fairness,
He is condemned with a short reign.

As he takes his place on the royal throne,
Wolf and sheep drink from the same source.
He says, "O illustrious, wise, noble, worldly men,
You have accomplished many mighty deeds!
Since Yazdan, Giver of virtue, has brought me joy
And adorned my head with the royal crown,
I shall make every effort to spread kindness.
Happy is the man who follows his father's advice!
With benevolence, I shall make you loyal friends
In the hopes that you withhold no secret from me.
The unruly character of a defiant, disagreeable man
Will steer him down the wrong path,
Where his needs will never be satisfied.
He will be the target of the sword of envy
And the everlasting mockery of providence.
On the other hand, the one who blushes at work,
Is content with a life of discomfort and poverty.
The heart of a vulgar man is an open door to greed.
Guard yourselves against his kind.
And if you do not find wisdom in a man,
Keep clear of his door for as long as you live.
The royal throne and crown will endure

◇◇◇◇◇◇◇◇◇◇◇◇◇
17 Ormazd day: In the ancient Persian solar calendar, each day had the name
of a deity instead of a number. Each name evoked a concept. The division
then was not based on a seven-day week but on a thirty-day month.

Through wisdom, tradition, and purpose.

"Revive your hearts with insight and reason,
And avoid hateful, vengeful acts.
Wisdom is like water; knowledge is like the earth.
These two elements are always connected.
Do not be surprised if a king's heart
Detaches itself from benevolence and dims.
May all my subjects live in bliss!
May they continue to worship the Creator!
May wisdom be my guide in all my endeavors!
A sage who speaks of the king
With a virtuous man must weigh his words,
For compassionate words never grow old.
Always choose gentle and gracious discourse.
No one listens to wicked language.
The king's heart will see into your secrets,
And his ear will listen to your voice.
The man who knows how to speak and to listen
Once proclaimed that walls have ears."

The assembly blesses the pure, awakened king.
The men in the noble gathering scatter,
Happy to live in the shelter of the tall cypress tree.
And this tree who welcomes learning
Follows the path of Shahpoor, son of Ardeshir,
As the entire world celebrates him.

What joy to see a just and generous king!
Ormazd governs fairly and with modesty,
But after some time, camphor replaces musk,
And the flower of Arghavan withers in the garden.

2 | Ormazd Turns Kingship Over to Bahraam, and His Last Wishes

Sensing that he has not the power to escape death,
His black eyes shed copious blood tears.
He asks for a carpet to be spread in the royal hall
And calls Bahraam, his proud son, to his side.

He says to him, "O child of pure race,
You shine with merit and knowledge.
Weakness has cast its eyes on me,
Forcing my cheeks to pale as white as my hair.
My cypress tree stature is now curved,
My roses have assumed the color of quince.
As soon as your day is here,
Take over governance of the world.
Always act with wisdom, never with malevolence.
Guard yourself from turning away justice-seekers,
And never forgive the crimes of oppressors.
Guard your tongue from aligning with falsehood
If you wish to render your crown brilliant.

"May wisdom guide you through life!
May decency be your advisor!
May your words be kind and your voice gentle!
May the Creator, Giver of victory, be your mate
And your subjects' hearts be your prey!
Renounce thoughts of vengeance and war.
Fend off cravings, they have a tendency to rule over you.
Do not give access to betrayers and ignorant men.
Shield your heart from them, as they will cause you harm.
Remember that a man deficient in decency
Has nothing good to offer you, and the one
With flowery speech does not merit your respect.

"Consider wisdom as your master, anger as your slave.
Do not treat a probing man with harshness.
Hold greed at bay, for it invites anger, fear, and need.
Remain always patient and upright,
And keep your heart away from perversity.
Take care that your fame never wanes,
For a man of ill repute will not access his desires.
Never deviate from the cautious, sensible path.
Your heart will repent if you make haste.
A slow resolution will bring just actions.
One must not digress from the path of duty.
The head of a patient man never heats up
As he rejects the superfluous.
But when patience surpasses all measure,
The man of heart will suspect apathy.

119

"Whoever is master of throne must turn to wisdom
To find the middle path between these two roads.
He must act neither with violence nor in weakness.
Best then to allow insight to guide your heart.
Pay heed to those who blame others;
They profit at the shah's expense and gain honor.
Do not seek to befriend the enemy,
No matter how eager his praise.
He is a green tree, but his fruit is poison,
And if you think you can grab him by the foot,
Your hand will come to hold his head.
Whether you are high or low,
Guard yourself against treachery.
Do not nurture evil thoughts in your heart,
For the fate of the deceptive man does not bode well.

"A king who breaks the terms of a treaty
Is the object of ridicule in every assembly.
Cultivate wisdom, an attribute that will help you
Prosper and will watch over your words and actions.
Wisdom will organize your wealth, crown, and host.
Wisdom will show you the rotations of Sun and Moon.
Refrain from attaching yourself
To opulence and material things.
This passing dwelling will end one day for you.
Take counsel only from wise men.
Keep the tradition of ancient kings.
Strike with terror evil men with your host.
Reflect deeply on causes and consequences.
An able speaker who, with ambition, praises
Undeserving men, seeks your ruin with his words.
Do not then keep them in your memory.
But do not consider highly a man who abstains
From fraising others, for the Creator appreciates acclaim
And renders powerless those who talk idly of others.

"Anyone who closes his eyes on faults and easily
Suppresses his anger will see his fortune advance.
But the one who is impatient will suffer.
Anyone who puts up a fight against
Turbulent ocean waves is not a sensible man.
May your heart be the bow and your tongue the arrow!

Do not take lightly my words. Expand your chest,
Hold your arm steady, and mark your target.
When your heart and tongue conform to the truth,
You may then speak to your heart's desire.
The one devoid of brain will communicate
Insincere intentions and insincere words.

"Anytime you find yourself asking for counsel,
Speak to your guide alone, outside of the gathering.
If you combine experience with good advice,
Your fortune will expand each day.
Your mind will be more discerning than your foe's,
And your heart, brain, and head will expand.
The advice of a man guided by desire will not benefit you.
If you have a friend with a cheerful disposition,
You will increase his happiness by helping him prosper.
But to your enemy, present a frowning and pale face.

"Fulfill the wishes of virtuous men.
They are the ones who will procure your wealth.
Free your soul and heart from envy,
For envy will plunge you into anguish
And provoke you to shed bitter tears of blood.
When a king exhibits greed and jealousy,
He will be subject to the blame of virtuous men.
I had no idea that I would be on the throne
For no more than one year and two months.
I thought I would be secure in my position
With the crown for many years to come.
But my time on earth has come to an end,
And you must cinch your waist in kingship."

The blessed scribe writes the king's last words,
Takes them, and the vizier places them before Ormazd.
The world master exhales a deep sigh,
And his ruby cheeks pale like a yellowing leaf.
The face of the world dims for Bahraam.
For forty days he sits beaten down, in mourning,
While the powerful throne remains vacant.

Such is the revolving sphere for as long as life exists,
At times full of grief and at times full of affection.

121

If you have sense, do not assume it is your friend.
As soon as it wills, it will split your skin to burst apart.

The night of Ormazd is upon us,
The first night of the winter month.
Let us end all discourse and raise a cup of wine.

III. The Three-Year-Three-Month-and-Three-Day Reign of Bahraam, Son of Ormazd

1 | Bahraam Ascends the Throne and Advises His Leaders

Now let us turn to Bahraam's crown
And a reign that shines light on the world
But only for a very short time.
He takes his place on the golden throne,
Heart and mind mourning the loss of his father.

Iran's noblemen present themselves at court,
Shedding tears and dressed in armor.
They invoke divine grace on him, saying,
"May you live for as long as the world exists!
The Kianian crown sits well upon your head,
And the kingly diadem you inherit belongs to you!
May your enemies' cheeks pale!
May your soul forget your grief!"

Bahraam replies, "O brave warriors and valiant riders,
Never extend a hand to hurt others,
Whether they are farmers or the king's subjects.
Remember that the revolving dome never stops
Its rotation, neither for servant nor for master.
Enchain the hand of greed;
Guard your earthly yearnings from ruling over you.
Desire debases a man and will invalidate his life.
It renders him as powerless as a wingless bird.
Anyone who abstains from evil acts
And from defiling himself with misdeeds
Will live happily and will depart from the world
Without having to fear Ahriman, a potent adversary.

"The king must be the protector of his people's wealth.
He must treat righteous men with favor and act as
A champion of faith, for faith is the diadem on his head.
There is no safer shelter than religion;
From it you draw your breath.
Happy is the one able to rule over himself!
In a moment of anger, he will not suffer, and his heart
Will remain noble and joyous in times of distress.
May the world never be vacant of wise men!
They never trample beneath their feet a fallen enemy,
For they march down the path of wisdom.

"Quarrel does not suit a seeker of glory.
Contain yourself, and avoid discord.
An army, farmers, and a lazy disposition
Will not lead you to attain your goals.
An idle man is a drowsy, indolent man
Who, when he wakes up, will have cause for regret.
If you speak kind words but act in evil ways,
You will gain neither praise nor access to paradise.
Always speak the truth;
Always act with kindness and virtue;
Do not break the hearts of honest men.
I own wealth and vast amounts of dinars,
Power, kingship, and a strong arm.
Enjoy and spend what you possess, and believe
That poor men have a share in our vast reserves.
My treasure chests are open to draw from,
And no one must be left in need."

2 | Bahraam Hands Over Governance to His Son and Dies

After some time passes over his kingship,
Bahraam's crowned head is quite suddenly
Gripped by the talons of the birds of death.
He has a son who charms dim hearts
And whose name is Bahraam, son of Bahraam.
He summons him, asks him to sit below his throne,
And says, "O young and verdant branch,

I have not enjoyed the throne for long.
May your life be blessed with good fortune!
The crown and my destiny have not been loyal to me.
Be merry, outspoken, and prosperous.
Spend your days and nights in joy and delights.
March down a path that guards you
From turning away in shame before Yazdan.

"The world is created to be reveled in
And not with the goal of accumulating wealth.
Enjoy, give abundantly, and repress your soul.
Yank out with your hands the roots of evil.
Make the world prosper with
Your just ways and your generosity.
Bring happiness to your subjects' hearts.
Human existence does not last forever,
Not for anyone, not even for a king or for a wise man."

In this way, Bahraam abandons the world to his son,
Who furnishes him with the residence of a tomb.
You best remember that this is not an arbitrary,
Wrongful move from the revolving dome of sky,
For what passes like a breath is nothing but wind.
Such has been the rotation of the firmament
Ever since it came into existence.
Why should you weary your soul with worry?
Why run around in search of the future?
Where are you going? What have you to say?
You cannot invent a story for the end of existence.
Let us not cease to speak of all this.
Though your mind is free from greed
And you are not burdened by old age,
Still, your dwelling will be a narrow coffin.

Nevertheless, since death has a wolf's nature,
I request a large cup of wine and a woman
Blessed with the stature of a cypress tree,
A silver body, and an amiable nature.
Let her be soft-spoken, exude the scent of jasmine,
A moon-faced beauty with rosy cheeks,
Bright as the sun, charming, and scented like musk.
My subjects will think wine and rosebud have merged.

If your joy is curtailed, you will feel a decline
In your wisdom and your very soul.

Now we shall tell the tale of Bahraam, son of Bahraam,
And discover what events develop in the field.

IV. The Nineteen-Year Reign of Bahraam, Son of Bahraam, His Rise to the Throne, His Advice to the Leaders, and His Death

Because of his father's death, Bahraam refrains
From placing the crown on his head for forty days.
Concerned leaders full of wisdom visit him
To convey their complaints and lamentations.
They sit before him, afflicted and in mourning,
Their cheeks pale, their lips blue.

One wise man of sound counsel rises
And presses the king to take his place on the throne.
For one week, he insists with fervor
Until Bahraam finally assumes the position.

The king rejoices on the royal seat, lowers the crown
On his head, according to Kianian custom, then salutes
The Creator, who illuminates the dazzling spinning dome,
Giver of wisdom and righteousness, Inhibitor of injustice
And decline, Master of Saturn and the rotating sphere,
Who demands justice and charity from earthly servants.

Then he says, "O pure sages and wise men,
Honor knowledge, hold yourselves close to kings,
And labor in the name of virtue.
Take part in the Iranian king's joys and glory.
Anyone honored by Yazdan with wealth,
Eloquence and power must always act
Guided by justice and generosity.
May the world prosper with truth and integrity.
Heaven forbid we live in oppression,
Heaven forbid we walk the path of transgression,
Or that our greedy nature leads us to amass riches.
I shall fill my treasury only for the sake of charity,
For the banner of the king must be virtue.

At the end of nineteen years of rule,
Life has cause to weep for him. Once worthy of the crown,
He becomes the eternal companion of the dust,
Inheriting a narrow coffin from this beautiful world.
His only choice is to retreat inside the shelter of a tomb.

Such is the law and the disposition of the world;
It always hides its deepest secrets from us.

V. The Four-Month Reign of Bahraam Bahraamian, His Rise to the Throne, and His Death

Bahraam Bahraamian is seated on the throne,
Armed with justice and generosity.
People scatter chrysoprase over him
And recognize him as the King of Kerman.

He says, "May the just Creator give me
A share of wisdom, justice, and good sense!
May I follow my father's example in virtue.
He was a shepherd herding kings as sheep.
May the beautiful and the fair color my thoughts!
This passing dwelling remains for no one.
May excellence and purity be my guides!
Let us turn toward integrity and stay loyal.
Let us be the guarantors of justice and liberty.
Good and bad will remain as memories of us.
Better then to sow only seeds of excellence."

After a period of four months,
The throne and crown shed bitter tears for him.
Bahraam feels the approach of death like a whale
About to snatch the rhinoceros and elephant as prey.
Handing over world governance to his son,
He says, "May Yazdan's grace steer your reign!
Deck yourself and drink abundantly.
Enjoy life and give charity. Guard yourself from
Spoiling the good fortune of your crown and throne."

Kingship and fate having abandoned Bahraam,
He surrenders his crown and throne to Nersi.

Such is the way of this passing world.
Man in his eagerness does not count his breaths.

O auspicious cupbearer, bring me ruby-colored wine.
The poet has crossed the threshold of his sixty-third year.

VI. The Nine-Year Reign of Nersi, Son of Bahraam, His Rise to the Throne, His Advice to His Son, and His Death

Once Nersi takes his seat on the ivory throne
And dons the glorious shining crown on his head,
Noblemen approach him with offerings,
Dressed in mourning attire in respect to the father.

The king utters blessings over them and says,
"O dear friends, endowed with a sense of justness,
Know that this is the will of the Creator,
Who lavished me with, among the world's virtues,
Intelligence, humility, courage, prudence, and eloquence.
If my star of fortune protects me from adversity,
I shall bestow happiness upon you all.
Wise men are my friends. Learn wisdom from them.
Treat them as if you share your skin with them.
Learn from powerful men acts of kindness.
Courage is a consequence of insight,
And the brave man is worthy of praise.
Anyone who flees from the battlefield
Will strip himself of glory and honor.
Cowardice will weigh down on his mind.
A heavy mind and a petty heart go together."

Nersi rules cautiously for nine years,
Marking his place in the world with his words.
In the end, his days pull him down, his fortune dims,
The steel helmet on his head softens like wax.
Ormazd, the son of the illustrious king, bright
As the moon on a dark night, a tulip in the midst
Of verdant greenery, runs to the father's bedside.

Nersi says to him, "O my dear son,
You have enjoyed only favors from life.

Guard yourself from causing harm.
You are the soul of Nersi,
And the Bahraamian fortune belongs to you.
You are worthy of the crown,
You are the ornament of the throne.
Heaven forbid that, despite your tall stature,
Your majestic mien and limbs,
Despite your incomparable knowledge,
The crown would have cause to weep on your account
And the hearts of our people would be consumed by grief.
Govern the world according to royal custom
Just as you have learned from your virtuous father.
May your mind and your heart be always happy!
May your power and your treasure prosper!
Ultimately, your days will end as well,
And the turning wheel will trample you.
Walk the journey in a way that you can reply
When the Creator interrogates you
And your responses assure you a happy fate."

With these words, Nersi covers his face, draws a deep sigh,
And it is as if he never lived and never sat on the throne.

This is the way of the world.
Its greatest mystery is that we can only expect grief from it.

VII. The Nine-Year Reign of Ormazd, Son of Nersi, His Rise to the Throne, and His Death

Once the powerful Ormazd accedes the throne,
The wolf's claws hold back from catching its prey.
The king provides the world with a sense of security,
And Ahriman withdraws its wily hand.

Ormazd begins by paying homage to the Creator:
"The almighty, omniscient foster parent of all beings,
Creator of day and night and of the revolving sky;
Creator of Saturn, Mars, and Sun; Giver of victory
And majesty; Giver of the heart who worships justice
And of the diadem of the King of Kings.

"May we always turn to justice
So that our subjects' hearts may fill with joy!
Lowly, ignorant men will never be subject to praise.
Distance yourself from them as much as you can.
Do not seek advice from a malevolent man.
If you require guidance, summon a virtuous man.
If you praise others only to collect acknowledgment,
No pious man will call you generous,
For if you act to receive something in return,
You are neither big-hearted nor pious.
If the one on the receiving end fails to express gratitude,
You might as well not give him anything.

"The harsh man must tremble, for he is friendless.
A sensible man will not take guidance
From someone who acts weakly.
If you charge an unwise man with your affairs,
You might as well forgo world possession
And the loyalty of men.

"Try not to consider yourself a powerful man
And give into pride once you sit on the throne.
When a man of evil nature becomes poor and despised,
He sees it only as the consequence of misfortune.
He passes years being lazy and complaining of his fate
Without asking advice and lacking wisdom and virtue.
Once he loses his wealth, he is devoid of soul,
Head, heart, good sense, value, and faith.
He is good for nothing, only to perform evil acts,
Unhappy with the lot given to him by the Just Giver.
May you live in happiness, day and night!
May your enemies' souls and bodies perish!"

The noblemen praise him as world king.

Once the sky rotates over his head for nine years,
His face, which resembles the flower of the pomegranate,
Turns the color of a yellow flower,
His crowned head feels the anxiety of death,
And he expires without a son at his bedside.
This illustrious, soft-spoken king
Dies and passes this ancient world with a sigh.

For forty days they mourn,
Leaving the throne abandoned and vacant.

VIII. The Seventy-Year Reign of Shahpoor, Son of Ormazd, Named Shahpoor Zolaktaaf[18]

1 | The Birth of Shahpoor, Son of Ormazd, Forty Days After His Father's Death, and His Rise to the Throne

With the throne unoccupied for some time,
The heads of noblemen fill with concern.

The grand vizier examines the royal chambers
And finds a moon-faced beauty with tulip cheeks.
The edge of her eyelids are as sharp as Kabuli daggers;
The two curls of her hair twist like Babylonian script,
Forming chains braided one inside the other,
Rolled in knots and raised by the ends.

This fairy-faced queen hides a child in her womb,
And everyone rejoices. The vizier seats her joyously
On the Kianian throne and lowers a crown over her head,
Which they sprinkle with gold and silver.
After a short while, the queen gives birth
To a boy as dazzling as the sun.

A poet bard, son of a sage, who recites words borrowed
From tradition, has faithfully recounted to me this story.

The child is named Shahpoor.
He is celebrated with a splendid feast.
It is as if divine majesty shines in him
And the shadow of wisdom's banner shelters him.

◇◇◇◇◇◇◇◇◇◇◇◇
18 Zolaktaaf: Name for Shahpoor II; meaning he pierces the shoulder blades of his
captives.

For forty days, music resounds at court, wine is poured.
Then a royal throne is decked, and the heroes
Of golden belts suspend above it a golden crown.
The little prince is nourished with milk,
Swaddled in silken fabrics, and placed for forty days
On his glorious father's seat below the crown.
Noblemen salute him as king and scatter jewels over him.

There is a wise man named Shahrooy,
Insightful and of cheerful nature.
He sits on a golden seat but acts as the king's humble
Servant and a valuable guide to people in all things.
He governs the world with justice and prudence.
He expands the treasury and the army;
He decks his palace and his throne.

Five years pass in this way, during which time
The child acquires dignity and strength.

One night, the king sits in Ctesiphon,
With Shahrooy standing before him,
At the hour when the sun descends
And the dim veil of night spreads.
A sound of loud voices is heard by the River Arvand.[19]

The child says to the wise man, "What is happening?"

The wise man replies,
"O valiant, benevolent, auspicious young prince,
Merchants and hardworking men return from work
To their homes, and as they cross the narrow bridge
Over the river, each, fearing to be pushed
In the water, cries out as he runs across."

Shahpoor declares to his illustrious advisors,
"We must design and construct another bridge
So that there is a separate path to come and one to go,
So that my subjects, whether servants or warriors,
Need not be exposed to such worry every time.
We must draw much wealth from my treasury
For the completion of this project."

◇◇◇◇◇◇◇◇◇◇◇◇◇
19 River Arvand: Tigris River.

The wise men are delighted to see the young tree
Grow more verdant, and the grand chamberlain
Asks for the building of a second bridge
In accordance with the king's orders.

His mother's heart rejoices with the affair.
She brings many learned men to him,
And soon the child makes such fast progress
In his studies that he surpasses his masters.

At the age of seven years, he engages in sports,
Participates in wrestling, and learns to play polo.
At the age of eight years, he observes
The customs of the throne and crown.
It is as if he is King Bahraam himself:
He carries himself with royal grace
And settles on Estakhr as his place of residence,
Following the example of his glorious ancestors,
His noble family, proud and virtuous.

2 | Taaer, the Arab, Abducts Nersi's Daughter and Marries Her

After some time, the world-illuminating crown
Reaches the heights of its splendor.
Taaer, the Ghassanian,[20] of lion heart,
Whose sword is so mighty,
It would inspire fear in the sky,
Arrives in Ctesiphon with a vast host, warriors
From Rum, Pars, Bahrain, Kurdistan, and Kadesia.

He destroys and devastates the land.
Who could ever have the strength to resist him?
When he hears of Nooshah, the king's aunt,
As beautiful as spring, he enters her palace,
And this coarse, ignorant man takes her prisoner.
The city of Ctesiphon fills with reports of his actions.

◇◇◇◇◇◇◇◇◇◇◇◇◇
20 Ghassanian: An Arab tribe living in Sham, Syria, which at the time was part of the Rumi Empire.

After one year at the side of Taaer,
Nooshah's heart floods with anxiety.
She gives birth to his daughter, as beautiful as the moon.
She resembles Nersi on his throne and with his crown.

Taaer names his daughter Malekeh,[21]
For he finds her worthy of kingdom.

At the age of twenty-six,
Shahpoor is a valiant king, as bright as the sun.
He goes to the plain, reviews his army,
And selects twelve thousand brave warriors,
Each riding a camel of winded hooves.
Ahead of them march one hundred guides.

The heroes, the king's servants, climb on
Their horses, handling the reins with one hand.
In this way, Shahpoor marches toward
The Ghassanian king, Taaer, a voracious lion.

Shahpoor kills countless enemy warriors,
A great number take flight, including Taaer.
The sound of blows administered and received
Echoes through the land, and the Persians
Successfully seize a number of Taazian captives.

Taaer's warriors hide in a fort city in Yemen.
The cries of children, women, and men echo all around.

Shahpoor takes a host so vast that ants and flies
Cannot find a path through the multitude.
He finds Taaer with his troops in the fortress.
He attacks him and blocks his way of escape.

They fight for the duration of one month,
Day and night, and the warriors inside the fortress
Run out of supplies and provisions.

◇◇◇◇◇◇◇◇◇◇◇◇◇◇
21 Malekeh: Meaning Queen.

3 | Malekeh Falls in Love With Shahpoor

One early morning, the valiant Shahpoor
Climbs on his horse and departs full of ardor,
A bow in his hand, dressed in a black coat of mail,
A shiny black banner billowing over his head.

Malekeh observes, from atop the ramparts,
And sees the banner of the illustrious leader.
Her cheeks are like rose petals, her hair is black,
Her lips are as red as blood and exhale the scent of musk.

Sleep and rest evade the beauty.
Her heart full of love, she says to her nursemaid,
"This powerful, sun-faced king,
This vengeance-seeker is the blood of my essence.
He represents to me everything in my world.
Take a message from me to Shahpoor.
He came to battle, but I wish to invite him to feast.
Tell him,
        'I am of your race, the race of the valiant Nersi.
        I am your ally in vengeance,
        For I am your relative, daughter of Nooshah.
        If you wish to marry me, I will give you this castle.
        If you choose to conquer the castle, I am yours.
        Make arrangements with my nursemaid,
        And give your royal word as pledge.'"

The nursemaid replies, "I shall obey your command.
I shall bring you the news as soon as I obtain it."

Night takes possession of the world,
And darkness seizes the earth from sea to sea,
Staining it pitch black, the mountains in hues of indigo.
Stars twinkle like three hundred thousand lanterns
Suspended from the eighth sky.
The nursemaid departs, shaking with fear,
For her heart breaks at the thought of Taaer.

At the king's tent pavilion,
She approaches one of the guides and says,
"If you assist me in an audience with the king

I shall reward you with a crown and a ring."

The discreet and shrewd man leads her to the king.
The nursemaid enters, sweeps the floor with her lashes,
And recites the words of her mistress.

The king is delighted with the message.
He smiles and offers her one thousand dinars,
Two bracelets, a necklace, a diadem,
And a veil of Chini brocade. He replies,
"Relate many kind words to your beautiful mistress.
Tell her,
          'I swear by the Sun and Moon,
          By the belt of Zoroaster, by kingdom and crown,
          That never will she hear a hint of refusal from me.
          Never will I be unfaithful to her.
          I shall accept her and promise
          To surrender treasury and army to her!'"

The nursemaid leaves the tent enclosure
And runs to the fort of the silvery cypress tree,
To whom she assures that Venus
Is now the welcomed companion of the sun.
She describes in detail to the dazzling moon
The stature and mien of King Shahpoor.

4 | Malekeh Entrusts the Fortress to Shahpoor, and the Death of Taaer

As the sun's crown fades on the side of dusk
And raven shades stretch across the earth,
Malekeh reaches for the treasury key.
The king's minister opens the food supplies
To catch hold of some jugs of wine.
He sends provisions, an abundance of wine, and
Perfumes scented with narcissus and fenugreek
To all the noblemen of the castle,
Valiant heroes and leaders tested in battle.

Malekeh summons the cupbearer
And speaks softly to him: "You are to serve tonight.

Give Taaer only pure wine.
Make sure that no one is holding an empty cup.
May they all be inebriated and fall into a slumber!"

The cupbearer replies, "I am your slave.
I live to execute your command."

As the sun pales in the western horizon and
The dark night expels day, Taaer asks for royal wine
And drinks to the health of the Ghassanians.

After some time, he grows fatigued,
And they march off to their chambers.

Malekeh commands the servants to speak softly
And to quietly open the castle gates.

This is what Shahpoor is waiting for.
He had listened disapprovingly to the voices
Of the drunken men, but once he spots the light
Of the candle beneath the castle door, he says,
"I shall now be united with good fortune!"

He offers the moon-faced lady
Lovely accommodations in his tent pavilion.
He gathers his host, selects glorious and brave warriors,
Takes warring infantrymen and horsemen,
Enters the castle and engages in fighting
And killing to avenge ancient hostilities.

Taaer's army is with him in the fort.
Many are knocked out in their intoxication,
Others who are sleeping awaken astonished
And instantly engage in battle on every side.
None of them turns his back in cowardice,
And the King of Iran kills a great number of them.

Taaer falls captive to enemy hands, his head bare,
Advancing toward Shahpoor reluctantly.
The castle, its contents, and many foes
Submit to the clutches of the Iranian king.

This night passes, and in the morning,

141

When the sun parades its golden headdress,
A turquoise throne is placed solemnly in the castle,
According to custom, and visitors are granted an audience.

Once everyone leaves, Malekeh, a spring rose,
Approaches Shahpoor, a diadem of garnet on her head,
Dressed in lush, jewel-encrusted Chini brocade.
The king seats her before him on a golden throne
And calls to his side the shackled Taaer.

The latter arrives, head bare.
His glance falls on his illustrious daughter.
He understands that she is the author of the ruse
And says to Shahpoor, "O King of free men,
Reflect on the way my child behaved toward me.
Expect a similar treachery from her as your mate."

Shahpoor replies to the man of ill repute,
"When you seized Bahraam's daughter
From the women's chamber, you dishonored our family
And reignited the dormant hostilities."

He commands the executioner to strike him
On the neck and to burn his body.
Taaer's head is wretchedly severed off.

Shahpoor forbids the Taazian prisoners
To ever utter Taaer's name in his presence.
And if they do, he reprimands them
By dislocating their shoulders.
The world is stunned by his deeds,
Which lead the Arabs to call him Zolaktaaf.

From there he returns to Pars,
And the entire world pays homage to him.
He forgives anyone who begs for mercy.
Those who owe tribute and royalty fees are quick to pay.

In this way, the revolving dome spins for some time,
Until it shows Shahpoor a different face.

5 | Shahpoor Travels to Rum as a Merchant and Is Captured by the Caesar

Despite his crown, treasure, and possessions,
Shahpoor's soul, one day, grows weary of life.
As a third portion of night passes,
He summons astrologers and questions them
On his throne's future, his hardships,
And the happiness that may or may not be his share.

The astrologers bring their astrolabes
And make projections relative to his state of peace.
They study indications of threats to his kingship.
They study the prosperity and glory
Bestowed upon him by the Divine Creator.

After having made their observations, one of them says,
"O virtuous world master of serene heart,
A treacherous and painful affair threatens you,
Yet no one dares speak of it."

Shahpoor asks, "O truth-seeking man,
What means do I have to escape a calamity
And to evade the crush of misfortune?"

The astrologer replies, "O King, no one is able
To escape the spinning of this unstable wheel,
Not even by means of either valor or wisdom,
No matter how informed or belligerent he may be.
All that is about to occur is certain to unfold.
Let us not argue with the rotations of the sky."

The noble king says, "Yazdan is our shelter
In misfortune, Creator of the firmament,
Creator of the powerful and the weak."

The king spreads justice over his kingdom.
A period of happiness ensues, free from grief.
But once his land prospers through his efforts,
He sets his sight on Rum, wishing to go and assess
The Caesar's splendor, his army, his treasure and power.

Shahpoor opens up to his just and wise minister.
He confides in him his secret thoughts and adds,
"Govern this realm with justice,
For justice will bring you happiness."

The king asks for ten rows of beautiful camels,
Each to be led by a camel driver.
He loads many of them with silk and jewels
And thirty more camels with dinars.
He departs full of worry from his prosperous land
And continues in this way until he reaches Rum.

He finds a village inhabited by farmers and townspeople.
He enters the house of a landowner to ask for lodging.

The master of the house greets him graciously, saying,
"Never have we received such an eminent guest!"

Shahpoor spends one night there.
He dines and distributes gifts, which the owner
Receives with effusive blessings and praise.

In the early morning hours, he loads up the luggage
And travels as fast as the wind to the Caesar's palace.

At the door, he salutes the guard and offers him gifts.
The guard asks, "Tell me who you are, for you bear
The stature and the countenance of a king."

Shahpoor replies, "I am a simple, honest man from Pars.
I come from Djaz[22] to trade, hoping to see the Caesar.
I have a caravan full of furs and fine cotton.
May the ruler accept from his humble servant
Anything that pleases him, whether merchandise,
Jewels, or weapons, to be secured in his treasury.
I shall be delighted to have him accept my goods.
The rest I shall sell for gold and silver.
The Caesar is my shelter, and I fear nothing.
I shall buy all that I need in the land of Rum
To take with me to the flourishing land of Iran."

◇◇◇◇◇◇◇◇◇◇◇◇◇
22 Djaz: Name of a region in ancient Rum.

The old man leaves his post in haste, enters
The chambers of the Caesar, and recounts the affair.

The Caesar commands the curtain be raised
To allow the merchant to make his way to him.

Once in the Caesar's presence,
Shahpoor salutes him in a proper way.
The Rumi ruler looks him over
And surrenders his eyes and his heart to him.
He asks for banquet and wine, as well as for the palace
To be decked and everyone at court to be dismissed.

There is, in the land of Rum, an Iranian,
Experienced, though unjust and vile.
He says to the Caesar, "O proud emperor,
Learn something new from me in secret.
I suspect this notable merchant and brocade vendor
To be none other than Shahpoor, King of Kings.
My assumption is based on his speech, his stature,
His royal features, and his refined manners."

The Caesar is troubled by these words.
His eyes dim at the sight of the king.
He places a watch guard to keep an eye on him
And reveals his secret thoughts to no one.

Once intoxicated, King Shahpoor rises,
But the Caesar glances at him.
The guard approaches, seizes him, and says,
"What marvel! You are Shahpoor,
Son of Ormazd, son of Nersi!"

He takes him to the women's palace and ties him up.
No one may escape the snare of misfortune,
Not even the bravest man.
Why waste time asking astrologers to make
Calculations since their knowledge serves no one.

A candle is burned before the drunken king
Who is sewn miserably inside donkey skin.
Everyone considers him the most wretched man
For having traded his royal throne for donkey skin.

They throw him in a small, obscure room.
They bolt the door with a padlock
And hand over the key to the mistress who is
To guard Shahpoor's body thus dressed in foreign pelt.

They tell the Caesar's wife, "Give him enough
Water and bread to keep him alive.
If he lives for some time longer, he will then
Understand the value of his crown and throne.
He will cease to long for the Caesar's throne,
As his lineage originates from a different race."

The Caesar's wife closes the door to this room.
She resides in another wing of the palace,
But she has a treasurer, a moon-faced woman,
Who is her advisor on all matters and who remembers
Her lineage from a long line of Iranian nobility.

The Caesar's wife entrusts her with the key and
The guard of the valiant Shahpoor entrapped in skin.

The same day, the Caesar sets his army in motion
And travels from the land of Rum to Iran's border,
Where he asks his troops to draw the sword of vengeance.

The Rumi ruler takes back Iranian prisoners,
For these men do not have a leader.
He leaves the land of Iran
Deserted of men, women, and children.
He plunders all the wealth, great and small.

No one has news of Shahpoor Shah,
His whereabouts, whether he is dead or alive.
All of Iran sheds tears on the deeds of the Rumis
As the uninhabited empire falls into decline.

Countless Iranians convert to Christianity
And present themselves to bishops.

6 | A Young Lady Liberates Shahpoor

Some time passes.
The Iranian population and the troops scatter.
The Caesar holds Shahpoor in Rum,
Awarding him no freedom, day or night.
The young female guarding him, being of
Iranian descent, is miserable for his condition.
She weeps inconsolably over his state of torture,
Thus incased in donkey skin.
Her heart is consumed by pity.

One day she says to him,
"O handsome young man, who are you?
Have no fear confiding in me.
Your graceful body is trapped in donkey skin,
And you can enjoy neither rest nor sleep.
You were a lofty cypress tree haloed by the moon,
Your head covered with musk-black curls.
Now your tall stature is curved over,
And your elephant-like body is a bent reed.
My heart bleeds for you, day and night.
My two eyes profusely shed tears for you.
What are you thinking in your wretched state?
Why do you not share with me your secret?"

Shahpoor replies, "O moon-faced beauty,
If you are moved by affection for me,
I ask you to pledge an oath that you will
Never disclose my secret to my enemies.
Furthermore, promise to always remember
The weak and withering state you find me in.
Then I shall share with you my predicament."

She swears: "By the Just Creator,
By the clerics' belt that loops seventy-two times,
By the soul of the Messiah and the mourning of the cross,
By the King of Iran, the fear and affection he inspires,
That I shall never share your secret with anyone,
And I shall never attempt to benefit from it."

Shahpoor confides in her, leaving her in the dark

147

With neither the good nor the bad.
Then he adds, "If you execute my command,
If your heart is the guarantor of my secret,
I shall lift your head above the heads of queens.
I shall place the world at your feet.
At the hour of dinner, bring me warm milk,
And get to work, slowly, very slowly.
With the milk soften the donkey leather,
Which one day will be the object of many a tale.
Many years after my death,
Countless wise men will recount the story."

The young lady asks for milk, discreetly and quietly.
Upon her return, she places the pot over a strong fire.
She then takes it to Shahpoor without uttering a word.

After the span of two weeks, the donkey casing
Is finally mollified, and Shahpoor can free himself,
With a bleeding heart and an aching body.

He secretly tells the young lady,
"O pure maiden, you are foreseeing and kind.
You must now make use of all your acumen to leave
The land of Rum. May it be forever cursed!"

The young lady replies, "Tomorrow at dawn,
All the noblemen will march off to a feast
That draws everyone to it, men, women, and children.
When the Caesar's wife marches from city to plain,
The palace will be deserted. I shall then design
A scheme to flee without cause to fear misfortune.
I shall happily bring to you horse, mace, and bow and arrow."

Shahpoor extols the valiant and foreseeing young lady.

After a moment of deep contemplation,
She selects two noble steeds from the stables.
She allows reflection to fortify her intent
And wisdom to guide her heart.

At the moment the sun sets and
Night deploys its head beneath a pitch-black veil,
Shahpoor's soul fills with worry at the thought

Of the next day and the actions of the young lady.

But when the sun appears in the house of Leo,
When day takes over and slumber disappears,
Everyone in the city departs to rejoice in feast.
Happy are the ones who can take part in revelry!

The young lady heads toward the house,
Having taken the necessary precautions.
Once alone and mistress of the castle, she feels
As if she has a lion's heart and a leopard's claws.
She leads the two noble horses out of the stables,
Grabs the riding armor that she had selected,
And takes as many dinars as she deems necessary,
Along with pearls, garnets, and all sorts of gems.

Once everything is ready for the departure
And night descends, they execute their escape.

7 | Shahpoor and His Rescuer Run Away to the Land of Iran

The two happy beings ride off to Iran
With peace and contentment in their hearts, traveling
Day and night without wasting time on food or sleep.

In this manner, they leave Rum by way of a land
Covered in brushwood until they reach a city.
Horses and riders are exhausted from the race.
Shahpoor searches for a place to rest.
On the road, he finds a cheerful town,
Full of gardens, pavilions, and festival halls.
He enters, body shattered by the exertion
Of the journey to escape the grips of misfortune.

He knocks at the door of a gardener's home.
The hospitable, kind-hearted man
Rushes to open, sees the two young people
Armed with spear and dressed in armor,
And asks Shahpoor, "What is happening?
Where do you come from at this undue hour

And thus equipped for an expedition?"

Shahpoor replies, "O benevolent man, does one
Interrogate people who have lost their way?
I am an Iranian in distress who fled to come here.
I have suffered at the hands of the Caesar and his host.
May I never lay eyes on his head and crown again!
If you offer me hospitality for the night,
If you show sense and act as suits a border guard,
It will be to your benefit, and the tree that you plant
Today will one day bear the sweetest fruit."

The gardener replies, "This dwelling is yours,
And the garden master is your host.
I shall do everything in my power; I shall fulfill
All your desires and speak of this to no one."

King Shahpoor dismounts; the young lady follows suit.
The gardener's wife prepares various fares.
Once they have eaten their fill, they are offered wine,
And a humble lodging is prepared for them.

The gardener brings a jug of wine,
Places it on the table and takes a cup.
The presence of his guest makes him happy.
He offers wine to Shahpoor, saying,
"Drink to the health of whomever."

Shahpoor says, "O my dear host,
O prudent and insightful gardener,
The one who brings the wine must drink first
When he is the older and wiser one.
You are a little older than me,
You must then drink, since you offer it to me."

The gardener replies, "O valiant man,
The more illustrious man must drink first.
You must show the example as you are
Older in intelligence and younger in years.
The glory of the crown shines on your face,
And your hair exudes the scent of musk."

Shahpoor smiles and takes the cup,

Then he sighs deeply and says to the gardener,
"O pure man, what news have you from Iran?"

The other replies, "O man of shining royal soul,
May evil men's misfortune never touch you!
May your enemies be struck by calamities
Just like those the Caesar inflicts upon the Iranians!
Iran's inhabitants have fled and scattered.
Nothing remains of this land, neither seed nor harvest.
So many men and women have been ravaged
And killed that this great people has lost its way.
Many have converted to Christianity
And have appeared strapped before bishops.
Many have turned to priesthood and wear the bonnet
In order to acquire land and a place of rest."

Shahpoor tells him, "May you always shine
As bright as a flower amid new grass!
How could the Caesar get away with such deeds?
How could the glory of Iran tarnish?"

The gardener replies, "O illustrious man,
May power and happiness be yours!
Never did Iranian noblemen receive a hint
Of their king's whereabouts, dead or alive.
Everyone who once lived in this fertile land
Has now been captured and is in the land of Rum."

The man of the house weeps bitterly at the thought.
Then he continues, "Remain here for three days.
You will make my home shine like the dazzling sun.
A wise man long ago said that the one who fails to show
Courtesy to a guest is deprived of sense and reason,
And his gloomy fate will bring him misery.
Remain here, rest, drink a cup of wine, and when I have
Gained your trust, you will reveal to me your name."

Shahpoor says, "It is good and right;
The keeper here is my temporary master."

8 | The Iranians Recognize Shahpoor

Shahpoor spends the night, eats, speaks, and listens.
In the morning, as dawn reveals itself
And a golden banner spreads across the plain,
The garden master nears his guest and says,
"May your day be joyful and your head
Rise beyond the rain-dropping clouds!
My home is not worthy of your status.
It is not a suitable place for you to rest."

Shahpoor says, "O blessed man, I much prefer
This dwelling to the throne and crown.
Bring me the *Zand Avesta* and the barsom[23],
And reply to all my questions."

The host obeys, and once he has prepared
The barsom and the place of prayer,
Shahpoor whispers to him, "Tell me the truth:
Where is the grand wise master?"

The gardener replies, "O illustrious,
Pure-hearted, soft-spoken man, he is nearby.
From here, I can see his house with my two eyes."

The king murmurs, "Ask the village chief
To bring some clay, the kind used for seals."

The gardener rushes to bring him the clay.
Shahpoor prints his seal into it,
Gives it To the gardener, blesses him,
And says, "Take this to the grand wise master,
And listen well to what he has to say."

At the first light of day, the gardener visits
The grand wise master with the king's seal.
Nearing his home's entrance, he finds
A group of armed warriors by the bolted door.
He calls for the door to open, he enters,
Finds himself in the presence of the grand wise master,

◇◇◇◇◇◇◇◇◇◇◇◇◇
23 Barsom: Sacred twigs from the pomegranate tree used in ancient Zoroastrian
prayers and rituals.

And, bowing low, he exhibits the seal.

The wise master takes one look at it
And his heart leaps with joy. He sheds tears
And asks the gardener, "Who is this man?"

The gardener replies, "O illustrious one, the seal
Belongs to the rider lodging in my house.
He has with him a moon-faced beauty,
Slender as a cypress tree, smart, graceful, and dignified."

The grand master says, "Describe to me
The stature and mien of this fame-seeking man."

"Anyone who has not witnessed spring
And a cypress tree on the edge of a stream
Can glance at his visage and frame
And his heart will rejoice at the sight.
His upper arms are as wide as camel thighs,
His chest is as strong as a lion's trunk,
And his face is the color of blood.
He makes you blush with his kindness.
The majesty of his crown gleams over his face."

9 | The Wise Master and the Warrior Learn of the Arrival of Shahpoor

The gardener speaks and the other listens.
The insightful wise man understands that the man
Of lion heart described, with a stately appearance,
Can only be the king, master of the throne.
He seeks an intelligent messenger,
Sends him to the warrior to say,
"The glorious Shahpoor has reappeared.
Mobilize a host on every side."

The envoy departs immediately and reports
To the warrior, who is delighted by the news.
He brings his eyes to the ground
And addresses the Just Creator:
"O World Master, besides You

There is no one being worthy of worship.
Who would have thought that King Shahpoor
Would once again catch a glimpse of his army?
Praise be to You, O sole Creator,
Our Guide on the road to happiness!"

As night deploys its black banner and
The stars and the sphere of the moon emerge,
Troops travel toward the king's hiding place.
Everywhere, the noble leaders raise their heads
And appear alone or in pairs.
They arrive at the gardener's gate and in the presence
Of the joyous king, who orders that they be received
No matter how poor the condition of the dwelling.

In the presence of the glorious ruler,
They bow down, head low to the ground.

The king embraces all the noblemen.
He laments over his misfortunes in Ru,
Describes his suffering inside the donkey skin,
Repeats his discussions with the Caesar,
Praises the beautiful young slave,
And recounts the devotion she showed him:
"I owe my life to her and to the Creator.
May her fate be a happy one!
You may be king and a favorite of fortune,
When you have a valiant slave,
You become his or her captive.
I am the servant of this fearless woman,
Holder of my secret, whose heart is open.

"You will dispatch envoys in every direction
Where there are troops and where my rule
Is recognized to give news of my condition.
You will send armed forces to occupy the roads.
You will block the paths leading to Ctesiphon.
We must not allow the news to spread.
Were the Caesar to learn of my whereabouts,
Were he to find out that the authority
Of the King of Kings is on the rise once again,
He would rush to destroy my host;

He would break the hearts and backs of Iranians;
And we would not be able to resist him.
We would have to give into his shining fortune.

"When the grand wise master arrives,
He will bring a vast army
That will block the way to ants and flies.
We shall prepare, devise new plans
To rid our garden of unwanted weeds.
In every corner, there will be a sentinel,
Patrols will be on guard day and night,
And Rumis will no longer have the chance
To rest with a sense of security and free of armor."

10 | Shahpoor Captures the Caesar in a Night Attack

Before long, Shahpoor gathers around him
A unit of six thousand soldiers.
He sends experienced leaders to Ctesiphon to spy
On the Caesar's actions and to report back.

The observers depart in secret to covertly
Evaluate the affairs of the world.
Having seen all there is to see,
They return to the renowned king and say,
"The Caesar, busy with feast and hunt, has no time
For thoughts of anything else, let alone waging war.
His army has scattered on every side
And is busy ravaging the borders.
There are no patrols by day and no guards by night.
Their host is a herd in the absence of its shepherd.
The Caesar does not suspect having an enemy
And enjoys his life of pleasures and delights."

Shahpoor rejoices at the news.
His past suffering appears to him as a gush of wind.
He selects among the Iranians three thousand
Shield-bearing men riding adorned horses.
At nightfall, he slips into a dark armor
And drives his troops to Ctesiphon.

They march swiftly during the dark hours
And hide during daylight.
In this way, they cross deserts and mountains
Through uncharted roads, and, whether there is
A path or not, he asks for the way to be lit
From the front for more than two farsangs.

He continues in this manner to Ctesiphon, preceded
By teams of riders, and he arrives at the Rumi camp
After two-thirds of the night has passed.
He does not fear the Caesar since he hears
Neither the sound of timpani nor the cry of sentinels.

The plain is covered with tent enclosures,
But who would suspect a surprise attack?
The Caesar is drunk with wine in his tent,
And the land is encumbered by his troops.

Upon seeing the situation, the valiant Shahpoor
Releases the reins of his royal charger,
Launches his troops to attack the camp,
And extends his hand to unhook his heavy mace.
The blare of trumpets rises to the clouds.
From here to there, to the edge of camp,
One can hear the crash of mace,
The ringing of bells, and the clattering of weapons.
It is as if the vault of sky is raining blood from the sun.

The Kaaviani banner shines in the dark night,
And the blue blades of steel twinkle.
It is as if a shower of swords is plummeting down
And a fog envelops the world.
Mountains disappear in the dust, and the stars
Raise the rim of their robes for protection.

Shahpoor overthrows the Caesar's worthless tents.
Fires are set in every corner.
Rumi warriors are killed, more than twelve thousand,
And the entire field is covered with body parts.
It is as if the sky has tumbled down onto the earth.
In the end, the Caesar is seized,
As his star of good fortune is decidedly extinguished.

Many Rumi noblemen are captured, and many
Valiant, choice cavaliers are bound up and taken.
Such is the rotation of the sublime firmament,
At times it raises one, at times it plunges one;
At times it awards one with joy, at times with grief.
It is best to show a human face
And abstain from causing others pain.
Only then will the Creator be our support.

As day shows its face and night retracts the edge
Of its dark cloak, the sun's banner rises high.
Shahpoor summons a scribe
With pen, paper, musk, and amber.
They address letters to every ruler
And every nobleman in the provinces.

The letter begins: "May my soul's grace
Be with the World Creator, Guide to virtue,
Who saves the observers of righteousness
And necessitates the help of no single being.
The Caesar, who scorned divine command
And sowed in our land seeds of animosity,
Is now bound up, for his soul did not honor wisdom.
He was forced to abandon the royal crown to us
And surrender his infamous name to the world.
His army and his throne are shattered
By the force given to me by my divine Guide.
Anyone who encounters a Rumi man in this land
Must destroy him at the point of his sword.
Seek justice, follow my command,
And renew your pact of duty to me."

Race camels take the letters throughout the empire
Ruled by King Shahpoor of serene heart.

Shahpoor travels from camp to Ctesiphon
And settles there without difficulty as ruler.
He places on his head his ancestors' crown
And addresses prayers to the Giver of good.

He commands a scribe to go to the prison
And write on paper the names of the prisoners.
They count one thousand one hundred and two

Noble Rumi warriors, parents and allies of the Caesar,
And the mightiest lords of the land.

The world king asks for the hands and feet
Of the instigators of violence to be cut off.
Then he summons the Rumi Caesar,
Leader of the Rumi army.

An executioner seizes the Caesar by the hand
And drags him lamenting from his cell.
At the sight of Shahpoor's crown,
Copious tears flow down the tyrant's cheeks.
He rubs his face to the ground
And praises the throne and crown.
He sweeps the floor with his lashes,
And bows down, face and body in the dust.

The king says to him, "O wicked man,
You claim to be a Christian,
Yet you actions oppose Yazdan.
You ascribe a son to someone with no mate,
With no beginning and no end.
You are only capable of lies,
But a lie is an evil flame without glare.
You are a traitor and a cheater.
You are foolish, evil, and of an evil race.
If you are a Caesar, where is your sense
Of generosity? Where is your sense of reason?
Where is the path indicated by compassion?
Why did you detain me in donkey skin
And fling me on the ground like a vile thing?
I came as a merchant ready for feast,
And not with timpani and host to engage in war.
You chose to thrust your guest in animal skin
So that you could depart for Iran with your troops.
Now you will witness the deeds of valiant men.
You no longer have the power to seek battle in Iran."

The Caesar replies, "O King,
Who is able to evade divine will?
The royal throne deprived me of reason
And turned me into the mercenary of a deev.

But if you trade good for evil, you will be celebrated
In the world, our glory will never grow old,
And all your desires will be approved.
If you show mercy and grant me life, I shall not
Place value on dinars or on my golden treasury.
I shall be one of your majesty's slaves at court.
I shall only wish to be the ornament of your throne."

The king says, "O malicious, wicked man,
Why did you completely ransack our land?
In the first place, I demand the return
Of all the prisoners you have abducted
As well as all the wealth you have seized.
May you never set eyes on this cursed land again!
You will bring them from your palace
And hand them over to my illustrious people.
You have converted every region into a desert,
Allowing leopards and lions to establish their lair.
You will lift the ruins at your own cost
And you will in this way pay for your misdeeds.
Furthermore, for every Iranian you have killed,
You will summon and hand over as compensation
Ten members of the Rumi royal family.
You will pledge to me their souls and their lives.
But I demand men only from the Caesars' race
So that they may stay with me in this delightful land.

"Finally, every tree you have uprooted in Iran
Must be replaced by planting a new one.
Never does a good man cut the tree of another.
You will raise the walls in the hopes
Of diminishing my people's anger.
Now that you are bound in chains,
How shall I forgive you for the donkey leather?
If you do not obey all my commands,
I shall split your skin from head to toe!"

After enumerating all the steps forcefully,
Shahpoor cleaves the Caesar's two ears with a dagger,
Pierces his nose, and threads a strap through the hole
Like a camel's bridle in memory of the donkey skin.
Then he ties up his feet with heavy chains,

And the executioner leads him to a prison cell.

11 | Shahpoor Drives a Host to Rum to Battle the Caesar's Brother

They pass the troops in review,
Ask for the key to the treasury, prepare the palace,
And distribute the balance of fees to the army.

Shahpoor's head is riddled with thoughts of vengeance,
His heart fixed on retribution.
He and his host march out of Iran to the border of Rum
And begin to slay everyone who comes their way.
They burn homes, lighting the world with massive fires.

As the Rumis receive the news that their border
And their beautiful land have been invaded,
And the Caesar has been taken captive at night,
They weep and tremble at the sound of Shahpoor's name.
Each one says, "Who else is the source of this calamity
But the selfish, thoughtless Caesar himself?"

The Caesar's father is dead, but his mother lives,
And he has a brother, a young man named Janus,
Ambitious, generous, and of a joyous nature.

An entire army assembles at his door,
And his mother, eager for battle, gives him coins.
She says to him, "Avenge your brother.
Do you not see that an Iranian army is advancing?"

Janus boils with anger and exclaims,
"It is my duty to avenge my brother!"
He asks for the beat of timpani
And the drawing of a huge cross,
As well as a formidable army of horsemen.

Once the two hosts come face to face,
The warring combatants no longer rely on rest.
They form their ranks, and the clatter of war resounds.

Janus charges at the head of his contingent.
Black clouds rise, and the dust is so thick
That the sun dims and eyes lose their way in the dark.
The army is supported on one side by the mountain
And on the other by a body of water.
The winds of battle blow from every side.
Sparks fly from swords, mace, and arrows.
The air turns purple from the dust of riders.
Spears shimmer, banners surge and billow.
The stars witness this brutal battle.
It is a battle of hatred, vengeance, and contention.

The Rumi warriors strap their belts like wild lions.
You would think the air is thick with a cloud
That rains down honed diamonds.

On the other side, the Iranians are cinched for battle,
Ready to shed rivers of blood. Until the sun
Begins its yellow descent, the winds of war
Alternate and waver from one side to another.

So many men are slain that the surface of earth,
Covered with armor, appears to be made of iron.

Shahpoor advances from the army center.
He calls his loyal friends from right and left.
They spur their horses,
Making the earth quiver and the army stir.

He leads a massive strike against the Rumis.
Strong and weak are of equal importance to him.
Janus realizes that he has no power over him,
And he turns around to flee with his troops.

The valiant Shahpoor chases after him,
Raising dust that chokes the translucent air.
Everywhere he leaves heaps of cadavers.
Everywhere he sullies the ground with Rumi brains.
He kills so many adversaries that the plain
Is covered with heads robbed of limbs and trunks.
The field empties of army and cross.
Castles empty of bishops and crucifix.
Shahpoor plunders so much wealth

That the troops remain confounded.
He distributes the lot to his host, keeping only
The Caesar's hard-earned treasury for himself.

Once this wealth has disappeared,
The hardships of the Caesar do not stop,
For the Rumi army gathers to speak of him:
"We no longer wish to have such a ruler!
May the name of the Caesar perish in Rum!
There remains not a single altar in our land
And not a single cross or school.
The bishops' belts have been consumed by flames.
Whether Rum or Ghennooj, it no longer matters to us,
Since the path of the Messiah's cult has been extinguished."

12 | The Rumis Place Bezanoosh on the Throne; His Letter to Shahpoor

There lives a sensible man named Bezanoosh,
Descendant of the Caesars and of noblemen.
He is wise, spirited, and of good advice.
The army leaders tell him, "You should be the Caesar.
You should rule over this land and its citizens,
Glorify the crown and throne! The troops will obey you."

Bezanoosh climbs on the ivory seat majestically,
With the crown gracing his head.
The Rumis proclaim him the reigning Caesar.

Bezanoosh reflects on the affairs of Rum,
On the state of the battlefield and of war.
Mindful that contention can destroy a powerful king,
He selects a prudent and respectful envoy,
Able to speak gently, able to write, a man who is
Eloquent, agreeable, intelligent, learned, and worldly.

He summons him, offers him a seat next to him,
And speaks to him in an amiable tone.
He dictates a letter invoking Yazdan's grace
On the world king: "May your crown endure!
May famed princes stand as your slaves!

You know that illustrious men always
Condemn destruction and devastation,
The attack, looting, and bloodshed of innocent men,
No matter where, whether in Iran or in Rum.
Iraj's murder caused the rise of this enmity,
But Manoochehr put an end to it with his courage.
Salm perished in the struggle, and the world
Was freed from the tyranny of Toor.
As for the war of vengeance between Eskandar
And Dara, much time has passed over Rum since.
Dara's fortune abandoned him when
His two evil viziers killed him viciously.
Though the Caesar renewed the old hostility,
He now pays dearly with chains in your prison.
The land of Rum must not be converted into a desert,
For there is no region more beautiful.

"If your intention is set on devastation and bloodshed,
This land is powerless in the face of your force.
As of now, women and children are either taken captive
Or have been wounded at the point of your blades.
It is time to shed all thought of retribution:
Hatred and religion do not blend well.
May our treasury be the ransom,
For animosity reduces the soul's strength.
Appease your heart, cease to burn down this land.
The days must not follow one another unchanging.
The World Creator does not approve
Of the world master pursuing an unjust requital.
May divine grace bless the king!
May his star of good fortune rise to the moon!"

The scribe stamps the royal letter with the Caesar's seal,
And the intelligent envoy takes off
In the direction of the king.
He arrives, delivers the message
To Shahpoor, prince of illustrious birth.
Once the letter is read and the gentle words are uttered,
Shahpoor forgives the Rumis, his eyes fill with tears,
And he relaxes, no longer frowning menacingly.

The king immediately writes a reply

163

In which he relates what occurred, good and bad:
"Who sewed up a guest in donkey skin?
Who renewed the old hostilities by doing so?
If you have any sense, rise and come to me
With your men of pure intentions.
Since I show you mercy, I shall no long seek war.
The world is not a threat for a reasonable man."

The emissary takes the reply to the Caesar
And repeats all that he has heard at the court of Iran.

13 | Bezanoosh Signs a Treaty With Shahpoor

Upon discovering the contents of the letter,
Bezanoosh's pure heart blossoms with joy.
He commands one hundred Rumi noblemen
To depart with him to Iran.
They take sixty kharvaar[24] loads of dirham,
Jewels and festive attire, stallions, and dinars,
About one hundred thousand, as offerings.

The noblemen appear at the side of the king,
Heads bare, and they scatter dinars over him,
Which they top with precious gems.

Shahpoor exonerates them, receives them amicably,
And kindly assigns each a seat according to his rank.
He says to Bezanoosh, "An unjust and vile man
Has arrived from the land of Rum.
He has converted Iranian cities into thickets.
I now ask for reparations for the land
That lies barren as the lair of leopards and lions."

Bezanoosh replies, "What is your request?
Since you have granted us mercy,
Guard yourself from turning your back on us."

The illustrious king says, "If you wish me
To pardon your people's past missteps,

◇◇◇◇◇◇◇◇◇◇◇◇◇◇
24 Kharvaar: A unit of measure equivalent to about 300 kilograms.

I require a tribute of two hundred thousand
Rumi dinars disbursed three times a year.
In addition, if you wish to curtail vengeance,
The city of Nassibin[25] must be mine."

Bezanoosh replies, "The land of Iran is yours.
Nassibin and the plain of brave men are yours.
I consent to the tribute you impose upon me,
For we have no way of contesting your wrath
And your acts of vengeance."

A treaty is drawn in which Shahpoor promises
To refrain from traveling out of Iran with a host
Until it is agreed by both parties and in friendship,
So that Rum would have no reason to suffer.

After that, Shahpoor treats the Rumis honorably
And cordially, extolling their noble heads.
He dismisses them so that they can return home.

Upon their departure, Shahpoor retreats with his host,
All the while praising profusely the Creator.
He travels joyously to Estakhr, the glory of Pars.

Hearing the news about their city of Nassibin,
The inhabitants prepare for battle, saying,
"We must not allow King Shahpoor and his host
To seize our land, for they do not observe
The traditions of the Messiah and will not listen to us.
They will wish to spread the faith of the *Zand Avesta*,
And we have no desire to adopt an ancient religion."

Noblemen of high rank are demoted.
Because of the hate, religious men climb on horseback.

Shahpoor Shah is furious with the Christian faith
When he finds out that access to Nassibin is barred to him.
He dispatches a vast host, saying, "One cannot approve
Of the religion of a prophet condemned to death by Jews."

They battle for one week.

◇◇◇◇◇◇◇◇◇◇◇◇◇
25 Nassibin: A city in northern Iraq.

The city gates are too narrow for the combatants.
A great number of Nassibin leaders are killed,
And the survivors are burdened by heavy chains.
They ask for mercy by way of a letter to Shahpoor.
The glorious king accords them pardon
And commands his troops to retreat.

Shahpoor's reputation spreads throughout the world
As he takes hold of power everywhere.
He is proclaimed a victorious king and
Maintains his position as master of crown and throne.
He gives the name of Delafroozeh Farrokhpay
To the young lady who rescued him
And helped him reach such heights of power.
She becomes his heart's appeal among the beauties.
He gives abundant wealth to the gardener
And grants him an honorable leave.

The Caesar remains enchained in prison,
Lamenting, despised, wounded, wretched.
He asks for all the wealth he owns in Rum,
Amassed with great pain from everywhere,
To be released and handed over to Shahpoor.
He lives in this way for a long time, lips full of sighs.
In the end, he dies in prison and in bondage,
Abandoning to another Caesar the royal crown.

Shahpoor sends him to Rum in a coffin
With a crown of musk on his head and says,
"Such is our end, and one never knows for certain
Where one's resting place will ultimately be.
One may be all greed and foolishness, another may be
All reason and grace, but the days pass over both.
A wise man never experiences sorrow."

Once King Shahpoor restores order
And satisfies the Iranians' need for vengeance,
He climbs on the Kianian throne
And remains world master for a long time.
He sends many men to Khuzestan.
He builds there a city for the prisoners
And fills the region with affection.

The name of the city is Khorram Abad.[26]
But who benefits in joy from this place?
It is the dwelling of those whose hands
Have been cleaved and who have been given a rank.
Every new year, each resident receives a new robe.

Next he founds another great city in Syria,
Which he names Pirooz-Shahpoor.[27]
Finally, he builds a third city in the district of Ahvaz,
Where he erects a palace and a hospital.
This one is called Khoonehye Asiran,[28] a place
Where the captive can live in peace and serenity.

In this way pass fifty years of his rule.
He has no equal in all the world.

14 | Mani Appears and Avows to Be a Prophet

An eloquent man arrives from Chin,
A painter the likes of which the world has never seen.
He is an ambitious man named Mani,
Able to obtain by his skills his heart's desires.
He says, "The beauty of my paintings
Prove that I am indeed a prophet,
Greater than any who has preached thus far."

He presents himself at King Shahpoor's court,
Asks for an audience, and hopes to turn the king
Into a supporter of his vocation of prophet.
His eloquent words prompt the king to reflect.
His mind stirred, he summons his wise men
And speaks to them at length of Mani:
"This articulate, eloquent man from Chin
Has inspired in me doubts about my faith.
Speak to him and listen to him.
Perhaps you will adopt his doctrine."

◇◇◇◇◇◇◇◇◇◇◇◇◇
26 Khorram Abad: A city in northwestern Iran.
27 Pirooz-Shahpoor: A city in Syria.
28 Khoonehye Asiran: Meaning the dwelling of prisoners.

They reply, "This man is a painter of the human face,
And not on the same level as the grand wise master.
Listen to Mani, but summon the wise man,
And when Mani sees him,
He will not dare open his mouth to speak."

Shahpoor summons Mani,
And they sit with the wise master
To discuss at length every subject imaginable.
Mani cuts short the discussion with the wise master,
Who says, "O worshipper of pictures,
Why do you foolishly raise a hand against Yazdan,
Whose essence is superior to everyone and everything,
The Creator of the sublime firmament,
Creator of time and space,
The arena for the play of light and dark?
The glorious revolving dome spins day and night;
From it one attracts both security and danger.
How then can you derive trust from mere images
And refuse to listen to my advice and my faith?
The preacher says that the pure Yazdan is unique,
And one's only option is to submit devotedly.

"Does the movement of your drawing serve as proof?
You must know that this demonstration has no foundation
And that no one will value as truth this doctrine.
If Ahriman was equal to Yazdan, the dark night
Would be as bright as day, and all year the days
And nights would be perfectly equal, no more, no less.
The Creator, above time and space,
Cannot be contained in one place.
You speak foolish words indeed,
And no one will pay heed to you."

He further speaks, for he is a wise and valiant man.
Mani is confused by the speech, and his affairs,
Which once appeared so successful, begin to decline.

The king grows angry with Mani,
And the rotation of fate constricts the world for him.
Shahpoor orders him to be taken and expelled from court:
"This image worshipper cannot dwell in our world.

He is a source of discord for everyone alive.
We must strip him of his skin from head to toe,
Fill it with straw, so that no one allows himself
To get carried away with similar ambitions.
We shall suspend the filled skin at the city gates
Or, even better, on the walls of the hospital."

The king's orders are obeyed, and the remains are hung.
The crowd invokes divine blessings on the king
And tosses dust on the skin of the deceased.

15 | Shahpoor Names His Brother Ardeshir as Regent

The state of the world is such under Shahpoor's reign
That garden roses are free of spiky thorns.
He is just, prudent, intelligent,
Ready to work, to give and to fight.
He does not have a single enemy,
And evil finds no shelter on earth.

The day he has nothing more to hope for,
After he has exceeded the age of seventy,
He calls a scribe to his side, the grand wise master,
Along with Ardeshir, his youngest brother,
Who sports a diadem of justice and wisdom.

Shahpoor has a very young son, also named Shahpoor,
Who was not blessed with the right timing at birth.
The king says to Ardeshir in front of his noblemen
And the scribe, "If you wish to do me the honor
And give me your word as guaranty that
When my son Shahpoor attains the age of maturity,
When the winds of power blow on him,
You will release to him treasury, crown, and army.
Promise me that you will act as his kind and caring advisor.
If you give me your word, I shall entrust the crown,
The treasury, and the royal army to you."

Ardeshir agrees to the king's words and takes the oath
In the presence of the noble assembly, men young and old.
He swears that, upon the child reaching an age

Worthy of the royal throne and Kianian diadem,
He would surrender the kingdom to him
And act in every way to his benefit.

Shahpoor hands over the crown and seal
To Ardeshir before the noblemen and says,
"May you not take lightly the affairs of the world!
I am entrusting you with the crown and throne of power."

Ardeshir replies, "I shall obey you like a slave!"

The king continues, "Know, O dear brother,
That an unjust king cares little about sovereignty.
He is greedy and wishes to fill his treasury
And behaves as a coarse ruler to illustrious men.
We must honor a just king, a Yazdan worshipper
Who is the source of his subjects' happiness.
He makes things prosper with justice and charity:
Two virtues by which he guides the world.
He guards his land against enemies,
Raising his head and his crown to the clouds.
He fills his treasury calmly and dissipates
Grief by spreading justice and peace.
He forgives the faults of others
And takes great care to show his humanity.
Anyone who strains to acquire these virtues
Will attain wisdom, vigilance, and sound judgment.

"The king must be intelligent
And able to teach men, young and old.
Subjects give into vice if they are not pious.
If hatred rules the king's heart,
It will destroy his faith and his sense of justice.
The heart and the brain are the two rulers of the body,
The rest of the body is merely the army troops.
If the heart and brain are sullied, if despair has stripped
Them of reason, then the mind will grow confused,
For how could an army prosper without a warrior?
When it lacks knowledge and direction, it dissolves,
Overturns a body deprived of soul into the dust.
Conversely, the actions of an unjust king
Will shake up and upend the world. After his death,

He will be cursed and will be named a faithless ruler.

"Place your hopes in devotion,
And keep your anger for religious violations.
Yazdan is Master of wrath and eyes.
Any king who does not follow this path
Will have to renounce world governance.
His subjects will desert the land,
And his once loyal court will abandon him.
Are you not familiar with the wise man's advice
To banish perversity from your heart?
When a king is blessed, his affairs prosper,
But the tyrant is a damnable man; for that reason
Keep away from the door of greedy men.

"Know, my dear brother, that sensible men
Ask a king for many things.
First, they ask that he be victorious and refrain from
Turning his back on the enemy on the day of battle;
Second, they ask that he treat his army with justice
And he recognize the superiority of highborn men,
For the one who is worthy of royalty
Would not wish a nobleman to serve in ranks;
Thirdly, they ask that the king model a righteous heart
And never infringe upon justice;
Fourthly, they ask to keep the door to the treasury
Tightly closed before subjects and aging servants
So that the fruits of the tree may rain down.

"The king's court must not be without an army,
And the king must keep his wealth for the troops.
If you fill your treasury with just means,
You and your host will enjoy the results.
Consider your armor as your body's ornament;
You may need it in a dark night.
Do not blindly trust your administrators.
Settle your affairs yourself if you wish to feel secure.
In the end, death is certain to come for you,
Whether you are a fading light
Or the light shining bright upon the world."

Shahpoor's words stir tears in his brother.

He lives for another year after having written
His last wishes, then he dies whispering these words:
"Guard yourself from sowing seeds rooted in avarice,
For in the end, your days will pass,
And the enemy will enjoy the fruits of your labors.
As long as the rules of Ormazd and Bahman
Are followed, this lofty palace will be a residence
That will propagate good fortune."

O cup-bearer, bring me ruby-colored wine,
Drawn from a jug that never empties.
Since I am sixty-three years old and going deaf,
How will I seek in the world honor and dignity?

Now I shall tell the tale of King Ardeshir.
Pay attention to what I have to say and learn.

IX. The Ten-Year Reign of Ardeshir the Benevolent, His Rise to the Throne, and His Speech to the Iranian Leaders

King Ardeshir ascends the throne of King Shahpoor.
He straps his royal belt, assembles the Iranians,
And seats them on the steps of the golden throne.
He says, "I wish not for the skies to bring harm to anyone.
If the world conforms to my desires,
You will enjoy only peace under my rule.
But if the world resists us, we shall merge into its flow.
My brother trustingly handed over to me
The empire because his son was too young.
We must invoke blessings on his soul,
For he freed the world of evil men.
When Shahpoor, son of Shahpoor, grows up,
And when he is able and worthy of crown and throne,
I shall hand over to him kingship, host, and treasury
As stipulated by his father in his last wishes.
I am merely the temporary master of the throne.
I am merely the prince's father's delegate.
You must all keep your eyes on justice,
Attempt in every way to make it prevail.
Know that we enjoy life and it passes, and when
We die, all our labors drift away in the wind."

For ten years, he maintains world order.
He enjoys and shares his pleasures with all.
He asks for neither tribute nor royal fees.
He occupies the ivory throne without making demands.
His people call him Nikookaar,[29]
Since no one has cause for complaint.

Once Shahpoor is of age to assume crown and throne,

◇◇◇◇◇◇◇◇◇◇◇◇◇
29 Nikookaar: Meaning the benevolent.

Ardeshir, following a path of courage and loyalty,
Bestows on him the diadem of fortune
In observance with the terms of the agreement.

X. The Five-Year-and-Four-Month Reign Of Shahpoor, Son of Shahpoor, His Rise to the Throne, and His Speech to the Iranian Leaders

As Shahpoor ascends his uncle's throne,
The population of Iran is divided:
Some are delighted while others are afflicted.

The new king says to his leaders,
"O illustrious, worldly, sensible wise men,
Anyone who lies to me will disgrace himself.
The path of falsehood is not a prudent path.
Only through reason does one maintain power.
You will not find a friend in a vile man.
Do not sow weeds in the garden.
Anyone with sense will abstain
From unjustly accusing another.
One must guard one's tongue.
One must avoid honing one's mind with poison.
The one who speaks excessively will ruin his name.
But if a wise man speaks, listen to him, for a word
Based on science and knowledge never grows old.
The heart of a greedy man is filled with bitterness.
Maintain yourself at a distance from greed.
Do not form a friendship with a liar
Or a man who displays impure intentions.

"The nobleman's nature unites four necessary qualities:
First, he must be valiant, modest, and just;
Next, he must always display nobility in his actions;
Thirdly, he must take the middle road in his affairs
And content himself with the blessings of providence;
Fourthly, he must neither speak in vain
Nor foolishly seek glory in excessive praise.

175

"The nobleman will be happy in both worlds,
But the heart of a wicked man will never find happiness.
His name in this world will be odious,
And in the other, he will not have access to paradise.
The vain man who foolishly dissolves his possessions
Will not leave a good name behind.
Conversely, the man who selects the middle path
And is showered with blessings will be celebrated.
May fortune always watch over you!
May the World Creator always come to our aid!
The throne of power remains eternally for no one."

He says this, and the noblemen rise before him
To acclaim him and pay tribute to him.

Five years and four months pass in this way.
One day, the king is on his way to hunt.
The world fills with falcons, cheetahs, and dogs,
Some animals flying, others running eagerly.

A canopy is dressed above the king's bed.
He dines, rests, drinks three cups of royal wine,
Daydreams, and falls into a deep slumber,
At which time his friends disperse.

During the king's restful sleep, a fierce wind rises,
The likes of which no one has ever witnessed.
It plucks the pole supporting the canopy
And flings it on the head of the powerful king.

The valiant Shahpoor, world seeker, dies instantly,
Leaving the Kianian headdress for another to enjoy.

This is the way of the rotating world:
Nothing remains except the world itself.
It plays tricks on us while it snatches
The throne from one to give to another.
Work and enjoy life; play and do not tire yourself.
Why would you concentrate on hostility?
Why would you boast about your wealth?
Such is your lot in this somber globe.
Stay valiant and do not attempt
To discover this world's mysteries.

Should you find out, you would tremble in grief.
Refrain from inquiry; refrain from spying on its secret.

XI. The Fourteen-Year Reign of Bahraam, Son of Shahpoor, His Rise to the Throne, and His Speech to the Iranian Leaders

King Shahpoor has an only son,
Old in wisdom but young in years.
Bahraam, wise and decent, mourns for some time.

Once he climbs on the imperial throne, he declares:
"If a king fills his treasury by just means,
You must know that he will never lose it.
May Yazdan, the pure, approve of my person!
May the hearts of my enemies fill with worry!
Wisdom belongs to the Creator,
And we stand as lowly and mere divine servants.
We are exposed to either being belittled or elevated.
The World Master represents Justice.
In kingship, Yazdan is never a subject
To be glorified in domination or to be debased.
Anyone who is rich in generosity and intelligence,
Anyone who is vigilant and wise,
Must not close the door to his treasury,
Especially if he is the master of crown and throne.

"If you spread the treasures of speech, be lavish,
For wisdom can never be exhausted.
Address Yazdan in good and bad fortune
If you wish your happiness to endure.
If you learn goodness and evil from the Creator,
You will receive a reward in happy paradise.
But if you favor conceit and vanity,
You will be a prisoner without ransom.
If Yazdan does not support you,
You will live in a state of suffering and pain.
My hope is that when I rest my head in the dark dust,
The Creator will treat me as a victorious king

178

And a man whose eternal glory shines in the world.
Spreading justice throughout the world is more esteemed
Than filling your treasury through wicked means.
The fruit of our labors will remain here,
And our riches will fall into enemy hands.
Good and bad will endure as a memory.
Guard yourself, as much as you can,
From spreading the seeds of evil."

Once his reign exceeds fourteen years,
Bahraam falls ill, and his graceful stature bends.
He remains unwell for a long time.
The hearts of his people fill with grief.
He does not have a son, but a daughter and a younger
Brother named Yazdegerd, a proud and willing man.

The king summons the brother and gathers his host.
He remits to his brother treasury and army,
The empire's seal, throne, and crown.
Then Bahraam, young world master,
After twice seven years of rule, expires.

And you, old man of sixty-three years,
Until when will you sing the praises of wine?
Your last day will arrive unexpectedly.
Enter then through the door of repentance
And march down the road of reason.
May the Creator be happy with his servant!
May wisdom be my wealth!
May my words benefit me!
I am able to split hair with my speech
And draw in the obscurity the plot of a poem.
Do not be surprised if I complete, in my old age,
What I began in honor of the King of Kings,
The one who strikes with his sword
And whose head rises above the noble assembly.
May the world be at his command!
May his throne lift to grace the moon as its crown!
May the royal seat rejoice of his presence!
We receive from him the fulfilment of every wish,
For our king is tall with fame and grace!
May power and wisdom be his path!

May his enemies' hands be ineffective against him!
May the reign of Mahmoud endure!
May his throne be the diadem on the head of generosity!

XII. The Thirty-Year Reign of Yazdegerd, the Wicked

1 | The Beginning of Yazdegerd's Reign

Upon rising to world kingship, Yazdegerd
Gathers the army from every corner of the land.
He places on his head the royal crown, and,
Instead of mourning, his brother's miserable death
Is a source of considerable pleasure to him.

He turns to his court's eminent figures:
"Any of you who nurtures a sense of justice
May address prayers to Yazdan.
May our just ways delight your hearts!
I shall not allow wicked men to live
Unless they listen to my advice and obey me.
I shall honor those who perform righteous acts
And abstain from falsehoods and causing trouble,
By banishing hostility toward them from my heart.
I shall ask guidance only from noblemen,
Men of sense, sages of awakened mind.
But those who surrender to vice,
Whose wealth makes them insolent,
Who oppress the defenseless,
Or who raise their heads because of their wealth,
I shall fight them, crush their arrogance,
And make life peaceful for the poor.
Anyone who does not guard against our fury,
Anyone who passes before me with insolence,
Wishes only for a bed of dust
And an Indian sword at the neck.
Observe carefully my commands, and protect
Yourselves with the armor of wisdom."

The men who place their hopes in mace and sword

181

Begin to shake with fear like leaves on a willow tree.
Once the king's authority on the world is secure,
His power expands and his kindness diminishes.
Sensible men are despised by him;
He neglects important royal duties;
Governors, warriors, border guards,
Learned men, able and skilled, are nothing to him
As his soul dims driven by a fierce and acute tyranny.

Any remaining sense of tenderness and justice
Dissolves from his heart.
He never welcomes a subject's wish or desire.
No one has a higher rank in his eyes.
He soon undertakes to punish crimes hastily.
His court's ministers, who make his crown and star
Prosper, agree to never speak to him of state affairs.
Everyone trembles in terror before the King of Kings.

When a minister learns of the arrival
Of an ambassador or a subject to plead for mercy,
He quickly dismisses him and his business,
His tone gentle, his words warm:
"The king is not available for this affair,
And you may not see him at the moment.
I have submitted your demands,
But he did not consent to give orders."

2 | The Birth of Bahraam, Son of Yazdegerd

In this way he passes seven years of his reign,
With his wise men in a state of pain and anguish.
At the start of the eighth year,
On Ormazd day, [30] during the month of Farvardin,
When the sun, the object of devotion,
Bows down to the earth, under a lucky star
And omens that light the world, a son is born.

The father gives him the name of Bahraam
And is delighted at the sight of the child.

◇◇◇◇◇◇◇◇◇◇◇◇◇
30 Ormazd day: The first day of the month, see footnote 13.

PART TWENTY-FOUR

Able astrologers gather at court,
Including a renowned Indian mystic,
A majestic, intelligent man named Sooroosh.
Hoshyar, another sage from Pars has the ability
To rein in the sky, so vast is his knowledge.

The king summons them to court.
They arrive full of caution and precaution.
They look into their astrolabes and their Rumi tables
To uncover the mysteries and to calculate the future.

They observe that the child will rise one day
As the world king, master of the seven realms;
That he will mature to be a pure and good-natured man.

They run to court with their tables
And tell the crown-bearer Yazdegerd:
"We combined our talents and knowledge and
Discovered that, according to the sky's position,
It will favor the child with affection.
The seven realms of the earth will be his,
And he will be a magnificent and glorious king."

Upon the astrologers' departure from court,
The wise men and virtuous royal viziers deliberate:
"Should the child not inherit his father's nature,
He will prove to be a king who will spread justice.
But if he does show signs of greed and tyranny,
He will overturn the land, and neither wise man
Nor fierce warrior will have the chance to enjoy life
While he will never have a moment of peace."

The wise men present themselves to the king,
Their hearts open and full of benevolence.
They tell him, "This child of good disposition
Is sheltered from reproach and quarrel.
The entire world is at your command,
Everyone pays tribute to you,
Every subject is at your feet, firmly loyal to you.
Find a place where there is instruction and cheer.
The land will welcome a learned king.
Select an experienced man from a wealthy
Family, and the world will bless him.

183

This good-natured prince will acquire skill,
And his reign will bring joy to the world."

Yazdegerd listens to the wise men
And gathers envoys from around the realm.
At the same time, he sends worldly men to the lands
Of Rum, India, Chin, and other civilized nations.
He sends an emissary as well to the Taazian,
To determine what belongs to them, good or bad.

Inquisitive emissaries travel to various lands
To search for eloquent, learned star observers
Who would be suitable to raise Bahraam.
From every region arrives a worldly, wise scholar,
Guided by fortune and gifted with intelligence.

Each makes his way to court and to the king's side.
Yazdegerd receives them graciously,
Questions them, and assigns them proper dwellings.

One night, Noman and Monzer, King of Yemen,
Arrive with a number of spear-wielding noblemen.
Once they are gathered in the land of Pars,
They appear before the illustrious king
And say, "We are your slaves.
We have rushed here at royal command.
Who among the noblest men will be blessed
To embrace the world king's brilliant son?
Who will have the honor of teaching him and
Of shining a light into his heart's darkness?
We journey from the lands of Rum, India, and Persia.
We are astrologers, mathematicians, learned
Philosophers, rhetoricians, sages, and scholars.
We are the dust beneath your feet,
Eager to serve as guides toward learning.
Look and see which one of us suits you best."

Monzer adds, "We are also your slaves.
We live in the world only to serve the king.
His majesty knows our skills, for he is
Our shepherd and we represent his flock.
We are riders and warriors; we launch our steeds
And the most powerful foes cannot resist us.

We do not have among us an astrologer
Who knows much about counting,
But our hearts are full of affection for the king.
We have climbed on speedy Taazian stallions.
We are here as the slaves of the king's son,
And we celebrate and extol his grandeur."

3 | Yazdegerd Charges Monzer and Noman With His Son's Instruction

After this discourse, Yazdegerd gathers
All the men of reason and sense.
He entrusts Bahraam to the noble Monzer.
He commands that a present be prepared
And that his head be raised to the sky.

They dress Monzer in a robe of honor.
They bring to the king's door
The horse of the King of Yemen.
The land, from palace to plain, is covered
With passing horses, camels, and litters.
Countless servants and nursemaids crowd the area
From the marketplace to the palace door.
The bazaars are decked for feast
From the city gates to the court.

When Monzer arrives in Yemen, everyone,
Men and women, advance to greet him.
At his residence, he calls a number of women
From the most powerful and influential families,
From the landed gentry and from the wealthy,
High-ranking Taazian community.
He narrows them down to four women
Of renowned, noble birth, two of them Arab
And the other two from the Persian Kianian family,
Who are willing and eager to serve as nursemaids.

They take care of the child in this way for four years.
Once he has adequately grown, they wean him
With difficulty and raise him delicately on their knees.

At the age of seven, he challenges Monzer:
"O noble leader, is this the proper way
To treat a prince, like a breastfed baby?
Entrust me to the care of erudite masters.
The time has come for my education to begin."

Monzer replies, "O gallant child,
You need not yet learn and be educated.
When the time of instruction has arrived,
I shall no longer allow you to indulge in game.
Right now, it is through play that you learn best."

Bahraam retorts, "Do not make an idle child of me.
Though I may be young and my chest
And limbs have not yet the might of a warrior,
I am gifted with intelligence.
You are old, yet you lack wisdom,
And my nature does not agree with your plans.
Are you not aware that the one who knows
How to search for the right moment
Always picks the affair that has priority?
What we accomplish outside of time
Does not bear abundant fruit.
The head is the best part of a man's body.
Teach me what I must learn to be a just king.
The start of righteousness has to be learning.
Happy is the one who holds his sights on the goal
From the moment the journey begins."

Monzer observes him with astonishment
And murmurs the name of Yazdan.
He dispatches an envoy on camelback to Sorsan.[31]
The envoy assesses three wise, educated men
Who enjoy a favorable reputation.
One is able to instruct the prince in the letters
And dissipate the obscurity from his heart.
Another is able to hunt with falcon and cheetah,
Play polo with mallet, draw his bow and arrow,
Fight with his sword against the enemy,
Do aerobatics left and right, and hold

◇◇◇◇◇◇◇◇◇◇◇◇◇
31 Sorsan: Or Shorsan, a village in central India.

186

His head high in the company of eminent men.
The third master is to instruct Bahraam
On subjects dealing with world affairs
And the duties of the King of Kings,
As well as the duties of an administrator.

These three wise men arrive, explain to Monzer
All that they know, and he, a valiant friend of instruction,
Entrusts them with the care of the prince.

Bahraam's skills soon reach such heights
That he can complete his manly duties.
Upon hearing of a high deed,
His mind aspires to forge a similar path.
At the age of eighteen, he is brave and kind.
The sun-faced king sees that his son no longer
Needs the aid of the wise men to learn
Or to play polo, to hunt with cheetah and falcon,
To handle the reins on the battlefield,
Or to launch his horse on the attack.

He says to Monzer, "O man of pure intentions,
You may dismiss the masters."

Monzer distributes many gifts to each of them,
And they joyfully take their leave.

Then the prince says to Monzer,
"Tell the spear-wielding riders to exercise before me
And to threaten each other with their weapons.
They will determine the price of the horses;
I will reward them with dirhams, beyond their need."

Monzer replies, "O valiant, glory-seeking prince,
The chief of this stud farm is at your command,
The master of these stallions is your kin.
If you wished to purchase Arabian stallions,
Why did I have to work so hard to obtain strong ones?"

Bahraam says, "O honored man,
May the world always fulfill your desires!
I wish to select a horse that I can launch on a descent
Without having to fear that he may fall.

Once I teach him to have a sure stance,
I will make it the rival of the wind in battle.
But one must not force an untested horse."

Monzer commands Noman to gather a herd
Of the most valiant horses in the stud farm and to cross
The desert of spear-riders to search for battle steeds.
Noman departs and returns
With one hundred stallions picked by warriors.

When Bahraam sees them, he goes to the plain,
Marches left and right, and circles the horses.
But the ones that equal the wind in speed
Buckle beneath Bahraam's heroic weight.

In the end, he selects a black-maned chestnut
Of winded hooves and expansive chest,
And a brown bay with a black tail
That resembles a whale emerging from the sea.
Its hooves ignite sparks,
And ruby-red blood drips from its chest.

Monzer pays for them according to their value,
As they come from the Forest of Kufah.[32]

Bahraam receives from him the two steeds,
Each as bright as the flame of Aazargoshasp.
Monzer holds them in his attentions
Like fresh apples so that nothing can hurt him.

One day, the young prince says to Monzer,
"O wise and serene man, you keep me without reason.
You never leave my side in your excess of care.
But among all that you witness in the world,
There is not a heart that is without a secret.
Men's cheeks turn yellow with worry,
And it is through joy that a noble nature prospers.
Nothing evokes more cheer
Than the sight of a beautiful woman.
A woman can ease one's suffering
And calm a young man's passion,

◇◇◇◇◇◇◇◇◇◇◇◇◇◇
32 Kufah: A city in Iran on the banks of the Euphrates River.

Whether he is a hero or a crown-bearer.
She can inspire him to have faith in Yazdan;
She can guide him toward all that is good.
Summon five or six young women,
Gracious and graceful sun-faced beauties.
I shall select one or two of them and summon divine grace
In the hopes of watching the birth of a child,
Something that will soothe my restless heart.
The king will be happy with me,
And the entire court will glorify me."

Monzer commends him. He orders a good runner
To dash to the yard of a slave merchant
And bring back forty young Rumi girls,
All desirable and able to seduce the heart.

Out of the beauties presented to him,
Bahraam selects two of tall stature,
Gifted with rosy skin, ivory bones, and
Slender waists, and full of charm, grace, and dignity.

One of these two stars plays the lute, and the other
Has tulip-like cheeks and resembles the star of Canopus.
Her stature is that of a cypress tree,
The curls of her hair appear to be threadwork.

Monzer pays the fee, Bahraam smiles and thanks him,
His cheeks turning red as a ruby from Badakhshan.
He engages in the game of polo and in the hunt.

4 | The Story of Bahraam and the Lute Player

One day, Bahraam marches off, without an escort,
To hunt with the lute player named Aazaadeh,
Whose cheeks are the color of coral.
The source of his desires, she charms his heart,
And he continuously parts his lips to utter her name.

He asks for a camel dressed in a cover of brocade
With four stirrups hanging from its back,
A beast able to run nimbly in climbs and descents.

Two of the stirrups are in gold, and two in silver,
All four are inlaid with precious jewels.

Bahraam carries a crossbow in his quiver,
For he is proficient in every skill.

As two pairs of gazelles approach,
The young man says to Aazaadeh with a smile,
"O moon, when I have bound my bow
And seized the arrow with the ring,
Which gazelle do you wish me to bring down?
Here stand a young female and an old male."

Aazaadeh replies, "O lion warrior,
It does not suit a hero to slaughter gazelles.
Convert with your arrow this female into a male
And turn the old male into a female.
Launch your camel when the gazelle flees.
Then fling a ball to bring its ear to its shoulder.
The ball will tickle the ear without causing harm.
You will pin its head, foot, and shoulder
With your arrow at once
If you wish to be called light of the world."

At these words, Bahraam remembers an old saying.
Still he binds his bow and shouts a cry that slices
Through the silence and echoes on the plain.
He has in his quiver a two-pointed arrow.
As soon as the gazelles move to bound away,
He plucks off with the two-pointed arrow
The black horns on the head of the male,
And he instantly turns him into a female.

The young lady is in awe of his abilities.
Next, the hunter sticks two arrows
Into the female's forehead that take on
The appearance of two horns on her head.
Blood floods down her chest.

Then Bahraam charges his camel to the other pair,
Places a bullet in the hollow of the crossbow,
Sends it flying to the ear of one of the gazelles,
And is thrilled with the precision of his strike.

The gazelle immediately scratches her ear.
Bahraam binds an arrow of poplar wood to his bow,
Fires it, and stitches her head, ear, and foot together.

Aazaadeh feels a sense of pity for the creature.

Bahraam asks her, "O moon, what is it?
Why are you shedding tears?"

She weeps bitterly and says, "This is a coldhearted act!
What you are exhibiting here is not power but folly."

Bahraam extends his hands to push her
Violently off the saddle and onto the ground.
He marches over her with his camel, and blood
Soaks her breast, her hand, and her instrument.
He says, "O imprudent lute player,
Why did you make use of ruse with me?
If I had missed, my family would have been humiliated."

Aazaadeh dies, trampled by a camel,
And Bahraam never again takes a woman to hunt.

5 | Bahraam Exhibits His Skills at the Hunt

Another time, Bahraam departs to hunt
With a noble escort, cheetah and falcon.
He notices a lion on a hilltop who proceeds
To tear apart the back of an onager.
He hooks the rope with a black end to the bow,
Leaps on the saddle, and sends a three-fletched arrow.
The shot pierces the back of the lion
And the heart of the onager.
The lion's corpse, covered in blood,
Is sprawled on top of the other.

One day, Noman and Monzer join him on the hunt,
Along with a number of illustrious Taazian men
Able to point to the road of prosperity and perdition.
Monzer asks for Bahraam the hunter to show
His horsemanship and his strength.

They come upon a flock of sprinting ostriches,
Each as large as a liberated camel.
At the sight, Bahraam lunges like a hurricane.
The valiant young man rubs his bow, adjust four arrows
Of poplar wood to his belt, aims at the ostriches,
And fires them one after the other.
At every attempt, his shot brushes against the fletches
That adorn the previous arrow, so precise it is.
This is the display of a true hunter.
No arrow strikes either higher or lower
Than the other for the width of one needle.

The renowned men advance to take a closer look
And estimate that the rider's shots do not deviate,
Not even by a hair.

Monzer and the spear-bearing riders praise Bahraam.
Monzer says to him, "O King, I am as delighted
With you as with a blossoming rosebush.
May your moon face never wrinkle!
May your stature never slump!"

Once in his palace, Monzer,
Who lifts Bahraam all the way to Saturn,
Searches through Yemen to find a number of painters.
The best of them gather at his court.
He commands one of them to paint on silk
The story of Bahraam's hunt.

The picture is as clear as life itself.
It displays with black ink on silk
Bahraam riding a powerful camel,
With his mighty arms and shoulders
Drawing his bow with skill and force, illustrating
His crossbow, the gazelles, the lions and onager,
The ostrich, the plain, and the piercing arrow.

Monzer dispatches a rider to the king
And sends him the painting.
As the messenger reaches Yazdegerd,
The entire army assembles around the letter.
The noblemen are astounded and acclaim Bahraam.

Since that day, they rush to paint every skill
And activity of the prince to send to King Yazdegerd.

6 | Bahraam Travels With Noman to Yazdegerd

Bahraam, a vanquishing sun, a lion,
Wishing yo see his father, one day says to Monzer,
"I shall gladly stay longer with you,
But I nurture the desire to lay eyes on my father.
Since I will be free of worry at his side,
My heart pushes me in that direction."

Monzer prepares all that is necessary, royal presents
From Yemen, Taazian stallions of golden bridle,
Valuables, striped fabrics, swords from Yemen,
All sorts of precious stones mined in Aden.[33]

Noman, for whom Yazdegerd has the greatest esteem,
Accompanies the prince, and in this way they trudge
To Estakhr, discussing matters relating to kingship.

At the news that his son and Noman, the Arab,
Are on the way, the court's wise men march off to greet them.
The king is astonished at the sight of Bahraam in the distance,
His limbs and his imposing stature, his striking mien,
So stately, so well educated, and so handsome.
He questions him at length, receives him graciously,
And asks that a dwelling be prepared for him nearby.

Then he selects a residence in the city for Noman,
A palace that would have suited Bahraam,
And sends him slaves and servants worthy of his rank.

Bahraam remains day and night at his father's side,
Serving him attentively, with no time to scratch his head.

After one month passes in the king's company,
Noman expresses his wishes to return home.
Yazdegerd calls him one evening, sits him next to him

◇◇◇◇◇◇◇◇◇◇◇◇◇
33 Aden: An ancient port city in Yemen that is today the temporary capital.

On the royal throne, and says, "Monzer has taken
Tremendous care in raising the noble Bahraam,
And I must find a way to reward him.
Your friendship is the star of my fortune.
I appreciate his good judgment and his insight,
For I see that in all matters he acts with wisdom.
You remained at this court for a long time,
And your father most probably has his eyes
Fixed on the road, awaiting your return."

The king offers him fifty thousand dinars
Along with a magnificent robe.
Ten splendid horses are elected from the royal stables
With gold and silver bridles, and from the royal coffer,
Mehran, the treasurer, draws carpets, slaves,
And all sorts of valuables to give to Monzer and Noman.

A delighted Yazdegerd opens the door to generosity
And gives presents to Noman's companions.

Then the ruler dictates a royal letter to Monzer,
To praise the King of Yemen and thank him
For all the kindness he showed his son, adding,
"I shall attempt to acquit myself of this debt,
For my offspring is a source of tremendous pride."

Bahraam also composes a letter in which he says:
"My position here is hollow and disagreeable.
I did not think that my father, the king,
Would watch over me with such precision.
I am not here as a son or as a servant.
I am unable to enjoy life at my own court."

Then he divulges his secrets to Noman,
Issues relating to the poor path followed
By the world king and his undesirable behavior.

Noman takes leave of the king and his court
And makes his way back to Monzer's palace.
He hands over the world king's letter.
Monzer kisses it and rubs his forehead to it.
He expresses his delight at the sight of the presents,
And he extols Yazdegerd numerous times.

Then the envoy speaks for some time, secretly,
To Monzer describing Bahraam's predicament.
Once Bahraam's letter is read out loud by a scribe,
The face of the nobleman turns as yellow as turmeric.

Monzer immediately composes a reply
In which he relates suitable, auspicious advice:
"O illustrious prince, do not disobey your father.
Approve of the king's actions, whether good or bad.
Serve him and follow the path of wisdom.
Misfortune can be avoided through patience.
The revolving dome has willed it thus,
And we cannot contest its wishes.
It holds the heart of one full of affection
And the heart of another full of fury.
This is the way the world was crafted
By the World Creator from the beginning of time,
And we must follow the path laid before us.
From now on, I shall send you all that you need
In terms of coins and jewels worthy of a king.
You must not remain in a state of distress.
My amassed wealth has no value next to your needs.
I send you ten thousand dinars as offering
As well as the slave from the women's quarters
That was the advisor and the delight of your heart.
I send her to you so that your dim heart
Can gain a semblance of serenity.

"Every time you make use of dinars,
Do not cause yourself trouble with the king.
I will send you so much more wealth from my land.
Double the ardor of your service to your father,
And shower him with abundant praise.
You cannot, in your soul, separate
The bad character of a world king."

Monzer dispatches ten Taazian cavaliers,
Eloquent men, insightful and devoted.
They arrive at the side of Bahraam
With crates of gold, slaves, and a friend.
The prudent prince is filled with joy,
And the distress he previously felt dissipates.

From this moment on, he applies himself,
Day and night, to serving the king,
Strictly following the advice of the Arab ruler.

7 | Yazdegerd Imprisons Bahraam

One day, Bahraam stands for a long time
At the side of the king in the hall of feasts.
As day turns to night, he grows sleepy.
While still on his feet, he closes his eyes.

At the sight of him, the king is infuriated
And screams to the executioner:
"Take this man away. He may no longer
Set his sights on the royal crown and belt.
Turn his palace into a prison and return to me.
This man is not worthy of a position
Where one gains honor in battle."

Bahraam is confined to his palace, heart wounded,
And for one year he does not see his father, except
On the day of Nowruz and for the feast of Saddeh,
Where he presents himself amid a crowd.

It happens that Teynoosh, the Rumi,
Arrives at the king's court as the Caesar's ambassador,
With cases full of gold, slaves, and tribute from Rum.
The King of Kings receives him graciously
And orders a dwelling be prepared worthy of him.

Bahraam sends him a message:
"O shrewd man who always reaches his goal!
The king's anger toward me is unfounded,
For I am innocent, and I am kept away from him.
Ask him to show mercy toward his son; he will grant it,
And perhaps my withered fortune will shine again.
Perhaps he will send me to the one who raised me,
For Monzer treated me better than a father or a mother."

Teynoosh receives this message
And succeeds in having his wish granted.

Bahraam, whose heart was so troubled,
Is released from his wretched captivity.
He gives alms to the poor and prepares to leave.
He calls to his side his friends and departs at night
With them, declaring, "Praise be to Yazdan,
We are finally on the road and exempt from fear."

As he approaches the land of Yemen,
Men, women, and children come out to greet him.
Noman and Monzer take the road
With spear-riding loyal warriors.

Monzer approaches Bahraam, raising the dust.
These two free noblemen dismount,
And Bahraam recounts to him his suffering.

Monzer, tearful at the account, questions Bahraam,
"What is the meaning of the king's star?
Never will he walk down the path of wisdom.
I fear that he may resort to retribution."

Bahraam replies, "Heaven forbid
That he discovers his misfortune!"

Monzer takes him to his palace
And treats him with kindness and affection.
Bahraam occupies himself with feast and game,
With acts of generosity and with battle.

8 | Yazdegerd Visits Tous

Some time passes.
The father is in his palace, the son in the desert.
But soon the stars of swift rotation put an end
To the joys and sorrows of King Yazdegerd.
He begins to despair on the fate of kingship.
He unites wise men from the provinces,
Commands astrologers to glance into the stars
To assess when, where, and how his cheeks may wither
And his head may tumble into the darkness of death.

One of the astrologers says, "Heaven forbid
For the world king to speak of death!
When his majesty's fortune turns sour,
He will march from here to the fountain of Soo.[34]
He will take an escort with clarion and timpani
To travel cheerfully to Tous to visit the fountain.
There his fate will be determined, a fate never heard of.
But he must not speak of this to anyone,
For this secret is sheathed in a veil of divinity."

The king swears by the flames of Barzeen and
By the brilliant golden sun that his eyes will never
Perceive this fountain, neither in joy nor in sorrow.

After three months, the world is touched by the fate
Of the king who develops a nosebleed.
Physicians come from every corner to offer advice.
They treat the condition with medicinal herbs.
The king appears to be cured for one week,
But the following week, blood flows again like tears.

9 | Yazdegerd Is Killed by a Hippopotamus at the Fountain of Soo

A wise man says to him, "O King,
You no longer have faith in the Creator.
You claim that death is not your ultimate purpose,
That you have the ability to escape death.
It appears you have one way out left,
And that is to travel in a litter
To the fountain of Soo by way of Shahd.
There you can pray to the pure Yazdan.
You will meander through the burning sands
And lament, "I am a weak, unskilled servant
Who entrapped his soul with an oath.
I present myself before you, O Justice Giver,
To uncover when my end is to come."

The king approves of this speech,

◇◇◇◇◇◇◇◇◇◇◇◇◇◇
34 Fountain of Soo: Must be a fountain near or in Tous.

Finding it beneficial in his distress.
He asks for three hundred litters
And takes the road to the Sea of Shahd.
He travels day and night hastily in the litter.
Blood flows from his nose from time to time.

Once at the source of Soo,
He exits the litter and observes the sea.
He draws some water to wet his head while
Invoking the name of the Creator, Giver of good.
Immediately, his nosebleed stops.
He lies down to rest with his advisors.
He grows overconfident and says,
"I accomplished what I set out to do.
Why should I stay here longer?"

While the king reclaims his pride and
Attributes everything that is good to himself,
A white hippo emerges from the waters.
He has round buttocks like an onager,
A short rump, and he leaps like a mad lion.
Massive, with black testicles, his eyes are indigo,
His tail drags on the ground, his mane drapes
Around his chest, and his hooves are black.
His mouth foams as if he were on the verge of killing a lion.

Yazdegerd says to his noblemen,
"My escort must surround this horse."

A valiant shepherd departs with ten trained horses,
A saddle, and a long, rolled-up noose.
What does the king know of the secrets of the Creator
Who made this dragon appear on his path?

The shepherd and the retinue are surprised.
But seeing them unable to obey his order and reach
The hippo, he is furious, grabs the saddle and reins,
And approaches the white beast who remains still.
He quietly allows the king
To restrain him with bridle and saddle.
The king straps it firmly, then passes behind
To attach the crupper to the unmoving beast.

At that very moment, the hippo of stone hooves
Shouts a cry, nickers and snorts,
Then strikes the king with its two hind legs.
Both head and crown fall into the soil.
The king, who emerged from dust, is thus returned to it.

What can you ask of the sky's seven revolutions?
You cannot escape its rotations,
But it does not serve you well to worship them.
Address the Creator, who is your shelter,
Who is Master of shining Sun and spinning Moon.

Upon the death of the king, the hippo returns
To the blue source from which it emerged
And disappears beneath the surface.
No one in the world has ever witnessed
Such an awe-inspiring marvel.

A cry rises from the royal host, as loud as timpani:
"O King, destiny brought you to Tous!"

Everyone tears apart their clothing;
Everyone tosses dust on their necks and arms.
Then the wise man cleaves the chest,
The midsection, and the brain of the king.
He fills the body with camphor and musk,
Wraps it up with bandages to keep it dry,
Covers it with a beautiful, shiny, silky robe,
And places on the head a diadem of musk.

Then they take the master of crown to Pars
In a golden casket placed in a litter of teakwood.

Such is this passing dwelling.
One finds in it joy, another grief.
When the powerful revolving dome grants you
Rest on this dim earth, have fear of misfortune.
You are full of good will, but it is not reciprocal
As the world bears none for you.
Once you have finished your meal,
There is nothing more welcoming than a cup of wine.
But if one has the strength for it, following
The rules of faith is far better than transgressing.

10 | The Noblemen Place Khosrow on the Throne

With the world king in his tomb,
Leaders come from all over Iran to mourn.
Governors, accompanied by wise men and warriors,
Sages and insightful viziers, all gather in the land of Pars
Around the grave of King Yazdegerd.

Gostaham, able to kill an elephant on horseback;
The valiant Ghaaran, son of Goshasp;
Milaad and border guard Aarash;
Pirooz, the cavalier from Gorzban;[35]
All the powerful Iranian leaders arrive, world masters,
Whom Yazdegerd had considered with scorn.

The eloquent and erudite Goshasp says,
"O illustrious men, young and old,
Since Yazdan created the world,
There has not been such an unjust king.
He excelled only at killing and inflicting pain,
Always hiding from his subjects
Both his intentions and his wealth.
No one remembers a king so corrupt.
We no longer wish to place on the throne
A man from his lineage.
We continue to complain to Yazdan.
The highborn Bahraam is his son;
He inherits his essence, his heart, will and family,
Yet he only speaks of Monzer.
We no longer wish to have an unjust king."

The Iranian leaders take a solemn oath:
"We shall not have a descendant of this race
Climb on the throne of the King of Kings!"
Having agreed, they rise to find a new king.

As the news of the king's death spreads,
The King of Alaan,[36] the army warrior;

◇◇◇◇◇◇◇◇◇◇◇◇◇
35 Gorzban: Unclear location.
36 Alaan, or Alaanan: Region northwest of Iran, north of the Aras River; a part of the
Caucasus.

Bivard; and Shaknan of golden diadem;
Behzaad of Barzeen, from the lineage of Rostam,
The brave Saam, from the seed of Kay Ghobaad;
All say, "Kingship belongs to me from the earth
To the moon's highest summit!"

Everyone is moved with emotion
To see the throne vacant of his master.
Every nobleman, warrior, and learned man
Gathers in the land of Pars to deliberate at length.
They say, "Who is worthy of the royal throne?
Look and see who can fill this empty seat.
Nowhere do we find a just man able to climb
On the throne and strap the golden belt
To calm the troubles that stir the world,
A world which, without a king, is just a pasture."

There lives an old man named Khosrow,
A valiant man of serene and joyous soul,
Born of a most noble and wealthy family.
The leaders hand over to him throne and crown,
And an army gathers around him from everywhere.

11 | Bahraam Learns of His Father's Death

Bahraam the hunter receives the news
Of the misfortunes fate has inflicted on the throne.
Someone says to him, "Your illustrious father is dead,
And with his passing, royal glory fades.
The entire population has sworn never to accept
Another member of his family as ruler,
Convinced that his son Bahraam resembles him,
Having inherited traits, skin, and marrow from him.
They have placed a man named Khosrow
On the throne and have acclaimed him as king."

At the news, Bahraam claws his cheeks,
His heart afflicted by the death of his father.
For two weeks, laments rise from the land of Yemen.
Everyone mourns: sages, men, and women.

After a month of mourning, the prince
Decks his palace at the start of the new moon.
Noman, Monzer, and Arabs from Yemen,
Great and small, come to him weeping
To express their affliction, consumed with grief.

They unravel their tongues and say,
"O powerful King, full of virtue,
We all come to this world to turn into dust.
We arrive without hope for a remedy.
Anyone who is born from a mother is destined to die.
If one looks at the path of life as a violation of nature,
Then death is a just, natural, and divine consequence."

Bahraam the hunter says to Monzer, "Now that the day
Has dimmed for us, if kingship does not continue
From our lineage, our glory and grace will wane.
We must address the king, no matter how violent he is,
He has always been the friend of this desert land.
If the dignity of the King of Kings
Is plucked from this family, a great glory will perish.
They will destroy the plains where live the spear-riders,
And the Taazian land will become a lowland.
Think about that and come to my aid.
Prove to me that you mourn my father."

Monzer listens to Bahraam and replies valiantly,
"This is my destiny. I pass my days hunting.
Climb on the throne and be foreseeing.
May crown and bracelet be yours forever!"

All the noble riders agree
That Monzer has hit the mark.
They rise before the prince, wishing
To prepare for war and to possess the world.

Monzer commands Noman to leave:
"Gather a host of young lions from the tribe of Shayban.
Take ten thousand troops from the tribe of Gheyssian.[37]
I shall show the Iranians who is king,
Who possesses name, treasury, and army."

◇◇◇◇◇◇◇◇◇◇◇◇◇
37 Shayban and Gheyssian: Arab tribes.

Noman musters a vast host, armed with sword and spear,
And commands the troops to invade Iran
And trample the land beneath their feet.

On the road of Assyria[38] to the gates of Ctesiphon,
The earth is stunned beneath the horses' hooves.
Women and children are taken captive.
The world is consumed by devastation and fire,
As the throne of the King of Kings is vacant.

The news spreads through Rum and Chin,
India and Mokran, all the way to the Turks,
That there is no king on the throne of Iran
And that there is no one worthy of kingship.
All the lands prepare to invade,
Rising to pillage and commit unjust acts.

12 | The Iranians Send a Letter to Monzer

The Iranians discover what is happening
And learn of Bahraam's intention to invade Iran.
They rush to convene and propose a solution.
They say, "These attacks from Rum, India,
And from the desert riders surpass all measure.
We must find a way to free our hearts
And our souls from incoming hardships."

They select an envoy, a Persian man of open mind,
Erudite, powerful, and articulate, named Javanooy.
He is to relay the following message to Monzer:
"O renowned man, the world needs you.
You are the protector of Iran and Tooran.
In every way you are the support of valiant men.
When the throne became vacant of king and crown,
A spew of blood rippled like a pheasant's wing.
We proclaimed you the ruler of the land,
For we deemed you worthy of its borders.
But now you are the one destroying everything
And spilling blood as you plunder and pillage.

◇◇◇◇◇◇◇◇◇◇◇◇◇
38 Assyria: Mesopotamia.

Never did you employ such vicious ways.
Do you not fear curses and confrontations?
Reflect on the matter, if it suits you.
Reflect and see whether your actions
Will be to your advantage once you reach old age.
There is a higher ruler besides you whose nature
Is far beyond anything our minds can access.
The envoy will relate to you what he has seen and heard."

Javanooy travels to the land of spear-riders.
He delivers the letter and the words of the Iranian leaders.

The Arab King listens to him but refuses to reply.
He says, "O wise man, seeker of the true path,
Repeat all this to Bahraam, King of Kings.
If you wish to obtain a response, he will give it to you."

He sends an illustrious man to accompany Javanooy.
At the sight of Bahraam, the learned emissary
Invokes the name of the Creator, in awe over
His stature, his legs, his arms and shoulders.
It is as if wine drips from his cheeks,
As if his hair exudes the scent of musk.

The eloquent, intelligent envoy loses sense
Of himself and of the message he is to impart.
Bahraam notices his confusion
And the fact that his appearance troubles him.
He receives him kindly, questions him formally,
And invites him to sit before the throne.

Once he sees him regain his composure,
The king asks, "Why did you put yourself
Through the hardship of traveling from Iran?
Later I shall reward you and fill your treasury."

At this point, the messenger hands over the letter
And acquits himself of the message.

Bahraam urges him to heed his message,
Then sends him back to Monzer with an escort.

Javanooy departs and speaks to Monzer,

Whose cheeks blossom at Bahraam's wisdom.
He composes the reply to the letter and says,
"O wise emissary, anyone who causes harm
Will suffer grave consequences.
I have listened to what you had to say
And the greetings you relay from Iran's noblemen.
Tell me who instigated this?
Tell me who is the cause of this foolish struggle?
The King of Kings, Bahraam the hunter, is here,
Endowed with royal majesty, power, and army.
If you draw out the serpent from his hole,
You will drag your robe's hem through blood.
If it were up to me, if I gave you my counsel,
The Iranians would never have to be challenged."

Javanooy, having seen the king's face, having spoken
To him at length, and having questioned him to see
If he is worthy of throne, power, good fortune,
And victory, designs a brilliant idea and replies,
"O famed man, you require no one else's wisdom.
If the Iranians lost their senses for a moment,
A great number of brave men have perished.
I am an old man who seeks a good name.
Do you wish to listen to what I have to say?
In all trust, we can place you and Bahraam
In possession of land and throne.
Travel to Iran with falcon and cheetah,
As suits a king who spreads light across the world.
You have heard the words of the Iranians.
You may journey there without fear.
You will tell them what is necessary, for you are
An intelligent man who keeps stupidity at bay.
Turn your mind away from ill intentions
And from condemnation and quarrel."

Monzer listens to him, offers him gifts,
And allows him to leave satisfied from his visit.

13 | Bahraam the Hunter Travels to Jahrom

Monzer and Bahraam sit with an advisor
And discuss without the presence of a council.
Monzer selects thirty thousand Taazian,
Armed with spear and suited for battle.
He elevates them with dinars
And fills their heads with the winds of vanity.

As news reaches Iran, Javanooy returns
To the side of the valiant leaders, who,
Weary of this affair, go to the flame of Barzeen.
They plead with the Creator to grant them mercy
And convert fight to the joys of feast.

Monzer drives his host from the dry plains to Jahrom.
Bahraam asks for the tent enclosure to be set up,
And the troops settle all around.

Bahraam says to Monzer, "O sensible man,
You have marched to Jahrom from the land of Yemen.
Now that the two hosts are present,
Shall we battle or shall we negotiate?"

Monzer replies, "Call the noblemen.
When they arrive, dress the banquet spread.
Listen to their words, and do not allow another's
Anger to fling you into a state of irritation.
We shall attempt to uncover their secret thoughts and
The identity of the one they wish to nominate as king.
Once we hold the information,
We shall evaluate a proper course of action.
If it is an easy task, we shall not resort to hate.
But if their hostility leans toward battle,
If they stir and expose their leopard nature,
I shall turn the plain of Jahrom into a bloodbath,
Convert the sun into the constellation of the Pleiades.
I think that once their eyes fall on your features,
Your lofty stature, your wisdom, your education,
Your patience, your knowledge and deportment,
They will not call any other to accede and to reign.
You are master of crown and ornament of fortune.

207

"But if they stray and attempt to seize the throne,
I shall, with the aid of my horsemen and
Their honed swords, turn the world upside down.
Then you will witness furrowed brows.
May I be the ransom for your body and soul!
When they see my vast host, my manner of being,
My customs, and the path I follow,
When they realize that bloodshed is our occupation,
When they think of Yazdan, the just, our support,
They will call you and only you world king,
As you are, from father to father, the legitimate
Master of crown, worthy of the royal throne."
The prince smiles at Monzer; his heart opens with joy.

As the sun raises its head over the mountain crest,
A host of Iranian leaders and noblemen
Prepares to travel on the road to meet Bahraam.
It is an assembly full of wisdom.

Meanwhile, an ivory throne is decked for Bahraam.
He sets on his head the magnificent crown and,
As world master, commands a reception
In line with imperial ceremony.
On one side is Monzer, on the other Noman,
Sword in hand, and all around the royal pavilion
Stand the Arab leaders and warriors.

The well-intentioned Iranians present themselves
At the opening of the tent enclosure.
Bahraam asks for the curtains to be raised
And for them to be announced in a loud voice.
They arrive in front of Bahraam Shah,
Observe his crown and glorious throne,
And exclaim, "May you always be happy!
May the hand of misfortune be kept at bay!"

The King of Kings asks them the customary questions,
Receives them graciously, and positions them
According to their respective rank.

Then Bahraam says, "O brave men of Iran,
As leaders and aging men, you know the world well.
Kingship belongs to me as a succession from father to son.

Tell me, why have you taken it
Upon yourselves to decide otherwise?"

The Iranians reply in a common voice,
"Do not keep us in a state of adversity.
We are unanimous in our choice:
We do not desire you to be our king.
The land is ours, though you have an army.
Your family inflicted on us deep wounds.
We spent days and nights writhing
And sighing in pain and agony."

Bahraam replies, "It is all very well.
Desire reigns supreme in each heart.
If you do not wish for me to rule,
Why do you place someone on the throne
Without having first consulted me?"

A wise man says, "Neither subject nor the son
Of a king must evade what is right and fair.
Best you be one of ours and help us
Select a king we can receive with blessings."

Three days pass during which time
They search throughout Iran to find a proper ruler.
In the end, they write the names of one hundred
Illustrious men, owners of crown and belt.
One of them is Bahraam,
A prince who charms every heart.
They narrow down to fifty with a desire to succeed
With Bahraam still positioned at the lead.
And if he demands his father's seat,
He is only asking for what is rightly his.

The names are narrowed down to thirty
Glorious, prosperous, elected Iranian men.
Again, Bahraam is at the lead as a valiant prince.
And once they reduce thirty to four,
His position remains unchanged.

As they approach election day, the older Iranians
Speak: "We do not wish to select Bahraam.
Though he is brave, he is light of mind and will."

A great sound rises from the leaders,
And the hearts of many flame up.
Then Monzer says to the Iranians,
"I am eager to know what this is about and how
The prince, so young, so brave, has filled your hearts
With concern and your souls with wounds.
There is no king equal to him in glory.
He has no equal in beauty, not even the moon.
His arrow of poplar wood pierces anvil.
His power can uproot a mountain.
He is young in age but old in wisdom.
He is skilled and insightful, a true seeker."

The noble leaders are ready and quick to reply.
They summon a great number of wretched Iranians,
Men mutilated and hurt by Yazdegerd.
Some are deprived of hands and feet,
Others are missing feet but still have their hands.
Others' hands, ears, and tongues have been maimed.
They appear to be soulless bodies.
Yet others are without shoulders.

Noman is confused at the sight of the maimed.
He perceives a man whose eyes
Have been removed with a nail.
Monzer loses his temper.

Bahraam is similarly troubled.
Addressing his father's dust, he says,
"O miserable King, you could have just
Been happy by preventing me to enjoy life,
Why burn your soul in the flame of these reprimands?"

World seeker Monzer says to Bahraam,
"You cannot hide these misdeeds from them.
You have heard their words; now reply to them.
A king must not remain in a state of indecision."

14 | Bahraam Affirms His Ability to Serve as King

Bahraam says, "O worldly, skilled leaders of Iran,
You speak the truth, and I do blame my father.
My heart fills with bitterness on this subject.
He is the one who tarnished my subtle mind,
For his court became my prison cell
Until Yazdan came to my rescue.
Teynoosh freed me from his bonds,
And I was able to escape the king's fishhook.
After that, Monzer's desert became my refuge.
Never did the king show me a hint of kindness.
May no one exhibit such a wicked nature!
If there existed more men like him,
Any remnant of humanity would disappear.

"Praise be to Yazdan, who endowed me with wisdom
And nourished my mind with sense and reason.
May Yazdan be my Guide toward all that is good
So that I may expunge my father's crimes!
Let us, together, seek peace and justice.
I shall be the shepherd and you the flock.
I shall live to satisfy all my subjects,
As a proper worshipper of the Creator.
I am gifted with good will, integrity, and virtue.
An unjust king is surely deprived of these qualities.
Injustice and deceit are the greatest sources of misery.
One must weep bitterly for those who are unjust.
I am the heir of my father's throne:
Greatness, valor, and supremacy are mine;
Wisdom, benevolence, and kingship are mine.

"From Shahpoor, son of Bahraam, to Ardeshir,
Kings, young and old, from father to son,
Are my ancestors and my guides in faith and conduct.
On my mother's side,
I am a descendant of Shah Shemiran,
Identical in race and intelligence.
I own the same faculties of prudence, power,
Horsemanship, bravery, and strength.
I see no one equal to me in battle or in feast.
I inherited a secret treasure from royal supporters.

211

I have many illustrious, devoted friends,
I shall make the earth blossom with justice,
And you will have much cause to rejoice."

15 | The Iranians Make a Royal Pact With Bahraam

Bahraam continues, "I shall make an agreement
With you, holding Yazdan as my witness.
Let us deck the ivory throne of the King of Kings.
Let us bring two wild lions from the forest,
Place the crown between them.
Let us attach the lions on both sides,
And the one desirous to be king will seize
The royal crown and place it on his head.
He will sit as king between the two lions,
The crown on his head and the throne beneath him.
We shall not seek any other king but him
Should he remain a fair and faithful ruler.
We shall name him king provided he is just and pure.
But if he is not, we shall replace him with another.
Monzer and I will be there with mace and sword
And Taazian warriors who know not how to flee.
We shall annihilate your king,
We shall toss your heads above the sphere of the moon.
I have spoken. Give me your reply.
Apply wisdom to this cause,
For wisdom cultivates good luck."

After speaking, he rises and enters his tent.
Confused by his words, the noble and wise Iranians say,
"Here is an example of divine majesty
Bestowed upon a man by the Creator.
There is no perversity or foolishness in his words.
He does not say anything that is not just,
And for that reason, we have cause to rejoice.
As for the two fierce lions and the Kianian crown
And throne that we would place in between them,
If they devour Bahraam, the Justice Giver
Would not find a reason to reprimand us
Since Bahraam himself proposed the plan.
If he dies, we can rest at ease and live in joy.

If he succeeds in seizing the crown,
He will be more glorious than Fereydoon.
We shall then recognize no other as king.
We shall make our final decision
According to his own suggestion."

16 | Bahraam and the Noblemen Discuss How to Proceed

The night passes, and the next day at dawn,
The king arrives and climbs on the throne.
He summons the Iranians and speaks at length
On the subject discussed the previous day.

The illustrious and sensible men reply out loud,
"O King, wisest among judicious men,
What will you accomplish in your royal seat
Once you conquer it with your boldness?
How will you exhibit justice and righteousness
To reduce the harm that has been done?"

He replies, "I shall accomplish more than I promise.
I shall abstain from unjust acts and extortion.
I shall distribute the world to those worthy of rule.
I shall govern guided by justice and wisdom.
Once I have succeeded in giving a sense of security,
I shall be happy with the outcome of my deeds.
I shall distribute wealth from my treasury to the poor.
I shall advise those who stumble and err.
If they fall back, I shall bind them in chains.
I shall pay the army's wages on a timely basis.
I shall fill with joy the hearts of sensible men.
My intentions will be in agreement with my words,
My mind repudiating darkness and perversity.

"If a rich man dies without an heir, I shall offer
His inheritance, no matter how vast, to the poor.
I shall not attach my heart to this passing dwelling.
I shall always consult those with knowledge
Of world affairs, and, by the order established,
I shall annihilate greed.

With every new matter concerning justice,
I shall resort to the counsel of my vizier,
Without the need to raise the assembly.
I shall give justice to anyone who claims it.
I shall punish evil men according to royal tradition.
I hold Yazdan, the pure, as my witness
And reason as the master of my tongue."

The vizier, the wise and worldly noblemen,
And the skilled warriors cry out, "We are your slaves.
We lower our heads at your command and at your will."

Bahraam Shah says, "O sensible men,
You shed light on the true path!
Were one hundred years to pass over us,
I shall not turn away from my words.
I reject my inheritance, my right to crown and throne,
And will sit among those whose fortune is unclear."

At these words, the wise men, leaders, and sages
Repent their words of long ago and seek a solution.
They declare, "Who is more worthy of kingship?
Never has there been a man greater in courage,
In eloquence, in intelligence, and in birth.
No one more pure was ever born.
The Creator molded him with justice.
May misfortune evade him!
We shall receive great happiness from him.
We shall have the chance to enjoy life.
No one in the world equals him in stature,
In strength of chest and arms.
Behind him is a vast Taazian host,
And Monzer is his ally in good and bad.
If he occupies his family's throne,
Who will be superior to him on earth?
Furthermore, why should he fear the Iranians?
What are we to him but a fistful of dust?"

They turn to Bahraam and say, "O glorious prince,
Our souls welcome you and acclaim you as our king.
None of us was apprised of your qualities,
Your speech, your wisdom, your intentions.

But we paid homage to Khosrow as king
And as descendant of Kay Pashin.
We are bound to him by an oath
That allows him to cause us harm.
If he continues his reign as King of Iran,
The land will be destroyed by wars
As one half of the population will greet you with joy
While the other half will support Khosrow.
In all justice, your proposition is worth more.
From now on, the world will be at your command.
This battle with lions is a good excuse
To dismiss certain contenders for power."

Bahraam is in complete agreement,
Since he is the one who designed the scheme.

The ritual of noble kings dictates that
Upon the arrival of a new ruler,
The grand wise master is to appear before him,
Attended by three wise men. Together they are
To settle the king on the throne, utter blessings,
Then lower the golden crown on the royal head,
Thus conferring on him glory, grandeur, and majesty.
After adjusting the Kianian crown, the vizier
Would happily rest his face on the ruler's chest.
Then the king would distribute alms to the needy.

The grand master is given the crown and throne,
And this man of awakened fortune goes from city to plain.
The valiant Gostaham has two enchained lions
That he hands over to the vizier, who fearfully
And with great effort leads them to the throne
Where they are attached to the ivory foot.
The crown is placed in the corner of the seat.
The crowd gathers to observe how the auspicious prince
Will handle the precarious, perilous situation.

17 | Bahraam Kills the Lions and Ascends the Throne

Bahraam and Khosrow arrive on the plain
And approach the lions with wounded hearts.
At the sight of the two wild beasts
And the crown raised between them,
Khosrow says to the wise men, "In the first place,
The crown suits the one who seeks kingship;
Furthermore, Bahraam is young, and I am old
And incapable of contesting with such fierce claws.
It is best for him to execute the deed first
In view of his youth and his body's strength."

Bahraam replies, "It is all very well.
You are right, and we have nothing to hide."
He grabs a bull-headed mace,
And the crowd watches in astonishment.

The wise master says to him,
"O pure and prudent king, full of knowledge,
Who asked you to battle the lions?
What more do you want than royalty?
Do not surrender your life for the sake of the throne.
Do not foolishly offer your body to be crushed.
We are innocent, yet you put yourself at risk,
And the world is in agreement about your fate."

Bahraam replies to him, "O faith-seeker,
You and the people are innocent in this affair.
I am the worthy rival of these male lions.
I am responsible for the plan to engage
In a fierce battle with bold warriors."

The vizier says, "The Creator is your shelter
If you wish to absolve your soul of sins."

Bahraam Shah obeys the grand vizier.
He purifies his heart and repents for his sins.
He washes his head and body with fresh water
And finds a secluded place of prayer on the field.
He bows down to the pure Yazdan to pray,
His face and eyes resting on the dark dust:

"O Creator, allow your humble servants
To succeed in all their endeavors.
Help this slave of yours who seeks justice
And wishes to cleanse the world of evil.
In this war, have mercy on my life
And give me the strength to overcome the lions."

The wise king returns and departs for battle
Wielding his bull-headed mace.
When the warring lions see him approach,
One of them breaks free of his chains
And lurches toward the lofty king.
The valiant Bahraam strikes him on the head
With his mace and robs him of his eyes' glint.
Then he walks over to the other lion
And sends a sharp blow to its head.
Blood flows from its beastly eyes onto its chest.

The world ruler sits on the ivory throne
And lowers the glorious crown on his head.

Khosrow bows respectfully before him and says,
"O highborn King, may you find peace on the throne!
May world heroes stand as your slaves!
You are king, and we are your servants,
Prosperous only through your benevolence.
Our shelter is Yazdan, our Protector,
Who shows drifters the proper path to follow."

The noblemen scatter jewels over Bahraam
And joyously bless the new throne.
A great cry rises over the world.
A feast on Sooroosh day in the month of Aazar[39]
Commemorates the day Bahraam claims supremacy,
Intent on performing acts of justice and generosity.

A black cloud passes over the moon
From which a dense snow falls,
Covering river, sea, plain, and mountain crest.
I find myself unable to distinguish a raven's wing.
I wonder what the revolving dome expects to achieve

◇◇◇◇◇◇◇◇◇◇◇◇◇◇
39 Sooroosh day, Aazar month: November seventeen.

With this interminable and blinding snowfall.
I have no salt left, no wood, no smoked meats,
And hardly any barley to harvest for next year.
In this darkness of day and the fear of tribute to pay,
While the snow turns the earth into a mountain of ivory,
All my affairs appear to be on the decline,
Unless a friend, the governor of Tous,
Is able and willing to come to my aid.

Now I shall turn to tell an astonishing tale
Of which nothing can exceed the wonders.

XIII. The Sixty-Three-Year Reign of Bahraam the Hunter

1 | The Beginning of Bahraam's Reign

Bahraam sits upon the throne of authority,
Allowing the sun to pay homage to his majesty.
He begins to worship the Creator,
Omnipresent World Master who never rests;
Master of victory and power, of growth and decline;
Master of Justice and Master of Wisdom,
Who nurtures, nourishes, and guides all beings.

Then Bahraam says, "The Creator of good fortune
Has endowed me with this throne and crown.
My hope rests in Yazdan, whom I fear,
Giver of all that we have; the One to be exalted.
Make every effort to observe our divine pact."

The Iranians open their lips to say,
"We are cinched in service to you.
May this crown bring good fortune to the king!
May his heart and his good will live eternally!"
After celebrating him, they scatter gems over him.

Bahraam adds, "O illustrious leaders,
You have experienced good and bad days.
We are all servants, and Yzad is one,
The only One to be worshipped.
I shall guard you from the fear of unhappy days
And will never expose you to an adverse destiny."

He speaks in this manner, then the Iranians rise
And summon new blessings upon him.
They spend the dark night discussing the events.
Once the sun reveals its shining face in the sky,
The king sits peacefully on his throne

219

While his people ask for an audience.

Bahraam says, "O illustrious, auspicious
Noblemen, let us turn to the divine.
Let us rejoice in the light of Yazdan.
Let us relinquish pride
And the vanities of the physical world."

The horses are brought in,
And the heroes form a court worthy of a Kianian.

On the third day, he sits on the throne and says,
"We must not neglect the customs of worship.
Let us affirm the existence of Yazdan.
Let us connect our hearts to the path of faith.
There is paradise, hell, and resurrection,
And we cannot escape the good or the bad.
A man who does not believe in the day of retribution
Cannot be considered a believer or a wise man."

On the fourth day, as he sits on the ivory throne
And places the venerated crown on his head,
He declares, "I have never attached myself to wealth,
But I have attached myself to the joy of my subjects.
I do not hold on to this fleeting dwelling.
I feel, without grief or fear, that I must depart.
The other world is eternal; this one is transient.
Abstain from greed, and do not dwell in worry."

On the fifth day, he says, "The pain I would inflict
On others to aggrandize myself would crush my joy.
Let us make every effort to gain access to paradise.
Happy is the one who scatters seeds of righteousness!"

On the sixth day, he proclaims,
"Heaven forbid that we must suffer a defeat.
We shall guarantee the army against the enemy.
We shall make it formidable to evildoers."

On the seventh day, he takes his seat and says,
"O wise men full of vigilance and experience,
Since battle with wicked men debases us,
Let us befriend only judicious men.

Anyone who does not enthusiastically help us
Will have more reason to suffer under my reign
Than under the reign of my father.
But anyone who obeys our command
Shall endure neither worry nor sorrow."

On the eighth day, after climbing on the throne,
He singles out Javanooy from his court's assembly.
He says to him, "Write a judicious, benevolent letter
To all the noblemen in the provinces
To communicate the following message:
    'Bahraam has happily ascended the throne.
    He is a master of kindness and righteousness,
    He is able to keep perversity at bay.
    He is glorious and powerful, benevolent and just.
    He speaks only of the pure Creator.
        "I shall favor those who obey me," he says,
        "But offenders will be deemed culpable.
        I sit on the throne of my glorious father
        And observe the customs of Tahmures.
        I shall show virtue toward all, good or bad.
        I shall surpass my ancestors in justice
        And will be your guide toward faith.
        I am of the religion of Zoroaster, the prophet.
        I shall not stray from the path of my forefathers,
        Who held before their eyes the ancient law
        And the path of Ibrahim, the truthful prophet.
        Every one of you is king of his own domain,
        Defender of his borders, guardian of his faith,
        And master of his wife and children.
        Happy is the one who is pure and wise!
        I wish not to accumulate more gold,
        For treasures leave the poor in distress.
        May Yazdan give me life and guard me
        From the wrath of adverse stars!
        Read this cheerful letter that will confirm
        The preservation of your honor and wealth.
        Greetings to the rulers, especially those for whom
        Benevolence is the weft and warp of life."'"

The seal is affixed to all the letters.
Bahraam selects illustrious emissaries

And prudent riders of awakened minds.
And they ride off with the correspondence.

2 | Bahraam the Hunter Forgives the Iranians' Back Taxes

The next morning, as the sun begins to light
The mountain crest and stirs awake the sleepy heads,
A group of anxious men gather at Monzer's hall
So that he may intercede in their favor
And influence the king to forgive them of their crimes.

They say, "Our actions resulted from the evil deeds
Of Yazdegerd who made the blood run cold
In our hearts with his countless misdeeds,
With his nasty words, his unjust acts, his afflictions
And the abuse he subjected us to during his reign.
The reason why our hearts grew cold toward Bahraam,
Was because, in fact, we detested his father."

Monzer appears before the king and softens him
With sweet and gentle words.
The king forgives even the most culpable ones,
For he is just and compassionate.

Bahraam prepares the royal hall, and powerful
And highborn men present themselves before him.
Once everything is in order, seats are assigned.
Banquets are spread with wine, music and singers.

The next day comes another group and a long time
Passes before they grow weary of drinking wine.

Three days of banquet, wine and feast pass
With worry kept away from the king's palace.
The king recounts all that Noman and Monzer,
Men of pure race, have accomplished for him.
All the noblemen shower with praise
The blessed, sandy land and its two just rulers.

Then the king opens the door to his treasury

And fills his palace with gold and brocade,
Horses, bridles, battle armor, scents and colorful gems,
Giving the lot to Noman and Monzer.
Javanooy takes the list to them and counts the goods.

No one is as generous as Bahraam,
And no one has the power to resist his will.
In a similar manner, he gives abundantly to the Arabs,
And they joyously take their leave.

He asks for a horse, a royal robe, and a warrior's attire
Which he offers to Khosrow whom he receives graciously
And whom he seats on an auspicious throne.

After the ruler Khosrow, Bahraam climbs down
His throne and approaches his brother, Nersi,
With whom he shares a heart and a tongue.
He gives the younger illustrious man
The command of troops and nominates him
Army leader so that he may bring peace and order.

The king gains everyone's heart through his generosity.
He opens his treasury and makes the delight
Of the troops by paying their salaries with gold coins.

Then, the benevolent king summons Goshasp,
The scribe, and the vigilant Javanooy, his treasurer,
And commands them to clear all the back taxes.
The learned scribes go to the offices
And speak on the subject of the dirhams to Kayvan,
The most educated man of this time
Who is in charge of the world accounts.

They add up all the payments owing the empire
And estimate that ninety times one hundred dirhams
Are missing from the treasury funds.
Bahraam forgives the unsettled payments
And throws the registers into the fire.

The entire population of Iran rejoices,
And everyone showers the king with blessings.
They travel to the fire temples and to the palace
To celebrate Nowruz and the festival of Saddeh.

They sprinkle musk on the flames
And invoke divine grace on Bahraam.

Then the king sends skilled agents around the world
To search for those Yazdegerd once exiled.
He gathers them in a city to receive a royal letter,
That asks the liberated men what their hearts desire.

He sends a robe of honor and crates of gold
To every nobleman and offers each a province to rule.
The illustrious men and border guards
Who hear the praises of Bahraam arrive at court,
Open-hearted and with cheerful faces.

The king tells those who seek justice
To address the grand wise master.
At his order, he places heralds at the doors
To proclaim, "O subjects of the vigilant king,
Forget your worries and keep away from sin.
Bless those who make the world prosper.
Seek protection in the Creator, our Savior.
Anyone who wishes to obey our command,
Anyone who walks down our path
Without deviating from his pact to us,
I shall double my kindness to him,
Casting hatred and greed out of my heart.
But anyone who abuses his duty to justice
Will submit to severe punishment.
If the Creator gives us strength,
If fortune fulfills our wishes,
Our acts of kindness will multiply
And you will have cause to celebrate us."

Those who hear these words depart in joy,
Willing to follow the true path.
Once his kingship is firmly established,
Happiness takes over and worries vanish.

The king only occupies himself with feast and hunt,
With riding his horse, and playing polo on the field.

3 | The Adventure of Bahraam With Lambak

One day, Bahraam is on his way to hunt with a number
Of valiant men when an old man, cane in hand,
Says to him, "O King and Yazdan worshipper,
There are two men in our town: One is Beraham,
A prosperous Jew, rich in gold and silver,
A selfish man of ill character who lacks integrity;
The other is Lambak, carrier of water,
A noble, hospitable man, amiable of speech."

The king asks "Who are these people?
Are they truly as this old man describes?"

An honest man replies, "O illustrious King,
Lambak is a pure and kind carrier of water.
He is young, cordial, and soft-spoken.
Half of the day, he busies himself with his task,
The other half, he searches for a guest or companion.
He does not keep anything from one day to the next.
On the other hand, Beraham is useful to no one
And is extremely miserly.
He owns coins, golden treasures, carpets of brocade,
And all sorts of riches and valuables."

The king commands a herald to proclaim
At the marketplace that if someone buys
Water from Lambak, he must not drink it.
He awaits the descent of the sun,
Then he climbs on his charger and, as swift as wind,
Gallops to Lambak's home, knocks on the door,
And calls: "I am an army leader from Iran.
Night has fallen, and I have been delayed.
Let me pass the night in this home.
I shall be discreet and act honorably."

Lambak, delighted with the voice and friendly words,
Says, "O rider, be quick to enter my home.
May the King be pleased with you!
I wish you had brought ten companions with you.
Each one of you would be far superior to me."

225

King Bahraam dismounts, and the water carrier
Takes care of his horse, rubs him down gaily,
Removing the dust, and attaches him to a halter.

Once seated, Lambak places before Bahraam
A game of chess and procures him a meal,
Presenting him with all sorts of fare.
Then he says to his guest, "O venerable lord,
Leave the pieces of the game and keep me company."

Once they have dined, Lambak brings a cup of wine.
The king is in awe of the way he is received by his host,
His politeness, kind words, and friendly face.

Bahraam sleeps soundly through the night.
In the early morning, his host's voice awakens him:
"Your horse was poorly nourished during the night.
Remain one more day as my guest,
And if you wish I can invite another visitor
To keep you company and satisfy your needs."

The king replies to the carrier of water,
"I do not have much to do today.
I shall not refuse your offer."

Lambak departs, carrying some buckets,
But no one approaches him to buy water.
Disappointed, he strips off his tunic,
Takes a leather bucket under his arm
And a stole he places under the bottles, and walks
To the market, where he buys meat and whey.

Upon his return, he places the cauldron on the fire
While his guest observes his efforts.
Lambak cooks the meal. They eat, drink wine,
And enjoy each other's company.
Bahraam spends the night, cup in hand,
With Lambak the water carrier delighting in wine.

As night makes way to day,
Lambak rushes to Bahraam's side and says,
"May your days and nights be happy!
May you live free of worry, fatigue, and hard work!

Grant me one more day of your presence.
It will give me energy and bring me good fortune."

Bahraam replies, "Heaven forbid
That we enjoy each other for some time longer!"

His host blesses him and says,
"May your heart maintain its awareness
And your fortune remain loyal to you!"

He goes to the market with some buckets
And utensils and pawns them to a rich man.
He buys the necessary items and runs back
Quite joyously to Bahraam, saying,
"Help me cook, for a man subsists on meals."

Bahraam cuts the meat and roasts it over the flame.
After dining, they drink to the king's health.
Then Lambak prepares the king's bed
And places a candle at his bedside.

On the fourth day, as the sun begins to shine,
Bahraam the hunter awakens, and his host
Approaches him to say, "O illustrious man,
Without a doubt you have not found comfort
During the night in my narrow and somber home.
If you do not fear the wrath of the King of Iran
And if it is your heart's desire, remain for two more
Weeks here, though it is quite an inferior dwelling."

Bahraam Shah acclaims him and says,
"May you spend months and years happily!
We have enjoyed each other's company for three days.
We have drunk to the health of world kings.
I shall sing your praises everywhere to your delight,
For your hospitality is praiseworthy.
You will receive vast rewards
And perhaps a throne and crown."

As swift as dust, he saddles his horse
And departs in the direction of the hunting grounds.
He chases prey until nightfall dims the mountains.
Then he abruptly separates from his escort.

4 | The Adventure of Bahraam With Beraham

Without his army being aware of his movements,
Bahraam knocks at Beraham's door and says,
"I drifted away from the king
Upon his return from the hunt and lost sight
Of the royal escort when night descended.
If you wish to give me lodging for the night,
I shall not be a burden to anyone."

The servant announces the visitor to his master.
Beraham replies, "Do not bother yourself.
Tell him that he may not find shelter here."

The envoy tells Bahraam,
"There is no lodging for you here."

Bahraam replies, "Tell your master
That I have no intention of leaving.
I ask for shelter for only one night,
And I shall not cause further trouble."

The servant listens and returns to Beraham:
"This rider is most stubborn and refuses to leave.
He has explained his reasons at length."

Beraham replies, "Go right away and tell him
That this home is small, that the master is wretched,
And sleeps hungry and naked on the floor."

The servant relays the message, but Bahraam insists,
"I shall recline at the door and ask for nothing."

Beraham says, "O belligerent man,
You are a source of great trouble.
If you choose to sleep here, someone will come
And steal your belongings; this fact concerns me.
Enter my dwelling, if the world is restricted for you
And if you are in a state of despair.
Only promise that you do not ask for anything,
For, I swear on my life, I possess neither towel nor coffin."

Bahraam says, "O righteous man,

I promise not to be a bother to you.
I shall recline by the door and keep watch
Without making a sound."

Concerned, Beraham reflects deeply:
"This man will not leave so quickly,
And there is no one to take care of his horse."
He says out loud, "O noble man,
Your speech exhausts me.
If your charger, who is your companion,
Requires feed, or if it performs its business,
Or breaks the bricks of the house, then it is your duty,
In the early morning hour, to take out the refuse.
You will have to sweep the house
And throw the dust into the fields.
Then you will turn to my firebricks, and,
Upon awakening, you will pay for the broken ones."

Bahraam replies, "I promise to obey, and may
My head be the guarantee for any damage incurred."

He dismounts, attaches his horse by the bridle,
Draws his sword from its sheath,
Spreads on the floor his charger's felt covering,
Makes use of his saddle as a pillow, and lies
Down to sleep, extending his feet on the bare floor.

The Jew closes the door behind him,
Brings a table and sits down to eat.
Then he says to Bahraam,
"O rider, remember the story I tell you.
Anyone who has something to eat, eats.
Anyone without food observes the others eat."

Bahraam replies, "I have heard this old tale
From the mouth of a wise sage,
And I now see it unfold before my eyes."

After his dinner, the Jew brings wine,
Which makes him joyous as he cries,
"O weary traveler, lend an ear to these old words:
Anyone who has money will enjoy saving it
With a sense of gratitude.

A rich man is assured a serene heart,
For the dirham is his armor of shelter.
Those who possess nothing have a parched lip,
Like you who is hungry in the middle of night."

Bahraam replies, "I have seen this astonishing thing
And will guard myself from forgetting it.
If the end of this cup brings you good luck,
Long live the drinker, the wine, and the cup!"

As the sun raises its dagger over the mountain,
Bahraam the hunter shakes away his slumber.
He saddles his hungry horse, but really
It is his firm pillow that he places on the horse.

Beraham comes to him and says,
"O rider, you do not keep your word.
You promised to sweep away your horse's droppings.
You must do so and take them away from here.
I find myself pained to have such a dishonest guest."

Bahraam says, "Go and bring me your servant.
He will take these droppings without aversion.
I shall give him gold to take them to the field."

The other replies, "I have no one to sweep
And take the remains into a ditch.
Do not avoid your duty by way of duplicity,
For you accepted the agreement we made.
I wish not to call you unjust."

At these words, a brilliant idea comes to Bahraam.
He has in his boot a beautiful silk handkerchief
Perfumed with musk and amber.
He pulls it out, places the droppings inside,
And throws it into the ditch with the swept dust.

Beraham runs to retrieve it, and the king, surprised,
Says to him, "O pure man, if the king learns
Of your decent actions, he will put you above need
And raise your status above the noblest noblemen."

5 | Bahraam Offers Lambak Beraham's Treasure

Bahraam returns to his palace
And searches all night for a way to proceed.
He cannot sleep, so preoccupied is he.
He laughs but does not share his secret with anyone.

In the early morning, he places the crown on his head
And gives an audience to the army leaders.
He summons Lambak, the carrier of water,
Who presents himself arms crossed over his chest.
Beraham, the wicked, is brought in and seated.
Then they call upon a man of integrity to whom
The king says, "Take with you loaded horses
And depart, making sure to avoid unjust actions.
Go without delay to Beraham's home,
Inspect his belongings, and bring them all here."

The pure emissary departs, finds the home of the Jew
Full of brocade and gold, clothing, carpets,
Hangings, and all sorts of valuables and collectibles.
The house is reminiscent of a caravan depot
With merchandise so abundant,
It fills the space from ceiling to floor.
There are pearls, rubies, all sorts of gems, and in
One place, crates full of gold covered with diamonds.

The wise man cannot accurately estimate the lot.
He brings one thousand camels from the desert
Of Jahrom, and, once they are fully loaded,
There is still more wealth inside.
Then the emissary joyously sets the caravan in motion.

As the bells ring out at the palace court,
The intelligent emissary relates to the king:
"There is as much wealth as in your treasury,
And more remains, about two hundred kharvaar."

Astounded, the King of Iran reflects on the excess
Of greed: "This Jew has amassed so much!
But what good is it to him,
Since he does not take his share every day?"

He gives the carrier of water one hundred camels
Loaded with gold and silver, carpets and other objects.
Lambak departs, grateful for the valuables.

Then he calls Beraham and says to him,
"A loss brings you down into the dust!
You say that your prophet has long lived here.
I grant you an extended life.
Why do you cry over the superfluous?
A rider once shared with me an ancient saying:
        'The one who prospers enjoys,
        And the one who has nothing wastes away.'
        Withdraw your hand from these pleasures
        And observe from now on the water carrier's joy."

Then he reminds the miser of the horse's droppings,
The gold-embroidered handkerchief, and the bricks.
He gives the impure man four dirhams and says,
"Here is your capital. More than that would be unwise.
I give the money to the poor and, to you, your head."

He distributes the wealth to men worthy of it,
And the Jew departs weeping and lamenting.

The king plunders what remains in Beraham's home,
For strangers are more worthy of it than this man.

6 | Bahraam Kills the Lions and Prohibits Wine

One day, Bahraam has the idea to hunt with cheetah.
He rises and climbs on his speedy stallion
To charge into the plain, a falcon perched on his fist.

He reaches thick woods, the sojourn of fortunate men,
A site as verdant as paradise, vacant of men and beast.
He thinks, "This must be a place where lions roam
And not the sort of forest where men can rest."

He crosses the woods and glances in every direction.
He spots a male lion through the trees, and while
Aware that a true weapon would be a sword,

He hollers a shout as he binds his bow.
The lion attempts to bolt, but Bahraam
Is able to suspend its flight with an arrow
That bores through its flank and its heart.

A raging female lion charges at Bahraam.
Roaring madly, she digs her claws into his body.
The cavalier strikes its midriff with his sword,
And the creature weakens, unable to struggle.

A peasant, named Mehrbandad, a Yazdan worshipper
Who dwells nearby, emerges from the woods
To greet Bahraam, exalt him, and speak gently to him:
 "O powerful, illustrious King,
May your star of fortune be favorable to you!
I am a farmer, O man of pure intentions;
I am the master of these lands and fields.
I own oxen, donkeys, and sheep, but lions
Terrify me more than anything and cause my downfall.
Now the Creator has placed you here to free me
From the lions' threat with the tip of your sword
And the ring of your bow.
Why don't you settle in this forest for some time?
I shall offer you milk, wine, and honey,
As much lamb as your heart desires while you rest
Beneath the cool shade of fruit-abounding trees."

Bahraam dismounts, looks around the forest,
And finds it full of greenery and fresh water,
A suitable place for a young man.
Mehrbandad summons musicians
And some notable men who live in the borough.
He has a number of hefty sheep slaughtered
And returns with a golden cup in hand.
After dining, they are offered wine, roses, and fenugreek.

Mehrbandad takes one cup and hands Bahraam another,
Making every effort to treat the king most courteously.
Cheered up by the wine, the host says to his guest,
"O hero of good fortune, you have the mien of a king
Or that of a two-week-old moon at midnight."

The king replies, "You are right.

233

The one who molded my face is the Supreme Ruler,
Who creates to divine wish and is never
Subject to decline or expansion.
And since you say that I resemble a king,
I give you ownership of this forest and this dwelling."

Bahraam pronounces the words,
Positions himself on horseback,
And returns drunk to his palace.
He enters the golden women's chambers
But does not succumb to sleep.
He spends the night in the company of joyous friends,
Recounting to them his fascinating adventures.

7 | The Adventure of Bahraam With Kebrooy

At dawn, Bahraam climbs on the throne and asks for wine.
The army leaders arrive joyously,
And a village chief presents himself with camels
Loaded with all sorts of fruit: pomegranates, quince,
Apples, and flowers worthy of the King of Kings.

At the sight of him, the world master receives him
Most graciously and assigns him a place of honor.
The bearer of fruits and flowers is utterly charmed
By the sight of king, noblemen, and audience hall.
He sees a crystal cup of wine,
Which sends a shiver of trouble down his spine.
He reaches for the cup, grabs it, and rises
To drink to the health of the King of Kings:
"I am Kebrooy the wine drinker," he says,
Boastfully revealing his Pahlavi name.

At that moment, right before the king,
He drains his cup in one stroke and adds,
"I shall empty seven times more,
Then I shall return sober to my village.
No one will witness me stammer like a drunken man."

After saying this, he drains the cup seven times,
To the astonishment of those present.

With the king's permission, he exits the town and
Enters the plain to see how the wine has affected him.
But as soon as the wine ferments within him,
He drives his horse outside the crowd and crosses
The plain to the mountain, where he dismounts.
He searches and finds a remote shady location,
Where he reclines to rest for some time.

A black crow descends from the mountain
And plucks out his two eyes during his sleep.

Soon after, people find him dead at the mountain base,
Two eyes torn out of his head by the black bird,
His horse standing idle nearby on the road.
His servants lament at the sight of him
And profoundly curse the assembly and the wine.

As Bahraam exists his bedroom,
One of his friend recounts to him the tale
Of the black crow and the fate the drunken Kebrooy
Encountered at the mountain base.

The king's cheeks pale, the wretched end of Kebrooy
Fills him with sorrow, and he immediately proclaims:
"O illustrious men, glorious and wise, I prohibit the use
Of wine to everyone, warrior, merchant, and artisan."

8 | The Adventure of the Young Shoemaker and the Lift on the Ban

An entire year passes. Everyone observes the ban,
And the king, when he is holding an audience,
Asks for the recitation of ancient books.
He refrains from drinking wine, previously customary.
Neither its color is seen at court, nor its aroma is sensed.

Life unfolds in this way for some time
Until a young shoemaker marries a rich woman
From a renowned and respectable family.
But he finds himself powerless in the conjugal bed,
And his mother weeps over his misfortune.

It so happens that she has hidden a little wine.
She summons her son to her home and says,
"Drink seven cups of this wine so that
You may become confident, strong, and joyful.
Then perhaps you will break the seal tonight.
How could a pickax made out of felt
Successfully rupture a stone quarry?"

The shoemaker drinks seven or eight cups of wine,
And he feels his feet and skin firm up.
The drink emboldens the young man, who marches
To the entrance and pierces through the bolted door.
He returns to his mother happy
To have found a way to achieve success.

It so happens that one of the king's lions
Breaks out of its chains and exits the enclosure.
The young shoemaker is still drunk on wine.
His prowess converts his fingers
Into a wide net that could capture fish in the sea.
He assails the lion and climbs on top,
Extends his hands, and grabs the animal's two ears.

The lion, having had a meal, is satisfied.
He does not struggle beneath the shoemaker.
The lion guardian rushes in,
Chain in one hand and noose in the other.
He perceives the shoemaker on top of the lion,
Seated like a valiant cavalier riding a donkey.
He runs to the palace, enters boldly at court,
And recounts to the king the marvel he witnessed,
A sight never seen or heard before.

Astounded by the tale, the king summons
His wise men and his court's noblemen.
He says to the grand wise master,
"Find out the shoemaker's lineage.
If he is the son of a warrior, it is understandable,
For such valiant behavior suits a conquering hero."

They question the mother to assess
Whether his birth is nobler than his profession.
The mother, after much discussion,

Rushes to the king and divulges to him her secret.

She begins by invoking blessings upon the king:
"May you live eternally in the world!
This son who has not yet reached manhood
Wished to marry and act as master of the house.
But he found himself powerless in the marital bed,
And his wife said to him,
        'It is because of your lowborn state.'
So I secretly offered him three cups of wine,
At which time his cheeks turned the color of ruby,
And a thing that was the consistency of felt
Became rigid and as hard as bone.
His grandfather was a shoemaker,
So was his father, and no one in our family
Was able to rise above the profession.
It is only through the act of drinking three cups
Of wine that he is now able to extend his lineage.
Who would have thought the king would find
The account of my son's activities so fascinating?"

The king smiles at the old lady's tale and says,
"This is a story for the ages, never to be forgotten!"
He turns to the grand wise master and adds,
"We must allow everyone to indulge in wine.
Anyone who drinks enough to climb on a lion
Will never be overtaken by such a beast.
But one must not drink so much that one falls asleep
And gives the chance to a black crow
To swoop down and pluck out one's eyes."

A proclamation is declared at the royal gate:
"O world heroes of golden belts,
You may drink wine, but do so in moderation.
It is up to you to reflect in the end.
When wine drives you to mirth, then recline
To rest so that your body does not suffer."

9 | The Grand Wise Master, Roozbeh, Destroys a Village

On the third day, at dawn, the king marches
Onto the plain to hunt with his army.
On his left is Ormazd, his vizier, and on his right is
Roozbeh, grand wise master, a man of good counsel.
Both recount stories to him and speak
On the subject of Jamsheed and Fereydoon.

Dogs, cheetahs, gyrfalcons, and falcons
Saunter and fly freely ahead of the group.
Bahraam dashes across the plain, but when the sun
Arrives midpoint in the sky, they still have not
Spotted the trail of a single deer or gazelle.

The king finds it hard to tolerate the heat
Of the blistering sun beating down on him.
He leaves the hunting site in a state of fury.
He comes upon a happy, cultivated place full
Of greenery, homes, men, and four-legged creatures,
A place where one can rest and forget one's worries.

A great number of villagers are on the road ready
To catch a glimpse of the world king, who, red-hot
And angered, wished to dismount in this borough.

None of the inhabitants gives him homage.
It is as if donkeys are chained to the ground.
The king grows more incensed with these people.
He casts on them a look that bears little kindness.

Bahraam Shah addresses the wise master:
"May a place with such an unlucky star
Be the lair of wild animals and game!
May the water flowing through it turn to tar!"

Roozbeh understands the king's wishes
And departs for the borough.
He convenes the notable men and says to them,
"Listen to the king's message:
Bahraam, King of Kings, has taken a liking to this lush

And verdant land full of fruit, men, and cattle.
He has conceived a most beneficial plan.
He has distinguished each of you as a lord,
Which means you no longer need obey anyone.
Servants and masters no longer exist,
As everyone is now on equal footing.
All of you, women, men, and children, are masters,
With each of you governing as ruler of this borough."

Great cries of joy surge over the village.
From here on, men and women have equal authority,
With servants and hired people
Rising to the same level as their masters.

No longer restrained by fear, impure people
Cut the heads of their former masters and lords.
They attack each other, kill each other,
And spill each other's blood in faraway places.

As these upheavals ravage the town,
The inhabitants rush to leave.
The old and the weak remain, but the instruments
Of culture, the tools, and the harvests disappear.
The entire land offers the aspect of desolation.
Trees wither, the river dries up, the ground is barren, and
A great number of men and four-legged creatures have fled.

A year passes. Spring returns, and
King Bahraam passes the village on his way to hunt.
This place once verdant and cheerful is in ruins,
The land has been leveled, the trees have dried up,
The homes are deserted, and there are hardly any men
Or four-legged creatures walking the grounds.

At such a sight, the king's face pales.
He fears the Creator and grieves deeply.
He says to the grand wise master,
"O Roozbeh, alas, this beautiful town is now barren!
Go quickly to repopulate it with my wealth.
Find ways to stimulate the prosperity of its inhabitants."

The wise master leaves the side of the king
And takes the direction of the borough.

He travels from street to street
And finally finds an idle old man.
He dismounts and approaches him courteously,
Sits next to him, and says,
"O aging master, who is the cause of turning
This once populated land into a barren desert?"

The other replies, "One day, the king passed by
With a foolish wise man, one of these high-ranking
Noblemen who never accomplishes a good deed.
He told us that we were all lords,
That we no longer had to obey anyone,
That we were all the masters of the village,
And that the women and the men were even
More distinguished than the greatest rulers.
Following this discourse, chaos rained down,
Along with pillage and murder.
People left; everything wasted away.
May the Creator reward him according to merit!
May grief, suffering, and misery
Never cease to plague his life and being!
Everything here took a turn for the worse.
Know that you must bitterly weep over our fates."

Roozbeh is afflicted by the old man's words.
He asks, "Who is the village chief?"
The old man replies, "Who can lead a land
Barren of any sort of seed, herb, or fruit?"

Roozbeh says, "Why do you not take on the role
Of chief, as if you are the diadem of the land?
Ask for dinars and treasure from the king;
Ask for seeds, cattle, donkeys, and provisions;
Draw into the village idle people. They will
Be your subordinates, and you will be their chief.
Do not accuse the old wise man;
He did not speak with ill intentions.
Should you require a man from court to lean upon,
I shall send him to you. Ask and you shall receive."

These words delight the old man,
Whose mind is freed from worries.

He instantly enters his home
And brings men to where there are water reservoirs.
He takes great pains in repopulating the land
And redistributing the fields.

They ask their neighbors for cattle and donkeys;
They toil to cultivate the fields.
He and the other residents work very hard,
Planting trees everywhere, and when a field
Has been sown, hearts rejoice.

At the news that the borough has been repopulated,
Those who fled the land shedding blood tears
Return to reestablish the streets and the streams.
Hens, cows, donkeys, and lamb multiply.
In one year, the old man rebuilds three villages.
Everyone plants many trees, and this land,
Once deserted, becomes a verdant paradise.

The chief organizes the town in the third year.
Everything that had been sown prospers,
And once cheerful spring arrives,
The king travels through the plain to hunt,
Accompanied by Roozbeh, grand wise master.

Nearing the village, the brilliant Bahraam the hunter
Looks around and sees the cultivated fields and cattle.
He sees large homes, the borough full of cows and lamb,
Everywhere are gardens and springs of water,
Fields of barley, meadows dotted with tulips and fenugreek,
Sheep and goats scattered on the mountainside.
The entire area appears like a beautiful paradise.

Bahraam says to the wise man, "O Roozbeh,
What did you do to make the barren land flourish again?
What did you give to disperse men and herds
And to reestablish the village?

The wise master replies, "This lush and prosperous place
Fell to its demise by one word only.
Similarly, one idea repopulated it,
So that the heart of the King of Iran may rejoice.
The shah had commanded me to make this land

Disappear with the dinars in his treasury,
But I feared the World Creator,
And I feared the blame of men, great and small.
I observed that one heart can conceive two ideas.
These ideas can destroy them in no time.
In the same manner, if two rulers govern a city,
Nothing will remain of the land.
A sensible man would be astonished to see
Two men do the same work peacefully.
I went to the borough and told the old men
That there no longer exist superiors in their land,
That women, children, servants, and employees
Are all equal in the eyes of their masters.
Those who were inferior became lords,
And the heads of once powerful men fell soon after.
It is only through words that this beautiful land
Was razed and reduced to a desolate, barren region.
May reproach and fear of Yazdan's retribution
Never reach your majesty!

"Later, the king forgave them.
I went there and showed them another path.
I placed an old, intelligent man as village chief.
He is eloquent, educated, and able to lead.
He took great pains to repopulate his province
And has brought joy to his subordinates.
Once there was only one ruler, a man of sense,
Good deeds multiplied while evil deeds dwindled.
I showed them secretly the road to perdition,
Then I opened for them the divine gates.
Words are more precious than royal jewels
If one makes use of them wisely.
In order for the mind to evade grief,
Judgment must rule as king, and speech as warrior.
May the heart of the king be forever joyful
And free from being harmed by crime and corruption."

The king says, "Well done, Roozbeh!
You are worthy of sporting a crown."
He offers a pouch of dinars to the insightful man,
Along with a royal robe of honor.
Roozbeh's head rises as high as the clouds.

10 | Bahraam Weds the Miller's Daughters

A few weeks later, the world king departs
To hunt with his wise men and noblemen.
He plans to spend one month in pursuit
Of game and drinking wine with his escort.

Freely and in an unbounded way,
He engages in hunting in mountain and plain.

Upon his happy return to the city with his men,
Night descends and the world fills with darkness.
The noblemen dismiss the escort
And recount stories of kings to Bahraam.

The King of Kings observes in the distance
A magnificent blaze reminiscent of the ones that burn
During the celebrations of the Feast of Bahman.[40]
On one side is a beautiful village with a windmill
At its entrance and village leaders seated in front of it.

A number of young ladies who have organized
The feast stand on the other side of the flame.
Each has a crown of flowers on her head,
And musicians are seated all around.
The maidens sing songs relating to royal battle,
Each taking a turn in beginning a new song.
These moon-faced beauties with curly hair
And soft voices exude the scent of musk.
They form a line on the grass
To sing in front of the windmill's door.
Each holds a bouquet of flowers in her hand,
Each half drunk with wine and joy.

One of them raises her voice and cries,
"May this be a memory of King Bahraam,
Whose majesty is incontestable in his tall stature,
His handsome face, and his kind heart.
The dome of sky revolves over him as a slave.

◇◇◇◇◇◇◇◇◇◇◇◇◇◇
40 Feast of Bahman: Reference to the Feast of Saddeh, which marks 100
days before the start of spring, or Nowruz. It is a celebration of overcoming
darkness.

It is as if wine drips in droplets over his cheeks,
And the fragrance of musk escapes from his hair.
He disdains all prey except for the deer and the lion.
This is why he is called Bahraam the hunter."

At the sound of their voices,
The world king swings the reins of his horse
And rides in the direction of the village.
As he draws near the maidens, he takes a closer look
And notices that the entire field is full of moons,
A sight that restrains him from continuing his trek.

He commands cupbearers to bring wine
And summons drinkers as well.
The cupbearers obey and hand him a crystal cup.

The four principal maidens emerge from the group.
One is named Moshknaz,[41] another Moshkenek,[42]
Another Nazyab,[43] and the fourth one Soossanek.[44]
They advance toward the king holding hands,
Cheeks like spring, tall of stature,
And singing a ballad about the high deeds
Of the wise and mighty Bahraam, King of Kings.

Bahraam is excited at the sight of them and asks,
"O rose-cheeked maidens, who is your father?
Are you responsible for lighting the fire?"

One of them says, "O rider of cypress stature,
You resemble the king in every way.
Our father is an old miller who is hunting
With his bow and arrow on the mountain slope.
He will soon return, for night will be deep
And the obscurity will hinder his vision."

At that moment, the miller arrives from the hunt
With a group of his companions. At the sight of Bahraam,
He presses his cheeks into the dust and holds

◇◇◇◇◇◇◇◇◇◇◇◇◇
41 Moshknaz: Pure musk.
42 Moshkenek: Partridge.
43 Nazyab: Flirtatious.
44 Soossanek: Small lily.

Himself before him, full of respect and fear.

The king offers him a golden cup and asks,
"Why do you keep your sun-faced beauties?
Is it not the time for them to marry?"

The old man invokes divine blessings on him
And says, "There are no worthy husbands
For my daughters, who are still pure virgins.
Besides, they own nothing, neither gold nor silver."

Bahraam replies, "Allow me to have all four of them,
And deprive yourself of their presence."

The old man says, "O brave rider, do not think of it.
We have neither bolts of fabric nor silver,
Neither land nor home, neither cattle nor donkey."

Bahraam says, "This is all just as well.
I have no need for any such things."

The old man replies, "All four are your wives then
And the servants of your secret chambers' dust.
Your eye spotted them and approved of them
With all their faults and their qualities."

Bahraam says, "I accept all four of them
From the hand of the father who raised them."

Upon rising, he hears in the plain the whinny
Of horses and commands the eunuchs in the escort
To lead the idols to the royal chambers.

The procession gradually heads out of the plain,
Riding throughout the night.

Surprised at the events of the day, the miller
Reflects to his wife, "How did this illustrious man
Who resembles the moon, so tall and so powerful,
Happen upon our village at night?"

The wife replies, "He saw the blaze from a distance
And then heard the song of the maidens.
He sat and asked for wine and musicians."

The miller asks, "O wife, give me your advice:
Will the end of this matter be good or bad?"

She replies, "It is evidently the work of the Creator.
When he saw them, he did not ask about their births,
And his heart did not deliberate on dowries.
He has been searching the world for a moon
And not for wealth or for the daughter of a king.
If a Chinese idol worshipper would see one of them,
It would be the end of idol worshipping."

They continue to discuss in this manner,
At times of evil men, at times of righteous ones,
Until the sun appears at the tail end of the black crow
And the world shines resplendent with its light.

Once night gives way to day, the village chief
Arrives at the home of the old man and says,
"O valiant, prosperous warrior,
Fortune reached your bedside last night,
And the green limb of your tree has borne fruit.
King Bahraam arrived after dark
From the plain where he was hunting.
He saw the festivities and the fire,
Swung his horse's bridle, and rode the distance.
Now your daughters are his wives,
Living securely in his secret chambers.
You made your daughters worthy of a king by giving
Them their attributes, their hair, faces, and virtues.
Bahraam, King of Kings, is your son-in-law,
And you will be the subject of talk in the land.
He has offered you this province and this district.
Do not afflict yourself, for you are above worry and fear.
We are all inferior to you; what am I saying, inferior?
As your devoted servants, we shall follow you to any end.
Give your command, for you have the right to do so.
We depend on you, and to you belongs authority."

Stunned, the miller and his wife murmur Yazdan's name.
The village chief declares, "These faces and manes
Have attracted a husband from the fourth firmament."

11 | Bahraam the Hunter Finds Jamsheed's Treasury

A few weeks later, Bahraam drives the hunt
With his wise men and his army's favorites.
A devoted man advances, as swift as wind,
A stick in his hand, and asks for the position
Of the king among the members of the escort.

The wise man tells him, "What do you want?
Tell me. You may not just see the world king."

The other replies, "Until I perceive his majesty's face,
I shall not utter another word to this company."

They prepare an audience for the eloquent seeker,
Who, at the sight of Bahraam, says,
"I have to speak to you in private."

Bahraam sways the bridle away from the crowd.

The stranger says, "O King, world master,
You must pay heed to my words.
I am a wise landowner in this region.
This earth, this harvest, and this house are mine.
I irrigated these parts so that I could plow
And extend the value of the dirt.
As the water flowed, it became difficult to contain,
And a hole deepened in the field.
A great sound struck my ear,
Filling my heart with fear and anguish.
A loud rumble rose from the water,
The beat of timpani to indicate a treasure."

Bahraam listens to him, travels with him
To the plain, and, noticing that it is covered
With greenery and water, he requests
A workforce of men with shovels.

The powerful king dismounts.
A tent is set up for him in a sown field,
And once night descends, the warriors
Light up the surroundings with candles.

247

As the sun raises its banner over the sea
And the blue atmosphere shines with light,
Workers arrive from every direction.
Assembled, they are as numerous as a vast host.
They proceed to search the grounds,
And this part of the field becomes a ditch.
At the moment they grow weary of digging,
A structure appears beneath the ground
Similar to a mountain, a house built of fired bricks,
Stucco-clad, and as beautiful as paradise.

The excavators poke around it with pickaxes,
And soon a door is revealed.

At the sight, the king's wise man enters,
And with him another man, an uninvited guest.
They find a room, vast and deep, a few fathoms high,
With two golden bulls standing before a golden crib
Full of stones, a mix of chrysoprase and ruby.
They appear as the double sign of the Taurus.
Hollow, their bellies are filled
With pomegranates, apples, and quinces.
In the quinces are fine pearls,
Every seed resembling a droplet of water.
The eyes of the bulls glitter with rubies,
And their heads are eroded by time.
All around are lions and onager,
Some with ruby eyes and others with crystal eyes.
There are golden partridges and male peacocks
With chests and eyes of precious stones.

The vizier, whose deep intelligence makes him
The diadem over the moon's head,
Fills his eyes with the sight, then turns to the king:
"Rise, for we have found wealth to endow all treasuries.
We have discovered a chamber full of precious stones.
The dome of sky had kept its key until now."

The king says, "When one wants to amass wealth,
One must always write one's name on it.
Look and see what name is written on this treasure
And how much time was spent to accumulate it."

At the command, the grand wise master descends
To observe the bulls and returns to say,
"I have seen the name of King Jamsheed
Inscribed as a seal on the two bulls."

Bahraam replies, "O chief wise man, wisest among sages,
Why should I embrace a treasury
Put together by Jamsheed for his own profit?
May any treasure perish that is made rightfully mine,
Outside of what is acquired by justice and sword!
Distribute the lot to men who merit wealth.
Please Yazdan that calamity does not befall me!
If my destiny is to become famous,
I shall accumulate a treasure by my own just labor
And at the point of my blade.
My host has no need for this ancient prize,
For the world is mine due to my courage.
These valuables must be estimated
According to Kianian custom.
Sell the stones for gold and silver.
Bring from deserted and inhabited lands
Widows, orphans, poor men who carry a name,
Those with broken, disenchanted hearts.
Then make a list, one by one,
And distribute to them a wealth of gold and silver,
All for the good of Jamsheed's soul.

"Why should I go after his treasure
As long as I am young and of sturdy health?
Give one-tenth of it to the one who showed us the way
And who singled out the king out of his escort.
May the one who steals Jamsheed's shroud
Never find contentment in the world!
I shall amass treasure from Rum and Chin
With much effort, perhaps with my army.
I alone, with my horse Shabdeez and
My sharp sword, shall never surrender
To either ruse or the urge to take flight."

He draws from his treasury, amassed
With his own hands, with much sweat and tears,
Summons the brave men of the land

And pays them the balance of one year's earnings.
He organizes a feast in the early spring
And refines an audience hall with inlaid stones.

With ruby-colored wine shining through crystal cups,
Bahraam feels joyous and says to his friends,
"O highborn men, well-versed on royal traditions,
See what remains of the powerful kings,
From Hooshang to the noble Nozar, Fereydoon's heir,
All the way to Kay Ghobaad,
Who placed the crown of power on their heads?
Who now sings the praises of their just ways?
The sky revolved over them, and no other memory
Remains of them but the words of men who say
That one had a noble soul and the other had not.
Some are condemned while others are celebrated.
Why would I seize the fruits gathered
With the labors of a deceased king?
Why would I open my heart to a longing for gold?
I have no attachment to this passing dwelling;
The crown does not enchant me in any way;
Treasures and wealth have little appeal to me.
When their day unfolds happily,
Why would men surrender to worry and grief?
May my head, throne, and treasury be cursed
Every time one of my subjects, whether farmer
Or one of my court's noblemen, complains
About some harm I may have caused him!"

Maahiar, an older man, over sixty-four years of age,
Rises at these words and says, "O master of justice,
We have heard of the ways of Fereydoon, Jamsheed,
And other illustrious kings, but never has anyone
Heard the tale of a king like you.
You are the hope of lowborn men
And the glory of noble ones!
With a heart as vast as the sea, you stirred up such waves
That your mind diffused light in the manner of Sooroosh,
A light that overshadowed the wisdom of learned men.
You distributed a wealth so vast throughout the world
Such as men, great and small, had never seen before.
Such abundance in the times of Jamsheed

Was referred to as the treasury of bulls,
But no one knew where it was hidden,
Whether beneath the ground or in a dragon's jaws.
When you found it, you did not even glance its way,
For you scorn this passing existence.
No living being has ever seen in the sea
So many pearls, yet you lavished on the poor
The pearls and the contents of the golden bulls.
May the throne and belt never be deprived of you!
May you prosper, and may your fortune sustain you!
Many a book on the history of kings
Will be filled with black ink on your account,
A subject that will never be exhausted.
After your departure, your name will be celebrated.
The narrator of history will never cease
To recount tales of your life and your high deeds."

12 | The Adventure of Bahraam With the Merchant and His Apprentice

The following week, the king prepares to hunt again.
He is ill-disposed as he departs with quiver and bow.
The plain is heated by a blazing sun,
And later he sluggishly returns from the hunt.

He arrives at the residence of a merchant, looks around,
And, not seeing anyone, says to the merchant,
"Can you lodge me for the night?
I promise not to be a burden on you."

The merchant helps him dismount
And prepares a bed for him.

Bahraam suffers from stomach pains.
He gives the merchant a number of dirhams
And says, "Roast some old cheese with almonds.
I also have a craving for eggs, if you have any."

The merchant fails to serve the king's request,
For he has no almonds in his home.
But after nightfall, the master of the house

251

Comes quietly with warm roasted poultry.
He fixes the spread and places it before Bahraam.

The valiant king says, "I asked you for old cheese.
I insisted upon it, but you did not bring me any,
Even though I gave you money
And complained about my stomach."

The merchant replies, "O foolish man,
Does intelligence not stimulate your mind?
I am offering you warm roasted chicken,
What more do you want from me?"

At these words, the king loses his appetite for cheese.
He regrets having spoken, and he dines
Without speaking further on the matter.
The time of sleep arrives, and he prepares to rest.

As the sun emerges from the simmering sea
And the pitch-black veil dissipates,
The rich merchant says to his apprentice,
"O clumsy man, why did you spend
More than one dirham at my expense
For a chicken that was worth far less?
Had you bought one worthy of our guest,
I would have avoided a scene last night.
You could have bought some cheese
For a quarter of a dirham.
It would have made him gentle with me today
And as sweet as honey and milk."

The apprentice replies, "It is all the same.
Know that the chicken is on my account.
Be my guest today, you and your cavalier,
And do not speak to me further of this chicken."

Meanwhile, Bahraam awakens from his sweet slumber.
He approaches his fervent horse to saddle him
And to make his way back to the palace,
Where he may raise his crown to Saturn.

At the sight of Bahraam, the apprentice says,
"Keep me, your servant, company today."

The king sits on his bed, surprised
At the generosity of the young apprentice.

The young man leaves, returns
With two hundred eggs, and says to his boss,
"O respectable man, do not remain inactive.
Heat up and grill these almonds
And prepare some old cheese with soft bread,
For that is what he desired last night.
Take this meal to him and display a proper table."

He goes to Bahraam and says,
"O rider, yesterday you asked for eggs.
We shall prepare and heat up what you desired
While you await the arrival of other small dishes."

After speaking, he goes to the market
And purchases other items: sugar, almonds,
Poultry and lamb, and to complete the meal,
He grabs wine, saffron, musk, and rosewater.
He returns home with a restless, eager heart.
This young man, full of good will and of pure mind,
Sets up a spread covered with delicate dishes.

At the end of dinner, he brings cups of wine
And presents the first cup to the king.
They drink slowly at first, then drain their cups
Until they find themselves full of cheer.

In the end, Bahraam says to his host,
"King Bahraam will require my services.
You keep on drinking and getting drunk.
Do not budge until you have shown
That you are true worshippers of wine."

He grooms Shabdeez and saddles him,
And says to the merchant, still enlivened by wine,
"Do not take such great pains for profit.
Yesterday you sold me for a quarter of a dirham.
You made your apprentice lower his eyes in shame
For having bought an overpriced chicken,
And you delivered me to the dragon's breath."

At these words, he takes his leave
And gallops swiftly to the royal palace.

As the sun beams its golden crown on the sky's throne,
The world guardian sits on the ivory seat
And commands his vizier to summon the merchant.

They bring him, along with his apprentice.
One is happy, the other morose.
The king receives the apprentice graciously
And seats him among his noblemen.
He is offered a pouch full of gold,
Rendering his dim heart as bright as the moon.

Then Bahraam says to the merchant,
"Know that as long as you live,
You will be the servant of the apprentice.
Twice a month, you will pay him sixty dirhams.
He will exercise hospitality with your money
And will bring joy to the hearts of generous men."

Then he says to the grand wise master,
"If the king did not roam the world,
How would he know who is worthy of leadership?
How would he distinguish between
Well-intentioned men and evil ones?"

Now, O shrewd reader, if you respect wisdom,
If you have any sense, listen to my words:
If you have heart, never commit acts of avarice,
For it is quite probable that the dividend
Will be at the expense of your joy.

13 | Bahraam Kills a Dragon and Visits a Farmer

Bahraam spends some time
In the company of his noblemen,
Distracting himself with wine, cup, and singers.

Spring arrives, the earth becomes a paradise,
And the air sows tulips on the ground.

The land fills with game; the waters flowing
In streams and rivers taste like wine and milk.
Onager and antelope roam the fields,
And form everywhere dots on the greenery.
All the sources of water exhale the scent of musk,
And wine shines in jugs like a pomegranate blossom.

The noblemen remind Bahraam the hunter:
"It has been a long time since our last hunt."

He replies, "We must single out a host
Formed of one thousand riders and gather
Cheetah, falcon, hunting thong, and gyrfalcon.
We shall journey from here to Tooran
And spend one month occupied in the hunt."

The eager king and his valiant lords
Find the land of Tooran full of color and scent.
They take on the task of depopulating
The world of onager, wild ram, and antelope.
They spend two days in this way,
During which time the king holds a cup of wine.

On the third day, as the dark night flees
In fear before the spread of daylight's glow,
As the sun gradually deploys its dazzling crown,
Daubing the earth in golden tones
And the mountain and sea in hues of ivory,
The king departs to engage in the hunt.

He sees a dragon that resembles a male lion.
The fur on its head reaches the ground,
And it has two female breasts on its chest.

The king binds his bow and immediately delivers
An arrow of poplar wood into the dragon's chest
And another shot into the center of its head.
Blood and poison gush out of the torso.
The king dismounts, draws his sword,
And splits its chest from top to bottom.

The dragon had consumed a man whom the king
Finds frozen in a mix of blood and poison.

Bahraam sheds bitter tears on the deceased,
But his own eyes dim with the effect of the poison.
He extracts the body out from the creature's side.
He runs on the road, confounded and writhing,
Searching for water and a place to rest,
Until he arrives at a field and a populated place.

He runs toward the door of a house where he sees
A woman carrying a jug of water on her shoulder.
She quickly covers her face at the sight of him.

He says to her, "Would you offer me hospitality,
Or should I journey on, though I am quite weary?"

The woman replies, "O valiant rider, you are welcome.
Make use of this home as if it were your own."

Bahraam enters the dwelling with his horse,
And the woman calls her husband, to whom she says,
"Bring some hay, and curry the horse.
If you do not have a currycomb, use a woolen bag."

She enters her private chamber after having diligently
Swept the house, spread a mat, placed a cushion on it,
And uttered countless blessings on Bahraam.

Then she retrieves water from the tank,
All the while secretly cursing her husband:
"This lazy old fool remains inactive
Every time he sees someone enter our home.
It is not the wife's business to serve a warrior."

Bahraam rinses his face, for he feels unwell
From the effect of the dragon's poison.
Then he sits on the mat while the old husband
Stands motionless at the entrance.
The woman places a table carefully and dresses it
With watercress, vinegar, bread, and curdled milk.

Bahraam eats a little, reclines moaning,
And covers his face with a silk handkerchief.

Once she awakens, the wife says to her husband,

"O wicked man, you did not wash your face!
You must slay a lamb, for this rider
Is a noble lord of royal lineage.
He has a Kianian stature and shines like the moon.
I find in him a striking resemblance to King Bahraam."

The despicable husband replies to his wife,
"Why must you speak so much?
You have neither salted meat nor wood or bread,
And you do not spin like other women.
You would kill a lamb, have the rider eat and depart.
What will you gain from such an act?
The cold, the heat, and the storm will not hit you less."

The husband speaks thus, but his wife fails to listen.
She is a good woman of good counsel.
In the end, the husband slays the lamb
As requested by his wife, who cooks it in a pot
With wheat and vinegar, with wood and cinder.

Then she places a spread before the king
Consisting of eggs and watercress from the riverbank.
She brings the roasted leg of lamb
And a dish boiled in a starter.

After eating, Bahraam washes his hands.
Feeling uneasy, he has no wish to sleep.
As night begins to blend with day,
The woman brings a jug of wine and the fruit of jujube.

The king says to her, "O quiet woman,
Entertain me with an old story while I drink my wine.
I wish to chase, for a moment, sorrow from my heart.
I give you the freedom to speak of your king,
Whether it is to praise him or to blame him."

The woman of few words says, "It is well.
He is at the source of the beginning and end of all things."

Bahraam replies, "It is so,
But no one finds in him justice and kindness."

The resolute woman says, "O pure warrior,

This village has many men and many homes.
Yet all the time, either cavaliers pass through
Or employees of the king's court.
One of them accuses a man of theft, which brings him
Much grief, for the employee poisons his happy life
To extort five or six dirhams.
Or else he wrongfully calls an honest woman
By disgraceful names to abuse her as her master.
These are insults, for the money does not make it
Into the treasury, and the king, world master,
Is the cause of the suffering inflicted on his subjects."

Her speech and the idea that his name suffers from
His servants' actions send Bahraam into deep reflections:
"A just king and Yazdan worshipper has nothing to fear!
I shall for some time exert harsher power so that,
Through hardship, they will welcome clemency and justice."

Tortured by such dim thoughts, he finds himself
Unable to sleep, his heart pondering matters of oppression.

At the time when the sun tears apart the black veil
And exposes its glorious face to radiate in the sky,
The wife exits the house and says to her husband,
"Bring the cauldron and the fire from inside.
Soak all sorts of grains in water,
Cover them to protect them from the sun's heat,
And do not neglect the cauldron.
I am on my way to milk the cow."

She brings the cow from the field,
Grabs a bunch of grass to toss in front of it.
She rubs the cow's udder saying, "In the name
Of the Creator without equal or companion."

Her heart drops when she notices that the udder
Is empty of milk. She says to her man,
"O master, the king's intentions have changed.
He has become the oppressor overnight.
His heart has taken a different path."

The husband asks, "Why do you say that?
What need have you for these bad omens?"

258

The wife says, "O my noble husband,
I do not speak like this without reason.
When the world king turns to unjust acts,
The moon no longer shines in the sky,
Milk dries up in the cows' udders;
Musk loses its scent in the pouches of gazelles;
Adultery and hypocrisy make a comeback;
The softest heart becomes as hard as rock;
The wolf devours men in the desert;
The sage takes flight when faced with foolishness,
And the egg lies sterile beneath the hen.
All this happens as soon as the king forsakes justice.
Our cow's pasture has not been reduced,
The basin from which she draws water is the same,
Yet her milk has dried up in the udder, and her fur,
Once pitch black, has lost its sheen and luster."

At these words, the world king instantly repents.
He addresses Yazdan: "O almighty Master of fate,
May I never occupy the royal throne
If my heart recoils from the path of justice!"

The fortunate wife, pure and pious,
Passes her hand over the cow one more time
And gets to work invoking the name of Yazdan:
"May the milk emerge from its hidden place!"

At that moment, milk pours out of the cow's udder.
The mistress of the house exclaims, "O divine Rescuer,
You must have rendered just the unjust king
For this miracle to manifest."

Then she turns to her husband,
"The unjust one has found the right path again.
Rejoice, for the Creator showed us compassion."

Once the milk is cooked in the cauldron
And the married couple complete their tasks,
The clever woman approaches her guest.
The husband follows her with a tray on which
Is a bowl of milk soup that would taste even better
If it were cooked with some cumin.

The king eats a few spoonfuls of soup,
Then addresses the daring woman,
"Hang the whip outside in clear sight of passersby.
Take care to suspend it on a thick and strong branch
So that the wind may not damage it.
Then observe attentively the people going by."

The master of the house obeys
And quickly hangs the object onto a tree.
He keeps his eyes on it for some time.
Innumerable soldiers pass on the road, and each one,
At the sight of the crop, blesses Bahraam.
Everyone takes turns to step down from their mounts,
Approach the whip, and honor it with a salute.

The husband and wife say to each other,
"This man must be the king, for his face can only
Belong to the one who occupies the throne."

They return inside confused, running to Bahraam
And saying, "O powerful ruler, noble and astute
World master, highest sage among wise men,
In this home, your hosts have been poor people,
A woman without resource and a gardener husband.
Yet your servants did not expend great effort,
Never suspecting that their guest was the monarch.
They never thought a man of his standing
Would ever lower himself to accept a welcome here,
In the wretched home of a modest couple."

Bahraam says, "O man blessed with good fortune,
I offer you this land and this village.
Occupy yourself with hospitality and nothing else.
Forgo your occupation of gardener."

He says this, then exits their home smiling,
Climbs on his charger of winded hooves,
And, leaving the poor village behind,
Takes the road to his gem-studded palace.

14 | Bahraam Weds Barzeen's Daughters

Three days later, the king departs with escort and gear
In the direction of the hunting grounds.
Three hundred Iranian noble riders accompany him.
Every horseman brings thirty servants of various origins:
There are Turks, Rumis, and Persians.
The hunting procession thus exits the king's palace.

There are ten dromedaries with brocade covers,
With golden stirrups and spurs trimmed with pearls.
Ten camels carry the king's tent and his quilted bed.
At the head march seven elephants who transport
The throne, a deep turquoise blue,
Reminiscent of the waters of the Nile;
Its base is a mixture of gold and crystal.
It is the royal seat of Bahraam the hunter.

Every sword-bearing rider is accompanied
By thirty slaves cinched with golden belts
And mounted on camels of golden bridles.
There are one hundred mules for the musicians,
All bearing gem-encrusted diadems.

The falconers transport one hundred and sixty falcons,
Two hundred gyrfalcons, as well as other noble birds.
Among them is a black bird, a favorite of the king,
The most valuable one in his eyes.
His claws are black, and his beak is yellow,
Like brilliant gold on a backdrop of lapis lazuli.
His name is Toghrol. His eyes are like cups of blood.
The Emperor of Chin offered him to the king
With a throne and a crown pieced together with garnet,
Along with a golden torque inlaid with emeralds,
Forty bracelets, thirty-six earrings,
Three hundred loads of camels full of gifts
From Chin, and three hundred ruby rings.

After the falconers leading the royal procession,
Come one hundred and sixty cheetahs bearing
Necklaces and golden chains inlaid with precious gems.

The King of Kings advances in this manner,
Raising his crown above the sphere of Jupiter.
The hunters drive to the shores,
A place Bahraam, world master,
Visits every seven years under favorable auspices.

Once the convoy arrives at the water's edge,
The king sees that the surface is full of birds.
He asks for the drumbeat and sends off
Toghrol to swiftly soar high through the air,
For this royal bird is not gifted with patience.

The crane is game unworthy of its claws,
Since leopards are his true and favorite prey.
An eagle falls beneath its talons,
And it climbs and disappears into the air,
Flying like an arrow shot out of the bow.
A falconer runs after the bird.
The king's heart constricts at the momentum,
And he chases after him, guided by the sound of bells.

He arrives in this manner at a beautiful garden.
In a corner rises a palace. The king sprints, followed
By a few people, while his escort engages in the hunt.

As Bahraam enters the verdant garden, he sees
A palace and, beyond, the crest of a steep boulder.
In the middle of the garden is a pool of water
With an old man seated on its edge.
The ground beneath him is covered in a carpet of brocade,
And the garden is full of slaves and beautiful things.

His three daughters, white as ivory,
Are seated beside him sporting turquoise crowns.
Their cheeks are like spring, their statures slender,
Their brows arched, and their hair is as long as a noose.
Each holds in her hand a crystal cup.

Bahraam the hunter observes them.
His sight is troubled by their appearance, while his heart
Remains deeply moved by Toghrol's disappearance.

At the sight of Bahraam, the rich landowner's face

Pales with fear to a shade of fenugreek yellow.
He is a wise old man named Barzeen
Who is not happy to see the king.
He rushes from the edge of the pool, as swift as wind,
Approaches Bahraam and kisses the ground at his feet.
He says, "O moon-faced King, may the sky
Revolve according to your heart's desires!
I dare not invite you on my land
With your two hundred bold cavaliers,
But Barzeen's good fortune would rise to the moon
Were the king to take some delight in this garden."

The ruler replies, "Toghrol flew away today,
And my heart is anguished for this chaser of birds.
I followed the sound of his bells."

Barzeen says, "I just spotted a black bird
With golden bells, pitch-black feathers and claws,
And a beak the color of turmeric.
He fell on the walnut tree, and, by your good fortune,
You can easily snatch him this moment."

The king commands a slave to examine the tree.
The obliging slave exclaims,
"May the world king dwell in happiness!
Toghrol is hooked on a branch,
And the falconer can now retrieve it."

At the reappearance of Toghrol, the old man says,
"O King, you have no equal on earth!
May my hospitality bring you good luck!
May crown-bearing men be your slaves!
In your contentment, drink a cup of wine,
And since you have recovered peace of mind,
Surrender yourself to joy and revelry."
The old man is pleased to see
The King of Kings dismount by the pool.

At that moment, the vizier, the army leaders
And the treasurer arrive.
Barzeen asks for cups and red wine,
And begins to drink to the king's health.
Then he searches for a crystal goblet

And places it in the hands of Bahraam the hunter.
The world master takes the cup and drains it.

Barzeen is delighted and places jugs of wine
Everywhere in the garden, and, once drunk,
He says to his daughters, "O my skillful children,
King Bahraam is our guest in the garden.
You, the one who sings, sing us a song.
And you, my moon-faced daughter,
Pick up your lute and pluck at its strings."

The three maidens appear before the king,
Jeweled tiaras on their heads.
One can dance, the other plays the lute,
And the third one is graced with a voice so beautiful
It can chase grief away from hearts.

The King of Kings drains his cup and, feeling elated,
Says to Barzeen, "Whose daughters are these beauties?
Do they reside with you?"

Barzeen replies, "O King,
May the world never be deprived of your being!
Be assured that they are my daughters.
They are the joy of my life, my heart's enchantment.
One sings, the other plays the lute,
And the third one dances gracefully,
For she is apt at keeping the beat with her feet.
O King, I lack nothing. I have gold and silver,
Gardens and lands, and three beautiful daughters,
Each resembling the most glorious spring."

Then he says to the singer, "O moon-faced beauty,
Take courage and sing the king's song."
The young maiden surmounts her timidity
And prepares to perform to the melody of the lute.

The singer recites to Bahraam,
"O King, you resemble the moon in the sky.
The royal throne is the only worthy seat for you.
With your beauty and your plane tree stature,
You bring pride and glory to the throne and crown.
Happy is the one who sees your face in the morning!

Happy is the one who smells the scent of your hair!
Your waist is as slim as a tiger's, your arms are strong,
And the splendor of your crown rises to the highest heights.
Your face resembles the flower of the pomegranate.
Men smile with joy for your affection.
Your heart is as vast as the sea,
Your powerful hand captures only leopards and lions.
You split a strand of hair with your arrow's tip,
And water converts to milk with your just ways.
At the sight of your noose and formidable arms,
The hearts and brains of the most belligerent warriors
Tear apart, no matter how numerous they may be."

Bahraam listens to the song and drains his cup.
He says to Barzeen, "O illustrious man,
You have experienced life's ups and downs.
Nowhere will you find a son-in-law more worthy
Than me, chief of kings, master of the land.
Offer me your three daughters
And raise your crown to the heights of Saturn."

Barzeen says, "O King,
May cup and cupbearer please you!
Where else can one find such a singer?
Since you allowed me to worship your throne
Like a slave, I shall extol your crown and seat,
Your majesty, your glory, and your good fortune.
Similarly, my three daughters are your slaves.
They stand before you to serve you.
The king approved of the three moons
The moment he spotted them from afar,
Admiring their statures as high as plane trees
And their complexions as white as ivory.
They certainly are worthy of the throne
And will be additional ornaments to the crown.
I shall now reveal to the world king
What I secretly possess, good and bad.
I have, behind closed doors,
Two hundred camel loads, if not more,
Of fabrics, beds, blankets, and carpets.
In addition, I have countless bracelets, torques,
Crown, and thrones, all to my daughters' delight."

The king smiles at Barzeen and says,
"Leave everything you have in your home.
Abandon yourself to me and to the joys of wine."

The old man replies, "I give you my three
Moon-faced daughters in accordance to the customs
Of world kings Kiumars and Hooshang.
The three beauties are the dust beneath your feet
And will live only to serve your will."

The eldest is named Maah-Aafareed;
The second, Faraanak; the third, Shambeleed.
They please the king from the onset.
He includes them among his legitimate wives.
He commands one of the convoy leaders to bring four
Golden litters and to summon sixty Rumi ladies-in-waiting,
Who surround the maidens and sing their praises.
As the three moons depart for the golden chambers,
The king remains to indulge in drink and inebriation.

A slave takes Bahraam's whip and hangs it at the door.
Until then, the escort ignores the king's whereabouts.
Those who perceive its handle now run to bow before it.

Bahraam remains until he is duly intoxicated.
Then, feeling cheerful, he climbs in a litter
And departs for his home's golden chambers:
Apartments perfumed with the scent of ambergris.
He spends one week there, taking and giving pleasure,
As well as speaking and listening at length.

15 | Bahraam Displays His Hunting Skills

On the eighth day, Bahraam marches off to hunt
With Roozbeh and an escort of one thousand riders.
He sees the plain full of onager, draws his Kianian bow
Out of its case, attaches the rope to the two black ends,
And invokes the victorious Creator.

It is spring, a time when male onager search for females.
They have gathered there from around the world

266

To tear each other apart in a way that their spilled
Blood has turned the ground the color of tulips.

Bahraam proceeds until he sees a male onager
Heatedly wrestling another.
The moment the valiant beast mates with a female,
Bahraam binds his bow and smiles at the sight.
He hits the back of the male with his arrow,
Which entirely penetrates the creature
And pins the two, male and female, together.

The company witnesses the blow in awe
And showers the king with praise:
"May the evil eye keep away from your glory!
May every day be a celebration for you!
Your merit is invaluable, as you are both king and warrior."

16 | Bahraam Kills the Lions and Weds the Jeweler's Daughter

From there, Bahraam launches his horse Shabrang
And finds a forest on his path.
At the entrance of the woods, he spots two fierce lions.
He binds his bow, stretches it and shoots.
The arrow strikes the chest of the male lion,
Penetrating the body from tip to fletch
And pinning it to the ground.

He quickly approaches the female,
Releases the thumb ring that holds the arrow,
And strikes the animal in the chest.
He says, "It was nevertheless an arrow
Without fletches, an arrow with a blunt tip."

His escort sings his glory:
"O illustrious world king, no one has seen
Nor will ever see a ruler of your stature
Seated on the imperial throne!
You have the ability to bring down a lion
With an arrow bare of plumes and can uproot
A boulder with one adorned with fletches."

Bahraam dashes across the field with his escort.
They find a forest full of sheep and shepherds
Who saunter away, fearing a calamity.
One of the chiefs, a man who never rests
For fear of wild beasts, approaches the king.

Bahraam says to him, "Why are the sheep
Congregating in such an unfavorable location?"

The chief shepherd replies, "O illustrious man,
I am the only one daring to enter the field.
The sheep belong to a merchant jeweler.
I carried them down from the mountain
To the plain yesterday. Their owner is rich
And does not retreat at the threat of loss.
He owns loads of precious jewels, gold, and silver.
He only has one daughter, who plays the lute
And whose head is framed with a cascade of curls.
The father drinks wine only from her hand.
No one has ever seen an old man like him.
How could he have held onto his wealth
If Bahraam had not been a just king?
But the King of Kings is not greedy for gold,
And his wise master is not an unjust man."

Then the chief shepherd adds, "O renowned lord,
You are brave, intelligent, and a valiant horseman.
Could you not tell me who killed these wild beasts?
May the World Master always be his support!"

Bahraam replies, "The two lions succumbed
To the arrows of a most courageous hero.
The brave rider killed them
And rode off with his seven companions.
Where is the home of the merchant jeweler?
Show me the way; do not hide it from me."

The chief shepherd says, "If you take the road,
You will encounter a beautiful new village.
Its reputation must have reached the city,
And the king is at the palace by now.
Once the sky dons its garment of black satin,
This wealthy man prepares for feast.

If you wait a bit, you will hear the sounds
Of cups clinging and lute playing."

At these words, Bahraam asks for a horse
And an attire worthy of the king.
He takes leave of his vizier and the company,
His head filling with need and desire.

Roozbeh says to the noblemen,
"The King of Iran is going to the village.
He will knock at the jeweler's door.
Listen to what I have to say:
He will ask the father for the daughter's hand
And will place, without a doubt,
A golden crown upon her head.
He will settle her in one of his golden harems.
He never tires of women, and in the dark night
They find themselves running away from him.
He now has more than one hundred women.
It is a calamity for a king to behave in this way.
The eunuch has counted nine hundred and thirty
Young women in the royal palace, each bearing
A heavy diadem, each having been offered great wealth.

"He asks for tributes from all the lands, and in
A single month squanders the taxes paid by Rum.
Alas, his chest, his shoulders, and waist!
Alas, his face, once the assembly's delight!
No one will ever set eyes on a man of his strength,
A man able to pin two deer together with a single shot.
He will perish from so abusing his women
And will soften like an ailing man.
His eyes will dull, his cheeks will pale,
His body will weaken, and his face will dim.
The scent of women will whiten his hair, and
When one has white hair, one loses hope in the world.
Though still young, his lofty stature will bend,
And his misfortune will derive from women.
Cohabiting more than once a month
Is equal to spilling the blood of others.
A young and prudent man must save his strength
For his children, for if one exceeds the limits,

One exhausts oneself, and a weak man produces men
Whose hearts fill with the blood of anguish."

Speaking in this manner, they reach the palace
Just as the sun disappears from the vault of sky.

Bahraam departs at dusk, accompanied
By a lone man to tend to his horse.
Near the jeweler's home, he hears the lute.
He launches his steed Golgoon in the direction
Of the music, nearing the merchant's house.
He knocks at the door and requests entrance,
Invoking the name of the Master of the Sun.

A benevolent servant asks who it is
And why someone knocks at this time of night.

Bahraam replies, "This morning, the king went to hunt.
My horse began to limp beneath me, and I fell behind.
I fear the theft of this beautiful charger of golden bridle,
In which case I wouldn't know what to do."

The young woman approaches her master and says,
"There is a man at the door who seeks shelter.
He fears his horse and golden bridle may be stolen,
Which would make him terribly miserable."

The jeweler replies, "Open the door and usher him in.
Have you never seen guests enter our home?"

The young woman rushes to invite Bahraam in.
She says, "Enter, young man, you are welcome."

At the sight of the beautiful home and
The servants standing all around, Bahraam reflects:
"O incomparable Yazdan, Justice Giver,
You guide your servants down the path of righteousness.
May my actions follow your ways and never cast them off!
May greed and pride never dictate to me!
May my subjects' hearts be happy with their king!
The greater my wisdom and my just ways,
The brighter my name after my death.
May all my subjects enjoy, like this jeweler,

270

PART TWENTY-FOUR

The sounds of the lute and clinking cups!"

The King of Kings enters the main pavilion.
From the entrance, he spots the merchant's
Celebrated daughter, who at the sight of him
Rises eagerly and dips her straight stature.
He says, "May this night be propitious to you!
May the hearts of your adversaries be torn apart!"

The master of the house asks for a carpet
To be laid out with a cushion for comfort.
He delights at the sight of Bahraam's face.
A sumptuous array is displayed,
An abundance of delicious dishes, cold and warm.

A servant enters. The master commands him
To tie up the horse and prepare a meal
And a bed for their guest's helper.

A chair is set up for the master of the house,
And he sits next to the king, excusing himself:
"O benevolent lord, you are master in this home.
Comply here to our coarse customs and ways.
Once dinner is complete, let us grab our cups,
Then seek respite in sweet slumber.
The night is dark, and the wine worthy of a king.
You will sleep well once you are inebriated.
In the morning, you will awaken
And will then travel in a royal manner."

Bahraam replies, "Whoever is so lucky to find
At night a host with a face as fresh as yours?
You must not forget to give thanks to Yazdan,
For the heart of an ungrateful man is full of fear."

The young woman brings a bowl and a jug
Of water for him to wash his hands.
She is surprised at the sight of the stranger.
Once his guest has washed, the jeweler asks
For a cup of wine, calling for music, comfort, and rest.

The young woman brings a cup full of a crimson
Wine crowned with roses and fenugreek.

271

The jeweler takes the first cup, drains it,
And washes it with musk and rosewater.
Then he gives the heart-charming cup to Bahraam
And asks, "What is the name of our guest?
I will make an oath with you to seal our friendship.
We shall propose King Bahraam as guarantor."

The king laughs heartily at these words and says,
"My name is Goshasp the rider.
I came here drawn by the sound of the lute.
I did not come to drink and spend the night."

The master of the house says, "My daughter,
Whom you see here, is my greatest source of pride.
She is my cupbearer, my lute player,
My singer, and my most comforting companion.
The name of this heart charmer is Arezoo.
She pours me wine and is my heart's delight."

He says to the lofty cypress tree, "Take your lute
And approach Goshasp in all your beauty."

The lute player walks majestically to the king,
Tall as an elm tree, and says to Bahraam,
"O elite rider, you resemble the ruler in every way.
Know that this dwelling celebrates you.
My father is your host and your treasurer.
May the dark nights be joyful for you!
May your head rise above rain-filled clouds!"

Bahraam says to her, "Pick up your instrument.
Play for me. I must hear a song without delay.
Your father, Maahiar, will be renewed with youth.
He pledges his soul for the sound of your music."

The young woman presses the lute to her chest
And begins a song on the subject of mages.
As the silk cords vibrate and sound, it is as if
The house fills with the scent of jasmine.

The next song is in honor of her father, Maahiar:
"You are like a tall cypress tree on the river's edge;
Your hair is like camphor framing a blooming rose;

Your speech is full of warmth, your heart full of love.
May your enemy be always afflicted with grief!
May wisdom always expand in your soul!
You are like Fereydoon of noble character,
And I am your humble servant, Arezoo.
You are just as happy in the company of your guest
As the king is at the sight of his victorious army."

Then she moves closer to her guest,
Plucking at the strings and singing,
"O man of royal mien, your star is powerful,
Your heart is sincere, your hand is prompt in battle.
Anyone who has not seen Bahraam,
The celebrated rider and heart charmer,
Might as well look into your face,
For you resemble him more than anyone else.
Your waist is as slender as a reed,
Your stature is that of a tall cypress tree,
An elegant, graceful tree with a pheasant's stride.
The nature of your heart is that of a male lion
And your body that of a fierce elephant.
In battle you toss your javelin a distance of two miles.
Your cheeks resemble the flowers of the pomegranate,
As if rose petals have been washed with wine.
Your two arms are as wide as camel thighs.
You can uproot Mount Bisootoon.
May Arezoo's body be the dust beneath your feet!
May her life unfold in accordance to your will!"

This song, the lute, her demeanor, her height,
Her intelligence affect the ruler in such a way
That it is as if her heart were the prize for his agony.

The king says to Maahiar, who sits before him drunk,
"If you wish to be praised for your just ways,
Give me your daughter according to your rites."

Maahiar says to Arezoo, "What gifts
Do you desire from this man of lion heart?
Look at him well to see whether he suits you,
Whether he is good enough to live at your side."

Arezoo replies, "O noble and kind father,

273

If you wish to give my hand to a man,
Goshasp the rider is worthy of me, and that is that.
Who would not, at the sight of such a man,
Tell Bahraam to move aside?"

Maahiar is not satisfied with his daughter's reply.
He says to Bahraam, "O valiant cavalier,
Observe her attentively from head to toe.
Assess her energy, her knowledge, her wisdom.
See if your heart admires her attributes.
It is better to gain information than to remain idle.
With all her virtues, she is not poor.
I do not make it a habit of boasting,
But if you estimate Maahiar's jewels,
You will find that their value exceeds royal riches.

"Nevertheless, guard yourself from acting
In any way hastily or carelessly.
Rest for the duration of the night,
And, if necessary, drink another cup of wine.
Powerful men do not sign treaties drunk
And neither do wise women.
Wait until the sun returns to the sky
And the heads of noblemen emerge from sleep.
We shall then bring some learned, old men
Who are literate and endowed with patient hearts.
The dark night does not agree with the customs
And the rites of King Fereydoon.
Asking for someone's hand in marriage
Or engaging in a new project while inebriated
Cannot be a harbinger of good fortune."

Bahraam replies, "It is absurd and wrong
To consult fate when one follows Yazdan's path.
It pleases me to wed, on this night, your lute player.
Do not bring us misfortune if you can do otherwise."

The father addresses his daughter, "O Arezoo,
Observe this man. Does he please you?"

She replies, "Yes, I was enthralled by him
The moment I set my eyes on him.
Allow me to marry him,

And leave the rest in Yazdan's hands.
The sky has no reason to disagree with Maahiar."

The father tells her, "I offer you to him as his wife.
Always remember that you are under his watch."

He gives her to Bahraam the hunter, who weds her.
As day replaces night and the ceremony is complete,
A servant hangs the king's whip at Maahiar's door.
Arezoo withdraws to her room
At the time when the world is asleep.

Maahiar prepares another room for Goshasp the rider.
He says to his servant, "Close the doors,
Send someone to my sheep's shepherds.
Our spread tomorrow must include
A juicy, plump, and tasty lamb.
When Goshasp awakens, bring him beer and ice.
Place a cup of camphor and rosewater in his room
To diffuse a pleasant fragrance throughout.
As for me, I am fatigued and in need of rest."
After these words, he reclines to sleep.

As the sun displays its glittering crown
And the earth brightens in a dazzling shade of ivory,
Squires and javelin carriers look for hints
Of the king's whereabouts by the location of his crop.
Bahraam's escort assembles at Maahiar's door,
As if before the king's palace,
And all those who recognize the whip approach
At the sight of it and bow down in respect.

When the guardian of the door sees the crowd
Of squires and javelin holders, he enters the house
And approaches his sleeping master.
He awakens him, attempts to dissipate
The effects of wine still troubling his mind,
And says to him, "Rise and shake yourself.
This is not the time to sleep or to be lying still.
The world king is your host in this humble home."

The guardian's words move the jeweler.
He asks, "Why do you say such a thing?

Where do you see indications of royalty?"

The drunken man listens to his guardian's report
As he quickly slips down from the bed.
Angry, he exclaims, "A sensible old man
Must not speak in this manner."

The servant replies, "O worldly master,
Who would make up a story about the world king?
There is such a vast host at your door that,
If you wished to pass through,
The space would be too constricted.
Anyone who wanders by
Reveres the old felt of your door's hanging drapes.
A servant came before the rising sun
And hung a whip at your door in clear sight.
It is braided with gold and inlaid with fine stones.
You would think the entire population
Of the world has gathered here.
Now do as you must.
Attempt to drive your sluggishness away,
Even though you drank last night."

The old man, now fully awake, shakily says,
"How could I get drunk with the King of Kings?
How could I make my daughter serve him wine?"

He runs to Arezoo's room and says,
"O moon of noble soul, Bahraam, King of Kings,
Is the one who knocked at our door last night.
He came from the plain after the hunt.
Now rise, don your dress of Rumi brocade,
Place the diadem you wore yesterday on your head,
And select three rubies out of my cache of jewels
Worthy of the king to offer him.
At the sight of his sun-like face, bow deeply,
Cross your hands at your chest, and lower your eyes,
Refraining from peering directly at him.
May he be yours, body and soul!
If he asks you questions, reply in a gentle voice.
Talk to him with deference and humility.
As for me, I shall show myself only if he asks to see me,

276

Only if he counts me among his most humble servants.
I cannot believe I sat at the table with him
As if we stood on equal footing.
May the bones in my body shatter to pieces!
How could I be so free with the king?
How could I dare bring myself to drink with him?
Wine brings out the worst in men, young and old."

A servant rushes in to announce
That the king of serene heart has awakened.

Bahraam exits from his bed chamber in good health
And walks into the garden to wash his head and body.
He turns toward the sun and prays hopefully.
Then he enters the main hall
And asks a cupbearer for a cup of wine.
He learns that people have convened
At the door and commands them to be dismissed.
Then he asks for Arezoo, whom he wishes to see.
She arrives humbly, decked in diadem and earrings,
Holding wine and an offering for the king.

She bows deeply and kisses the ground.
His heart enchanted by her, the king smiles
And says to her, "How did you conduct yourself?
You gave me wine to intoxicate me, and then you left.
Your enchanting songs and your delicate fingers
On the lute suffice for me.
I have no need for gifts from women.
They are better given to other men.
Sing to me again about the hunt, the blows of spear,
And the battles engaged by the King of Kings."
Then he adds, "What became of the jeweler
With whom I drank last night?"

At these words, the young woman calls her father,
Surprised at the king's kindness.

The father presents himself before the sun-like king,
Hands crossed at his chest, and says, "O King,
You are noble, smart, powerful, strong, and valiant.
May the world always turn to your will!
May every crown be inscribed with your name!

A man of my status who drank the fruit of the vine
With you has only one option: to remain quiet.
My error derived from my ignorance.
You must think that I am possessed by a deev.
Could you possibly choose to forgive me?
Could you return its sheen to my face
And light up the path before me?
I stand at your door a senseless slave
Whom you will not wish to include among men."

The king says, "A sensible man
Never accuses a drunken one.
When one is aggrieved by the effects of wine,
One must avoid the color and scent of drink.
Never did I witness you, in your inebriation,
Display the slightest hint of irritability.
Now listen to Arezoo, and in lieu of a defense,
Listen to her sweet song about tulips and jasmine.
We shall listen and engage in drinking wine.
We shall not lend a thought to the days to come."

The prudent Maahiar kisses the ground and sets a table.
This man of pure intentions summons
The noblemen stationed at the door of his home.
But Arezoo, at the sight of strangers,
Withdraws to her room with a frowning face.
She remains there until the sky dons its black mantle
And the stars appear around the sphere of moon.

After dining, Maahiar calls Arezoo, seats her
On a golden chair ornate with golden figurines,
And entreats her to pick up her lute
And recite the song the king had requested.

She sings, "O valiant King, at the sound of your name,
The lions in their forest dens swiftly run away.
You are the victorious ruler, army destroyer.
Your face is a blooming tulip on a bed of jasmine.
No world king reaches the heights of your stature,
And no moon in the sky is your equal in beauty.
At the sight of your helmet on the battlefield,
Every heart, every bone marrow, splits in fear,

And every head loses the sense of highs and lows."

They drink slowly at first, but once they achieve
A state of cheer, they pour larger cups of wine.

Roozbeh makes an appearance before the king,
And a dwelling is prepared for him in the village.
He brings a litter and forty moon-faced,
Charming females from the king's following.
The cheeks of these Rumi maidens are like lush brocade,
And the entire land is revived by their appearance.
Arezoo leaves for the king's harem
With a jewel-encrusted diadem on her head.

17 | Bahraam's Adventure With Farshidvard

The king, his open heart filled with joy,
Takes his leave from the village chief with Roozbeh.
They spend the night sleeping, and in the morning
At dawn, they go to the plain to hunt.

The procession crosses the land by way of roads
And pathless terrain to settle on the plain.
Their tents are pitched, their enclosures set up.
For one month, they chase various beasts and birds,
And clear the land of game.
No one gives a thought to sleep,
For the wine pours freely
And countless wild animals roam the fields.
Furthermore, the delightful sounds
Of the lute and rebec fill the air.

Fires are lit to burn green and dry wood.
Many people come from the cities,
Most of them in need of dinars.
Things are bought and sold,
And the ground dazzles beneath the mass of men.

Merchants buy and sell: The price of ten antelopes
Or one onager is equal to one fourth of the price.
Anyone who asks for it receives so much roasted

Game and water birds that he takes donkey loads
Back to his family, his children, and his guests.

After the duration of one month,
Bahraam grows impatient to see his women.
He leaves the hunting preserves with his company.
The road disappears beneath the riders' dust.
The escort marches swiftly until the face of day
Is obscured by the advent of indigo night.

Bahraam finds a borough in front of him
Full of guesthouses, streets, and markets.
He commands his escort to stay there
And not leave anyone behind.

He enquires after the home of the village chief,
And he finds a large, thick dilapidated door.
The master of the house greets him, and Bahraam asks,
"To whom belongs this battered, run-down home,
And why this desolation in the middle of the village?"

The master replies, "This home belongs to me,
And, regrettably, ill fortune is my guide.
I have neither cow nor clothing, neither courage
Nor knowledge, neither foot nor wing.
You have seen my dismal mien.
Now take a look at my somber dwelling,
A home more deserving of curse than benediction."

The king dismounts and visits the house,
But his hands fall to his side and his legs fail him.
He is astonished to find a vast, arched palace,
Though it is littered with sheep dung.
He says to the proprietor, "O respectful host,
Bring something for me to sit upon."

The master of the house replies,
"You are wrong to mock me, O border guard!
If I had a carpet, others would celebrate me,
But I have neither carpet nor food,
Neither clothing nor bed to recline upon.
You better look for another lodging,
For everything here is lowly and lacks comfort."

Bahraam says, "Search for a pillow
So that I may rest for a short while."

The other replies, "This is not a place
Where one should seek comfort.
You might as well ask for bird milk
Instead of a pillow in my home."

The guest says, "Bring me warm milk
And a piece of soft bread, if you can find some."

The other replies, "Assume that you have dined
And that you have departed in a joyous state.
If I had bread, there would be life in my body,
And if I had life, it would be more worthy than bread."

Bahraam says to him, "If you do not own sheep,
How come your place is littered with sheep droppings?"

The other replies, "It is now pitch black,
And my head is weary of your discourse.
Select a house with a felt gate,
And its master will bless you for going to him.
Why do you insist on lodging with a wretched man
Who rests his achy body at night on a bed of leaves?
You have a golden sword and golden stirrups,
And you must not spend another moment here.
You have cause to fear thieves,
And a dilapidated home such as this one
Serves as shelter to bandits and lions."

Bahraam says, "If a thief could seize my sword,
I would not be in possession of one today.
Give me a place in your home, just for tonight,
And I shall not trouble you for anything else."

The master of the house replies, "Do not insist.
No one is ever welcome in my home."

The king says to him, "O wise old man,
Why are you so troubled by my presence?
I still have no doubt that you will be kind
Enough to offer me a glass of fresh water."

The master says, "Did you not notice the reservoir
Nearby, two arrows' length from here?
Drink your fill and take with you what you please.
But what do you want in this bare and lowly house?
Have you never seen a poor man
Rendered incapable of work by the effects of old age?"

Bahraam says, "If you enjoy a higher rank,
Do not seek quarrel with an armed man
For the sake of a small sip of water.
What is your name?"

He replies, "Farshidvard. I have neither land
Nor clothing, neither water nor food to eat."

Bahraam says, "Why do you not seek
To earn some bread and procure yourself some rest?"

Farshidvard replies, "Yazdan, the Nurturer,
Will perhaps put an end to my sorrowful fate.
If I see my home free of your presence,
I shall give thanks to the Creator.
Why do you insist on staying in an empty house?
May you never enjoy either power or happiness!"

As he says this, he begins to weep so bitterly
That the king leaves and takes the road,
Laughing at the fate of this old man,
And his escort joins him little by little.

After exiting this noteworthy village,
He comes upon a land covered in thorns.
A man is slashing the barbed stems with an ax.
Bahraam drifts away from his escort to approach him.
He says to him: "O enemy of thorns, do you know
Who is the most influential person in this town?"

The other replies, "Farshidvard is a greedy man
Who does not allow himself to either sleep or eat.
He must have one hundred thousand sheep,
A tenth of that number in camels,
And quite as many in horses and donkeys.
The gold he amasses is buried deep in the ground.

May his body be devoid of skin and bones!
His stomach is empty; his body is bare and weak.
His avarice bars him from nourishment.
He has neither children nor allies,
Neither friends nor dependents.
Were he to sell his plowed lands,
The sum obtained would fill an entire home with jewels.
His shepherds cook their meats in milk.
As for him, he eats millet bread with cheese.
Never has he owned two sets of clothing,
For he is harsh even when it comes to his own body."

The king says to the lumberjack,
"You are familiar with the count of his sheep
But do you know where his herds of horses
And his caravans of camels roam free?"

The lumberjack says, "The location
Of his camels and his sheep is close by,
But my heart dreads what he may do to me."

The king gives him some dinars and says,
"Do not fret. You will become an honorable man."
He summons a learned horseman, valiant and charming,
From his escort, named Behrooz, and dispatches him.
With one hundred illustrious and able riders.
A conscientious scribe is meant to oversee the affair
And to chronicle the transactions.

Then the king turns to the lumberjack:
"You came in search of thorns;
You may now collect gold.
One-hundredth part of the wealth will be yours.
Go and show others the way."

Delafrooz[45] is the lumberjack's name.
He is a man of proud bearing and strong body.
Bahraam offers him a horse and tells him
To ride as fast as wind. Delafrooz becomes
Guitiafrooz[46] and departs triumphantly

◇◇◇◇◇◇◇◇◇◇◇◇◇◇
45 Delafrooz: Name meaning "light of the heart".
46 Guitiafrooz: Name meaning "light of the world."

To guide the troops through mountain and plain,
Where they find innumerable herds of sheep.

There are ten caravans of camels on the plain,
Each with a camel driver. The scribe composes
A list of twelve thousand plow oxen and milk cows,
Two times ten thousand horses and camels.
The entire field is burrowed with marks
From horses' hooves, jars are full of cow butter,
And in the mountains are three hundred
Thousand loads of whey and yogurt.
Everywhere on the plain, mountain, and desert
Are dwellings unknown to people.

Behrooz, son of Hoor, writes a letter to Bahraam,
King of Kings, beginning in praise of the Creator,
Victorious and nurturing, then invoking blessings
On the king who eases his subjects' suffering:
"O world ruler, men great and small
Dwell in happiness during your reign.
Your just ways surpass all measure.
Your humble servants can only remain silent.
Everything in the world has its place,
And the king's heart delights in the order of things.

"Farshidvard is foreign to banquet and battle.
No man, great or small, knows his name.
He recognizes neither king nor Creator.
He does not exhibit gratitude for anything.
While he covers the earth with his wealth,
He hides, empty-handed, in a state of anguish.
His unjust ways are equal in measure to the king's justice.
May you not find offense in my boldness
When I propose you establish a treasury with his wealth.
It will require three years to sort through.
I have brought in scribes from the outside
And settled them on Mount Alborz.

"The worth of this wealth has not yet been estimated,
And already the backs of the scribes are weary.
I have been told that even more gold and
Priceless jewels are buried in the ground.

I remain on the mountain, eyes fixed on the road,
Awaiting his majesty's command.
May blessings be showered over the King of Iran!
May his highness live as long as his name
Weaves into the world's warp and weft!"

He charges his speedy camel on the road
To deliver the letter to the king.
Bahraam the hunter is troubled by its contents.
He grows somber, his eyes fill with tears,
And he arches his eyebrows into a frown.

He summons a scribe with a Rumi reed and Chini silk.
Beginning in praise of the Creator, victorious Ruler,
Master of wisdom and guidance,
Master of the crown of the King of Kings,
He continues: "You write to me that,
If I were righteous, I would immediately
Extract this man from the list of the living.
But he did not amass wealth by theft or murder;
He never engaged anyone to commit evil acts.
He is a man devoid of respect for anyone
And devoid of divine fear or gratitude.
He has acted only as the guardian of his treasury.
His heart and soul perish in the process
And in the fierce yearning to accumulate more.
What difference if wolves or sheep wander
Through the plains if they serve no one?
What difference if there are gems and jewels
Beneath the ground if they furnish men
With neither food nor clothing?

"I shall not use what has been accumulated
With such great pain to establish a treasury.
I wish not to attach my heart to this passing dwelling.
Fereydoon disappeared from the world, and Iraj, Salm,
Toor, Kay Ghobaad, Kay Kaavoos, all succumbed to death,
Along with many illustrious ones we remember well.
Consider the end of my father,
A man who filled my heart with grief,
A man without justice and generosity.
None of these famed rulers survived, and no one

Can blame the World Master for their departure.

"Gather all the wealth, distribute it,
And do not even keep a hair for yourself.
Give to those who hide their needs,
Those who find it hard
To escape their own wretchedness.
Give to the elderly no longer able to work,
Who are scorned by rich men.
Give to those who once owned wealth
But spent it all and now dwell in sorrow and sighs.
Give to those who are indebted and have
Neither dinar nor friend among merchants.
Give to orphaned children whose fathers are deceased
And who have neither wealth nor gold.

Finally, give to widows who own
Neither clothes nor craft or profession.
Give all this wealth to delight
The hearts of poor, wretched beings.
Upon your return to town,
Do not worry about hidden treasures.
Leave the dinars buried by Farshidvard
To him as consolation.
Gold and jewels are as worthy as dust to him.
He only knows how to bury them deep in a trench.
May the revolving dome spin in your favor!
May you always act with justice and awareness!"

The royal seal affixed to the letter,
The messenger returns on the road.

18 | Bahraam the Hunter Kills Lions on the Hunt

Bahraam commands his slaves
To take his throne to the spring garden.
They obey and place the turquoise seat
Beneath a blossoming tree raining down petals.
Wine and cups are set in the rose garden;
Musicians and the court's noblemen are summoned.

The king says to his intimates,
"May this day bring happiness to men!
No matter how high we rank, we shall one day
Lie in solitary confinement in our graves.
Death wipes out everything:
It brings down palaces and audience halls.
Whether you are king or pauper, you may
Only take a good or a bad name with you.
All the effort you have exerted is pointless,
For your suffering and pain will die with you.
If one lacks gratitude for Yazdan,
Another will inherit one's crown and belt.
Refrain from causing another grief;
Always follow the path of righteousness
If you wish to ward off your own suffering.

"I have reached my thirty-eighth year,
And all my days thus far have been spent in joy.
Once a youth reaches his fortieth year,
The fear of death will decidedly lodge in his heart.
If one of your strands of hair grows white,
You have to give up all hope for happy times.
A crown is not appealing on a mane of camphor.
I shall spend the next two years in feast and revelry,
As my body will not sustain much after that.
I shall soon have to appear before Yazdan
In tattered clothes, yet I shall always appreciate
The divine gifts and good fortune bestowed upon me.
I have spent many a day rejoicing under my Kianian crown.
I now sit beneath the blossoms of the pomegranate,
The apple and the quince trees, holding a golden cup
That must never be empty of wine.
When I glance into the ruby face of the apple,
The skies appear spotted like leopard skin
As they prepare to rain down on us.
Spring is auspicious to us, with its colors and scent,
And the crimson wine chases away our sorrows.
The air is a perfect temperature,
Neither too cold nor too hot.
The earth is renewed and refreshed
While the waters turn a shade of deep blue.

"At the time of Mehregan, we shall don attires of fur.
We shall travel to the plains of Jaz to engage in hunt;
We shall leave a memory of ourselves in the world.
The onager will be endowed with a strong neck,
The heart of a male lion, and the color of a tiger.
We shall travel at length with our dogs, cheetahs,
Falcons, gyrfalcons, and hunting thongs.
Such is the place where we shall endlessly
Launch our steeds in the hunt with bow and arrow.
On the plain I have seen below Jaz,
Where the plant of tamarisk grows as tall as reed,
We shall chase lions, which will make it
A grand hunt, though our stay may not be long."

He awaits the arrival of August clouds.
The world fills with armed warriors.
From every province, hosts eager to fight
Travel to the side of the King of Iran.

Bahraam selects the proudest and most expert hunters
And takes a procession of ten thousand
Sword-bearing riders to the hunting grounds.
Around the king's tent enclosure
Are stationed the stables and the stallions.
The servants march ahead of the army.
Everywhere, they dig up wells to which wheels
Are adjusted to draw enough water rations
To accommodate such a vast troop of men.

After the caravan rides the king,
Along with his most intimate friends.
He sees the entire plain abound with onager,
The woods resounding with lion roars.
He says, "This evening we shall chase the wine,
But tomorrow we shall follow their trails,
For there are lion imprints on the ground.
Today, let us rest happily and in good health.
We shall engage in drink until the dawn of day,
When the sun's crown lights up the shining world.
We shall knock down the valiant dragons with our swords,
And when the forest is rid of lions, the onager will be ours."

He remains still for the night, and the next morning
He goes into the forest with his procession.
As soon as he sees a lion emerge from the woods,
One that is full of courage, having dined on an onager,
The valiant Bahraam says to his friends, "I am expert
At the use of bow and arrow, but I shall capture the lion
With my sword to evade being deemed a coward."

He dresses in a damp woolen tunic
And climbs on a battle horse.
As soon as the lion catches sight of him, he leans back
On his hind legs and pounds with his front legs,
Hoping to hit the horse on the head.
But the hunter prompts his charger with his heel
And strikes the lion's head with his sharp sword.
The female lion quickly absconds.
The blade pierces her mate from head to loin,
Filling the hearts of other male lions with dread.

Another roaring lion advances boldly with a lioness
Who is in the process of feeding her lion cub.
The king raises his sword and strikes it on the neck,
Sending the head flying away from its body.

Someone says, "O sun-faced King,
You bear no pity for your own person.
The entire forest is full of lions with
Their lion cubs hanging on their mother's teats.
We must beware of the female lions,
For they have their young in the fall.
This forest is three farsangs deep, and even
If you spend an entire year capturing lions,
The world still would not be free of them.
Why then would you take such great pains?
Once you took possession of the throne,
You sought to battle lions, as it was agreed upon.
But today you are king; the world belongs to you.
You came here in pursuit of onager.
Why then insist on chasing lions?"

The king replies, "O wise old man, tomorrow
Will witness the sight of onager, arrows, and me!

The proud riders of ancient times
Did not gain fame with bow and arrow.
If we wish to fulfill our duty to bravery,
We shall speak only of mace and sword."

The wise man says to him, "If you went to battle
With ten riders as strong and powerful as you,
There would not remain throne and crown
In either the land of Rum or the land of Chin.
Prudent men would take shelter on the sea
With all their belongings and valuables.
May the evil eye never access your glory!
May your dwelling be in the rose garden of feasts!"

The king returns from the forest to camp
With the grand wise master and the army warriors.
Everyone showers him with blessings: "May diadem
And seal never be deprived of your presence!"

He enters his tent as soon as the troops depart
And washes off the sweat from his arms and hands.
His butler, a border commander,
Extends a silken spread across the tent's interior.
He calls for camphor, musk, and rosewater,
And sprinkles musk around the sleeping quarters.
In all the tents, he places golden tables
Decorated with crockery and vases from Chin.

The kitchen master fills them with plates of lamb
And other dishes to complement the meat.

Once dinner is complete, King Bahraam the hunter
Asks a fairy-faced cupbearer for a large crystal goblet.
Cup in hand, the king, giver of justice, says,
"King Ardeshir, whose good fortune reenergized men,
Was our home's master, and we stood inferior to him,
Even though assigning ourselves lower rank
May exhibit, in some way, a sign of impudence.
In battle and in feast, in council and in banquet,
He was the only one entitled to be world ruler.
At the time, Eskandar traveled from Rum to Iran,
Converting our land into a barren desert.
But he was harsh and lacked generosity,

290

For he sentenced to death thirty-six kings.
Princes continue to condemn him.
The entire world still holds his actions against him.
We cultivate only blessings for Fereydoon
While Eskandar is cursed by those who hate him.
May I dispense happiness throughout
The world among men, great and small!"

He continues, "Bring me a silver-tongued herald,
One of our illustrious warrior leaders,
To make the rounds of camp and to proclaim:
"If someone takes what is not rightly his
From cities, mountains, or the town of Jaz,
Whether it be jewels, gold, brocade,
Lush fur, valuables, or worthless trifles,
I shall tie him up on a horse, facing the rear,
And will have two armed men drag him
And send him to the temple of Aazargoshasp.
There he will spend his time in prayer
And in worship to Yazdan, the Holy,
Seated in the dust, facing the flame.
I shall donate and return his belongings
To those he stripped and violated.
Furthermore, if someone places a horse
In a freshly sown field or causes damage
In a fruit garden, he will go to prison for one year,
Whether he is a noble rider or a poor man.
It is of utmost importance to us to gain what we must
From the plain so that we may return to the city in joy."

The merchants and half of the inhabitants
Of Jaz and Barghoveh rush over, and the desert,
On the side of the king's position, resembles
A Chini bazaar with the influx of merchandise.

19 | Bahraam Displays His Skills in the Hunt and Travels to Baghdad and Estakhr

The next morning, as the sun displays its shining crown,
The world master engages in the hunt.
All the members of his company bind their bows,
And the king shadows them into the fields.

He says, "Anyone who rubs his bow
And releases an arrow on an onager
Must aim at the breech so that the tip
Of the shaft emerges from its chest."

One of the warriors says to him,
"O King, observe this illustrious escort
And determine to whom belongs the expertise
Of bow and arrow to realize such a deed.
Such a blow may be easy for you.
May your head and diadem live forever!
When you grasp your arrow, your sword and mace,
The troops are filled with immeasurable awe
And respect for his majesty's arms and tall stature,
Embarrassed by their own weakness
When it comes to archery."

The king replies, "It is indeed a divine gift.
What would Bahraam be if he were
To be deprived of his divine strength?"

Bahraam the hunter launches his horse Shabdeez.
As soon as he approaches a male onager,
He seizes the moment, releases the ring,
And strikes the creature to pierce the rear
All the way through to pin his legs to his chest.

The onager instantly drops to the ground,
And the warriors of golden belts rush over.
They remain quite astonished by the blow
And, in a common voice, invoke blessings on the king.
One could no longer perceive the arrow,
From tip to fletch, so deep it sank into the beast's flesh.

The warring cavaliers and the vengeful combatants
Bring their foreheads to the ground.
After singing his praises, one of the heroes says,
"O King, may your eye never perceive fate's misfortune!
You are a bold cavalier while we are seated on donkeys;
We do not even merit the title of donkey driver."

The king replies, "It is not my arrow; it is Yazdan,
The victorious, who came to my assistance.
The one who fails to receive aid from the World Master
Is the lowliest creature on earth."

He launches his charger as if it were the flying Homay.
A female onager appears, its offspring sprinting ahead.
Bahraam strikes it with his piercing sword,
And the onager, split in half, tumbles to the ground.

The proud and noble swordsmen, great and small,
Run over and, at the sight of the wound,
A stunned wise man says, "What a sword! What force!
May the king, so alike to the moon,
Be forever protected against the evil eye
Or else the celestial orb would disappear from the sky!
The heads of the world's rulers are beneath his feet.
The firmament submits to his arrows and his sword."

The troops follow in the footsteps of the king
And carry on in order to rid the desert of onager.
Bahraam orders the creation of golden rings
On which his name is engraved and which
He hangs on the ears of onager as he releases them.
He similarly marks a herd of three hundred,
Which he then proceeds to release,
Sending them free to benefit his name's glory
For his own pleasure and entertainment.

A man makes the camp's rounds and announces:
"No one on this plain is to sell a single onager.
They are to be given to the merchants free."

The famed inhabitants of Barghoveh and Jaz
Bring an abundance of brocade and furs to the king,
Who demands that taxes be withheld,

Even if they are able to pay them without effort.
All the poor people of the region
And those who gain their living through hard work
Obtain wealth through the king's largesse,
And many of them accede to thrones and diadems.

Bahraam returns from the hunt to his palace
And furnishes the city and the army
With seven days of joy.
He holds a plenary court in the public square.
Present are eloquent speakers, wise men,
Poor men, and the army standing rank.

One of the wise men says, "O justice seekers,
Find shelter at the side of Yazdan
Rather than at the side of the king's servants.
Those who were unable to sleep because
Of some wrongdoing I may have caused them,
Those who did not have a share of my wealth,
Go to the public square to see if the king
Can establish for you a more prosperous fate.
Furthermore, if there are older men, weary men,
Men incapable of performing their work functions
Or young men who have fallen ill,
If there are among this crowd some who are
Indebted and fear the pursuit of creditors,
Or children deprived of fathers who dare not
Ask anything of wealthy men
And whose mothers are secretly in need
While they attempt to hide their misery,
Or if there are the small children of a deceased
Wealthy man whose shameless, fearless overseer
Attempts to take possession of his fortune,
May no one hide any such a case from me,
For I cannot help someone who conceals a secret.

"The king wishes to render the poor wealthy,
Return the soul of the impious to faith,
Pay the debts of the destitute and of the worried.
I shall open the royal treasury and offer wealth
To the poor who live in a state of shame.
If my administrators give rise to grief

And strip orphans of what is rightly theirs,
I shall attach these evil oppressors alive at the gallows."

The door to the treasury is opened,
And those in need gain wealth.

Bahraam, upon leaving the hunting grounds,
Heads toward the city of Baghdad,
Having gained wisdom, his heart full of joy.
The illustrious noblemen, strangers and relatives,
Appear before him, but he commands everyone
In his escort to return while he enters his palace.

A golden bedroom is prepared,
And servants request musk and wine.
Idols sing songs and play the lute.
Visitors are dismissed as the air
Rings with the sound of music, flute and song,
And blends with the scent of wine.
In every room, young women execute dances
In the night to bring joy to the king's dim heart.

For two weeks, he surrenders to revelry,
His treasury door open, day and night.
He distributes gold and silver freely.
Then he travels to the city of Estakhr,
Where he places on his head the glorious crown.
He opens the women's palace of Khorraad
And gratifies the idols with a silver treasure.

If the king finds a young woman in the golden chambers
Who does not bear a crown on her head
Or is not seated upon an ivory throne,
He murmurs with anger, bites his lip,
Quite displeased with Roozbeh, and says to him,
"I shall give them the tributes from Rum and Khazar
When you bring them to me.
Immediately ask for an abundance of dinars,
Ask them from the treasuries of Rey and Isfahan.
From the way you behave, the women's chambers
Are in ruins and not worthy of the King of Kings."

New tribute is demanded from various provinces,

The earth is decked in brocade, and the world
Rejoices in this manner for some time
In the absence of war, grief, dispute, and battle.

20 | The Tarkhan of Chin Attacks Iran

Some time later, word spreads through the lands
Of India, Rum, Chin, Iran, and among the Turks
That Bahraam occupies himself only with worldly
Pleasures, disregarding his subjects' needs.
He fails to dispatch patrols, spies, and sentinels.
The borders are vacant of border guards.
He spends his time in revelry,
Oblivious to what is happening around him.

At the news, the Tarkhan selects troops
From Chin and Khotan, pays the tribute,
And marches to invade the land of Iran,
Where Bahraam is no longer deemed relevant.

While troops from Chin and Khotan trudge eastward,
The Rumi Caesar dispatches a vast host to march west.

News of the armies marching from the east
And the west reaches the land of Iran.
The Iranian leaders, young and old illustrious men,
Present themselves before Bahraam the hunter,
Full of anger and anguish, heads in a state of rebellion.
They speak to him harshly:
"Your shining fortune has abandoned you.
The rulers have their minds set on battle,
Yet your heart dreams only of games and feast.
The treasury, the army, the borders of Iran,
Its throne and crown have lost their value in your eyes."

The world master replies to his wise advisors:
"The Creator, Distributor of justice on earth,
Wiser than the wisest beings, is my support.
By the victorious power of Yazdan, highest Emperor,
I shall safeguard Iran from the claws of wolves.
By my fortune and army, by my sword and wealth,

I shall protect my land from a calamity."

He continues to entertain himself as before.
Blood tears spring in the proud leaders' eyes
As each one laments, "The hearts of men
Of good faith must turn away from the king."

The news awakens Bahraam's heart.
Concerned, he secretly shapes his host,
And no one in the world knows what he hides.
All of Iran trembles to see him occupied as he is,
All hearts split painfully in sorrow, despairing
Of the king, cursing him and his government.

Meanwhile, Bahraam Shah receives the news
That an army from Chin is occupying Iran.
He calls Gostaham and speaks to him at length
About the Tarkhan and his belligerent host.

Gostaham is a warrior and a vizier
Who equates battle to feast.
He calls Mehr Pirooz, son of Behzaad;
Mehr Barzeen, son of Khorraad;
Bahraam of Pirooz, son of Bahraamian;
Khazarvan; Rohaam and Andman,
One is King of Gilan, the other King of Rey,
Two warriors who never give up in war.
Next he summons Raam Barzeen,
The governor of Zabolestan, a tested warrior;
Ghaaran, son of Borzmehr;
And Daad Barzeen of scowling face.
An army forms of six thousand Iranians,
Prudent and skilled warriors.

Bahraam entrusts Nersi with the throne and crown,
Charging him with the custody of his treasury
As well as the army's command.
Nersi, his pure brother of noble features,
Accepts the appointment.
He is a wise, majestic, and just believer.

Bahraam departs with troops toward Azerbaijan.
He selects a small cavalry of men,

Great and small, eager and ready to fight.
Two lines of six thousand mail-sporting riders
Wielding bull-headed maces fall into place.

Since he fails to take troops from Pars, people form
The impression that their king flees to avoid battle
And to take shelter in the temple of Aazargoshasp.

As Bahraam marches onward, an envoy
Sent by the Caesar arrives as swift as wind at court.
Nersi takes him to his palace and assigns him
Sumptuous accommodations, fitting his rank.

The army flocks around the grand wise master
To obtain news of the king, saying, "Since Bahraam
Has vacated the throne, our fortunes have dimmed.
If he does not waste away his wealth on us, then why
Should he not form a treasury in the manner of kings?
He distributes gold everywhere,
Not paying heed to the value of youth.
The land and the army are in a state of disarray,
And everyone seeks to aggrandize himself,
To climb to reach a higher status and position."

After further discussion, they agree to send
An illustrious man from Iran to the Tarkhan,
To provoke assaults on all sides as a shield
Against the advent of misfortune
And the onslaught of enemy troops.
This is to safeguard Iran from the prospect of pillage,
Destruction, and annihilation while the ruler abandoned
His home and engaged in wandering the world.

Nersi replies, "This is not a just course of action.
This is a body of water for which there is no river.
Never shall I ask the ruler of Chin for protection.
I shall cover the earth with elephants and troops.
We have weapons, treasure, valiant warriors who will,
With their swords, extinguish the flames of hostility.
Why should we despair of King Bahraam
Just because he has left with a small battalion?
What on earth inspired such wicked thoughts?
Twisted reflections can only give rise to tragedy."

The Iranians reply, "Bahraam did not
Take an army from here with him,
And one must not surrender one's soul to grief.
If the Tarkhan arrives to attack Iran,
He will destroy this beautiful land.
The army and Nersi will vanish as well,
And we shall be trampled beneath their feet
Without concern for either worth or distinction.
We must find a way to safeguard our homes
And to avoid the erasure of our imprint."

There is a wise man named Homay,
A man of sense, wisdom, and good counsel.
The Iranians single him out to find a solution.
They write to the Tarkhan in the name of Iran,
A letter of submission beginning thus:
"We are your slaves, bowing low to your will.
We shall send you presents crafted in Iran-Zamin
With requests for forgiveness and your blessing.
With these gifts, we offer you tributes and royalties,
For we cannot resist a war with the Turks."

The blessed Homay departs from Iran
With noblemen of good counsel.
He relays the message to the Tarkhan,
Whose heart blossoms like a flower with joy.
They speak of King Bahraam's sudden
Departure with his small retinue.

The ruler of Chin says to the Turks, "We have imposed
A saddle on the courier of the revolving dome of sky.
We are the only ones able to seize Iran without engaging
In war, for we have wisdom, acumen, and infinite patience."

He offers the envoy many gifts, dirham and dinars
In abundance, then writes a reply to the message:
"May the souls of pure men be the allies of wisdom!
I completely approve of your envoy's message.
When I reach Marv with my army,
I shall render the face of the world as shiny
As a pheasant's wing with my justice,
My good intentions, and my magnificence.

I shall make milk take the place of water
To richly and gently stream into rivers.
We shall remain until tribute arrives from Iran.
I shall march to Marv and not further,
For I wish not for my army to cause you harm."

The messenger returns in haste to Iran.
He recounts all that he has seen and heard.

The Tarkhan drives his host to Marv,
And the world darkens with the dust of riders.
Once he has rested, he revels in life,
And no one gives a further thought to Bahraam.
In Marv, the incessant sounds of lute and rebec
Do not afford the residents a chance to rest or sleep.

The Tarkhan scatters his army on the plain.
There is neither patrol nor guard for the horses.
There is only the hunt, wine, gathering, flute, and lute.
They feel protected against an attack, day and night.
The Tarkhan awaits tribute from the Iranians,
And his fury mounts with each delay.

21 | Bahraam the Hunter Attacks the Tarkhan of Chin

Bahraam, on his side, keeps watch.
He protects his army against an enemy attack.
Day and night, he sends out spies
And refrains from engaging in feast and drink.

Once aware of Tarkhan's presence in Marv
With his host, Bahraam drives his troops
To Aazargoshasp without loads and baggage.
Each man is equipped with two horses,
Chain mail, shield, quiver, and a Rumi helmet.
Day and night, they ride, advancing as swift as wind,
Like a torrent rushing down the mountainside.
They arrive in Amol by way of Ardabil, and from Amol
They reach Gorgan, tormented by the suffering of noblemen.
From Gorgan, they enter the land of Nessa,
Preceded by a loyal guide, crossing mountain,

300

Desert, and roadless regions, and marching
During the undue hours of night until dawn.

King Bahraam sets up sentinels during daytime
And watch guards during the night.
He advances in this manner to Marv,
Faster than a pheasant can fly.
There he finds one of his spies, who tells him
That the Tarkhan neglects his royal duties,
That he occupies himself with the hunt
In Coshmaihan[47], and that, day and night, he holds
Company with Ahriman, his partner and advisor.

Bahraam rejoices at the news
And overlooks his exhaustion.
He takes a break from travel for one day,
And once host and horses have rested,
They march off at dawn to Coshmaihan.
As the illuminating sun rises over the mountaintops,
Their ears fill with the sound of clarions
And the clatter of weapons.
Their eyes reflect the sheen of banner tops.

The King of Chin and his army hear the tumult
Growing so thunderous it tears apart the lions' ears.
It is as if hail is plummeting from clouds.
The battlefield floods with copious blood
As if the moon showers down a crimson rain.

The Tarkhan, weary of the hunt, is barely awake
When he is taken captive by Khazarvan.
Three hundred illustrious Chini fighters are seized
And tied up to saddles on the backs of horses.

Bahraam marches from Coshmaihan to Marv.
He has become as thin as a reed from
The strenuous exercise on horses of winded feet.
There are no Chini men left in Marv
As they have either bolted or have been killed.
No armed man survives the attack.
Bahraam hastily chases the ones who attempt to flee.

◇◇◇◇◇◇◇◇◇◇◇◇◇
47 Coshmaihan: A region around the city of Marv, near the River Jayhoon.

He dashes through thirty farsangs,
Trailed by Ghaaran the Persian.
Then he returns to the hunting site
And distributes the booty to the troops.
Raising his head higher with his victory,
He recognizes that all power belongs to Yazdan,
Who endows one with the ability to perform
High feats and who is Master of Sun and Moon.

22 | Bahraam Seals a Pact and Marks the Border Between Iran and Tooran

Bahraam the hunter takes some time to rest in Marv.
Once king and war steeds have regained their strength,
He becomes a combatant, despite the pacifist that he is,
And decides to raise an offensive on Bukhara.

He reaches the Jayhoon in one day and one night.
Instead of game and hunt, he thinks only
Of rising to the status of world sovereign.
He and his company cross the River Jayhoon
And travel through the sands of Farab.[48]

When the sun dispatches its golden shimmers
Through the air and rejects the indigo tunic of night,
Dust turns the world as black as a falcon's plumage.
The king passes through the lands of Maimargh.[49]
The Turks are defeated, and the blaze consumes their lands.
The stars take refuge beneath the folds of the moon,
And fathers trample their sons in their haste to flee.

The leaders of the Turks, men old and young,
Skilled sword-wielding warriors,
Appear on foot humbly before Bahraam.
Their hearts swelling with grief, they plead,
"O glorious King of fortunate star,
O prince, ruler over the noblest in the world,
Do not spill the blood of innocent men

◇◇◇◇◇◇◇◇◇◇◇◇◇
48 Farab: An ancient city on the Silk Road in present-day Kazakhstan.
49 Maimargh: A village in the region of Bukhara.

Just because the Tarkhan committed an error
And was tired of his dependence on the world master.
It does not suit a king to be implacable.
If you demand tribute from us, we consent.
Why should you sever the heads of noblemen?
We are all your slaves, men and women.
We accept our loss and submit to you."

The king's heart is moved by these words.
He closes the eye of fury with the hand of wisdom.
He forbids his warriors to further spill blood.
His pious soul fills with grief.
The king's mercy is affirmed, fearful men find peace,
The leaders appear and offer a sizable annual tribute.

As this affair concludes according to the king's desire,
Aside from the tribute he imposes on the Turks
And in lieu of redemption for the pillage,
He takes with him a number of hostages.

Then he departs toward the land of Farab
With a cheerful face and a smile on his lips.
He rests there with his troops for one week.
He calls to his side the famed Chini men and asks them
To build a column made of plaster and limestone.
He declares that no one among the Turks
Or any member of the tribe of Khalaj is allowed
To pass him and travel in the direction of Iran
Without having been granted royal consent.
He further declares that the Jayhoon River
Is to mark the border between the two lands.

There is a man named Shohreh in the army,
Who is sensible, highborn, well known, powerful.
Bahraam Shah appoints him King of Tooran
And raises his throne to be the diadem of the moon.

Shohreh sits on the silver throne,
Fastens the royal belt, acts generously,
And places the golden crown on his head.
The entire land of Tooran rejoices.

303

23 | Bahraam the Hunter Writes to Nersi About His Victory

Once the affairs of Tooran-Zamin are organized
And Bahraam's heart is freed from worry,
He summons a scribe, musk, pen, and Chini silk.
The king composes a letter to Nersi, describing
The struggle with the Turks and his army's high deeds.

The letter begins with expressions of gratitude:
"To the World Creator through my humble lips:
Master of victory and power, Saturn, Mars, and Moon,
Creator of the revolving dome of sky,
Creator of the dust scattered upon the earth;
To Whose will all things, large and small, submit;
In Whose hands the future lies.
I am sending a letter written on silk
From the border of Chin to my brother in Iran-Zamin.
This letter is addressed to the famed leaders of Iran.
Anyone who did not witness our fight with the Tarkhan
Must hear the account as told by my warring allies.

"The Tarkhan's army was so vast
The dust it stirred obscured the face of the sky.
The land turned into a sea of blood,
And the throne of the unjust king was toppled.
He was taken prisoner in battle, evidence
That the revolving sky was weary of his rule.
I bring him now tied to a camel, his heart wounded,
His eyes brimming with blood tears.
The necks of the proudest warriors are bent,
Their words are now soft and gentle,
And their hearts are swollen with warm blood.
The enemy has promised to pay tribute,
And those who were lost are now on a straight path.
I shall arrive soon after this letter with my army,
According to the desire of those who wish me well."

Camels of winded feet and foaming mouths depart,
As swift as a stormy wind, to deliver the letter.
Nersi's heart blossoms with joy at the news.
The grand wise master appears with warriors,

Members of the king's relatives.
A great cry of joy rises over the land of Iran.
Everyone listens for the hum of his arrival.
Yet noblemen's hearts tremble in shame
For having disrespected the king.

More than one hundred and thirty warriors
Approach Nersi to express their apologies,
Seeking the proper course and a return to reason:
"Perverse thoughts and the deevs' command
Turned certain souls away from the divine path.
The manner in which he vanquished an army was
As if Yazdan opened the gates of the firmament to him.
It was a marvel that surpasses the imagination.
Knowledgeable wise men find themselves disconcerted.
Once you reply with the actions executed, good and bad,
We shall write to the glorious king asking forgiveness.
May he excuse our trespasses,
No matter how dreadful they may be."

Nersi promises to proceed in a way as to make
The king abandon all thoughts of vengeance.
He immediately writes a reply in which
He reveals good deeds and poor judgment:
"The Iranians, in their grief and worry, and in the hopes
Of saving their land, their children, and their wealth,
Asked the Tarkhan of Chin for protection.
It was a time when they despaired of their glorious king.
It was neither because of enmity nor weariness,
Neither for hatred nor for longing for another ruler.
If now the victorious king agrees to forgive them,
He will convert their dark night into a glorious day.
They charged me, as their friend, to pardon them
And to intervene in their behalf."

Borzmehr, a wise man, is elected to make the trip.
He travels to the world king to reveal the secrets.
The king is delighted, and, in this way,
The ardent flames cease to emit smoke.

The warriors of Chaghan, Khatl,[50] Balkh, and Bukhara,
Along with the wise men from Gharchehgan,
Arrive in silence holding in their hands the barsom.
They execute the prayers before the servants of fire,
And, from then on, anyone who has the means
Travels to court every year with tributes and royalties.

24 | Bahraam the Hunter Returns to the Land of Iran

Once the fire temple is set up as the site of Nowruz
And the feast of Saddeh, Bahraam takes the direction
Of Azerbaijan with his illustrious noblemen.
They take their positions in front of the fire
To execute their prayers, and these wise men
Assist at the ceremony, hands on their heads.

The king gives generously to the temple servants,
Departs from there with pomp and grandeur,
And travels toward Estakhr,
A city that is the glory of the King of Kings.

He draws one thousand one hundred and sixty quintals[51]
In dirham and dinars out of bags made out
Of buffalo skin and lugged ahead by elephants.
This is a currency that Persian wise men call pandavsi[52]
In Pahlavi and that is tossed at the crowd.
He asks for cowhide, stretches it,
And, in his joy, pours coins of silver and gold into it.

Firstly, if he encounters a run-down bridge
Or the indication of a dilapidated caravan depot,
He refurbishes each one at his own expense,
Without imposing hardship on anyone.

Secondly, if he comes across a destitute person,
Anyone who painstakingly earns his keep,
He distributes a number of dirhams to him,

◇◇◇◇◇◇◇◇◇◇◇◇◇◇
50 Khatl: Unknown location; perhaps in southern Iran.
51 Quintal: An historical unit of mass; 0.01 quintal (metric) is equivalent to 1 kilogram
or around 2 pounds.
52 Pandavsi: A Pahlavi currency, each coin equal to five dinars.

Never growing weary of the act of giving.
Thirdly, he weighs silver in large scales
To give to widows and orphans.
Fourthly, he distributes vast wealth to the elderly
Unable to work and whose days of battle are long gone.
In the fifth place, he gives to men of noble birth
Who are overlooked by rich men.
In the sixth place, he gives to those
Who come from afar and hide their poverty.
In every aspect, he strives to act with kindness,
Glancing around with a benevolent eye.

He abandons the loot to the troops
And no longer thinks of accumulating wealth.
He commands a wise man of pure faith
To bring the crown of the Tarkhan of Chin.
The fine jewels inlaid within are plucked out
And used to decorate the walls of the fire temple and
The throne of Aazar, to which they add gold and gems.

From there, Bahraam travels to Ctesiphon,
Where Nersi and his advisors reside.
All the great leaders and governors of Iran
Come to meet and greet him on the road.

Nersi observes his head and the royal crown,
His heart-enlightening banner, and his vast host.
He dismounts to salute the king and the leaders,
And the illustrious grand wise master follows suit.

Bahraam commands them to climb on horseback.
He takes Nersi's hand into his, and together
They enter the palace. He sits on the golden throne
And accepts an audience with the noble leaders,
Who arrive with offerings and bow low to him.

Bahraam distributes an entire treasure to the needy
And unlocks the prison's narrow doors.
The world fills with joy and justice.
The hearts of the afflicted are liberated from worry.
The king keeps grief and suffering at bay
And plans a magnificent feast for his court's patricians.
Anyone present is to receive a worthy robe of honor.

25 | Bahraam the Hunter Advises His Administrators

On the third day, a great feast is prepared,
And a scribe is placed before the king,
Who, in a state of clemency and joy,
And about to drink some wine,
Composes a letter beginning with:
"May praise fall on those
Who purify their minds with knowledge;
Who adorn their hearts with wisdom
And valiantly acquire their fortune
Through their own bodies' hard work;
Who recognize that all things come from Yazdan;
Who cultivate wisdom assisted by learned men;
Who banish vengeance and enmity from their souls
And take, in all matters, wisdom as their advisor,
And who, knowing that justice brings happiness,
Do not knock at the door of malfeasance.

"If someone complains about my administrators
Or about my proud and valiant cavaliers,
He will have to expect either prison or the gallows,
Or to be executed and flung scornfully into the dust.
Attempt to diminish the suffering of men;
Attempt to appease the affliction lodged in their hearts
By infusing joy and affection into them.
The world does not and will not remain for anyone.
Seek to refrain from causing harm,
And seek to remain on the path of justice.

"I am a perfect example of what I speak about,
And my fate is motivation for me to act rightly.
My famed warriors and I were attacked by a vast host.
I left with a small cavalry, overthrew the enemy,
And now, every foe has converted into a friend.
A glorious prince such as the Tarkhan of Chin,
World master, possessor of crown, throne, and seal,
Is now my prisoner, and the Turks' fortune has faded.
Yazdan the pure has endowed me with victory,
And the heads of my enemies lie in the dust.
May I always remain the Creator's servant!
May my attention always aim at the execution of justice!

"For seven years, I did not demand taxes,
Neither from a subject nor from an equal.
I address this letter in Pahlavi to every administrator
And every powerful ruler so that he may treat
His subjects according to custom and just ways,
Never lending a thought to an evil act.
If there are poor men in your city,
Men who do not take part in joy, share their names
With us, and we shall satisfy their desires.
Next, reaching into my treasury,
We shall attempt to place above need
Men of good name who lost their fortunes.
We shall elevate the heads of intelligent ones,
Pay the debts of those who are treated
Everywhere with scorn and disrespect,
And write their names on your lists.

"Pray to Yazdan that our hearts pursue the path of faith.
Happily apply yourselves to execute this accord,
Treat your subordinates tenderly,
And abstain from scorning slaves,
For they are the servants of the Creator.
Anyone who has a fortune and a serious mind
Must send his children to learned teachers
To empower their brains with study
And crown their intelligence with faith.
Avoid touching the property of others;
Avoid committing any other misdeed.
Always serve Yazdan faithfully,
And seek shelter in divine affiliation.
Take great pains to follow my instructions,
To eradicate evil to the last trace,
Tearing out the root of every link.

"Refrain from oppressing your neighbor,
Especially the noble and the illustrious.
When a poor man becomes rich and has risen
Above a base condition, do not view him as superior,
For his greatness will soon enter into the void.
Wash your hands clean of evil deeds and injustice.
Do not keep anything that is destined
For a poor man, for you are above need.

309

Affiliate yourselves to pure men, and be generous.
Do not break the backs and the hearts
Of those who ask for something.
Every act disapproved will meet its just punishment.
May the grace of the World Giver enfold
The soul of the one who weaves compassion
Into the warp and weft of his existence!"

Once the letter is written on shiny silk,
The scribe dips his reed in musk and, at the top,
Inscribes the name of the world king,
Who is the heart of justice, who recognizes good and evil,
Master of bounty, majesty, and power,
King of Kings, the generous Bahraam the hunter.

Messengers on foot, on horseback, and on camelback
Depart in every direction, accompanied by guides
To carry the letters to border guards, powerful men,
Intelligent and learned men, and valiant chiefs.

Once rulers, in their respective provinces,
Are in possession of the letter in their
Respective provinces, each one says, "Thanks to Yazdan,
We have a king who believes in divine existence!"

Men, women, and children travel to the plains.
In every region, they emerge from their homes to offer
Praise and their soul's benedictions to the just world king.
Then they ask for a feast, wine, music and musicians.
They revel for half the day and work the other half.

Every day at dawn, a proclamation is declared:
"May all those who possess wealth
Appreciate it and share with others,
And may they express gratitude for their joy!
May those who are in need appear at my treasury
And receive five royal dirhams of legal weight
And three mahns of clear, shiny wine, aged
And the color of gold or the flower of pomegranate."

Everyone gets prepared to celebrate.
Cities and streets resound with the voices of the revelers.
In the end, they ask two dinars for a coronet of flowers.

People easily buy a stem of narcissus for one dirham.

Joy renews the hearts of the elderly,
And the water in springs converts to milk.
The world seeker gives thanks to the World Creator
For the happiness pervading throughout the world.

26 | Bahraam the Hunter Sends His Brother Nersi to Khorasan

One day, Bahraam says to Nersi,
"Take the seal and diadem; I offer you Khorasan.
Settle there, make the land prosper,
And bring joy into our subjects' hearts.
Take care to always act with justice, and never
Interrupt others who travel through the region.
Our father committed many wrongful acts,
But he had cause to tremble like a naked man
Trembles when standing in an autumn wind."

He orders a robe of honor and an abundant treasure
For his brother and says to him, "May the Creator
Be your shelter and the sun's throne be your dwelling!"

Nersi passes two weeks on the journey and easily
Takes possession of the land of Khorasan.

One week after Nersi's departure, the king,
Free of worry, summons the grand wise master
And a few noblemen, to whom he says,
"We have neglected the affairs of the Caesar.
His envoy receives his leave with much delay.
What sort of a man is he, and how far reaches
His wisdom, for wisdom is the soul's support?"

The wise master replies, "May you remain eternally
World master, surrounded by divine majesty!
He is an old sage, reserved, soft-spoken yet eloquent,
A sensible man from the school of Plato,
Learned and of high standing.
Full of energy after his arrival from Rum,

311

He now lives weary from his stay in our land.
He appears as numb as a serpent in winter.
His body is weak, and his cheeks are pale.
His servants are like sheep found by a hunting dog,
But he considers us with pride and anger,
And counts our men for nothing."

Bahraam says to his wise master,
"Yazdan endows us with majesty, crown, and strength.
Yazdan made me victorious, converting to day
The dark night that weighed heavily on my life.
But the Caesar, ruler of Rum, lord of a grand nation,
Is a powerful man and moreover a descendant of Salm,
On whose head Fereydoon placed the crown.
He remembers his ancestry from father to father.
Until now he has behaved well and wisely,
Having not succumbed to folly like the Tarkhan.
I shall call the envoy at the time of the audience
To see if he is able to speak reasonably.
Then I shall dismiss him graciously,
For I find myself indifferent to the opinions of men.
One hopes for battle and musters a host,
Another wishes to revel in feast,
Handing me a golden headdress.
I am left to assess the value.
Happy is the one who knows how to deal with lords!"

The wise master blesses him affectionately:
"May you live in joy for as long as the sky revolves!
May your tongue always utter kind words!
May you be the greatest among the most renowned!"

27 | Bahraam Summons the Rumi Envoy to Court

The next day, as the sun exhibits its crown launching
Its flames across the vault of sky, the world king
Sits on the ivory throne and summons the Rumi envoy.
A worldly old man enters,
Sage, learned, eloquent, and observant.
Hands crossed at his chest, he bows deeply
And sits on his heels before the imperial throne.

Bahraam addresses him with the customary questions,
Receives him graciously, offers him a seat,
And says, "You have been here for some time.
Are you not weary of the sight of our land?
Our battle with the Tarkhan kept me away from you,
It stuck to me like an inseparable companion.
Now my days are renewed, and the credit is yours.
But your stay has been prolonged beyond measure.
I shall reply to all of your questions.
I shall draw good luck from your sound words."

The old man utters blessings on the king:
"May era and world never be deprived of your being!
You are a shrewd king who appreciates sensible men.
You recognize that the wise man is close to Yazdan
And the day dims for his enemy.
You are the greatest among the world's rulers,
For you are illustrious, you are emperor, and you are kind.
Your tongue is a scale, and your words are jewels,
But jewels that cannot be evaluated against gold.
You are endowed with knowledge, judgment,
Prudence, and more majesty than any winning king.
You are blessed with wisdom and pure intentions.
You are the master of wise men.
Although I am an emissary of the Caesar,
I am the servant of the king's servants.
I relay greetings from the Caesar to King Bahraam.
May his majesty's head, crown, and throne be eternal!
My king has instructed me to address
Seven questions to your wise men."

The king says, "By all means, speak your mind.
Nothing is more worthy of glory than speech."

He summons the grand wise master,
Sages, and illustrious noblemen.
The king's lips are for some time full of sighs,
So worried is he about the seven enigmatic questions.
The sages and wise men, well versed in the sciences,
Arrive, and the eloquent envoy unravels his secret.
He repeats to the wise master the words of the Caesar:
"O guide to wisdom, what is it that invites you inside

313

And what is it that invites you outside,
Something for which you have no other word?
What is above, O my master, and what is below?
What has no limitation and what is despicable?
What has many names and is present everywhere?"

The grand wise master replies to the savant,
"Do not make haste, and do not turn away
From the path of knowledge.
O sensible man, listen to my replies from beginning to end.
There is only one response to your questions.
The one about outside and inside is of little importance.
The outside is the sky, the inside is the air.
Above is the splendor of the all-powerful Yazdan,
Who is omnipresent, universal, and limitless in the world.
It is a crime to turn away from Yazdan in favor of science.
Above is paradise, and below is hell, the den
Of the wicked who rebel against the Creator.

"As for the thing that has multiple names
And everywhere shows its actions,
Know, O old man, that wisdom has many names.
Wisdom helps a ruler reach his desires.
One may speak of it as clemency
And also as good faith, for without wisdom
One is left with grief and tyranny.
The eloquent man refers to it as righteousness;
The fortunate man believes it to be artfulness.
At times we ascribe it as patience,
At times as the guardian of our secrets,
Since words do not lose their way with it.
Wisdom encompasses all these attributes.
Its glory surpasses all measure,
And nothing takes precedence over it.
It is the first and most precious of all our assets.
Wisdom is the conduit to the discovery
Of worldly mysteries, inaccessible to the human eye.

"Finally, the wise man can easily access the mysteries.
He is like a star shining in the glorious dome of sky.
But our naked eye is incapable of assessing the number
Of stars in the limitless, sublime firmament.

You might as well avoid counting them and
Seeking to understand the imprint of their rotation
On the world, for no one can attain such knowledge.
The wise man who does not know where the arrow
Originates from will not be surprised.
It is useless to count the stars in the sky.
Here is the extent of my knowledge,
And if your questions have another answer,
It is because divine mysteries are unlimited."

The wise messenger of the Caesar listens,
Kisses the ground, and declares himself defeated.
He says to Bahraam, "O world master,
Do not ask the Creator for more than you have.
The entire earth is at your command;
The proudest heads are your devoted subjects.
You are the object of the admiration of every illustrious man.
The world has no memory of a ruler like you.
Furthermore, your vizier surpasses in knowledge
All the world's sages and wise men.
Philosophers drop at his feet as slaves
And lower their heads before his erudition."

Bahraam is hardly able to conceal his joy
As light infiltrates his heart with these words.
His glory intensifies in his own eyes.
He offers a robe of honor to the wise master
Along with valuables:
Ten cases of dirhams, clothing, and horses.

The illustrious Caesar's envoy prepares to travel
From the king's court back to the Rumi palace.

28 | Bahraam the Hunter Dismisses the Caesar's Envoy

As the sun raises its hand in the revolving dome,
The King of Kings sits on his golden throne.
The Caesar's envoy and the skilled wise master
Appear gaily at court to discuss all sorts of things.

The king's wise master says to the envoy,
"O wise man without equal, tell me,
What is most baneful in the world,
That which provokes a man to shed bitter tears?
And what is most beneficial in the world,
That which elevates men to the highest status?"

The envoy says, "The savant will always be the greater,
Most influential man, while the ignorant man
Is as dreadful as mud and unworthy of joy.
You wished to speak of learned and ignorant men,
And you have received, I believe, a just reply."

The wise master says, "Reflect well before acting,
And do not set a fish down on dry ground."

The envoy replies, "O prized leader,
If you know things that we ignore, speak,
For knowledge increases one's reputation."

The wise man says, "Observe and ponder,
For reflection gives substance to words.
Know that the nobler a man's heart,
The more tragic his death,
But rejoicing over the death of an evil man
Is acceptable, for such a person is execrable.
Besides, we are all born to ultimately die.
One is necessary, and the other awful.
May your wisdom decide between the two replies."

The Rumi listens and approves of the discourse,
Drawing benefit from it.
He smiles and pays his respect to the king:
"Blessed is Iran-Zamin, a land that houses
A ruler with such infinite knowledge.
You are more learned than the most learned sages.
It is fair for you to claim tribute from the Caesar,
For your vizier is the king of wisdom.

Pleased, the ruler's heart blossoms like a spring flower.
The envoy, also delighted, leaves court
Just as night rolls out its black banner.
Bahraam heads toward his harem.

Soon after, the musk-scented veil appears,
Turning the face of the sun a shade of amber.
The impatient dome of sky does not cease its rotation
And before long stirs the sleepers from their slumber
When the sun's fountain floods down on the earth.

The world king awakens.
The grand chamberlain gives access to the court.
Bahraam takes his position on the golden seat,
Commands the preparation of presents,
And summons the Rumi emissary.

There are more golden and silver trinkets,
More noble chargers and bridles, golden dinars
Imprinted with the name of Bahraam,
Indian swords in golden sheaths, brocade,
Jewels and gems, musk and amber,
More than the old man can dare to dream.

29 | Bahraam Addresses the Leaders on the Subject of Justice

As the king closes his business with the Rumi,
His mind turns to the state of his army.
Worried, he calls his wise master and noblemen.
He distributes lands to warriors, keen on battle,
Offering them dirhams, horses, seals and diadems,
And to the most renowned: territory, crowns, and thrones.

He spreads righteousness throughout the world.
Men great and small are happy under his rule.
He distances unkind souls who do not
Give liberally and are cold of speech.
Then he says to his wise men, "O skilled friends,
You are endowed with sense and with pure hearts.
Remember our heritage,
And remind the noblemen of it on every occasion,
Retelling the high deeds of kings, just and unjust.
Many sovereigns have lent a hand to wicked acts
While they made themselves invisible.
They gained little and barred themselves

317

From the ability to indulge in comfort and luxury.
Greedy rulers spread terror throughout the world,
Splitting the hearts of good and righteous men in half.
All hands turned to perform wicked actions,
And no one fought for the work of the Creator.
Many souls were depraved beyond measure.
There was no one to rule over women and children.
The hearts of pure men filled with sorrow.

"Deev claws extended their reach in every direction.
Beings lost any remnant of fear of the World Master,
Everything rests on the king: the source of good,
The hand of malfeasance, the door to learning,
The efforts of wisdom, everything.
It is through the king that either perversity
Or righteousness reigns supreme in the world.
If my father committed certain misdeeds,
If he lacked virtue, wisdom, and piety,
Do not be astonished, for his mind's shining steel
Had been eroded by the rust of folly.
Look at what we have accomplished
From the era of Jamsheed to that of Kay Kaavoos;
Look at those who held fast to the guidance of deevs.

"My father followed the same path and
Did not wash his dim soul in the waters of wisdom.
Thus he sent tremors of fear through his subjects,
For, in his fury, he precipitated the deaths of many.
He is now departed; nothing remains of him
Except a poor reputation. No one remembers him.
I am left to utter blessings over his soul,
May he rest in peace. Yazdan forbid that the hatred
He left behind make people tremble in fear.
Now that I sit upon my father's throne,
I hope that his soul finds its way to heaven.

"I implore the World Creator to always grant me
The strength to be kind to my subjects, in private
And in public, and to convert the vile dirt into
Pure musk so that, when my body lies in the dust,
No one will blame me for having acted unjustly.
You as well, cover yourselves with the cloak

318

Of righteousness and wash your hearts of falsehood.
We are born from a mother only to die one day,
Whether we are Persian, Taazi, or Rumi.
Death will pounce on us like a ferocious lion,
And no one is able to evade its hook.
The lion, able to shred everything, and the dragon
Are both its prey; neither one can evade its snare.

"Where are now the crowns and thrones
Of the illustrious kings of yore?
Where are now the happy princes, the riders,
The illustrious men from time immemorial
Who have left no visible trail behind?
Where are now the fairy-faced beauties
Who charmed the hearts of noblemen?
Anyone whose face is in a shroud
Has united with dust as its eternal companion.
Let us attempt to reach what is pure and good,
And let us not surrender the world to evil deeds.

"I swear by Yazdan, who granted me the splendor
Of the throne and crown, of birth and royal race,
That if someone affects the loss of even a fistful of dust,
Whether he is high ranking or not,
I shall have his body burned,
And I shall hang him by the neck on a high stake.
If a thief steals the attire of felt from a poor man,
No matter at what time of night,
I shall compensate the poor man with gold coins
From my treasury and free his afflicted heart.
If someone snatches sheep from a herd,
Whether at night or during a windy, foggy day,
I shall compensate with a pricey charger and give thanks.
When battle is engaged against an enemy and
A rider is wounded, I shall send him a year's wages
In royal dirham and not allow his children to suffer.

"Give thanks to Yazdan, Justice Giver,
Who knows for all eternity what is good.
Refrain from touching water and fire,
Unless you are a clergyman devoted to fire worship.
Do not shed the blood of plow oxen,

As it is a disgrace for a nation to kill cattle
Unless it is found is too old to work
And loses its value in his master's eyes.
Similarly, one must not kill pack cows;
The honor of the land would suffer from it.
Consult learned men, and guard yourselves
From breaking the hearts of fatherless children.
If you are old, guard yourself from getting drunk.
It is not advisable for an aging man to drink wine.
Keep yourself distant from thoughts that inspire deevs.
Do not seek a feast on the day of battle with a foe.

"If I demanded taxes from my subjects,
Yazdan would abandon me and my ivory throne.
If my father, Yazdegerd, committed evil acts,
I expiate his misdeeds by spreading justice,
Hoping the reward is divine exoneration
That would grant him access into paradise.
When you are young, live in joy
And break not the hearts of your inferiors.
Guard yourselves from committing sinful acts;
Your provision for departure,
Once you are old, will be more praiseworthy.
If the Justice Giver approves of us,
We must not worry about a future life.
May my actions bring you happiness!
May you attach yourselves nobly to the cult of fire!
May my subjects' hearts be joyful,
And may the heads of leaders be free of grief."

The noble leaders, eyes brimming with tears,
Turn their hearts toward good deeds.
They are touched at the sight of this king
Endowed with such a conscious and lively mind.
They praise him loudly and salute him as world king.

30 | Bahraam the Hunter Writes a Letter to King Shangal of India

One day, the wise vizier rises before Bahraam
And says, "O just and righteous excellency,
The world no longer fears wicked men,
And our land is freed from outside threats.
Shangal of India is the only one left
Who refuses to walk the path of justice.
He holds the world in a state of fear from India to Chin
By protecting bandits who cause harm to Iran.
You are the only one able to take care of this matter.
You are king, and Shangal is merely India's governor.
How does he dare demand tribute
From the lands of Chin and Sindh?
Reflect on the matter, and try to bring order to it.
This situation must not lead to our decline."

In his contemplations, the universe appears
Like an obscure forest to the king, who says,
"I shall fix this affair secretly, without involving anyone.
I shall observe alone his army, his royal court and throne.
I shall go to him as an envoy without telling my men.
As for you, O wise master of pure faith, write a letter
To Shangal, its tone at once friendly and threatening."

The pious vizier departs with a scribe,
Excluding anyone who may be extraneous.
They consult at length on all sorts of matters.
They reach for paper, musk, and reed.
The vizier composes a letter full of good sense,
Kind words, and homage to the Creator.

The missive begins with divine blessings:
"On the one who is worthy in the eye
Of the Master of being and non-being,
All things find their equals while Yzad is one.
Wisdom is the most precious divine gift to man,
Whether he is a slave or bears the crown.
Wisdom brings clarity to the tiniest and the largest.
When one appreciates wisdom, one finds himself
Incapable of committing misdeeds in the world.

When one is addicted to wisdom, one never repents,
For the waters of wisdom sustain all that is good.
Wisdom saves man from calamity.
May everyone always evade hardship!
The first indication of wisdom is fear of drifting.
Let us delve within; let us observe
The world through the eye of wisdom.
Wisdom is the diadem of kings,
The ornament of noblemen.
The sage knows good and bad;
He acts with justice and moves away from evil.

"You are not aware of your own power's limitation.
You often dip your soul in blood, thirsty for it.
Since I am the one bearing this era's crown,
It is only through my permission
That clemency and perversity can be exercised.
But you wish to act as an emperor, and justice suffers,
As on all sides crimes proliferate.
It is unfit for a king to make inroads
And gang up with malicious bandits.

"Your grandfather was my servant;
Your father stood as a slave before our kings;
We never consented to deferring India's tributes.
Consider the fate of the Tarkhan of Chin,
Who left his land to invade Iran-Zamin.
He lost everything he brought with him, and
His misdeeds fell back on him in painful retribution.
I take in your appearance, your fortune,
Your grandeur, and your faith.
I own weapons of war, treasure,
And an army united in heart and ready to fight.
You will never resist my warriors.
There is no man able to lead in all of India.
You have a false idea of your strength.
Next to me, with power as vast as the sea,
You appear as a tiny, insignificant stream.
I am dispatching an eloquent and noble envoy.
You may send us tribute or prepare for war.
May blessings be showered on the soul gifted
With wisdom and justice as its warp and weft!"

Once a breath of air dries up the musk,
The scribe folds the sheaf and writes at the top:
"From the intelligent world ruler, master of empire
And power, world owner Bahraam the hunter,
Yazdan worshipper, who generously donates to all,
Who inherited the Kianian crown from Yazdegerd
On the day of Ard[53] in the month of Khordaad,[54]
Commander of borders and protector of lands,
Whom the Slavic and Rumi peoples serve as slaves;
To Shangal, commander of India from
The Sea of Ghennooj to the frontier of Sindh."

31 | Bahraam the Hunter Travels to India With His Letter

Once the seal is affixed on the letter,
The king makes preparations for the hunt.
No one in the army is aware of his secret plan
Except for a few noblemen in his company.

He travels to India and crosses the Indus River.
At Shangal's palace, he is impressed by the lofty structure.
At the door he sees a vast supply of weapons and war gear,
Riders and elephants, and much noise is heard inside,
Along with the sound of clarions and Indian bells.

A surprised Bahraam grows increasingly worried.
He says to the guards and servants of the king
Positioned at the curtain entrance,
"An envoy of the victorious King Bahraam
Has arrived for an audience with the King of India."

The chamberlain leaves his station to approach the king.
The latter commands him to welcome and introduce
The visitor with all the honors due his rank.

Bahraam the hunter enters solemnly.
He observes the elaborate ceiling made of crystal

◇◇◇◇◇◇◇◇◇◇◇◇
53 Ard: The name for the 29th day of any month.
54 Khordaad: The name of the third month of the year.

And Shangal, sitting on his throne,
Proud and majestic, the crown on his head.
The leveled steps of the throne are made of crystal
And upholstered with silver cloth drapery,
Embroidered with gold and pearls.

His brother occupies a seat nearby
And wears on his head a diadem of fine gems.
Next to him sits the king's advisor,
And near the throne stands his son.

Bahraam approaches the king in greeting.
He remains at length before him, then loudly declares,
"I bring to the King of India a silken letter
Written in Pahlavi from the great ruler,
World master Bahraam, Yazdan worshipper."

Shangal offers a golden seat to his guest.
They invite Bahraam's companions,
Who had remained by the door, to draw closer.

Once seated, Bahraam loosens his lips to say,
"O powerful King, I shall speak if you permit.
May power and virtue never be deprived of your being!"

Shangal replies, "Speak, for the sun
Grants its blessings to the most eloquent men."

Bahraam says, "I bring news from the King of Iran.
No mother has given birth to a son of his standing.
The illustrious ruler, who brings joy to his land,
Whose justice turns poison into its antidote,
To whom sovereigns and princes pay tribute,
To whom lions fall prey in the hunt;
A valiant warrior who draws his sword
To convert the plain into a sea of blood,
Whose generosity is like a spring shower,
And who considers a golden treasure as a vile thing;
The revered one who sends to the King of India
A letter written on silk in Pahlavi."

32 | Shangal Receives Bahraam's Letter

Shangal, in awe of the presence and the words
Of the alleged envoy, noble cavalier, asks for the letter.

Once a blessed scribe delivers the contents,
The king's cheek turns a pale yellow,
And he says, "O eloquent envoy,
Do not hasten to speak and remain calm.
Your travels here and your descriptions give us
The sense of a king who is quite presumptuous.
If someone allows the misguided notion
To enter into his head to demand tribute from us,
Wise men would not approve.
If your king speaks of his army or treasury,
Or of trampling beneath his feet cities and provinces
And subsequently surrendering them to misery,
Know that kings are cranes and I am an eagle,
Or perhaps I am a body of water while they are dust.
No one attempts to lead an attack on stars.
No one seeks fame and glory in a fight with the sky.
Better employ virtue, for vain words
Would only inspire sages to further condemn you.
You have neither courage nor wisdom.
You have neither land nor city.
You retain from kingship nothing more than its speech.

"My land is full of hidden treasures,
Riches never accessed by my ancestors.
Furthermore, I have stores of caparisons
And coats of mail, so numerous that
When my treasurer has need for them,
The keys alone must be carried not just
By any elephant but by a war elephant.
If I were to enumerate my swords and armor,
You would find the number of stars scornful
Next to the quantity of this vast equipment.
The earth cannot bear the weight of my host,
My war elephants, and my throne.
Multiply thousands of men by thousands of men,
And you will calculate the number of those
Who recognize me as their king.

Gems concealed in mountains, pearls in the sea
Are mine, for today I am the support of the world.
My land has an abundance of gold, silver, jewels;
It has fountains of amber, aloeswood, and musk,
Remedies for the ill, and anyone who suffers;
Its air carries the scent of fresh camphor.

"Eighty rulers bearing golden crowns
Seize their weapons at my command.
With its mountains, rivers, and gorges,
A deev would not dare traverse my grounds.
From Ghennooj to the border of Iran,
And from there to the land of the Slavs
And to the Sea of Chin, every prince is my subject,
Every single one is forced to pay homage to me.
Sentinels in India, Chin, and Khotan
Never cease to glorify my name.
Everyone celebrates my crown;
Everyone exceeds in his devotion to me.

"In the women's chambers, the Faghfoor's
Daughter invokes divine grace on me.
She has given birth to my son, a youth of lion heart
Who splits with his sword the hearts of boulders.
Since the time of Kaavoos and Kay Ghobaad,
No one has spoken of tribute in my land.
An army of three hundred thousand warriors
Salutes me as their rightful king, and one thousand
Two hundred allies, who are mine from father to son,
Stand before me in service to the land of India,
Forbidding people to approach me with hostile intentions.
No secret stands between us.
They are men who, at the time of battle,
Spread such terror that, at the sound of their voices,
Forest lions fearfully gnaw at their claws.
If custom permits a noble man
To sentence an envoy to death with his fury,
I would separate your body from your head,
And your shirt would have cause to shed tears!"

Bahraam replies, "O crowned King, if indeed
You are a prince, do not sow seeds of rage.

My emperor commanded me to tell you:
>'If you are a sensible man,
>Do not follow the way of deevs.
>Summon two of your sages, the most eloquent.
>If one of them exhibits superiority in wisdom
>And intelligence to one of my noblemen,
>I shall renounce any claim to your territories.
>The wise man never disdains another's words.
>Should you prefer to select in India
>One hundred valiant, mace-wielding riders
>Able to overcome just a single one of ours,
>If your courage and your skills are proof,
>I shall abstain from demanding tribute from you.'"

33 | Bahraam Displays His Courage in a Fight With Shangal's Warrior

Shangal replies to Bahraam,
"Your discourse discounts reason.
Remain here for some time and unwind.
Why utter such worthless words?"

A festival hall is set up and arrayed.
Bahraam rests until midday.
Once the throne of the world-illuminating sun
Arrives at its apex, zealous servants prepare
A glittering feast concurring with the king's orders.

Shangal sits before the spread and commands:
"Beckon the eloquent Iranian envoy
Who came to conclude an affair.
Beckon his companions as well,
And seat them at the table with our leaders."

Bahraam hurries to the hall, sits before the spread,
And begins to eat, lips closed to speech.
Once the meal is complete, an assembly is formed,
And musicians and wine are summoned.
The guests sip the musk-scented wine
And recline on carpets of golden brocade.

The assembly, soon in a state of merriment,
Abandons all thought and worry for the morrow.
Shangal asks for two skilled warriors
Able to wrestle and overcome a deev.
Two young men arrive, prepared for the game.
They tighten their breeches around their waists
And begin to tussle and bend each other.

Bahraam picks up a crystal cup.
His mind somewhat troubled by the wine,
He says to Shangal, "O King, allow me to prepare.
When I wrestle with a powerful man,
I no longer give a thought to revelry or wine."

Shangal smiles and says,
"Rise, and if you can defeat him,
I give you permission to spill blood."

At these words, Bahraam rises and proceeds
To bend the stature of the contenders.
He reaches for one mid-waist,
Like a lion pouncing on a wild deer.
He flings him to the ground and breaks his bones,
Draining all the color from his cheeks.

Shangal is astounded at the sight
Of Bahraam's stature, his strength and shoulders.
He invokes the name of Yazdan in Hindu
And estimates that Bahraam
Is worth the weight of forty men.

Once inebriated, they exit the jewel-encrusted room,
And when the sky dons its cloak of blackness,
Everyone, young or old, king or warrior,
Withdraws to prepare for a restful night.
Shangal retreats to his sleep chambers,
Heart and vision altered by the King of Iran.

Gradually, the musk-scented mantle colors the dome
Of sky in golden shades as the sun reveals its face.
Shangal, mallet in hand, climbs on his stallion
And charges in the direction of the city square.
His servants carry his bow and arrows.

He jousts for some time with great delight.
Then he commands Bahraam
To climb on horseback and to seize his royal bow.

Bahraam replies, "O King, I have in my company
Many Iranian cavaliers whose only desire
Is to draw arrows and play polo with a mallet.
What command does the noble king wish to give?"

Shangal replies, "The arrow and the bow
Are definitively the foundation of a rider.
You, with your chest and your strong arms,
Raise your hand, bind your bow, and shoot."

Bahraam the hunter binds his bow,
Turns loose his keen stallion's reins,
Places an arrow on the string, aims, releases the ring,
And shatters the goal with a single shot.

The riders present and all the warriors
Shout cries of admiration for him.

34 | Shangal Suspects Bahraam's Origins

Growing increasingly suspicious of Bahraam,
Shangal reflects, "With his majesty, his strength, and skills,
This man does not resemble a simple employee,
No matter whether he is Indian, Persian, or a Turk.
But if he is a relative of the king or a lord,
It is appropriate for me to call him brother."

He smiles and addresses Bahraam, "O noble prince,
Your ambition, your strength, and your skills
Force me to believe that you are the king's brother.
With the majesty of a Kianian and the strength
Of a lion, you are not a simple illustrious hero!"

Bahraam replies, "O King of India,
Do not treat an emissary as illegitimate.
I belong neither to a royal race
Nor to the race of Yazdegerd.

You would be committing a serious offense
To consider me as the king's brother.
I am an Iranian, a stranger to his family.
I am neither a learned man nor a reputable one.
Dismiss me, for the road is lengthy,
And we must not stir up the king's wrath."

Shangal says, "Do not rush to act.
I still have some things to say to you.
You must not depart in haste, for haste has no value.
Remain here with me, appease your heart,
And if you care not for aged wine,
I shall offer you some new wine."

He summons his vizier, a sage relative,
And speaks to him on the subject of Bahraam:
"I must secretly confer with you.
It would be an astonishing fact
Were this envoy not a relative of Bahraam
And thereby superior to Iran's warriors.
We must not settle for what he tells us.
Suggest to him that he extend his stay in Ghennooj.
Speak to him artfully, for if I do,
He will grow fearful or suspicious.
Make him understand that the best course of action
Is for him to put himself more and more
In the good graces of the King of India. Tell him,
          'If you remain at King Shangal's side
          And accept his sage advice,
          The most beautiful regions will be yours,
          For he highly values your being.
          There are lands where spring is eternal,
          Lands that exhale a floral breath.
          A man favored by fortune does not leave Ghennooj,
          Where trees bear fruit twice a year,
          Where there are jewels, treasures, dinars and dirhams.
          A man is never displeased in possession of wealth.
          This benevolent king, because of his affection for you,
          Smiles the moment he perceives your face.
          Therefore, you may ask for anything
          Your heart desires when you see him.'

"Once you tell him, ask for his name,
I will be happy to know who he is,
And if he wishes to settle in our nation,
The evidence of my favor will surpass rank.
I shall name him before my army leaders.
I shall place him at the head of our land
And will shower him with much honor."

The king's worldly vizier relates the words
To Bahraam and gives him sound advice.
Then he asks him for his name and identity.

Bahraam's face drains of color
As he knows not how to answer.
In the end, he says, "O eloquent man,
Do not cover me in shame before the two lands.
I shall not trade the King of Iran for treasure,
Even if poverty reduces me to a state of misery.
Our religion teaches us otherwise;
Our ways, our customs, and our paths are different.
Anyone who turns his back on the king
And rebels loses his way.

"A wise man does not seek to aggrandize himself,
For the good and the bad that affect us pass.
Where is the master of Fereydoon's throne,
Who was the support of his era?
Where are the powerful branches of the royal race,
World masters Khosrow and Kay Ghobaad?
Furthermore, you are familiar with Bahraam,
Who is young and eager to possess the world.
I swear that if I disobeyed him, he would
Make the world tumble down on my head;
He would destroy the land of India
And would take its sorcerer dust into Iran.
It is best for me to make my way back home,
To allow the victorious king to set eyes on me.
If you wish to know my name, it is Borzooy,
A name given to me by my father and mother,
A name by which the king calls me.
Relay my response to Shangal in haste,
For I have stayed far too long in a foreign country."

The vizier listens to him and reports to the king.
The king frowns and says,
"This light-shining man strays off his path.
I shall now find a way to end his days."

35 | Bahraam Battles and Slays a Rhinoceros

There dwells in India a rhinoceros so massive
That he bars the wind from flowing through.
Male lions flee the forest where he resides,
And swift-winged vultures avoid the skies above.
He dips the entire region into a state of turmoil.
The strongest ears are deafened by the tumult.

The king says to Bahraam, "O esteemed man,
Only you can bring this affair to a favorable conclusion.
There is near my city a forest that causes me grief.
In it roams a rhinoceros as fierce as a whale,
Who tears apart the lion's heart and the leopard's skin.
You must near this beast, pierce its skin with arrows,
So that this land of ours can find some peace.
At that moment, your glory will expand
And will reach a high rank in my esteem
And in the esteem of our illustrious assembly.
The people of India and Chin will bless you eternally."

Bahraam, whose intentions are pure, replies,
"I shall require a guide, and at the sight of the beast,
You will see that I shall bathe its skin in blood
With the strength given to me by the Creator."

Shangal selects a guide familiar
With the whereabouts of the creature's lair.
The two take the direction of the woods,
Hearts swollen with blood, and discussing at length
His massive figure, his weight, and his stature.
Bahraam marches rapidly into the forest
Followed by a number of Iranians
Heavily armed to fight the rhinoceros.
But at the sight of the beast's muzzle from afar,
At the sight of his weight bearing down to bend the earth,

They cry, "O King, go no further! Abstain from action,
Else you will surpass the limits of courage!
No one dares engage in a fight with a mountain.
No matter how valiant you may be, stop here!
Tell Shangal that such a thing is not reasonable.
Tell him that you do not have your king's permission
And that if you were to fight for someone else,
Your king would severely punish you."

Bahraam replies, "If the Creator assigns me a grave
In the dust of India, how could I die elsewhere?
It would be foolish for us to think so."

The fearless young man binds his bow
As if he cares little of life.
He advances swiftly to chase the rhinoceros,
Head full of wrath, heart resigned to die.
Kianian bow in hand, he draws
An arrow of poplar wood from his quiver
And sends a shower of shots to hail down.

Soon the rhinoceros weakens.
Bahraam sees the end closing in.
He replaces his bow with his sword
And slices off the head of the beast, saying,
"In the name of the Creator with no equal
And no mate, Giver of power, force, and glory,
By whose order the sun shines in the dome of sky."

Bahraam requests an ox-drawn cart
To carry the head of the beast out of the forest.
At the sight of it from afar,
Shangal asks for a banquet in the great hall.
The king, full of magnificence, climbs on the throne
And seats Bahraam in front of him.
The leaders and noblemen of India and Chin
Shower him with offerings and benedictions:
"O illustrious hero, no high deed is worthy of you,
And the eye dares not look in the direction of your seat."

Shangal finds himself wavering between
A state of happiness and one of concern
Regarding the occurrences of the day.

36 | Bahraam Slays a Dragon

There is a dragon who lives on water and land.
At times he is in the river and at times in the sun.
He envelops with his tail a war elephant
And raises the waves of the River Nile.

Shangal says to his friends and confidents,
"I am either happy to have this envoy of lion heart
Or terribly anxious as my heart fills with worry.
If he remained here, he would be a support for me,
And I would make him army commander.
But if he returns to the land of Iran,
Bahraam will turn Ghennooj into a wasteland.
With a servant like him and a ruler like Bahraam,
Everything of beauty here will perish.
I have reflected throughout the night on this.
Let me share with you my idea for a new approach:
I shall send him to battle the dragon.
He will undoubtedly not return safe and sound.
Yet no one will blame me for the action
If indeed he is keen on fighting the wicked beast."

He speaks in this manner and summons Bahraam.
He praises his courage at length and adds,
"Yazdan, Creator of life, brought you from Iran
To protect India from harm as suits an illustrious man.
A project awaits you, full of pain and fatigues
That will conclude with the acquisition of wealth.
Once the deed is complete, you will no longer
Be retained here and will be free to return home."

Bahraam replies, "I have only one option,
And that is to submit to your will.
The sky would turn the wrong way
If I were to disobey your orders."

Shangal says, "Our nation has been cursed
With the presence of a dragon, in water and on land.
It chases its prey, the breath-conquering whale.
If you succeed in liberating us from him,
You would return to Iran with the tribute

From India, to the agreement of our people.
In addition to the fees, you would receive
Countless gifts: Indian products, aloeswood,
Swords, and all sorts of valuables."

Bahraam replies, "O King and governor of India,
I swear by Yazdan, the holy, that I shall erase
The dragon's imprints from the earth.
But I am not aware of the location of its lair
And wish for someone to show me the way."

Shangal sends him a well-informed guide,
And Bahraam departs with thirty famed riders,
Iranian sword-brandishing leaders.
They travel swiftly until they reach the river.
Despite the darkness, Bahraam spots the dragon,
Its massive frame, its movements, its wrath,
And the fire shimmering in its furious eyes.

There is an outcry among the noble Iranians.
Moved by the awe-inspiring sight, they say,
"O King, do not consider this dragon
As harmless as the rhinoceros of the other day!
Let us not throw the land of Iran into the wind
With an adventure that promises to be a catastrophe.
Let us not bring joy to your enemies in this land."

The valiant Bahraam tells the Iranians,
"One must surrender life to the Justice Giver.
If my time must end at the hands of this dragon,
I have no power to either prolong it or curtail it."

He binds his bow and selects arrows
With points dipped in poison dissolved in milk.
He dispatches a hail of shots to fall on the dragon,
Assailing him on the right and on the left,
As one does with a combatant in battle.
He sews its jaws with a steel arrow tip,
And the spewed poison is consumed.

Next, Bahraam strikes the beast on the head
With an arrow of quadruple layers of wood.
The dragon's body flexes and bends with a jolt.

A river of blood and poison flows out of his chest
To flood the earth.

Bahraam draws his damascened sword and quickly
Pierces the dragon's heart with all his strength.
Then he severs his head with the sword and battle ax
And flings the lifeless, headless corpse into the dust.

Once the affair of the dragon is complete,
He turns to the World Creator in prayer:
"O Justice Giver, you annihilated the dragon,
For no man alone would have had the strength to do so.
You are the shelter of your most humble servants."

Then he returns to the Indian court
And parades the head in a chariot before Shangal.
Bahraam says to him, "With Yazdan's help, the struggle
With the dragon has reached a triumphant end."

Shangal is distressed by the news that Bahraam
Succeeded and will soon leave his sight.
He orders the enormous corpse
To be hauled away by plow oxen.
He invokes blessings on Iran for having produced
A cavalier of such glory, able to battle dragons and who,
By his force, stature, limbs, and chest, rivals his king.

37 | Shangal Offers His Daughter to Bahraam to Wed

Everyone rejoices, but Shangal's heart is pained.
His face is pale from Bahraam's daring act.
As night descends, he summons sages,
Relatives and strangers, and says to them,
"King Bahraam's envoy, so strong of limb,
So powerful and so valiant, cares not to remain,
Although I have tempted him with many things.
If he returns to Iran and to his king,
He will accuse my warriors of cowardice.
He will declare that India has no skilled rider,
And my enemy will swell with pride.
Therefore, I wish to get rid of him secretly.

What do you say? What advice have you for me?"

One of the sages speaks up to say, "O King,
Avoid causing your heart further grievance.
If you sentence the king's envoy to death,
You engage on a path of folly and iniquity.
No one has ever conceived of such a thought!
Your name will be cursed among noblemen.
A king must be honored and respected.
If you sever his head, troubles will be upon us
As an army will arrive instantly from Iran
With a commander as fierce as Bahraam the hunter.
He will not allow a single one of us to survive.
In addition, you will have to relinquish kingship.
Do not turn your back on an honest path!
He saved us from the dragon's breath,
And his labors must not be rewarded by death.
He slayed both rhinoceros and dragon in our land,
Thus meriting a long life and not a quick end to it."

A troubled Shangal spends the night in anguish,
And the next day, at dawn, he secretly
Sends someone to summon the envoy without
The knowledge of court, vizier, and counsellor.

He says to Bahraam, "O charmer of hearts,
You have always been a powerful and wealthy man.
Do not attempt to reach higher or to extend further.
I wish to offer you my daughter.
Once the deed is done, you will remain at my side,
And you will never have need to leave my land.
I offer you the army's command and governance of India."

Confounded by the offer, Bahraam reflects
On his throne, his birth, his glorious battles.
He thinks, "I cannot argue with this offer.
It is not shameful to have Shangal as a father-in-law.
I shall save my own life by marrying here
And will perhaps once again see the land of Iran.
I have stayed in India longer than needed.
It feels as if the lion has fallen into the fox's snare."

He replies to Shangal, "I shall obey your command.

337

I shall adopt your words as my soul's dictates.
Select one among your daughters worthy of praise."

The King of India is pleased with the exchange.
He has the room's walls quilted in Chini silk.
Three maidens enter, resembling spring
In their adornments, scent, color, and beauty.

Shangal says to Bahraam the hunter,
"Prepare your heart for a new sight."

Bahraam rushes to the hall, takes a good look,
And selects one of the moon-faced young ladies,
Sepinood, as beautiful as a verdant spring,
Full of grace and modesty, sense and desire.

Shangal offers him Sepinood, a tall cypress tree,
A slender candle burning free of smoke.
The father puts together a vast treasure
And hands the key to his daughter.
He summons Bahraam's companions,
Elegant and powerful cavaliers, and distributes
Dirhams and dinars, and all sorts of valuables,
Amber, camphor, aloeswood, horses of golden bridles,
And belts; and to high-ranking men, golden crowns.
He gives Bahraam a turquoise crown and an ivory throne.
He prepares a gem-paneled hall and invites
All the illustrious lords from Ghennooj to his court,
And they proceed in pomp and ceremony.

They sit in the reunion hall in good humor,
With cups in hand for one week.
Sepinood shines next to Bahraam the hunter,
As bright as wine in a crystal cup.

38 | Bahraam Receives the Faghfoor's Letter

The Faghfoor of Chin receives news that a man
Full of majesty was sent to Shangal from Iran;
That he has the bearing of a king or a nobleman;
That he has accomplished some astonishing feats,

And that Shangal has given him his daughter,
Raising his diadem to the sphere of the moon.

The Faghfoor writes a letter to the supposed envoy:
"This letter is composed by the world king,
Leader of illustrious men and crown of noblemen,
To the Persian envoy who arrived in Ghennooj
With his thirty companions."

Then he adds, "We have heard of you at length,
O illustrious and glorious one.
We have heard of your prudence,
Your courage, and your vast intelligence.
We have heard that anywhere you plant your foot,
Its imprint firmly remains.
We have heard that the rhinoceros and the dragon
Could not evade your piercing sword.
Shangal has offered you his daughter, who is my kin
And whose beauty mark is worth the entire land of India.
You raise your head to the clouds with this alliance with
A most powerful king, and the King of Iran only gains
In eminence, his crown elevated to heights above the moon.
His emissary has united with a worthy mate.
He came to Ghennooj to embrace the moon.

"Now give us the pleasure of your visit,
And remain with us for as long as you desire.
Our vision will brighten at the sight of you.
Your wisdom will be my soul's protective armor.
You may stay and leave whenever you please.
I will offer you gifts and wealth to your delight
As well as to the members of your escort.
This will not be a source of shame for you.
I invite you in amity, lending no thought to war.
I hope you will grace us with your presence
And not further linger in India."

As the letter reaches Bahraam the hunter,
His heart grows more anguished.
He summons the scribe to compose a reply,
Thus planting a tree of hatred:
"I have read your letter, but your eyes

339

Travel no further than the borders of Chin.
You wrote as the world king,
To someone who is the pride of noblemen.
I do not accept the grandeur you offer me.
Our King of Kings is Bahraam the hunter,
Who has no equal in all the world
In valor, wisdom, knowledge, and lineage.
He is the victorious world ruler,
Above all other rulers, past and present.

"Next, you speak of my feats and the fatigues
I endured in the land of India, all of which came
To fruition thanks to Bahraam's star of good fortune.
He is the master of majesty, of throne and glory.
The Iranians perform the greatest deeds, and that is that.
They deem fierce lions as of no threat, of no importance.
They are sincere in the recognition of Yazdan.
They do not give thanks to stars in their happiness.

"Furthermore, if the king offered me his daughter,
It is an honor I conquered through acts of courage.
Shangal is a powerful ruler who, by means of bravery,
Chases wolves away from sheep.
When he saw that an alliance with me
Is convenient to him, he offered me his graceful daughter.

"Next, you tell me,
          'Rise and travel to my court.
          I shall be your guide to happiness.'
The King of Iran sent me to India only for me
To travel to Chin to obtain silk and satin?
The king would not approve of such words and acts.
Then you tell me that you will send me back to Iran,
Satisfied with gifts and wealth,
But the Creator raised me above the need
To extend my hands toward the riches of others.
I have only gratitude to Bahraam for bounty.
I pray to Yazdan during the day and three times at night.

"Finally, as for the praise you lavish upon me,
Which vastly surpasses my accomplishments,
I accept it from you, O Emperor of Chin,

340

And I shall make them known to the Iranian king.
May Yazdan grant you so many benedictions that the sky
No longer distinguishes between warp and weft!"

He embosses the letter with the imprint of his seal
And sends it to the ruler of Chin.

39 | Bahraam Flees India
With King Shangal's Daughter

After living with Bahraam for some time,
Shangal's daughter realizes that he is the King of Iran.
She weeps day and night, witness to his affection,
Eyes fixed on him with tenderness.
Observing her love for her husband, Shangal discards
Any suspicion he may have had toward him.

One day, the happy couple sits together in joy,
Discussing all sorts of matters, great and small.
Bahraam says to Sepinood, "I know you wish me well.
I shall tell you my secret, but keep it between us.
I yearn to leave the land of India with you
And hope that you will be in agreement.
I wish to take you with me, but no one
At court must be apprised of our plan.
My position in Iran is greater than here.
The World Creator is my Protector.
Should you decide to accompany me,
Your wisdom will have inspired you well.
Everywhere you will be greeted as queen,
And your father will kneel before your throne.
The most worthy women are the ones
Who put a smile on their husband's face."

Sepinood replies, "O highborn man,
Seek the wisest path and do not drift from it.
Here is my option: Should I disagree to your plan,
I shall lose any remnant of happiness.
Even if my entire being trembles at your proposition,
I shall never fail to rise to follow you."

Bahraam says, "Find a way to do so,
But without uttering a word of our secret."

Sepinood replies, "You are worthy of the throne.
I quickly shall prepare all that is necessary.
If fortune conspires with us, there is, not far from here,
About twenty farsangs away, a blessed site,
A forest where my father prepares a festival.
Idols are grouped, and a particular idol
That will cause you to sob.
It is a feast for the riders of Ghennooj
Who are given the opportunity to hunt deer,
A place that welcomes Yazdan worshippers.
When the king and his army travel there,
The throng is so dense that one cannot pass through.

"Now, if you wish to leave, seize this occasion.
Though it is an ancient feast,
You will be renewed with youth.
Have patience for five days,
And when the world-illuminating crown
Appears in the dome of sky and the king
Begins his exit, then prepare for departure."

Bahraam is delighted by his wife's words
And finds himself unable to sleep.

The moment the sun raises its hand in the firmament,
Forcing night to pack up its assets and withdraw,
Bahraam Shah sits on his charger
And gallops in the direction of the hunting fields.
At the river's edge, he spots Iranian merchants
With their cargoes of goods exhibiting
Their valor on water and on land.

The chief's eyes, in turn, fall on Bahraam,
Who bites his lips, gesturing him to keep silent.

The chief refrains from revealing
The king's identity to his cohorts.
As a result, no one bows low before Bahraam,
Who says to the chief, "Be discreet.
Only your silence can save us,

But your idle talk will be our demise.
If my secret is known in the land of India,
Blood will flood Iran, convert the land into a sea.
The one who knows how to keep silent succeeds.
You must seal your lips and open your two hands
So that I may reclaim my place on the throne.
I shall fasten your tongues with a binding oath.
You will swear to never disobey King Bahraam
And to always keep his secret, or else we shall drift
From Yazdan's path and commune with deevs."

After the Iranian merchants take the pledge,
Worry releases its grip on the king's heart.
He says to them, "Guard my secret in your hearts
As the most precious valuable you possess,
More precious than your own lives,
If you wish to turn my bonds into a crown.
If I fail to reclaim the throne,
Eager armies will advance on all sides,
And no one will remain, neither merchant nor king,
Neither farmer nor host, neither headdress nor throne."

They march away, faces flooding with tears,
Exclaiming, "May the life of noblemen be your ransom!
May youth and royalty be your ornaments!
If the treasure of your secret is discovered,
Our land will turn into a sea of blood.
Who would dare think of such an occurrence?
Who would dare turn his wisdom into an ax
And his intelligence into a bat?"

Bahraam blesses the illustrious men of pure faith.
Then, in a state of anguish, he travels to his palace,
Surrendering his body and soul to Yazdan.

They hold tight until the site of the feast is decked,
And the noblemen take leave of the court.
As Shangal prepares to take the road to the plain,
Bahraam's wife tells her father, "Borzooy is ill.
He expresses his excuses to the king
And entreats him not to worry about his state.
He says that a feast is an unfortunate thing

343

When one is not in top health. He hopes
That the glorious king will understand."

Shangal replies, "How unfortunate.
He must not devote a single thought
To a festival if he is unwell."

Shangal exits Ghennooj at dawn,
Traveling in haste to the site of the feast.

As night deepens, the wife says to Bahraam,
"My dear husband, now is the moment to leave."

He dresses in his coat of mail and climbs on his steed.
He hooks equipment to the saddle, grabs his mace,
Assists Sepinood to her mount, murmuring
Yazdan's name, and launches his horse
To the river's edge, where he finds his friends asleep.
He awakens them to urge them to launch a ship
And a small boat for Sepinood.

They sail to the opposite shore by the light of dawn
And arrive at the time when the illuminating sun
Gradually brightens the world.

40 | Shangal Pursues Bahraam and Discovers His Identity

A cavalier takes the road from Ghennooj in haste
To carry and deliver the news to the king.
Shangal takes leave of the feast, as swift as a flame.
He gallops away toward the river's edge,
Where he catches sight of Sepinood and Bahraam.

Wrathful, he crosses the water and shouts:
"O wicked, impudent girl, you navigated the river
Like a lioness with this insolent, deceitful man!
You wish to secretly travel to Iran,
Abandoning our merry paradise for a barren desert.
You will now be the recipient of my javelin's blows,
Since you dared leave my side without a word!"

Bahraam says to him, "O miserable prince,
Why have you launched your horse like a madman?
You put me to the test, and you know that I am
As valiant in battle as when I revel in banquet.
Are you aware that one hundred thousand Indians
Are less worthy in my eyes than a single rider?
My thirty famed companions and I,
With our coats of mail and our Persian swords,
Shall fill with blood the eyes of the Indian people
And not allow a single one to remain alive."

Shangal knows that he speaks the truth
And must not underestimate the other's courage.
He replies, "I set aside my daughter,
My parents, and allies for your sake.
I saw more value in your being than in my own eyes.
I kept you like a diadem over my head;
I offered you the woman of your dreams;
I acted with righteousness, yet you deceived me,
Going down the path of iniquity instead of loyalty.
When did you ever hear that a violation
Is a just return for devotion?
What shall I say of a man that I treated like a son,
A man who appeared reasonable to me,
A man who decamps now like a valiant rider
And thinks that he can do as he pleases?
Is the heart of a Persian capable of commitment?
As he utters the word yes, his mind is locked on no.
You are like a lion cub who causes grief
In the hearts of those who raised him:
Once his teeth have matured and his claws are sharp,
He seeks a fight with his foster parent."

Bahraam tells him, "Once you get to know me,
You will no longer call me an adversary
Or regard me as a wrongdoer.
You will not seek to quarrel with me over my departure.
I am the King of Kings of Iran and Tooran.
I am the chief and the support of brave men.
From here on, I shall treat you according to merit;
I shall cut off the heads of those who offend you;
I shall acknowledge you in Iran as a father;

345

I shall exempt your land from having to pay tribute.
Your daughter will be the flame of the east;
She will be the diadem on the heads of queens."

Confounded by these words,
Shangal removes his Indian headdress,
Strikes his horse, lurches to the head of his retinue,
And nears the king to ask forgiveness.
In his joy, he embraces the King of Kings
And asks him to pardon his words.
He is happy to see Bahraam, and he asks
For a table to be dressed and cups to be brought.

Bahraam reveals to him his secret,
The events that occurred,
And how he alone devised the adventure.
They drink, then rise to excuse themselves.

The two kings, one idolatrous
And the other a Yazdan worshipper,
Shake hands and promise that, in the future,
They will no longer crush the heart of righteousness.
They pledge to pluck out the roots of deception, always
Remain in good faith, and to heed the words of wise men.

Shangal takes Sepinood in the folds of his arms,
Bids her farewell, and takes his leave.
They turn their backs on each other,
Having flung into dust their hearts' hostilities.

One ruler departs toward the river,
The other toward dry land, happy to return home.

41 | The Iranians Advance
to Greet Bahraam the Hunter

As news of the king's return from Ghennooj reaches Iran,
Festival halls are decked on the roads and in cities,
And every Iranian contributes in any way he can.
Dirhams are dispensed from one border to the next,
Along with musk, dinars, and saffron.

Everyone gives in to joy.
Every tongue acclaims the king.
Every soul yearns for his presence.

When Nersi is apprised of the situation,
He unites the dispersed troops and,
With the grand wise master and other wise men,
They advance to greet the king.
Bahraam, at the sight of him, dismounts and bows low,
Rubbing his forehead to the dust.
Nersi and the grand wise master approach him,
With dusty cheeks and joyous hearts.
Everyone celebrates his glory
And the favors of his good fortune.

Bahraam enters his palace,
Entrust his body and soul to Yazdan's care.
He reclines to rest as dark night descends
And the moon gains its silvery shield in all its splendor.

As soon as day tears apart the robes of night
And the world-illuminating torch appears,
The King of Kings sits on his golden throne,
Opens the doors to the audience hall, and keeps silent.

The wise men, noblemen, and the empire's leaders arrive.
The world owner rises and utters words
Full of piety and righteousness.
He begins his speech on the subject of Yazdan
And in this way pays his debt to wisdom:
"One must fear the World Creator,
Who is fully aware of the visible and the hidden.
Glorify and pray to the Giver of Victory and power,
Master of shining Sun and Moon.
Anyone who wishes to have access to paradise
Must keep evil and misdeeds at bay.
As much as his heart is replete with generosity,
Righteousness, and justice, he must, in equal measure,
Turn away from falsehoods, lies, and vice.

"You never will have cause to fear,
Whether you have a mountain of gold
Or a deep and rich silver mine.

Reject dread from accessing your hearts,
And proceed to augment your possessions.
The plowman and the farmer's descendant
Are equal in my eyes on the day of justice.
The one to whom we offered crown and throne
Owes his fortune to Yazdan and to justice.
If it is the will of the almighty Creator,
His heart will rejoice, and his fortune will smile.
I shall increase his wealth.
I shall show him the way to happiness.
I shall not work to increase my assets.
I do not wish to cause division among my people.
I only desire to amass a fortune that is just and fair
And can benefit others after my death.

"Should a person be oppressed by my troops
Or by an employee, a relative, or a bold cavalier,
He must let me know. Should he hide this fact,
His suffering will be fueled by his own doing.
How can one consent to affliction by his own cowardice?
I, for one, will implore Yazdan to execute justice on the one
Who hides the moon behind a veil of clouds.
You may have other wishes,
For every one of us has a unique disposition.
Tell me boldly, and I shall hope to fulfill
The longings your heart nurtures.
Lend your ear to my words, obey my command,
And adapt my advice as your souls' ruling."

Having thus spoken, he takes his seat happily
And places the crown of power on his head.
The noblemen summon blessings upon him:
"May seal and diadem never be robbed of your being!
When the king is wise and his fortune victorious,
The earth, crown, and throne gain in glory.
You have knowledge, courage, and splendor.
Your power, your bloodline, and your birth
Surpass the requirements of the imperial throne.
The world does not remember a king of your status.
It is impossible for us, young and old, to refrain
From invoking blessings on your person.
We glorify you before the Creator, before free men.

We proudly declare: On this throne of venerable kings
Sits a fair ruler, victorious and powerful.
You resurrect the dead with your justice,
Your generosity, and your pure words.
May the almighty Creator come to your aid!
May the star of fortune rest in your arms!"

The noblemen, full of wisdom, favorites of fate,
Leave the king's court in joy.
Bahraam climbs on his charger and rides toward
The temple of Aazargoshasp with his host.

He distributes gold and jewels to the poor,
And those who hide their needs receive the most.
A priest of the fire of Zoroaster, quietly praying,
Arrives with barsom in hand.
The king brings Sepinood to him
And teaches her the faith, the rites, and the true path.
He purifies her with the doctrine and the holy waters.
He clears her of the dust and rust of idolatry.

The king opens the narrow prison doors
And distributes dirhams to everyone he meets.

42 | Shangal Travels With Seven Rulers to Bahraam the Hunter

At the account of Bahraam's high deeds,
Shangal yearns to visit Iran,
The home of his daughter and the noble king.
He sends an Indian messenger, an eloquent,
Honest man, and asks Bahraam for a new treaty
To keep as testimony of their friendship.

The world master composes a pact,
Shining like the sun on a verdant paradise.
The envoy takes the road, carrying
The missive written by the king in Pahlavi.

As soon as he reaches the ruler of Ghennooj,
As soon as Shangal reads the letter,

He undertakes the preparations for his departure
While concealing it from his Chini relatives.

Seven rulers arrive to accompany him.
The King of Kabul, the King of Sindh,
A glorious monarch respected by the yogis;
The renowned King of Sandal;
The King of Jandal, victorious in every venture;
The powerful King of Cashmere;
And, finally, the illustrious King of Moulton.[55]

Seated on tall elephants, whose necks are bedecked
In strands of bells and their bodies in brocade coverings,
They are shaded by parasols made of peacock plumes.
Bearers of crowns, torques, and earrings,
They desire the acquisition of glory and crown.
It is a procession of noblemen, troops, and war apparatus
That shines for miles as they march with pomp and glory,
With heavy loads of gifts and offerings.
Next to them, dinars appear to be of little value.

Shangal advances from station to station
In this manner with his seven influential kings.
As news reaches Iran of their approach,
Bahraam organizes a convoy to take the road.
In every city and town, illustrious men rise
And prepare to greet Shangal.

The King of Kings, holder of ancient wisdom
And youthful good fortune, travels to Nahravan.[56]

The two powerful rulers, two friends,
Reach each other and come face to face.
They dismount with lavish apologies and salutations.

Two highborn kings, masters of crown
And royal majesty, embrace each other.
Their escorts follow suit and dismount,
Surrounded by a rowdy crowd.

◇◇◇◇◇◇◇◇◇◇◇◇◇
55 Kabul, Sindh, Sandal, Jandal, Cashmere, Moulton: Various regions in Afghanistan
and India.
56 Nahravan: Village in northwestern Iran.

In each other's company, the two kings
From two lands discuss all sorts of matters,
Great and small, then climb on their horses,
Their valiant hosts mirroring them.

Bahraam asks for a golden throne
To be placed in the audience hall,
Covered according to royal custom.
He asks for a spread with a shiny, delicate covering;
Its length equals the distance traveled by an arrow.
On it, they place roasted lamb and poultry.

After the meal, he holds a royal assembly
In a hall full of scent, color, and art.
He asks for wine and musicians,
And the sound of music and song
Spins through the air from one end to another.
Servants stand about.
The palace resembles a paradise;
The cups are made of crystal;
The plates and platters are made of gold.
The drinkers sport golden diadems
And jewel-embroidered boots.

Shangal is astonished at the sight of the palace
And reflects as he sips his wine on the fact
That Iran is akin to a lush garden
And that his friends exude the scent of musk.

He secretly speaks to the Iranian king:
"Find me a way to fill my eyes
With the sight of my precious daughter."

Bahraam commands one of his eunuchs
To escort the father to the moon's apartment.
The illustrious king follows him
Through the stately halls, as beautiful as spring.

Shangal finds Sepinood on her ivory throne,
A crown of rubies on her head.
He walks over to her, kisses her head,
And presses his cheek against hers.

The father sheds copious tears of tenderness.
His fair-faced daughter also weeps with the emotion
Of finding herself in the presence of her father.

Shangal takes Sepinood's hand into his.
He extols the palace, the audience hall,
And the chambers: "You were lucky
To escape a dismal home, a vile place,
To take up residence in paradise."

He presents her with many gifts, crates of gold,
Crowns and slaves, along with offerings for the king.
The priceless jewels, colorful bolts of fabric,
And precious crowns bring gaiety to the hall.

From there, Shangal makes an appearance at court.
He joins the noble assembly gathered,
And, once they are merry with drink,
They withdraw to their homes to rest.

As the musk-colored veil spotted with stars,
Like the hide of a leopard, appears,
The drinkers seek a sweet slumber while the servants
Remain standing, arms crossed in service.

Some time passes until the golden cup called sun
Comes to light, peeling off the dark shroud of night
And scattering jewels of topaz across the plain.
The valiant Bahraam marches off to hunt,
Taking with him the King of India and a gathering
Of cheetahs, falcons, thongs, and proud gyrfalcons.

They spend one month released from pain and worry,
In pursuit of onager and deer.
At the end of the month, they return,
Eager to reengage in feast and wine.

King Shangal does not lose sight of him for a single day,
Whether on the square or in assemblies,
Whether in the hunt, in feast, or in games of polo.

43 | Shangal Returns to India

Much time passes in this manner until
One day Shangal prepares for his return to India.
He arrives on the square, climbs to find his daughter,
Asks for a reed, paper, and ink made of crushed musk,
And composes a letter with Hindi characters.
It is a letter full of justice, as if written in Pahlavi.

He begins with a declaration of blessings
On the One who frees the world from sorrow,
Who puts forth virtue and righteousness,
Who abandons to the deev perversity and vice.
"I am the servant of the path of faith.
I renounce the path of fury and hatred.
By uniting Sepinood to the illustrious Bahraam,
I bestow upon him so much more.
May the King of Kings live eternally!
May the noblest noblemen be his servants!
Once I depart from this passing dwelling,
King Bahraam will be Rajah of Ghennooj.
Follow his command, carry my corpse to the fire,
And surrender to Bahraam treasury, land,
Palace, throne, and headdress."
He hands over the investiture of India,
Written on satin, to his daughter Sepinood.

Shangal, having passed two months in Iran,
Has one of his leaders ask permission from the king
To return home with his auspicious companions.

The King of Kings consents to his request.
He asks his vizier to select a cache of valuables:
Dinars, fine jewels, silver and gold objects,
A throne, a crown, a sword, and a belt;
To his noblemen he distributes horses
And Chini brocade according to rank.
Then he dismisses them, happy and content,
And accompanies them for three stations.

Not taking into account the presents he handed them,
Bahraam furnishes them with provisions for the journey.

44 | Bahraam Returns Taxes to Landowners

Upon his return, Bahraam sits on his throne
In peace and reflects on death and misfortune,
His heart fills with grief and his cheeks pale.
He summons a scribe, the powerful vizier,
And commands the latter to inspect his treasury
And to estimate the gold, the jewels, and the attire,
For astrologers predicted some troubling events.

They once told him that he would live
Three times twenty years
And that in the fourth period he will be mourned.
He then reflected, "I shall have a joyous time for
The next twenty years and plant the tree of happiness.
In the second twenty-year period,
I shall spread justice and generosity
Throughout the world, openly and privately.
I shall not allow a single corner of land
To be vacant and desolate, and I shall make sure
That, under my care, everyone finds nourishment.
During the following twenty-year period,
I shall hold myself in prayer, in the hopes
That Yazdan will agree to be my Guide."

The astrologers had given him sixty-three years,
But the period of three years remains unclear to him,
Though he owns vast treasure, the predictions worry him.
Happy is the sober man free of distress,
Especially when he is king!

As soon as the treasurer receives the vizier's order,
He proceeds to assess the accounts in the treasury.
He works for some time,
Then provides the vizier with various lists.
The latter, preoccupied, takes the lists to the king
And says, "For twenty-three years,
You will have need for nothing.
I estimated the food, the alms, the army's earnings,
The expense of envoys who visit your court
Sent by different rulers in your provinces.
Your wealth will suffice for so many years.

It is full of gold, silver, and precious items."

Bahraam listens and reflects.
His wisdom guards him from feeling sorrowful.
He thinks, "My reign draws to an end.
Ultimately, life only lasts for three days.
But since yesterday has passed
And tomorrow has not yet arrived,
I shall not allow myself to be bent by worry today.
Since I am able to give to others
And since I possess throne and crown,
I shall no longer ask for tribute from the world."

Then he puts the edict into effect that all rulers,
Great and small, are no longer required to pay tax.
He places a leader in every city to stir sleepy heads
And to prevent quarrels from erupting,
Quarrels that could have dire consequences.
He gives the necessities to the men full of wisdom,
From provisions to clothing to carpets,
And tells them, "You must hide nothing from me.
I wish to know everything, good and bad.
Act as mediators in disputes,
Ask for nothing, and always be courageous.
Guard my mind from having ill-founded suspicions.

The wise men disperse throughout the world,
And nothing is kept hidden, neither good nor bad.
They take the affairs into their own hands.
Yet, letters arrive from provinces, declaring
That the king's gifts, lack of work, and abundance
Have shaken reason out of people's minds,
That in the middle of struggles and bloodshed,
Young people disregard the value of highborn men,
That their hearts are solely set on the acquisition of wealth,
No longer respectful of noblemen and of the king.
They stray off onto the path of greed.

Deeply afflicted by the news of spilled blood and conflict,
The king selects an administrator in every province
Who is just and wise, furnishing him with all the means
To act generously and to distribute the necessities,

Such as clothing, food, and carpets.
He commands them to open offices for six months
And to collect dirhams from their subjects
That are to be stamped with the legend "taxes."

Crown-bearing receivers are positioned in offices.
For six months they distribute to the needy
As well as to men of noble lineage.

The goal is to prevent idle men from shedding blood
And dragging others to commit evil acts.
The agents write to the king to report
That trust in justice has vanished from the world,
That those who have dirhams do not pay taxes,
And the desire to fight has only grown,
That they make use of fraud for their own benefit
At the expense of persecuting others.

Bahraam's heart is deeply troubled by the news.
He selects a border guard, each with a just heart,
To apply the law of Yazdan to every province
To anyone who spills blood or perverts justice,
So that men can ultimately live in peace and harmony.

For one year he feeds and nourishes his subjects,
Then he turns to Yazdan in gratitude.
A long time passes. The king writes a letter
To truthful, observing men scattered everywhere,
And asks them what would cause harm to the empire.

They reply, "The result of the king's gifts
Is that people no longer observe the customs
And have deviated from the proper path.
Work and the care for crop production have ceased.
Yet it is a fact that man acquires value only through work.
We notice the plow cattle have disbanded
And weeds grow among the wheat and sown fields."

The king says, "The plowman, by profession,
Must not take time to rest from working the land
Before the afternoon, before the sun reaches its zenith.
The other half of the day belongs to either rest
Or to dining, pleasure and entertainment.

If an idle man retreats before plowing,
Do not seek to find value in him.
His indolence derives from his ignorance,
And one must shed tears for ignorant men.
If someone does not own seed and cattle,
Do not show him anger and do not be demanding.
Help him kindly with money from the treasury
So that no one has to suffer for lack.
Act in the same manner when the atmosphere
Brings about a disaster, as no one is master of time.

"Supposing locusts cover a nation
And remove the greenery of sown fields,
Compensate the residents at our expense
And proclaim this command in the province.
If there exists a sterile plot of land
Or a gravesite that are impossible to cultivate,
Do not have expectations from such places.
If one of my servants, or perhaps my foster father,
Asks even for the most minute contribution,
I shall bury him alive and curse his dwelling."

The king's seal is affixed to the letter.
Bahraam sends it to all the provinces
By way of messengers on camelback.

45 | Bahraam Summons Gypsies From India

Later, Bahraam writes a letter to every wise man
In order to ameliorate the condition of the poor:
"I must know who can live without having to work
And who is poor and deprived of wealth.
Observe the state of the world,
And direct my heart toward clarity."

He receives the same reply from every wise leader:
"We are witness to the world prospering.
Continuous benedictions rise everywhere.
However, the poor complain about the king
And about their misfortune. They say,
        'The rich drink wine, bearing flower crowns

On their heads and rejoicing to the sound of music.
They do not hold men like us in high esteem,
For we are destitute and deprived, and are left
To drink in the absence of music and flowers.
Meanwhile, their prosperous hearts and souls rejoice.'"

The king heartily laughs at the contents of the letter.
Then he launches a speedy camel to Shangal
With a missive to be relayed:
"O helpful King, select ten thousand gypsies,
Men and women, expert lute players."

Shangal's head proudly reaches Saturn
And he quickly obeys the command.
The gypsies travel to the king,
Who receives them in his audience hall
And gives each one an ox and a mule,
Hoping to make farmers out of them.
He asks his collectors to deliver one thousand
Ass-loads of grain so that they may
Cultivate the land with their oxen and mules,
Use the grain to sow and produce harvest,
Play music for the poor and freely serve them.

The gypsies depart, consume beef and corn,
And, after one year,
They appear at court, their cheeks yellow.

The king says to them, "You did not need
To squander seeds, grain, grass, and harvest.
Now your mules remain yours.
Load them up with luggage, prepare your musical
Instruments, and spin the silk into thread."

Still today, according to the king's just words,
Gypsies wander the world in search of life and lodging,
With dogs and wolves as companions.
They travel on the road, stealing day and night.

46 | The End of Bahraam the Hunter's Life

In this way, Bahraam's life exceeds sixty-three years,
During which time he has no equal.
But at the start of a new year, his vizier, a wise man
Who serves him as scribe, appears before him and says,
"The treasury of the king of noblemen is drained.
I have come to receive your command.
The wealthy are not paying tribute to us."

The king replies, "Do not exert yourself
To increase our wealth. We no longer have need for it.
Abandon the world to the Creator,
Who manifested the revolving dome of sky.
The era will pass, and Yazdan will remain
And will guide you and me on the road to happiness."

He sleeps, and the next morning at dawn,
A vast host marches to the palace gate.
They gather all those whose presence is invaluable.
Yazdegerd appears before his father, Bahraam,
Who hands him the crown, a torque, bracelets,
And the ivory throne in the presence of noblemen.

Wishing to devote himself to divine service,
The king rejects the crown and renounces the throne,
For he has become disgusted with worldly affairs.
As night deepens, he longs for sleep.
But when the sun reveals its face at the horizon's edge,
The heart of the king's wise man fills with terror
At the fact that the world master does not appear.
He fears that he may have taken flight
To avoid confrontation with tenacious subjects.

Yazdegerd enters his father's chambers
And finds him lying still, his breath congealed,
His cheeks discolored, wrapped in gleaming brocade,
Having yielded his existence.

Such is the way of the world, and such
It has been since the beginning of time.
Do not consume your soul with greed.

A heart of stone and steel fears death,
And you have not the power to avoid its snare.
If you wish your past life to protect you from danger,
You must take care in being a kind human
And avoiding causing harm to others.
What is the point of amassing a treasure
If in the end you must abandon your possessions?

Alas, such a king, alas his sense of integrity!
I wish to eternalize his generosity
And his sense of justice never besmirches
The memory of Bahraam the hunter.
Fifty rulers of Kianian lineage have sat on the royal throne.
Not one of them was equal to Bahraam
In justice, majesty, valor, custom, and power.
His vizier called him the Rostam of kings, for he shattered
The hearts of mountain and steel with his mighty arrow.
What is the benefit of mace, strength, and heroism
When the days of your existence come to an end?

The new king grieves his father's death for forty days.
The army stands by him, dressed in blue and black.
Once the valiant ruler is placed inside the tomb,
It is as if generosity has been eclipsed from the world.
Neither the sun nor the moon, neither Venus nor Saturn,
Neither throne nor crown will ever witness such a ruler.
Alas, his Kianian majesty, his demeanor and stature!
Alas, this king of powerful star, his hand and mace!
He was the adornment of throne and crown.
The lands of Rum and China paid tribute to him.
Ultimately, the wretched poor lacking bread and water
No longer yearned to fight to earn their keep.
Since the destitute have little to boast about,
Their ruler's departure is painless.

What good are royalty and grandeur
Since one cannot hold on to kingship forever?
Happy is the dervish who has faith and wisdom.
Fate may have mistreated him, but when he departs,
He leaves behind a good name and a good memory.
He will have a share in the other world
And will be honored by the Creator.

PART TWENTY-FOUR

Never will he be despised and miserable like me.

I prepare, in great despair, to enter the gates of hell,
Expecting nothing from a future in the other world,
As I receive little of value from this life.
No matter which path I followed, I have been shaken
And shattered, flung aside, plastered like a drunken man.

Now, if I find myself able to gather my thoughts,
I shall recount the reign of Yazdegerd, world seeker.

PART TWENTY-FIVE

From the Eighteen-Year Reign
of Yazdegerd, Son of Bahraam the Hunter
to the Forty-Year Reign
of Ghobaad, Son of Pirooz

I. The Eighteen-Year Reign of Yazdegerd, Son of Bahraam the Hunter

Yazdegerd becomes world king
And gathers his scattered army.
Wise men and noblemen, brave, illustrious,
And worthy of praise, sit around him.

He climbs on the golden throne,
Closes the door to pain, and ties up the hand of evil
As he proclaims: "The one who renounces his sins
Will not have to fear the reprisals of an avenger.
Anyone who allows his heart to dim with envy
Will suffer grievances that will compel him
To seek a cure from a wicked deev.
Envy gives birth to greed, suffering, and need.
A sinful man resembles a deev who breeds hatred.
Do not wish upon your enemy
What you may not wish upon yourself.
Avoid causing harm to others
Or attracting something that displeases you.
Patience is wisdom's brother,
And wisdom is the crown on the head of knowledge.
If you touch someone with a good deed,
Do not reproach him, to avoid breaking his heart.
If you are benevolent and patient,
You will never be scorned in the eyes of wise men.
If triumphant fortune comes to my aid,
It will satisfy my desires in the world.
I shall act with righteousness so that the book that
Lists my actions detects no perversity among my deeds."

He governs the world with justice for some time,
Rendering the era happy as he himself dwells in happiness.
He sends innumerable troops on all sides
To protect the empire against a possible enemy.

Once ten plus eight years pass over his head,
He feels his star dimming, he sighs deeply,
Summons the noblemen and sages,
Seats them on the heels of the golden throne, and says,
"The wheel of the endless, timeless firmament
Knows neither foster parent nor child.
It shows little respect for the crown of mighty kings.
It hunts any sort of prey that comes its way.
Now my days are coming to an end,
And my strength has been exhausted.
I give the diadem and seal, treasury,
And the land of Iran to my son Hormoz.
Listen to my words and obey.
May my commands give your soul some respite.
It is true that Pirooz is powerful and strong
And has a few years over Hormoz,
But there is a certain gentleness in the latter,
As well as insight, modesty, and merit."

He speaks in this manner and lives for another week.
Then he expires, and the throne bitterly weeps for him.

Whether you live for one hundred years or for twenty-five,
You must leave this passing dwelling.
Anything that can be counted
Must not be deemed as a durable or lasting thing.

II. The One-Year Reign of Hormoz, Son of Yazdegerd

Hormoz climbs on his father's throne
And places on his head the golden crown.
It is as if his brother Pirooz is all anger,
And his eyes brim with envy's tears.

Pirooz takes his escort, his valuables, and a few noblemen
And travels to the King of Hephthalites,[57] one of the rulers
Of the land of Chaghan,[58] an ambitious man
Named Faghanish, owner of army, treasury, and power.

He says to Faghanish, "O benevolent King,
We were two sons worthy of kingship.
Our father offered the crown of royalty to the youngest,
And, having accomplished this unjust act, he died.
If you wish to give me an army, I have treasury
And weapons, power and a strong hand."

The Chaghani replies, "It is all very well.
The son of the world master is king himself.
I shall entrust an army to you and come to your aid
So that you may obtain what is rightly yours,
But under the condition that Tarmaz and Viseh-Guerd[59]
Remain under my jurisdiction, according
To the promise sealed under the rule of Yazdegerd."

Pirooz replies, "Yes, those cities belong to you,
And you deserve a kingdom even larger."

The king offers a glorious army to Pirooz,

◇◇◇◇◇◇◇◇◇◇◇◇◇
57 Hephthalites: Residents of a region in central Asia during the 5th to the 8th centuries
CE.
58 Chaghan: A region in Afghanistan north of the Jayhoon River.
59 Tarmaz and Viseh-Guerd: Ancient cities in northern Afghanistan.

Thirty thousand sword-bearing Hephthalites,
And the circle of the moon dims with the dust they raise.

The battle does not last long.
He attacks King Hormoz, who cannot sustain the fight.
In the end, he is captured and taken prisoner,
And all the crowns of the world gain little value in his eyes.

At the sight of his brother's features,
Pirooz's heart leans toward love and brotherhood.
He rushes to him, takes his hand into his, tells him
To climb on his horse, and sends him back to his palace.

Later, he reads him a treaty and adds,
"Give thanks to Yazdan.
The man who recognizes Yazdan is the wiser man.
My brother seizes the crown and throne.
May Pirooz's fortune be victorious!"

III. The Eleven-Year Reign of Pirooz, Son of Yazdegerd

1 | Pirooz Ascends the Throne, and Iran Endures a Seven-Year Drought

Once Pirooz's heart finds some peace and his mind
Frees from worry, he climbs on the Kianian throne,
As suits a king who is a Yazdan worshipper.

He addresses his court: "O valiant, skillful,
And highborn noblemen, I implore the Creator,
Who is above all need, to grant me a long life
So that I may discern the subject from the ruler,
And to grant me wisdom and good fortune.
Our highest achievement is the exercise of patience.
Haste always attracts contempt.
Justice and clemency are the columns of wisdom,
And the door of generosity serves as their ornament.
The art of speaking gently is wisdom's glory,
Courage and virility are its feathers and wings.
How could a prince who lacks wisdom
Enjoy the throne of power?
Not even the wise man remains eternally.
There is no glory greater than that of Jamsheed,
Yet he died at a time when his crown reached the moon,
Leaving the Kianian throne for another.
No one endures forever on the dust of earth.
Every man must seek refuge in the Creator."

Pirooz governs for one year with justice and sagacity,
Displays vast intelligence and evades misfortune.
The following year, the face of the sky dries up,
And drought paints the rivers as black as musk.

The lack of rainfall persists through the third and

369

Fourth years, plunging everyone into a state in distress.
The mouth of air dries up like dust.
Water in streams is as rare as theriac.
So many men and animals perish
That the space of passage becomes constricted.

Witness to this calamity, the King of Iran
Exempts the world from paying taxes.
He distributes grain to people, great and small,
In every city and home supplied with attics.

A proclamation is announced at the king's door:
"O illustrious, powerful men, sell your grain
And amass a golden treasure marked with my name.
Anyone who possesses in secret grain, cattle,
Or sheep in the pastures may sell them,
As men are perishing from lack of nutrition."

In haste, he dispatches a letter to every administrator
And every independent man thus conceived:
"Open your storerooms for those in need.
Should someone die from a lack of bread,
Whether he is young or old, male or female,
I shall spill the blood of the storeroom master
For failing to perform his divine duties.
I shall cut him in half with my sharp sword
As if the day of resurrection is upon him."

He commands people to leave their homes, to travel
To the fields and raise their hands to the Creator.
A great clamor rises to the sky, the sound of weeping,
Cries of distress, pain, and restlessness.
Prayers pleading Yazdan for mercy ascend
Over mountains and plains, deserts and caverns.

For seven years, one cannot find greenery in the world.
In the eighth year, during the month of Farvardin,
A glorious cloud emerges that rains pearls
Upon the parched earth, and the scent of musk
Drifts through gardens and fields.
The cups in the grasp of rosebushes fill with dew
Like jugs brimming with wine.
A colorful rainbow shines above,

And the world is freed from the oppression
Of evil men standing with bows drawn.

Once freed from this period of famine,
Pirooz sits calmly on the royal throne

2 | Pirooz Battles the Tooranians and Is Killed

Pirooz builds a great city, which he names Pirooz-Ram.
The eloquent world master declares,
"Here is another Rey, a place of tranquility
And rest for glorious kings of blessed imprints."

Then he founds the city of Baadan-Pirooz
In a joyful land, peaceful and beautiful.
It is the city that today we call Ardabil,
Where the Caesar rightly erected
The column that marks the border.
With the foundation of these two cities,
Pirooz makes all the nations prosper.
He brings happiness to the hearts of wise men.
He pays the balance to his glorious army
So that it may prepare for a war against the Turks.
Hormoz leads the frontline and departs with new legions.

Ghobaad commands the rearguard
And marches as swift as wind with his troops.
He is Pirooz's son, an intelligent fruit
On the fertile branch of the royal tree.

Next the king seats Balaash on the throne,
His youngest son, a man full of dignity and justice.
The king commands Soofraay, an illustrious youth
From Pars, to stay put as Balaash's loyal vizier.

Then he marches against the Turks with his host
And takes with him the royal crown and throne.
He departs with troops, treasury, and the necessary
Gear to make war and to attack Khoshnavaz.

There is a column erected by the hero Bahraam

Out of stone and plaster, of great height, on which
Is engraved a royal treaty by the Turks and Iranians.
It declares that no one is allowed to cross the frontier
Or to set foot beyond the Jayhoon River.

As Pirooz, lion vanquisher, arrives and notices the mark
Agreed to by the King of Iran, he says to his noblemen,
"I shall similarly raise a tower before the Turks
With the aid of my sword and my treasury,
So that Hephthalites cannot cause us any harm.
Once this round column stands before Terek[60]
And the noblemen of the land bring me a written pact,
I shall say that Bahraam the hunter
Accomplished the deed with his worth,
His knowledge, his authority, and his power.
I shall not allow a single trace of Khoshnavaz
To remain among the Hephthalites or the Turks."

3 | Khoshnavaz's Letter to Pirooz

Khoshnavaz, the son of the Tarkhan,
Learns that Pirooz has crossed the Jayhoon
With his host, that he has violated the treaty,
And that the land is storming with battle and trouble.

He calls an expert scribe to write a letter in which
He invokes divine grace on the world king,
Then he adds, "You stray from the deal
Sealed by just rulers, and I shall no longer
Deem you a descendant of Kianian kings.
This was not the custom of your ancestors,
Noblemen and pure world rulers.
But since you violate the treaty that bound the Persians,
Since you cast into the dust the mark of glory
Established by powerful men long ago,
I shall break it as well and, against my will,
Bring my hand to the hilt of my sword."

◇◇◇◇◇◇◇◇◇◇◇◇◇
60 Terek River: A major river north of Iran in today's Russia that flows into
the Caspian Sea.

Khoshnavaz explains the entire affair in the letter
And sends it along with many presents.
An eloquent, noble cavalier departs with letter and loads.

Upon reading the letter, Pirooz grows infuriated.
He says to the envoy, "Rise and return to this vile man.
Tell him that Bahraam sent you a piece of writing
In which he fixed the border beyond the River Terek.
And now you occupy every part leading to the Jayhoon.
Everything belongs to you, heights and shallows,
Mountains and plains, all the way to the river's edge.
I lead a vast host of warriors, proud and ready for fight.
I shall not allow you, not even your shadow,
To linger on earth for long."

The envoy departs as swift as a dust storm,
Reports all that he heard and speaks at length
To Khoshnavaz of the proud and conceited king.

Khoshnavaz listens to him, reads the letter,
And calls his dispersed troops.
He guides his army to the battlefield
And attaches his ancestor's treaty, the one
Received from King Bahraam, to the point of a spear,
Which mandates that the Jayhoon marks the border.

Then he selects a sagacious, soft-spoken man
From his host, one honored by everyone,
And tells him, "Approach Pirooz, speak to him gently,
And listen to his reply. Tell him,
       'I shall carry your grandfather's treaty.
       He was a king of powerful star
       Who should now be your guide.
       I shall brandish it before the army
       On the point of my spear, like a sun
       That brilliantly shines on the road, so that men
       Of sense observe the command of this just king.
       I shall be praised while you are cursed
       And are referred to as the faithless king.
       Neither Yazdan nor Yazdan worshippers,
       Nor the very last subject on earth,
       Approves of this sort of unjust action:

The repudiation of treaties executed by kings.
Never did a ruler as just and brave as Bahraam
Place the royal crown upon his head.
I attest before the World Creator that your attack
Calls for a war that is inexcusable and unjustifiable.
Regardless, you will be certainly defeated,
For your good fortune will not assist you.
I shall not send a messenger to you again.
The Creator is my support in this fight,
And that is all that I need.'"

The messenger travels with the letter, as swift as dust,
And reports the message to an irate Pirooz.
He retorts, "An aging man who knows the world
Would not speak in this manner. Tell him that if he takes
A single step from Chaadj[61] in the direction of the river,
I shall send him a greeting with the tip of my spear."

The envoy returns and secretly reports to Khoshnavaz:
"Not only did I find in Pirooz little fear of the divine,
But he fails to receive guidance from wisdom.
He seeks only vengeance and combat,
With complete disregard for Yazdan's command."

At these words, Khoshnavaz takes shelter
In the Creator, praying, worshipping, and saying,
"O Supreme Judge, you created earth and wind.
You know that Pirooz, the unjust,
Is not more valiant than the famed Bahraam.
He utters falsehoods, he seeks power with his sword.
May his imprint be erased from the surface of the earth!
May his force perish, along with his mind and heart!"

He asks for a ditch to be dug up around his camp
And disguises it by concealing the opening.
It is deep, the depth of a noose,
And the width of twenty arrash.[62]
Once the task is complete, he invokes Yazdan's name
And leads his army out of Samarkand.

◇◇◇◇◇◇◇◇◇◇◇◇◇◇
61 Chaadj: A city near Tashkent.
62 Arrash: Unit of measurement corresponding to the length of the
forearm, from fingertip to elbow.

4 | The Battle of Pirooz and Khoshnavaz, and Pirooz's Death

Meanwhile, Khoshnavaz feels disquiet in his heart
As he marches toward the completed ditch.
King Pirooz, who has lost his mind,
Swiftly travels on the other side with his troops.

The sound of clarions and timpani rises over the hosts.
The air dims, as black as ebony from the dust,
And on each side falls a fierce shower of shots,
Making the rivers overflow with blood.

King Pirooz springs into action, as swift as a storm,
With his mace and Rumi helmet.
He approaches Khoshnavaz, but the leader of Turks
Withdraws, swings the bridle, and turns his back on him.

Pirooz presses his charger and gallops with a small
Number of companions, pursuing Khoshnavaz ardently.
He falls and tumbles into the ditch along with a few men
Who exhibit the courage of lions on battle day.
Included among them are his brother Hormoz,
His illustrious son Ghobaad, and other highborn princes.

In this way, seven rulers, bearers of golden helms,
As well as some warriors eager for battle
Are destined to perish in the ditch.

Khoshnavaz dismounts on the other side,
His heart full of joy, and calls the ones who are still alive,
Men whose thrones have cause to weep for them,
To be extracted from the ditch.

Pirooz, the king, leader of noblemen, master of crown
And throne, is found, his head and back shattered.
None of the princes remains alive except for Ghobaad,
And this once glorious army and kingdom
Are, just like that, delivered to the wind.

Khoshnavaz in this way attains the object of his desire.
He springs proudly and follows his keen army

To destroy and pillage the Iranians and their loads.
One no longer is able to distinguish
Between the left wing and the right wing.
A few Iranians are taken captive, and many more
Are abandoned, lying in the dust, riddled with shots.

A man who seeks world control must not act wickedly,
For a wicked heart is the companion of the dark dust.
Such is the way of the endlessly spinning dome,
Whether king or subject, whether foolish or the very
Foundation of reason, no one remains eternally on earth.
Act in a way that your provision of travel
Is righteousness, and that will suffice.

Khoshnavaz passes over the ditch,
And his army's wealth expands with the Iranians' goods.
Iron bonds are attached to Ghobaad's feet
Without regard for his throne or his lineage.

As the warriors of Iran receive news of the events
And the battle fought by Pirooz Shah,
A great cry of anguish rises over the entire nation,
Anguish over the fate of the princes, free men.
When, with time, the news is confirmed,
Balaash descends from the golden seat,
Tears his hair out of his royal head,
And scatters dark dust over the throne.

Iranian people and troops grieve painfully.
Women, men, and children lament.
Everyone pulls his hair, scratches his cheeks;
Everyone calls the king, wishing to see him;
Everyone sits in a state of affliction;
Men, great and small, reflect on ways
To take the road and march out of Iran
To properly take vengeance on the desert people.

IV. The Five-Year-and-Two-Month Reign of Balaash, Son of Pirooz

1 | Balaash Imparts Advice to the Iranians

After one month of mourning,
Head powdered with dust and cheeks scratched,
Balaash opens his hall to an assembly
Consisting of the grand wise master,
Sages, noblemen, and warriors.

They give him much advice,
Address to him helpful words,
Seat him on the imperial throne,
And proceed to scatter gold and gems over him.

Once on his seat, he says, "O brave noblemen,
Conform to the counsel of sensible leaders.
Once my somber position gains in brilliance,
Your influence will lend luster to my faded thoughts.
Encourage anyone who is prone
To accomplish good deeds in the world.
Alternatively, discourage and disavow anyone
Who is evil and whose intentions are malevolent.
I shall crown with a diadem of his blood
The head of anyone who exerts his power
Contrary to royal decree and rejects our advice.
If one of my subjects complains to me
About a member of my devoted host,
I shall break the heart of the unjust man,
Deracinate his tree, branch and root.
Do not take liberties with the king,
Even with those who are irreprehensible.
A king plays at times the role of poison
And at times the role of its antidote.
Better for you to seek theriac than venom.

"If you wish to be welcomed by the king,
Present yourself to him with a smile on your face.
If he is angry, ask forgiveness and bless him,
Whether his sentiment is fair or unfair.
Each time you boast about your wisdom,
Each time you assert that you are strong in every science,
Know that you have never been so idiotic
Than at that moment; do not be your own enemy.
If you follow my valued advice,
You will obtain treasure from the benevolent king.
Knowledge has never worked to anyone's detriment."

The noblemen pronounce benedictions on him,
Astonished at the level of his sagacity.
The troops speak to each other:
"Thanks to this glorious ruler,
The throne and crown shine resplendent.
May the evil eye be kept at bay!
May his enemies' bodies endure eternal pain!"

They depart from the palace content,
Imploring Yazdan to protect his soul and body.
Their hearts are full of affection and
Their tongues pray for him to live eternally.

2 | Soofraay Learns of Pirooz's Death

Earlier, while preparing himself for war, Pirooz
Searched for a determined warrior of good counsel
To act as temporary guardian of throne and diadem
And kindly care for his younger son, Balaash.

The most able to fit the position was Soofraay,
A wealthy man of honest intentions.
Full of experience, this highborn,
Famed military leader from Shiraz is the governor
Of Kabolestan, Bost, Ghaznein, and Zabolestan.

Once apprised of the way Pirooz fell into a trap
And perished in the absence of counsel and guide,
Tears spill from Soofraay's lashes onto his cheeks.

He shreds to bits his hero's garb.
Brave men around him remove their headdresses
And continue to mourn the king for one month.

Soofraay unceasingly says, "How could Balaash,
So young, take upon himself to avenge the king?"
He knows that it is a useless effort.
He knows that the imperial crown has lost its luster.

Soofraay convenes his scattered troops,
Asks for the beating of timpani and the rising of dust.
One hundred thousand sword-striking men assemble,
Avid for battle and eager to implement reprisals.

He pays their salaries and equips them, bringing joy
Into hearts that exhale the breath of vengeance.
He summons a soft-spoken messenger,
A man of intelligence, awakened mind, and serene soul.

Grieving, his heart wounded, his eyes
Replete with blood tears, and his cheeks pale,
He writes a letter full of sound advice drawn from
The reigns of Jamsheed, Kay Khosrow, and Kay Ghobaad.
He sends the letter to Balaash and adds,
"O King, do not concern yourself with death.
Everyone suffers one way or another.
One must be patient and care for his fame.
What comes with the wind vanishes with a breath.
One may call it justice, another oppression.
Now, if the king permits, I shall prepare
For war with my men eager for battle,
For the sun and moon weep bitter tears
Of vengeance for the spilled blood of Pirooz Shah."

The envoy takes the road on one side,
And on the other, a vengeful Soofraay departs.
He decks his army like the wing of a pheasant
And marches from Zabolestan to Marv.

Soofraay selects a perceptive man,
Able to soften hearts with his words,
And says to a scribe, "It is time for you to rise
And set in motion the tip of your reed.

Write a letter to Khoshnavaz and say,
"O foolish, deceitful fox,
You have been fostered by Ahriman.
Your shirt will have cause to weep for your body
For the crimes you have committed before Yazdan.
Who in the world do you know
Who has acted so deceitfully and disloyally?
You will witness the anguish in the sword of tyranny.
You killed the innocent King of Kings,
The grandson of Bahraam Shah.
You have given birth to new retributions on earth,
A flare of vengeance that will never be extinguished.
Why did you not present yourself before him
At the sound of timpani, crawling like a cunning dog?

"Your grandfather was a poor man.
Your father stood before Bahraam like a slave.
Here I am in Marv to execute vengeance, and I shall not
Allow the Hephthalites to hold on to their wealth.
I demand your prisoners with the sword of vengeance.
I demand all the booty that has fallen into your hands,
Anything that you have picked up on the battlefield.
With my vengeful sword, I shall drag to Marv
The dust from the land of Tooran.
I shall not leave the world to your sons,
And I shall burn your relatives and allies.
At Yazdan's command, I shall cut off your head
And flood your land with an abundance of blood.
Hatred will not be my guide. The blood of Pirooz
Or Khoshnavaz will perish beneath the black dirt.
Their souls will seek justice in the flames of hell."

The envoy departs, as valiant as a lion, with the letter.
He presents himself to Khoshnavaz
Like a man devoid of sense, steps up to the throne,
Refrains from bowing low to express respect,
And delivers Soofraay's letter.

The army leaders exit the audience hall,
And Khoshnavaz hands over the letter to a scribe
With the order to secretly share its contents, good or bad.

The scribe says to the king,
"This letter is full of sword, mace, and arrow."

The king, having led many a battle,
Is broken by Soofraay's eloquent letter.
He instantly begins a reply to its every point,
Good or harsh, beginning thus,
"We fear the Creator and the uncertainty of fate.
When one professes to be a divine worshipper,
One does not violate treaties sealed by kings.
Yet I had sent to Pirooz a letter full of advice
In addition to the treaty of the mighty King Bahraam.
But he did not take into account any of my points
And failed to remember the old agreements.
He is the one who initiated the war,
While I was simply defending myself.

"When the two armies came face to face,
The stars fell into a state of indignation.
Your monarch succumbed to death against my wishes.
He violated the convention drawn by just kings.
And since then, he did not enjoy a youthful day.
The World Creator did not approve of his actions.
It was as if the earth was clinging to his feet.
Anyone who misses devotion due to his ancestors
And tramples righteousness beneath his feet
Will succumb on battle day just like Pirooz,
Vanquished in a dusty ditch, smeared in dirt.
If you decide to come, you will meet a similar fate,
For I lack neither treasure nor valiant men."

The messenger departs in haste with the letter
And returns in seven days at the side of Soofraay.
The hero warrior reads the letter and curses heavily.
The sound of trumpet and timpani booms.
He takes such a vast host to Coshmaihan
That the sun loses its way in the sky.

They cross the River Jayhoon,
And it is as if they are home on the road.

3 | The Battle of Soofraay With Khoshnavaz

Khoshnavaz receives the news of the army's motions.
He enters the desert and prepares for battle.
He marches to Baikand[63] and establishes a camp
In a way that the vault of sky no longer
Perceives the surface of the plain.

On his side, Soofraay, heart pounding
With vengeance, advances as swift as wind.
As night deepens, the army leader
Bars access to camp with a row of elephants.
On both sides, patrols make the rounds.
The world fills with the clatter of avenging men,
And in the distance, one hears the cry
Of watch guards and the ringing of bells
Both at the vanguard and at the rear.

Such is the state of things until the sun's blade
Makes its appearance, until valleys and fields
Grow resplendent as white crystal.
At that moment, the two hosts
Deploy their imposing banners.

The fierce shouts of warriors eager for battle
Tear apart the hearts of dragons.
The plumes of arrows turn the air into a vulture's tail,
And the blood of leaders turns the earth into a lake.
No matter which side one's head turns,
One sees bits and pieces of corpses and limbs
Maimed and shattered by warrior blows.

Soofraay emerges from the army center
With his troops stirring to action behind him.
On the other side, Khoshnavaz advances,
Battle sword in hand, closing in on him.

Soofraay hands him a blow of mace on the head.
It is as if the sky is shaken by it.
But Khoshnavaz steps aside with a leap

◇◇◇◇◇◇◇◇◇◇◇◇◇
63 Baikand: Must be a fictional region on the border of Iran.

And launches his horse toward the hillside.
Anyone who notices his own fate turning adverse
Must swing the reins and offer a view of his backside.

Soofraay, as swift as a hurricane, chases after him,
Brandishing his life-destroying spear.
He takes a great number of illustrious men captive,
And many others are killed by swords or arrows.

Khoshnavaz gallops toward Kohan-Dej.
He sees countless bodies,
Dead and wounded, on the road.
He observes from above his troops
Dispersed on the hillside and desert shallows,
The road littered with corpses and booty,
And the plain shining like a garden in bloom.

Each person takes items to Soofraay: armor, belts,
Bridles, lances and helmets, horses, and slaves.
The goods pile up to form a heap
As high as the peak of Mount Alborz.
Soofraay distributes it all to his troops,
Keeping nothing that belongs to the Turks.

He says to his brave men, "Our affairs today
Unfolded according to our hearts' desires,
Thanks to the favors granted us by fate.
But we must not linger on this plain.
When the sun reveals its hand above the sky,
We shall go to avenge the Iranian king,
We shall depart like lions to seize the castle."
The troops place their hands on their chests,
And each man utters his opinion.

As the gem on the sun's crown
Begins to shine in the canopy of sky,
The sound of drums rises over the encampment.

At the moment Soofraay climbs on his charger,
An envoy dispatched by Khoshnavaz arrives at his side.
The envoy says, "War, battle, and bloodshed
Only serve to further pain and spur new conflicts.
Is it right for two wise and brave youths

To mutually send their souls to hell?
If you return to the path of reason, you will recognize
That Pirooz's death occurred by divine command.
It is not the wind that caused his demise
But the stars that sliced off his years and months.
He was at fault; he violated the treaty, favoring
The bitterness of quince over the sweet taste of honey.

"What was meant to be has already unfolded.
Let us not walk a path contrary to the dictates of fate.
Happy is the one who keeps misfortunate at bay!
I shall send to the royal army leader prisoners
And all sorts of valuables, gold and silver,
Raw gems, weapons, steeds, crowns and thrones,
And all the loads discarded by the misfortunate Pirooz.
I shall send everything that once belonged
To him and to his troops to the treasurer.
I shall proceed so that you may return victorious
To the land of Iran and to the king of brave men.
I shall not undertake any action against Iran,
And you will observe the terms of Bahraam's pact.
The King of Kings divided the world fairly:
To me the land of Turks and Chin, to you Iran."

After hearing the missive, Soofraay immediately
Summons the army into his tent and says to the envoy,
"Repeat to the warriors your fighting master's words."

Khoshnavaz's delegate reveals all the points,
Public and private, then Soofraay asks his troops,
"What is your opinion on this affair?"

They reply, "It is up to you to conclude the peace treaty.
No one in Iran is more capable than you.
You are our leader and our master."

Soofraay says to his highborn leaders,
"Today my advice is to end the war
And to return without delay our troops to Iran.
Ghobaad, Pirooz's royal son, is held captive by them,
Along with the grand wise master, Ardeshir,
And many other army leaders, young and old.
If we continue the war with Khoshnavaz,

384

The struggle will be a lengthy one,
One that will have no benefit for us.
They will kill the Iranian prisoners;
Ghobaad, world seeker; and Ardeshir.
Still, if Ghobaad was not among them,
My heart and mind would forget the wise master,

"But if, by some calamity, Ghobaad
Has fallen into the hands of the Turks,
The land of Iran would resound with clamor,
And humiliation and blame would prevail.
Such actions would never be forgotten,
Not until the day of resurrection.
Let us charm the messenger with kind words,
And let us accept the peace accord
So that we may set our sights on Ghobaad.
May kingship never be deprived of him!
The same goes for the grand wise master Ardeshir
And all the prisoners, young and old."

The troops shower him with praise:
"Here is a suitable peace accord!
Here is a proper royal manner and faith!"

The noble leader summons an envoy
And speaks to him gently:
"It was Yazdan's will, and that is that.
When fate strategizes misfortune, it does so secretly.
You may send to me in pomp and circumstance
All the noblemen of Iran taken prisoner,
Ghobaad, Ardeshir, the enchained warriors.
Next, you will send to me all the wealth
You have seized, dinars, crowns, and all.
I will receive them in the presence of my court.
We shall abstain from further killing and raiding,
For we are above need as the Creator's servants.
We shall cross the Jayhoon again on the tenth day,
And from here on, we shall refrain
From trampling the earth in pursuit of each other."
Soofraay adds to the envoy,
"Pay attention to what I told you, and,
When you arrive, repeat everything to the king."

The envoy returns without delay
And presents himself proudly to Khoshnavaz.
He recounts everything word for word.

Khoshnavaz is absolutely delighted.
He instantly removes the chains binding Ghobaad,
The wise master Ardeshir, and all the Iranian prisoners.
He gathers the loot collected on the battlefield,
As well as the throne and crown of King Firooz
And all that was scattered among the Turkish troops.
He sends the lot to Soofraay
To be delivered to him by a virtuous man.

4 | Ghobaad Returns to the Land of Iran

The army leaps in joy at the sight of Ghobaad,
The wise master Ardeshir, and prisoners, young and old.
The leaders emerge from their tents
And raise their hands to the sky in gratitude
To see the king's son return safe and sound
With his highborn and valuable company.

The chief leader asks for pavilions
To be disassembled so that they may set off.
He climbs on his horse, and,
In the company of Ghobaad and the others,
They cross the Jayhoon River in joy and victory.

News spreads through the land of Iran:
The auspicious and glorious leader has returned
After a battle with Khoshnavaz and a successful,
Elaborate plan that reached a triumphant resolution.
Cries of joy echo as if they intend to deafen ears.
The wise leaders rise and prepare to greet the others.

After the river crossing, the Iranian troops journey on,
Their vast numbers occupying mountain and plain.
The clatter is loud as the land's noblemen
Prepare to receive them.

Balaash asks for a golden throne for Ghobaad

To share with Soofraay, who soon arrives.
All the renowned men take the road to greet him
As the king and the warriors march on.

In the presence of Ghobaad happy and free of chains,
Balaash holds him close to his heart, strokes his head,
Cursing the Hephthalites and the Chinis.

They wander off the road and enter the palace,
Hearts aggrieved and desirous of vengeance.
Balaash asks for tables, wine, music, and singers,
But the scene is not a merry one.
Pirooz's death casts a shadow over it.

Singers celebrate Soofraay with a song of war,
Its melody accompanied by the lute.
The noblemen hold their gaze on Soofraay,
Who is the reason for their return to peace and trust.
The affairs of Iran are reinstated, thanks to him.
And thanks to his high deeds,
Anyone who holds a grudge against Khoshnavaz
Now enjoys a happy heart and a carefree spirit.

Soofraay has no equal in the world.
Four years pass in this manner.
Everything unfolds according to his will.
He shapes the world in accordance with his ideas.
Once his power is recognized by all,
He pushes Balaash away from the throne
And says, "You do not know how to be king.
You cannot make the distinction
Between good people and malicious ones.
You make a game of kingship
With perverse acts and joy in your heart.
Ghobaad is more knowledgeable on matters,
More able to govern the kingdom than you are."

Balaash returns to his private palace,
Not daring to chase Soofraay away, and says,
"Here is a throne that I shall occupy free of hardship,
For it does not require hard work, does not cause pain,
And does not bring me adversity."

V. The Forty-Three-Year Reign of Ghobaad, Son of Pirooz

1 | Ghobaad Climbs on the Throne and Addresses the Noblemen

Once the blessed Ghobaad ascends the throne
And places the crown of power on his head,
He departs from Estakhr in the direction
Of the city of Ctesiphon, the glory of noblemen.

He sits on the turquoise throne and declares,
"Guard yourselves from keeping secrets from me.
My door is always open, day and night.
The only worthy man is the one
Whose tongue speaks only the truth,
The one who does not seek perversion.
If he forgives, even in a bout of fury,
Fair men will take him as a guide,
He will raise the throne of contentment in the world,
And powerful men will praise his just ways.
If you bar hatred from your hearts,
Men, great and small, will pay homage to you.
Should a king embark on the pronouncement of lies,
He is sure to fall into the trap of war.
He must first listen to everyone, and if he is learned,
His reply will directly reach the goal.
But when a knowing man becomes greedy,
His knowledge cannot bear fruit.
If the wise man acts in haste, his wisdom
Will be as worthless as water in a salty marsh.

"The one who seeks the army's affection
Takes a modest tone, even when he gives reproof.
The powerful man, when he shows a harsh face,
Degrades himself to the level of a poor man.

But if a poor, ignorant man exercises power,
His governing will lead to madness.
The one who is aware of his own shortcomings
Does not speak much of the fault of others.
The support of wisdom is patience,
But if you give in to anger, you will defile yourself.
If you conform to divine justice, you will be powerful,
Constant in your moods, and pure in your intentions.
Avoid pain and weariness, for a man free of greed
Is more valuable than the one who hordes wealth.
The one who is generous takes with him an allowance.
His body will perish, but his name will live on eternally.
In conclusion, guide everyone on the path of virtue,
And guard yourselves from navigating
This inconstant world by way of evil acts."

All the court's noblemen acclaim Ghobaad
And scatter emeralds over his crown.
He is a youth of three times five plus one
Who takes only a little part in governing.
He is untried and inexperienced,
While Soofraay is the real master of Iran,
The one who tends to the affairs of the world.
The warrior performs all the royal duties
And allows no one to approach the king.
In the absence of a formal vizier,
Ghobaad refrains from exerting his command
And is not consulted on various matters.
The world is in the grips of the rule of Soofraay.

2 | Soofraay Travels to Shiraz, and the Iranians Disparage Him

Some time passes in this manner
Until the king reaches the age of twenty-three.
One day, as the wine colors the royal cup like a tulip,
Soofraay presents himself before the master of crown
To ask permission to return to his homeland.

The leader and his escort make the preparations,

They sound the timpani and happily march away
In the direction of Shiraz.
All of Soofraay's wishes have been fulfilled,
All of Pars is under his dominance.
Everyone stands before him as his slave.
He has everything except the royal crown.
He reflects on the fact that he was the one
Who placed Ghobaad on the throne,
The one who celebrated him as king.
Anyone who would speak against him
Would receive a cold answer and be chased away.
He accepts taxes from all notable and noble rulers.

Ghobaad receives news from Shiraz
Of the events unfolding there, just and unjust.
He hears everyone say, "Ghobaad holds in Iran
The mere title of king and nothing more.
He is not the master of either army or treasury.
He gives neither command nor advice to us.
The world is subject to the will of Soofraay."

Some of Ghobaad's confidants relay the words:
"O powerful King, why have you settled for title?
This man's treasury is vaster than yours.
You must free the world from a festering wound.
All the inhabitants of Pars are his slaves,
All the noblemen are his servants!"

These words rattle Kay Ghobaad's heart.
He discards the memory of Soofraay's labors
And says, "If I send a host, his head will spin
And he will wish to engage in war.
I have spent my wealth to create such an opponent,
And he will cause me much grief and pain.
Everyone remembers his high deeds,
But no one is aware of his secret scheming.
I do not know of any Iranian warrior
Bold enough to march against him."

One of the advisors says to him,
"Do not fear. He will never be recognized as king.
You have servants and an army leader

Who will seize the revolving sphere,
And when Shahpoor in Rey marches off,
The heart of the wicked Soofraay will tear apart."

With this speech, Ghobaad regains hope.
He discounts Soofraay's merits, fixing only on his flaws.
He commands a worldly man to mount
On a charger and pretend to go falcon hunting,
Though he would go instead to Shahpoor's side.
There he would have him quickly saddle a horse
To travel from Rey to court.

The messenger departs with a spare horse,
As swift as autumn wind, to apply the king's command.
When the chamberlain sees him,
He addresses some questions to him,
Takes hold of the royal letter,
And presents it to his master Shahpoor.

Shahpoor, descendant of Mehrak,
Reads Ghobaad's letter and laughs,
For he is Soofraay's fiercest enemy in the world.
He gathers servants
And leads his army to Ctesiphon.

The moment he arrives with troops at court,
He is allowed access to the palace, and the king,
Upon seeing him, receives him graciously,
Seats him at the side of his turquoise throne,
And says, "I receive nothing from this crown
But a royal name, worthless in the world.
Soofraay seized all the power from me,
Leaving me with only the title of King of Kings.
In the end, I wish to rebel against this weight
Around my neck, whether it is fair or unfair.
If my brother had remained King of Iran,
It would have been a better outcome
Than being bound in oppression by Soofraay."

Shahpoor replies, "O King, do not grieve over this affair.
We must compose a serious letter right away.
You have the support of the throne's splendor,
You have your title and your birth. Tell him,

'I have gained from the royal crown
Only fatigue and an empty treasury.
You receive taxes, but I am the one to blame.
I would rather you cease to call me king.
I have sent to your side a warrior,
Because I am left in a constant state of worry.'
Once he receives the letter,
And once I am near him with my eager host,
I shall not allow him a moment of reflection;
I shall address him only with heated words."

A scribe is summoned to sit next to Shahpoor,
Who dictates the words he spoke to the king.
The scribe's reed moves as fast as wind.
The king affixes his seal to the letter,
And Shahpoor departs with a host
Consisting of the most brilliant royal troops.
He and his noblemen, hearts keen on battle,
Take the direction of the city of Shiraz.

Soofraay receives the news, quickly musters a host,
And marches off to greet Shahpoor with an escort
Of selected cavaliers dressed in armor.

They meet, and these two highborn men dismount.
Shahpoor sits next to Soofraay, and they discuss
At length various affairs, good and bad.
Then Shahpoor hands over the king's letter,
At which time the discussion turns argumentative.

After scanning the contents, the warrior pales,
His heart constricts, and his mind is troubled.
Shahpoor says to him, "We must not hide anything.
The world king commanded me to bind you in chains.
He has lamented at length before the assembly,
But you have read his letter, and you know
That the King of Kings is keen on holding on to his wishes."

The warrior replies, "The world ruler knows me well.
I have endured fatigues and hardships for him.
I journeyed from Zabolestan with an army.
I freed him from iron bonds with my courage,
Sheltering him from further calamity.

I exerted influence on the king and on noblemen.
Since I am being rewarded with chains
And since resisting you would upset you,
I am not asking for more time.
You may tie up my feet; royal chains are to my favor.

"I am innocent and feel no shame
Before the Creator and before the king's host
Since I have shed blood for him.
When the king was enchained, I swore by Yazdan
To maintain my hand clutched to the hilt of my sword,
To bring the sun down to the clouds
In the struggle until I either sacrificed my head
Or bravely severed the head of Khoshnavaz.
After having plucked him off the throne
And abandoned him to the shears of death,
Now he commands you to tie me up?
Do you think I deserve such shackles?
Are injurious words meant to be my reward?
Still, do not deviate from his command in any way.
Iron anklets are the ornaments of a brave man's feet."

Shahpoor listens, shackles Soofraay's feet,
Taps the timpani, and climbs on his horse.
He takes him away from Pars and to Ghobaad,
Who remains silent on the past
And who commands his men to take him to prison
And fling him amid the reckless captives there.
Then he asks for all of Soofraay's wealth, in terms
Of savings, treasure, and products of the earth,
To be hauled from Shiraz to Ctesiphon,
Where the man charged with the convoy
Is to hand over the lot to the treasurer.

After seven days, the king holds council
With the grand wise master on the fate of Soofraay.
The advisor says, "All of Ctesiphon is in his favor,
The army and the people, the farmers and the court.
If he remains safe and sound in Iran,
You must resign yourself and abandon kingship.
It is best to sentence to death the enemies of the king."

393

The king listens to his vizier and follows the path.
He realizes that he must keep the new, let go of the old.
He commands his men to put Soofraay to death,
Thus distressing the hearts of his family members.

3 | The Iranians Shackle Ghobaad
and Place His Brother Jaamaasp on the Throne

Once the Iranians learn that the mighty Soofraay has ceased
To breathe, a deep cry of anguish rises over the territory.
Men, women, and children lament,
Their tongues spewing a string of curses.
The land of Iran shudders; a dense fog of dust lifts
From the ground as everyone prepares their battle gear.

Each person says, "Ghobaad may not occupy
Iran's imperial throne in the absence of Soofraay."

Warriors and townspeople are in agreement,
No longer wishing to hear the name of Ghobaad.
They march to the kingly palace,
Complain about the wicked men who disparaged
And slandered Soofraay, and demand justice.
They execute the malicious evildoers
And drag their corpses out of the palace.
Then they go on the hunt for Jaamaasp,
The young brother of the king, a youth of tall stature
Whom Ghobaad raised with tenderness.
They single him out, place him on the throne,
And acclaim him as King of Iran.

They tie up Ghobaad's feet with iron chains,
Without concern for his royal rank or his birth.

Soofraay has a valuable son, intelligent, pure,
And glorious, a harmless young man named Zarmehr
Whose rank and stature make his father proud.
Ghobaad's foes hand him over to him, bound up,
Hoping that Zarmehr would avenge his father's murder.
But the gentle and pious Zarmehr
Does not raise a hand to Ghobaad to hurt him.

He bows low to the king and speaks to him,
Avoiding the subject of the crime
For which he has a right to retribution.

The world master is rather surprised,
And praises him for his compassion.
He asks forgiveness and says, "My adversaries
Shook up the motions of my star and my moon.
If I ever regain my freedom,
I shall compensate you for the wrong you suffered.
I shall liberate my heart from these afflictions,
And my eyes will shine brighter at the sight of you."

Zarmehr replies, "O King, do not distress yourself.
If my father did not fulfill his duties, it is up to his son
To endure the pain caused by his untimely death.
I am your slave, stand before you as your servant.
Should you ask, I pledge an oath never to diverge
From the loyalty that binds me to you."

Ghobaad's soul is appeased by Zarmehr,
Whose words return a sense of joy to him.

4 | Ghobaad Flees With Zarmehr and Takes Shelter With the Hephthalites

Ghobaad reveals his secret: "I do not wish to conceal
From you what I have on my mind, my strategy.
Five people are aware of my secret,
And I shall speak of it to no one else.
We shall include the five should the need arise.
If you free my feet from these metal bonds,
I shall be assured that you approve of my designs."

Zarmehr, whose intentions are pure,
Immediately obeys and takes off the chains.
They leave the city during the dark night and
Advance into the desert, away from hostile eyes.

They journey to the land of the Hephthalites,
Tormented by worry and searching for their way.

In this manner, seven distraught men
Travel as fast as dust and arrive in Ahvaz.
They enter the rich borough in haste
And dismount at the house of a noble landowner
To finally rest and breath at ease.

The farmer has a beautiful daughter
Who wears a diadem of musk on her head.
The sight of her moon face confuses the young king,
And his mind empties of sense and reason.
Rashly, he says to Zarmehr, "I need you to communicate
The secret I hold in my heart to our master.
Ask him for her hand in marriage."

Zarmehr relays the message and says,
"If this lovely maiden is not yet promised,
I can propose an excellent husband for her.
Such a union will bring you many rewards,
One of which is the rulership of Ahvaz."

The distinguished landowner replies,
"My daughter is not committed to anyone.
She will receive in marriage any man enthralled by her."

Zarmehr returns to Ghobaad's side and says,
"This moon may be yours with good wishes!
You found her unexpectedly, and she pleased you."

The valiant Ghobaad calls the moon-faced beauty
And seats her on his lap. Though he has only
One ring on him, it has a priceless stone set into it.
He hands it to her and says, "Keep this ring.
The day will come when I shall come to claim it."

Ghobaad remains in the village for seven days,
And on the eighth day, he takes the road.
He travels to the King of the Hephthalites
And recounts to him all that occurred
And the Iranians' wicked acts.

The king says, "It appears that your crime
Against Khoshnavaz brings you distress today.
I shall give you an army of crown-bearers provided that,

If you enter into possession of treasure and crown,
The land of Chaghan, its wealth and throne fall under my rule.
Chaghan will be mine, while Iran will be yours.
And you will observe the terms of our accord."

Ghobaad replies to the oppressor with a smile,
"I have no wish to ever claim this land.
I shall send you an innumerable army when you so desire.
What do I care about the land of Chaghan?"

The King of the Hephthalites offers the world master
Herds, weapons, and all the riders in his army.
Ghobaad accepts thirty thousand
Sword-bearing, illustrious heroes and cavaliers,
And marches from the land of the Hephthalites to Ahvaz,
Filling the world with the rumors of his adventures.

5 | Ghobaad Returns From the Land of the Hephthalites

Approaching the house of the landowner,
Ghobaad sees groups of men rejoicing, who say,
"May your child bring good luck to your majesty!
Your mate has given birth tonight to a son
Who appears identical to the moon."

At these words, he joyously enters the home.
The child is given the name of Kesra.
Ghobaad asks the farmer, "O blessed man,
Tell me about your lineage; reveal your origins."

The other replies, "I am a descendant of Fereydoon,
The hero, who snatched royalty from Zahaak's race.
Both my father and my grandfather disclosed it to me.
We particularly revere Fereydoon."

Ghobaad grows happier than the day when
He lowered the Kianian crown on his head.
He asks for a litter to be equipped in which
He places the queen, and they take the road.

He guides his convoy toward Ctesiphon,
Irritated with the way the Iranians treated him.

Aging noblemen of the land gather,
As well as men celebrated for their wisdom.
They say, "We are subject to endless challenges
As we are between two highborn kings.
Armies from Rum and Chin will soon arrive
To shed copious blood in our land."

One man emerges to address the assembly:
"O noblemen, illustrious and famed warriors,
We must present ourselves before Ghobaad
In the hopes that he will forget the past.
We shall bring Jaamaasp, a ten-year-old child,
So that he may convert the threat of a grail
Falling over our heads into a shower pearls.
Let us attempt to, together,
Fend off pillage, bloodshed, and war."

They approach Ghobaad and say,
"O King of regal lineage, if you have
Wounded many hearts, if men have washed
Their eyes in the waters of temerity, you may now act
As you please, for the world king is world master."
Everyone rushes to him with dim hearts,
On foot and covered in dust.

The king forgives the crimes of the noblemen,
And their pleas save them from a death sentence.
They praise him for showing mercy to Jaamaasp.

Ghobaad sits on the Kianian throne,
And Jaamaasp stands by to serve him.
He hands over the affairs of the kingdom
To Zarmehr and seats him next to him.
The empire submits to his sovereignty,
And the world fills with justice and prosperity.

Some time passes thus until Kesra matures
And becomes a valiant and proud young man.
Ghobaad entrusts his son to learned men
As the bright new branch is fit to bear fruit.

He organizes the affairs of Iran and Tooran,
Raising the diadem of power to the vault of sky.

Then he leads his army to Rum, which he fashions
And molds to his will as easily as a ball of wax,
Turning everything into a wasteland.
The inhabitants of two cities plead for protection:
One city is Hendia and the other Faarghin.[64]
He teaches everyone the *Zand Avesta* and the true faith,
Erects fire temples, establishes his power,
And institutes the festivals of Nowruz and Saddeh.

He fixes the royal palaces in Mada'in[65]
And performs many deeds, good and bad.
He builds a great city between Ahvaz and Pars
And lays the foundation for a hospital.
He names the city Ghobaad,
Which the Arabs today call Awan.
Everywhere water canals are designed,
And the earth becomes a place of peace and serenity.

6 | Ghobaad Adopts the Religion of Mazdak

An illustrious physician arrives by the name of Mazdak,
Eloquent, learned, intelligent, and ambitious.
The valiant Ghobaad lends an ear to his speeches.
Intrigued, he makes him royal vizier and treasurer.

Clouds disappear from the sky, and the land of Iran
Endures the absence of any form of precipitation.
The great drought causes famine and desolation.
Noblemen continuously knock at Ghobaad's door
To beg for water and bread. Mazdak assures them
That the king will show them the path to hope.

He runs to Ghobaad and says, "O virtuous King,
I shall address you a question, hoping you will reply."

◇◇◇◇◇◇◇◇◇◇◇◇◇
64 Hendia and Faarghin: Two ancient cities in Rum situated in today's Turkey; Hendia is today Diyarbakir.
65 Mada'in: An ancient city on the Tigris River between Ctesiphon and Seleucia.

Ghobaad says, "Speak and enlighten me."

Mazdak says, "A man bitten by a snake
Finds his life threatened, having no access to the antidote
That may cure him. Another man is in possession
Of a supply of twenty dirhams[66] worth of antidote."

The king replies, "The one with the antidote
Is a murderer to be executed at my gates.
The family of the bitten man must seize him
So that they can avenge the death of their kin."

Mazdak rises and goes to the people seeking help
And says, "I have spoken to the king.
I have addressed him many questions.
Tomorrow I shall show you the path to justice."

The brave men depart to return the next morning,
Mouths full of words, hearts full of anguish.

At the sight of them in the distance, Mazdak rushes
To Ghobaad: "O victorious King, eloquent, vigilant,
Powerful and majestic, you are worthy of the throne.
I revealed to you a case yesterday,
And your reply reopened the door of wisdom.
May I address you again? For you are my guide."

Ghobaad replies, "Speak!
I reap the benefit of your words."

Mazdak says, "O renowned King, suppose someone
Is enchained and barred from eating, he will certainly
Have to die and give up his sweet life in utter misery.
How will you punish the one who, having bread,
Refuses to share it with the prisoner?
Tell me, what is your verdict for a wise and virtuous man?"

The king replies, "He is a wretched man.
It is just as if he is responsible for someone's death."

◇◇◇◇◇◇◇◇◇◇◇◇◇
66 Dirham: In this instance it is not the gold coin but a unit of measure equivalent to
160 grams.

Mazdak kisses the ground, leaves the king's side,
Positions himself at the palace gate, and says to the crowd,
"Wherever you find hidden grains of wheat or corn,
You may take your share, and if a fee is demanded,
You have the right to destroy the village."

Everyone who is famished engages in plunder
And snatches a ration of corn for himself.
Soon not even a grain of wheat remains either
In the city's storehouses or in the royal stockpiles.
The supervisors approach the vigilant world king
To tell him that the royal attics are being looted
Upon Mazdak's insistence and offense.

Ghobaad summons the eloquent man
And questions him at length on the pillage.

Mazdak replies, "May you always live in joy!
May your words serve as nourishment to wisdom!
I only gently repeated to the Iranians
What I heard from his majesty's mouth.
I recounted to the world king
The story of the serpent's bite and the venom,
And of the city man who possesses the antidote.
The king replied that if the man bitten by the serpent
Dies without having received a portion of the antidote,
The one who spills blood must be held accountable.
When there are starving people, bread is the antidote,
But no one will ask for the cure when one is well fed.
If you are a just king, the grain in your attics is worthless.
Many men died of hunger with full stockpiles of supplies."

Mazdak's just words agitate Ghobaad's head.
The king questions him and listens to his replies.
He finds his mind and heart full of words
Spoken by prophets, sages, and righteous leaders.
The effects of his discussion surpass all measure.
Large crowds gather around him
Of men who strayed off the right path.

He says to them, "A man who is empty-handed
Is equal to the most wealthy man.
No one must possess in excess.

401

The rich must be the warp and the poor the weft.
Equality must reign across the world.
The superfluous in wealth is an illicit thing.
We must share women, homes, and properties.
The poor man is equal to the rich man.
I shall reconcile all of this with my pure faith
So that we can distinguish the good from the vile.
Yazdan will curse anyone who follows a different path."

He treats the poor as equals, whether old or juvenile.
He takes from one and gives to another.
Wise men are distraught by his actions.
But the king, under the influence of Mazdak,
Adopts his faith, thinking that
It will make the world a better place.

He is happy to seat him to his right,
And the army knows little about this new vizier.
The poor, those who earn their keep by their labor,
Gather around him as his doctrine renews the world,
And no one dares complain or seek vengeance.
The wealthy, forced to relinquish their fortunes
To the poor, discard the path of virtue.

7 | Kesra Executes Mazdak and His Followers

One early morning, Mazdak marches to the king
And says, "A great number of our loyal chiefs
And pure-hearted subjects arrive from different provinces.
Shall I bring them to you, or shall I dismiss them?"

Ghobaad commands his vizier to welcome them.
Mazdak says to the powerful king,
"This place is rather inadequate for such a big crowd.
They will have a hard time carving a path to the king.
It is better to go into the field to review them."

The king asks for his throne to be carried
From the kingly palace to the plain.
Three thousand followers of Mazdak arrive
And present themselves in joy before the king.

Mazdak says to the world king,
"Your majesty is above wisdom and benediction!
Know that Kesra does not share our faith.
What right does he have to stray?
We must demand a handwritten pledge
Of his renouncement to his own wicked beliefs.
Five things provoke us to deviate from rightness,
And the wise man cannot find more to add:
They are jealousy, hatred, fury, need,
And the fifth, greed, which governs men.
Should you effectively vanquish these five deevs,
The path to the World Creator will manifest for you.
These five elements contribute to the fact
That women and wealth condemn men
And lead them to squander the true faith.
One must combine them to avoid perdition.
Through them arise jealousy, greed, and need,
Traits that covertly join anger and vengeance.
At that moment, the deev will take advantage
And turn the heads of sages away from virtue.
Therefore, we must unite women and wealth."

After speaking thus, Mazdak takes Kesra's hand,
Confounding the latter who withdraws in anger and
Indignation, and moves his gaze away from Mazdak.

Ghobaad smiles and says to Mazdak,
"Why do you pay attention to Kesra's wrath?"

Mazdak says, "He has adopted a different religion."

The king tells Kesra, "It is not right
For you to deviate from the true belief."

Kesra replies, "If you allow me time,
I shall prove the falsity of such an opinion.
Once pretense and perversity are exposed,
The truth will shine brightly in your eyes."

Mazdak says to him, "How many days
Do you ask of the world-illuminating king?"

Kesra replies, "I require five months.

I shall provide a reply during the sixth month."

Everyone agrees, and they return.
The noble king enters his palace.
Kesra dispatches learned men to assist him.
One of them goes to Khorreh-yeh Ardeshir
To summon the aging Hormoz to court.
Mehr Aazar, who dwells in Pars, travels
From Estakhr with thirty companions.
These wise and mature sages, seekers of knowledge,
Sit together to deliberate at length
And to communicate to Kesra their thoughts.

Kesra listens to them, then goes to Ghobaad
And speaks to him of Mazdak:
"The time has come for me to study the true faith,
And if Mazdak is on the right path
And if the doctrine of Zoroaster is false,
I shall adopt the religion of Mazdak.
If the path of Fereydoon is not the right one,
The world will be freed from the *Zand Avesta*,
Mazdak's doctrines will prevail,
And men will have no other guide but him.
But if his words are replete with falsehoods,
If he does not walk the path of Yazdan, the holy,
Then you must turn away in disgust from him
And reject his unfavorable rules.
Deliver him to me, with those who share his principles,
And may they be stripped of their brains and skins!"

He takes Zarmehr, Khorraad, Faraaeen, Bandooy,
And Behzaad as witnesses and returns to his palace,
Determined to observe his commitment.

At daybreak, when the sun displays its crown
And the earth is a vast sea of ivory,
The son of the eloquent world king
Departs with wise and noble men.
They proceed to the palace,
All the while discussing, in search of the true path.

One of the wise men, able to charm hearts,
Presents himself before Ghobaad and the assembly

And opens the door of discourse with Mazdak:
"O truth-seeker, you have introduced a new world faith.
You have grouped together women and wealth.
But how will a son know his father,
And how will a father recognize his son?
If men are equal in the world,
If no distinction is made between the meek and mighty,
Who will wish to serve or to exercise power?
Who will work for you and me?
How will virtuous men keep the malevolent at bay?
What will happen to the fortune of the deceased
If king and craftsman stand on equal footing?

"The world will become a barren desert,
And such a calamity must not be the fate of Iran.
When everyone is master, where are the wage earners?
When everyone has wealth, where are the treasurers?
Never has the founder of a religion spoken
On subjects of this nature, so radical and strange.
You must secretly be out of your mind
For leading men into hell, discounting evil acts."

Angry, Ghobaad speaks on the subject of justice.
The noble Kesra joins him,
And the heart of the faithless man
Grows disquieted as the gathering shouts,
"May Mazdak find his way into exile!
May this destroyer of Yazdan's religion
Be banished from the illustrious court!"

The world master is disgusted by the doctrine.
His head fills with grief for past deeds.
He abandons Mazdak to Kesra,
Along with three thousand notable men
Who follow Mazdak's law and deceitful faith.

The king says to his son, "Proceed as you deem fit
On this matter, and never speak Mazdak's name again."

There is in Kesra's palace a garden,
Its walls rising higher than the mountain crests.
He asks for a ditch to be hollowed out along the walls
Where the faithless men are to be planted like trees,

Feet in the air and heads below, firmly buried.

Then Kesra says to Mazdak, "Go to my beautiful garden.
The seeds you have sown are bearing bitter fruit.
You will see trees like no one has ever seen."

Mazdak opens the garden door,
Hoping to find an orchard of fruit trees.
But at the sight of the scene before him, he cries loudly,
Loses consciousness, and falls to the ground.

Kesra asks for high gallows to be erected
From which dangles a coiled rope.
He hangs the wretched man alive from it, head below.
Then he kills him with a shower of arrows.
If you are a sensible man, avoid Mazdak's path.

The court's noblemen are relieved to return
To life with their women and wealth,
And to hold on to their most precious belongings.

Ghobaad feels ashamed for a long time and
Only speaks Mazdak's name alongside a string of curses.
He gives generously to the poor
And sends offerings to the fire temples.

The king is so delighted to witness his offspring, Kesra,
Bearing the fruits of wisdom that he consults him
And follows his guidance on all matters.

8 | Ghobaad Makes Kesra His Successor, and the Noblemen Name Him Anushiravan[67]

After forty years of rule, the anticipation
And the sorrow of his dying day
Seeps into Ghobaad's heart.
He composes a letter on silk
In beautiful and elegant Pahlavi lettering.
He begins in praise of the Justice Giver,

◇◇◇◇◇◇◇◇◇◇◇◇◇
67 Anushiravan: Meaning gentle soul.

"Who grants faith, wisdom, and skill;
Under Whose command all things flow unfailingly,
Whether beneath the gaze of men or secretly.
No one knows the limits of Yazdan's power;
No one fails after having submitted to divine will.
Once you see Ghobaad's note, consult the sages.
I surrender my glorious throne to Kesra.
He will be, after my death, fortune's favorite.
I hope that the World Creator is pleased with him.
May his enemies' hearts fill with anguish!
By this seal, we ask our wise men, our subjects,
Our celebrated leaders, never to stray from my command.
It will aid you on the path to happiness and wealth."

He affixes his golden seal on the letter
And hands it to the wise Raam Barzeen.

At this time, Ghobaad is eighty years old.
And as old as he is, he does not desire death.
Who in the world is ever content with its prospect?
Who is ever cognizant of his own fate?

He expires and leaves the world vacant of his presence,
His pains, his joys, his splendor having passed.
Who can ever profit from his amassed treasure,
Since he must leave the world empty-handed?

They wrap the king's body in brocade.
They call for rosewater, musk, camphor, and wine.
They build a royal tomb and bring
A gilded throne and a kingly crown.
They place the king on the golden throne
And permanently wall the entrance to the vault.
Ghobaad's face disappears forever.
It is as if he traveled the world as a breath of air.
How can you trust this ancient dome of sky?
In the end, infallibly, it will destroy you.

At the end of a period of mourning, the grand
Wise master places the royal letter on the throne.
The noble and wise men of Iran gather to read the letter,
And Ghobaad's designated successor accedes the throne.

Kesra takes his new seat, observes his father's rites
With dignity, splendor, grace, and royal majesty.
Everyone acclaims him as the new king;
Everyone offers him faith and homage;
The era and the earth submit to his rule.
The world is renewed by his crown,
Sheep and wolf drink at a common spring,
The resplendent throne spreads joy,
And men shower him with blessings:
"May this king occupy the throne eternally!
May his glory surpass the glory of Jamsheed!"

Because of his kindness, his justice, his dignity,
His vast knowledge, and his piety,
He is given the name of Anushiravan.
Young is his face, and new is his affection.

The story of Kay Ghobaad comes to an end.
I shall now celebrate Kesra's name and memory.

9 | The Poet's Lament Over His Old Age

"Alas, O slender cypress tree, seducer of hearts,
Why have you surrendered to poverty?
You were once happy, majestic, beautiful.
How did your shining heart allow entry to fear?"

The cypress tree replies,
"I was happy as long as I was young.
But I now surrender to my enemy's force.
At the age of sixty, I have relinquished my power.
Be wise and do not put up a struggle.
Old age has a dragon's tail and a lion's claws.
It grinds and mangles its prey.
Its voice is that of thunder;
Its force is that of a rhinoceros.
In one hand it holds the necessities of life,
In the other it clutches death.
It bends the waist of the once-charming cypress tree,
It brings hues of amber to a lily complexion,
It converts the flower of Arghavan to saffron.

After the saffron comes intense suffering.
It burdens with chains the feet of runners
And degrades the most beautiful body.

"My freshwater pearls have tarnished;
My noble cypress waist is now curved;
My eyes of narcissus, once black and brilliant,
Shed tears of languor and weariness.
My heart, once happy and carefree,
Is filled with grief and causes me great misery.
The moment the child is weaned of milk,
Death rears its head, and we must call him old.

"The reign of Anushiravan lasts forty-eight years.
You have crossed the threshold of sixty years,
Leaving youth behind. Consider the end in all
That you take on, and do not tear your heart apart
With the senseless need to glorify yourself."

PART TWENTY–SIX

The Forty-Eight-Year Reign
of Kesra Anushiravan

1 | Anushiravan Speaks to the Iranian Leaders

Once Kesra is settled on the ivory throne
Bearing the heart-dazzling crown on his head,
The leaders of the earth gather to confer.

The king begins by celebrating the Just Giver,
Who spreads joy through the world:
"May our hearts be full of homage and affection
For the Creator of sky, Giver of joy and misery,
Shame and glory, grief and happiness;
By Whose order the sun shines in the sky;
From whom we attain power and majesty.
Let us follow divine guidance and respire divine will.
Anyone seated on the throne of power,
Anyone who rules with justice will profit himself.
Anyone who surrenders to evil thoughts
Will ultimately suffer from evil himself.
No one is aware of the heart's inner reflections,
And I cannot find my way on this narrow path.
I shall reply to your requests as best I can.
When a king acts with justice, everyone benefits.

"Do not postpone today's work for tomorrow.
Who knows how fate will unfold?
The rose garden may be in full bloom today,
But if you wish to pluck its flowers,
They may start fading tomorrow.
When your body is at its optimum strength,
Think of illness, pain, and misfortune.
Remember that the day of death follows life
And that in the face of death we are as weak
And hopeless as an autumn leaf
Drifting in the wind.

"Every time you act halfheartedly,
You will execute your plans poorly.
Should jealousy rule over your heart,
You will succumb to a deadly illness.

Should material longings straddle your wisdom,
No witness is required to avow for your folly.
The idle man who speaks endlessly earns little respect.
Corruption further obscures your path,
While the road to righteousness is a narrow one.
The work you excel at will not prosper
If you put weight and sluggishness into it.
Should your tongue espouse lies,
The sky's throne will not share its sparkle with you.
Lies and deceit stem from privation,
And all we can do is weep for them.

"Should the king always be the first to rise,
He will be secure and safe from the actions
Of his adversaries and will enjoy good health.
Should the king exhibit justice and generosity,
The world will fill with beauty and abundance.
But if he infuses perversity into his strategies,
His nourishment will have to be bitter squash
And his beverage will be blood.
Each of you in this assembly
Who has heard what I said out loud,
Understand and pay attention to every point,
And fortune will always attend to you.
We have witnessed many a crown-bearer;
We have opted for the path of wisdom and justice.
Yet in all matters, you must obey the vizier
Who is a mediator in all our deeds, good and bad.
I shall blame the vizier should he hide from me
The fact that he has barred entry to my court
To someone who rushed here with a fair demand.

"I shall not refuse wages to my court's workforce
And my army's valiant cavaliers. They must be paid
In a timely, proper manner to maintain name and honor.
Humanity and righteousness must infuse all actions,
And we should never consent at the expense of justice.
Any Iranian who comes to my court
To tend to me with sense and discretion
Will be rewarded gently and with vast wealth.
Conversely, should he inflict
An unjust act to one of my servants,

Should he not behave with sense and piety,
He will suffer the consequences.
Moreover, one must not be concerned or feel sad
For the fate of a man who lacks benevolence.

"Apply yourselves to obey the Creator's command
And have no fear for us.
The Creator is a sovereign king above all kings,
Victorious and commanding World Master;
Crafter of the blazing Sun and the shining Moon;
Our Guide on the path of justice;
World Owner and ultimate Judge
Who is above and beyond all thought;
Who crafted time and space, earth and sky;
Who has infused our souls and hearts with affection;
Thanks to whom we spread justice and generosity.
Support of your crown and throne; our mate in prayer.
Your hearts shine bright with our affection.
May the hearts and eyes of our enemies
Be fixed on the king's command!
Good health and happiness originate from divine order;
Everything from a strand of wood to the seven skies,
Fire, water, and the dark earth, witnesses divine existence
And thus bring peace and connection to your soul.
Everything that is worthy of praise is by divine order.
Every worship must be addressed to Yazdan."

The assembly is astonished at Anushiravan's declaration.
The leaders rise and shower him with renewed blessings.

2 | Anushiravan Divides His Empire Into Four Sections and Regulates Tax Collection

The King of Kings summons his wise men
And discusses world governance with them.
He divides the world into four sections
And attributes a flourishing nation to each section.

At first he speaks of Khorasan
In a way that brings joy to the hearts of noblemen.
The second section consists of Ghom and Isfahan,

The seat of powerful men and the home of leaders.
It includes a portion of Aazar Abadegan,[68]
Which the Persians take pride in expanding.
The insightful king annexes Armenia
All the way to Ardabil and the land of Gilan.

The third section covers Pars and Ahvaz
To the edge of Khazar,[69] from east to west.
The fourth section is formed by the lands
Of Iraq and Rum, a beautifully cultivated empire.

Any man who labors with his hands
In these four sections is offered a treasure,
And everyone profusely blesses the king.

As for other rulers, whether they consider
Themselves more or less powerful,
They withdraw their parts in the harvests,
And no one escapes paying tribute.

While the king's portion consists of either a third
Or a quarter, Ghobaad had fixed it at one tenth.
He wished to reduce it to less than that,
For he sought to render the poor equal to the rich.
But fate did not give him the chance or the time.
Do not trust the waters of the sea,
For the whale dwells there.

Once on the ivory throne,
Kesra quickly forgives the tribute of one tenth.
Sages and noblemen, leaders and wise men,
Ultimately the entire empire convenes,
And the king distributes the earth.

A tax is raised for every product dirham,
So that farmers will not fall into a state of distress.
Should there be a shortage of seed or cattle,
Those in want receive from the royal treasury,
Thus preventing their plots from becoming wastelands.
No taxes are demanded for unsown fields,

68 Aazar Abadegan: Same as today's Azerbaijan.
69 Khazar: Caspian Sea.

And old customs are abolished on this point.

The value of the tax for six fruit vines is one dirham,
And the same decree is applied to palm tree plantations.
Olive trees, walnut trees, and fruit-bearing trees
In autumn are valued at one dirham per every ten trees.
One is then exempt from further duty
For the span of one year. Fruit produced
From spring to the month of Khordaad
Does not fall subject to taxation.

Those who have money but no land
And who do not endure the hardships of seeding
And harvesting pay four to ten yearly dirhams.
Gardeners pay easy tribute three times a year,
And envoys carry a part of the contribution
To the royal treasury four times a year.

Scribes, secretaries, and employees
In the treasury's office also pay tribute.
Once a list is drawn of all the taxes,
Three registers are given to the grand wise master.
The latter authenticates the first one with a stamp
And returns it to the treasurer. The second is sent
To district administrators and chiefs in the provinces.
The third one remains in the possession
Of the grand wise master, who finds in it
The general account of capitation and taxes.
Everything falls under his command,
From taxes to tributes, from seeds to harvests.

Agents are scattered throughout the empire
To keep him apprised of all actions, good and bad.
Everywhere he makes justice reign;
Everywhere he cultivates untilled lands.
Men, great and small, sleep soundly in the desert.
Wolf and sheep join each other at the water trough.

3 | Anushiravan's Letter to His Workers

Anushiravan writes a letter in Pahlavi.
I await your gratitude as I share its contents with you.
It begins thus, "From the hand of the mighty
King of Kings, Kesra, worshipper of Yazdan,
The One who proffered the throne and crown on him.
This fertile branch of the tree of Ghobaad
Placed the crown of power on his head.
The Just Creator endowed him with glory,
And as a result, nations flourish under his authority.
I address countless greetings to the administrators
Of tributes and taxes, as well as to those who serve
Beneath the shelter of his majesty and his crown.
I shall reward them if their merit matches their births.
I begin my discourse in praise of the World Creator.
Know that a sensible and insightful man
Is the one who worships the Justice Giver,
The one who knows that Yazdan does not need us,
The One to whom all secrets are revealed,
The One Who places above need
Those who are meant to accede to grandeur.

"Yazdan, supreme Just Ruler for all eternity,
Above most things sublime,
Commanded me to spread justice.
King and subject stand on equal footing
Before Yazdan, as slaves of divine will.
From the depths of the earth to the glorious sky,
From the sun to the dark and somber dust,
Everything must submit to divine rule.
The ant's imprint is testimony to the fact that we are
Servants of Yazdan, Who is our ultimate Sovereign.
We are directed on the path of righteousness.
The culpable one is the deev who led us astray
And tempted us on the road to perversity and ruin.

"If my part in this vast world
Had been a garden, a field, and a palace,
My heart would only seek justice and affection.
I would lead all my affairs with awareness.
But since Yazdan the holy entrusted me

With, as my kingdom, the surface of the earth,
From west to east, from above to below,
From the shining sun to the dark dust on earth,
I shall exert only justice and affection,
No matter how irritating my affairs may be.
I shall never allow a frown to crease my brow.

"When the shepherd is careless and the field is vast,
The sheep cannot be extricated from the wolf's grasp.
The sun must shine in the celestial vault
Only with justice and tenderness on its subjects,
Whether they are farmers, servants, or fire-worshippers,
Whether they are on firm land or on ships on the sea,
In the light of day or at the hour of sleep.
Whether they are merchants, bearers of loads of dirhams,
Dripping with pearls or musk,
The sun must shine in the dome of sky
Only with justice and affection.
Such has been the custom of our race and our family:
The son received the crown from his father,
Justice and generosity reigned in the world
And no less in secret than in public.

"I established taxes on trees
For the needs of the throne and crown.
May life be auspicious to you upon receipt of this letter!
I swear by Yazdan, who gave me diadem and majesty,
That, if one of you asks for a single dirham more,
If one of you commits an unjust act for the duration
Of even one breath, I shall have him sawn in half.
In this way, the Creator's wrath will shake
The one who brings fruit to the seed of evil.

"Hold this rule and this letter before your eyes.
Do not deviate from the law and the faith.
Every four months, ask for tribute kindly and fairly.
You will not demand taxes from certain lands:
Lands lain to waste by locusts, lands where the sun
Beats down on naked ground, lands where snow and
Wind raze sown fields, or where spring rains fail to fall
And drought casts a gloom over the countryside.
You will take from the treasury and pay the salaries

Of farmers who have lost their crops.
If there are fields abandoned due to a death
And there is no family member or ally able to work,
Lest it should remain uncultivated
Beneath the shadow of the King of Iran,
My enemy will drag my name in shame reproaching me
That, under my rule, my nation is desolate and in ruins,
And the shadow of my wings has failed to protect.

"Draw the necessary aid from my treasury.
Thank heavens I have no need for it.
If the one responsible for the distribution neglects
This difficult task, I shall hang him alive at the gallows,
At the place where he stands,
Whether he is a powerful man or a humble subject.

"Influential kings of long ago had other customs.
The good and bad was in the hands of employees,
And the world was trampled by horses' hooves.
They foolishly discarded wisdom
And continuously sought to amass more wealth.
Justice is my most prized possession,
Farmers are my fighters,
And the sight of dinars does not draw my gaze.
I would rather acquire the affection of the world
Through my justice and reward highborn men
Who deserve it than to battle evildoers
Who wish to seize my provinces and my seat.

"An army leader who sells his men for gold
Will never find access to my court.
Places of honor are reserved for just and merciful men
Who abide by the law and follow the righteous path.
I shall deem unworthy one of my shrewd workers who lies.
I care not for those who lack justice.
There is no difference between a leopard and a tyrant.
But anyone who seeks the path of the Creator and purifies
His soul in the waters of wisdom will obtain power
At my court and will be honored by wise men.
Yazdan will reward him with access to paradise
For having sown the seeds of righteousness.

"We have no need for wealth

That makes one curse and lose his soul.
When one lives from the flesh of others,
One devours even their skin.
The leopard is more worthy than such a king
Who has no shame and does not observe the law.
The door of righteousness is open to us.
Why then knock at the door of perdition?
Performing evil acts in secret and kind acts
In public to aggrandize your esteem before me
Will not receive divine sanction
And will not be a title of distinction at court.
Yazdan and I applaud the hearts in which justice
And affection are interwoven as warp and weft.
O King, if you are just, you will leave a memory behind.
A ruler who brings prosperity on earth
Will be eternally praised and blessed.
The wise and awakened man is the one
Who expresses gratitude to the World Creator."

4 | Anushiravan Asks the Wise Babak to Report on the State of the Army

Of all the kings, possessors of thrones and crowns,
Powerful by virtue of their treasures and hosts,
None has proved himself more just than Anushiravan.
May his manes remain young forever!
None has been mightier, more worthy of throne
And crown, and none has been more insightful.

He holds a wise man near, named Babak,
Who is prudent, foreseeing, and joyful.
He puts him in charge of reviewing the army
And reporting back to him at court.
He commands him to build a tall and wide
Pavilion to exceed the height of the palace gate.
A carpet worthy of a king is spread out
On which sit the indispensable staff members.

A proclamation rises from Babak's pavilion:
"O illustrious men, skillful in battle,
Prepare to mount your stallions!

421

Those of you who receive wages from the king,
Present yourselves at the palace gate,
Braced in helmets of steel and coats of mail,
And wielding bull-headed maces."

Crowds gather before Babak's enclosure.
The air turns dark with the riders' dust.
Babak reviews the troops, but failing
To see the king's banner and the crowned head,
He exits, mounts his horse, and dismisses everyone.

The sky continues its rotation, and as the brilliant sun
Reveals its face, a voice is heard at the king's door:
"O mace-bearers of Iran's army,
Come one and all to Babak's gate in full attire,
Equipped with armor, bow, and noose."

They arrive with their spears, helms, and mail.
The dust of their motions climbs to the clouds.
Babak looks around at the troops,
But aware of the king's absence, he says,
"Despite the good will and affection
You have displayed in your duty today,
Return victorious and happy."

On the third day, someone proclaims, "O illustrious,
Glorious noblemen, no one may present himself
At this door without helmet or breastplate.
Come so that the inspector may confirm your name.
Those of you who enjoy crowns, royal honor,
Power, and high thrones, know that this affair
Is not one of airs and lordliness,
And you must not feel ashamed to participate."

Kesra, King of Kings, lends an ear to Babak's call.
He smiles, asks for his armor and headdress,
And appears before Babak with his royal standard,
His Rumi helmet of steel, and his coat of mail
Attached to the collar with a multitude of knots.
He wields a bull-headed mace and
Displays four arrows of poplar wood.
His bow hangs on his arm, his noose on the saddle's hook,
And he sports a golden belt around his waist.

He leaps on his horse, flexes his thighs,
Presses his heavy mace to his shoulder,
Swings the reins to the left and to the right,
And flaunts his equipment and his equestrian skills.

Babak observes him with delight.
He approaches the King of Kings and says,
"Greetings, O King! May you live forever,
And may wisdom be your soul's provision!
You bring world order with your sense of justice.
We shall remember the way you fulfill your duty.
It is a bold discourse on the part of a servant,
But I do not believe you will act against justice.
Now swing the reins once again to the right
For a new testimony of your brilliance."

Kesra launches his horse right and left,
With the vigor of Aazargoshasp.
Babak continues to watch him in wonder,
Invoking the name of the Creator multiple times.

One cavalier earns one thousand dirhams,
Another two thousand, but no one
Receives in excess of four thousand.
Babak allocates one dirham more to the king.

A shout is heard at the office door:
"Bring the horse of the leader of brave fighters,
The world cavalier, the illustrious king!"

Anushiravan laughs heartily,
For young he is and young is his fortune.

Babak presents himself before the illustrious prince
Once again and says, "O noble King, today
I may have taken some liberties as your servant,
But my heart clung to righteousness and a sense of duty.
May his majesty disregard my harshness!
The virtuous man is allowed to show some callousness!
Happy is the one in search of virtue!"

The king replies, "Never stray off the path of honesty.
When one minds oneself, one breaks the heart of virtue.

423

I honor your actions, and my mind refers to the self.
I ponder the best strategies to overcome our foes in battle."

Babak replies, "Never will the seal and diadem
Witness a ruler of your stature.
Never did a painter see in all of Iran
Hands and reins like those of your majesty.
The sublime dome of sky turns according to your wishes.
May your heart always dwell in joy
And your body remain free of suffering!"

Anushiravan says to his wise master,
"Old men are returned to youth by my justice.
A king must always seek to leave behind
A memory of his piety and virtue.
Why should we exert so much effort?
Why should we amass vast amounts of wealth?
Why should we attach our souls to this transient dwelling?
Better enjoy life, since our stay may not be long.
World affairs have burdened me with much worry,
Yet I have kept my trepidations private.
I reflected on the fact that my royal crown has enemies
And that Ahriman prevails all around me.
I told myself,
          'If I call my troops from the provinces,
          No host will unite in the absence of wealth,
          And I will gain nothing but further hardship.
          But if the poor must suffer,
          I shall have to renounce my own desires.'

"After much inner reflection,
I have sent a letter to warriors, insightful sages,
And independent, illustrious noblemen so that I may
Urge them to raise their sons with the intent to serve
And the intent to send them to the battlefield
In war armor in order to gain honor and glory.
They must learn to master their hands, their bridles,
And their stirrups in climbs and descents.
They must know how to battle
With mace, sword, bow and arrow.
A youth who learns nothing is as good as nothing,
Even if he were a descendant of Aarash.

424

I have sent a review inspector from my court
To every province to distribute money to noblemen.
The evaluations lasted forty days.
Ambitious youths presented themselves with weapons,
Seized the money, and spend many days in joy.
I was forced to cover the world with armed men
To determine who would come to my attack.
I have more weapons, more knowledge,
And more power than any of the ancient kings."

The wise master listens to the words
And blesses the throne and crown.

5 | Anushiravan Advises the Iranians and the Rulers to Accept His Directions

As the sun displays its dazzling face
And the revolving dome of sky opens its garden gate,
Chasing away the two black loops of night's mane,
Anushiravan sits on his throne smiling,
Joy in his heart along with fervor for his new empire.

A voice proclaims at the royal gates:
"Anyone who seeks the path of justice
May come to the court of Anushiravan,
A blessed king who inspires his subjects to rejoice."

Justice seekers from around the world flock to the court.
The king speaks to them in a loud voice:
"Hold Yazdan the pure as your sole support,
For Yazdan is Creator and Guide in both worlds.
May my throne and crown fail to instill fear!
Everyone has free access to my person, always.
Anyone, at any time of day and night,
May come to me and speak unreservedly.
Whether I entertain myself with wine or I am
In consultation with advisors, whether I play
A game of polo or am engaged in the hunt,
You may always approach my seat.

"Whether I am asleep or awake, whether I am at work
Or at play, never dismiss a person who seeks my help.
No one must go to bed displeased with his king,
Having failed to obtain the object of his desire.
My heart will be most content on days
When I have extracted someone
From pain or from any form of persecution.
Heaven forbid one of my workers,
Troops or servants falls asleep aggrieved,
For such a thing would bring me misfortune.
Yazdan will demand an account of my deeds,
No matter how insignificant or how undisclosed.
Aside from accepted taxes and tributes
Recorded by my wise master in his books,
I shall not demand any gold or silver.
Therefore, you may go to sleep
With your mind at peace, having nothing to fear."

A great cry of acclaim booms in the audience hall,
Rising from the dark earth and surpassing the shining sun:
"May Anushiravan live eternally in all his majesty,
Always wearing the crown of the King of Kings!
May the throne and palace never be deprived of him!"

They depart in joy and happiness.
The surface of the earth resembles the garden of Eram.[70]
Sadness is swept away from the world, and rain showers
Down from clouds at the right times to sow tulips
In the ground, converting the world into a sunny paradise.
Valleys, plains, and rose gardens resemble lamps,
While fields are the sun and mountains are the moon.

News spreads through the west and through India
That the land of Iran is as colorful as Rumi silk,
That the king, with his justice and his army,
Has rendered the earth as dazzling as the moon,
That no one, except the king, knows the number of troops,
All full of good will, equipped with weapons,
And glorifying the world with name and honor.

◇◇◇◇◇◇◇◇◇◇◇◇◇
70 Eram: A Persian garden located in Shiraz, Iran; also a heavenly garden in the desert said to appear to the traveler like a mirage.

In all the nations, rulers' hearts grow troubled,
Their souls dimming at the thought of Anushiravan.
From China and India, people arrive
And sing the praises of the king.
They realize their inability to resist his force
And resign themselves to paying tribute.
They recognize themselves as inferior
And gather many slaves and crates of gold.
Their envoys take the road
With golden mace and golden crown.
They attend the world king's court,
Bearers of royalties and heavy tribute.
The slaves and the golden crates with their visitors
Make the court take on
The appearance of a decorated paradise.

The sky marches on thus for some time,
Covering the Iranian king with unceasing affection.

6 | Anushiravan Makes the Rounds of His Empire

The wise Kesra decides to leave his court
To make the rounds of this world full of joy
And draw knowledge from hidden affairs.
He asks for the sound of timpani and sets his army
Into motion, stunning the Moon and Sun with his pomp.

There are so many banners with emblems,
Such an abundance of troops, jewels, gold and silver,
Golden belts and golden shields
That it is as if the mines have been exhausted
And the seas are empty of freshwater pearls.

He departs for Khorasan with ease,
Leading his army in the Sassanian manner.
When entering an inhabited land,
He would erect his camp and tent enclosures
In the countryside, and at the sound of the trumpet,
A herald would precede him to proclaim:
"O subjects of the world king,
Who would secretly cause you harm?

427

Sleep peacefully, trust your king, and refrain
From tormenting yourselves with worry!"

In this way they march to Gorgan,
Taking with them the crown and throne.
Know that never does justice produce damage.
Yet a king must be skillful, wise, and of noble birth.

From Gorgan, they march to Sari and Amol.
It is the season of the nightingale's song.
Valleys and plains are covered with forests,
The King of Iran falls into deep reflections at the sights.
He climbs from the plain to a lofty mountain,
Seated on an Arabian bay horse.
He observes the mountain crest and the forests,
Noticing roses, hyacinths, springs, and wild beasts.

He says, "O victorious World Creator,
You are every creature's foster parent;
You have crafted the Sun and the Moon;
You have opened the true path to us;
You have made a world so beautiful
That one cannot distinguish heaven from earth.
Anyone who worships another leads his soul to hell.
For this reason, Fereydoon, Yazdan's servant,
Made his home in this part of the world
Where the waters flow with rosewater
And the dirt is made of amber."

A man replies, "O justice giver, if the Turks
Were barred access to this land, our hearts would
All the more rejoice for its wealth and magnificence.
But we dare not raise our heads,
So frequent are the murders, ravages, and invasions.
They destroy everything, whether of value or not,
Everything, including birds, men, and cattle.
It is the only road through which ailments
Spread from province to province through Iran.
In ancient times, this gave rise to battles and wars.
But the road to Khaarazm has always served
As passage for the Turks. Today, a farmer
Or a merchant would surely sacrifice his head

Should he boldly raise it against them.
Now, since you have brought an army,
Turn misfortune away from us and bar the road.
Our suffering will not diminish from it
But rather increase every day.
Now is the time to show generosity."

Tears flow from the king's eyes as they plead for aid.
He says to his vizier, "We face a challenging matter.
It would be unfitting for us to surrender to revelry
Or to make do with the occupation of the throne.
Yazdan would not approve for us to dwell in joy
While farmers are overcome by heartache.
I shall not allow this region to go to waste
With its beautiful mountains and vast plains
That should be edged by gardens, public squares,
And palaces, abounding with cattle, wild beasts,
And freshwater springs that refresh the soul.
I shall not allow for these lands to be destroyed
And for Iran's cities to be plundered.
My duty as a king endowed with wisdom,
Honor, and integrity forbids me from such an act.
No one will ever praise me again if the land
Of Iran were to turn into a barren desert."

He gives his command to the vizier:
"Select the most able, ingenious men
From India, Chin, and various regions
To build a strong wall that emerges out of the water.
It must have a wide base and a height of ten nooses.
It must rise from the depth of the sea,
Be made of stone and mortar, and climb to the sun.
I hope that by constructing such a dam,
We shall protect and safeguard our land.
We must not make use of forced labor.
Open my treasury to pay the demanded fees.
The worker, the farmer, and the highborn man
Must be equally guarded from the gusting wind."

An aged wise man executes the handiwork,
Placing the desert behind the wall. A strong iron door
Is built to protect sheep from the attacks of wolves.

The king positions guards in these parts, and once
Everything has been secured, he drives his army away.

7 | Anushiravan Admonishes the Alaanans, the Baluchis, and the Gilanis

From the sea, the king travels to the land of Alaanan,
Which he finds deserted and lacking in culture.
He says to the Iranians, "What a shame
That what belongs to Iran must turn barren.
We must not allow our enemy to reproach us."

Anushiravan selects a wise, eloquent, suitable envoy
From his army's men and says to him,
"Depart from here at dawn and speak
To the leader and his people, in my name:
> 'My spies and the rumors, public and private,
> Have informed me that you boast
> About your lack of fear for Kesra
> And the fact that you regard Iran
> As nothing more than a fistful of dust.
> Now we have reached your side.
> We have raised our camp,
> Our tent pavilions, and our throne.
> Your deserts are vast, and your mountains are lofty,
> But our host makes quick use of arrow, mace, and noose.
> Valleys and caverns are ambushes for you.
> Your land is all mountain, and the earth is yours.
> Meanwhile we are stranger warriors.
> Neither host nor commander feels at home here.'"

The envoy departs and relates the discourse,
Telling the others the goal of the Iranian king.
An army forms of residents of Alaanan,
Mostly noblemen and notables able to deliberate.
They are people who have no other occupation than pillage
And who give little consideration to kindness.
They terrorize the border of Iran,
Depriving its residents of clothing, gold and silver.
Men, women, children, and cattle are forced

To take shelter in the plains and dare not stay in one place.

The envoy relates the message of the world king,
Hiding nothing from the Alaanans.
The noblemen's features obscure.
Their hearts are troubled by Anushiravan's fame.
Chiefs and leaders depart with dues and owed heavy taxes,
Taking with them slaves, bolts of fabric,
Gold, silver, and countless stallions of noble race.

The oldest, most eloquent and wisest among them
Appear at the king's court, weeping over past deeds.
But when courage weds with wisdom, one no longer
Needs to feel shame or to plead for forgiveness.

They arrive at the royal tent enclosures
With their presents and offerings.
They shout and roll in the dust,
With tearful eyes and swollen hearts.

The insightful king takes pity on them
And forgives them their past deeds.
In this land that turned into a barren desert,
A place that is the lair of tigers and leopards,
He commands them to swiftly build
A vast city in which there would be grounds
To seed and harvest, surrounded by a tall wall
To protect the inhabitants from an enemy advance.

They reply to the illustrious king:
"We stand as your slaves with ring in our ears.
We shall raise a wall and a beautiful residence,
Just as the king commands."

Anushiravan travels to India with his troops,
Where he stays for some time.
The noblemen, respecting his order of appearing before him,
Arrive, desirous to obtain his help.

From the edge of the Indus River and for two miles,
The land fills with silver and gifts, horses and elephants.
All the noblemen present themselves to the king,
Hearts full of joy and good will.

Kesra receives them graciously, asks them the common
Questions, and assigns them seats according to rank.

He marches off from there with a happy heart.
The world fills with horses, elephants, and troops.
He continues his trek until he reaches
A land that appears to be in a state of chaos,
Having been depopulated by the Baluchis
With an excess of slaying, pillage, and plunder.
In Gilan, the desolation is even more acute,
And blessings disappear beneath setbacks.

Anushiravan's heart is deeply afflicted,
His joy eclipsed by an onslaught of worry.
He says to the Iranians, "Alaanan and India are now,
For fear of our swords, as soft and malleable as silk,
Though we cannot yet return satisfied.
We must attempt to chase the wolf away from the sheep."

A man speaks up: "O King, the garden rose
Always bears a thorn that may prick one's finger.
Similarly, since the beginning of its existence,
This land has been an embarrassment,
With the sole purpose of devouring wealth.
The noble Ardeshir struggled with his old advisors
Against the Baluchis, but neither deceit nor ruse,
Neither walls nor battle have had a chance to succeed.
Furthermore, he even disregards the deeds he is told."

The king, infuriated by these words,
Marches toward the Baluchis.
Once at the foot of the tall mountains,
He makes the rounds with his escort and,
So dense is the mass of troops encircling them
That neither the wind nor the ant can carve a path.
Akin to swarming locusts, they occupy the land
From mountain base to arid plain.

Heralds run through the host,
Their voices sharp echoes as they proclaim:
"You will not grant any resident of Baluchistan
The permission to get away,
Whether a child or a valiant sword-bearing man,

Whether they run in great numbers or few."

As the troops grow cognizant of the king's wrath,
Cavaliers and infantrymen bar the road.
No one survives, neither woman, nor warrior, nor child.
Everyone succumbs to the sword's blade.
Iniquities among the Baluchis come to a definitive end.
The world no longer has cause to fear their evil acts
As nowhere is a single Baluchi person to be found.
On the mountain, herds roam freely
In the absence of guide or shepherd.
All past suffering is forgotten, and the valleys
And mountains feel as secure as one's own home.

After that, the king departs, aware of the damage
That has been executed in Gilan and Deylam.[71]
The army spreads from sea to mountain crest.
The air fills with banners and the earth with troops.

Anushiravan says, "We must not allow the trace
Of a lion or a wolf, great or small, to remain."

He scatters his army throughout Gilan,
Dimming the light of both the sun and the moon.
So many men are killed in this land
That the entire province is inundated with blood.
In the middle of these massacres, pillages, and fires,
The cries and lamentations of men and women rise.
They tie up their own hands, place the women
Behind them and the children in front.
So many dead that no matter where one looks
There are heaps and heaps of corpses and limbs.
Plants take root in combatants' expiring brains.

All the warriors of Gilan, sensible and notable men,
Visit the king, shouting and crying,
Chests torn apart and heads peppered in dust.
They assemble at the palace door, hands bound,
Bodies wounded, and they moan,
"We have abandoned the wicked path in the hopes
That the king will give up his vengeful actions.

---
71 Deylam: A port city in southwestern Iran.

If the king's heart is wounded by the people of Gilan,
We shall cut off our heads with our own hands.
Maybe then, at the sight of a mound of severed heads,
The king's soul will be satisfied."

The king hears the proclamations and laments
Rising at his door and takes pity on them.
His heart forgets the past. He calls for
Two hundred hostages from Gilan and Deylam
So that no one veers onto the path of violence.

He positions one of his warriors in place.
Once everything is finished to his satisfaction,
The king takes the road with his host.

8 | Monzer, the Arab, Asks for Aid to Fight the Caesar

From Gilan, he marches toward Mada'in
With an army so vast its count and spread are inestimable.
On the road, they spot in the distance
A huge host of spear-wielding warriors.

A cavalier emerges out of the company,
Advances as swift as wind, dismounts
And announces: "Here comes Monzer the Taazi."

The leaders make room for Monzer to approach.
The king asks him the customary questions
And expresses his delight,
For the sight of him brings a gleam to his eyes.

The worldly Monzer speaks to him of Rum
And of the Caesar: "If you are the King of Iran,
Guardian and support of brave men,
Why do the Rumis make claims to kingship?
Why do they drive through the desert of spear-riders?
If the Caesar were our legitimate ruler,
Our heads would lower in shame.
However, if the powerful king consents,
We shall cease to voice our objections.
The desert riders are more skilled and valuable

Than Rumi cavaliers, whether at work or at war."

Monzer's words send Anushiravan into a fit of rage
Toward the Caesar who dares raise his diadem.
He selects an eloquent warrior able to understand
The Rumi language and instructs him:
"Travel westward to Rum without stopping.
Tell the Caesar, "If you show a lack of wisdom,
Your brain will have cause to repent.
If a valiant lion assails an onager, he will
Devour it even if its lair is in salty waters.
If you obtain from Monzer what you are due,
It is already quite a bit, for his mount is a vulture.

"First distinguish between your right and left hand,
And once you are aware of your rights,
You may claim the land that belongs to you.
Since I am the one who distributes domains,
Since I hold the highest seat as the master,
I shall act in every way as suits my position
And not allow the wind to blow on Monzer.
If you seek battle with the Taazian,
Attempt to know yourself first.
Next, reflect on the fact that kingship belongs to me;
To me belongs all that exists between the bull,
Support of the earth, and the house of Pisces.
If I were to send an army into Rum,
Your sword of steel would turn into pliant wax.'"

The envoy takes his leave of Anushiravan,
As swift as a tornado, and travels to the Caesar
To acquit himself of the message.

The vile Caesar turns away from the path of justice
And manages to reply with deceitful words
Since he believes that dishonor would be far worse
Than the heights of his present position.
He says, "We must take the words
Of the unwise Monzer at their value.
If he laments foolishly and exaggerates
In this way the suffering he has endured,
Or if, from one border of the desert to the other,

Comes a single one of the spear-wielding warriors
With evil intentions, I shall level the mountains
In the entire nation and turn the barren desert into a sea."

The envoy listens and departs as swift as dust
To repeat all that he heard to Kesra.
The king grows angry and says to his vizier,
"Wisdom has not united with the Caesar's brain.
I shall show him who is master and who has
The right to engage in wars, conquests, and treaties.
He will soon repent for his claims, his pride,
His murders, his pillages, and his invasions,
Which will lead him to foolishly
Shove his hands into nightly flames."

He commands the ringing of bells,
And the army sets in motion on all sides.
The sound of timpani rises over the palace gate.
The earth turns the color of tar,
And the mountains merge with shades of ebony.

The king selects thirty thousand sword-striking
Warriors to form his host, entrusts them to Monzer,
And says, "Lead these troops from the desert to Rum
So that they may consume and devastate the land.
As long as I am your king and protector,
You have nothing to fear from the Rumis.
They are for me nothing more than a fistful of dust.
I shall send a gentle message to the Caesar in which
I consent to leave the land of Rum to the Caesar.
From now on, you need not suffer from his actions."

9 | Anushiravan's Letter and the Caesar's Reply

The king summons a palace scribe
And commands him to write a letter:
"On the part of Anushiravan of illustrious birth,
World master, successor of King Ghobaad,
To the noble Caesar of Rum, to whom
The border and cultivated lands are bestowed."

He begins by invoking benedictions on Yazdan,
"The Source of grandeur, Master of the rotation
Of Sun and Moon, Giver of victory and power,
Above the intentions of the revolving dome,
Whether they are for war or for mercy.
Since you are the Caesar and ruler of Rum,
Do not seek quarrel with the Taazian.
You must know that, if you wish to seize
A sheep from the grips of a wolf,
You will end up with injury and loss.
If you send a host against Monzer,
I shall leave you with neither troops
Nor treasury, neither crown nor throne.

"If one of my subjects becomes too willing,
I shall punish him with the tip of my sword.
Do not advance to the border, not even by one step,
If you wish to adhere to the terms of our treaty.
However, if you override it, I shall follow suit
And trample your head and throne beneath my feet.
Greetings from the master of crown and power
To those who refrain from sowing seeds of injustice."

The royal seal is affixed to the letter.
A cavalier is selected from court,
A suitable man who is soft-spoken, experienced,
Valiant and lays claim to a serene mind.
The envoy departs with the king's letter
And makes his way to the illustrious Caesar.
He greets him, hands over the letter,
And relays Kesra's intentions.

The proud Caesar listens to his discourse
And reads Kesra's letter.
He turns pale; his face twists into a frown.
Confounded and angry, he summons a scribe
To record his thoughts, good and bad, in a reply.

Once the top of the sheaf is blackened with ink,
He invokes benedictions on Yazdan,
"Who has starred the surface of the skies;
From whom we receive struggles, rest, and affection;

Who establishes a single ruler on the earth
And elects a more worthy person as the king's servant.
Even if the revolving firmament is under your command
And Jupiter's head beneath your sword,
Study your books of taxes and observe that
Never has a man of Rumi race paid tribute
To any member of the Kianian family.
Though you are king, I am not less admirable.
I own a head, a crown, and a host as well.
Why would I accept your vain propositions for fear
Of your elephants' feet and the beat of timpani?

"I shall be the one to demand tribute from you.
Who is able to stand up to the Rumis in battle?
You are aware of the high feats of Eskandar in Iran.
He was the king of free men but one of ours,
And his sword has not been lost.
Why then must you impose your supremacy on us?
Cavaliers armed with spears seized our goods
During times of pillage, and we shall no longer
Suffer from oppression. We shall ravage the desert plains
Of the Taazian from one border to another.
Anushiravan is not the creator of the Sun.
Neither is he the holder of the keys
That unlock the mysteries of the revolving dome.
He does not recognize anyone
Among the most noble as high placed,
And alone, he imposes his will on the world."

He refrains from giving an answer to the envoy.
In his anger, he pronounces the name of Kesra.
As he dips his seal in musk, he exclaims,
"The Messiah and the cross are my allies!"

The envoy does not respond,
Realizing that the reply is full of hostility.
Unhappy, he hastily makes his way back to
The King of Iran to report the affair of the Caesar.

10 | Anushiravan Marches Against the Caesar of Rum

The king reads the letter and finds himself
Bewildered by fate's rotations.
He convenes all the wise and noble men
And speaks to them at length of the letter.
He remains three days to deliberate
With advisors and army-destroying heroes.
On the fourth day, he is determined to execute
His plan of leading his host into war against the Caesar.

The sound of trumpet, timpani, and drum
Resonates at the palace gates.
The king does not take time to rest.
Resolute, he departs to engage in war to set things right.
He musters up his army, loads up the gear,
And invokes the Creator, Source of happiness.

A great dust rises, and it is as if the sun
Has dipped its face in a sea of tar.
Horses' hooves cover the earth,
And silken banners tint the air in hues of ruby.
So thick is the air with the shielded riders
And the dust stirred by elephants
That neither the fly nor the wind can pass through.
The world resemble the rolling surface of the River Nile.

The world owner departs with the Kaaviani banner,
Wearing the crown and golden boots.
The racket of the troops is heard for two miles,
Preceded by the sound of timpani and elephants.
Following is the king, trailed by the noble leaders.
They march swiftly to Aazar Abadegan.

Spotting in the distance the temple of Aazargoshasp,
The king dismounts and abandons his horse.
He asks a holy man for barsom,
And his face floods with tears.
He silently enters the fire temple, where there is
A golden throne on which rests the book of *Zand Avesta*.
A wise man recites out loud, according to custom.
The cleric and the nobles roll in the dust before the book

And tear apart the hems of their tunics.
The leaders toss precious gems on the book
And whisper divine blessings.

The king approaches, assumes a stance of prayer
To glorify the Creator, and pleads to be granted victory,
To be given strength, and to be shown the path of justice.
He distributes goods to the temple worshippers
And wherever he encounters people in need.

He sets up a tent in front of the temple,
And the army forms ranks on both sides.
He summons an intelligent scribe and dictates to him
Suitable words, composing a letter full of dignity,
Addressed to the commanders of Iran's borders:
"Nurture fear of Yazdan and remain vigilant.
Guard the world from the entry of the enemy.
May governors and heroes exercise justice.
May enough troops remain standing
To push the enemy into retreat.
In the absence of my banner,
Abstain from surrendering to a sound sleep."

As he leaves the fire temple and marches toward Rum,
The report of his travels spreads, and his loyal subjects
And warriors make their way to join the army.
The earth empties of valiant men.
Princes arrive with presents and offerings.

Wherever Anushiravan pauses,
He receives messages and amicable greetings.
Wherever he leads his army, there is celebration and hunt,
And every night, one thousand brave men gather
Around the king to engage in banquet and feast.

Anushiravan approaches the enemy and readies for battle.
He first pays the troops' wages, then selects leaders:
Army commander is Shirooy, son of Bahraam,
A prudent man, calm in battle;
The king entrusts the left wing to Farhaad,
Counseling him at length.
He places Ostaad, son of Barzeen,
At the lead of the right wing, and Goshasp,

Ambitious leader, in charge of the loads.
The center corps is handed to Mehran,
Whose heart is fixed on vengeance.

The king calls to his side the worldly army leaders,
Exhorts them, and gives them much advice.
He charges Hormozd, son of Khorraad, with the rounds,
Speaking to him at length on the subject of wisdom.
He sends spies everywhere so that nothing escapes him.

He declares, "O army troops, warriors, and noblemen,
If one of you strays from my command,
If one of you scorns my advice, even for a moment,
If he brings harm to anyone, whether destitute or
A noble owner of vast wealth, if he tramples beneath
His feet sown fields or if he advances before the ranks,
If he attacks fruit trees or commits any misdeed,
I swear by Yazdan, who gave me diadem and power,
I swear by the Master of Saturn, Mars, and Sun,
That I shall cut him in half with my sword,
Even if he were to hide behind clouds like stars.
I make the rounds of camp; I am an ambitious ruler
Always positioned in the army center;
I watch over elephants, troops, and gear.
At times I stand at the right wing, at times at the left.
I tread dry land, I cross waters, never taking time
To rest or sleep when I am engaged in war."

A herald by the name of Shirzad
Memorizes the king's words and,
Running through the troops and the tents, proclaims,
"O vast host, here is the order of the vigilant king:
We shall make blood flow into the dark dust
Of anyone who strays from divine command,
Anyone who walks and acts in any way
Contrary to mercy, justice, and wisdom."

But the king is not content with the proclamation.
He makes the rounds by daylight and by night,
Inquiring about the good and the bad,
Learning about world events, neglecting nothing.
If a warrior dies on the road, they bury him in place.

441

Should a deceased leave behind gold and silver,
Noose and helm, belt and bow, whether good or bad,
These items are interred with him.

Men are astonished at Anushiravan's power.
At the thought of an imminent fight,
He displays prudence and patience.
He assigns an eloquent messenger
To entreat the enemy to push back.
Should they choose to enter the path of justice,
The wise king would not cause them harm.
But if they prefer battle, he would willingly
Engage with the rage of a daring whale
And plunder land and fertile ground.
He seeks to possess the world not only
By means of justice but also by means of blade.

His wisdom is akin to the sun shining upon all things,
Indiscriminately, its light never dying
As it chases clouds out of the sky.
It is all the same for the sun, whether dust or sand,
Dry or wet, color or scent; whether pearls or river water,
It is pure justice and giving. The sun never hides its splendor.
It charms every heart and offers assistance everywhere.

The King of Kings, with his grandeur, majesty,
And justice, shelters the world beneath his royal wings.
Because he holds his head so high,
Battles and bounty are games to him.
Everyone in Iran acclaims and reveres him.

Should an elephant or a wild lion face him,
He would not delay a fight for a single day.
Should a host of warriors with helmets and mail
Advance resolutely against his host, the victorious king
Would either destroy them all or burden them
With chains and banish them behind prison bars.

11 | Anushiravan Seizes Forts in the Land of Rum

Anushiravan advances in this manner
Toward the busy city of Shooraab,[72] a site of battle.
When Goshtaasp made his way to Rum long ago,
He resided in this city for some time.
Situated on a rock, it plunges into deep waters
And is full of men, weapons, and wealth.
The top of its walls are so high they reach the clouds.

The Iranian army surrounds the fort
But cannot find a way to near its gates.
The king plants mangonels on four fronts,
Fires, and the Christian wall collapses.
A great commotion rises from the castle's four corners,
Where men cannot find a way of escape.

As the dazzling sun withdraws from the dome of sky,
The castle wall is as flat as the plain.
The cries of cavaliers and the dust of troops,
Smoke, and flames climb to the moon.

Strewn throughout the fort are heads and limbs,
While the matching bodies lie at a distance.
The shouts for mercy and the women's laments
Pierce the sound of the pounding of drums.

Wealthy men and those who distinguish themselves
Through their courage are captured,
Tied up, and placed atop war elephants.
One hears their cries and their pleas for mercy.
But they are not given a show of clemency,
Neither in battle nor for gold in times of feast.

The king continues his march with his host.
They find another fort on the road that houses
The Caesar's treasure guarded by a powerful man.
This fort is called Aarayesheh Rum.[73]

The vigilant King Kesra strategizes a calamitous end

◇◇◇◇◇◇◇◇◇◇◇◇◇
72 Shooraab: A city in northwestern Iran.
73 Aarayesheh Rum: Meaning the ornament of Rum.

To this castle that has escaped capture until then.
He orders a shower of shots to fall upon it,
Fierce as a pounding spring hail.

The Persian leaders storm the walls
And toss fire at the city and the fort.
Not a single survivor remains from the army.
Not a single thorn or bramble subsists.

Kesra abandons it to plunder the Caesar's treasure
And to give his troops the crates of gold and crowns.
He destroys the city, forcing its inhabitants to take flight.

The cries of children, men, and women resound.
Young and old approach the mighty king.
They moan and plead for mercy:
"The Caesar's vizier, treasurer, and wealth are yours.
Gain and loss await you in Rum. We beg you for our lives.
We shall endlessly worship the majesty of your crown."

The king commands the end of the massacre
And distributes great wealth all around.

12 | Anushiravan's Battle With Farfoorius, and the Capture of Ghalinus and Antiochus

From there, Anushiravan leads
His host out of Aarayesheh Rum.
He learns that the Caesar has dispatched a vast host
Of spear-bearing, armor-sporting warriors.

He communicates the news to his army so that it may
Prepare to bear the appearance of a mountain of steel.
The wail of brass trumpets rings.
A messenger sent by spies rushes to the king and tells him
That the Caesar's approaching host comprises
His most illustrious warriors, as avid for battle as wolves.
At its command is the wild and illustrious Farfoorius,
Preceded by the call of clarions and the beat of timpani.

Almost instantly, the world king notices

PART TWENTY-SIX

The dust of the approaching host in the distance.
He smiles and tells the envoy, "We expected it.
We have made all the necessary preparations."

The crowned king moistens his lips to speak
And commands the troops to form rank.
The two hosts come together in a dust so thick
The wind finds no passage through.

On one side is the glorious Persian army
Of proud, sword-striking warriors,
Their blood-stained blades tearing clouds apart.
Their waists girded for a fight, they are powerful men,
With many members of the Kianian clan.

This host holds back as much as a leopard
About to pounce on its prey.
On all sides are scattered body parts
Of Rumi fighters either killed or wounded.
Farfoorius is injured and moves away from the brawl,
His banner torn apart, his timpani flung to the ground.
The Iranian riders take the stance of leopards
Falling upon mountain sheep on the plain.
They leap in pursuit of the Rumis
And free the valleys and fields of their presence.

Anushiravan gets back on the road with his warriors,
Spear, mace, and sword in hand.
He drives his army onto a large field, where they come
Across the tall walls that enclose the castle of Ghalinus.

The top of the walls is higher than the eagle's flight,
And a water-filled trench encircles it.
The city forms an enclosure around the fort
Consisting of palaces, squares, gardens, and structures.
It is protected by a vast Rumi army, eager for battle.

The king settles at a distance of two farsangs.
The world turns black with the army's dust.
The Rumis begin the battle from the gates,
Tossing arrows and flinging petrol-filled bottles.
A booming clatter rises over Ghalinus,
Buffering the sound of timpani.

The king observes as a great number
Of his troops enter the city.

By the time the shining sun pales and half the sky
Has been obscured, much of the wall has disappeared,
And the city is leveled to the ground.

A proclamation is announced at the king's entrance:
"O illustrious warriors of Iran's army,
Emerge from this city and return to the plain,
And if, in the dark night,
I hear the cry of a woman or an old man,
The sound of pillage and plunder, blows administered
And blows received, or if a single plaintive voice echoes,
The one culpable for such cries will be flayed
And his skin stuffed with straw."

As the sun draws its sword in the house of Cancer,
Erasing rust from the world and dissipating sleep,
As the drumbeat resounds at the royal door,
The most significant people take the road,
Men and women, residents of the castle
Gather at Kesra's court to say,
"Not a single one of our warrior riders
Or illustrious men remains in our city.
They have all been either killed or wounded
Without having committed any crime.
It is time for the king to show mercy,
For justice does not approve of children,
Women, and old men being restrained.
The castle and the city are in such a state
That nothing will ever grow there but brambles.
If the Caesar is at fault, why must we be punished?
What have you to reproach the residents of Ghalinus?"

The king forgives the Rumis who escape,
Whether they are guilty or innocent.
He leaves them much wealth
And continues his travels in haste.
He loads up the men able to carry weapons,
Enchained and placed on elephants.

In Antioch,[74] news spreads that the king
Is on his way with host and elephants.
In this city, there is a vast army of valiant Rumis.
The king stops there for three days
To give them time to surrender.
But on the fourth day, the companies forming
The Iranian army advance one after the other.
Rumi cavaliers exit to defend their women,
Their children, their treasures, and their land.

They engage for three days in three mighty battles.
On the fourth day, at the rising sun,
The borders of inhabited regions open to the king
As not a single Rumi cavalier remains.

The Persian army enters the city,
Finding little space to walk through.
The noblemen, owners of throne and diadem,
And the Caesar's treasurers hand over
Their hard-earned wealth to the king.
The able warriors are placed on the backs of elephants.
Anushiravan sends the prisoners
And the spoils of war to Mada'in.

Anushiravan roams the city, which he finds
More dazzling than the sphere of the moon.
Gardens, squares, sources of running water
Renew old men with youth.

The king says to his wise men,
"Is this Antioch, or is it a new spring?
Anyone who has not yet seen this merry paradise
Must stop here and visit. It is a place
Where the earth is made of musk and bricks are of gold,
Where trees bear rubies and streams ripple with rosewater,
Where the ground is the sky and the sky is the sun.
We must take good care of this region.
May the entire land of Rum prosper!"

◇◇◇◇◇◇◇◇◇◇◇◇◇
74 Antioch: Ancient Greek city that would be in today's Turkey, near the city of Antakya.

13 | Anushiravan Builds a Replica City of Antioch for the Rumi Captives

Anushiravan commands the building of a city
Similar to Antioch, furnished with running water;
Filled with grounds, gardens, palaces, and squares;
Shining like a lantern.

The serene noblemen name the city Zibeh Khosrow,[75]
And once it is decked and adorned like spring,
A paradise full of scent, color, and beauty,
The king asks for the prisoners held captive
And the wounded to be liberated,
And to be settled comfortably in the new city.
He adds, "I have founded these grounds, gardens,
And residences so that each person may
Find a suitable dwelling worthy of his name."

He distributes wealth all around.
The land is as beautiful as paradise.
There are so many homes and streets,
So many markets that it is as if
The wind may not find space for passage.

A loquacious shoemaker presents himself
And says, "O unjust King, in my home in Ghalinus,
I had a white mulberry tree in my courtyard.
I gain nothing if I settle in Zibeh Khosrow,
Where there is no mulberry tree near my door
To provide me with comforting shade."

The king asks for the planting of fresh trees
At the door of the wretched man.

Then he selects a Christian man and entrusts him
With the command of treasury and troops.
He says to him, "I nominate you chief of this city,
Of its visitors, and of its new palace.

◇◇◇◇◇◇◇◇◇◇◇◇
75 Zibeh Khosrow: A city founded by Kesra Anushiravan to house the Rumi prisoners, built after the ancient city of Antioch.

Make the city prosper and bear fruit
By alternately playing the role of father and son.
Beautify it with liberality; keep away from villainy.
All things must be performed in moderation."

The king leads his army out of Antioch,
Leaving the skilled Christian to govern the city.

14 | The Rumi Caesar Asks for a Peace Accord

At this time, Farfoorius brings news to Rum
And recounts the fate of Ghalinus.
He says to the Caesar, "World ruler Kesra,
His host, elephants, and thrones arrived.
So commanding is the army that mountains
Tremble in fear at the sight of the dust."

The Caesar shudders at the memory of his words
And gathers his sages and noblemen.
His heart filled with trepidation,
The Rumi ruler holds counsel three times at night.

One of the wise men says to him,
"This is not a prudent course of action.
You cannot stand up to Kesra.
His host will destroy our beautiful land,
And all the work of the Caesars will go to waste.
The voice of your interlocutor and his reasoning
Reflect only the possible dangers that threaten our empire."

The Caesar listens to him, his heart troubled,
His mind dimmed at the thought of Anushiravan.
Among the Rumi philosophers, he selects
A learned, eloquent man of pure character.

Sixty wise men, whose souls and intellect
Are free of the dust of greed, offer to escort him.
He sends the envoy to the king.
The noblemen take the road with Mehraas at the lead,
A valiant man, mature in wisdom but young in years.
He is preceded with all sorts of wealth,

Its value reaching beyond the imagination.

The Caesar, regretting his previous correspondence,
Sends a profusion of excuses, advice, kind words,
Valuable offerings, and tributes.
In addition, members of his family
And notables are dispatched as hostages.
Mehraas understands that he has the key
To undo the chain of ill-fated events.

They arrive at the side of Anushiravan,
Tongues and minds as sharp as diamonds.
Mehraas presents himself at court,
Greets the king in the Rumi language.
The clarity and integrity of his words
Make it seem as if stars flow out of his robe's sleeves.

He says to Kesra, "O King,
The world is not worth what you think it is.
You are now in the land of Rum, leaving Iran vacant.
The land is without merit and without glory,
Rum would not even be worth a fly
In the absence of the Caesar.
All goods are the products of men, and if the number
Of men diminishes, the goods diminish as well.
If this great commotion is for the acquisition of wealth,
Which is stronger than the desire for modesty
And learning, I bring you all the treasures of Rum.
A pure soul has more value than all the nations
Of the world and their assets."

The king, happy as a spring garden to hear these words,
Accepts Mehraas's offerings of gold and slaves.
He covers the messenger with praise
And extols the beautiful gifts.
He says to Mehraas, "O envoy of superior intelligence,
Anyone endowed with wisdom is a true warrior.
You are more valuable than the land of Rum,
Even if its dirt were to turn into gold."

They set the tribute at one hundred yearly sacks
Of buffalo skins full of dinars to be sent
Along with presents and offerings.

They agree that his army would never come
Near the land of Yemen or disturb its people.

The envoy is given a robe of honor,
A headdress, a ring, and a belt.

At the blare of trumpets and timpani,
The vigilant world master marches off with his host
To Syria and remains there for some time.
He takes so many weapons and troops,
So many crates of gold, slaves, thrones, and crowns
That his elephants bearing the weight of silver goods
Make the spine of the earth buckle.

Upon departure from this border,
He gives command to Shirooy, son of Bahraam,
And says to him, "Always ask tribute from the Caesar.
And do not worry if there is a delay of a month or a day."

Shirooy bends to kiss the ground.
He blesses the king and says, "May you be victorious!
May your fortune always shine,
And may this Kianian tree never fade!"

The sound of drums rises at the king's door
As he marches off to Armenia with banner and host.

15 | The Story of Nooshzaad

World ruler Kesra shines as bright as the sun,
And everyone at once fears him and trusts him.
He walks like the sun in the sky, in one hand
Clutching a sword while the other hand engages
In acts of benevolence, refusing to forgive when
He is angered and banishing anger when he is giving.

Such is this ruler of Kianian lineage.
He brings order to the world with justice.
A man, whether he is a king or a subject,
Or a pure-hearted worshipper of to Yazdan's cult,
Knows that he needs a mate, clothing, food, and lodging.

If his wife is pure and of sound counsel,
She is a treasure that multiplies, particularly
If she is of tall stature, with black curls that graze
Her ankles, with intelligence, wisdom, chastity, caution,
And endowed with an eloquent and gentle voice.

Now the noble king has such a wife gifted with
The height of a cypress tree and a bright moon face.
She observes the religion of the Messiah,
And the city is full of rumors on her fame and beauty.

She gives birth to a sun-faced son,
More dazzling than Venus in the sky.
The illustrious mother names him Nooshzaad,
And her affection bars the wind from attaining him.

He grows up like a slender cypress tree.
He is gifted and the ornament of kingship.
He is aware of the paths to hell and paradise,
The doctrine of Ezra, of the Messiah, and the faith
Of Zoroaster, but he does not approve of the *Zand Avesta*
And washes his cheeks in the waters of Christianity.

Instead of his father's faith, he adopts
His mother's, to everyone's surprise.
The king is deeply irritated that this rosebush
Is only able to bear spiky thorns for him.
They close the doors to his palace and turn
Nooshzaad's shiny audience hall into a prison.

His residence is in Gundeh Shahpoor, but
He is blocked from contacting either Iran or the East.
At the same time, the city holds captive
Many criminals burdened by chains.

The king, as he returns from Rum, complains
About the continuous motion and fatigues of the road.
In the end he grows so weak that his body bends,
And his state prevents him from giving audience.

Someone brings the news to Nooshzaad
That the empire's glory has tarnished,
That Kesra, vigilant world master, has died

And that fate is entrusting the earth to another.

Nooshzaad is delighted over his father's death.
May he never be called *noosh*, which means gentle!
A man who rejoices over the death of a just king
Must certainly have an evil nature.

An elder once spoke on the subject: "If you rejoice
Over my death, attempt to avoid a similar demise."
The knowledge that death is unavoidable
Will not change whether it comes earlier or later.
Only the one whose life is virtuous before
Yazdan will not be troubled at the prospect.
But a son who strays off his father's path
Must either be a scoundrel or devoid of sense.
Whether the sowing of the quince is fresh or dry,
Its fruit will never have the scent of musk.
Why then must the fruit be the nature of the seed
That the gardener plants to begin with?
If it leans toward the dust,
It will back away from the sun and fresh water,
And will not provide you with proper fruits and leaves.
It will grow, live, and die in the dust."

16 | Anushiravan's Illness and Nooshzaad's Dissent

I shall now tell you the story of Nooshzaad.
It will remind you to always act with a sense of justice.

If the skies nurture a full moon,
It would embody the being of Anushiravan.
Why did the son have to stray off his father's path
To usurp his throne and royal dignity?

Listen to me, dear son, as I recount
This tale from beginning to end.
By setting the story of the peasant bard to verse,
I work to leave an imprint in the world,
A memory of me that will endure.
May praise bless the one who honors me!
As poet, I seek eternal fame with my work.

A Persian bard who lived four times thirty years
Once said, "The enemy of the just king
Is not a descendant of the human race
But comes from the lineage of Ahriman."
The story of Nooshzaad reminds me
Of the peasant bard's words.

Once the son of Kesra hears that the throne
Escapes the branch of the royal tree,
He opens the palace door and from all around
Gathers companies of men of little sense,
Once captured and imprisoned by Anushiravan.

Nooshzaad returns freedom to the demented men,
Bringing an aura of fear over the population.
Christians, whether secular or clerics, illustrious,
Sword-bearing riders, unite around him in great numbers.
With money given to him by his mother from her treasury,
Once filled by the king, he is able to muster a host
Of thirty thousand skillful, spear-bearing warriors.

He captures all the surrounding towns,
And everyone speaks of him and of his deeds.
With dark intentions in his heart, he writes
To the Caesar, his relative: "You are the supreme ruler,
My friend and kin, and we share a common religion.
The entire region is like Rum and belongs to you,
Whether Azerbaijan, Iran, or other inhabited lands.
My father passed away from illness,
And my fortune, once asleep, is now awake."

In Mada'in spreads the news of the prince's actions.
The governor of this province sends a rider
To the king to communicate what he has heard
And all the secret reports he has received.

The envoy arrives at Anushiravan's court,
Running like gushing water, relates the rumors
About Nooshzaad, and hands over the letter.

The king is deeply afflicted by the letter.
He consults at length with his renowned vizier.

17 | Anushiravan's Letter to Raam Barzeen, Governor of Mada'in

Once the king fixes a resolution,
He summons a scribe and dictates a letter.
His features twisted in a frown, his lips emit cold sighs.
The letter, addressed to Raam Barzeen,
Reveals his grief and his heart's deepest wounds.

He begins in praise: "Of the One Who created
Sky and earth, time and space; the one responsible
For lighting up the heavens with Sun, Saturn, and Moon;
The one who glorifies the crown and the throne of majesty.
From a worthless scrap of wood to the mighty lion
And elephant, from the dust raised by an ant's path
To the turbulent flows of the River Nile, every object,
Every being, everything lives under Yazdan's command,
Even if it were to hide beneath an anvil.
No one can find a limit to divine authority,
Nor can anyone seize divine power.

"I am familiar with my son's cursed letter,
A great calamity that I must endure.
I am aware that the criminals who shattered
The prison doors are united with Nooshzaad.
If someone is destined to witness such a day,
Better his journey on earth be curtailed.
One is born from a mother only to ultimately
Face death, from Kesra to Nooshzaad.
No one, neither the fly's head nor the ant,
Neither the elephant nor the rhinoceros, is able
To evade the scavenging beak and claws of death.

"If the earth wished to show its beginning and its end,
And allow its deeds to be measured,
One would find its lap full of crowned heads
And its bosom full of the blood of riders,
The hem of its robe full of learned men,
And the slits of its tunic full of rosy-cheeked women.
Why should you cover your head with a diadem?
Why should you sport a helmet?
The fletches and the arrow of death will drill through them.

No matter how much we insist that no one may stay
On earth for long, few men rejoice for the death of a son.
May Nooshzaad evade misfortune!
His allies are associated with him
Only to murmur their longing for Kesra's death.

"If you are able to evade the claws of death,
Then you can rejoice over the death of others.
Furthermore, it is a man of ill race
Who seeks the death of a just king.
If Nooshzaad has turned his back on me,
It is only because he united with the deev.
He has risked everything to gain nothing.
Now that he is consumed by such a flame,
My words will have little consequence.
As long as my head wears the crown,
No other man will be world king.
He should not have so lightly declared vacant my place.
There is no doubt that Nooshzaad would rise as master
Of royal crown if I were to vacate the throne.
But his behavior did not conform
To a belief worthy of his evil soul.

"There is no reason for me to harbor fear,
Even though my son's path proves to be impure.
The treasures that he has wasted do not weigh heavy
On my heart, and all those who have acted covertly
With him and have shown little respect to me
Are evil, malicious men of wicked lineage,
Unworthy of being my subjects.
All this has little effect on me, and you must
Not trouble yourself over their actions.
I fear and shudder before the World Creator,
Who surpasses the wisest men in wisdom.
May my soul never abstain from expressing gratitude.
Yazdan bestowed on me victory and royal majesty,
Prosperity and the empire's crown.
If my gratitude had equaled divine kindness,
My prosperity would have increased tremendously.

"This lifegiving droplet passed through me
To rest in another person in peace.

456

It was the seed from which my son awakened
And arose to become my worst enemy.
I fear therefore that I may be
The instigator of all my troubles.
But if the World Master does not hold it against me,
I shall not worry about the affair.
If fortune shelters me, I shall not perish.
All those who united with Nooshzaad
Are despicable and worthless in my eyes.
The dark waters that troubled the river
Came from the Caesar's letter to him.
We believed that he was related to my son
As he is his friend and shares his faith.
He is a man of little sense who does not
Respect the beliefs of his ancestors.
The most earnest son is the one who accepts
His father's religion and refrains from attacking it.

"Although this foolish man turned away from justice,
One must not defame him, for the injury would
Fall back on me since he is my flesh and blood.
Gather an army and prepare for battle.
Proceed slowly and patiently.
If we reach extreme ends and he rejects our terms,
Do not act with haste or violence.
It is better to capture him than to kill him.
One must always nurture hope for redemption.

"Here is your position: The dust on the cypress tree
Must be washed away with the waters of wisdom.
But if the prince despises your advice,
If the powerful cypress tree stoops,
If his head rises from its soft bed,
Spare neither mace nor sword on him.

"When a nobleman takes a liking to vile things,
It is impossible to cure him.
Furthermore, he will become vile himself
By seeking war with the world king.
You need not have qualms about killing him
Since he is after spilling his own blood.
A man who gives into the Caesar's religion

457

And turns his back on my diadem
Is loathsome, contemptible, and weak in my eyes
And will rush the lofty sky to hasten his demise.

"Mehrnoosh, a wise and pious man
Dressed in wool, once said on this subject:
        'May the person who rejoices over
        His father's death be deprived of life's joys.'
Searching for light in the darkness is equivalent
To finding water and fire flowing in the same river.
Never has anyone enjoyed rest without labor.
It is the rule of fate, and that is that.
Do not befriend the turning dome of sky;
At times it gives you an almond, at times its shell.
Why chase after the color and scent
Of the flower of the pomegranate tree?
Better not to expect anything good from the world.
It hands you something only to quickly snatch it away.
At the moment you reach the heights of glory,
Your suffering, your troubles, and your fears begin.

"The troops gathered around Nooshzaad
Have abandoned their sense of duty and justice.
You may view their movements as wind,
The object of mockery, and will not last long.
As for the Christians who are members of this army
And who have strayed because of their faith,
Know that the Messiah's religion is such
That if its followers go against its rulings,
The end result to their hostility will be crucifixion.
The others, people gathered from everywhere,
Are wicked men aiming their attention
Solely on the execution of evil deeds.
They hold no fear in their hearts and will change
Their ways and beliefs upon a shifting gust of wind.

"If Nooshzaad is taken captive in war,
Do not speak to him on these matters.
His soul must not be wounded by grief
If he renounces the path to perversity.
His body must not suffer at a time
When his tunic is torn by the blows he receives.

In that instance, all the veiled women
In the world would secretly rise in his favor.
It is better for his palace to serve
As a prison to him and to his servants.
Never close the treasury door to him,
Even when he is stripped of his dignity.
He must not be lacking in clothing,
Food, wall hangings, and carpets.
In the absence of these requisites,
My words would be meaningless.
As for the Iranian leaders armed to defend him,
Once you have gained a victory over them,
Do not hesitate to slash them in half with your sword.
It is right and fair to seize those hostile to the king
And to forsake them to the dragon's jaws.

"Once you are victorious, you may use
Your dagger to slay Iran's border governors,
Supporters of Nooshzaad.
Any adversary of the king and of the kingdom
Must be sent away to meet the jaws of the whale.
Other than Nooshzaad, any secret foes I may have
Must surely belong to the race of Ahriman.
They never speak of my kind deeds.
They are distinguished by their behavior
In regard to Nooshzaad. In my presence,
They were full of virtue, for fear of retributions.
But once they saw what was happening,
Those who spoke slander behind my back
Turned their tongues in friendship toward my son.
That is when they seized the occasion to blame.
Do not agree with these spiteful men who make up fibs.
Even though Nooshzaad has become wicked,
He is nevertheless my son, and my heart attests to it.

"You may pierce before the assembly the ones who
Speak evil of Nooshzaad and are unjust toward him.
Cursed be their tongues; cursed be their mouths!
Those who seek war to demean the king,
Those who employ deceitful and devious means
And who surrender to the hateful precepts
Of Ahriman's faith must not reside in my kingdom,

For they are the enemies of the king."

The royal seal is placed on the letter,
And the messenger departs in haste.

18 | Raam Barzeen Prepares to Battle Nooshzaad

Once the envoy reaches Raam Barzeen, he repeats
The king's words, then hands over the letter containing
The royal wishes on the matter of Nooshzaad
And commands him to gather a host and to engage
In war without regard for the respect due a king's son.

The old man reads the letter
And listens to the messenger's long account.
At the hour of the rooster's call,
The sound of timpani rises at the palace gate.
A vast host departs from Mada'in,
And Raam Barzeen instantly takes off for war.

The news reaches Nooshzaad,
Who musters troops and pays their earnings.
All the Catholics and patricians of Rum
Who dwell on the border of this beautiful land,
With Shammaas at the lead as chief commander,
Form an army of men accustomed to shedding blood.

A great sound rises from Nooshzaad's door
As the troops fall into motion like a wind-whipped sea.
They exit the city in the direction of the plain,
Heads full of battle, hearts full of venom and vengeance.

At the sight of the dust rising from the troops,
Raam Barzeen asks for the blow of trumpets
And the formation of army lines.
The dust whisked by the motion of warriors,
The leader's spilled blood, the blows of mace
All contribute to tear apart the hearts of boulders.
One can no longer distinguish the face of the sun.

Nooshzaad positions himself at the army center.

He places a Rumi helmet on his head.
His troops, consisting of Rumi Catholics, are so many
That the ground disappears beneath the horses' hooves.
It is as if the earth beneath them is on the boil
And the air above is howling its affliction.

A brave warrior by the name of Pirooz the lion
Advances boldly, dressed in a coat of mail.
He cries, "O illustrious Nooshzaad,
Who is guilty of turning you away from justice?
Guard yourself from fighting with the king's host.
You will soon repent from such a struggle.
You have abandoned the faith of Kiumars,
The path of Hooshang and Tahmures.
The Messiah, himself an impostor, was killed
When he rejected the path of Yazdan.
Do not take the way of the founders of religion
Who do not know their own fate.
If divine majesty had shone on him,
How could the Jews have vanquished him?

"Have you heard of the actions of your noble father
In his dealings with Rum and with its Caesar?
Now you dare engage in war?
You dare to raise your head to the sky?
Despite this moon face, majesty, and stature,
Despite your limbs and chest, your hands and mace,
Your obscure soul is so troubled
That I see little intelligence in you.
A father living while his son yearns to displace him,
How does that fit with faith, rule, and reason?
If he dies, it is fair for you to claim the throne,
But to contest him today is a reprehensible crime.
Alas, this head, this crown, this name and birth
That you are about to throw into the wind!
You are not in a state to fight King Kesra
Unless you are a lion or an assailing elephant.

"O prince, I did not see in the king's palace
An image that has hands and reins,
Feet and stirrups, chest and neck,
A warring movement and a mace like yours.

461

Never did a painter see such a painting.
Never did the world have a more glorious king.
Do not burn the soul of Kesra Anushiravan.
Young as you are, do not tarnish the radiant crown.
Even if a son, enemy of the king, dies,
His father will lament and desperately grieve.

"Dismount, ask the king for forgiveness,
Cast aside your mace and Rumi helmet.
If far from here a cold wind touches your face,
The king's heart would be consumed by grief
And the sun would shed tears at the sight of you.
Do not spread seeds of greed throughout the world.
One must never rise against a king.
If you stray off the path I show you,
If you adopt the path of violence and pride,
You will have cause to remember Pirooz's advice,
Giving your heart reason to sigh deeply."

Nooshzaad replies, "O decrepit old man,
Your head is full of wind. Do not believe
That a host composed of illustrious warriors
And the son of a king will ask forgiveness.
I do not care for the faith of Kesra.
My heart leans toward my mother's beliefs.
The faith of the Messiah is her religion and mine.
I shall not deny her glorious example.
If the Messiah, who initiated this religion,
Was sentenced to death,
The majesty of the world did not abandon him.
The saint returned to Yazdan the holy,
Raising his status to celestial grandeur,
Which he favored over this obscure earth.
I have no fear if I must die. Death is a poison
Against which the antidote does not exists."

19 | The Battle of Nooshzaad with Raam Barzeen and the Death of Nooshzaad

Nooshzaad, having spoken to the aging Pirooz,
Covers the sky with his arrows' fletches.
Warriors stir to the sound of timpani and clarion.

Nooshzaad launches his horse, as swift as fire,
Advancing as fast as Aazargoshasp.
He overthrows the left wing of the Iranian host,
Allowing no warrior to advance to face him.
So many valiant men fall that Raam Barzeen
Grows concerned and orders a shower of shots
To fill the air like a raging spring hail.
Warriors keen on battle fight fiercely on both sides.

Nooshzaad is wounded in the melee
And remembers the advice of Pirooz.
He runs to the army center, body pierced by shots,
Cheeks pale from intense pain, and covered in dust.
He admits to the brave Rumis, "One engages in a vile,
Sad, and deplorable exploit when battling one's father."

He laments, weeps, and summons a bishop.
He confesses to him his heart's deepest secrets:
"I am responsible for the unfolding of this sad day.
Now that my head is about to be buried in dust,
Send a rider to my mother to tell her
That her son, Nooshzaad, has left this world,
That the days of justice and injustice end for him.
O dear mother, do not grieve for me!
I suffer the laws of this passing dwelling.
My part in this dismal life was such
That I did not enjoy a share of happiness,
That I did not shine light upon the world.
All living creatures are born with the purpose to die.
Since you will one day endure such an end,
Do not afflict yourself on my account.
My death does not cause me anguish.
What is worse is my father's discontent with me.
I wish not to be given a tomb and a throne,
I care not for lengthy ceremonies.

I prefer to be offered a Christian grave.
I require neither camphor nor musk nor amber,
Since I exit the world wounded by an arrow."

The illustrious Nooshzaad speaks, seals his lips,
And this man of lion heart soon expires.

At the news of the prince's death, the army disperses.
Raam Barzeen rushes to Nooshzaad's side, lamenting.
The Iranians no longer engage in killing on the battlefield.
They are unable to rejoice or to collect the spoils of war.
They find the prince dead, fallen like a vile thing,
A Rumi priest holding the head of the deceased.
The battlefield echoes with cries of grief.
Raam Barzeen is deeply afflicted and moved.
He asks the bishop about Nooshzaad's last wishes.

The bishop replies, "Only his mother
Is allowed to glance at his uncovered head.
When he felt the wound of the arrow, he forbade us
To build a mausoleum
And to make use of musk and amber.
His mother will prepare a tomb and a shroud
According to Christian rites and custom.
She will wrap his head, divested of a diadem,
And he will lie in rest without brocade or throne,
As the wretched one has seen it done for slaves.
Now his soul has united with the Messiah,
Although he did not perish on the cross."

All the Christians of the land scratch their cheeks.
A cry of mourning rises, and men and women assemble,
Declaring, "He is dead. This valiant young prince
Who was the heart and eyes of Anushiravan is dead!"

They take him away from the plain in a coffin
That travels from hand to hand for three farsangs.
Two mules carry him the rest of the way to his mother.

At the news of her son's demise,
She lowers her head and her diadem to the dust.
She exits the women's apartments
And advances on the road, face uncovered.

The crowd in the marketplace surrounds her.
A canvas enclosure is raised around her.
Everyone covers his or her head with dust.
The body is entrusted back to the earth.
One day, the wind brought him to life, and now,
Unexpectedly, the wind carries him away.
All the residents of Gundeh Shahpoor are in tears,
Their hearts consumed in sharing the king's grief.

Why do you writhe foolishly in the chains of greed?
You know that your visit here is not a drawn-out one.
Seek a passage, but do not seek the world,
Its flower is poison; do not attempt to smell it in a daze.
Do not turn away from faith and righteousness,
For the wrath of the Creator would precipitate your end.

The Taazian prophet once said, "If you stir up
Your father's wrath, it will be harmful to your soul.
When a father is discontented with his son,
Know that the son originates from a bad seed.
Never seek to distress your father in any way,
Even if he abandons you to intense pain.
When you have peace of mind,
Release sorrow from your heart,
Do not allow the flames of grief to consume it.
Do not allow your desires to conquer your wisdom.
Complete every action in due time, according to its value.

If you hold affection for Ali in your heart,
You will have, on the day of judgment,
A support for your demand for grace.
He is the only one who can open the door to salvation for us.
If you hold doubts in your heart,
Your place will not be secured in paradise.
May the heart of the world king be happy!
May my words be celebrated!

The throne of Mahmoud, world master,
Who desires splendor and glorifies every heart,
Has become the support of the glorious skies.
The sun forever shines from the brilliance it lends to it.
If you have a golden cup in your hand,

Pour golden wine and enjoy drinking.
Always dwell in happiness, rejoice with music and song,
Drink wine, but refrain from inebriation.
Always pay heed to the spoken word;
It is never in vain.

20 | Anushiravan's Dream
And Bozorgmehr's Journey to Court

We shall now turn to relate a more joyous account:
It is the story of Bozorgmehr.
Guard yourself from disregarding dreams;
They bring news to you, sort of like prophecy;
Especially when it is the dream of the world king,
A dream chosen by his luminous soul.
The stars hold counsel in the circle of the moon
And in the skies, scattering words on their path.
Serene souls dream of the future,
Like the reflection of a flame in water.

One night, while Anushiravan sleeps, his mind mature
And aware, his power young, he sees in dream
A charming royal tree rising before his throne,
A vision that enchants his heart.
The king calls for wine, lute, and singers.
But in this place of rest and delights sits a boar
With sharp tusks who, eager to take part in
The banquet, asks to drink from Anushiravan's cup.

As the sun raises its head in the house of the bull
And the song of the lark is heard on every side,
The king climbs on his throne, worried,
His heart aggrieved by his dream.

They summon a dream interpreter, and noblemen
Of good counsel take their seats around the throne.
The king recounts to them his dream.

The dream interpreter fails to answer,
For he has never heard of such a dream.
When one confesses one's ignorance,

One is sheltered from reproach.

In the absence of a response from the learned man,
The king, his heart full of worry, seeks other means.
He sends wise and sensible men everywhere.
He offers each one a pouch of gold
And promises much more upon his return.
Each pouch contains ten thousand dirhams,
A reward for finding a learned dream interpreter,
A man well-versed in the sciences, who could explain
The king's dream, unravel its unseen mysteries.
A man who would be the recipient of the reward
Along with the king's profuse expressions of gratitude.

The worldly sages, intelligent and learned cavaliers,
Depart in every direction.
One of these noblemen is named Aazaad Sarv.
He goes to the region of Marv, surveys the city,
Searches left and right until he encounters a wise man
Who holds the *Zand Avesta* in his hands, rudely teaching
Its principles to children, with outbursts and a loud voice.

In front of him is a young man, older than the others,
Who applies himself diligently to his studies.
Named Bozorgmehr, he comes from a learned family.
He holds the book before his eyes with passion,
Surpassing the other children in knowledge.

The wise envoy steers his horse his way, enters, and
Questions the master on the subject of the king's dream.

The teacher says, "This is not my domain.
As far as learning goes, I restrict myself to the *Zand*.
I teach it but dare not further my knowledge."

Bozorgmehr is struck by the words of the master.
He raises his eyes and says to the wise man,
"This is prey for me to catch.
I have the gift of dream interpretation."

The master shouts to him, "Have you yet finished
The book that you attempt to proudly stretch your neck
And make such outlandish claims?"

467

The envoy says, "O wise man,
Perhaps he is indeed in possession of the science.
Do not treat him with scorn.
What do you know of the rotations of fate?
Perhaps this youth's fortune is about to shine
And it is not you but providence that teaches him."

The master, angry with Bozorgmehr, cries,
"Speak and reveal your knowledge!"

The young man replies,
"I shall only speak in the presence of the king
And at a time when I stand before his throne."

The envoy gives him a horse, dirhams, and equipment.
They travel together from Marv,
Sprinting like francolins beneath rose bushes.

In this way, they march, discussing subjects
Relating to the king, his power, his majesty,
His command, his crown and throne.
They march until they arrive at a water source.
As it is the time to rest and dine,
They dismount beneath the shade of a tree.

After a meal, Bozorgmehr falls asleep beneath
The tree's canopy, his head covered with a cloth.
Deep reflections keep his road companion awake,
So moved is his mind by this learned youth.
He looks around and spots a serpent
Slithering around the sleeper.
It removes the piece of cloth covering the sleeper's head
And smells him from head to toe.
Then it glides away to hide on a treetop.

Once the black serpent reaches the highest branch,
The young man awakens. The serpent, seeing him
Stirring, vanishes behind the leaves of the tree.

The envoy is surprised and invokes
The name of Yazdan numerous times,
Understanding that this intelligent youth
Is attaining a high level of power.

21 | Bozorgmehr Interprets the King's Dream

Abandoning the forest, they continue on the road
Until they arrive at the king's court.

The envoy leaves the young man behind,
Presents himself before Kesra's throne,
And says to him, "O King Anushiravan,
May your fortune always be youthful!
After I left the royal palace, I rushed to Marv
Like a francolin dashing through a rose garden.
I found a youth among the learned men
And have brought him back here in haste."
Then he recounts what he heard him say
And the wonder of the black snake.

World master Kesra summons Bozorgmehr
And speaks to him at length of his dream.

The youth listens to Anushiravan,
His head full of words, his tongue eloquent.
He replies, "In your palace and among your idols
Dwelling in the night chambers,
There is a young man disguised as a woman.
Dismiss all the visitors from this hall
So that no one uncovers our scheme.
Command your women to walk before you
As you count each of their steps.
We shall ask this daring intruder
How he made his way into the lion's den.
With your heart aligned on the divine path,
You will have to access the hidden realm."

The king sends away all the visitors
And closes the imperial palace doors.
The members of the king's harem enter,
Full of beauty, color, and scent.
These gorgeous, proud, and modest creatures
Exhale the scent of jasmine as they pass before their king.
Failing to see a man among them,
Kesra grows as infuriated as an enraged lion.

The dream interpreter says, "This is not possible.
There has to be a young man among these women.
Have them pass before you one more time,
Face uncovered, and you will expose the ruse."

The king commands the eunuch to swiftly
Bring back the idols, to whom he says,
"Walk by me once again, but this time
Lift the veil of modesty that conceals your faces."

As they obey the command, they recognize
The dream interpreter's shrewdness,
For there appears in their midst a young man
Of cypress stature and Kianian visage.
His body shakes like a willow tree,
And his heart despairs of his sweet life.

In the apartments live seventy young women,
Each comparable to a noble cypress tree.
One of them, the daughter of the ruler of Chaadj,
Is svelte of stature and boasts ivory cheeks.
A young man of jasmine face and musk scent
Once loved her in her father's palace.
He now stands before her as her servant,
Following her every step.

The king asks for the identity of the young man,
Bold and strong favorite of a slave,
Who dares bring such shame to the royal court
By infiltrating Anushiravan's night chambers.

The woman says, "He is my younger brother.
We were born from the same mother
But different fathers.
He cannot act in improper ways with me.
My brother has dressed in this way
And covered his face in bashfulness,
For he dares not raise his eyes to his majesty.
Do not view it as an excuse."

The moon-faced woman fearfully pleads for mercy.
But she is merely uttering deceitful lies,
Her heart urged on by the flames of grief.

Anushiravan frowns, confused by the situation.
His fury breaks out, and he bellows at the young man:
"O filthy dog, you contaminate my pride and my lineage!"
Then he turns to the executioner and cries,
"The bodies of these guilty ones must be buried in dust!"

The executioner drags them outside,
Behind the curtain of the women's chambers.
He hangs them to teach a lesson,
So that others refrain from committing such a sin.

Anushiravan gives the dream interpreter
A pouch of gold, horses, and attire to his heart's desire.
He is stunned by his knowledge,
And his words give him cause to reflect.

His name is inscribed in the king's registers
Alongside wise men and advisors.
The affairs of Bozorgmehr prosper
As the revolving dome favors him.
His fortune increases every day,
And the king is delighted to have him by his side.

The heart of Kesra Anushiravan is full of justice,
His soul and head ennobled by wisdom.
He holds many wise men at court as well as
Learned men versed in all the sciences.
At all times, there are seventy eloquent men
Who reside and dine in the royal palace.
Every time he is in need of making decisions,
Giving alms, ordering banquets, or engaging in battle,
He would consult the wise men
So that they may guide him with new words.

Bozorgmehr is young and eloquent.
His mind is subtle and his face is fair.
His knowledge soon surpasses
The illustrious wise men, astrologers, and sages,
His head reaching higher than all the philosophers.
No one knows the secret of the stars as well as he does.
He is superior in the art of medicine
And is continuously praised for his articulate discourse
And his counsel on government and state affairs.

22 | Anushiravan Gives a First Feast for the Wise Men

One day, the king asks for tables to be set up
And invites the wise men, eloquent, smart,
And observant holders and seekers of knowledge.
Sages of awakened mind, noblemen searching
For the path of science, appear at court.
After the meal, they ask for wine to enliven their souls.

The vigilant king says to them,
"Reveal to me the secret treasury of wisdom.
Each of you may elaborate on the science
He is most familiar with and thereby enlighten us.
It will make everyone in this assembly quite happy."

The learned men, young and old,
The ones daring and knowing how to speak,
Share their knowledge with the king.

Bozorgmehr, upon hearing their speeches
And noticing that the king is keen on listening,
Blesses him, rises to his feet, and says,
"O master of justice, may the earth
Be the slave of your ivory throne!
May the sky draw its gleam from your crown!
Since you command your humble subjects
To unravel their tongues, I shall be next to speak,
Although I am a man of little consideration,
Owning the lowest level of knowledge.
One cannot blame a learned man who attempts
To unravel his tongue in front of Anushiravan."

King Kesra looks at him and says,
"Why should wisdom remain hidden?"

The youth develops a powerful language,
And his words render the world more luminous.
His eloquence and his advice
Have the power to enchain the hearts of sages.

He begins his discourse in praise of Yazdan,
Then he adds, "Brilliant is the mind of the one

Who makes use of a few profound words.
The person who has a thoughtless mind
Speaks at length without making much sense;
Excess speech makes him despised by other men.
Do your duty and avoid the path of ambition.
The earth offers us a fleeting journey,
And all we do is pass through life.
If our days were eternal, many men
Would hungrily seek world possession.
Nothing is better in life than humanity.
On this point, science will not contradict.
The first step to righteousness is awareness of the divine.
It is a state of being that propels one to fear Yazdan,
A fear that is just and right. Everything in man
That is luminous originates from righteousness.
One must shed tears over darkness and perversity.
Each heart is a slave to individual desires,
And for that reason each person has a distinct mood.
Furthermore, since there are different temperaments,
You must accommodate them all.

"The one who is first in his sphere
Takes great pains to rise even further.
But the sensible and wise man is the one
Who surely finds inner contentment in this world
With his body and in the other with his heart.
Do not torment yourselves
For the things you have not yet attained;
It is an illness for the soul and a pain for the body.
Strength gives man honesty;
Lies and perdition originate from weakness.
If your mind is devoid of wisdom,
Your most valuable ornament is silence.
If you take too much pleasure in your knowledge,
It will snatch governance from your intelligence.

"Wealthy and happy is the one who sheds all greed
And decidedly rejects its company.
Tenderness is wisdom's brother;
Wisdom is the diadem on the soul's head.
An intelligent man as your mortal enemy
Is far more worthy than an idiotic friend.

Wealthy is the one who dwells in happiness;
He is able to shackle greed and worry.
If you have enough humility to want to learn,
You will listen to those who have knowledge.
When a man enunciates a confused opinion,
He will not succeed in the action.
Anyone who forgets what he once knew
Must deny his tongue the right of speech.
If you hold wealth, gold and silver, and adorned horses,
Prepare your expenses in a convenient manner,
And abstain from either waste or avarice.

"When a sensible man keeps away from his foes,
The foes become his servants.
If you take the middle road, you will always
Stay true to yourself, with virtue as your guide.
If you perform your duty at your own risk,
You will triumph over the battle of life.
Avoid pronouncing meaningless words,
For then your share of a fire will be its smoke.
Do not attempt to undertake
A task that may not be completed:
You cannot pierce iron with water.
A learned king will always have humility,
But his knowledge will make him powerful.
Anyone who knows the works of the Creator
Is above the misfortunes of fate.
He will worship the Supreme Judge more and more
And will bar deev temptations from entering his heart.
He will abstain from improper acts
And never trouble those who must not be troubled.
In the end, we must turn to Yazdan,
Our foster Parent and Source of our daily bread."

Bozorgmehr's beautiful words
Light up the faces of the learned men.
The assembly is astonished to see such
A young man elevate himself to such heights.

Kesra Anushiravan, world master, is stunned.
He summons the heads of the processing offices
And asks for his name to be inscribed at the top

Of the list so that the register begins with him.

Bozorgmehr's fortune at court
Is that of a dazzling sun in the sky.
The leaders rise before the King of Kings
And salute Bozorgmehr with renewed acclaim.

Then they question him on his discourse, since
They see that his head and heart are the allies of wisdom.

The young man of pure heart and shining mind
Speaks again: "You must never, not even in thought,
Turn away from the king, distributor of justice.
We are the herd, and he is our shepherd.
We are the earth, and he is the lofty firmament.
We must not violate the pact that binds us to him.
We must not stray from his path or disobey him.
We must celebrate his joys
If we wish to establish justice in the world.
We must spread the fame of his merit
And watchfully guard his secrets.
Express your respect to him without intruding.
Though he may grow irritated,
Even the male lion's heart fears fire.

"If a mountain scorns his command,
We would call it foolish of heart and weak of mind.
Everything comes from the king:
Misfortune and good fortune, crowns and thrones,
Iron bonds and underground prisons.
The world is glorified by his affection.
Our blood boils when faced with his wrath.
His crowned head is Yazdan's grandeur.
Sensible men enjoy life under his rule.
The one who does not gain happiness
Through him originates from Ahriman.
His heart and head must be estranged from wisdom."

They listen to the young man's words, for they have
The power to awaken the decrepit minds of old men.
Then the assembly breaks up and disbands,
Tongues and mouths full of praise.

23 | Anushiravan Gives a Second Feast for Bozorgmehr and the Wise Men

A week later, the king of serene heart
Invites the learned men once again.
He sets aside world affairs to pay attention
To the discourse of the one who is honored
And whose knowledge is worthy of the king.

The eloquent sages, some youn,
Some insightful, and some worldly old men, arrive.
In their midst is the distinguished Bozorgmehr.
The men of science sit before the illustrious
Throne, their eyes fixed on Bozorgmehr,
Whose presence brings light to Kesra's face.

One of the most learned of them questions
Bozorgmehr on the subject of fate and destiny:
"What is the start and the outcome of fate?
Who is the instigator of its unfolding?"

Bozorgmehr responds, "The seeker dictates his path.
No matter how young he is and how hard he may work,
Day and night, the direction of his destiny will be unclear
And narrow, and water will slowly flow into his river.
Another, without value, will be reclining on the throne
Of good fortune, gently showered by rose petals.
The wise World Master, our foster Parent,
Has thus created the star of destiny:
One does not evade chance by one's own efforts."

Another asks, "Who is the one whose
Share of fortune and prosperity is highest?"

Bozorgmehr replies, "The one who cares for virtue
And whose labor bears the most fruit."

Another asks, "What feature is most worthy in us,
And who is most deserving of happiness?"

He replies, "Happiness originates from patience,
Clemency, nobility, and decency.

The modest man lowers his head and serves others,
Without contemplating a reward.
He strains himself to make way for the world.
He stays close to his companions at the hour of marching."

Another asks, "What must the wise man
Do in times of dispute and quarrel?"

He answers, "The one who recognizes his own faults
Must change his ways and his habits."

Another asks, "What can we do
To sustain the least amount of bodily harm?"

Bozorgmehr replies, "If a sensible man's heart
Is patient, he will attain contentment.
He will be equally fair when he trades,
In selling as well as in buying.
He will close the door to perversity and perdition.
He will forgive the fault of others
When he rises to the status of master
And will not cave into anger and impatience."

Another member of the assembly asks,
"Who is our individual protector?"

He replies, "The one who gives generously
And whose good deeds make him lenient and kind.
This one will not pursue his own longings.
Also, the one who exhibits indolence at work when
He sees that aggrandizement may lead to hardship."

Another asks, "Which is the better of the two:
A generous nature or a virtuous one?
How can we produce crops that would
Yield fruit for two springtides in one year?"

Bozorgmehr replies, "The one who, without being urged,
Surrenders his heart's happiness to giving
And expresses gratitude to the recipient of his act.
Should he expect a reward in return, he may as well
Be deemed a merchant and not a generous man."

Another asks, "What is the true ornament of a man,
And which is the ultimate high deed?"

He answers, "When the bighearted man performs
A good deed for someone who deserves it,
He gains in stature like a tall cypress tree
And never withers in the rose garden.
Conversely, handing musk to someone unworthy
Will result in a bramble that will never generate
Either scent or flower, just as it is quite futile
To question a person who is deaf and mute."

Another asks, "In this fleeting world,
The wisest cannot escape pain and suffering.
How can we acquire a good reputation
And drive life toward a happy conclusion?"

He answers, "Go and keep sin at bay.
Treat everyone like you treat yourself,
And do not wish anything on anyone, friend
Or enemy, that you may not wish on yourself."

Another says, "What is the better option,
Moderate or excessive work?"

He answers, "Nothing follows the path of wisdom except
For a thought or act that takes root in deep reflection.
If you wish for your labor to bear fruit,
Exert yourself with every opportunity."

Another asks, "Who is worthy of praise,
Since one must weep over the guilty?"

He replies, "The one who places his hopes
In the Creator whom he fears the most."

Another says, "O clear-sighted man,
Your head rises above the dome of sky.
Who does the sublime firmament favor most?"

The eloquent man replies,
"The one who holds neither worry nor need.
He will receive the most beautiful gifts from destiny

As long as he does not stray off the path of justice."

Another asks, "Which is the knowledge
By which we can attain happiness in the world?"

He replies, "The wisdom of the patient man
Who scorns the shameless and angry man,
And who closes his eyes on the guilty.
Also, the one who, though his brain simmers
With fury, is able to restrain himself and forgive."

Another asks, "O wise man,
What does the sensible man approve of the most?"

He replies, "The one who cultivates his wisdom
Never regrets when something evades him.
If someone he cherishes is cast in the dust,
He does not forsake his heart to regret, grief, and fear.
Furthermore, he extracts all hope for the impossible
From his heart, like wind plucking leaves off a willow tree.
He is always happy, his soul is serene,
And he does not mourn the passage of time."

Another asks, "What is faulty for a king
And will afflict the heart of an honest man?"

He replies, "The wise man says that the king
Can be at fault in four instances:
First, if he fears his enemy in battle;
Next, if a charitable act does not afford him joy;
Thirdly, if he neglects sage advice on battle day;
Finally, if he proceeds in haste in trying times
Without allowing for a break to rest or sleep."

Another asks, "Who is without reproach,
And what is there to blame in a free man?"

He replies, "The just man is the one for whom
Wisdom acts as a guarantor of his words.
But when a wealthy man lies and cheats, and seeks honor
By devious, unfair means, when he restrains
His selfishness and greed before the king,
And then foolishly wounds the hearts of pure men,

When he points the finger at others in blame or judgment,
Feeling the urge to dominate, all these are signs of vanity."

Another asks, "What is the most profitable
Disposition for a righteous man?"

He replies, "The one who speaks only the truth
And whose intentions lean toward virtue.
He makes use of his tongue in a way
That never gives him cause to shed shameful tears.
In the midst of shouts, he speaks in a soft voice.
The wisest is the one who never allows himself
To stray from the path by following his desires."

Another wise man asks, "Who in the world is able
To manage his affairs, enjoy life, and help his relatives
And his allies without causing any harm to anyone?"

He replies, "The one who, from the beginning,
Seeks the path of Yazdan, our shelter,
Master of day and night, Moon and Sun,
To whom we must express our gratitude.
One must submit one's heart in public
And in private to the command of the world king;
One must take care of one's body
And defend it against pain and greed;
One must watch over one's family
And increase the provisions for the poor;
Entrust young children to the care of teachers,
For we must not abandon the world to the ignorant.
If a child obeys, the father must treat him with indulgence."

Another asks, "What place must a good son
Take next to his father?"

He answers, "A son must be dearer
To his father than his own life.
After his death, the son must maintain
His father's name and reputation.
For that reason, he calls him his guide."

Another asks, "According to your knowledge,
What valuable things bring happiness to a man?"

He says, "A man is considered for his wealth.
The one who has nothing is scorned.
There are a few things in what I told you
That you must pay attention to: In the first place,
The thing that inspires you to acquire indicates,
By its nature, that your character is good.
Furthermore, if you have obtained it but do not use it,
A stone and a gem worthy of a king are of equal value."

Another says, "Which renowned king,
Master of the throne, surpasses everyone?"

He answers, "The ruler who assures the safety
Of the honest man, whose voice injects
Terror into the hearts of evil men,
And whose throne brings peace on earth."

Another asks, "How does a man gain power,
And who is poor and burned by grief?"

He replies, "Influential is the one who is grateful
For the gifts of the Master of the firmament.
For the one who is not the companion of good fortune,
There is no greater calamity than greed."

The leaders admire Bozorgmehr's acumen
And unanimously shower him with praise.

24 | Anushiravan Gives a Third Feast for Bozorgmehr and the Wise Men

Seven days pass, and on the eight day, at dawn,
The victorious king sits on the turquoise throne
And summons his wise men, skillful in their speech
And their knowledge, and they debate various subjects.

A dissatisfied Kesra says to Bozorgmehr,
"Remove the veil of modesty from your face."

The learned and eloquent youth unravels his tongue
And wisely elaborates on all sorts of subjects.

He begins in praise of Kesra Anushiravan:
"May the master of the crown, vanquisher of lions,
Most illustrious king, powerful, learned,
And virtuous, always, always be victorious!"

Then he adds, "Man can attain grandeur
Only by turning his back on evil.
Since you must grow by way of learning,
You need intelligence to help you find the right words.
Courage is the means to achieve fame.
Providence fends off heartless men.
If you yearn to sit on the throne,
You must be endowed with virtue and skill.
The tree will bear fruit when its limbs are verdant.
When someone asks about merit,
Refrain from alluding to your lineage.
Birth without merit is meaningless.

"A king once spoke on this subject:
        'If a rose lacks fragrance, do not speak of its color.
        Let us not demand river water from a blazing fire.'
A king's treasury grows with his generosity
Rather than by hording a hidden treasure.
One extracts merit from one's verbosity.
One brings words to justice through one's actions.
The sensible and wise man breathes humility;
His skies have been nourished with wisdom.
So is the man of simple heart whose noble soul
Preserves him from perversity.
Wisdom represents the tree of honesty,
And its first fruit is the king's heart.

"A sense of contentment for your fate
Will afford you with a sense of peace.
Giving into greed causes one tremendous fears.
Perform your good deeds away from the sight
Of others, or else you will not be rewarded.
Fortune is propitious to the generous.
Patience is recompensed by happiness.
Any man who seeks power needs merit.
He must first be prudent and intelligent,
Then he must acquire experience.

At the time of action, he must have friends
And calculate his chances, good and bad.
He must be endowed with wisdom and righteousness,
And rid himself of any hint of falsehoods and lies.
If you have strength, put in the effort:
It will only increase your power.
Your words must complement these qualities.
If a strong man does not apply strength,
He will not obtain the object of his desires.
But know that the one who exerts effort
Beyond measure has no hope of success.

"I shall first enumerate five traits that distinguish
The wise man and shield him from pain,
Followed by seven traits of the foolish man
Whose inclinations lead him to wicked acts.
To begin with, a wise man will not
Grieve over something that eludes him.
He will not rejoice for what he has not yet attained
And will refrain from bemoaning what passes by him.
He will not place his hopes on what has not yet occurred
And will not claim that a willow branch can produce fruit.
He fears the future at the moment
When he is free of pain and suffering.
If the harshness of fate exceeds all calculation,
He will move forward and not weaken in action.

"Let us turn to the seven behaviors of an unwise man:
In the first place, he bursts into fits of anger for no reason;
Secondly, he opens his treasury to unworthy people
And obtains neither reward nor reciprocity;
Thirdly, he does not give thanks to Yazdan
And is unfamiliar with the path of righteousness.
Fourthly, he broadcasts his secrets loudly;
In the fifth instance, he draws grief and hardship
Onto himself by uttering imprudent words;
In the sixth place, he depends on unreliable people
And searches for silk among the brambles.
Finally, he quarrels under false pretense and lies
On his path to shamelessly seek glory.

"Know, O mighty King, that evil acts

Only lead to pain and suffering.
When you hold your tongue in an assembly,
The reward for your silence is a peaceful heart.
When you lend your ear to the speech
Of a learned man, his words feed your soul
And bring clarity and awareness to your heart.
Try to remember these bits of wisdom,
For they are the crown on the throne of knowledge.
If you wish for knowledge to bear fruit,
Release the jewels of wisdom in your speech.
If you wish to glorify your name,
Draw words out of your tongue
Just as you extract your sword from its sheath.
You raise the status of low-ranking people
By sitting in the company of a learned man.
The heart and soul shine through wisdom;
Take care not to hover around deceitful lies.

"When an eloquent man speaks,
Stay patient and allow him to finish.
The words of the speaker will make you powerful,
And you may then speak as you heard him speak.
You may not search for independence in knowledge,
No matter how arduous the path may be.
In times of distress, wisdom guides your soul's tranquility.
The union between your tongue and your heart
Tightly shutters and seals the door to perdition.
May the soul of Anushiravan always yearn to learn!"

A sage of ingenious mind asks Bozorgmehr,
"What is beauty, and what are elegant words?
Where does one find the light,
And how can one remain free from hardships?"

He answers, "Anyone who possesses wisdom
Will find happiness in both worlds."

The wise man says, "What if he lacks wisdom,
Since it is a shining gift from the divine?"

He answers, "Knowledge is the ultimate goal.
A learned man will rise above the status of noblemen."

The wise man asks, "What if he fails to find the path
And cannot purify his soul with knowledge?"

He replies, "We must then humbly respect him
As a valiant warrior who leans on his body.
If he is strong on the day of battle and
Able to fling enemy heads into the dust,
He will be dear to the king's heart
And will be happy and mighty for life."

The other asks, "What if he lacks a warrior's body
And fails to search for the path of knowledge?
What if he has neither religion nor faith?"

He replies, "Then it would be better for death
To place a somber helmet on his head."

The wise man asks, "How are we to nourish
Ourselves with the fruit of the tree cultivated
By the sage in his spring garden?
How are we to benefit from it
As we walk beneath its glorious shade?"

He answers, "The man who bars his tongue
From uttering evil words will save his soul from pain.
The man who does not tear the skin of others
With his discourse will be viewed as a friend.
He will accomplish with ease the most challenging things,
And he will treat everyone equally, enemy or friend."

The wise man raises his voice again to ask,
"Can the one who distances himself
From the road of evil become powerful?"

Bozorgmehr responds, "Evil actions are like rotten fruit.
The ear of the one who speaks softly
Will rarely be stricken by harsh words.
Know that the tongue is the cause of human misery.
If you seek to avoid pain, weigh your words carefully.
The only suitable place for a man of a few words,
A man devoted to the king, is a seat near the throne.
He will not weep over future misfortune like a bird
Or a wild beast flails when trapped in a snare.

Furthermore, he stands strong against the wicked,
Whom he avoids as he strides the path of virtue.
He averts grievous matters and disturbing the peace.
He does not allow happiness to pass by him
Without delving into it with unrestrained joy.
He abstains from counting the steps of future days.
He eludes his enemy with vigilance, like on the hunt,
And holds on to his friends like the fletch to the arrow.
The sensible man has little wish for indulgence
When he is aware that the end result is regret.

"Reject inertia and laziness; work hard
And thus conquer, with your body's weariness,
The right to treat yourself to rest and feast.
In this world, there is no gain without fatigue,
And the lazy man will never acquire wealth.
May Anushiravan's sweet soul make the world prosper!
May his power always remain young!"

They continue to discuss this theme at length,
Awakening dormant hearts.
Wise men, border keepers, and enlightened sages
Praise Bozorgmehr, celebrate the king's glory,
And take leave of each other with joyful hearts.

25 | Anushiravan Gives a Fourth Feast for Bozorgmehr and the Wise Men

After two weeks, the king clears army matters and
Summons wise men, sages, and noblemen to court.
He questions them on a variety of subjects, including
Their bodies and their births, their fervor and their rest.
He brings up wisdom, justice, royalty, throne, and power.
He asks them about the beginning and end of prosperity.

Each one responds in measure to his knowledge,
But the king is not satisfied until addresses Bozorgmehr:
"Extract the dazzling gem from its hiding place."

Bozorgmehr returns the homage and says,
"O King of serene heart, O affectionate monarch,

Know that never has a crowned ruler reigned with
More justice, knowledge, glory, wisdom, and fortune.
Never has the world seen
A more glorious crown, throne, and royal face.
When a king cares for his affairs,
All hostility vanishes, and no one seeks war.
It is better to turn our backs on wicked deeds
Than to subject our hearts to grief and misery.
The learned man once related a beautiful story
About a king who had the wisdom of acting
On the path of virtue and shunning transgressions.
The king fears Yazdan at the time of judgment.
He suppresses his hunger for power
And rejects enmity and hatred.
He will control his urges with wisdom,
Even and especially in a moment of fury.

"The king never beholds a thought
That the Creator would disapprove.
He recognizes that joy and grief come from Yazdan,
With paradise as the reward for virtue.
The duty of the world master and honorable man
Is to be honest and conciliatory at all times.
His tongue will utter truths, and his soul will be serene.
World honor depends on it.
Those who counsel him will be held in high esteem.
With his eloquence, clear heart, and sense of justice,
He will treat each person according to his rank.
No subject of the king must be robbed of his rightful place.

"The crown will remain powerful,
And royal majesty will be preserved so long
As the king holds learned men in high regard.
If he listens to the counsel of ignorant men,
He will be responsible for the collapse of his throne.
The ignorant one evades knowledge
And seeks quarrel out of witlessness.
When the king has access to vast knowledge,
He will rule his realm with pride and glory.
He will observe what happens at court
And will lacerate his enemies' mouths with poison.
We must not allow anyone to endure a night of pain;

Such a thing would cause misfortune for the king.
Furthermore, he must keep at bay any criminal
Whose evil race and evil nature merit punishment,
So that the innocent have nothing to fear.
We must open the royal prison door to anyone
Who is held there, whether guilty or innocent,
At Yazdan's command, as dictated in the *Zand Avesta*.
But if he is someone evil, impudent, and depraved,
We must rid the surface of the earth of his presence
To prevent him from having a return to good fortune
Or committing his crimes in the homes of men.

"The world master must be connected
To faith and justice to attain a state of joy.
He must work in private and in public
To purify the world with his sword
From the deevs and their evil misdeeds.
If he commands his army wisely,
Men who need help will cease to suffer.
The hearts of those who strategize will fail.
Engage men to make repairs before the time of battle
To set the course right on any breach to the empire.
Any blame placed on the king falls back
On the throne and crown.

"Cherish your son as much as you can,
For he is like your reflection on water.
When you must part from him against your wishes,
Do so by making use of your wisdom.
One can only hope that his heart will be enlightened
By instruction and the teachings of knowledge.
You must open your treasury door for him
To alleviate any pain he may suffer.
A royal prince's heart must never be broken,
Even if he were to commit an unjust act.
Return him to the right path with affection,
And restrain his power from the beginning.
If you find a hint of enmity in him, you must
Pluck it as one plucks a weed from the rose garden;
If you allow it to grow, it will gain in strength
And will fill the royal gardens with brambles.

"A king who wishes to act with dignity
And caution must not lend an ear to slander.
Should he feel the need to punish evildoers,
He may spill blood only by divine command.
An ill-natured vizier who indulges in gossip
May cause the downfall of throne and kinship.
It is best not to heed the discourse of ignorant men.
When someone speaks poorly of justice,
Beware of pronouncing a judgment.
Your every act must be performed with righteousness,
And your heart must remain distant from perversity.
Only virtue befits the world king.
Surrendering to the deev is the cause of perdition.
The ruler who listens to these words
Will make wisdom his heart's witness.
The crown will bless the king,
And the throne will gain strength from him.
The king's crown and throne will be proud of him,
His enemies will lose trust in their fortunes,
And for as long as the revolving dome of sky turns,
A good memory of him will remain.
May the mighty soul and the glorious name
Of Kesra Anushiravan remain forever young!"

The assembly is confounded by Bozorgmehr's words.
The acumen of the sages appears dim compared to his.
Bozorgmehr's advice brings tears to the royal lashes,
And his grandeur expands in Anushiravan's eyes.
The king fills his mouth with freshwater pearls.

Everyone leaves the king's audience hall,
Lips pronouncing words of praise and blessings.

26 | Anushiravan Gives a Fifth Feast for Bozorgmehr and the Wise Men

Another seven days pass, and on the eighth day,
At the time when the world-illuminating sun
Begins to shine, rejecting the indigo veil of night
And decking the world in a mantle of gilded brocade,

The King of Kings sits in the presence of his wise men,
Aging, intelligent, and eloquent chiefs:
Ardeshir, leader of insightful and noble men;
Shahpoor and Yazdegerd, the scribe;
Astrologers, seekers, and insightful speakers.

The impassioned and young Bozorgmehr
Presents himself before Anushiravan
And praises the king, who is delighted with him.
The world ruler addresses the learned assembly:
"Whose soul among you holds so much knowledge
That he can be the support of Yazdan's faith
And safeguard the kingly throne from any form of evil?"

The grand wise master opens his mouth to respond:
"It is the king's sense of justice that brings
Luster to royal majesty, diadem, and throne.
Since he opens his treasury according to merit,
His name will remain powerful after his death.
Generosity is the gift that assigns great fame
To one, while wealth exists to be distributed.
Next, his name will retain glory after his death
Because his tongue is devoid of lies and he does not
Seek to acquire honor by fraudulent means.

"He is just and generous,
And his crown is the embellishment of his era;
The king's illustrious head does not boil with rage
Over the errors committed by his subjects;
He speaks in such a way that his name
Will never grow old in the world;
In all things, great and small, he speaks the truth
And never deviates from the rules of dignity;
He cares for his throne's servants as much as his fortune.
As learned and eloquent as is his speech,
His tongue ably infuses it with even more style;
His heart never ceases to learn,
And his brain is consumed by thoughts.
Anyone who has gratitude is endowed with wisdom.
Without it, man is left to complain about his hardships.
O King, never divorce your heart from your mind,
For the mind drives you to glory and to a happy end.

It is a poor mind of little integrity that claims:
       'No one equals me in knowledge!'"

Yazdegerd the scribe says, "O wise King
Who welcomes learning, it is shameful for a king
To shed blood and to display anger over trivial things.
If he acts lightly, without first reflecting, he will
Find himself in opposition to the intelligent man
And will grow bitter as a result of his ignorance.
If the king's heart abandons itself to greed,
It is because the deev has united with his mind.
If the mind of the judge is bitter,
His words will not expedite the affair.

"A warrior who, at the time of battle, fears for
His own life with no qualms of being humiliated,
And a wealthy man with a narrow, avaricious heart
Are one and the same, and might
As well disappear into the dust.
Power does not suit a poor man,
For the destitute is not fit for command.
An old deceiver who presents himself as odious
Will remain unhappy, and after his death,
His soul will be consumed by fire.
If a young man displays laziness in action,
The world will be disgusted by him, and
He will lose his power, his health, and his vigor."

Once Bozorgmehr hears these words,
His brain fills with these pearls of wisdom.
He says, "O sun-faced King, may the starry sky
Be always propitious to your desires!
Act in a way that any intelligent man
May cultivate his mind with knowledge.
The hearts of boulders weep over the foolish man
Who, because of his ignorance, inspires scorn.
He cannot discern the beginning and the end of things,
Or the difference between the base and the honorable.
He is despised by the working crowds
And still more despised by wise men: First, the judge
Of bad faith, to whom the sage grants no respect;
Then the army leader who guards his treasury,

His soldiers refuse to listen to his command;
The learned man who does not retreat in fear
When faced with an offence
That only appears to him as something distasteful;
The physician who has fallen ill
And finds himself incapable of curing the ailing;
The poor man who takes pride
In the acquisition of wealth of little worth;
The king whose subjects are unable
To rest because of their unsettled hearts;
The sweet breeze of dawn that strokes your cheek
And you forget to express your gratitude;
The intelligent man who grows infuriated
And fixes his eyes on the wealth of others;
Finally, the one who favors guidance from
The ignorant and abandons power to the lazy.
A man without talent but endowed with wisdom
Repents when he commits a wicked act.
But the heart of a foolish man ignites with desire
Like the fire that finds sulphur as nourishment
Or feeds on a parched field of reeds.

"May Anushiravan's heart remain forever valiant!
May the leaders of the earth stand as his servants!"

27 | Anushiravan Gives a Sixth Feast for Bozorgmehr and the Wise Men

The king allows another seven days to pass,
Then commands the servants to deck the court.
He sits on the golden throne
With bracelet, crown, and golden belt.
On one side is his wise vizier,
On the other is Yazdegerd the scribe;
Around him stand the clerics
And the eloquent Bozorgmehr.

The king first addresses Bozorgmehr:
"Why should one hide the gems of wisdom?
They are words able to heal the soul

And give grandeur to a man of little worth.
The listener's heart finds delight in the discovery
Of the mysteries concealed in words
While the loquacious speaker is deaf to them."

The wise man says to Bozorgmehr, "O friend,
More illustrious than the revolving dome of sky,
What do you know that reduces you when it grows
And allows you to grow when it declines?"

Bozorgmehr replies, "The less you eat, the stronger
Your body will be and the more your mind will benefit.
As you engage in the act of performing good deeds,
You will surpass your equals."

Yazdegerd the scribe says, "O eloquent speaker
And learner, what are the three flaws hiding
In one's heart that serve or benefit no one?"

He replies, "The first is the desire to blame others;
You must first wash your heart of it.
No one in the world is without failing or without flaw,
Whether one's actions occur in private or in public.
If you are raised on a pedestal, you are subject to envy;
If you succumb to a decline, you will shed tears.
The informer and the double-faced man
Toil at extracting even dust out of water.[76]
A speaker who is out of line
Loses his dignity and his reputation.
The one who fails to listen to the end also fails
To learn and thereby will fail to conform.
The wise man does not fix his eyes on his fortune;
In the absence of wealth, he does not bend in anger."

The grand wise master says, "Let me ask you this,
Since you surpass the most intelligent in wisdom:
No one exists in the world who does not have desires,
Whether he reveals them to others or conceals them.
Man pursues the fulfillment of his longings
By means that display his strength and worth.

◇◇◇◇◇◇◇◇◇◇◇◇◇
76 Extracting dust out of water: A nearly impossible task, unusual and almost supernatural.

Which path is most profitable and which path
Is most laborious, painful, and pernicious?"

Bozorgmehr replies, "The road splits into two paths:
Think of which one you wish to take.
One is the path of those who are fearless,
Full of ill intention and ill deeds;
The other is the path of virtue and wisdom.
Only one road in the world leads back to the dust,
A long and arduous path full of dread and terror.
You may direct your questions to wisdom,
Your guide for the why and the how of things.

"The wise man owns a gift from Yazdan:
Look and see who is worthy of such a gift.
No one in the world wishes to employ
A man who has a strong body yet lacks wisdom.
Where there is no wisdom, there is no soul.
Wisdom is the soul of the soul, Yzad is its witness.
Without wisdom, there might as well be no life.
When man attains the foundations of knowing,
He becomes suited for life's trials and tribulations.
The first use of knowledge is to come face to face
With the Creator, who lives on eternally.
By placing your faith in the Creator, you attain the object
Of your desires and may effortlessly attain your goal.

"The second tenant of knowing is to adequately
Fulfill your needs of food and nourishment.
In food and clothing, maintain purity
And closely observe divine command.
When you find yourself in need,
Never seek the aid of a miser.
Select a profession that honors your name.
Develop a friendship with someone
Who can help you in times of danger.
If you seek praise, maintain silence in assemblies.
When you are given the chance to speak,
Repeat what you have painstakingly learned.

"Weigh your words rather than your dinars,
For a wise man cares little for wealth.

Bring ease and eloquence into your speech,
Making wisdom your bow and words your shafts.
If you must engage in battle, exercise vigilance
And protect your body from enemy blows.
When ill-intentioned troops form ranks,
Maintain your composure and a sense of caution.
When you come face to face with a combatant,
Guard yourself from turning pale with fear.
You will conquer him with an assault,
But if you show the slightest hint of weakness,
Your head will be slashed.
Launch your horse with caution,
And beware of your adversary's weapons.
If he behaves in a rash manner,
Guard yourself from turning your back on him.
Select prudent battle companions.
If you are not up to an enemy in strength, do not test him,
For prudence calls for a warrior to return from war alive.

"Nourishment must not cause you harm:
Eat in moderation and avoid excess;
Overeating will not be to your advantage.
It will make you swell and grow
In weight as much as in height;
Consume food to conserve your appetite.
Your forces will increase with abstinence.
Drink wine to cheer up a bit but in moderation,
As a drunken man will never hear a word of praise.

"If you devote yourself to serve Yazdan,
The world will be the head, and you will be its eyes.
Continuously utter the name of the Creator,
Making divine reflection the basis of your worship.
Pay attention to moments when you must take action.
Set aside some time to rest, day and night.
Select the middle path in all your endeavors,
In worship, battle, and war. You are a breath of wind;
You are water kneaded with a piece of clay.
Do not forsake Yazdan's path.
Do not curtail your prayers to indulge in meals.
Keep renewing yourself; the law is an ancient one.
Seek happiness through good deeds; consider them

A booty, a divine offering, a source of gratitude.
Keep at bay the wicked and the contemptible.
A sensible man will adorn his head
With the laurels of benevolence.
The one whose actions are righteous, in private
And in public, will be celebrated everywhere.
If you allow your desires to overcome sense and caution,
Wisdom will turn its back on you.

"Teach your children the art of writing as soon
As you secure your life and your family's life.
If you want your work to bear fruit,
Stay facing your masters and teachers.
The art of writing may lead a youth to sit upon a throne
And allow an incompetent man to be worthy of fortune.
It is the most honorable of professions;
It restores the power of a fallen man.

"If the expert writer combines his writing skills
With his mind's acumen, he will certainly
Gain the right to sit before the king.
If his body is accustomed to labor,
The king will give him treasure beyond measure.
If he combines eloquence with writing skills
And if his mind expands with reflection,
He will gracefully select the shortest expression
And reproduce it in elegant handwriting.

"The scribe must be a sensible man,
Indefatigable and endowed with a keen memory.
He must indulge in the king's moods, abstain from slander,
Display a nature that is chaste, patient, wise,
Truthful, loyal, and of good faith and integrity.
These assets will elevate him at court
And grant him a seat before the throne."

Kesra's heart blossoms like a spring rose.
He says to the grand wise master,
"Go and confer on him a new distinction.
Give him silver and a worthy robe of honor,
For his speech brings joy to the soul."

28 | Anushiravan Gives a Seventh Feast for Bozorgmehr and the Wise Men

Seven days later, as the sun's crown faintly gleams,
The king takes his place upon the ivory throne.
Before him stand the grand wise master,
The noblemen, and the enlightened, ambitious sages,
Such as Saabeh, Yazdegerd the scribe,
And, in front of them, the intelligent Bahman.

The king addresses Bozorgmehr:
"Enlighten our hearts and show us the true path.
Tell us everything you know about righteousness,
Avoid gaining favor by telling lies.
How should my command be observed?
How should my path and my pact be preserved?
How should my subjects express their loyalty?
Speak freely and hold nothing back.
Avoid disguising meaningless words
Beneath embellished discourse.
The leaders gathered here from around
The empire will spread your teachings."

The wise man replies to the enlightened king,
"Your seat is loftier than the azure skies above!
The path of obeisance to the king can be likened
To the path indicated by faith, says a wise man.
One must never fail, not for a moment,
In the execution of royal command.
One must not cede the king's heart to unrest.
Anyone who is the enemy of the king is,
In his soul, a worshipper of Ahriman.
A man who disavows friendship with his king
Deserves to be stripped of brains and skin.
Know that world peace depends on the king.
If we act with the common good in mind,
Kesra Anushiravan will grant us advancement,
For he has access to good and bad fortune,
Never acting with hostility or with favor.
Do not seek to see his son take his place.
Worship his heart-charming face like your soul.

"Distress is barred entry to a nation
Where the love of the king reigns.
His glory has the power to shelter you from harm,
For his fortune assures you peace and happiness.
Under the influence of the king, the world's heart
Smiles on the face endowed with divine majesty.
If he is gracious toward you,
Always pay heed to his order.
If you turn away from him in thought,
Fortune will turn its back on you.
If you are held close to him, do not show pride.
If you are far from him, do not cause harm.
If the king imposes strain on a servant,
He must reflect upon the fact that it is
Matched with good rewards and salary.
He must never be repelled by work
And must display his valor in battle.

"Gratitude to the king is a gift from Yazdan,
And gratitude to Yazdan blesses the king.
One must entrust the king's secret to his heart
And confide it to neither Sun nor Moon.
When one exhibits sluggishness in the execution
Of royal command, one becomes one's own critic.
Cursed be the flowers of the tree that fails
To scatter its fruit on the throne and crown!
Never vilify the king's close companions,
For that would diminish the favors he would grant.
Anyone who lies will never be honored by kings.
Take care never to pronounce before the king
Words that would be at odds with wisdom.
If he questions you, tell him everything you know,
And nothing more, or else you will disgrace yourself.
There are many things to learn in the world
That the ear hears in private and in public.

"The soul of someone scorned by the king
Will always be stricken by grief.
But the one smiled upon by the king
Will be respected in the entire world.
If you are welcomed to the kingly court,
Do not assume proud and pompous airs,

498

Though you may be an old servant.
No matter how long your service,
Know that you are not indispensable to the king.
If he favors another, he must, without a doubt,
Be as devoted as you have been.
If he blames you for something,
Ask forgiveness and do not complain.
But if you know you are innocent of the crime,
Reveal what is in your heart to the king.
If you harbor deceitful thoughts in your heart,
Refrain from showing him your face and move away.
By the grace of the Creator, he can see your soul;
With his glory, he can peer into your heart's perversity
And witness your soul's gloominess.
From then on, you will no longer
Be the recipient of his loving kindness,
You will no longer hear him utter friendly words.

"Consider the royal court like the sea:
His servants are the sailors, their skills are the vessels,
Speech is the anchor, wisdom is the sail.
When the sage navigates, he fortifies the sail,
For it protects him and shelters him from the sun.
When skill and talent fail to unite with intelligence,
It is best not to venture into court.
Were the king a mountain on fire,
His servants would have to adjust to live there.
In an outburst of rage, the flames burn you;
In times of contentment, they shine light on you.
Court may offer you milk and honey,
But beware, for at times its elixir can be deadly venom.

"The king's action is akin to the motions of the sea:
The moon shines in the sky at its command.
One draws from the flows a fistful of sand,
The other plucks pearls out of shells.
May the revolving dome always spin at the will
Of Anushiravan, who rises above all other rulers
And whose good deeds make the empire flourish!"

Kesra pays attention to Bozorgmehr,
Whose voice revives his heart.

He once promised to pay him four pouches
Of silver for each exclamation of praise.
He follows through and rewards him in kind.
There are so many acclaims that, in the end,
The sage receives forty pouches of royal dirhams.

The treasurer keeps the score before the king.
Each pouch contains ten thousand dirhams.
The King of Kings says, "Bravo, bravo, and bravo!"
As the sum corresponds to the promise made.
The sun-faced treasurer brings the pouches
And places them in front of Bozorgmehr.

29 | The Story of Mahbood, Anushiravan's Vizier

Having weaved sufficient words into this story, I turn
To another tale, one of Mahbood, the king's vizier.

Never chose the option to rest over the chance to learn,
And never surrender your mind
To the illusion that you know everything.

If you say, "I have paid my debt
To acquiring knowledge,
I have learned all that was necessary,"
Fate will play a fascinating trick on you
And will force you to sit before a master.

Listen to this adventure, according to the words
Of a peasant bard who read it in an ancient book.

A wise man said, "Never has a king of Kesra's stature
Sat on an ivory throne and placed the crown on his head.
No one holds the memory of a king as mighty
In war and feast, as able to master his desires, and as just.
He clings to learning to enlighten his mind
And adorn it with the pearls of knowledge.
He sits in the company of wise men at meals and at rest.
Just as Anushiravan improved his discourse
Through learning, you too must intensify your studies.
You may not know yourself if you make claims

To be learned and to have the power to act as you wish.
At that point, you are the most ignorant of all
Because you are incapable of listening to others."

Learn from this story, and keep in mind
The words of the aging poet bard.
I posed him questions on times gone by,
And he related to me that Anushiravan
Has an honest and attentive vizier, his treasurer.
Righteous in his intentions,
Of simple nature and excellent counsel,
His mind and heart full of gentle words,
He seeks only to acquire a good name in the world.
With these qualities, he finds
Access to the king, who honors him.

He has two sons akin to joyous paradise, always
At the service of the king, whether during prayer
Or at the moment one receives barsom from a cleric.

Anushiravan eats only from Mahbood's hand
And considers his two sons with equal respect.
The kitchen features in Mahbood's house,
Where the king is always a welcomed guest.
The two young, illustrious, and pure men
Carry the meals to the king.

The noblemen at court shed bitter tears of jealousy
In regard to Mahbood and his high-ranking position.
Specifically, there is a man named Zarvan,
Whose sole desire is to attend the king's court.
He is old, and he functions as the king's chamberlain
And as his palace attendant in times of feast.
His consuming sense of envy for Mahbood and his sons
Provokes tears to flood his face through the year.
He seeks a pretext to turn the king
Against these virtuous and innocent men.
But he cannot find a means to slander them
And to alienate them from Anushiravan's mind.

The wise Mahbood is not aware of having an enemy
In the palace and does not concern himself
With the words and deeds of the wretched man.

One day, a Jew borrows money from Zarvan
To assess its value. He comes and goes, his influence
Grows, and he befriends the possessor of a dark soul.
Gaining familiarity with the chamberlain,
He is granted access and frequents the royal palace.

One day, he secretly brings up various subjects to Zarvan,
Speaking of court and king, incantations, sorcery,
Secret arts, and iniquities meant to serve evil intentions.

Zarvan, attentive to the Jew's discourse,
Reveals to him his own secret:
"Only speak on this subject with me.
You must design a work of sorcery
To free the world of Mahbood.
His power reaches such heights
That he seeks world possession.
He respects no one in the world.
It is as if he is Anushiravan himself.
The king takes his meals only
From the hands of Mahbood's sons.
His indulgence has made them so powerful
That the sky kisses the hem of their robes."

The Jew replies to Zarvan, "Do not distress yourself.
At the time when the king holds the barsom,
Inspect the dishes and search them for milk.
Find the one who carries and smells the food.
It is enough to see milk in it, even from afar.
You will never again find Mahbood or his sons alive.
If the taster eats from a plate of bronze or stone,
He would instantly fall to the ground."

Zarvan's heart rejoices at the Jew's words.
He does not attend court without him and
Shares his meals, his secrets, and his joys with him.

Some time passes, and the evil instigator
Adopts the habit of walking to the palace.
The two sons of Mahbood happily
Visit the king's court every morning.
In Mahbood's women's chambers,
Lives an honest and wise woman who fixes

PART TWENTY-SIX

King Kesra's golden tray at the time of dining.
She places the food on three bowls of fine jewels,
Which she covers with a golden cloth.

The tray then makes its way to the lofty king
In the hands of the valued vizier's sons.
After dining on meals made with honey,
Milk, and rosewater, the king reclines to rest.

One day, the two youths escort a servant
To whom the food tray is always entrusted.
As they enter Anushiravan's vestibule,
Zarvan, the chamberlain, notices them.
He smiles and says: "O trusted confidant
Of the king, let me cast a single glance
So that I may assess the color of the royal fare.
What a delicious, mouthwatering aroma!
Remove the napkin for a moment."

The young man uncovers the bowls innocently
As Zarvan observes from afar.
The Jew fixes his gaze on the contents, then,
Having discerned the color of the food,
He turns to the chamberlain and says,
"The tree you have planted is about to bear fruit."

The two young men of open minds
Place the table before Anushiravan,
But behind them enters Zarvan, as swift as dust,
And says to the pure-minded ruler,
"O King of fortunate star, giver of justice,
Do not touch this food without having it tasted first.
May the skies smile down on you!
May your throne's gleam shine on the world!
The wicked cook has mixed poison in the milk.
May your enemies have a share of the venom!"

Anushiravan casts a calm glance at the youths,
Knowing that his meals are prepared
By their wise and loving mother.

The young men, full of innocence and virtue,
Pull up their sleeves to take a bite of honey and milk.

503

As soon as they do so, they both fall to the ground,
As if struck by arrows, and exhale their last breaths
In full sight of King Anushiravan.

The world king is stricken by terror, his face
Turns as pale as the flower of the fenugreek.
He orders the destruction of Mahbood's palace,
Sparing no one, and the beheading of Mahbood
So that there remains no trace of him or his relatives.

He curses him, curses his wife, who prepared the meals.
The king delivers Mahbood's wealth, his women,
And his children to pillage and plunder.

In this way, Zarvan attains the object of his desires
And for some time enjoys fame at Kesra's court,
All the while holding the Jew in high honor
And raising his head above the lofty clouds.

In this way, the sky turns for some time
While the truth is concealed behind a veil of deceit.

30 | The King Finds Out About the Spells of Zarvan and the Jew, and Sentences Them to Death

One day, the world king organizes a hunt in Gorgan.
Kesra summons a great number of hunting horses
And notices Mahbood's brand on two of the horses.
His cheeks color at the sight of the Taazian steeds,
For his soul is consumed with his friendship
With Mahbood, who left an imprint on his heart.
He sheds tears of grief at his memory and says,
"How could the damned deev corrupt
A man so glorious, so honored?
He was a true and sincere friend.
How did his soul find its way to perdition?
Only the World Creator, pure and unique,
Can distinguish the hidden truth from appearances."

From there, he drives his retinue to the hunting site,
Bearing in his heart a deep wound.

He engages everyone to speak on the road,
Hoping that conversation would distract him.
He is accompanied by a great number of storytellers,
Whose entertaining tales lighten their march,
Making the distance appear considerably shorter.

On one occasion, the scribes, Zarvan, and the vizier
Plod along the road, deep in conversation.
They speak at length of spells and sorcery,
And of magicians serving the pernicious Ahriman.

The king says to the wise man,
"Do not concern yourself with sorcery.
Only speak of Yazdan and our faith.
Do not give credence to the marvels of sorcerers."

Zarvan replies, "May you live eternally!
May your words remain nourishment for wisdom!
Everything we hear about sorcery is real, though only
Those skilled in magic arts are privy to its mysteries.
When a meal contains a part of milk,
It is possible, with one glance, to convert it to poison."

Anushiravan immediately recalls the past event.
He remembers Mahbood and his two sons.
He exhales a deep, cold sigh, observes Zarvan,
Remains silent, and suddenly launches his ardent steed.

His mind is troubled by suspicions
As he discovers Zarvan's hostility toward Mahbood.
He thinks, "I do not know what this distrustful man
Was doing on the day that I proclaimed
A death sentence on Mahbood and his family.
I hope that the Creator will reveal to me the truth
To appease my heart and mind with a resolution.
I suspect that the crime originates from Zarvan,
And this past affair fills me with grief."

The king continues on the road, heart full of concern,
Cheeks strained, eyes awash with tears.
He arrives at a station where they set up
His tent pavilion on the river's edge.

Zarvan enters the royal tent, and visitors are dismissed.
The king once again speaks to him of magicians,
Of milk and honey: "It is a topic that enchants me."

The king questions him on the subject of Mahbood
And the circumstances leading to his sons' death.
He notices that Zarvan is shaking,
An obvious indication of his guilt.

Kesra says to him, "Tell me the truth.
Do not resort to lies and falsehoods, which
Only lead to the execution of wicked deeds.
Even a kind heart is perverted
Under the influence of a malicious friend."

Zarvan relates the affair from beginning to end,
Thus unveiling his secret.
He places all the blame on the Jew and presents
Himself as burdened by grief and anguish.

The powerful king instantly chains his feet.
Then he sends a rider with a spare horse
To travel as swift as wind to the Jewish sorcerer.
When the latter arrives at the lofty palace,
The powerful king interrogates him warmly:
"Tell me how the affair unfolded.
Do not attempt to utter lies."

The wicked man asks the world king for mercy,
Promising to unveil the mystery of the sorcery.
He recounts all that Zarvan had told him
And all that occurred in secret.

The world master listens to him, confused.
He summons his noble wise men and army leaders
So that they may witness the interrogation.
Then he commands an executioner to raise at the door,
In plain sight, two gallows from which hang two nooses.

The executioner drags Zarvan to the foot
Of one of the gallows and the Jew to the other.
He brutally hangs them, and they both
Perish beneath a shower of stones and arrows,

All for having cast a spell on the milk.

One must not trample the earth with poor intentions,
For a calamity will inevitably befall the criminal.
The king orders an extensive search
For any surviving relative of Mahbood.
He finds his veiled daughter and three illustrious men.
He offers them Zarvan's treasures
As well as the valuables belonging to the Jew.

He is consumed by the memory of Mahbood.
He weeps the entire night until daylight,
Asking for Yazdan's aid for the injustice
And flooding his chest with tears of blood.
He distributes generous alms to the poor,
His mouth constantly invoking the Creator's name,
Hoping to be forgiven for having fallen into a trap
And having acted as an oppressor.
If one is a sincere worshipper of Yazdan,
One does not extend a hand to perform a misdeed.
As easy as it may appear,
In the end, the heart will shudder with terror.

If your heart were made of solid stone,
Nothing within would remain hidden.
No matter how gentle your voice may be,
Time will ultimately reveal your secret.
Although the world cannot see your life's riddles,
It is far better to lean toward virtue, even in private.
If you lead an innocent and pure life,
You will be rewarded in this world and the other.

31 | In Praise of Anushiravan's Wisdom and His Founding of the City of Sursan[77]

Now that the story of Zarvan and the Jew is complete,
Let us sing the praises of eternal wisdom.
If you distribute justice, O King, your glory

◇◇◇◇◇◇◇◇◇◇◇◇◇◇
77 Sursan: A city, whose name means "place of feast," on the way to Rum. It is no longer in existence.

Will endure, although your body may not.
On the other hand, an unjust king will collect
Only curses and a tomb as the fruit in his life.

If your heart makes claims to righteousness,
You will spread happiness throughout the world.
If you wish to be celebrated after your death,
You must, O crown-bearer, don the helmet of wisdom.
For that very reason, long after he is gone,
I am able to revive and renew Anushiravan
And his just ways through the verses I compose.

From the moment the earth surrendered to him,
His only goal became to obtain blessings from power.
In his reign, men, great and small,
Are able to enjoy a peaceful and undisturbed sleep;
Sheep and wolf come together to drink at a common trough;
Higher-ranked men pay attention to their inferiors,
And the king's name is glorified more than his diadem;
Brave warriors are freed from the restrictive
Clasps of their coats of mail and have
The chance to unfasten their armor's buttons.
Shoulders are relieved of the weight of mace,
And songs of joy reach people's ears.
No one can resist the world ruler, as he receives
Tributes and royalties from every province.

The king easily carries out difficult tasks.
He loves indulging in hunting
And playing games in the royal square.
He sits in his audience hall, which is inlaid with jewels,
And holds counsel while drinking with his guests.

He builds a vast city on the road to Rum,
Extending over two farsangs;
A city consisting of palace, square, and gardens.
It is bordered on one side by a river
And by verdant hills on the other.
There are in Rum a number of such cities.
Kesra adopts their design, asks for the plans to be drawn,
And constructs tall palaces admired by everyone.

The king's palace has an audience hall

With ornaments of gems and jewels.
Arches are fashioned out of gold and silver,
Trimmed with precious stones of all kinds.
The dome is paneled with ebony and ivory,
And decorated with ivory figures and teakwood.

From Rum and India, he gathers masters skilled
In their art and carriers of their teachers' tradition.
From Iran and the province of Sistan,
He calls for the most renowned artists and artisans.
He brings them together to show off their skills
In this great city, which is to be the residence
Of prisoners captured in Barbarestan,
Rum, and a number of fallen towns.
This city becomes the ornament of hearts
And the center of government affairs.

Once it is built and complete, surrounding
Villages are designed on its outskirt.
The king asks for fields to be sown and fertile land
To be cultivated and planted with fruit trees.

He brings hostages from Kooch,[78] Gilan, and other
Devastated regions, builds a home for each of them
And, in this way, populates the city with strangers.
He assigns a job or a task to each one, and he unites
Those who are isolated with a companion in the same field.

There are artisans, plowmen, surveyors, merchants,
Men devoted to worship, masters, and subordinates.
He adorns the city like paradise,
And the eye cannot find an unpleasant sight.

Kesra names this delightful place Sursan,
For a prince finds satisfaction in feast.
He has no other desire than to spread justice
And make the world prosper in private and public.
Yet fate snatches such a man from kingship,
Relinquishing his crown to another.
You, as well, will not remain in this world forever.
Keep yourself at a distance from committing wicked acts.

◇◇◇◇◇◇◇◇◇◇◇◇◇
78 Kooch: A village in today's Iran; a tribe.

The world is nothing but deceit;
It offers one neither grandeur nor weakness.

Now listen to the tale of the fight
Between the emperor and the Hephthalites.
When you have no choice but to face battle,
Make sure to seize your mace.

32 | The Battle of the Emperor of Chin with the Leader of Hephthalites

What will the glorious poet reveal
On the subject of the King of Iran,
The Hephthalites, and the Emperor of Chin?
Hear the tale of an ancient, famous peasant bard;
Pay attention and learn from it.

He says: There does not exist on earth,
Among illustrious princes, givers of justice,
Celebrated for their hosts, treasuries and high births,
A ruler comparable to the Emperor of Chin
Except perhaps for King Kesra Anushiravan.

From Chin to the banks of the River Jayhoon,
Everyone honors the emperor for his kingship.
The army leader is positioned at the Golzarioon,
Near Chaadj, with army, treasury, and crown.

Words of praise spread through the land for Kesra,
For his courage, his wisdom, his majesty, his birth,
And the integrity of his royal manners.

From the moment he hears about the king's eminence,
The wise emperor seeks to cement a friendship.
He summons his advisors, a gathering of famed men.
He opens space in his heart to welcome amity
And speaks to his noble and wise leaders.
Then he prepares countless gifts, priceless
Keepsakes, Rumi stallions, Chini brocade,
Thrones, crowns, swords, and seals.
He gathers valuables typical to his land

In abundance to load up on one hundred camels.
He commands his treasurer to add one hundred thousand
Chini dinars to the gifts as an offering to the king
And to pack ten camels with dirhams.

Among the noblest, he selects an eloquent, wise man,
Worldly in that he has traveled extensively.
He calls a scribe and composes a letter on silk
Addressed to the king, filled with one thousand blessings
And as beautiful as a painting in the book of *Arjang*.[79]

The letter carrier is to travel
Through the land of the Hephthalites,
But he finds his path blocked by mace and arrows.
An army spreading from Soghd to the Jayhoon
Has lined up in support of the Hephthalite King,
Ghatfar the valiant, renowned for his past battles.

Upon hearing of the emperor's designs
And the presents he dispatches to the King of Iran,
Ghatfar calls to his side his most skilled warriors
And recounts to them the proceedings:
"The stars threaten us with a grim calamity.
If the King of Iran and the Emperor of Chin get along
And develop a strong bond, it will be to our detriment
And would incite a deep sense of fear in us.
Our land would be attacked from both sides.
We must plan an expedition to annihilate the Chini envoy."

He selects a notable army man, illustrious and valiant,
Delivers him to plunder the wealth, the camels and
Adorned horses, and asks him to cut off the envoy's head.
Only one Chini rider is able to escape the massacre.

At the news, the emperor's heart fills with grief
And his head fills with a keen desire for vengeance.
He sends his host off, consisting of leaders from Chin
And Khotan, on the path to Ghajghaarbaashi,
Allowing no descendant of Afraasiyaab or Arjaasp

◇◇◇◇◇◇◇◇◇◇◇◇◇
79 *Arjang*: Also known as *The Book of Pictures*, is the beautifully illustrated holy book of Manichaeism written by Mani, the Iranian prophet who preached to Iran in the third century BCE.

To remain in a state of rest or inaction.
They are forced to leave the banks of the Golzarioon,
Hearts full of wrath, heads full of thoughts of bloodshed.

The commander of the emperor's host is Fanj,
Able to send dust to the sky like smoke.
His cavaliers satisfy their fury in Chaadj,
Tinting the waters of the Golzarioon red with blood.

Ghatfar learns of the emperor's actions.
He musters a host of Hephthalites
Fierce enough to eclipse the sun.
He sends for arms, troops, and dirhams from Balkh,
Shaknan, Aamooy, Zam, Khotlan, Tarmaz, and Viseh-Guerd.
His army stirs the dust everywhere.
His troops emerge from mountains and plains,
From sandy desert and barren ground,
Like a swarm of ants and locusts.

Once the emperor crosses the Terek River,
It is as if the sky sends down a shower of swords.
He unites the army in Mai and Margh,
And the sun turns as black as an eagle's plumage,
So numerous are the spears and purple blades,
So dazzling are the colorful banners.
Bukhara, where King Ghatfar is positioned,
Is crowded with troops and a mass of weapons.

Ghatfar departs with an army as large as a mountain,
Having assembled the entirety of the Hephthalites.
The soldiers battle on all fronts,
Thus obstructing the passage of the wind.
A great windstorm rises, with clouds so dark
The light of both sun and moon disappears.
The swords of leaders gleam, heavy maces twirl.
It is as if iron is endowed with a tongue
And the air is the interpreter of the arsenal.

The people of Koshan and Soghd gather,
Men, women, and children, cheeks flooding with tears,
To witness the outcome of this battle
And in whose favor sun and moon would spin.

For seven days, these ardent troops struggle.
Everywhere heaps of cadavers rise,
Blood reddens the ground and the stones
Like the flower of Arghavan.
So many blows fall of spear, mace, sword, and blade,
It is as if the clouds send down showers of stones.
The dust hides the face of the sun
And obstructs the eagle's eye in flight.

On the eighth day, the dust turns toward Ghatfar.
The world darkens as deep as the indigo night.
The Hephthalites endure a massive defeat,
One that will not be forgotten for years to come.
The survivors invoke the name of Yazdan;
The wounded are scattered here and there,
And the entire plain is strewn
With the deceased and with prisoners.

One says to another, "Never have we witnessed
A more unendurable and willful battle.
It is obvious that this is not an army of men.
One dares not look at them: Their faces appear
To be the faces of deevs and wild beasts;
Their hearts do not distinguish between good and bad.
It is as if, at the sight of sword, spear, mace, and blade,
They are unable to search for a path of escape.
They possess dragon faces;
Their spears can pierce through mountains.
Their hands are shaped into leopard claws.
Never do their hearts grow weary of battle.
Never do they relieve their mounts
From the bearing of their saddle.
Their steeds feed only on brambles, and their riders
Never sleep, always assuming the stance of battle.
They spend the night chasing prey and engaging in pillage.
It is as if they fling their bodies into blazing flames.
They know not the meaning of eating and sleeping.
Only deevs can contend with them.
We shall never resist the Emperor of Chin.
We shall be forced to immigrate to the land of Iran.

"If Ghatfar acts upon our demands,

He will plan to surrender to Kesra Anushiravan.
He will deliver to him the land of the Hephthalites
And will forget the use of mace and blade.
Otherwise, we shall select a man of the lineage of
Khoshnavaz, illustrious and agreeable to Anushiravan,
Who alone will renew our ancient empire and to whom
He will recount the actions of the Emperor of Chin.
The world will then bless Kesra, for he is endowed
With majesty, might, generosity, and wisdom,
And his intelligence favors the right path.
He has imposed tribute and royalties to the Caesar,
And no one dares to ever challenge him."

The Hephthalites, men, women, and children,
Emit a unanimous cry of agreement.

In the land of Chaghan lives an illustrious young,
Ambitious, generous, wise warrior named Faghanish.
He possesses treasure and army, and noblemen of
The lands of Hephthalites and Chin acclaim him as king.

33 | Anushiravan Learns of the Actions of the Hephthalites and the Emperor

The noble King Kesra receives news
Of the Emperor of Chin, a formidable ruler.
The reports say that the emperor has triumphed
Over the Hephthalites and their leaders,
And that the King of Chaghan, favored
By a young fortune, now sits on a new throne.

The world king decks a hall in the palace
And sits, surrounded by his vigilant, loyal men,
His thoughts fixed on their speeches.

A feast is prepared, and royal supporters counselors
Arrive, including Ardeshir, the grand wise master;
Shahpoor; and Yazdegerd the scribe.

Kesra says, "O wise and worldly men, O performers
Of high deeds, I have learned painful and disturbing news

About the Hephthalites, the Turks, the Emperor of Chin,
And the leaders of the borders of Tooran.
Vast hosts of helmet-covered, sword-striking warriors
From Chaadj, Chin, Turkestan, and Khotan have gathered.
For seven days they battled without removing
The saddles from their steeds' backsides.
In the end, the Hephthalites were defeated
And two-thirds of them were wounded or killed.

"The Hephthalites once enjoyed great fame.
Their sword-striking skills were held in high esteem.
For these reasons, their defeat is quite astonishing.
May a populace never have a leader of corrupt mind!
If Ghatfar had exercised some caution and sense,
Not even the sky could have wished his army to fail.
The Hephthalites, in a state of deep trouble, have sought
A prince from the family of Bahraam the Hunter.
They have placed a new ruler, Faghanish, on the throne,
Unanimously acclaiming him as their king.

"The emperor settled on the side of Chaadj,
Proud of his army, treasury, and crown.
He is a descendant of Arjaasp and Afraasiyaab,
And dreams only of invading the border of Iran.
Having vanquished Ghatfar's army,
He now ascends above the sun.
We must not allow the emperor to speak as he does.
The land of Kushan, from which the Chinis
Now draw their strength, belongs to me,
And their subjects have fallen prey to oppression.
Their bodies, their properties, and their treasures
Have fallen into the hands of the emperor.
What do you conclude from all of this?
How shall we proceed in the face
Of the actions of the Turks and the Emperor?"

The wise noblemen rise to offer a unanimous answer.
They bless the king and say, "O foreseeing, blessed King,
The Hephthalites are Ahrimans, men of lowly faith.
They are our mortal enemies who deserve hardship.
Yet the king must always express eloquent words.
We endured enough grievance from them

515

With the murder of Pirooz, a great ruler and light
Of the world, whom they killed so treacherously.
It was a vicious act and sufficient reason for us
To pray they never enjoy a day of happiness.
Never has an act of injustice produced just results.
Such is the retribution inflicted by the almighty
Justice Giver: Wrongdoers will suffer a grim demise.

"Furthermore, if you wish to speak about the emperor,
Who nurtures an ancient pain and a strong yearning
For vengeance, he may have found ill advisors in
The descendants of Afraasiyaab whose eyes still shed tears.
He may have regained courage as a result of his victory.
It does not surprise us that you dread his person.

"Do not trouble yourself about the Hephthalites
And Ghatfar's army or about the descendants
Of Arjaasp and Afraasiyaab or the Emperor,
Who has now settled on this side of the river.
You are the powerful world master, provider
Of light to our minds, our spirits, to wisdom itself.
May the one who cultivates wisdom live eternally!
You have more knowledge than this vast assembly.
You have no need for advisors and counselors.
The world's throne and crown belong to you,
For you possess majesty, glory, insight, and fortune.

"If his highness travels to Khorasan,
He will have cause to fear the land of Iran.
As soon as the Rumis see that the king has left,
They will come with a vast host to exercise vengeance
And to destroy our beautiful Iran-Zamin.
Until now, no one has set foot on our soil,
No one has threatened our empire.
If the king prepares for war,
The whales will emerge from the sea to assist."

With this discourse on peace, war, and battle,
The world master understands that none of the sages
Wishes to engage in a conflict.
They prefer to continue their feasts and revelry.

He replies, "Thanks be to Yazdan,

Whom I fear in both worlds.
The lions who are accustomed to rest and food
Will forget about struggles, and you will, too.
The dust of battle and the idea of a battlefield
Weigh on you by excess of sleep and banquet.
May the one who fought take time to rest,
And may feast return after battle.
I swear by the power given to me by Yazdan
That we shall prepare to march by month's end.
I shall muster the troops from every province,
Lead a host into Khorasan,
And, as long as we are illustrious warriors,
We shall attach timpani to the backs of elephants.
Neither the Hephthalites nor the Emperor of Chin
Will survive; neither one will be granted life
And the opportunity to pay homage to Iran.
I shall free the world of evil men by plucking out weeds
And renewing our land with justice and generosity."

The noblemen stand in awe of him.
They ask forgiveness and acclaim him:
"O victorious King, majestic and just,
May the world gain joy from your command!
We are your noblemen and your slaves.
We bow our heads to your will and wisdom.
Every time the king commands, we shall fight.
Never will he witness sluggishness on our part."

The king asks for counsel from his advisors.
He continues in this way until the beginning
Of the new moon, at which time he sits on a new throne.
The moon shines above the king's face,
And a cry of admiration emerges from the palace.

As the dazzling torch of sun rises over the mountains,
The earth glows like a golden bowl.
It is as if a topaz chalice has been placed
On a cloth the color of lapis lazuli.
The cry of men and the wail of trumpets are heard.
Timpani are fastened to the backs of elephants,
And the army heads toward camp,
Division by division, marching to the beat of drums.

Yazdegerd, the scribe, presents himself at court
With wise master Ardeshir, a man of sound counsel.
They write a letter to every illustrious nation
To announce that the king is marching off
With army and war apparatus, and that they must
Abstain from feast as a show of devotion to him.
The king addresses a letter to the Emperor of Chin
With praise and greetings to the Afghanis.

34 | The Emperor of Chin Receives News of Anushiravan's Departure to Gorgan

Anushiravan directs the army out of Mada'in,
Obscuring the land all the way to the sea.
The eye wearies at the sight of so many armed men
Dimming the space from one mountain to another.
In the middle shines the king's banner as they march
Toward Gorgan, obscuring the face of the sun.
At their destination, they rest for a while
And hunt, crossing mountain and plain.

During this time, the emperor is stationed in Soghd,
Where the entire spread of land is submerged
In the billowing waves from the motions caused
By the descendants of Arjaasp and Afraasiyaab.

The emperor says, "The ground buckles
Beneath the weight of my troops and throne.
I shall lead you into the land of Iran
And from there to the city of valiant warriors.
I shall take the dust of Iran into China
And with my war bring the sky down to earth.
I shall not allow anyone to have throne and crown,
A royal state, territory, and high fortune."

He holds himself in this manner for some time,
Speaking and dreaming of possessing the world
With the aid of his army and his glory,
Until the rumor spreads that the King of Iran,
A ruler of victorious fortune and power, has left
With his vast host, which spreads from sea to sea.

Troubled by the news, the emperor
Swears off his eagerness to engage in war.
Concerned, he says to his vizier,
"We cannot hide this awful news.
I have learned that Kesra has arrived in Gorgan,
His troops dispersed across the surface of the earth.
He obviously does not know where we are.
He is a foolish man, devoid of sense.
My army covers the land from Chin to the Jayhoon.
The world is under the protection of my diadem.
I must go toward him to engage in battle,
And any delay would tarnish my name and glory.
He believes that we cannot surpass him
Or that there is no other king but him in the world.
But he will learn that there are bold men like me.
I shall advance against him with Chini riders."

An intelligent man says to the Emperor of Chin,
"O King, do not speak of war with the ruler of Iran.
Do not pitch your kingdom and army into the dust.
No king disputes him his rank, unless he has lost
His mind and, with it, his intelligence.
There exists no more majestic and glorious king,
And the moon in the sky does not even compare to him.
He raises tribute in India and Rum, and everywhere
One can find treasures and cultivated land.
He is master of the crown and ornament of the throne.
He is a vigilant world master whose fortune triumphs.

The emperor listens to the worlds of his wise man and,
Adopting a sensible resolution, he says to his loyal minister,
"What does your wise mind offer for advice?
We have to decide between two courses of action,
For it would be foolish to remain inactive.
Since war with Kesra would bring us grief, there is
Nothing better for us to do than to spend our wealth.
Dinars help us with neither food nor carpets on battle day.
We must first assure our safety, then we can turn
Our attention to food, beautiful clothing, and carpets.
When one fears misfortune,
One spends money to gain a sense of peace."

35 | The Letter of the Emperor of Chin to Anushiravan

The emperor selects ten eloquent men from his army corps
Able to speak and understand what they are told.
A Chini savant writes a letter as beautiful
As the book of *Arjang* and according to custom.
Ten intelligent cavaliers depart with the letter
Toward the king's court, their mouths full of words.

They ask to be announced to Kesra, who prepares
An audience hall worthy of the King of Kings.
He commands the curtains be raised
And the visitors be admitted graciously.

The ten Chini men appear with their letter
And a multitude of presents and golden offerings.
The king receives them well, asks for news
Of the emperor, and offers each a seat.

They touch the floor at his feet with their foreheads
And relay to him the emperor's message
Contained in the letter and written in elegant
Chini characters on a fine sheet of silk.

One of the envoys places it before Yazdegerd,
The king's scribe, who reads it to everyone's astonishment.
The letter begins by invoking blessings
From the Justice Giver to the King of Iran.
Then it boasts to the king of the emperor's grandeur,
His treasures, vast troops, weapons, and power.
Next it expresses the homage paid by the Tarkhan of Chin
To the Emperor of Chin, to whom he offered his daughter
Without having been asked and whom the army obeys.

Finally, it recounts the story of the presents he has sent
To the king, which the Hephthalites intercepted:
"Intent on vengeance, I left the land of Chaadj
And seized treasure and throne from Ghatfar.
I left the edge of the Golzarioon, fought in a way
As to color the Jayhoon River in tints of ruby.
I honored those who spread through Chin and Maachin
News of the king's victory, his courage, his intelligence,

His modesty, and his knowledge.
In my heart, I wish to be the world king's friend."

With the understanding of the power, courage,
And intentions of the emperor, Kesra calls
For a suitable residence to be assigned to the envoys.
They are complimented and treated well.
Every time the cupbearer prepares the spreads
And the wine, the king invites them to join in.

They remain one day at the royal court,
Taking part in hunting and drinking.
The king holds his audience in the plain.
The air turns dark with the dust of riders.
All the border guards gather with golden belts,
The Baloochis and the Gilanis with golden shields.
They present their homage to the king,
Offering him three hundred chargers
Of golden reins and swords in golden sheaths.
Blades, javelins, and short spears shine
As if iron has been petrified with gold.

A brocade cover and a turquoise throne
Are placed on the back of an elephant.
The earth is full of noise, the air full of turmoil.
The finest ears are deafened. They cross the desert
Of spear riders traveling straight to the king.
Envoys from Bardah, India, Rum, and other
Cultivated lands present themselves at court.
The king wishes to show the Chinis the true
Meaning of kingship and to whom belongs the world
From the sun to the back of the fish holding up the earth.

Once the boundaries of the battlefield are set on the plain,
The warring cavaliers launch onto it,
Stirring dust and covering the earth in thick armor.
Full of pride, they engage in a tournament
With mace and sword, bow and arrow.
The plain disappears beneath the multitude
Of men armed with javelin and spear.
On one side are infantrymen, on the other riders.
Envoys from various lands, sent by princes and kings,

Are stunned by the army and its war apparatus,
And by the aspect, the glory, and the voice of the king.

Anushiravan secretly receives the news from the envoys
And commands his treasurer to collect weapons and gear,
And to bring to the field armor, helmet, and chainmail.
The king asks for the buckles to be unfastened.
A strong wrestler with wide shoulders attempts the task,
But no matter how much effort he exerts,
He is unable to strip off the chainmail.
Only the king's chest and limbs can support
The weight of the helmet, the coat of mail, and the mace.
No archer can shoot an arrow as he can,
No one can fight with his strength and skill.

Anushiravan advances on the battlefield like
A drunken elephant, waving a bull-headed mace
And riding an ardent steed,
Its mere stature astonishing the assembly.

A great sound rises, trumpets wail,
Bells jingle on the backs of elephants,
Musicians precede the king with cymbals and drumbeat,
And the earth trembles beneath the horses' hooves.

The King of Kings, topped with his helmet, his horse
Shielded in armor, gallops left and right, handling the reins.
His envoys praise him and bow low to the ground.
He makes his way back from the plain to his palace,
Accompanied by his retinue of noblemen.

The envoys murmur to each other,
"This illustrious king is not only a seeker of virtue,
But he is skilled in the expert handling of the reins
And is able to snatch spears from army warriors.
We must remember in our hearts the talents
He deploys before us and our companions
When we return to our princes and rulers.
Anyone who goes back to their kings
Takes with him conversations heard and actions observed.
We must declare that neither old nor young
Has ever witnessed a king like Anushiravan."

36 | Anushiravan's Reply to the Emperor of Chin

King Anushiravan summons his scribe
And the grand wise master Ardeshir.
He composes a royal letter in Pahlavi.
Having dipped his reed's two sides into amber,
He begins by giving thanks to the Justice Giver:
"Who created sky, Sun, and Moon, along
With everything above and everything below.
We are all the slaves of the World Master.
Wisdom is witness to divine power.
A breath is taken only by divine command.
The foot of an ant does not trample the earth
Without having been given divine permission.
I address my prayers so that my blessings
May reach the Emperor of Chin.

"As for the matter of the Hephthalites, who strapped
Their waists to commit crimes, as you describe it,
They have foolishly and unjustly spilled blood,
Consequently falling into their own traps.
A wrongdoer, even if he has a lion's strength,
Will never withstand or defy Yazdan's will.
The Hephthalites behaved like leopards,
And you vanquished them in battle.

"Next, you speak of your army and treasury,
Of the power, throne, and headdress of the Faghfoor.
But a wise man does not approve of someone
Who boasts about his own power.
You are in awe of the army and the border of Chaadj.
A man who considers himself superior
Will always find someone ranked higher,
Just like each star has a star above it.
You can speak of this to someone who has never seen
Or experienced treasure, army, battle, or hard work,
But most of the noblemen in the world
Have either seen me or have heard of my feats.
The Sea of Chin is shallow and insignificant to me,
And mountains tremble at my unyielding resolve.
The earth is beneath my treasury.
I exert myself any place there is water or land.

"Next, you ask for my affection,
You wish to secure our bond with friendship.
Since you propose feast and revelry,
I do not wish to engage in battle,
For no one would opt for battle over feast.
No sensible man would seek to struggle
With an illustrious or warring ruler,
Particularly if he is accustomed to launching
Into war without a moment's hesitation.
Because he has seen many a battlefield,
He has no need for a master at the hour of fight
And is able, at the height of the struggle,
To maintain peace in his heart just like
When he is in possession of crown and throne.
May the World Creator come to your aid!
May your diadem and seal forever shine!"

The king's signet is affixed to the letter.
The royal crown and throne are prepared,
Robes of honor are brought, according to Kianian custom,
And the envoys are summoned before the king,
Who relays a verbal message to be added to the letter.

They cheerfully depart from the kingly court,
Their tongues full of praise, and arrive at the emperor's
Palace gates pronouncing benedictions on him.

The worldly Emperor of Chin empties the room.
His vizier sits before the throne.
The envoys are summoned, and they advance
To speaks about Kesra and deliver his message.
The emperor questions them first on
His intelligence, his knowledge, his way of being,
His language, his demeanor, and his stature.
Then he asks about the number of his troops
And the people in possession of seals and diadems,
About his just and unjust actions, his army,
His provinces, his treasury, and his crown.

The most eloquent envoy unravels his tongue
And recounts all that he has seen.
He says to the Emperor of Chin, "O King,

You need not consider him your inferior!
In the span of one hundred years,
The world has not witnessed a mightier ruler.
He appears in banquet hall, battlefield, or hunt
Always with the same cheery, wise, and intelligent
Disposition, his heart content, his face fresh.
He has the stature of a cypress tree
And the strength of an elephant.
His hand is as generous as the flows of the Nile.
Upon the throne, he resembles the sky in his devotion.
On the battlefield, he is a destructive whale.

"In a state of fury, he thunders like the clouds,
His commanding voice able to tame a lion.
When he drinks wine, he subjugates hearts
With the warmth and affection of his words.
On the throne, he is like the blessed Sooroosh,
A fertile branch of the majestic tree.
The entire population of Iran forms his army
And reveres his diadem.
When he holds court in the plain,
The world cannot contain his vast host.
His mace-bearing warriors wear golden belts.
His servants are full of grace and dignity.
Only the Creator can estimate the number
Of his elephants, the steps of his ivory seat,
The number of his thrones, bracelets, torques,
And crowns that serve to magnify his splendor.
If a mountain of steel wished to resist him,
It would be, faced with his wrath, like the eye
Of a needle, and anyone who is weary of life
Has only to seize courage and to contend with him."

37 | The Emperor of Chin Offers His Daughter to Anushiravan

Upon hearing these accounts, the emperor
Pales and turns the color of fenugreek.
His heart is full of fear, his brain split apart
Beneath the blows of new thoughts and worries.

He sits full of grief with his advisors
And says to the illustrious assembly: "O sages,
how shall we proceed under these circumstances?
What grief is worse than the worries
Of a man struck like me?
After our victory, we must not allow
Our glory to be replaced by shame."

The wise men propose various courses of action,
Speaking left and right, and debating.

In the end, the emperor declares,
"Here is what we shall do:
We shall send a valiant man to the king.
I shall have the upper hand
With this idea, which just came to me.
I shall resolve the matter by embracing the king.
I have in my chambers many daughters
Who are diadems on the heads of queens.
I shall engage one of them to the King of Kings
And thus free myself from worry.
Once he is linked to me with an alliance,
No one will ever advise him to cause me harm.
He will be proud and glorious,
And the other wars will be mere games to us."

The noblemen, in a common voice, approve of his plan
And his strategy to effectuate a peaceful resolution.
The emperor then selects three great army leaders,
Able to speak eloquently and to understand the reply.
He opens the doors to his wealth of dinars
And says, "What is the use of jewels if not to acquire
Glory and fame, and dispel a sense of shame,
Or to be offered as gifts, music, and feast
In order to reclaim a state of peace?"

He gathers a cache of presents so vast no one,
Neither great nor small, had ever seen its like before.
Then he summons a skilled scribe
And dictates to him his heart's contents.

He begins in praise of the Creator, "Almighty,
All-knowing, all-encompassing, Master of Saturn,

Sun and Moon, Master of victory and power,
Who asks only righteousness from divine servants
And Who protects the just man from perishing.
May divine greetings reach the King of Iran,
Master of sword, mace, and helmet, master of knowledge,
Crown, and throne, whose wishes and good fortune
Are granted by the Giver of victory.
World master Kesra, son of kings, distinguished
By his solemnity, his knowledge, and his justice.
He knows that a man, no matter how great
And powerful, needs to be honored by others.

"My wise envoys, who are my kin and allies, have,
Upon their return to my court, spoken of the king
At length, of his wisdom, his sense of justice,
His fortune, his crown, his pride, and his throne.
The thought of his glory has given me the idea
Of finding shelter beneath the shadow of his wings.
Our most treasured asset is our heart's blood,
And an intelligent child is tied to his or her father.
Well, if it pleases you to ask me for the hand
Of one of my pure daughters, the most gentle,
Most beautiful, the most perfect in behavior,
If it suits you, and perhaps you deem it beneficial,
Iran and Chin would no longer be separate entities,
And we could spread blessings across the world."

Once it is written on Chini silk,
The letter and royal seal are taken to the vizier.
The emperor selects three noblemen, soft-spoken relatives.
They take leave of the lofty court
And travel toward Iran and its mighty king.

At the news of their approach,
Kesra takes his seat on the throne and dons the crown.
The three intelligent men present themselves at court
With a gift of thirty thousand dinars wrapped in scarves
And place it at the king's feet as an offering,
Along with objects of gold and silver, and Chini brocade,
Making the earth appear more brilliant than the sky.

The envoys are offered seats of honor,

And they greet the king in their language.
The royal vizier prepares for them
A residence worthy of their ranks.

The sky revolves for one night.
As soon as the sun exhibits its shining face
Over the mountains, the king climbs on
His turquoise throne, dons the ruby diadem,
Commands his wise and noble men to sit
Before him in the presence of illustrious sages,
And says, "Bring me this letter
Written on satin and place it before my scribe."

The noble leaders form a circle,
And Yazdegerd gracefully approaches the king.
Once the reading is complete, the assembly appears
In a state of wonder at the emperor's expression
Of good grace, courtesy, and respect for their king.

The virtuous noblemen celebrate Anushiravan:
"Let us give thanks to Yazdan, our shelter,
For having placed on the throne the most victorious,
Most majestic, most glorious king, most renowned
For his gentleness, kindness, solemnness, and grandeur.
In battle he is a mad elephant;
In feast, he is the moon cherishing his guests.
His enemies are far inferior to him,
Even if they are blessed with a title.

"We had cause to fear this army from Chaadj
And the emperor, master of treasure and crown.
But we find that all the valiant and sensible men
Who cultivate rest and righteousness befriend us,
Thanks to the majesty of the glorious king.
They grow closer to him, and now the emperor
Understands that he could not resist him
And therefore seeks to form an alliance.
We must not delay this affair's conclusion.
No one will find such a union humiliating
Since it is with a ruler whose army
Occupies a vast stretch from Chin to Bukhara
And who is the refuge of the greatest in these lands."

Having listened to the words of the intelligent,
Wise men of lucid mind, Kesra dismisses the visitors
From his hall and summons the emperor's envoys.

The King of Kings receives them amicably
And offers them seats near his throne.
They repeat to him the message of their prince,
Assuring him that they speak only the truth.

The army leader, with his host, crown, and treasure,
Sees the king and reveals the message of the emperor.

The king pays heed to their cordial conversations
Murmured softly and says,
"The emperor is a mighty, eminent, and wise man.
He wishes to fix an alliance and seal a friendship
With me by offering me his daughter in marriage.
Any sensible man must consume his affairs
With the eye of wisdom. I shall apply myself
And reach a conclusion that will bring us happiness.
I shall answer his questions, but the emperor
Must lighten my heart with a choice made in good faith.

"I shall send a smart man who will enter
The emperor's night chambers, select the most
Illustrious daughter and her father's dearest one,
And will assure himself that the mother
Is of royal blood and of equal birth to the father.
Once this matter is settled,
The emperor will have approved
The conditions for the union that I propose."

The envoys pronounce benedictions on the king:
"Our master is happy with the king's favors.
Although the women's chambers are a cloud
That only showers down pearls,
He will not refuse Kesra his selection.
Pick one of your wise men to travel to Chin
And to the women behind the veil.
They will uncover their faces before him."

With these words, the old era is renewed
For the King of Kings.

38 | Anushiravan Sends Mehran Setaad to See the Daughter of the Emperor of Chin

The king summons a scribe
And speaks to him at length of the emperor.
He commands him to carefully select fancy,
Flowery words to write a reply to his letter.

He begins in praise of the Creator,
"Victorious World Master, foster parent to all creation,
By whose order the world endures,
Who is the Guide to good and righteous deeds,
Who grants honor to the one favored,
Raising him from a low status to the lofty sky,
While another is holed up in misery.
I wish to express my gratitude
For the divine acts that benefit me.
If I have ever behaved in wicked ways,
My heart will tremble before the divine.
I wish not to have life in my body
If I must give up hope and fear in the Creator.

"An illustrious envoy has arrived, a carrier
Of kind words, on the part of the Emperor of Chin.
I know of the prospect of an alliance and
Of the pure maidens concealed in your harem.
I rejoice at the idea of uniting with you,
Especially if it is by way of a marriage
With one of your veiled daughters.
I send a sensible man your way,
A man whose soul I hold in high esteem.
He travels to you to convey my secret intentions
In regard to the conclusion of this alliance,
And how I wish to engage in it.
May your soul maintain its modesty!
May your heart always remain joyous
And your back be the support of our friendship!"

Once the scribe completes his task,
He folds the sheaf of paper.
They wait for the air to dry the reed's tears,
Then affix a seal of musk to the letter.

The procession is in a state of awe at the sight
Of the gifts lavished by the king on the envoys.
Anushiravan selects an intelligent, noble old man
Named Mehran Setaad,
And one hundred illustrious Iranian cavaliers,
Famed, eloquent men gifted with good manners.

He says to Mehran Setaad, "Leave in joy and victory,
Your heart full of affection and a sense of justice.
May your soul inspire you and your tongue be gentle!
May reason serve you as guide
And your heart retain its charms.
Begin by observing the emperor's harem
And assessing the good and the bad within.
Guard yourself from being duped by their toilette
Or by their attire's excess of gold and adornments.
Behind the veil the emperor hides a daughter
Who is tall of stature, bearer of a diadem.
The daughter of a slave does not suit me,
Even though her father is a ruler.
Inquire respectfully and precisely into their mothers,
Whether any one of them is from the lineage of emperors.
If she is as beautiful as her birth is illustrious,
She will bring joy to the world and to herself."

Mehran Setaad listens to the king's words,
Utters blessings on his crown and throne,
And leaves the world-illuminating court
At a propitious hour on the sixth day of Khordaad.

At the news of his approach,
The emperor sends a cortege to meet him.
With pomp, Mehran reaches the Emperor of Chin
And greets him by kissing the ground at his feet.

The world seeker receives him amicably and asks
For the preparation of a sumptuous dwelling.
Still, his mind is troubled by this affair.
He walks over to his wife's apartment
And confides in her Anushiravan's message.

He speaks of treasure and army in these terms:
"The king is valiant, aware, and young of fortune.

531

I wish to offer him one of my daughters
In the hopes of furthering our glory.
I have, behind the veil, a daughter
Who is the diadem on the heads of all the queens.
There is no more beautiful woman in the world.
Many times rulers have asked for her hand in marriage.
I love her so much I wish not
To deprive my eyes from her sight.
Servant women have given me four daughters,
Servants themselves and slaves of awakened minds.
I shall offer him one of them
And thereby remain free of war and quarrel."

The noble matron replies, "No one in the world
Surpasses you in intelligence and wisdom!"
On these words, he retires for the night.

As the sun reveals its face over mountain crests,
Mehran Setaad presents himself at court,
Advances toward the throne, and delivers the letter.

The emperor reviews it and smiles at the contents,
Revealing the choice he is to make for the alliance.
He gives Mehran the key to the women's chambers
And says, "Go and see what you discover."

Four of the most trusted servants accompany Mehran.
He opens the door to the secret apartments,
And they enter as the servants retell stories:
"The one you are about to meet
Has never been seen by stars, Moon, or Sun."

The women's chambers are as beautiful as paradise,
Full of moons, suns, and opulence.
There are five fairy-faced young ladies,
Seated on thrones with crowns on their heads,
And beneath each is a wealth of jewels.

The daughter of pure lineage sits apart, bearing
Neither diadem nor bracelet, neither necklace nor gem.
A simple dress covers her body, and her head
Is adorned with a black mane, a gift from Yazdan.
Her cheeks are free of rouge, and her only finery

Is the one given to her by the Creator.
She is a tall cypress tree topped by a moon
That lends its sheen to a new throne.

At the sight of her, Mehran concludes
That no other maiden compares to her.
This insightful and noble soul understands that
The emperor and the princess strayed from justice.
The young lady covers her eyes with her scarf
And her hand, and Mehran's fury mounts.

He says to the servant, "The king has a multitude
Of bracelets, crowns, and thrones.
I select the one who has neither crown
Nor jewels and who still has time to mature.
I have endured this difficult voyage to make
The right choice, not to purchase Chini brocade."

The princess says, "O old man,
Your speech does not sit well with us.
Here are illustrious princesses, graceful,
Intelligent, adept at igniting hearts.
They have reached the age of maturity.
Tall as cypress trees, cheeks as bright as spring,
They would happily serve the king.
Yet you select instead a youthful child?
You are not a sensible man."

Mehran Setaad replies, "If the emperor is fair,
He will recognize that the king, world master,
Would not call me an old and foolish man.
I select the one seated on the ivory throne,
Free of adornment, necklace, and crown.
If the masters of this land do not consent,
I shall return empty-handed as soon as you allow."

The princess reflects on these words,
Astonished by his sense and his decision.
He takes leave of the deceitful matron,
Who quickly approaches the emperor
And tells him of the unfolding developments.

The emperor sees the worry on her face.

He recognizes that the clear-minded old man
Is powerful and well-suited to handle delicate matters.
The wise ruler sits with his advisors, dismisses the crowd,
And summons leaders, chiefs, and astrologers,
Who come to his audience hall with their Rumi tables.

The emperor commands his friends
To calculate the position of the stars.
One of the wise men observes the firmament
Relative to the emperor's intentions
And the alliance he is about to make with the king.

In the end, he says, "Your excellency, there is
No reason to worry about future misfortune.
The will of the sublime firmament,
Indicated by the favorable rotation of the stars,
Dictates that this affair can only have a promising
Outcome, that your ill-intentioned enemies will not prevail.
That a prince worthy of the throne will emerge
From the union between the emperor's daughter
And the king, a prince to whom all the world rulers
And the valiant leaders of Chin will pay homage."

39 | The Emperor Sends His Daughter to Anushiravan

The emperor's heart is calmed by these words,
And the sun-faced princess smiles.
Their minds liberated from worry, they seat the envoy
Before them and relate to him all that is suitable
On the subject of the daughter of a princess
Who has, thus far, been hidden from sight.

Mehran Setaad accepts her from her father
In the name of the victorious King of Kings.
In agreement with the intermediary, the emperor
Gives away his only daughter born into full royalty.

Servants arrive joyfully with offerings for the king.
The emperor calls for a prepared treasure
Containing a variety of precious goods:
Dinars, jewels, torques, thrones, a turquoise litter,

An ivory throne, and yet another of aloeswood
Inset in gold and inlaid with countless fine stones.
They bring one hundred bridled horses
With ornate saddles and one hundred
Pack camels loaded with crowned jewels.
There are forty bolts of brocade embroidered in gold
With stones of chrysoprase weaved through them.

The emperor calls for valuable, finely crafted carpets
To be loaded atop one hundred camels.
He calls for three hundred servants
And waits for them to climb on the saddle,
Each holding a banner in her hand
According to Chinese custom.
The emperor of victorious fortune asks for
The turquoise throne, inlaid with gold and
Silver threads and framed by raw fine jewels,
To be placed atop an elephant.
One hundred men raise a dazzling banner
Of Chini brocade, beneath which the ground disappears.
A golden litter covered with golden brocade
Enfolds the daughter, a priceless untouched pearl.
The three hundred chambermaids depart
Happily and swiftly with the moon-faced maiden.

In this way, the emperor sends his child to the king
Accompanied by an escort and preceded by forty
Eunuchs, who trudge ahead, hearts full of joy.

Once freed from this affair, the emperor summons
A scribe holding musk, rosewater, and a sheet of satin.
They compose a letter to Kesra in the manner of *Arjang*,
Full of embellishment, scent, and color,
Beginning in praise of the Creator, World Master,
"Aware and vigilant, all-seeing,
Who directs the movements of divine
Creation toward divinely predestined goals.
The world king is the diadem over my head.
I do not seek an alliance because of my daughter.
Since sages, noblemen, and insightful wise men
Have spoken to me of the king's magnificence,
His power and his glory, I have pursued

A means of uniting with his majesty.
He spreads justice throughout the world,
And never has a ruler displayed such power.
No one compares to him in courage, victory,
Supremacy, splendor, stature, throne, and crown.
Yazdan, the pure, nourished him with justice,
Wisdom, faith, and intelligence.

"I send my daughter, the light of my eyes,
To King Kesra, in line with our customs and our ways.
I have commanded her to stand as your slave
Once she enters the royal women's chambers.
I have commanded her to mold her mind
In line with the king's splendor and sagacity,
To learn his customs and his ways.
May fortune and wisdom be your guides!
May power and knowing be your support!"

The seal is dipped in Chini musk and applied
To the letter, which the king hands to his envoy.
Then he prepares a gift for Mehran Setaad, a gift
So sumptuous that no one holds the memory of an envoy
Having received such an offering in private or in public.

The emperor distributes presents of dinars and musk
To the envoy's traveling companions.
He departs with his daughter and his treasures,
With cavaliers and adorned elephants,
Marching toward the River Jayhoon,
Tears of blood flooding his lash.
He remains until the procession has crossed the river
And reaches firm land on the opposite bank.
Then he marches away from river's edge,
His wistful heart mourning the loss of his daughter.

At the blessed news of Mehran Setaad's joyful approach,
People offer the travelers presents and offerings,
Wishing to express their hospitality and friendship.
They pronounce words of praise on both
The King of Iran and the Emperor of Chin.

Welcome pavilions are set up along the road.
Dirhams are tossed over the emperor's daughter.

In Amu, on the road to the desert, and in Marv,
The world is decked like the plumage of a partridge.

Once the escort reaches Bastam[80] and Gorgan,
It is as if the earth no longer perceives the sky,
So numerous are the bedecked pavilions and cupolas
In cities and in the countryside, and along the road
Traveled by the cortege for the duration of one month.

The palace children, men, and women
Crowd all the paths to catch sight of the Chini beauty.
They toss dirhams from balconies;
They sift musk and amber over her head;
They bring out trays of aromatic herbs;
The world fills with the sound of clarions and timpani;
The horses' manes are soaked in musk and wine,
And sugar and coins are scattered at their hooves.
The sound of flute, harp, and rebec is constant
And steals any chance anyone has to rest or sleep.

Once the beauty enters the women's lodging,
Kesra sneaks a peak into the litter, where he spots
A tall cypress tree surmounted by the moon's sphere
And bearing a diadem of amber on her head.
Beneath the diadem is a second diadem of black curls,
Loop on loop, woven, entwined and braided artfully.
These tresses form a ring of musk
That covers a face as bright as Jupiter.

King Anushiravan is astonished at the sight of her
And utters the name of Yazdan many times.
He selects a residence worthy of her stature,
And they prepare a throne for the moon.

◇◇◇◇◇◇◇◇◇◇◇◇◇
80 Bastam: A city in the province of Semnan, in north-central Iran.

40 | The Emperor Withdraws, and Anushiravan Drives His Host to Ctesiphon

The emperor receives news from Iran and from its king
Of the joy with which his daughter is received.
In his delight over the alliance, Anushiravan
Swiftly evacuates Soghd, Samarkand, and Chaadj,
And sends his crown to Ghajghaarbaashi.
In addition, the king places border guards in these cities.

Anushiravan's sense of justice renews the world.
Everyone, young and old, sleeps more peacefully.
Everyone everywhere raises hands to the sky,
Invoking blessings on the king and exclaiming,
"O Creator of space and time, maintain King Kesra
On the path of justice and deflect misfortune from him.
Protect his body and soul from danger.
Keep the world under his command, for his majesty
And splendor have chased away all acts of evil."

When Anushiravan arrives in Gorgan to hunt,
He finds no trace of the emperor.
As battle and fight no longer prevail,
As saddles come off their steeds, three hundred
Chini and Turk riders scatter to take their rest.
In the absence of the enemy,
The Iranians need not bind their bows.

Kesra the formidable, owner of majesty
And Kianian stature, launches into the hunt.
The royal star keeps his name company,
And fortune is his throne's mate.

The land's noblemen, from Amu to Chaadj and Khotan,
Gather to declare, "These vast regions, full of gardens,
Public squares, homes, and palaces,
From Chaadj to Samarkand and Soghd,
Have been greatly devasted, converted into owl lodgings.
In the lands of Chaghan, Shaknan, Khotlan, and Balkh,
The light of day has dimmed for everyone.
We speak of Bukhara, Khaarazm, Amu, and Zam
With great chagrin and affliction.

Afraasiyaab's sense of injustice and his oppression
Awarded people no place to rest or sleep.
But Kay Khosrow came to save us,
And men were able to put an end to discord.

"Later, Arjaasp grew more powerful,
Filling our lands with ailment and misery.
Then Goshtaasp came to Iran to battle him
And Arjaasp, and found no safe hiding place.
The world overcame the hardships he caused.
May the sky curse him forevermore!
Then, under the rule of Nersi, these lands
Once again succumbed to destruction.
But Shahpoor, son of Hormozd, seized power,
Overthrew Nersi, and brought the world back
On the path of justice and security.
The hand of Ahriman weakened.
When the emperor seized world governance
From Yazdegerd, violence once again cracked down.
World master Bahraam the Hunter came
To overwhelm and confuse the emperor.
His justice converted the world into paradise,
And evil and shameful acts disappeared.

"Khoshnavaz, at the time of Pirooz,
Filled the world with violence, anger, and anguish.
May Faghanish, his son, be cursed,
As well as his family and his unjust allies!
Now world ruler Kesra is in charge of our lands
And has restored and raised our sense of dignity.
May his reign last for all eternity!
If the earth is the recipient of his justice,
We shall be free of vexation and bloodshed."

The Hephthalites, the Turks, and the people of Khotan
Gather and settle at the edge of the Golzarioon.
Anywhere there is a wise man expert in the affairs,
A noble man of pure mores, intelligent and learned,
The Turks, full of advice, gather around him
In great numbers, and the people form the opinion
That they must travel to Anushiravan with presents.

Once in the presence of the king,
Unanimous in their intentions and words,
This crowd fills the royal court so tightly
That ant and fly cannot carve a path to cross.
They bow low to the ground and utter blessings:
"O King, we are your slaves.
We live on earth to reflect your will.
We are all noblemen, armed for war,
And we can tear the skin of leopards on the steppes."

The King of Kings accepts their offerings.
They take leave, preceded by Faghanish,
Forming an army of young warriors.

Since the king is pleased with the brave men,
The great chamberlain appears at the palace door,
Asks them the customary questions,
Receives them amicably, and prepares lodging.

The pious king exits his residence and bows down,
Addressing his prayers to the Creator:
"You are above the rotations of fate.
You have given me majesty, glory, and wisdom.
You are my Guide in good and bad fortune.
Act in a way that those who hear my name
Renounce the hope of seizing the royal crown,
That they resign in submission to kingship
And no one dares engage in a hostile quarrel.
Birds in the mountain and fish in the sea
Peacefully fall asleep at the time I recline.
Beasts, wild and tame, are my night guardians.
The earth's noblest men stand as my subjects.
The one you have selected is not a vile being.
There is in the world no other master than You.
The power you have endowed me with is such
That not even the ant suffers from oppression.

He weeps for a long time before Yazdan.
Look and see if you can find a more worthy king.

41 | Anushiravan Returns Victorious to Iran

Anushiravan exits the site of devotion,
Climbs on the throne and, with his host,
Prepares to depart from Gorgan.
He invokes Yazdan, Giver of good,
From whom all joy originates.

Trumpets and timpani resound at the palace gate.
The troops mount their stallions and hoist the loads
Of dinars, brocade, crowns, belts, reserves of dirhams
And precious stones, horses, veiled women,
Diadems, a turquoise litter, and an ivory throne.

Heart-charming attendants and all sorts of servants
Climb on their chargers, and the king sends them off
To Ctesiphon preceded by the Chini daughter.
They leave at a propitious hour, serene of mind,
The queen surrounded by eunuchs.

Mehran Setaad, the grand wise master,
Accompanies the queen, daughter of the emperor,
On the journey to Aazar Abadegan.
The treasures and the loads are being taken
To Ctesiphon, leaving no warrior behind.

A crowd of people from various lands gathers.
Men from Gilan and Deylam,[81]
From the mountains of Baluchistan,
From the desert of Saroj[82] and from Cootch,
Skilled swordsmen, arrive at the royal tent enclosure,
Bearers of presents and offerings.

The noble king is happy to see that the wolf's claws
No longer have the power to touch the sheep.
Since the beginning of time,
There has not existed a single man from Baluch
Who has not been a source of anguish and grief.
But with the influence of Kesra's majesty,

◇◇◇◇◇◇◇◇◇◇◇◇◇
81 Deylam: A city in the Gilan Province of Iran near the Caspian Sea.
82 Saroj: Region in Iran, unclear location.

The world has changed to be kind, respectful, and gentle.
In the land crossed by the army, farmers enjoy
Their bounty and the abundance of bread or water,
And at night the troops camp on the road.

In this way, the king travels around the world,
Observing the state of affairs in city and countryside.
Everywhere in the world he finds sown fields,
Valleys, and plains full of cattle and sheep.
He observes lands that had never been fertilized,
Where one had never witnessed a seed or a harvest.
He finds them now abounding with the earth's fruits,
He finds all the homes full of children.
Branches bend with the weight of bounty by the grace
Of the world master on whom fortune shines.

After the sky and moon turn in this way
For some time, an envoy dispatched by the Caesar
Arrives, carrier of gifts, clothing, gold and silver,
Rumi brocade, Rumi gems and fineries,
Offerings that cover the surface of the earth,
Along with a tribute unique in size from Rum.

The Caesar sends ten buffalo skins full of dinars,
As tribute and royalties to cover three years,
And a letter to the king attached to an offering of gold.

They seat the envoy before Kesra, who listens to him
Attentively as he reads the letter containing
Warm greetings, enumerating the gifts sent, consisting
Of the tribute to which they are to add crowns.

The king accepts it all and entrusts it to his treasurer.
Then he rises from his throne, climbs on his horse,
And travels in the direction of Aazargoshasp.
He spots the holy site from afar,
His cheeks flooding with tears.
He dismounts, grabs the barsom, murmurs a prayer,
Advances silently and respectfully toward the flame,
And begins to give thanks to the World Creator.

He hands over a great quantity of the gold and jewels
To the temple treasurer, providing wealth

And jeweled attires to the wise men.
They appear before the flame for prayers
And murmur benedictions on the just world king.

Anushiravan travels to Ctesiphon with his host,
Turning the earth into Mount Bisootoon.
In every city, this just man distributes gold and silver
To the poor, and the fortune he spreads
Fills these lands with treasures and wealth.

From there he takes the road to Mada'in,
The seat of the key to his treasury.
At the lead of the procession is Mehran Setaad,
Who escorts the Chini beauty and her forty servants,
Maidens who have attained mastery in their art.

42 | The World Enjoys Peace Under the Rule of Anushiravan

Kesra Anushiravan solemnly climbs on his throne
And believes himself to be fortune's mate,
Since the world shines like a paradise, full of wealth
And abundance, due to his kindness and his just ways.
Rulers rest from their battles
And cease to engage in unreasonable bloodshed.
The world is renewed by divine majesty
Accorded to Kesra Anushiravan by Yazdan.

It is as if the hand of evil is bound.
No one even remembers what it is like to pillage,
Invade, or to raise a hand to perform wicked deeds.
Men mold their behavior in line with the king's command,
Opting for the righteous path,
And renouncing perversity and darkness.

Thieves run away from the sight
Of a cache of coins spread across the road.
Villains refuse to cast a glance on brocade
Or on dinars, on the ground or in the waters,
By day or by night, for fear of the king.
The world is decked like paradise;

Valleys and plains come alive in their lushness.

Letters arrive from every land, from every noble,
Powerful man, every merchant from the lands of
Turks, Chin, Saghlaab, and other kingdoms.
There are so many letters of musk, bolts of Chini silk,
So many beautiful things from Rum and Indian perfume,
That Iran truly resembles a most splendid paradise.

The earth is of amber, bricks are of gold.
It is as if the tears of clouds are made of rosewater,
And suffering and the need for medicine has vanished.
Men turn their gaze to the land of Iran,
Free from aches, pains, and quarrels.
Water showers down on the flowers at the right time,
And the farmer no longer suffers from drought.
Valleys and plains brighten with bursts of blossoms,
As well as countless new homes and palaces.
The world fills with greenery and cattle.
Rivers expand as wide as seas,
And garden flowers resemble the Pleiades in beauty.

In the land of Iran, people learn foreign languages
To enlighten their souls with knowledge.
In all the lands, from Turkestan to Chin, from India
To Rum, merchants celebrate the king's glory.
Animals multiply, thanks to the abundance of grass.
Eloquent men learned in a number of sciences
Attend the king's court, where noblemen,
Wise men, and sages are highly honored.
Evil men tremble from fear of reprimand.

Every day, as the sun rises over the world,
A voice resounds at the palace door:
"O subjects of the world king,
May you never hide the harm inflicted upon you!
Those who have exerted themselves at work
Will be paid according to the level of their labor.
You may address the royal chamberlain,
Who will request from me your salary.
If a creditor solicits money from an unresourceful man,
My treasurer will pay the debt to curtail suffering

And to avoid finding the hand of the laborer empty.

"If a man casts a glance at another's wife
And if she accuses him before the king,
We will not allow him to escape due punishment.
He will surely receive chains in the dungeon
And shots of arrows on the gallows.
If a landowner complains about a horse sprinting free,
The horse will be executed on the cultivated field
Where he was found roaming around.
The injured man will walk away with the flesh,
And the rider will remain on foot, without a mount,
Left to serve penitence at the temple of Aazargoshasp.
The army inspector will strike his name off the roll,
And his house will be razed.
For every crime, whether it is more or less,
The culpable will be demeaned and degraded.
A king will never approve of misdeeds.
A king only admits righteous men into his court.
Yazdan forbid that we sight in our halls
Men who oppose or denounce the right path."

43 | Bozorgmehr Advises Anushiravan

One day, the world master climbs joyfully on his seat
To receive the noblemen and the learned men,
And to speak to them with an open, smiling face.

Bozorgmehr takes his place by the throne
And utters blessings on the king,
Whose heart rejoices like a spirited spring.
He says, "O fair-faced ruler, may detractors
Never find ways to speak against your majesty!
O blessed King of Kings, victorious world master,
Learned and illustrious, I have written a few words
In the language of Pahlavi in a royal book.
I have handed the writing over to your treasurer,
Hoping that you will have a chance to read it.
But I am witness to the fact that the indolent
Vault of sky has no intentions of revealing its secret.

"A man may rise from the seat of feast,
Expose himself and his life to battle,
Purify the earth from his adversaries,
Protect himself from dangers instigated by Ahriman,
Rise to the status of world master,
Gain insight into one thing after another,
Have a strong hand able to perform high deeds,
Build flower beds, public squares, gardens, palaces;
Amass treasures, gather his children around him,
Count his days as happy ones,
Increase his troops and his wealth,
Own a dazzling palace and audience hall,
Offer work and goods to the destitute,
Collect crowns and riches from every corner,
Gather heaps of gold and silver,
Still his years will not surpass one hundred.

"He will return to the dust one day,
His forgotten labors no longer bearing fruit,
Forced to concede his wealth to the enemy,
Keeping neither son nor throne and diadem,
Neither royal hall nor treasury nor host.
When the wind of his prosperity falls,
No one will remember him.
When the final hour of his destiny comes,
Only his good name can outlive him.

"There are only two things in the world
That do not perish, and that is that.
Nothing else remains for anyone.
There are two things that never age,
No matter how long earth and sand endure:
These are gentle words and good deeds.
Neither sun nor wind, neither water nor dust
Can wipe out a good name and good words.
Such is the rotation of providence.
Happy is the man endowed with modesty and virtue!
O King, abstain from iniquity as much as you can,
For it would bring great shame to your soul.
Abstain from causing harm to others as much as you can,
And attempt to be of use to men.
These are the precepts of our path, faith, and religion.

As for me, I shall leave behind a few words,
A memory of me, which I believe will never age."

His heart brought to attention by these words,
Anushiravan questions him further: "Do tell me,
Which man dwells in happiness, his heart content,
Never having to sigh in fear or worry?"

He replies, "The one who does not transgress
And who remains staunch, despite Ahriman's efforts."

The king asks him about the path of perversity
And of the deev, as well as the path of the Creator.
Bozorgmehr replies, "The best course of action,
No matter what, is to obey Yazdan,
Giver of glory in both worlds.
The door to vice leads to Ahriman,
Who is the enemy of pious men.
Happy is the man who lifts his heart
And wraps himself in a tunic of chastity!
His knowledge being his body's guardian,
His soul will shine bright after his death.
He will never regret anything that belonged
To either his body or his soul.
One is the sheath, the other is the sword of life.
After his death, his soul will be uncluttered
Of all the things attached to the body.

"Do not listen to the worthless speech of cunning,
Selfish minds, for they injure serene souls.
Those who are not ready to enter the future life
By confessing their faults will be plagued by grief.
Furthermore, know that a man with no fear
Of Yazdan, the pure, is a wicked man indeed.
The one who watches over his body with greed
Will cease to speak of his desires.
He has no knowledge of the soul's wisdom
And fails to pay heed to the discourse of the sage."

Kesra asks, "Who among noblemen
Entertains thoughts of a modest and humble nature?"

He answers, "The one who is the most knowledgeable

And governs his urges in the best way."

The king asks, "Who is knowledgeable,
For wisdom rests in the soul's secret?"

He answers, "The one who rejects the deev's path
And remains on the path of the World Master.
He abstains from listening to the enemies of the soul,
Who are opposed to the essence of wisdom.
There are ten Ahrimans who have the strength
Of lions and who dominate the soul and the mind."

Kesra says, "What is the nature of these ten deevs
On which wisdom has cause to weep?"

"Greed and need are two proud and powerful deevs.
The others are fury, envy, a querulous nature,
Vengeance, slander, falsehood, and an impure faith.
The tenth deev is ingratitude toward
One's benefactors and irreverence for Yazdan."

The king asks, "Which of these ten Ahrimans,
Vile and harmful, is the most potent?"

Bozorgmehr responds, "Greed is the most tyrannical
Of all the deevs and the most persistent.
Greed can never be satisfied. Aggrandizement
Being another step to further acquisitions.
Need is a deev that we see in blindness
From the pain of suffering and from misery.
Let us turn to another, O King, and you will see envy,
An illness for which the physician has no remedy.
Envy makes one's soul suffer at the sight of a happy man.

"Next comes the quarreling deev, full of dispute,
Always honing his claws to perform wicked deeds.
Then is the deev of vengeance, loud and wrathful,
Keeping his gaze fixed on those he resents.
He is a cruel and devious deev, with a glowering mien,
Who never welcomes generosity or kindness.
Another is the defamer deev, familiar only with lies
And deceit, and who refuses to bestow praise.
There remains the informer, the double-faced deev,

Who plucks fear of the divine out of his heart,
Who gives birth to enmity between men
And schemes to shatter strong alliances.
Lastly, we have the ignorant and faithless deev,
Who recognizes neither wisdom nor virtue,
Who despises modesty and intelligence, and
To whose eyes, good and evil are one and the same."

The king asks the sage, "As Yazdan's servants,
What divine gifts do we have to protect ourselves
And shorten the deevs' reach?"

The faithful man replies, "O expert, glorious King,
Wisdom is a most impenetrable armor,
Able to shield us against the deevs' honed blades.
Wisdom purifies; it sheds light into hearts and souls.
Wisdom keeps the memory of the past
And nourishes the mind with knowledge.
May wisdom be your soul's guide,
For you still have a long journey ahead!
If wisdom becomes what we call second nature,
It eradicates any fear you may have of the deev.
Then your heart, full of good instinct and content
With the world, will not approach the door of greed.

"Now I shall speak hopeful words
That will guide you on the road to happiness.
The man who is endowed with reason always
Feels encouraged and sees joy in the world.
He never thinks to commit wicked deeds
And selects the straight path of the arrow
Rather than the crooked bend of the bow.
Furthermore, the one satisfied with his fortune
Will not extend a hand to exert himself.
He will not be burdened by worry
And will abstain from giving a thought to wealth.
All his days will unfold in contentment.
The one who is a loyal servant of Yazdan will not
Turn away from divine command to avoid pain,
To amass treasure, or to please someone else.
There is in his nature no evil element.
He is virtuous in all his deeds, as he will never

Sell the divine path, no matter what the price."

Kesra says, "Which virtue is most important
And reveals the path to happiness?"

He answers, "The path of wisdom, is,
Without a doubt, the most favorable path.
After that, an amiable disposition
Affords one honor throughout one's life.
I can conclude that of all the faculties,
The most solid one is contentment over one's fate,
The most gentle one is rest from one's labors,
And the most pleasant one is the faculty of hope.
Greed is a condition that leads to grief and anguish,
For no treasure is ever satisfying enough."

The king asks, "What is the best faculty,
The one that affords the most grandeur to a man?"

He replies, "Wisdom is the highest form of knowledge.
And the wisest man is the noblest among noblemen.
He will never throw himself violently on wealth
And thereby shields himself from weariness."

The king asks the nature of the most powerful foe
And how is one to defend oneself against him.
He answers, "Evil actions are the enemy
Of the serene mind and of wisdom."

The giver of justice asks the sage
Which is more worthy, learning or birth.
His guide replies, "Learning is more valuable
Than birth, for it is the ornament of the soul,
While there is not much to say about high birth.
In the absence of merit,
Birth is a sad and feeble thing of little value.
It is through instruction than the soul gains vigor."

The king says, "How can one polish his soul,
And how should the skills of the body be praised?"

He answers, "I shall say everything I have to say,
If you wish to follow me point by point.

Since wisdom is a divine gift,
It can be touched neither by doubt nor by evil.
But if a skillful man remains in awe of himself,
One must not have faith in his talents.
A good-natured man will not be scorned by a sage.
When a wise man unites birth with generosity,
Knowledge, and justice, he will always hold
On to power, wealth, and righteousness,
And will not succumb to a wicked nature."

Kesra asks, "O illustrious, knowledgeable seeker,
Do we gain power through our own efforts
Or do we do so as a result of chance arbitrarily
Bestowing the throne and crown to kings?"

He replies, "Fortune and talent form a couple
Intertwined like the soul and the body.
They are friends and mates. Their coarse parts
Are visible, and their spiritual nature is hidden.
If the fortune that watches over him is on the boil,
The body is the human instrument for effort.
But effort will not produce power
Without the assistance of good fortune.
Furthermore, the world is a fable and a breath of air,
A dream remembered by the dreamer,
Where one holds nothing upon awakening,
Whether the dream was pleasant or wrathful."

Next, the king draws out a new question,
From his mind's secret, and asks the sage,
"What person or thing is worthy of praise?"

He answers, "A king is the ornament of the throne.
His good fortune is the source of his power.
If he is just and has a good reputation,
His words and actions will attain their goal."

The king asks, "Who is afflicted in the world
With sorrowful days and a miserable life?"

"The poor and vile man who will attain neither
The object of his desires nor access to cheerful paradise."

The king asks, "What man is most miserable,
Forcing us to shed constant tears over his fate?"

"The learned man who pales for indulging in evil deeds."

"Which man is content with what he has
And has no need to seek a rise in his fortune?"

"The one without attachment to the dome of sky."

The kings asks, "What man is the most deserving?"

He answers, "The one who has the most dignity."

"What man is most dignified? For one
Has reason to weep over enraged men."

"The one who turns away from the judgment of others.
He is decent, gentle, wise, and intelligent."

"Who among men nurtures the most hope?"

He replies, "The one who is most attentive
And whose ears absorb the most wisdom."

The world king questions him on how
To assess the hidden good and the hidden bad.
He replies, "Those who claim to know everything
Are sure to possess empty brains.
They say our place is in this dust,
But no one has awareness of the other world."

Kesra says, "Which nation is the richest,
And what part do we have in its wealth?"

"Nations prosper from the justice of the world master."

Kesra asks, "Tell me which man is most aware,
Awake, and intelligent in the world,
So that he may glorify the world with his wisdom."

He replies, "An old, learned man
Who combines his learning with life experiences."

"What man is most satisfied
And is always supported by joy and happiness?"

"The one exempt from worry
And who possesses gold and silver."

The king says, "What quality is most worthy
Of praise, and who is worthy in the world?"

He answers, "The one able to hide his needs,
His desires, his vanity, and his longings.
He will not display a vengeful or jealous spirit
And will be agreeable to everyone."

The king asks which man, with his patience,
Bears the illustrious diadem of perseverance.
He replies, "The one whose heart, though he despairs,
Nevertheless shines bright as the sun.
Moreover, the one who has to count his days
And who works on a large venture."

He asks, "Which man is most afflicted,
So afflicted that he is weary of his own life?"

"The one who falls from the throne
And despairs in restoring his fortune."

The powerful king asks,
"Which man's heart is most mournful?"

He answers, "The one deprived of wisdom
And an influential man who has no children."

The king asks which man is most miserable,
For he is consumed by sorrow
Without having endured any misfortune.

He replies, "The man full of wisdom and virtue
Who has to patronize a frivolous king."

"Is there a man who despairs
Despite power and a vast fortune?"

"The one who is forced to abandon a large venture

Will remain bitter and displeased."

"O insightful sage whose fortune is young
Is there a man devoid of fame and distinction
Who is worthy of affection and charity?"

"The man who commits many a fault.
The poor guilty one who is without support."

"Tell me, according to the truth,
Who repents from the past?"

"A king who wears a black helmet on the day
Of his death will repent, and his heart will be full of fear
For having abstained from expressing thanks to Yazdan.
In addition, the one who has done much
For the ungrateful man who takes advantage of him."

"O intelligent man, you weave together all the talents.
Do you know anything that may preserve one
Against bodily harm and which is at the same time
Of great value to everyone's heart?"

He replies, "When we have good health,
The heart desires only joy. We yearn for health
When the body is beaten down by injury."

"What is the most urgent desire?
Tell me, O good-natured, wise man!"

He replies, "When we hold a high stature,
We desire mostly to be above all need.
When one is healthy and well, then one
Only has to seek the heart's contentment."

Next the king asks his advisor,
"What is the heart's principal worry?"

He replies, "The sensible man can indicate
Three worries to the one who consults with him:
First he worries about a day of misfortune,
Wishing to keep danger and harm at bay.
Next he fears the designs of untrue friends

Who would blame his head, his life, his blood and skin.
Thirdly, he is wary of an unjust king who cannot
Distinguish between a virtuous man and a scoundrel.
How happy would be the rotation of fate
If a friend full of wisdom would serve you as guide.
The world would be full of light and the king full of justice.
The sky could not give man a greater joy!"

The king questions him on the subjects of faith
And righteousness, elements that have the ability
To cast aside misfortune and perdition.

The sage elaborates, "O King, attach yourself
To a path that does not distance you from Yazdan.
Stay away from perversity and the path of the deev,
Live in fear of the World Master, pay close attention
To divine commandment, and never sell your faith."

Then he questions him on the nature of rulers
Who govern virtuous men, asking who among them
Has a triumphant fortune and who is worthy of the throne.

The sage replies, "The one who is just and endowed
With wisdom, finesse, intelligence, and ability."

The king questions him on old friends
With whom one can live and converse.

He answers, "A friend must have generosity
And a deep sense of justice,
Then he will not hurt you only to please another.
He will support you and help you in times of adversity."

"Who has the most friends
Who share common traits, and blood and skin?"

"Only an evil man will distance himself from a kind one.
The most welcoming, most accommodating one
Who performs good deeds has the most friends."

He asks, "Who has an excess of adversaries
Who stand staunchly against him?"

The sage replies, "The proud and querulous man,
As well as the harsh, frowning, tight-fisted one."

"Who is your friend forever,
For whom one weeps when separated?"

"The companion who is constant, kind, and caring."

Kesra asks, "What endures forever
And is never subject to diminishing?"

He replies, "A good deed is never forgotten
By a true friend and cannot be stolen."

"What is there that shines the most
And is the highest diadem on humanity?"

"The soul of the sage, mistress of his desires."

The king asks, "O affectionate man,
What is greater and more lofty than the sky?"

He replies, "A king with an open hand
And the heart of a Yazdan worshipper."

"What is the most honorable thing
Through which a sensible man gains pride?"

"O King, never offer wealth to impure men,
For giving goods to the ungrateful
Is as effective as tossing bricks into water."

The king asks, "What sort of effort causes
A distaste for the acquisition of wealth?"

He says, "May your heart always mirror spring!
The suffering of the servant of an ill-natured king
Will make him renounce riches, comfort, and life."

The king asks, "What marvel have you seen
That is inconceivable to the imagination?"

He replies, "The actions of the glorious firmament.
At times one sees a powerful man,

Whose diadem reaches the dark clouds,
While he cannot distinguish between his left
And his right hand. He has not the ability
To understand if his fortune increases or decreases.
At times one sees another who, by the skies' rotations,
Can predict the movement of the stars,
Yet fate subjects him to misfortune, and his share
Of the world is nothing more than a bitter destiny."

The king asks, "What weighs the heaviest?"

He replies, "The weight of iniquity."

The king asks, "Who is blamed by everyone,
Condemned, and treated like a wicked man
Because of his behavior, his words, and his actions?"

He replies, "A king who is parsimonious,
Who seeks dispute with innocent men;
A miserly rich man who saves by rejecting
Food, clothing, and nurturing;
A woman with no shame who speaks loudly;
A good man who acts in haste;
A man who boasts and affects grandeur.
Finally, lying is the most unseemly, vile, and abject
Thing to do, whether you are a servant or the king."

The king asks, "What is best in the world,
Whether in public or in private, that can function
As an armor and give the soul a sense of serenity?"

He replies, "The one who is serious in his faith
Will only find veneration in the world.
Furthermore, the one who is grateful to Yazdan
Is a wise man who understands true worship."

Kesra asks, "What are the best actions to take,
And what must we abstain from,
Whether we are a king or a commoner?
In what area is it best to command and dominate,
And what area must we overlook with scorn?
What must we abstain from touching,
And what must we hold on to tightly?"

557

He replies, "Guard yourself from anger
When someone closes their eyes on the guilty.
Also, stay vigilant, and as much as you can,
Forbid yourself from taking part in wicked deeds.
The soul of the one who rejects a grudge
And seizes hope shines like the sun.
No matter what reward you may obtain for a crime,
It is best to abstain categorically from committing it."

Thanks to the Master of Sun and Moon,
I complete here the discussions between Bozorgmehr
And the king, and, this matter that would have
Charmed your heart, having been exhausted,
I must turn to the story of the game of chess.[83]

44 | The Indian Rajah Sends Anushiravan a Game of Chess

A wise man recounts that one day
The king decks his palace with Rumi brocade
And hangs his crown above the ivory throne.
It is hard to equate the level of teakwood to ivory.
Everything shines like the sphere of the moon.
Everything is eclipsed by the royal throne.
The entire court is full of Kesra's armed procession.
The palace is crowded by wise men and border guards
From Balkh, Bukhara, and the various edges of the empire.

Anushiravan learns from his vigilant emissaries that
An envoy is on his way to court sent from the Indian ruler.
He comes with elephants, parasols, an escort of riders
From Sindh, and one thousand loaded camels.

At the news, the awakened king dispatches
A cortege to meet the visitor on the road.

◇◇◇◇◇◇◇◇◇◇◇◇◇
83 Chess: The game was invented in India in the eighth century and named *chatranj*.
Over time, the names of the pieces were changed by the Persians and the Arabs and
later by the Europeans. After it was introduced in Europe, the king remained king, the
minister or vizier became the queen, the elephant became the bishop, the horse became the knight, the chariot became the rook, and the foot soldier became the pawn.

The envoy of the illustrious, powerful prince
Enters the hall and greets the noble king
With gestures that honor his noble birth.
After giving thanks to the World Creator,
He presents the king with an abundance of jewels,
Elephants, earrings, and an Indian parasol
Decorated in gold and inlaid with fine stones.
He opens crates before the audience
And sets down their contents at the king's feet:
There is plenty of gold and silver, musk and amber,
Fresh aloeswood, rubies, diamonds, ornately carved
Indian sabers, and a variety of valuable objects,
Products of Ghennooj and Mai.

All of this is swiftly taken and placed before the throne.
The king of triumphant fortune looks at the wealth
Amassed with great effort by the Rajah
And entrusts it to the care of his treasurer.

Then the envoy hands a letter to Anushiravan
Written by the Indian Rajah on silk,
Along with a very rich and artful chessboard.
The envoy adds this message from his prince:
"May you remain king as long as there is sky!
Command the most learned men to place
The chessboard before them, to consult with each other,
And to determine the rules of the noble game.
They are to identify all the chess pieces,
Fix their movements and their squares,
Study the foot soldiers, the elephants, and the warriors,
The chariots and the horsemen,
And the march of the king and his minister.
If they discover the rules of this beautiful game,
They will surpass all the learned men of the world.
At that time, we shall gladly send to his majesty's court
Any tribute and fees demanded of us.
But if the illustrious men of the land of Iran
Are unable to solve the problem,
They must cease to ask us for tribute
Since they are not our equals in knowledge.
It will be conversely your turn to be tributary,
For knowledge is worth more than

Anything men may boast about."

Kesra lends his heart and ear to the words of the man
As he relays the message he was charged with.
They set up the chessboard in front of the king,
Who stares at the pieces for some time.
Some are made of gleaming ivory, others of teakwood.

The wise king questions the figures and the board.
The Indian replies, "O King, they represent the way of war.
Once you understand the game, you will find in it
The march to battle, its strategies, and its apparatus."

The king says, "I ask for seven days,
On the eighth day, I shall gladly play."

A beautiful residence is set up for the envoy.
Noblemen, wise men, and royal advisors gather,
Sit across the chessboard and attempt to unravel its secrets.
They play one against the other various moves.
They discuss, question, listen to each other.
But, unable to discover the game's rules, they give up
And depart, frowning over their disappointment.

Bozorgmehr appears before an irritated King Kesra.
Seeing a means to end this affair that began so poorly,
He says, "O King, vigilant and powerful world master,
I shall apply all the strength of my mind
To decipher the solution of this beautiful game."

The king says to him, "Success is worthy of you.
May your mind be clear and your body healthy!
I do not wish for the Rajah of Ghennooj to spread
The rumor that I do not have a man of good counsel.
Such a thing would bring dishonor
To my court, my throne and my wise men."

Bozorgmehr asks for the chessboard.
He sits before it to think deeply and apply himself.
He searches in every way for the rules of the game and
Does not give up until he finds the position of each piece.

Having spent one day and one night to discover the rules,

He runs to the palace and to the King of Iran,
"O victorious King, I have studied these black figures
And the board, and, by the fortune of the world master,
I have perfectly discovered the way of the game.
Summon the Rajah's envoy and anyone else
Who is curious, but not before the King of Kings
Has had a chance to learn the game.
It appears to be a faithful image of the battlefield."

The king is delighted by Bozorgmehr's words.
He summons the man of fortunate trail
And favorite of fate, and calls for the arrival
Of wise men, noblemen, and illustrious sages.
Then he calls the envoy of the Rajah
And seats him before the glorious throne.

Bozorgmehr speaks: "O sun-faced, wise man,
You were sent by the eminent Rajah.
What did your master say of these pieces?
May wisdom be your companion!"

The Indian replies, "My blessed Rajah
Told me before I left his side,
        'Take these pieces of teak
        And ivory to the master of the crown.
        Tell him to place them before the wise men,
        His advisors, gathered in the assembly.
        If they discover the way of this noble game,
        If they set it up correctly, their hearts will be joyous.
        We shall send pouches of gold, slaves, fees,
        And tribute for as much as we are able to.
        In knowledge rests the value of kings and not
        In their wealth, their subjects, and their lofty throne.
        But if his majesty and his advisors fail
        And if their minds do not solve the puzzle,
        Then Anushiravan may not ask us for tribute.
        His wise soul will mourn acquired fortune,
        And, recognizing the subtleness of our souls
        And our minds, he will send us wealth in abundance.'"

Bozorgmehr takes the chessboard
And places it before the throne.

He says to the noblemen and wise men,
"O illustrious and pure-hearted sages,
Pay attention to these words
And to the will of their prudent master."

Then the sage sets up the battlefield,
Places at the center the king, on the left and the right
The army soldiers, at the front the infantrymen,
The vizier next to the king to guide him in war;
On both sides, the elephants who observe the fight;
Beyond are the battle steeds,
Straddled by two skillful cavaliers; and finally,
Left and right, the chariots, rivals ready for battle.

Once Bozorgmehr sets up his army,
The assembly is in a state of awe.
The Indian envoy is chagrined,
Stunned by this magician on whom fortune shines.
He cannot overcome his surprise
And remains absorbed in reflection:
"He has nonetheless never seen a chessboard.
He has never heard of it from Indian wise men.
I never hinted at the role of these pieces,
Never facilitated it in any way.
How was he able to surmise the rules,
And master the game?
No one exists in the world with this man's abilities."

Kesra on his side is so proud of Bozorgmehr
That it is as if fortune turns over him.
He is blissful and treats him with favors,
Prepares for him a magnificent chalice full of gems
Worthy of a king, a pouch of dinars, and a strapped horse,
And he covers him with praise and blessings.

45 | Bozorgmehr Invents the Game of Backgammon, and Anushiravan Sends Him to India

The wise Bozorgmehr retires to his home,
Places before him a table and a compass,
And dives so deeply into his reflections

That his mind becomes jumbled.

He wants to invent a new and noble game that
Would astonish learned men and keep them guessing.
He reflects on the game of chess invented by the Indians,
And his mind applies itself to the point of weariness.
By joining his intelligence to his serene heart,
And with much thought and effort,
He creates the game of *nard*, or backgammon.

He has two dice made out of ivory
With the numbers marked in the color of ebony.
Then he forms an army of pawns or disks, similar
To those in the game of chess, placing them on two sides
In order of battle and distributing the troops,
Ready to assault the city, within eight boxes.

The ground is black, the battlefield square,
And two powerful kings of good disposition
Are to march without ever hurting each other.
They each have an army at their command,
Lined up on the battlefield and ready for war.

The two kings advance on the battleground.
Their troops circle around them, each in an attempt
To surpass the other, and they fight at times
On mountain heights and at times on the plain.
When two surprise a single opposite pawn,
They have the chance to overcome him.
The two armies face each other in this way
Until one of them is defeated.

Bozorgmehr sets up the game of backgammon,
Then appears before the king and explains it to him,
Elaborating on royal power and on the armies' battles.
He demonstrates the unfolding to Kesra, step by step.

The King of Iran is surprised, and he thinks deeply.
In the end, he says, "O brilliant man,
May you and your fortune always remain young!"

He asks for two thousand camels from the camel driver.
Riches are drawn from the royal treasury to load up

Camels with the products from the tributes of Rum and
Chin, the lands of Hephthalites, Mokran, and Iran.
The caravan prepares to march out of the king's court.

When the camels are loaded and the king has been
Rid of worry, he summons the Rajah's envoy,
Speaks to him at length on the virtue of knowledge,
And writes a letter to his master full of sagacity,
Playfulness, sense, and wisdom.

He begins the letter in praise of the prince who seeks
Shelter in Yazdan against the attacks of the evil deev,
Then he adds, "O illustrious ruler of India
From the Sea of Ghennooj to the border of Sindh,
Your intelligent messenger arrived with parasols,
Elephants, and his entire procession,
With the chessboard and your missive.
We have listened to him, and we have followed
The Rajah's instructions.
We have asked for time from the wise Indian.
We have summoned knowledge with our minds.
A pure sage, one of our most astute advisors,
Led extensive research and discovered the game.
Now this wise man will carry to the mighty Rajah
In Ghennooj two thousand camel loads, made up of
A variety of things acceptable as souvenirs from us.
I send also, instead of chess, the game of backgammon
To see if you wish to take a turn at this challenge.
There are many brahmins of good counsel who,
Through their vast knowledge,
Will be able to discover the rules of the game.

"The Rajah will hand over to his treasurer the valuables
Carried by my messenger with much effort.
If he and his advisors attempt to figure out the rules
And do not succeed, the Rajah from Ghennooj
Must prepare, in accordance to the terms of our treaty,
The same number of camel loads to send to me,
While at the same time returning what I send.
This is the convention and the bargain we have made."

Once the sun begins to shine at the top of the sky,

Bozorgmehr takes his leave from the king's court
With loaded camels, letter, and backgammon set,
His head full of strategies for conquest and battle.

He arrives at the side of the Rajah, and with the Brahmin,
His happy guide, he presents himself before the prince.
He sees his face, his diadem, and his fortune.
He greets him at length in Pahlavi, delivers the letter,
And repeats the message of the King of Kings.

The Rajah's cheek blossoms like a flower,
And the Indian guide recounts all that occurred
Relating to the game of chess and
The difficulties endured to penetrate its rules.

Then the learned Bozorgmehr explains
How he was able to break through the mystery,
The game, the movement of the pieces, and
The roles of the kings and their advising ministers.
Then he hands over the backgammon board
And adds, "May the ruler read the letter,
And may his mind remain on the just path!"

The Rajah's cheeks pale at Bozorgmehr's
Account of the games of chess and backgammon.

46 | The Indian Sages Are Unable to Decipher the Rules of Backgammon

An illustrious lord arrives
And assigns the envoy a suitable residence.
They set up a banquet hall,
Summon wine, music, and singers.

The Rajah asks for a delay of seven days.
He gathers his most glorious men of science
And the most learned and honored in the land,
Placing before them the board of backgammon.

For one week, the most sagacious of them,
Young and old, search for the way of the game,

Animated by ambition, vanity, greed, and the desire
For conquest and the acquisition of honor.

On the eighth day, the grand wise master
Says to the Rajah, "No one understands it.
We need wisdom itself to assist these noblemen
And to draw out a game from its pieces."

The ruler's heart is indignant,
His mind afflicted, his brow furrowed.

On the ninth day, Bozorgmehr arrives,
Heart full of passion, face deeply wrinkled.
He says, "The king did not authorize me to stay too long,
And I must not allow his heart to worry."

The noble savants together confess their ignorance.
Bozorgmehr, having listened to them,
Sits down to draw in the noblemen's attention.
He spreads out the backgammon set before them
And explains the rules of the game.
He shows them the leader and his valiant army,
The preparations for battle, and the king's command.

The Rajah, his advisers, and the assembly,
Consisting of the most illustrious men of the land,
Are deeply afflicted, yet they praise him
And call him the wise man of pure faith.

The Rajah interrogates Bozorgmehr on every science.
He instantly replies to all the questions.
The learned men who wish to gain,
Those who are able to read, all exclaim,
"Here is an eloquent man full of knowledge
Beyond the games of chess and backgammon."

The Rajah summons two thousand camels
On which they load all the tribute from Ghennooj.
They are dispatched to the court of Iran
With yearly fees, aloeswood, camphor and amber,
Gold, robes, pearls, and fine jewels.
Then the Rajah asks for a diadem from his treasury
And one of his full attires from head to toe.

PART TWENTY-SIX

He offers them to Bozorgmehr while praising him
And adding additional gifts for his companions.

Then he advances two thousand camels
And hands them over to him with tributes.
It is a caravan of insurmountable wealth,
More than anyone has ever seen before.

Bozorgmehr departs from Ghennooj,
Raising his head to the revolving dome of sky.
He is happy to be the carrier of a letter on silk
From the Indian ruler written in Hindu characters
And saying: "The Rajah and his noblemen declare,
And not out of fear or out of cowardice,
That no one has ever seen or heard
Of a more powerful king than Anushiravan,
That there exists no man more learned than his vizier,
Whose treasured wisdom is as vast as the dome of sky.
I am sending you a year's worth of tribute,
And if you ask for more, I shall send that as well.
Everything that I owe you for the game
Has been dispatched based on our convention."

The king is delighted to hear that his vizier is returning,
Having happily and peacefully reached his goal.
He commands all the city and army notables to prepare,
And many of them advance to greet
Bozorgmehr with elephant and timpani.
He executes his entrance into the city
With the pomp and honor due a victorious king.

Bozorgmehr enters the palace and approaches the throne.
The king showers him with praise, kisses him,
And questions him on the Rajah and on his voyage.

Bozorgmehr recounts to him what occurred
And speaks of the fortune that watched over him
And the favors the skies afforded him.
Then he produces the letter of the triumphant Rajah
And places it before the throne.

The king, eager to find out its contents,
Summons Yazdegerd, his scribe, to read.

The assembly is in awe of Bozorgmehr's mind
And the fortune of the sun-faced king.

Kesra says to Bozorgmehr, "Thanks be to Yazdan
For the intelligence and the piety you have shown.
Now kings are the servants of my throne and crown,
Their hearts and souls full of affection for me."

Thanks to the Master of Sun and Moon,
Giver of victory and support,
I am now able to compose a tale even more astonishing
Than the account of the prodigious Bozorgmehr,
To whom Yazdan granted such wisdom.
I am now about to relate the story of Talhand
And the invention of the game of chess.

PART TWENTY–SEVEN

The Continuation of the Reign
of Kesra Anushiravan

The Story of Gao and Talhand,
and the Invention of Chess

1 | The Beginning of the Story

One must pay attention to the words
Of the octogenarian Shahooy, who recounts
That there reigns in India an illustrious man,
Owner of treasure, army, and war apparatus.
Celebrated everywhere, more than any other
Indian ruler. His name is Jemhoor.

He is King of India, wise, sagacious, and calm.
He rules over Bost, Cashmere, and lands
That stretch all the way to the border of Chin.
Noblemen everywhere pay homage to him.
He dominates the earth with his courage.
He lives in Sendal,[84] the seat of his crown,
His treasury, army, seal, and diadem.
Jemhoor is a man of merit who seeks instruction.
He is powerful, learned, and glorious.
His subjects, whether city folk or court servant,
Live happily under his reign.

By his side lives a woman worthy of him,
Prudent, skilled, cultured, and harmless.
One night, she gives birth to a son
Indistinguishable from his father.
At the sight of the young prince,
The father assigns him the name of Gao.

Some time later, the king suddenly falls ill,
Relays to the queen his last wishes, and dies.
This just man leaves to Gao a just world to govern,
But the child is too young for throne, belt, and armor.

The leaders of the land cover their heads with dust,
Their hearts grieving over Jemhoor's death.
The world mourns him and his generous spirit,
His sense of justice and his feasts.

◇◇◇◇◇◇◇◇◇◇◇◇◇
84 Sendal: A village in northwestern India.

Warriors and townspeople, men, women,
And children gather to hold counsel and say,
"This small child is too young to command an army,
To spread justice, to exhibit fury,
And to climb on the throne and wear the crown.
Any kingdom lacking a powerful ruler will suffer."

The king has an intelligent and illustrious brother
Worthy of the throne, named Maay,
An idol worshipper whose residence is in Dambar.

Worldly men who seek a ruler travel from Sendal
To Dambar, and all the noblemen from Cashmere
And lands bordering Chin acclaim Maay as their king.

The powerful new ruler travels from Dambar
And climbs on the kingly throne.
He places Jemhoor's crown on his head
And begins to govern with justice and generosity.

As soon as he takes his kingly seat,
He marries Gao's mother and raises the son
Whom he adores as much as his own life.

The fairy-faced queen soon gives birth to another son.
His father, Maay, heart full of affection and love,
Gives him the name of Talhand.

Once the child reaches two years of age
And Gao, who is a brilliant and valiant boy,
Reaches his seventh year, Maay falls ill,
And the heart of his mate fills with grief.
Two miserable weeks pass, and the king dies,
Leaving the world and its rule to another.

The inhabitants of Sendal weep with misery,
Their hearts consumed by the pain of Maay's death.
They remain for one month absorbed in mourning,
But at the end of the month, a crowd of notables
And valiant, wise men from the land gathers
To discuss all sorts of plausible courses of action.

In the end, a sage stands up to say,

"This woman, companion of Jemhoor, has always
Held herself at a distance from poor actions.
She has always walked the path of righteousness
With her two husbands, always seeking justice.
She is of illustrious birth and inspires confidence.
It is best to hail her as our queen,
As she is the rightful heir to the kings."

The assembly agrees with this wise advice,
And a messenger is sent to the pure woman to say,
"Fill the seat of your two sons.
It is a necessary act to benefit the public good.
When your son has reached the age of maturity to rule,
You will hand over to him power, throne, and army.
You will be his guide, friend, advisor, and support."

The woman, blessed with good fortune,
Brings sheen to the crown and decks the throne.
She exercises power with moderation,
Kindness, and a great deal of justice.
The entire kingdom is thrilled to live under her rule.

She selects two virtuous and skilled wise men
Who have traveled the world extensively.
She entrusts to their care her two sons,
Two insightful princes with whom she never parts
As her joy emanates from the sight of them.

Once the princes have gained strength,
Once they have been well educated
And have mastered all the sciences,
They would come every so often, alone,
To their virtuous mother and say to her,
"Which one of us displays the best behavior?
Which one has a more virtuous heart
And works harder at his assignments?"

The mother would tell each son, "For me to assess
Which one of you has merit, you must exert effort
And show good sense, abstinence, and faith.
You must speak softly and eloquently, seek respect.
Since both of you are of royal race,
You must acquire wisdom, modesty, moderation,

And a sense of fairness and justice."

Upon a visit to his mother, the son would say,
"To whom belong land, throne, and diadem?"

The mother would reply, "The throne is yours.
You are wise, intelligent, and a favorite of fate."
She would repeat the same thing to the other,
In a way that each son delighted at the thought
That he would soon become heir to the throne,
The treasury, the army, to glory and prosperity.

In this way they attain the age of maturity,
Each under the guidance of someone
Who teaches him to act in wicked ways.
Each son is full of grief and jealousy,
Restlessly yearning for the crown and treasury.

The people and the army begin to split up,
And the hearts of virtuous men fill with fear.

2 | Gao and Talhand Discuss the Ascension to the Throne

The sons, agitated by the effect of poor instruction,
Approach their mother and continue to badger her
About who is most deserving and more patient.

The intelligent woman replies, "You must first
Deliberate with wise men of good counsel
In order to resolve the question in a peaceful manner.
Then you and your advisors will consult
The town's noblemen and principals.
Greed does not suit when it comes to state affairs.
When one aspires for the throne and crown,
One needs wisdom, intelligence, treasury, and army.
If an unjust man wishes to govern,
He will fill the world with wrath and ruins."

The sage Gao says to his mother,
"Do not seek to evade my questions.

If I am not in a state to do honor to this land,
Tell me without affecting ruse and falsehood.
Give the throne and diadem to Talhand,
And I will be his devoted subject.
But if my age and my wisdom give me the rights,
If being a descendant of Jemhoor elects me
As the lawful governing ruler, tell him not
To throw himself foolishly into a perilous venture
Only for the acquisition of the throne and crown."

His mother replies, "Do not get so carried away!
One must make use of measure in one's speech.
Anyone who sits on the kingly throne
Must be ready and willing to act,
To liberally open his two hands in giving,
Maintain his soul pure of any wicked intention,
And quietly walk down the path of wisdom.
He must guard himself against enemy attack
And pay attention to things
That afford one either glory or shame.
The Master of Sun and Moon will request
An account of the acts of justice or injustice executed
In the land and in the army, and should the king
Oppress a fly, his soul is sure to sadly dwell in hell.

"The world is more black than the dark night.
A king's mind must be more disentangled
Than a hair to maintain his soul and his body
Free from harm and to understand that
Perversity will never produce anything good.
If a king, seated on the throne of justice,
Places the crown on his head,
He will render the world joyous, but in the end,
Either his pillow will be of brick and dust
Or he will burn and perish in some ditch.

"Jemhoor was of the race of benevolent kings.
His mind and his actions always rejected ill advice.
He died prematurely and abandoned
The world to his younger brother.
The powerful Maay came from Dambar.
He was young, discerning, holder of pure intentions.

The inhabitants of Sendal gathered around him,
Hearts inflamed and desirous of finding a king.
He arrived, sat on the throne of power,
Ready for battle, hands open for giving.
He asked for my hand in marriage,
And we soon became husband and wife
So that all the affairs could maintain secrecy.
Now, since you are the elder brother,
You are the first in age and in maturity.
Guard yourself from being tormented
By a yearning for crown and treasure.
If I were to select one of you, I would offend
The other, who would be incensed with me.
Do not spill blood for the sake of kingship,
For this fugitive world remains for no one."

Talhand does not believe his mother's advice
Will benefit him in any way. He replies,
"You have chosen Gao because he is the oldest,
But that does not mean that he is more capable.
There are, in the army and in the city,
Many men as old as vultures[85] in the sky,
But they do not harbor ambition for dominion,
Diadem, treasury, throne, and crown.
My father died still young, having failed
To appoint a successor to the throne of power.
I see that your heart leans toward Gao
And you wish to place him ahead of me.
Yet I could build men like him out of mud.
Woe to me if I were to allow him
To dishonor my father's name."

His mother takes a solemn oath and says,
"I would be weary of the blue vault of sky
If I had asked such a thing from Yazdan,
If I desired it deep in my heart,
Or even I clung to the thought in my mind!
Take well what I have told you.
Do not grow irritated with the firmament;
It only grants happiness to whom it pleases.

◇◇◇◇◇◇◇◇◇◇◇◇◇
85 At this time, it was believed that vultures live for over 100 years.

Place your trust only in the Creator.
I have shared my advice as best I could.
If it does not suit you, then find out what
Course of action is preferable and proceed with it.
May my counsel calm your soul!"

Then she summons the sages, repeats the lessons
And opinions to them, asks for the key to the treasury
Of the two pure and wise deceased kings,
Lays open the contents before the noblemen's eyes,
And divides it all fairly between her two sons.

Gao says to Talhand, "O excellent man,
Seek new paths! You have heard how superior
Jemhoor was to Maay in age and in wisdom.
Your noble and virtuous father did not display
A desire to occupy the throne of Jemhoor.
He did not feel shame for being his inferior,
And did not ask to be placed above others.
Think carefully: Would Yazdan, Justice Giver,
Approve of me strapping my belt like a slave
Before my younger brother?
My mother only spoke of justice.
Why does your heart enjoy dwelling in injustice?
Let us call certain army leaders, intelligent, worldly men.
Let us listen to our tutors and our teachers.
We shall then conform to their command."

The two young people exit their mother's palace,
Deep in discussion, their hearts full of doubt.
They end up agreeing to discard the advice
Of noblemen, warriors, learned and ignorant men,
But to listen to their tutors,
Whose instructions Enlightened their minds
On all subjects, including the sciences.

The two learned advisors arrive
And discuss the matters among themselves.
Gao's tutor wishes him to be king
And ruler of Sendal, while Talhand's master,
The most intelligent learned man of the land,
Wishes for his student to rule.

They argue with each other for so long
That the two princes ultimately hate each other.

In the grand hall, someone places two thrones
On which sit the two princes of victorious fortune.
To the right are their two valiant masters,
Who disagree and contend with each other
Over the possession of the world.

The noblemen are summoned and seated
In the hall, on the right and on the left.
The teachers address them: "O illustrious ones,
You remember the government of their fathers.
Which one of these princes do you wish to see as king?
Which one do you think is the purest of the two?"

The wise men and sages of shining mind are stunned.
The two young princes remain seated on their thrones
While their mentors discuss, causing trouble.
City folk and warriors recognize that nothing
But bitterness and quarrel can result from this affair,
That the kingdom will remain divided and sensible
Men will succumb to the burdens of pain and terror.

Someone from the assembly raises his head,
Rises, and loudly addresses everyone:
"How can we, in front of two kings
And two viziers, discuss a proper course of action?
We shall organize an assembly tomorrow,
Where we shall privately consider each point.
Then we shall send a message to each, hoping that
The princes will find in it a means of satisfaction."

They take their leave, displeased and somber,
Mouths full of vain words, minds full of grief.
They say to each other, "This is an unfortunate affair.
It exceeds the power of men with more experience.
Never have we witnessed two kings come face to face
And two opposing viziers stand between them."

They spend the entire night with faces frowning,
And once the sun raises its head over the mountains,
The city's wisest noblemen, able to take
Matters into their hands, congregate.

All the intersections of Sendal fill with noise.
Everywhere there is an exchange of fervent words.
Some of the noblemen lean toward Gao,
Others speak in favor of Talhand.
Their tongues are weary of speech,
But they cannot agree on a distinct path to follow.
Some send a message to Talhand,
While they utter insults reserved for Gao.
Others appear at the side of Gao, armed
With mace and sword, declaring that
They are ready to sacrifice their lives for their king.

These friendships and enmities
Fill the land of Sendal with noise and clatter.
A sensible man declares that a house
Cannot remain standing with two masters.

3 | Gao and Talhand Prepare for Battle

Talhand and Gao are told that in every street
Stands a chief, that the city resounds with cries,
Exclamations that move men's hearts,
That the entire land will fall to ruin by disputes,
And that the princes must not consent to fight.
The news fills their hearts with terror
And they keep guard day and night.

One day, the two young princes meet
Without retinue and without warriors.
They discuss with frowning faces,
Their heads full of a longing for battle.

The illustrious Gao grows infuriated,
The talk making him simmer.
He says to Talhand, "O my brother,
Do not act in this manner. It is beyond measure.
Do not seek, imprudently and foolishly,
A course of action disapproved by the sages.
You know that when Jemhoor was alive,
Maay stood as his servant.
Jemhoor died and left me young and weak,
As the throne does not belong to a child.

My father brought prosperity to the world
Through his wisdom, and no one dared
Claim access to the line of succession.

"His brother was united with him
Like the soul is united to the body.
The people chose him to govern.
But if I had been of age to rule,
No one would have cast a glance at Maay.
Let us observe our ancestral royal customs.
Let us listen to the sages on what is right and fair.
I am above you in age as well as by my father,
And you know that I am more worthy.
Do not act in ways contrary to the royal path.
Do not seek the kingly throne and hence
Fill the land with trouble and turmoil."

Talhand replies, "Enough!
No one seeks to attain power through quibbles!
I inherit the throne and crown from my father.
It is the harvest of the seeds he has sown.
I shall assure my kingdom, throne, and army
With the help of my sharp sword.
Cease your speech of Jemhoor and Maay.
If you yearn for possession of the throne,
You may capture it by force."

Hearts keen on battle, they enter the city.
Warriors and townspeople, ready for battle,
Travel toward the princes' palaces.

One crowd of people is drawn to Talhand
While another is attracted to Gao.
A great sound rises from their two palaces.
There is in town no space to place one's foot.

Talhand is the first to prepare for war.
His courage does not tolerate the delay.
He opens the door to his father's treasury
And distributes helmets and armor to his troops.

The entire city is split in two,
And the hearts of sensible men fill with fear
For the possible outcome designed by the dome of sky

And which will determine the vanquished.

The nation hears of the affair with the princes.
On every side arrive troops of armed warriors.
Talhand is the first to dress in armor
And to prepare for bloodshed.
Then Gao asks for his coat of mail and helmet
And invokes benedictions over his father's soul.

In this way they rise with a great deal of anger.
They ask for the elephants to be strapped
And their seats placed on their backs.
It is as if the earth is armed for war.
All eyes are dazzled by the golden bells.
All ears are filled with the sound of clarions.

The two young princes march to their camps,
Each one thinking only of his own glorification.
The sky is hazy with these preparations for war,
Eyes are dimmed by the dust stirred by troops.
On both sides resound the blare of trumpets
And the drumming beat of timpani.

The right and the left wings form;
It is as if the earth becomes a mountain.
The army ranks stretch for two miles
With the princes mounted on their elephants.
Above each one drifts a shining standard:
One sporting the figure of a tiger,
The other the figure of a royal eagle.
Before them stand infantrymen
Suited for battle, armed with spear and shield.

4 | Gao Advises Talhand

Gao observes the battlefield and notices
The air streaked like a bold leopard's back.
Mouths fill with dust, the plain floods with blood,
And spears lead the way through the dusty haze.

His soul is consumed with pity for Talhand,
And his mind closes over the mouth of desire.

581

He selects an eloquent man, the first among
The noblemen present, and says to him,
"Go to Talhand and tell him,
        'Do not seek an unfair fight with your brother.
        You would be guilty of copious bloodshed
        And unnecessary warfare.
        Open your ears to Gao's advice,
        Avoid the words of wicked men that lead you
        Astray, for this struggle must not leave behind
        A memory of us riddled with blame.
        It would leave the land of India devastated,
        A desert, the lair of lions and leopards.
        Renounce the engagement in battle and attacks.
        Renounce plans to unjustly spill needless blood.
        Bring joy to my heart with a peace accord.
        Unload your neck of the debt of wisdom.
        We shall draw a peace treaty by which terms
        You will take possession of a stretch of land
        From this border to the border of Chin.
        Let us be friends of the heart.
        I shall think of you as the crown upon my head.
        Let us divide the kingdom as we divided the wealth.
        The throne and crown are not worth any such grief.

        'But if you are set on battle and injustice,
        If you scatter the herd that has been gathered,
        You will be blamed in this world, and, once in the other,
        You will have to provide an account for your acts.
        Do not surrender to iniquity, O my brother,
        For injustice cannot stand in the face of justice.'"

The messenger presents himself to Talhand,
Carrier of the prince's message and advice.
But Talhand replies, "Tell Gao the following:
        'Stop your excuses to evade battle.
        I reject you as a brother and as a friend.
        You are my kin neither by marrow nor by skin.
        You will convert this kingdom into a desert
        If you prepare to attack these courageous men.
        All the evildoers stand at your side,
        Pretending to be your support on Ormazd day,

While in reality it is on the day of Bahraam.[86]
You are the trespasser in the eyes of Yazdan,
For you are of ill repute, ill race and ill nature.
You will be cursed for the bloodshed in battle,
While I shall be blessed and praised.
Furthermore, you propose we share the crown,
This valuable border, and the ivory throne,
But power, throne, and majesty belong to me.
Everything, from the sun to the back of the fish
On which rests the world, belongs to me.
I would rather my soul exit my body than cast
A glance in the direction of the crown and throne
As long as you claim the title of king,
Assign me some land, and pretend to be my friend.

'Now that I have formed my army ranks
And the air is like a spread of golden silk,
There will be so many arrows, javelins,
And spear points that Gao will not be able
To distinguish between stirrups and reins.
I shall go on the battlefield to bring down heads.
I shall have your troops cry in anguish and pain.
I shall lead my warriors to battle in a way
As to discourage the most valiant leopards.
I shall capture Gao, hands tied.
His armies will witness the dust of defeat,
And none of the prisoners, not even the prince,
Will ever have the opportunity to don his battle armor.'"

The intelligent messenger listens to the reply
And returns to recount it, point by point, to Gao.
Gao is deeply afflicted to find his brother
Talhand so drained of sense and reason.
Greatly concerned, he summons his vizier,
Speaks to him at length of his brother's words,
And says, "O knowledge seeker, show me a way
To bring this affair to a rightful conclusion.
The plain is covered in blood, heads are deprived
Of bodies, and souls journey to the Supreme Judge.
This fight must not conclude in a disastrous end."

◇◇◇◇◇◇◇◇◇◇◇◇◇
86 Ormazd day and Bahraam day: Ormazd day is auspicious while Bahraam day is
inauspicious.

The wise man says, "O King, you have no need
For the counsel of a teacher, but since you ask me,
Do not stir cruelty into your struggle with your brother.
Send a high-ranking, soft-spoken man his way
With a message that could calm this quarrel.
Give him all the treasures you have inherited
Without having taken the pain to amass,
For a brother's life is preferable to any treasure.
As long as you maintain the crown and royal seal,
Do not seek a dispute with him over dinars.

"I have observed the rotations of the skies,
And I have seen that his life will promptly end.
Of the seven stars that spin in the firmament,
Not one of them will prove to be in his favor.
He will perish on the battlefield, but you must not
Be the one who plunges him to his death.
Do not surrender to him the royal seal, throne,
And diadem, for it will be a sign of cowardice.
Give him anything else he asks for,
Whether it is a horse or treasure and jewels, so that
You never endure the burden of guilt over his death.
You are king, the stars are in your favor.
You are more learned in the ways of the skies."

The king obeys his tutor and selects a different approach.
His face flooding with tears by grief caused by his brother,
He seeks a man of blessed fortune and gentle speech.
He says to him, "Go to Talhand and say to him,
        'Gao is all sorrow, pain, and suffering.
        His heart is afflicted, his mind is distressed,
        His body in a state of anguish.
        His soul is suffering from the fight
        And the rotation of the dome of sky.
        He prays for the Creator, Justice Giver,
        To infuse your heart with reason and affection
        So that you renounce contention with your brother.
        The tutor who stands by your side has corrupted you.
        Ask the twelve houses and the seven planets
        How the end of this affair will unfold.
        No matter how violent and valiant you may be,
        You cannot evade the rotation of providence.
        We are surrounded by enemies on all sides.

The world is full of malevolent men,
And if you and I engage in a fight,
I shall have cause to fear the King of Cashmere,
The Emperor of Chin, and the lion men of Iran
Who will constrict us on every front.
On three sides, we shall be looked upon with contempt.
The noble leaders, avid for battle, will blame us and say,
>"Why do Talhand and Gao engage
>In a battle for the throne and crown?
>Were they not born into the same family?
>Are they not of pure race by their fathers?
>Now these two brothers are after each other,
>Motivated by the words of a malevolent advisor."

'If you leave your troops and come to me,
You will shine light into my dim soul.
I shall give you gold, brocade, horses, and wealth.
I have no desire to cause you grief.
From me, you will receive my land as well
As seal, crown, bracelet, and ivory throne.
There is no shame for you to accept this from
Your older brother who has no desire to fight.
But if you do not obey me, point by point,
You will have cause to repent in the end.'"

As fast as running water, the messenger returns
To the court of Talhand, bearer of a dim soul.
He repeats to him Gao's words and elaborates
On the subject of rulership, treasures, and promised gold.

Talhand listens to the sensible discourse,
But the mysterious sky has contrary designs,
And he does not cede to his brother's advice.
He replies to the envoy, "Tell Gao:
>'You will continue to deceive, and for that reason
>Your tongue will be slashed by the sword of hardship
>And your body burned by the fires of Hirbad.
>I have listened to your worthless messages.
>I see your intentions are founded on ruse.
>Who are you among this vast assembly
>To offer me treasure and kingship?
>Power, fortune, and royalty belong to me.
>Everything, from the shining sun high above

To the back of the fish in the deep sea, is mine.
Evidently, your end is near,
Since you indulge in such lengthy reflections.
Here is an army with riders, horses, and elephants,
An army that captures two miles on the battlefield.
Bring your troops and begin the fight.
Why provoke a further delay?
I shall show you my power, so great that you will
Be left to count the stars in your darkest days.
When you see the precipice open at your feet,
You can use only tricks and sorcery.
You are far from the throne and crown,
And the sage will not say that fortune favors you.'"

The messenger returns, mouth full of sighs,
And reports all the words of the prince.
In this way, messages rush back and forth
Until the dark night reveals its somber face.

The princes dismount on the battlefield and
Ask for a great ditch to be excavated around them.
Patrols on watch dash through the plain,
And night unfolds in this way.

5 | The First Battle of Gao and Talhand

As the sun raises its head in the house of the lion
To roll out a gilded spread upon the vault of sky,
The earth shines like the glassy surface of the sea.
The sound of trumpets and the beat of timpani
Rise from the two princes' tent pavilions.
Their banners emerge as the right and left wings appear.

The two illustrious princes take their positions
At the center of their respective hosts,
With their learned viziers at their sides.

Gao commands his tutor to proclaim to the leaders:
"Plant your banners and draw your blue swords of steel.
No warrior must advance, no infantryman
Must leave his post, for the one who displays impatience
On the day of battle is neither intelligent nor esteemed.

I wish to observe how Talhand will appear with his host.
Everything that unfolds from the bright sun to the dark
Corners of the earth is at the will of Yazdan, the pure.
My hope is that I will be granted a victorious fate.

"We have made every effort, through advice
And tender words, but Talhand refused to agree.
If I am victorious, it is thanks to the Sun and Moon.
Try not to spill blood to gain wealth, for you will
Receive amassed treasures that are on hand.
If a valiant warrior from our host launches himself
From the center with ardor to face Talhand in the brawl,
He must not proceed to bury him in the dust.
We must advance against the war elephants,
Reins strapped, but driven by a sense of affection."

The army replies unanimously, "We shall obey you!
We shall assume your will as the rule for our souls."

On the other side, Talhand addresses the army vanguard:
"O keepers of the throne, to attain victory and
The fruits of happiness, draw your swords of vengeance,
Entrust your life to Yazdan, and strike the enemy.
If you come face to face with Gao, do not kill him,
And refrain from speaking harshly to him.
Remove him from the back of his war elephant,
And bring him to me, hands tied."

The sound of trumpets rises from the royal pavilion.
The cries of horses, the dust raised by the leaders,
The clanging of heavy maces fill the air
Through mountain, land, and sea.
It is as if the revolving sky is retreating further.
The clash, the clamor, and the crash of battle axes are such
That one cannot distinguish between heads and feet.
The shining tips and eagle feathers of arrows
Crowd the space, darken it,
Force the sun to fold the hem of its cloak in retreat.
The world becomes a sea of blood;
Heads and hands bend beneath the weight of weapons.

The two princes, sons of kings,
Emerge from the army centers like furious elephants.

587

Talhand, the hero, raises his hands to shout:
"Move away from my javelin's air line.
Do not advance to fight your brother.
Protect yourself against the harm I may cause you."

The world has turned into a sea of blood.
Sword-striking warriors encircle the battlefield,
And the blows of the two princes, eager for battle,
Make blood and brains flow freely into streams.
The struggle continues in this manner, surpassing
All measure, until the sun leaves the dome of sky.

One hears Gao's voice on the plain crying,
"O combatants and young warriors,
If someone asks for mercy, do not seek retribution,
So that my brother may withdraw from the fight
Once he sees himself alone on the battlefield."

Many men plead for mercy, many more are killed.
The entire army of Talhand breaks up and disperses.
It is a herd deprived of its shepherd
And a shepherd deprived of his herd.

Talhand remains alone, seated on his elephant,
And Gao speaks to him in a loud voice:
"O my brother, return to your palace.
Take care of your home and your court.
I have no desire to fight you anymore.
You will most likely not find many survivors
From this crowd of illustrious sword bearers.
Know that all good comes from the Creator,
And express your gratitude for as long as you live
That you emerged alive from this battlefield.
Now is not the time to consult and seek a delay."

Talhand listens and recoils with shame,
His face flooding with tears.
He leaves the battleground and heads toward
The verdant field where his troops gather.
He opens the doors to his treasury, pays the salary
To his troops, equips them, and satisfies their needs,
Offering all the worthy warriors robes of honor.

Once he has refitted his troops with dinars and freed

Their hearts from worry, he sends a message to Gao:
"You sit on the throne like a weed in the garden.
O brother, you will soon be consumed by fire.
Your soul will be pierced, your eyes sewn together.
Do you really think that I can no longer hurt you?
Do not fasten a belt of illusions around your heart!"

Upon receipt of the brutal message, Gao expels
All brotherly thoughts of affection from his mind.
His heart deeply chagrined by the words,
He says to his tutor, "Do you see the enormity?"

The tutor replies, "O King, you are the rightful
Heir to your father's throne.
You are more learned than all those who study.
You are more powerful than any crown bearer.
It is obvious to me, according to the rotations
Of the Sun and Moon, and I have already told you,
That your illustrious brother will not rest,
Nor will he cease to battle until he is killed
And squirms in the dark dust like a serpent.

"As for you, do not rush to battle. Be patient.
Do not send him a harsh reply, but approach him
Courteously with offers of a peace treaty.
All his efforts bring him closer to his wicked end.
What can you do about it? It is divine will.
If he pursues battle, we shall not refuse him.
He wishes to make haste while we seek a delay."

The prince summons a messenger and speaks
To him at length but gently: "Go and tell my brother:
        'No need to be so rude and so wrathful.
        Harshness does not suit royal princes.
        Your father was an illustrious man,
        And you bear his renowned name.
        I see clearly that you reject my advice
        And an alliance with me, yet I desire only one thing,
        And that is for you to attain glory as my friend.
        I shall tell you all that I hold in my heart
        And toward which my soul inclines.
        A wicked counselor turned your head
        Away from the wise and easy path.

Always attempt to utter, O brother,
Only just and kind words,
For the world is nothing but illusion and wind.
Clench your heart around thoughts of peace.
I shall then send all that I have in my treasury.
I shall send men who will remain devoted to you.
Your malicious mind will see that my soul
Is filled with nothing but a sense of justice.
May your heart refuse to reject this opening!
My intention is exactly as I tell you,
If you wish to listen to me in your obstinacy.

'But if you are resolved on battle,
If your inclinations drift off the path of amity,
I shall prepare my army for battle,
For my troops will require a vast space.
We shall advance from this cultivated land.
We shall drive our companies to the seashore.
We shall dig a trench around our camp
And close the road for these men keen on war.
We shall pour seawater into the trench
And quickly block any outlet for the water
So that the enemy, defeated, has no way of escape.
But those of us who are triumphant in battle
Will not spill blood in this constricted space.
We shall take the entire army prisoner.
Heaven forbid they use sword and arrow.'"

The messenger returns, as swift as wind,
And repeats to Talhand his brother's words.
Talhand listens, then summons his leaders.
He positions them according to seat and rank,
Communicates with them, revealing the secret:
"What are your thoughts on this new war?
How must we reply to my brother's suggestion?
If you agree with me, no one will refuse a fight.
If Gao wishes to measure himself against us,
There is no difference, whether sea or mountain,
As long as the armies can fight en masse!
If you agree to assist me in the battle,
The leopard will never have to fear the fox's cry.
Any of you who seeks to acquire glory
Will find the fulfillment of his greatest desires.

It is better for the ambitious man to fall gloriously
Into enemy hands than to live on
As an object of triumph for his opponents.
Now is the moment for the great day
That will determine who is wolf and who is sheep.
Those of you who exhibit ardor in battle
Will act at the same time in their own interest,
For you will receive from me much wealth,
Along with slaves and adorned horses.
All the lands will pay homage to us,
From Cashmere to the sea of Chin,
And I shall offer all the cities to my army
Once I am master of crown and throne."

The noblemen in his presence press their foreheads
To the ground and say, "We long for fame and glory!
You shall witness the rotation of fate as our king!"

6 | The Second Battle of Gao and Talhand

The clatter of war rises from Talhand's court,
And his army marches toward the sea.
On the other side appear Gao's troops.
The two kings come face to face, eager for vengeance.
A trench is dug up around each camp,
And once it is deep enough, they fill it with water.

On both sides they form their lines of battle.
The riders' mouths foam with rage.
They lay out the right and left wings
And place the loads on the shore.

The two powerful kings, full of grief and hatred,
Demand seats to rise on elephant backs.
Each occupies his army center.
Each commands his host.

The earth turns as black as tar, the sky a pale purple
From the reflection of blades and silken banners.
The air assumes a shade of ebony from the dust.
The blare of trumpet and the sound of timpani
Are such that it feels as if the sea is on the boil

And whales within screech for blood.
A red fog drifts off the surface of the sea
From the blows of battle axe, mace, and sword.
Before it, the sun folds the hem of its cloak,
And men no longer distinguish one another.
It is as if the air sends a shower of swords
And sows tulips across the battleground.

Cries and lamentations rise to the sky
As if it is the day of resurrection.
The eyes of the most expert warriors are stunned.
The entire world is dark with dust.
An enormous heap of corpses rises on the field,
Preventing vultures from flying above.

The plain is strewn with brains, livers, and hearts.
Horses' hooves are soaked and caked
With a viscous blend of blood and dust.
A mob is wrestling in the bloody trench.
A mound of headless corpses rises on the ground.
The wind stirs, whips and sweeps
The waves on the surface of the sea
As the army of Gao advances, division by division.

Talhand observes, from behind his elephant,
A world overturned and in a state of chaos,
A world more turbulent than the River Nile.
The wind turns against him,
And he finds himself in need of bread and water.
Between the wind, the sun, and the sharp blades,
He can afford neither rest nor a path of escape.
He reclines on his golden saddle and expires,
Conceding to Gao the land of India.

Men fix their gazes on aggrandizement,
Their hearts full of grief and an anger
Triggered by a decrease in their fortune.
O sage old man, nothing endures.
In all things, favor joy and happiness.
No matter how much you accumulate in treasure,
And no matter how much effort you put into it,
All the wealth in the world is not worth the cost.

Gao, who watches from the army center,
No longer sees the banner of the young prince.
He sends a cavalier to survey the surroundings,
To glide across the field, mile by mile,
And determine the location of the ruby-colored banner
That sends tints of violet upon the warriors' faces.

He says, "I sense my brother is no longer fighting,
Unless I am blinded by the flying dust."

The rider departs, looks around,
But he fails to spot the leader's standard.
He finds the army core full of noise
And full of riders searching for their prince.

The envoy swiftly returns and reports to Gao,
Who climbs down from his elephant
And marches the two miles weeping and sobbing.
He examines his brother's body from head to toe
And does not see a single injury on his chest or skin.
He hollers, tears apart his flesh, sits in grief
And desolation in front of his deceased brother,
And laments, "Alas, O valiant young man,
You left us in grief, your soul deeply wounded!
The rotation of an enemy star killed you
While you were never grazed by a hostile blow.
Your head turned away from your masters.
Your demise will break your mother's heart.
I gently gave you much advice,
But you did not wish to heed to it."

When Gao's tutor arrives at the site
And witnesses the once ambitious Talhand dead,
He rolls on the ground in front of Gao and cries,
"Alas, O new world master!"

Then he renews his counsel to Gao:
"O mighty King, what good does it serve
To mourn and remain in a state of distress?
What occurred was meant to happen.
You owe a debt of gratitude to the World Creator
For the fact that Talhand did not die at your hand.
I predicted to the king, after keen observation

Into the movements of Saturn, Mars, Sun and Moon,
All that was to unfold, how this young man
Would bend in battle and precipitate his own death.
Now he expired like a gust of wind, disappearing
As a result of his foolish and reckless actions.

"There is a vast host full of grief and anger
That has fixed its eyes on you.
Calm yourself to appease our hearts
And thereby elevate your wisdom.
If the army finds the king on foot on the road,
Weeping with grief, the respect due him will suffer
And the most insignificant men will grow insolent.
A king is a like a cup of rosewater and must
Take care not to be troubled by a gust of wind."

The intelligent prince listens to the sage's advice,
And a proclamation is declared loudly:
"O illustrious and valiant subjects of the king,
None of you must remain on the battlefield,
For now the two armies have united as one.
Every one of you must join to pay me homage.
You are all under my protection. You are for me
An inheritance from this noble soul, my brother."

He convenes the wise men,
The blood of his heart dripping from his lashes.
He prepares for Talhand a narrow coffin made
Of teakwood and ivory inlaid with gold and turquoise,
Caulked with bitumen glue, tar, musk, and camphor.
They secure the lid, cover it with Chini silk,
And this illustrious Indian prince disappears.

From there, Gao leads his army swiftly away
Without stopping on the road or at stations.

7 | Talhand's Mother Learns of Her Son's Death

The princes' mother is unable to sleep,
Unable to take part in either rest or food
Since her two sons left for the battlefield.

She maintains a sentry on the road to watch
And passes her days in a state of grave distress.

The vigilant sentry notices the dust raised
On the road, announcing the return of the army.
He notices Gao's banner, the land covered in troops.
He looks out into the distance for two miles,
Hoping to catch sight of Talhand's crown and elephant.
Failing to spot him in the midst of this troops,
He dispatches a rider from his post to tell the queen:
"An army composed of Gao and his supporters
Has traversed the foot of the mountain,
But neither Talhand nor his elephant appears,
Neither his banner nor his leaders of golden boots."

A torrent of blood spills from the mother's eyes.
She strikes her head many times against the wall.
She receives the news that imperial glory has eclipsed,
That Talhand, who aspired for world possession,
Is dead, abandoning his royal throne to Gao.
She runs to Talhand's palace, face drenched in tears.
She tears all her clothes, scratches her cheeks,
Tosses fire in the palace and to her treasury,
Burns down the crown and the throne of power.

Then she ignites a great pyre to cremate
Talhand's body according to Indian rites.
She bears witness to her faith by her grief.

At the news of his mother's distress,
Gao launches his speedy charger toward her.
He takes her in his arms, and, with tearful eyes,
He pleads with her: "O dear, affectionate mother,
Listen to me! We are innocent in this battle.
Neither I nor my friends have killed him.
None of my army warriors touched him,
As I had forbidden them to send his way
The slightest breath of hostility.
The rotation of an unfortunate star
Plunged him to his tragic demise."

The mother replies, "O wicked prince,
You have committed a wicked crime!

The sublime dome of sky will punish you for it.
You executed your brother for the crown and throne.
No man of pure heart will call you fortunate."

He replies, "O my tender mother, please,
You must not think poorly of me.
Calm yourself so that I may explain the battle
And how kings and hosts behaved.
Who would dare approach him to fight?
Who would instigate a quarrel with him?
I swear by the Justice Giver, Creator of Sun
And Moon, of day, night, and the turning skies,
From here on, I shall look upon neither seal nor throne,
Neither horse nor mace, neither sword nor helmet.
I shall make it clear to you that I am innocent
And in this way return softness to your bitter heart.
I shall make your lucid mind see that his death
Was not provoked at any warrior's hand.

"Who in the world can evade death?
Not even the one who shelters his life
Beneath a cask of solid steel?
When this torch is extinguished one day,
No one can prolong life, not even by a single breath.
If my words do not have the power to calm you,
I swear by Yazdan the Just, the Almighty,
That I shall burn my body in the fire
And make the souls of my foes rejoice."

His mother takes pity on him, admiring his courage
And his eagerness to bring a premature end to his body.
She replies, "Show me how Talhand died
On his elephant, or else my loving soul
Will be consumed by the blaze of sorrow."

Gao enters his palace in great distress.
He calls his tutor, who knows the ways of the world.
He recounts to him what occurred with his mother
And how she stirred in him the desire to perish.

Closing the doors to the audience hall,
Gao and his benevolent tutor sit to hold counsel.
The teacher says to his pupil,

"We shall not achieve our goals easily.
Let us call men, young and old, ingenious and studious,
From Cashmere, Dambar, Margh, and Mai.
Let us deliberate with seekers of truth on the subject
Of the river, the trench, and the battlefield."

8 | They Invent the Game of Chess to Comfort Talhand's Mother

Gao sends riders to every land where there lives
A distinguished wise man to summon him to court.
The world king sits with his powerful council,
Shining minds that are well educated.
The tutor draws the battlefield for them to show
How the fight of two kings and two hosts unfolded.
They speak of river, trench, and water intake.
None of them sleeps that night
As they open their lips to further discuss the matter.

At the rising beat of timpani over the square,
They ask for some wood of ebony.
Two powerful and kind men create a square drawing
Representing the trench, the battleground,
And the two confronting hosts.

They draw one hundred boxes through which
The troops and the kings are able to move.
Then they build two crown-bearing majestic kings,
One out of teakwood, the other out of ivory.
Infantrymen and riders form two lines of battle.
More figures are shaped as horses, elephants, viziers,
And warriors who are meant to assail the enemy.
Some fight with impatience and speed,
While others take their time.

The king is in the army center, his minister at his side.
Next to them are two elephants able to
Raise the dust like the flows of the River Nile.
Next to the elephants are two camels
Mounted by men of pure intentions.
The camels are followed by two horses

And two riders, eager to fight on the day of battle.
Finally, the line ends with two valiant chariots,
The horses' lips full of foaming blood.
Infantrymen are able to move forward and back,
Destined to come to the aid of others in war.
If one of them crosses the field to the other side,
He would take his place next to the king as advisor.

The vizier never advances in battle
For more than one square beyond the king.
The proud elephant moves three squares and observes
The battlefield for the distance of two miles.
The camel, similarly, could advance three squares,
While struggling on the ground.
The horse as well can move three squares
While one square is away from the direct path.

No one dares face the chariot to fight,
For it is able to cross the entire frame.
Each charges within the limits of its arena
And cannot make more than the motions prescribed.

When one finds himself within reach of the king,
One would say in a loud voice, "O King, beware!"
And the king would exit his box until the moment
When he can no longer make a move.
The opposing king, horse, advisor, elephant,
And infantrymen having blocked his way,
He looks around on four sides, sees his men
Overthrown, the trench barring his passage,
The enemy on his left and on his right, ahead and behind,
Dying of thirst and fatigue, he stands stunned, captured.
Such is the command given to him by the spinning skies.

The noble and benevolent King Gao is taken
By the chessboard so representative of Talhand's fate.
His mother studies the board, her heart in mourning.
She remains day and night full of pain and anger,
With two eyes fixed on the game.
She desires no other thing but this evidence
Of her son's death, for her soul is in great distress.
She ceaselessly weeps, and her only wish
Is to heal her pain through the game of chess.

She remains in this way, abstaining from eating
And from moving, until she meets her end.
Such is the nature of world affairs:
At times they fill you with grief, at times with joy.

I end here the story drawn from ancient sources.
The game of chess remains today a reminder of this tale.

9 | Anushiravan Sends Borzooy, the Physician, to India to Find a Magical Remedy

Pay attention to what Shadan, son of Barzeen, recounts
When he reveals the secret actions of Anushiravan,
King of Kings, may his name remain forever young!

The king is in the habit of calling wise men,
Versed in all the sciences, to make them his court's pride.
The whole world is under his command,
From noblemen to skilled men, from physicians to orators,
From valiant warriors to famed interpreters of dreams.

Among them is a celebrated nobleman
Who is the diadem over all their heads:
He is an eloquent physician named Borzooy,
Who has gained in years and loves to speak.
He is learned in all the sciences, though his knowledge
In merely one science would proffer him world fame.

One day he presents himself before the world king
At the hour of the audience and says,
"O King, you are the friend of erudition.
You study science and you remember it!
I have read an Indian book with a serene mindset.
It is written that on a mountain, in the land of India,
There grows a certain plant that shines like Rumi silk.
If a skilled man plucks it and blends it with science
And then applies it to a dead person, his faculty
Of speech will infallibly and instantly be restored.
Should the king grant me permission,
I shall undertake the arduous journey.
I shall make use of my knowledge to guide me,

And I hope to succeed discovering this marvel.
It would be only right for the deceased to be revived
Under the glorious reign of King Anushiravan!"

The king replies, "Such a quest is quite improbable
But must nevertheless be undertaken.
Direct a letter to the Hindu Rajah, and study
The nature of these Indian idol worshippers.
Ask an insightful friend to assist you in this venture.
Furthermore, appeal for fortune to watch over you.
If a mystical science were to emerge from what
You have read, the world would be quite astonished.
Take all that you need to the Rajah.
Without a doubt, you will require a guide."

Anushiravan opens the door to his treasury
And asks for three hundred camel loads
Of all that is worthy of a king in gold, brocade,
Royal jewels, bracelets, torques, earrings, crowns,
Furs, silks, diadems and seals, musk and amber.

The envoy takes leave of the court, marching to India.
He arrives at the Rajah's palace, hands him the letter,
And opens the lids of the crates before him.

The Rajah reads the king's letter and says,
"O man of pure intentions,
Kesra need not send me lavish gifts.
Our two peoples, our armies,
And our kingdoms are united as one.
Justice, majesty, royal glory, power,
And his fortune's splendor are so great
That no one would be bewildered
Were he able to resuscitate the dead.
All the brahmins who dwell in the mountain
Will come to your aid in this endeavor.
My fortunate vizier, idol worshipper, my treasury
And my treasurer, all that exists good and bad
In the land of India, everything is at your disposition.
All my power in great and small actions is yours."

They prepare a beautiful residence for him
Near the Rajah's quarters and send wall hangings,

Food, carpets, and clothing soft to the touch.
He spends the night in the company of wise men,
Sages, and noblemen of the region of Ghennooj.

As the brilliant day raises its head over the mountain
And the world-illuminating torch of sun is ushered in,
The Rajah summons the learned medicine men
With all those who, by their science, give guidance,
And commands them to visit the sage Borzooy
And to listen to all that he has to say.

The learned men, expert in the art of healing,
Arrive and accompany Borzooy to the mountain,
Which they cross on foot with a guide.
Borzooy selects a variety of dry and fresh herbs.
Some are wilted while others
Are at the height of their splendor.
He grinds the various species, dried and fresh,
And applies the herbal mixture to dead bodies,
But he is unable to revive any of them.

He treks around all the parts of the mountain,
With much effort, without generating results.
He realizes that resurrection can only be the work
Of the Eternal King, whose power never wanes.

His heart is restless, not only for fear of being mocked
By the king and the noblemen but also for having
Undertaken a painful journey, having brought lavish gifts,
And having pronounced foolish words, all to no avail.

His heart is heavy from what he read and believed in,
And from what the stone-hearted, ignorant man
Had stupidly written about something
That could only bring exertion and reproach.
He says to the wise men, "O noble, worldly,
Celebrated ones, is there anyone more learned than you?
Is there anyone who raises his head above crowds?"

The assembly replies unanimously,
"There is only one learned old man here.
He surpasses everyone in age and insight,
With more knowledge than any man of science."

Borzooy says to the Indians, "O perceptive men,
Add a new effort to the one you exerted for me.
Perhaps this aging and eloquent man can be my guide."

Borzooy, in a state of restlessness and worry,
Reveals to the learned man, to whom he recounts
His great efforts, what he heard, what he saw and read,
And the consequences of the damnable writing.

The aging sage speaks words full of science:
"I have also come across such a thing in books
And devoted myself ardently to the same pursuit.
But since all my effort afforded me little fruit as well,
We must, without a doubt, look at things differently.
I shall now tell you what I was able to understand.
The herb is the learned man, knowledge is the mountain
That always stands away from cities and crowds.
The dead body represents the ignorant man,
For an ignorant man is always devoid of life.
It is through learning that one is revived.
Happy is the one who relentlessly exerts effort!
There is, in the royal treasury, a book
Righteous men call *Kalileh and Demneh*.[87]
When men are numb with ignorance,
The *Kalileh* is the herbal remedy for resurrection.
Like the mountain, it is knowledge,
For it is your guide to learning.
You will find the book in the king's treasury."

Borzooy is happy to hear these words.
His worry dissipates like a gust of wind.
He acclaims the old man and, akin to a blaze,
Travels to the ruler's court.
He enters and greets the Rajah with praise:
"May you live as long as India exists!
O Rajah, your wishes have been fulfilled.
There is an Indian book called the *Kalileh*.
You preciously keep it under your treasury's seal.
It shows the path of science and wisdom.

◇◇◇◇◇◇◇◇◇◇◇◇◇◇
87 *Kalileh and Demneh*: An ancient collection of animal stories originally written in
Sanskrit but subsequently translated into Arabic and Persian.

The herb I was searching for is this book.
If it is not too much to ask, will his majesty be kind
Enough to ask his treasurer to hand it to me?"

The Rajah's soul is ill at ease by the request.
He shifts his position on his throne and says,
"No one has ever made of me such a request,
Neither now nor in times of yore.
Still, if Anushiravan, world master,
Would ask me for my body and soul,
I shall not refuse him, no matter what it is,
Whether he asks for one of my noblemen
Or one of my humble, devoted subjects.
I do, however, have one condition,
That you read this book only in my presence
So that evil spirits may not claim it has been copied.
Read it, understand it, and observe it from all aspects."

Borzooy replies, "O King, I require nothing more."

The Rajah's treasurer brings the *Kalileh*.
Borzooy stands to study it at court with his guide.
After reading one section, he would recite it
All day in his mind and commit it to memory.
Once he has read as much as his mind can absorb,
He abstains from further study until the next morning.
And once the book is returned to the king,
He secretly transcribes the chapter in Dari.[88]
In this way, he sends the entire book to Anushiravan.

Borzooy remains, heart content and in good health,
Flooding learning into his most serene soul
Until he receives a reply to his letter with the news:
"The ocean of knowledge has reached us."

At this point, he presents himself at the Rajah's palace
And asks permission to return home.
The Rajah showers him with kindness
And prepares for him an Indian robe of honor,
Two valuable bracelets, two earrings,

◇◇◇◇◇◇◇◇◇◇◇◇◇◇
88 Dari: An Iranian language that is a Persian dialect spoken today in Afghanistan
and Uzbekistan.

A torque of fine jewels worthy of a king,
An Indian turban, and an Indian saber of steel
Damasked on its entire surface.

He departs from Ghennooj with a joyful heart,
Clinging to the science in his mind and memory.
Upon arrival at court, he greets the king respectfully
And recounts to him all that he saw and heard:
How he found science instead of the herb
He was so desperately searching for.

The king says to him, "O blessed one,
The book of *The Kalileh* has revived my soul.
Take now the treasurer's key and select what suits you."

The sage does not give the treasurer much effort.
On the left and on the right,
There are many dinars and jewels,
But he asks only for a royal attire,
Which he wears in splendor,
And returns in haste to Kesra's court.
He praises the king and utters prayers in his favor.

The king says to Borzooy, "O weary traveler,
Why did you leave the site of the treasury
Without procuring yourself
Pouches of gold and priceless jewels?
Anyone who exerted such effort is worthy of wealth."

Borzooy replies, "O King whose throne
Is more elevated than the orbits of Sun and Moon,
A person who obtains a royal outfit has already
Reached the road of fortune and the royal crown.
Furthermore, the sight of me, unfit and unworthy,
Dressed in a royal robe will distress the hearts of my foes.
My friends' faces will gleam with pride.
But I must ask the king for one more thing,
One thing that will glorify my name in the world:
I wish that, when Bozorgmehr transcribes this book,
He agrees to acknowledge Borzooy's labors
In obtaining it, and, by order of the king,
To dedicate the first chapter to me so that,
After my death, learned men everywhere are aware

Of the challenges and hardships I have faced."

The king replies, "This is a grand ambition
That exceeds the demands of a man of your rank,
Someone who has the utmost respect for his king.
Nevertheless, it is equal in value with all
The challenges you have faced and endured."

The king turns to Bozorgmehr and says,
"We must not refuse Borzooy his wish."

The writer sharpens his reed and composes
At the start of the book a chapter on Borzooy.
It is transcribed on the king's copy, in the language
Of Pahlavi, the only characters used at the time.
The book is then deposited carefully
Inside the king's treasury, where access to it
Is forbidden to anyone who is unworthy.

In this way, the book could only be read in Pahlavi
Until the language of Arabic is adopted years later.
Once Mamoon,[89] a man of science well-verse in his time,
Returns its splendor to the world
And renews the appearance of sun and day
With his wise heart and Kianian intelligence,
That is when The Kalileh is translated
From Pahlavi to Arabic, as you can listen to it now.

The book remains in Arabic until the time of Nasr,[90]
Whose powerful vizier Abol-Fazl,[91]
His treasurer in the field of the letters and the arts,
Commands everyone to speak in Farsi or Dari.
But his power is short-lived.

Later, when Nasr hears the recitation of the book,
An idea guided by wisdom sprouts into his head.
He wishes by all means to leave a mark of himself.
He seats an eloquent interpreter before him

◇◇◇◇◇◇◇◇◇◇◇◇◇
89 Mamoon: Or al-Mamun (786-833) is the seventh Abbasid caliph.
90 Nasr, Amir: Samanid King who ruled from 865 to 892.
91 Abol-Fazl: Or Abul-Fazl al-Bal'ami, the vizier of Amir Nasr, died in 940.

Who reads the entire work to the poet Rudaki.[92]
Then the latter fashions the prose to metric verse,
Like a pearl pierced and strung into a necklace.
To a literate reader, this form adds to its value.
To an ignorant listener, it is even more of an advantage.
A simple account does not leave a clear imprint,
But one linked by the meter enchants soul and mind.

May the world master live eternally!
May time and Earth remain his slaves.
All hearts will be happy with King Mahmoud,
If the strategies of wicked men could be forestalled.

Do not distress your heart with the weight of worry.
You are far from a lasting destiny.
At times you are up high, at times you are low.
At times you live in joy, at times in fear.
Still, neither one fortune nor the other will remain,
As you have not the ability to cling to eternal life.

10 | Anushiravan Enchains Bozorgmehr in His Fury

Now pay attention to the fate of Bozorgmehr
And how he is exploited by providence,
Which at times elevates a man to the highest clouds,
Then reduces him to oblivion in the dark dust.
As long as you are alive, you will endlessly
Swing from one to the other, and when the end comes,
You have no choice but to surrender, even though
No one can assess the true nature of death.

It happens that, at this time,
Kesra exits Mada'in to hunt.
He pursues argali and antelopes on the plain.
The argali disperse, leaving him behind.
Bozorgmehr stands at the king's side,
As much out of affection as to offer his services.
Kesra arrives from the desert to the prairie, where

◇◇◇◇◇◇◇◇◇◇◇◇◇
92 Rudaki: Abu Abd Allah Ja'far ibn Muhammad Rudaki (859-940), the first great
poet of the Persian language.

He spots grass, a gurgling stream, and trees
Offering a welcomed canopy of shade.

The weary king dismounts to rest from the heat.
In the absence of servants, he sees Bozorgmehr.
He falls asleep in this sheltered place, leaning
His head in friendship on the young man's chest.

The wise king always sports a bracelet of fine stones.
At this time, the bracelet tears, the stones are released
And fall at the side of the sleeping ruler.
A black bird swoops down from the clouds,
Looks around, sees the bracelet,
And tears the link that retains the stones.
Then he begins to swallow, one after the other,
As many freshwater pearls as topazes.
After ingesting them, he flies away and disappears.

Bozorgmehr falls into a state of deep dismay
By this act from the revolving dome of sky.
He surmises that his fall is imminent,
That this is a day of sorrow and a time of deception.

The king awakens, looks at him biting his lips.
He glances at his arm and notices the jewels missing.
Since none of his men are around him,
He suspects that, during his sleep,
Bozorgmehr stole and swallowed his bracelet.
He says to him, "You dog, you have kept
Your ill nature hidden from me all this time?
I am neither Ormazd nor Bahman.
My body is made of air, mud, and fire."

But the world master is wearying his tongue in vain.
In reply he receives only a few mournful sighs
As Bozorgmehr pales before his ruler
In light of the actions of the turning skies.
Quickly recognizing the signs of his demise,
Terror suspends him in a state of silence.

The king's procession surrounds the prairie.
Kesra, in its center, climbs on his horse.
He does not look at anyone on the way back

And sucks his lip in anger until they reach the palace.
He dismounts and murmurs at length.
In the end, he commands his men
To put Bozorgmehr under house arrest.

The wise man remains inside his home,
Meditating on the sky's frowning face.
He has a young and valiant relative, a nephew,
Who is in the service of King Anushiravan.
He passes his days and night in the royal palace
In the company of the king, discussing all matters.

One day Bozorgmehr asks this man raised
By the sun-faced king, "How do you serve our ruler?"
Show me so that I can teach you better."

The king's servant replies, "O chief of wise men,
It happens that today, even Anushiravan
Cast my way a malevolent glance
That robbed me of the desire to eat and sleep.
I had poured clean water over his hands,
According to our daily habit, and when he rose
From the spread, I withdrew the pitcher,
Spilling water on the floor and the threshold.
The king was infuriated with me,
And in my fear I let go of the pitcher."

The wise man says, "Rise, bring some water,
And pour it over my hands like you did earlier."

The young man fetches warm water
And pours it gently over the sage's hands.
The latter says to him, "Let me show you how.
Avoid sudden motions. When the king
Moistens his lips with the scented water,
Then you must begin to pour."

The king's servant reflects much on this
Until he is asked to bring once again the basin.
He pours the water as instructed by the sage,
Neither too slowly nor to brusquely.

The king says to him, "Your devotion to me grows

Every day. Who told you to serve me in this way?"

He replies, "Bozorgmehr has taught me the art
Observed by the world master king."

The king says, "Go to the wise man and tell him:
     'You occupied such a place at my side,
     You enjoyed supreme honors.
     How could you, by your ill nature
     And unhealthy spirit of domination,
     Abase yourself instead of elevating your status?'"

The youth listens to him and runs off
To his maternal uncle, his heart wounded,
And repeats to him the king's words.

Bozorgmehr replies, "In every respect,
My place is much more worthy than the condition
Of the world king, whether in public or in private."

The nephew departs with the reply,
Deep in thought over his uncle's fate.

The king grows terribly angry and asks
For Bozorgmehr to be bound by chains and
Flung into a dim and cold underground dungeon.

Another time, the king asks his servant
How the foolish man endures his fate.
The messenger questions Bozorgmehr,
His face flooding with tears,
And the latter tells the devoted servant,
"My days unfold more peaceably than the king's days."

The messenger springs, as swift as wind,
And reports the reply to the king.
Kesra grows yet more irritated, wild as a leopard.
He asks for a narrow iron oven to be built,
The interior trimmed with the points of blades
And nails and secured with an iron top.
In it, Bozorgmehr can rest neither by day
Nor by night, for his body is tortured at all times
While his heart grows more and more restless.

A fourth time, the king says to his servant,
"Take a message to him and return with his reply:
    'How are you feeling now,
    Enveloped in this attire of nails and blades?'"

Bozorgmehr answers:
"My days are happier than Anushiravan's."

The messenger returns once more to the king, who pales
At the words, then selects an honest man from the palace,
Someone able to decipher the discourse of the sage.
A man armed with sword, an executioner at court
Is fetched to join him, and the king says to him,
"Go and tell this wicked man of ill fortune:
    'Either you give me a reply that pleases me
    Or the executioner will show you, with his sharp blade,
    The execution of the last judgment.
    You have declared that prison, nails, iron chains,
    And dark dungeon are better than the king's throne.'"

The messenger runs to the sage with the king's words.
Bozorgmehr says to his pure-hearted nephew,
"Fortune never shows me its face.
None of us will remain, good and bad,
We are all destined to rush forth to our end.
Whether we have treasury and throne or the most
Difficult life, we all have to ultimately pack up our bags.
It is easy to depart from a life of hardship
When the hearts of kings fill with fear."

The intelligent messenger and the executioner
Report to the proud king the last words uttered.
Anushiravan, dreading a stroke of bad luck,
Returns Bozorgmehr from his prison to the palace.

The skies turn in this way for some time.
Bozorgmehr's face deepens with wrinkles,
His heart constricts and weakens,
His eyes fade as a result of his worries,
And he wastes away with grief and sorrow.

11 | The Caesar's Envoy Brings an Enclosed Case, and Bozorgmehr Is Freed for Guessing Its Secret

Around this time, the Caesar sends a messenger
To the king with presents, a letter, an offering,
And a padlocked case with the message:
"O King, at your court you have countless sages
Of pure hearts. Reveal to me the contents of this box
Without touching the padlock.
If you are able to guess, I shall send customary
Tribute along with a wealth of presents.
But if the minds of your ingenious wise men
Are not able to assess what's hidden within,
Then the king must neither demand tribute
Nor dispatch an army to our kingdom.
This is the message. Respond as you please."

The king says to the envoy,
"This box does not contain a divine secret.
I shall gather pure men of good counsel who will
Help me, by heavenly grace, discover its contents.
Remain here with us for one week,
Enjoy life and wine in freedom and happiness."

The king is embarrassed by this affair.
He convenes all the wise and learned men,
And each examines the coffer and the keyless padlock
From every angle, but none is able to decipher the mystery,
And they have no choice but to admit their ignorance.

Faced with this powerless assembly,
King Anushiravan's heart fills with distress.
He reflects, "Only Bozorgmehr, with his sagacity,
May succeed in discovering the secret of the dome of sky."

The troubled king commands his treasurer
To bring a full attire and a horse of choice,
With a saddle worthy of serving the King of Kings.
He sends these to the sage with a message:
"We must forget the troubles you have endured.
The rotation of the skies above wished for you
To suffer harm at my hand, but your tongue incensed

My mind and caused me to wrestle with myself.
Now an urgent affair summons me,
Deeply wounding my aging heart.
The Caesar sends from Rum an illustrious wise man
With a golden box firmly shut
With a padlock and a seal of musk.
Learned men and Kianians are to discover
And expose the secret hidden within.
I reflect on the fact that only Bozorgmehr's mind
Is up to the task of unraveling this mystery."

Bozorgmehr's heart is renewed by these words.
He forgets the old suffering and the long sorrows.
He emerges from prison, washes his head and body,
And addresses prayers to Yazdan, the pure.
He fears the harm the enraged king
May cause him despite his innocence.

He is awake and alert as instructed by the king.
As the sun raises its crown at daybreak
To spread its dazzling light across the long
And lingering night, Bozorgmehr observes the stars,
Washes his heart's eyes with the waters of wisdom,
Selects a trusted man among the court's savants,
And says to him, "My affairs are not going well.
These misadventures have troubled my eyes.
Study the people we encounter, show them to me.
Do not fear anyone, and ask for their names."

Bozorgmehr exits his house.
A moon-faced woman rushes by him.
The intelligent man with clear eyesight
Indicates to the sage what he sees, and Bozorgmehr,
A path seeker, says to his companion,
"Ask if this moon has a husband."

The woman of pure intentions replies, "At home,
I have a husband, and I am expecting a child."

Hearing this, the sage on his white horse,
Is seized by a bout of emotion.

Another woman appears, and the guide asks,

"O woman, do you have a mate and a child,
Or do you live alone with nothing but wind in hand?"

She replies, "I have a husband but no children.
Now that you heard my reply, move out of my way!"

At that moment, a third woman appears,
And the benevolent servant approaches her:
"Who is your mate, O fair-faced woman,
For you walk with a proud and steady stride?"

She replies, "I have never married
And have absolutely no desire for a husband."

Bozorgmehr listens to these words,
And you will see what conclusions he draws.

He continues on his way in haste, frowning
And preoccupied, and once he arrives at court,
Kesra commands him to approach the throne,
His heart quite troubled upon witnessing
That he has lost the faculty of sight.

Kesra exhales a deep, mournful sigh, asks forgiveness
For past deeds and for the harm he caused the sage,
Then he speaks of Rum and the Caesar
And recounts the story of the padlocked box.

The innocent Bozorgmehr says to the world king,
"May you shine as long as the skies spin!
We must gather an assembly of sages,
Include the Caesar's envoy and the wise men.
Place the box before the king and the noblemen,
Seekers of the true path, and by the grace of Yazdan,
Who proffered wisdom upon me and assigned
Righteousness as a function of my mind,
I shall reveal the contents of the box to everyone
Without ever touching the box or its padlock.
Although my eyesight is weak, my mind sees clearly,
Since my soul is braced with the armor of science."

The king is happy to hear these words.
His heart blossoms like a spring flower.

Free from worry, he straightens up,
Summons the envoy and the box,
Summons the wise men and the noblemen,
Seats before the sage a great number of savants,
And asks the envoy to repeat his master's question.

The Rumi messenger reiterates the Caesar's words:
"The world master, victorious in battle,
Must have wisdom, knowledge, and a glorious name.
Now you possess majesty, power of rulership,
Grandeur, knowledge, and a formidable hand.
The wise men are full of insight and seek the true path.
Renowned warriors gather around you at court,
Or if they are away from court, they remain loyal to you.
If these great men of shining spirit take a look
At the box, the padlock, the seal, and the imprint,
They will reveal clearly the contents within.
This will be proof of their acumen,
And we shall consequently send tributes and fees,
For my land has the capacity to pay these.
But if they do not guess the secret, then
You have not the right to demand tribute from us."

Bozorgmehr listens, then begins with acclaim:
"May the world king always be happy,
Eloquent, and the companion of good fortune!
Thanks be to the Master of Sun and Moon,
Who shows us the path of wisdom,
Who knows all that is visible and hidden.
While I find myself yearning for learning,
Yazdan is in need of absolutely nothing.
In this box, there are three shining pearls
Hidden beneath more than three envelopes:
One is pierced, the second is pierced on one side,
And the third is untouched."

The clever Rumi envoy listens, hands over the key,
And Anushiravan takes a peek inside the box.
It happens that hidden within is a silken envelope
With three pearls, just as the Iranian sage described:
One is pierced, the other is half pierced,
And the third pearl is intact.

The wise men bless the learned one and scatter jewels.
The face of the King of Kings gleams with tears.
He fills Bozorgmehr's mouth with freshwater pearls,
But his heart constricts at the thought of the past.
He twists, and his features contract for his cruel treatment
Of the insightful man, though he never received anything
From him but acts and words of affection and devotion.

At the sight of the king's pale cheeks and his mind
Troubled by worry, Bozorgmehr brings to light
The hidden and speaks to Kesra of past events,
The bracelet, the black bird, the worry that he,
His loyal servant, suffered, and the king's sleep.

He adds, "It was the path of destiny,
And repentance will not serve you.
When the sky wills good or bad,
What can either king or wise man do?
What power does Bozorgmehr have?
Yazdan sowed the seeds in the stars,
And we must write their decree on our foreheads.
May the heart of King Anushiravan dwell in joy!
May he always live free of pain and worry!
As powerful as the king may be, the fact remains
That his vizier must be the ornament of his court.
The king may enjoy the hunt, banquet, and battle,
Engage in the distribution of justice and bounty.
But the effort of filling the stores,
Maintaining an army, condemning, speaking,
Listening to those asking for justice,
The concern for governance and the treasury,
All weigh heavy on the royal vizier's heart and mind!"

12 | On the Rule of Anushiravan

In this way we reach the end of Anushiravan's days.
He is a blessed king and warrior, a fighter
And wise man, a hermit and an army leader.
He has emissaries in all the lands
And does not abandon his empire to his ministers.
No one dares hide anything from him,

Whether great or small, whether good or bad.

One day, one of his emissaries, a kind and wise man,
Presents himself before the king with a letter
And says, "At times you pass over a crime
Without making an effort to blame the guilty.
At times you place the blame on someone
Who has an excuse for his wrongdoing."

The king replies, "When a man confesses his crime,
I am the physician and he is the patient who dismisses
The remedy and sheds tears when he is not cured.
It does not mean that we must do away
With the art of medicine."

Another wise man says, "May you live happily
Ever after, always preserved from harm!
The leader secretly left Gorgan one day
And entered a forest where he slept for some time.
His baggage was taken elsewhere.
He had nothing on him and was forced
To walk barefoot to find his belongings."

Anushiravan replies, "I have no need for such an escort.
The one who watches over the army
Must not worry over his own person."

Another says, "May you live eternally in joy
And in the company of your wise men at meals and rest!
There is a rich man here whose wealth exceeds yours."

The king replies, "That is all very well.
This man is the crown over my kingship.
I am the guardian of his life and his treasury,
And I shall attempt to increase his prosperity."

Another says, "O lofty King,
May you be happy and free from harm!
Among the Rumi prisoners are many small children."

Anushiravan assesses the cases and says,
"One must not count children among the captive.
We shall send them back to their mothers,

616

Happy and above need by our donations."

One person writes, "One hundred wealthy Rumi men
Wish to buy back their relatives with gold."

He replies, "If they wish to buy them back
Because they fear for them, sell each notable man
For a cup of wine and do not ask for more,
For we shall never want for anything.
With sword, we shall seize their jewels,
Their slaves, their pouches of gold and silver."

Another says, "Among the wealthy townspeople
Are two merchants who deny sleep to people
For two-thirds of the night
From the racket of their inebriated chatter,
And the sounds of lute, and rebec."

The king replies, "Do not complain about it.
You possess treasure and live in joy and delight.
Abstain from causing others harm,
And pass your time free from grief."

Another writes, "May you dwell in happiness,
And may the hand of evil be kept at bay!
The King of Yemen said in his audience hall
That when Anushiravan opens his mouth,
He remembers the deceased and thus
Fills the joyful souls of the living with sadness."

He replies, "Any man who is wise and
Of high birth will remember the deceased.
The one who discards them cannot be a sure friend."

Another says, "O King, your youngest son
Does not emulate his father's sense of justice.
He throws money on the ground upon purchasing
Something, thus offending the merchant."

He replies, "This is not a proper behavior.
Yet money tossed on the floor nevertheless
Falls into the merchant's hands."

Another says, "O King, your soul is so vast,
Neither reproach nor quarrels can touch it!
Long ago you respected the ways and customs.
Why do you now reject our attentions?
Why do you display a proud and pompous nature?"

He replies, "When I did not have teeth,
My only resource was sucking milk.
Then my teeth grew in, my back broadened,
And once strong, I asked to consume meat."

Another says, "I admit that you are the most powerful,
Intelligent, and learned man among us.
But how did you surpass the status of King of Kings
In a way as to fix your eyes only on your own designs?"

He replies, "My wisdom outshines anything seen by others.
Vision, vigilance, and knowledge are my ministers,
The earth is my treasury, and reflection is my treasure."

Another says, "O King, a falcon seized an eagle, your prey."

He replies, "Break his back for having attacked
A larger creature. Hang him at high gallows
So that he may expire for his crime.
A subject, inferior in rank, must not fight with the king."

One of the illustrious emissaries informs the king:
"Borzeen left early this morning with a host.
An astrologer appeared on his path and said,
            'O illustrious man, no one will ever see again
            This vast army and this vast war apparatus,
            Not since they left the royal court.'"

The king replies with authority,
"The sky, despite the opinion of the astrologer,
Watches over Borzeen with benevolence.
He commands army, treasury, and troops.
The stars of Sun and Moon will not spin
In a way as to plummet him to his demise."

Another wise man says, "O King, one day
You commanded us to select a highborn man

To make the rounds of the empire in justice
And to report to court on all the occurrences,
Good and bad, great and small.
Is Goshasp, the aging, illustrious scribe,
The right person to extend a hand in justice?"

The king replies, "He is avid for profit beyond his needs.
Select someone who does not boast about his efforts,
Who is wealthy and experienced, strict and righteous,
And whose discussions relate to matters of the poor."

Another says, "The chief cook complains
About the king and the noblemen, saying,
"No matter how much care and effort
I place in preparing meals for the king,
He barely smells them and refuses to touch them.
As a result, the king's servant is deeply troubled."

He replies, "Perhaps the sight of an abundance
Of food converts his appetite into disgust."

Another says, "Those who pay attention blame the king
For the fact that he departs without a vast escort
And fills with worry the hearts of his wise friends,
For an enemy could contemplate a devious attack
And make deceitful plans to instigate a raid."

He replies, "Justice and wisdom protect the king's body,
And when the ruler, justice giver, is all alone,
His righteousness avails to safeguard him."

Another says, "O companion of wisdom,
The governor of Khorasan declares on the square,
        'I do not know the reason why the king
           Recalled and dismissed Garshaasp, the rider.'"

The king replies, "He did not execute my orders
And chose to withhold my instructions.
I had entreated him to open the treasury door
In all circumstances to the destitute.
But the one who is a miser of skills
Hides to the world the king's majesty."

Another says, "The king is master of all.
He is generous and without reproach.
What did Mehrak, the old servant, do
For his salary to be reduced and his face to pale?"

He replies, "He became coarse and boastful.
He placed trust in his own services,
Came to court, and took his place drunk,
Always with a cup of wine in hand."

A wise man, one of his emissaries, says,
"If the king sends a host to fight the Caesar,
He calls to war the Iranians, and these wars
Against the land of Rum distress the land of Iran."

He replies, "This enmity is innate.
It is the struggle against the workings of Ahriman."

Another bold man says, "The king must ask
The feudal rulers for additional hosts.
Who are the warriors you need among the lion-men
Of sharp claws able to launch their steeds?"

He replies, "A valiant cavalier must not be weary of war.
He must be equally keen on battle as he is on banquet,
Whether by the light of day or in the dark of night.
He does not weaken at the moment
When he needs strength, and he does not worry
About the number of enemy troops, great or small."

Another says, "O King Anushiravan,
May you always dwell in happiness!
May your fortune remain young!
There was at court a pure man from Nessa[93]
Who served as the king's administrator.
When we came to draw his account,
He owed close to three hundred thousand dirhams
That cannot be paid, since they have been spent.
The noble wise men and villagers are sorry for it."

The king, seeing that the grand wise master

93 Nessa: A city in ancient Khorasan province.

Demands this payment, says,
"Do not afflict yourself for what has been spent.
Ask the accountant for the balance from my treasury."

Another says, "A valiant cavalier was wounded.
His injury kept him motionless for a long time
Until he launched an attack on the Rumi front
And was killed, leaving behind small children."

The king asks them to pay four thousand
Royal dirhams to the family of the deceased, adding,
"We must pay the salary of any man who falls
On the battlefield and leaves behind small children,
As often as the scribe pronounces his name.
The treasury must give the family the sum
Of one thousand dirhams four times a year."

Another says, "May your years and months be happy!
A warrior in Marv's army amassed a wealth of dirhams.
Since he has not spent a single coin,
The inhabitants left the land of Marv."

He replies, "They abandoned the land
Because of the money that was not spent.
Return it to those it was taken from,
And proclaim your action throughout Marv.
We shall set up gallows at this man's door,
In clear sight of troops and people, and hang
The oppressor alive, feet above, head below.
We shall make sure no other warrior is ever
Tempted to dissociate his heart from my orders.
Why should we draw a fortune
From the blood of poor people?
It is a sure way to bring hardship to the body
And extract joy from the soul."

Another says, "O King, Yazdan worshipper,
There are many subjects at your door
Who celebrate you for your sense of justice and
Who pray to the World Creator for your well-being."

Anushiravan replies, "I give thanks to Yazdan
For the fact that no one fears me.

621

One must take great care of men,
Whether they are innocent or guilty."

Another says, "O King, full of majesty and insight,
The world in its joy is full of lure, charm, and sweetness.
When night descends, the heads of noblemen
And their inferiors are drunk on the sound of song."

He replies, "Whether great or small, may everyone
Throughout the world be happy under my rule!"

Another says, "O renowned King,
Your detractors blame you for offering
Such beautiful valuables from your treasury,
As it did not take much effort to gather them."

He replies, "If I do not offer to those who are worthy
The wealth that abounds in my treasury,
It would be to my detriment and not to my benefit."

Another says, "O powerful ruler,
May your soul rest exempt from suffering!
Jews and Christians are you enemies,
They are two-faced worshippers of Ahriman."

He replies, "Anyone who asks for mercy
Will be the recipient of my compassion."

Another says, "O illustrious King,
Mardooy distributed more than three hundred thousand
Dirhams from your treasury to the poor
And allocated himself quite a bit."

He replies, "This act is congruent with our orders.
It is suitable to give to those who deserve it."

Another says, "O King, you have not suffered
The challenge of amassing. Our capital of riches
Is almost empty from the excess of your giving."

He replies, "The generous hand that took the wealth
Will make it sprout new leaves and limbs.
When the world master is a pious man,

All the doors in the world open for him.
We have observed the world constrict
Before a king of narrow character,
But I am not tempted by greed or avarice."

The grand wise master says, "O King,
Gharakhan, army leader, has raised with difficulty,
In the land of Balkh Bami,[94] three hundred thousand
Dirhams that he delivered to us to guard in the treasury."

He replies, "I do not wish to burden anyone
With the acquisition of dirhams.
Return the money to those who seized it
Along with anything else they may ask for.
A world master who reveres Yazdan
Does not wish to afflict his subjects' hearts.
Tear off the foundation of his beautiful palace,
Raze his vaulted chambers to the ground.
His home will fall to ruins.
He will have gained only pain and suffering,
And after that he will be at the receiving end
Of people's sighs, curses, and spite.
Cross his name from my list of employees.
Count for nothing the likes of him at my court."

Another says, "O noble King, you often speak
Of Jamsheed and Kaavoos, two glorious kings."

Anushiravan replies, "It is only fair,
For the world is witness to the virtues of my wisdom.
I speak of them so that after my death
No one forgets my helmet and my diadem."

Another says, "Why does the King of Iran
Hide his secrets to the highborn Bahman?"

He replies, "Because Bahman strays from wisdom's path,
And he cedes to the pleasures of his desires."

Another asks, "O King,

◇◇◇◇◇◇◇◇◇◇◇◇◇◇
94 Balk Bami: Bami is the old name for Balkh, a city in ancient Iran and in today's
Afghanistan, south of the Jayhoon River (Amu Darya).

Why do you avoid social interactions,
And why are you slow to nurture friends?"

He replies, "I hold myself in the company
Of wise men, for if Ahriman's voice strikes an ear,
The heart loses sight of the path of wisdom
And the mind strays from the path of caution."

A wise man questions the king on the nature
Of kingship and religion: "Is it not better for the world
To be without faith than to be without a king?
Any intelligent man can attest to that."

He replies, "Men of pure faith say the same thing.
No king has ever found the world without faith,
Although some may prefer one religion over another.
One is a worshipper of idols, another of the holy faith.
Another favors malediction over benediction.
The world does not fall to ruins by these words.
Always give a voice to your mind's secrets.
But if the king does not have the true faith,
No one in the world can attract blessings.
Faith and kingship are like the body and soul;
The world maintains itself through the union of the two.
And when the throne is vacant of a king,
Wisdom and faith alone have not the tools to serve."

Another says, "O King of serene soul,
You have spoken at length to noblemen.
Once you told them:
         'I am providence. I am the means
         By which I bring good and bad fortune.'
When you utter blessings upon the world,
We secretly fully reap the benefits."

He replies, "Yes, it is the truth, for the king's head
Is the crown on the head of providence.
The world is the body, and the king is its head.
This is why kings are the diadem of leaders."

Another says, "O King, you welcome your subjects.
May your reign and your life be everlasting!
O light of our minds, for five days now,

We have not seen the grand wise master at your side."

He replies, "This is not for me a source of affliction,
For he is quite occupied with the affairs of the nation."

Another says, "O sun-faced King,
The world will never produce a ruler like you!
We see a man who demands justice, attends court,
And occupies himself with his affairs.
We do not know the cause of his complaint."

Anushiravan says, "Thieves have taken
Countless valuables in Hejaz.[95]
I have replaced them with items from my treasury
So that he no longer feels the pain,
And I keep him at my court, hoping that
If a thief appears, he will recognize him."

Another says, "O noble and illustrious King,
Master of generosity and justice, never has
A ruler of your stature occupied the Kianian seat,
From the era of Kiumars to the present day."

He replies, "I give thanks to the Creator
That things unfold the way of divine will."

I complete here the maxims of Anushiravan.
The world is ancient, yet our thoughts are young.
My genius would not have blossomed
Had I not been endowed with the lyrical art of poetry.
Furthermore, my old age served to fuel the fire.
I started composing this book a long time ago,
Keeping it from Saturn, Sun, and Moon.
But once the name of Shah Mahmoud
Was inscribed at the opening of the book,
All the horizons rang with praise.

May the world prosper with the echo of his name!
May the sky rejoice with his resplendent crown!
When Mahmoud pronounces the prayer from above

◇◇◇◇◇◇◇◇◇◇◇◇◇
95 Hejaz: A region in ancient Iran located today in western Saudi Arabia, including
the cities of Mecca and Medina.

The pulpit, the cross bends toward the faith
Of Muhammad who, with his Rumi-damasked sword,
Seized the world from Indian idol worshippers.

Now let us read a letter from Anushiravan
And reflect on its contents with a clear mind.

13 | Anushiravan Advises His Son Hormozd

Kesra summons a scribe and commands him
To write a heart-warming letter full
Of knowledge, wisdom, advice, and disclosures.
"On the part of the powerful sun-faced king,
To whose will the firmament spins,
Just and benevolent world master,
Who distributes his wealth liberally,
Who has surpassed the glory of Kay Ghobaad
And exalted the royal throne; master of crown
And master of the mighty blade of justice;
Celebrated king, powerful, learned, famous,
Whose desires are fulfilled by the throne;
To his dear son, the pure Hormozd,
Who welcomes all of his heart's advice.
I find it a wise gesture to address this solemn letter
To my intelligent son, a disciple of our holy faith.
May the Creator give you joy
And may good fortune grant you victory!
May you remain master of world, crown, and throne!

"I place upon your head the golden crown,
Just as I received it from my father,
During the blessed month and day of Khordaad,[96]
Beneath a happy constellation and a bright augury.
I bless you just as the noble Ghobaad blessed my throne.
Remain vigilant, world master, wise and noble,
And never choose to cause harm to anyone.
Increase your knowledge, attach yourself to Yazdan,
And take the divine as your soul's guidance.

◇◇◇◇◇◇◇◇◇◇◇◇◇
96 Day of Khordaad: The sixth day of every month.

PART TWENTY-SEVEN

"I have asked an old man of good counsel
And mature wisdom which of us two is closer
To the Creator and which of us follows the path.
He replied to me:
>   'Abandon yourself to learning
>   If you wish to receive divine benediction.
>   Ignorance does not rise above the dust.
>   Learning cultivates a pure soul.
>   Learning makes a king worthy of the throne.'

"May you be learned and your throne be victorious!
Guard yourself from violating a promise,
For dust is the shroud of those who break their word.
Guard yourself from persecuting the innocent.
Turn your ear away from slanderers.
Act in every way according to justice,
For only justice will bring joy to your soul.
Never allow your tongue to encroach lies
If you wish to infuse the throne with splendor.
If one of your subjects possesses a treasure,
Act in a way as to lessen his worry over it.
The good that you take from others
Will be the enemy of your treasury.
Rejoice for wealth acquired through your own efforts.
In this way, if a subject is wealthy,
The king must be his support,
And everyone must fall under your protection,
No matter how proud or humble they may be.

"Reward those who commit righteous acts.
Fight fairly with your friends' adversaries.
No matter how much you are honored in the world,
Think of others: their fatigue, their pains and losses.
No matter which place we occupy,
This is a passing dwelling
In which we may not obtain a sense of security.
Seek to acquire merit and sit with learned old men
If you wish to be favored by fortune.

"Apply yourself to learning: It will give you
The power to bind your enemies' hands
If you wish to guard yourself from misfortune.

Honor the one who, before you,
Tramples his opponents' lives beneath his feet.
When you place the imperial crown on your head,
Favor the highest path among the righteous ones.
Always hold company with a wise man, and care
For him as you care for your own body and soul.
The city's noblemen and merchants
Must equally participate in justice.
Pay neither little nor too much attention
To a man whose merit does not equate to his birth.

"Do not entrust a worthless man with weapons,
For you will never find them again when you ask.
Your follower will give it to your enemy,
And you will find yourself knee-deep in challenges.
He will have given weapons to fight against you
And at the same time expect his pay from you.
Be charitable toward the poor, keep from evil acts,
And fear the damage you may incur.
Probe into your heart for its secrets,
And never exhibit a sense of nobility or justice
That would only skim the surface.

"Act with generosity in good measure with merit.
Listen to the advice of men with knowledge of the world.
Lean on pious men, but watch out for religions,
For they give birth to intolerance and anger.
Regulate your spending in accordance to your treasury,
And do not worry about advancing your wealth.
Keep an eye on past kings and how they have acted.
You must never lose sight of justice.
The share of an unjust king is malediction.
For that reason, always approve the just and fair;
It will guard you from misfortune.

"Where are the thrones of the Kings of Kings now?
Where are the powerful men, fortunate noblemen?
Only their words survive,
For this passing dwelling remains for no one.
Guard yourself from spilling blood lightly
Or rushing into war heedlessly.
Reflect on my letter full of advice.

Do not attach your heart to this passing dwelling.
I wish for my counsel to benefit you
And line your mind with a buffer of wisdom.
March down the path of the Master of Sun and Moon,
And keep at bay the influence of the deev.

"Hold this letter before your eyes, day and night.
Make wisdom serve as your heart's judge.
If your actions merit remembrance,
Your name will continue to be lauded.
May the Creator of all joy be your shelter!
May time and space be favorable to you!
May the wheel of the lofty dome of sky
Revolve to your will, and may it keep at bay
Wicked actions and any form of misfortune!"

He completes the letter and locks it into his cache.
He continues to live in this ephemeral world trembling.
The king, endowed with sense, justice, and wisdom,
Attempts to combine valor in war
And his arm's strength with modesty.
His faith is pure as he reveres the Creator.

Seek and find a man who possesses these virtues.
When you have found him, sing his praises.
Seek and find a king as dazzling as Jupiter,
Ambitious, armed with sword and armor,
One able to pluck idol worshippers from the world,
Able to enfold his heart's sanctuary
Onto the unsullied fabric of faith.

Today this glory is certainly found
In the person of King Mahmoud, world master,
A generous arbiter who is confident equally,
No matter where he is, in banquet or in battle.
How joyous is our era to be witness to the rule
Of Abol Ghassem, noble and victorious king!

14 | The Wise Men Question Anushiravan

An old man who speaks the language of Pahlavi
Informed me that a sage asked Anushiravan,
"What wish can the Yazdan worshipper
Secretly ask to be granted that, once fulfilled,
Will bring him good fortune?
Some men raise their hands toward the sky,
Pleading for something, and when they receive it
They remain frowning, their faces flooding with tears."

The victorious king replies, "Ask with restraint,
For a bold wish fulfilled will bring sorrow to the heart."

He asks, "Who is most worthy of a renowned name?"

The king replies, "The one who acquires wealth
Without effort and without the urge to distribute
Is not only not worthy of the throne,
But time will see his fortune fade.
One is powerful when one owns and gives liberally.
If you hold treasure in this world, always be generous
And bar yourself from accumulating in excess."

He asks, "Where does wisdom rest,
And who is the beneficiary of its leaves and fruits?"

The king replies, "Happy is the learned man.
After him, happy is the one
Who combines humility with a high birth."

The wise man asks, "How does one receive wisdom?
Are there men who, devoid of wisdom,
Are nonetheless free from suffering?"

He replies, "Anyone who cultivates wisdom
Will see his life improve tremendously.
The more wisdom one has, the more one gains.
The absence of wisdom leads to illness, grief, and loss."

The wise man asks, "What is more worthy,
Wisdom or royal majesty, since majesty
And power are ornaments of the throne?"

He replies, "Learning combined with majesty
Has the ability to conquer the world
And shelter it beneath the royal wings.
Wisdom, majesty, a name, and a royal birth
Are the necessary attributes
For a king to earn respect from the skies."

Then the wise man asks,
"Who among kings is worthy of the throne,
And what causes one's fortune to languish?"

He replies, "A king must first ask for help
From the World Creator; then he must have
Generosity, wisdom, adherence to customs,
Prudence, and a kind and just heart;
After that, he must assign a position of power
To those worthy by virtue of their assets;
Next, he must make sure nothing escapes him
In the world, nothing, whether good or bad;
Finally, he must be able to distinguish
Between a friend and an enemy,
For a king must not bring harm to others.
A prince who is endowed with dignity
And wisdom, faith and fortune's favor, is worthy
Of the crown and is the throne's most valuable asset.
If you cannot find in him these qualities,
You will see that he is deprived of glory and, after
His death, will leave behind a dishonorable name.
Furthermore, he will be denied access to paradise."

The wise man questions him on noblemen
And petty hearts, on kind men and spiteful ones.

He replies, "Greed and need are two
Of the most tenacious and ill-natured deevs.
Anyone whose passion is self-aggrandizement
Regulates his behavior on this evil deev.
When one gives into avarice and the effort
Of amassing wealth and a vast treasure,
One will suffer and will be a slave to his own needs.
At that point, man and deev are of the same nature."

The wise man asks, "How many ways are there

To speak, and which ones are they?
There are speeches that cause one to weep
While others are glory-giving treasures and crowns:
The first ones afflict us, the others delight us."

He replies, "Learned men have classified
The different manners of discourse
And have deepened our knowledge on the subject.
First, there are the customary addresses.
The soft-spoken man calls them inoffensive.
Next is the discourse we may refer to as confidential,
Uttered by skilled and enlightened men
Able to communicate only what is necessary
And that which leaves an imprint in the world;
Thirdly is the discourse of those who are able
To determine the right moment and thereby
Gain the utmost respect for the rest of their lives;
Next is the discourse the sage refers to as charming
And assigns the name of poet to the one able
To recite them in beautiful rhythmic meters,
Whether the story they recount is old or new;
In the fifth place is the warm discourse of the eloquent
Man who speaks gently, makes sweet sounds,
And attains with certitude his goal
As he weaves together a pattern of melodious words."

The wise man says, "Despite all that you have learned,
Despite all the wisdom shining in your mind,
You still question people of little value.
When do you think you will attain
The limits of knowledge and expertise?"

He replies, "The purpose of my learning
Has been to save my soul and my mind.
Pay attention: Learning is a guarantor against sin,
For it is more precious than crown and throne."

The wise man says, "I have never heard anyone
Boast or glorify himself about learning everything
Or anyone say that he has reached a point
Where he no longer needs to listen to masters."

He replies, "What man is ever satisfied with his assets

Unless his days end and he goes beneath the dust?
Still, the door to learning is more glorious,
More valuable to the sage than the door to his treasury.
Nothing will remain from us but the memory of our words:
Guard yourself from comparing wealth to wisdom."

The wise man says, "A man who learns
And remembers becomes a learned old man."

"A learned old man retains his youth
Through his knowledge of the sciences.
You will justly favor him to a young, frivolous man
Whose ashes' only value is the tomb resting upon them."

The wise man says, "You cannot become
King of Kings with only your good fortune.
You now utter the names of ancient kings more
And more, though you do so with deep sighs."

"I do not like to boast about my reign.
One must govern this world with the blade
Of justice, pass through life, and disappear."

The wise man says, "Long ago, you shared
Beautiful words with men more often.
Now you scorn them and speak to them
Of neither the present nor the past."

He replies, "I have sufficiently spoken.
I find myself now leaning more toward actions."

The wise man says, "Long ago, your prayers
At the fire temple were not quite as lengthy.
Today your time of worship has multiplied,
The echoes of your invocations are incessant."

He replies, "Yazdan, the pure, lifts believers
Out of the dust with the sky as servant
To the divine and the world as its slave.
If the slave does not appreciate divine value,
He does not merit to be exempt from hardship."

The wise man asks, "What new favors

Has the sky granted you since you are king?
Do you find yourself happier?
Are the hearts of your adversaries more anxious?"

He replies, "I owe the Creator a debt of gratitude
For my good fortune and for the fact that no one
Dared show ambition and drive in my presence.
My voice alone inspired men to renounce evil.
The sight of my mace and my warring ways
Caused my enemies to weaken and retreat in battle."

The wise man says, "In the war with the east,
You fought impetuously and valiantly but, faced
With a hostile west, you were patient and slow to act."

He replies, "In youth, one lends little thought
To the pain and suffering of others.
But upon attaining sixty years of age,
One becomes conciliatory.
Thanks to the Giver of good and bad days,
I was endowed with valor in my youth
And faced good and bad fortune with indifference.
Now I am immersed in old age with my assets
Of wisdom, vigilance, wealth, and generosity.
The world obeys my will and my prudence.
The marching dome of sky functions as my battle armor."

The wise man says, "The ancient kings
Required long speeches at every occasion.
You speak less and withhold more secrets.
You are well above illustrious men of yore."

"A king raised in the true faith
Refrains from working or from grieving unduly.
He knows that the Creator will take care of things."

The wise man says, "I notice that our king,
Instead of being in a state of joy, is full of worry."

"A sensible man will have no choice but
To allow the dust of anguish to permeate his soul."

The wise man says, "Ancient kings did not permit

The worry of future battles to disturb their feasts."

He replies, "In the act of drinking,
They did not fix their thoughts on glory.
As for me, I never sacrificed glory for wine.
I have always launched myself ahead of fate."

The wise man says, "Kings have always
Taken great care of their bodies with the help
Of remedies, medicine, and the art of physicians,
To avoid tears from streaking their faces."

"The nature of a fate that comes
From the sky's motions keeps a man healthy.
He has no need for remedies, for he is protected.
Once the time of departure arrives,
Abstinence has no power to delay the moment."

The wise man says, "How you praise the Creator,
Ceaselessly sending blessings and prayers to the skies,
And yet you never find peace and happiness,
Your mind always intent on dwelling in a state of worry."

He replies, "I have no concern, for the king's heart
And the spinning firmament are one, but I fear that
Those who commend me do so out of trepidation.
Praise must be handed out in measure with the truth.
I wish not to deepen the secret within my subjects' hearts."

The wise man asks, "What is the nature of the joy
Of bringing children into the world, and what
Does the desire to start a family stem from?"

He replies, "When one leaves the world to his child,
One cannot be forgotten; children give life
A certain flavor that protects us from vice.
The pain of dying is lessened by a son
Watching over you as your face gradually pales."

The wise man asks, "Who is the recipient of a good life?
Is there anyone who is repentant for his good deeds?"

He replies, "The pious man seizes the reins of fate.

If one does not seek aggrandizement,
One is allowed to enjoy peace and tranquility.
But when one yearns to climb higher,
One has cause to tremble in a state of fear.
As for what you say regarding good actions and
The secret wish of hearts and souls to spread kindness,
Know that there is no man more humiliated than
The one who is generous to an ungrateful person."

The wise man says, "The wrongdoer dies
And the world crosses his name off the list.
The caring man lives and fate counts his every breath.
Why should we celebrate virtue, since death
Equally harvests the benevolent and the wicked?"

He replies, "Acts of kindness are always rewarded.
The man who dies while spreading righteousness
Is not dead, he rests, and his soul returns to Yazdan.
Not only will the man who is not his equal in virtue
Never find rest, but he also will leave behind a sullied name,
And those he abandons will suffer from it."

The wise man says, "There is no greater tragedy than death,
And if this is so, how do we protect ourselves?"

He replies, "When you leave this somber earth,
You will embark on a beautiful sojourn.
Conversely, one must shed tears
For anyone who lives in fear and remorse.
No matter whether you are a king or a subject,
You leave behind this world's fear and suffering."

The wise man asks, "Which of the two is worse,
Fear or remorse, and which makes us most miserable?"

He replies, "Know that remorse that appears
In crowds weighs more than anything else.
What is our biggest fear if not remorse,
The most dreadful thing in the world?"

The wise man asks, "How do we escape remorse,
For the state of the world makes us weep bitterly?"

"We escape it by way of knowledge,
For a sage is always in a state of serenity."

The wise man asks, "Who among us is the most wealthy?"

"The one blessed with the least grief."

The wise man asks, "What is the most hideous and
Most humiliating vice that bars one access to paradise?"

"For a woman, it is immodesty
And an abrasive speech free of gentle words.
For a man, it is ignorance that enchains him for life."

The wise man asks, "What man is the most feared?"

"The one with the least remorse.
He will appear before Yazdan, his body guilty
And his soul dark from his misdeeds."

He asks, "Who is the honest man, whose wisdom
And mind form a shield of protection around his soul?"

"The one who applies himself in every way
And never arms himself to commit wicked acts."

The wise man asks, "What is the most valuable
Quality, a diadem over the head of humanity?"

"Patience is the highest quality,
For it closes the door to deceit and ruse.
A patient man benefits from his good nature
And will not use it for his own profit.
Furthermore, a noble man does not seek
Recompense for his noble acts.
He is generous, and his heart is free of darkness.
Finally, it is the one who engages in divine acts
According to his wisdom and his pure soul."

The wise man asks, "What do we fear the most?"

"The suffering we bring unto ourselves."

The wise man asks, "How can one be generous

And gain power and splendor through giving?"

"It is best to never refuse anything
To those who find themselves at a disadvantage."

The wise man asks, "Reveal to me the mystery
And the relevance of the actions of the world.
Should we respect and approve them
Even if they do not benefit us or our affairs?"

He replies, "The ancient dome knows everything,
Remembers everything, possesses everything.
The ancient dome is powerful, sublime,
Master Judge of all world judges.
Maintain your faith; maintain the true path;
Distance yourself from wicked acts;
Avoid gaining profit or suffering losses.
Know that good and ill fortune are decreed
By the One who has no companion, the One
Whose actions have neither beginning nor end.
The One who says, 'Be and create!'
The One who has always existed
And will always exist."

The wise man asks, "What part of us feels pain,
The body or the soul, since the body's only function
Is to be a passing dwelling for the soul?"

He replies, "The greatest source of suffering
Is for our round heads shielded by human skin.
It comes from the brains contained within.
When the soul disappears, the body becomes unfeeling,
For it requires a soul to pass through it."

The wise man asks the king about virtue:
"Who can one hide one's greed and desires?"

He replies, "A sensible man can, with much effort,
Repress his avidity. Greed is a vice that will
Make him miserable, as no treasure will satisfy him."

The wise man asks, "O world King,
Which of our ancient kings showed the most

Wisdom, prudence, dignity, and piety?
Name one such world ruler
Who must be celebrated after his death."

He replies, "Celebrate the king who is pious and pure,
Whose heart is full of gratitude for the Justice Giver,
Who does not inspire fear of oppression in anyone,
Who fulfills with hope the hearts of kind men
And with terror the souls of wicked ones,
Who equips the army with his own wealth
And diverts the threat of harm to his enemies,
Who questions wise men throughout the world
And secretly withholds good and bad from his foes."

The wise man asks, "How should we serve Yazdan,
And who fulfills acts inspired by divine will?"

He replies, "An obscure disposition drives
The mind down a path as narrow as a strand of hair.
When a man is aware of the existence of a unique Guide,
He is in some way pointed in the right direction.
He expresses his gratitude to the divine Creator,
Source of his happiness, whom he fears
Above all things and in whom he confides.
He fears Yazdan when committing harmful acts;
He trusts Yazdan when he is in a state of prosperity.
If you have a kind heart, if you seek the true path,
You will have a place of honor among men.
But if you are malevolent in any way,
You will pitch all of your baggage to hell.

"Do not place your trust in this audacious world,
For it hides its secrets from you.
Attach yourself to the work of prayer,
And do not value your present fortune over faith.
Make wisdom your heart's teacher,
And never fall into the trap of betrayal.
Abstain from helping the vicious man
In his designs, propagating quarrels and fights.
Never retain the concerns of this world secret
In your heart for the sake of the other world.
Maintain yourself as the companion of wise men.

Think of eternal bliss, for earthly pleasures pass
And wisdom does not count them as joy.
Attach yourself to learning and insight,
Which will guide you on the path to Yazdan.

"Abstain from hyperbolic discourse,
For you are a new being living in an ancient world.
Abstain from drinking the wine of fate
And from associating with evil men.
Turn your mind away from the impermanent.
Distribute what must be given.
Never refuse a friend your possessions,
May it be your eyes, your brain, or your skin.
And if two friends have an affair to settle,
A third one must never meddle in it.
If you must associate yourself with a wicked person,
Take care that he does not take a hold on you.
One must have merit, tact, and gentleness to befriend
Someone, but he must not boast beyond his worth.
The just man does not count false claims as virtue.
He does not regard another man's wealth as grandeur,
And he does not scorn another for his destitution.

"When a man who thinks poorly of others speaks,
Do not allow him to urge you to act in haste.
When a weak man shares his opinions with you
And his speech exceeds your patience,
Respond to him with measure, soft words,
And conceal your weariness.
If you bar yourself from speaking out of timidity,
You will repent in the end.
If you are idle, do not abandon yourself to pleasures;
An idle man, if sensible, is a lost man.
One must always work and listen to science.

"Abstain from taking part in affairs
That will lead you to remorse and anger.
Give to the wretched, for your heart must not rejoice
In the presence of others' pain and suffering.
A wise man with a patient nature is never
Considered vile in the eyes of the World Master.
He knows that his merit is recognized,

And he puts in every effort to work.
He knows that his Protector approves,
Contributes to his rising power and happiness,
And is pleased to see him accumulate wealth.
The wise man devotes himself to serving Yazdan
And keeps at bay the diverting roads and evil."

This is the wisdom. This is the path.
Attach yourself to Yazdan, who is your refuge.
O King, if you are just, you will leave behind a memory
Of yourself in the world, just as did Anushiravan.
He has turned into dust, but his glory is young
And his kind actions will, without a doubt,
Contribute to his name's lasting memory.
All the wise men will bless his soul
For as long as sky and earth subsist.

15 | Anushiravan's Letter to the Caesar's Son

I have witnessed in an ancient book,
Written according to the words of a true savant,
That Kesra, world master, receives news from Rum:
"May you live long and healthy!
The Caesar has passed away,
And his end leaves the land to another."

The news fills Kesra's soul with worry,
And his ruby-colored cheeks fade
To a pale shade of withering leaves.

He selects a worldly and noble Iranian envoy,
Sends him to the Caesar's son, issued from
The green, fertile branch of the ancient trunk,
And relays to him much good advice
On the hapless fate from which no one escapes.

In a state of mourning, eyes full of tears,
Cheeks pale, he writes the following letter:
"May the Creator grant you a long life!
May you find happiness after your father's death!
Every creature in the world is born to turn to dust.

The world is a place through which we pass.
Whether we wear a crown or a helmet,
We shall not escape the claws of death.
Whether one is the Caesar or the Emperor of Chin,
One will infallibly rest one's head on a pillow of dust.
May you receive good news from the Caesar!
May the Messiah protect your soul!
I learn that you sit on the illustrious throne
And have thereby renewed its glory.
You may ask me for assistance if need be:
Horses, weapons, treasures, and troops."

The envoy takes leave of Kesra
And travels in haste to the Rumi court.
The Caesar glances at the letter and the stamp,
And his heart leaps at the sign
That Kesra ascribes himself a superior rank.

The immature young man is new to the throne.
He takes his time to offer the envoy a seat,
Grudgingly asks him the customary questions,
Looks at him with pain without showing
Any desire of winning over his friendship.
Then he offers him a faraway dwelling
And decides to ignore the king's letter.

For one week, his advisors gather at his side.
In the end, the Caesar says to his minister,
"Reflect on the answer we must give the letter,
And write it as best as you see fit.
Insert all necessary elements, good and bad."

The wise man says, "I am his majesty's servant
And will never stray from his royal command."

All the bishops, the wise men, and advisors
Withdraw from the assembly to compose
In haste a reply as decreed by the Caesar.
They begin in the name of the Creator:
"The highest achievement is that of wisdom.
Such a letter may suit the king, but it lacks courtesy.
It is not a proper way to address an independent ruler.
Furthermore, the Caesar is young, new to the throne,

And, by birth, the rightful ruler of the land.
Guard yourself from irritating this young man
With claims of superiority or demands of tributes and fees.
The young king has written to each administrator
And to each independent prince a forceful letter, saying,
>'From the Caesar, the powerful ruler of Rum,
>Master of the empire and of the land.
>The envoy of the King of Iran has arrived,
>He will report to you openly the state of our affairs,
>What he has seen, heard, and spoken in sorrow
>And joy, things that may not remain hidden.
>The Caesar is deceased; his successor rises
>Above the noblemen with the people's support.
>He finds himself far above everyone's rank.'"

Once the Rumi letter is complete,
They summon the envoy to court.
The sage arrives and asks for the reply.
They offer him a robe not quite fitting his rank.

The audience hall is cleared, and the Caesar says,
"Tell your king:
>'I do not view myself as anyone's servant!
>My rank is not less than the Chinis or the Hephthalites.
>It is not appropriate to treat a powerful man lightly,
>Even if your king is a world ruler.
>Mighty is the one who has many adversaries,
>And I boast friends as well as enemies.
>How can you not recognize my power?
>How can you lower the sun into the dense fog?
>When I am in need of you, you will be my king,
>You, who are for me a memory of my father.'
O messenger, report in truth what you observed,
And do not seek to find ill intentions in my reply."

A present is prepared for the envoy,
And his charger is brought to the palace gate.
He departs, traveling swiftly,
Without taking time to stop at a station.

At court, he reports to Kesra the events
And all that was observed and heard.

The king grows anxious and says,
"You are weary from your journey.
I have always heard that the one
Who surrenders to vanity and does not think
About his affairs will have cause to repent.
He does not differentiate between enemy and friend,
And he openly reveals his heart's secret.
I believe that he is not one of our friends
And that his blood is impure.
The tips of our swords will emerge
From their sheaths to satisfy my heart's desires.
If I allow from here on a single Rumi man
To stand happy by the throne,
He will raise his head and claim to be the Caesar,
The most powerful among the greatest.
May people say that I am not the son
Of the valiant Ghobaad, and may there
No longer be question of me in the world.

"I swear by Yazdan, the pure, by Sun and Moon,
By Aazargoshasp, by throne and crown,
I shall destroy the glory of Rum.
I shall consume the land with fire.
Then he will strip himself of his land's
Ancient treasures; I shall fit inside buffalo skin
Everything he holds dear in his kingdom."

He asks for the blare of trumpets,
The din of cymbals and Indian bells.
Timpani are placed on the backs of war elephants,
And the ground surges and swells like the River Nile.

A vast host advances from Mada'in to the plain,
Stirring the green flows of the skies
With the sound of clarions, the colors of banners,
And the motions of riders with golden boots.
It is as if the stars are in the center of the water
And the spinning firmament finds itself in a daze.

16 | Kesra Drives a Host to Rum and Seizes the Fort of Saghilaa

At the news that the infuriated king
Marches out of Iran with a vast host,
The Caesar sets out from Amoorieh to Halab,[97]
And the world fills with noise and clamor.

Three hundred thousand Iranian riders
Engage in a siege in Halab and conquer the city.
They battle on both sides without pause.

The Rumi warriors, skilled in the use of war gear,
Raise catapults at each gate of Saghilaa
While the Iranians succeed in destroying the city walls.

Halab is a sea of blood; the army commanded
By Baateroon is reduced to pleading for mercy.
Innumerable Rumis are killed at arrow point,
And a multitude is seized in battle
And taken to the king, something like
Thirty thousand in the span of two weeks.

The Rumis dig a trench before their camp,
Fill it with water in the early morning hour,
And, in this way, cut off the path to the king, who,
With his army, remains confounded by the situation.

After some time, they finds themselves
Wanting of gold and silver.
The king summons the provision keepers
And speaks to them at length of the war:
"This affair is quite exhausting, for we are
Not able to cross the water and the trench.
Our host is in desperate need of money, materials,
Horses, armor, and Rumi headdresses."

The provision keepers, the scribes, and the king's vizier
Access the treasury and find that,
Considering the number of troops, they require

In excess of three hundred thousand dinars.

The grand wise master, as swift as dust,
Reports the situation to the king, whose face dims.
He calls Bozorgmehr and says to him,
"What is the purpose of my royal title?
Go and summon the camel leader.
Have him set his strongest beasts on the road
Loaded with more than one hundred pouches
Of gold from the treasure of Mazandaran."

Bozorgmehr replies, "O just, wise, and kind King,
The road to the treasury in Iran is long,
And your hand being empty, the army is powerless.
In the surrounding towns, live people with such wealth
That one out of one hundred would suffice.
If you wish to borrow from merchants
And landowners, they would not refuse you."

The king consents to the proposition.
Bozorgmehr proceeds to search for an intelligent,
Good-natured, kind-featured man, to whom he says,
"Leave on horseback with two spare mounts, and select
Among the town's merchants a renowned young man.
Ask him to lend you a sum of dirhams for the army.
The king will return the money without fail
Once he is able to access his treasury."

The soft-spoken messenger, young in years
And old in wisdom, departs.
He is an agent endowed with a subtle mind.
He arrives at nightfall in a city
And asks for a loan for the king.
A crowd of wealthy people gathers around him.
Among them is a shoemaker, a boot merchant,
Who opens wide his ears to the words of the envoy
And asks him how much is needed.

The valiant messenger says,
"O wealthy, wise man, we need the sum
Of forty times one hundred thousand dirhams."

The shoemaker says, "I shall give it to you in order

To obtain the good graces of the royal treasurer."

He brings a scale, weights, and dirhams,
Barring the need for slip and reed to write.
The merchant weighs the money,
And the work of the envoy is complete.
The shoemaker says, "O fair-faced man,
Would you mind telling Bozorgmehr that I am blessed
With one son whose future concerns me greatly.
Tell him that, should the world king consent for him
To be placed among lawmakers, it would bring me
Great happiness, for he is rich and intelligent."

The messenger replies, "I shall gladly do so.
You have spared me much grievance
And further travels by sharing your wealth."

At night the messenger reports to Bozorgmehr
The story and generosity of the shoemaker.
Bozorgmehr presents himself to the king,
Who is happy to have obtained the funds
And who says, "Thanks to Yazdan
For my virtue and piety allowing me to have,
In my land, a happy and prosperous shoemaker
Who was able to set aside some capital.
Heaven forbid he ever suffers from harm!
Inform yourself on his heart's deepest desires.
I would like to maintain his good will toward us.
When you return to him the loan, add to it
One hundred thousand dirhams as a royal souvenir.
May all my subjects be prosperous and powerful!
May they be owners of thrones and diadems!
May they never endure the reign of an unjust king!
May rulers always be glorious and content!"

Bozorgmehr says to the world master,
"O fair-faced King of auspicious star,
The boot merchant has one wish,
Should his majesty desire to listen to it. He said,
          'May wisdom be the companion of the world king!
          I have one son who has reached the age of maturity
          And who searches for a guide in learning.

647

If it pleases the king to make him a scribe,
I shall pray to Yazdan for his majesty's life.
May he live eternally, for he is worthy of the throne!'"

The king replies, "O sensible man,
How was the deev able to trouble your eyes?
You must go and return the camels to him.
Heaven forbid that I want his money and his gold.
A merchant's son, no matter how skilled,
How learned, or how attentive he may be,
Could never rise to the status of a scribe.
When my son sits on the throne,
He will require a scribe of victorious fortune.
If this bootmaker had any talent,
The king would only see through his eyes
And hear through his ears, while intelligent men
Of high birth would be left to sigh and grieve.
Worldly men would be treated with scorn
By this son of a merchant and would have
To thank him if he replied without waiting.
I would be cursed after my death if,
In my time, such a custom were introduced.
I do not wish to pay the army wages with his gold.
Return the camels immediately to him,
Do not ask for anything from this man,
And do not speak of our troubles to him.
You may request money from wealthy men,
But not from shoemakers."

The messenger returns with the money,
Deeply distressing the shoemaker's heart.

17 | The Caesar's Envoys Arrive at Anushiravan's Court With Apologies and Offerings

The advent of night finds the king anguished.
The din of bells rings as the camels march off.
The king sends patrols across the plain
To make the rounds of the army through the night.

As the sun reveals its crown in the house of Pisces

And spreads its ivory robe across the earth,
A sentinel enters the king's chamber to declare,
"A mission from the Caesar is on its way,
Full of worry and apologies on their behavior."

At the same time, the envoy rushes in.
He salutes Anushiravan, and a sigh escapes his chest
At the sight of the royal head and royal crown.
He reflects, "Here is a king worthy of the crown
By his majesty, his courage, and his vast host!"

Forty Rumi philosophers, mouths full of words,
Hearts full of vanity, advance, each bringing
An offering of thirty thousand golden coins.
Upon gazing into Kesra's face full of splendor,
They slither closer like snakes, shedding tears.

The King of Kings receives them graciously
And regally assigns them seats according to rank.
Their leader speaks out: "O King,
The Caesar is young and inexperienced.
His father just passed away.
He is not familiar with the ways of the world,
He has not the ability to distinguish
Between the apparent and the secret.
We stand loyal to you as your tributaries,
Your servants, and your protectors.
Rum is for you another Iran,
And Iran is as much yours as Rum.
Why must we make a distinction between the two?
The Emperor of Chin and the King of India
Equally owe their thrones and crowns to you.
The wisdom of the era resides in the King of Kings
And the Caesar's power is given by him.
If a child who has not yet attained the age of maturity
Speaks senselessly and without a guide,
The King of Kings would not hold it against him
And would not feel wounded in his heart.
He brings joy to the azure vault of sky.
We shall pay the tribute from Rum
As it was established in the beginning,
And our treaty will be faithfully observed."

Anushiravan listens with a smile
Until the envoy reaches the goal.
He replies, "The young prince is indeed illustrious,
But there is little sense in his words.
Who is the Caesar? Who is the foolish Baateroon,
So debased by their tongues' words?
All the wise kings from the race of Eskandar
Have been victorious and have occupied top ranks.
If someone strays from our command,
Renounces obeisance to us, I shall raise
The dust of destruction on his cultivated lands
And shall never fear his treasures and his armies."

The envoys bend down to kiss the ground,
As do flatterers, and say,
"O victorious and glorious King,
Do not quarrel with us over the past.
We are the dust at your feet that must be swept away.
We are the guardians of your treasury.
If the king wishes to show us his pleasure,
We shall no longer be worried and wretched,
And all the Rumis will deplore the efforts
And the weariness endured by the King of Kings.
We shall add to your treasure as tribute
Ten buffalo skins full of dirhams.
You can specify the quantity you require,
Although it may not be worthy of you."

He replies, "My skillful vizier controls my treasury."

The Rumis present themselves to the wise man,
Lamenting and under an inauspicious star.
They discuss at length all the points
And tell him all the Caesar's secrets.
They speak to him of dinars and buffalo skin
And on what elements the peace of Rum depends.

The wise man tells them, "You propose gold,
But how much brocade are you willing to include?
At the time when the king leaves this place,
I require one thousand bolts of golden fabric.
The king always needs robes of honor

To distribute to men, great and small."

The Rumis consent and return to the king,
Whom they greet in a state of humility.

The king remains in this camp for some time,
And after he and his troops have rested,
He selects a valiant man from his company,
One who knows how to count, write, and erase,
And gives him an escort, charging him to demand
Tribute and to take it to the rich land of Iran.

Then he departs for Ctesiphon, preceded and followed
By his troops, all quite satisfied with the abundance
Of gold and silver, golden belts, and silver restraints.
There are so many silken banners belonging to the leaders
That it is as if the air is made of silk and the earth of gold.
The gems on belts sparkle as bright as the Pleiades.

As he approaches the city, a great crowd advances
Toward Kesra on foot, strapped, their hearts full of joy.
The king's following accompanies them on foot
All the way to the palace gates.

The noblemen praise the foreseeing, glorious ruler.
Illustrious wise men shower him with rubies and pearls.
Nearing his residence, the king dismisses
His noblemen, who return home to celebrate
The widespread glory of King Kesra Anushiravan.

18 | Anushiravan Selects His Son Hormozd as His Successor

What says the world seeker, ambitious poet bard,
Of the furtive rotations of providence?
The wise man chooses not to attach his heart
To this misleading world.
One day we are up, another we tumble down;
At times we dwell in joy, at times in fear;
In the end, our bed of repose is beneath the dim dust,
For one to rest in honor, for another in disgrace.

Never are we to receive a sign from the departed
To let us know whether they are awake and happy
Or whether they have fallen into a deep slumber.

No matter how little there is in the other world,
The fear of death is no longer relevant there.
Whether we have one hundred years or twenty-five,
It is all the same when it comes
To that dreadful, painful day.

Whether one finds life joyous or one speaks
Of it with pain and misery, I have never
Encountered a person who longed for death.
Whether men respect the good or the evil path,
Whether worshippers of the faith, idol lovers,
Or Ahriman idol worshippers, everyone equally
Places his hands on his head in wonder.
O old man, when you pass your sixty-first year,
The wine, the cup, and the salt lose their appeal.
When you prepare for death, wine becomes a thin,
Silky tunic to wrap oneself in during a winter month.
Without it one would freeze in the midst of one's sins,
And the soul would lose the way to paradise.

Many friends are left behind, others have departed,
While you persist and stand in the desert,
A cup as a traveling companion.
If you do not think about your affairs from the start,
You will be sure to pay in the end.
When you commit a wicked act, you will suffer
The consequences and your grief will be
The one thing you take with you from this world.
Causing harm to another means self-harm.

Know that your end will arrive with certainty,
Even if you live in great joy for a while
And no matter how long your life may last.
Multiply your good actions during
Your passage through this transitory world,
For you will rejoice from them in the world beyond.
A souvenir of us lingers behind,
A record of our actions and our words.

I ask the Creator of Time to grant me a long enough life,
A joyous heart, and a clear mind so that I may
Collect these stories and many scattered tales,
Stories on which many years have passed
From the time of Kiumars to the era of Yazdegerd.
I wish to link them meter by meter,
Create an ancient garden free from weeds,
And renew the discourse of the Kings of Kings.
Then I shall leave this passing dwelling
With a clear soul, untainted by affliction.

Let me now return to the clear-minded poet bard's
Account of world master Kesra Anushiravan.

As the king reaches his seventy-fourth year,
His heart fills with concern for his imminent death.
He seeks a successor for the world empire,
One whose sole desire is to wear the robe of justice,
One who is endowed with a healthy body
And a serene soul, one who is kind to the poor.

Anushiravan has six illustrious sons,
All princely, intelligent, learned, and affable.
The eldest of them is the sagacious Hormozd,
A man with no equal, who is proud, cultured,
Handsome, and full of affection for Persians.

Over the following days and nights,
Kesra charges his agents to secretly assess
His words and his actions, good and bad,
And to report back to him.

Anushiravan says to Bozorgmehr,
"I am secretly tending to an important matter.
I have passed my seventieth year, my head
And beard, once black, are as white as camphor.
I shall soon bid farewell to this passing sojourn,
And the world will need a ruler
Who is as generous to the poor
And to strangers as he is toward his own kin;
Someone who gives liberally.
Someone who fears his heart's attachment
To his treasures and to his earthly life.

I give thanks to the Creator for giving me
Intelligent, well-educated, pious sons.
Hormozd is the dearest to me of the lot,
For he excels in wisdom and prudence,
And I think that his heart lacks nothing
In terms of kindness, generosity, and integrity.
His mind always leans toward acts of virtue,
And his place is on the seat of the King of Kings.
Now summon the wise men, noblemen, and
Those who spend their time in the study of sciences.
Put his knowledge to the test, and develop his skills."

19 | The Wise Men Question Hormozd

The wise men, seekers of truth in all matters,
Convene with the king's loyal advisors.
They summon Hormozd, the ambitious prince,
And seat him before the illustrious assembly.

Bozorgmehr is first to speak:
"O fair-faced prince of auspicious star,
What is it that brings light to the mind and soul
And stimulates the body to prosper?"

He replies, "The most prized value is learning,
For the wise man occupies the highest rank.
Knowledge gives one a sense of trust and security
And restrains Ahriman's power to commit crimes.
Furthermore, forbearance is an ornament of distinction.
Finally, one requires other assets, such as
Humility, justice, patience, devotion, and talent."

Bozorgmehr asks, "What is most useful,
And by what means does one gain power?"

He replies, "Gentleness and humility
Are most valuable in good and bad times;
Also making every effort to spare others pain;
Finally, when one acts with justice toward all,
One is able to gain self-contentment."

Bozorgmehr observes the stately and pure prince
And says to him, "Let us discuss various things:
Count on your fingers the subjects,
And note the questions I shall address to you.
Remember and reply to them accordingly.
Attempt not to invert the order one way or another.
Show yourself valiant and respond well.
If you learn and pay attention, you may hope
The door of the firmament will open for you.
If I overwhelm you with questions,
It is to obtain a greater number of answers.
May the World Owner inspire you!
May your wisdom shine
And your good fortune be your support!
I shall question you on all the parts of justice,
As well as I know them.
Respond with anything that comes to you mind.
An intelligent man reveals himself and attains
The object of his desires through his replies.
A question is like a padlock, and the answer is the key:
Through it one can access the good and the bad.

"Tell me, who is the son whose actions toward
His father are most noble and most proper?
Who is most worthy of touching the heart
To the extent of drawing tears for his suffering?
Who repents from a good deed in good faith?
Whose actions merit a great deal of blame?
Which part of the world is best left abandoned,
For it would bring our end should we stay there?
What has the power to infuse joy into life,
And what must we remember from the past?
At which times must we express praise,
And what things are most profitable to us?
Which of our friends is the most noble, most able
To convert the heart into a garden with his voice?
Who in the world has the most friends,
Whom he renders happy on every occasion?
Conversely, who has the most wicked enemies?
Where can one find the most peaceful place
To establish oneself and to fortify royal power?
What action is the most destructive, which

The perpetrator himself has reason to deplore?
What thing does man most firmly clasp onto
That will most swiftly waste away?
Who among shameless oppressors
Has the least affection and respect for men?
Who causes the most destruction with his words
And brings discomfort to his friends' hearts?
What sort of speech brings dishonor to one
And leads to greater misfortune?"

The wise man speaks without a show of weariness
For the duration of one day, until night descends.
As darkness forces them to fetch and light candles,
The heads of noblemen are weary and confused.
The king is tired of all the discussion
And remains silent as he listens to the replies.

The noble Hormozd rises to praise his father:
"May the world never be vacant of your presence!
May Kesra always sit on the imperial throne!
May we never see the crown, the ivory throne,
And royal pomp without his majesty!
May the elements be dust beneath his feet!
May the dome of sky be the remedy for our ailments!

"I shall reply to all the questions posed
And to that end apply my acumen as best I can.
The wise man addressed me a question
On the company that a son must have,
And I must touch on the goal in my reply.
If a son is full of affection, indulging in acts
Of kindness based on a deep sense of justice,
A father's heart will rejoice and be free from worry.
Furthermore, he speaks of a man who is the object
Of pity and for whom tears filter through his lashes:
This is the powerful man abandoned by fortune,
Who becomes the slave of a villainous person.
He has every right to shed tears on his fate,
For he is forced to labor for an impure master.
Also, the one who is kind to an ungrateful man
Will remain in a state of terror, since overlooked
Good deeds will hinder a deeper sense of wisdom.

"Then he asked me what is the best course of action
When one is faced with a choice between fight or flight.
The response is that it does not suit a wise man
To remain in a land ruled by an unjust monarch.
He must flee the king who will provoke
Chaos and destruction throughout the world.

"He asked me if I knew what brings us
The most joy in the world, a brother or a friend.
He addressed me a question on happy times:
It is right to celebrate, and above all,
To celebrate the times when one has no enemies.
Then he asked me about friends:
It is always best to give aid to a friend.
If he is rich, take shelter in his home;
If he is poor, work with him.
The most humble, most noble man is the one
Who infuses happiness into his friends' hearts.

"Next, he asked who is the enemy who fills
His heart perpetually with grief and pain:
The one whose tongue is always bold when
It comes to uttering words that incite others.
Then he asked me what is most painful
And what most troubles a serene soul:
Sitting next to a man evil in words and actions
Renders life as bitter as the biting taste of a quince.
He asked me to identify the true witness, whose soul
And intelligence are guarantors of his testimony:
There is no better, more eloquent,
More powerful witness than experience.

"He asked what is the most harmful, weep-inducing thing.
When desire dominates the soul and passes over it
Like a breath of air, regret follows close behind.
Guard yourself from touching the flowers of desire.
He asked what thing is so unstable that,
When you see its feet, your hand finds its head.
It is a friendly alliance with an ignorant man
Of ill nature and fluctuating disposition.

"Then he asked who is the unjust man,

And who washes his heart in the waters of shame.
The one who performs perverse acts,
May be called distressed and desperate.
If he is ashamed, call him unjust.
If he lies in his profession,
I refer to him as unfair and debased.

"He asked whose words provoke ruins
And who, without suffering himself,
Fills the lives of others with trouble.
The double-faced informer and the idle man
Bring grief into sensible hearts.
The wise man asked what brings on a sense
Of dishonor and makes a man regret his own words.
It is a frivolous, boastful speech before an assembly.
When one is alone and one reflects within,
One is chagrined by what one said.
Later, if he opens his mouth to speak,
Men of merit as well as unworthy men
Will reproach him for his boasting,
For no one escapes the consequences of one's actions.

"Those were all the questions and my replies.
May the world praise the king!
May tongues speak only according to his will!
May his noble heart dwell in joy and truth!"

Kesra Anushiravan, King of Kings, is stunned
And showers his son with blessings worthy of a Kianian.
The congregation is delighted by the youth's words,
And the ruler's heart is liberated from any worry.

A royal act is written at the king's command by which
He bestows the throne and crown to Hormozd.
A seal of musk is affixed, and once the writing
On Chini paper has air-dried, they hand it to the vizier
In the presence of illustrious noblemen and sages.

I have set to verse this act by Anushiravan
By order of the victorious world king.

20 | Anushiravan Writes an Edict for His Son Hormozd

In no way does the outer world resemble inner life,
And inner life is nothing but pain and sorrow.
Whether you possess a crown or grief and suffering,
This transient sojourn will without a doubt end for you.

The nature of the world lacks good faith
And hastens to harvest what it has sown.
Read the letter of the world king and think whether
There ever lived anyone equal to Anushiravan
In justice and intelligence, in banquet and in battle.
Yet, when his day comes, he is unable to find respite.

O unrepentant old man, select the true path,
And abandon revelry and worldly pleasures.
The world was new when you seized the cup,
When you turned your back on the door of regret.
If you have any sense, you would face it now,
For the pious man follows the path of faith.
You have little time left, a number of summers,
Autumns, and springs, and that is all.
Reflect carefully where your precious soul will go
Once your body finds its place beneath the dust.

What words does the eloquent old man speak
In regard to the last wishes of Anushiravan?
When Hormozd ends his speech,
The wise man pronounces a new discourse.
The king's advisor consults with the scribe,
And they compose upon silk a letter in which
Anushiravan addresses his young son Hormozd
In a manner that charms the heart.
After praising Yazdan, he writes,
"I shall give you advice from the son of Ghobaad.
O my dear child, listen well and scribble my words
Upon your heart; may they infuse life into it.
The world is a perfidious place,
Filled with lassitude, sorrow, and grief.
Anytime you are joyous and free of pain,
No matter how happy you may be,

No matter how free of worry your heart may be,
Your joy will be curtailed
As you are forced to leave this illusory place.

"I shall hand over the world to you
In accordance with justice, and you will have
To turn it over to another in the same manner.
When I started to think about death
During bright days and long nights, I searched
For a head on which to rest the Kianian crown,
A head that would itself be the diadem
On the forehead of humanity.
I am blessed with six sons who are intelligent,
Charming, and generous, and who lean on justice.
I have singled you out because you are the eldest
And because you are wise and worthy of the crown.
Ghobaad passed his eightieth year
When he first spoke to me of kingship.
I have now reached the age of seventy-four,
And I nominate you as my successor as world king.
By this action, I hope to receive my soul's peace
And blessings, and hope to benefit the public good.
May the Creator grant you happiness and prosperity.
If you provide security to everyone with justice,
You will sleep soundly and your fairness
Toward others will bring you happiness.
As a reward for your kind actions,
You will gain access to paradise.
Great is the one who sows seeds of virtue.

"Pay attention and always lean on patience,
For anger does not suit a king.
A world master of awakened mind who strives
To instruct himself will always be honored.
Hold yourself at bay from lies and falsehoods,
Or else your fortune will fall into the dust of deceit.
Distance haste from your heart and your head:
Wisdom is repudiated when one impels
His action with urgency and impatience.
Devote yourself to virtue and fight for it.
Listen to the advice of the sages
In times of happiness and misfortune.

Evil must be kept at bay,
For it would inevitably bring you bad luck.
Keep pure your clothing and your food,
And listen closely to the counsel of your father.

"Devote yourself to the Creator, who is
In all matters your shelter and your guide.
If you make the world prosper with your justice,
Your treasure will abound and
Your throne will be the seat of great joy.
When someone spreads kindness, reward him
So that he may forget the effort he expended.
Satisfy worthy men, and hold them near you.
Render the world black for wrongdoers.
Deliberate on every subject with a wise man.
Do not complain about the toils of kingship.
As long as intelligent men have access to you,
Your throne, treasury, and army will remain yours.
Make sure none of your subjects languishes in misery,
And make the land's greatest noblemen
Take a part in the execution of your good deeds.
Refuse to serve despicable people,
And never entrust an affair to an unjust man.
Lend your ear and your heart to the poor,
And tend to their concerns as if they are your kin.
When a powerful man acquits himself of his duty
With all his heart's justice, the world rejoices
And he himself dwells in happiness.

"Do not close your treasury door to the destitute.
Give liberally as well to pure, virtuous men.
If your enemy becomes your friend, guard against
Sowing the seeds of good deeds in salty ground.
If you follow my advice, your crown will be powerful.
May the Justice Giver be auspicious to you!
May wisdom be your throne and fortune your diadem!
May you never forget my words after I am gone!
May your head be pure, your heart joyous,
Your body untainted, and may evil be kept at bay!
May wisdom always be your guardian!
May you always have inclinations toward virtue!

"Once I make my exit from this vast world,
You must have a beautiful tomb built for me
In a solitary, distant place, free of men,
And above which swift-winged vultures fail to fly.
In the vault of the dismal, hollow chamber,
There will be a lofty door ten nooses high.
In this chamber will be inscribed my name,
The names of my noblemen, and my valiant warriors.
An array of lush and beautiful carpets will cover the floors,
An array of color and scent will fill the chamber.
You will embalm my body with camphor.
A crown of musk will grace my head.
You will bring from the treasury five robes
Of golden brocade that have never been worn,
And you will dress me in the Kianian manner
And the custom of the mighty Sassanian kings.

"Similarly, you will install an ivory throne
On which you will suspend my crown.
The gold utensils with which I serve myself;
Plates, goblets and casseroles; twenty cups of rosewater,
Wine, and saffron, and two hundred cups
Full of camphor and amber must be on my right
And on my left, but no less or more than I indicate.
You must empty the blood from my stomach
And fill the body with camphor and musk.
Then you will secure the entrance, and no one
Will have the occasion to see me ever again.
My door will have a completely different function,
For it will admit no one to my side.

"My children and my family members,
All those pained by my death,
Will abstain for two months from engaging in feast,
For this is the rule after the death of the king.
I hope pure men will weep upon receipt of the royal letter.
Do not ever disobey Hormozd! Breathe only to his will!"

Everyone sheds bitter tears on the letter.
Kesra survives one more year after
The nomination of his son, and then he expires.

21 | Anushiravan Dreams, and Bozorgmehr Reports on the Advent of Muhammad

One night, as Anushiravan falls asleep after prayer,
His enlightened soul has a dream:
A bright sun lights up the darkness, and next to it
Is a ladder with forty steps, its top step surpassing Saturn.
The sun rises from the city of Hejaz and gently advances.
The world, from mountain to mountain, fills with light.
Everywhere, grief and trouble quickly transform to joy
As the light reaches every dark corner of the world.

The king awakens at midnight.
He does not divulge his dream to anyone.
When the sun lifts its burka, he summons
Bozorgmehr, to whom he reveals his dream.
T contemplates the nature of the dream
And says, "O blessed King, the world conceals a secret."

The king says, "Tell me this secret, for I am restless."

Bozorgmehr says, "O King, your thoughts
And your hopes are beyond the Sun and Moon.
I have reflected on this dream from beginning to end.
Do not be too surprised by its interpretation.
Between now and forty years from now, a Taazi
Will advance whose path is that of righteousness.
He keeps wickedness at bay.
He will overthrow the faith of Zartosht
And will be able to split the moon with his fingertip.
No one will be able to replicate his action.
Judaism, Christianity, or any other religion
Will lose their appeal and disappear.
He will dominate from a three-legged throne,
And the world will fall under his rule.
Upon his departure from this earthly life,
His words and his teachings will remain deep-rooted.
The world will be full of joy for centuries to come,
Except for the royal court that will be cast to the wind.
A vast host with elephants and timpani, trumpets,
And bells will march toward you from Hejaz
And defeat your grandson and kill all your troops.

The festival of Saddeh will be abolished,
And all the fire temples will be razed to the ground.
They will worship neither the fire nor the sun,
And all of our warriors' fortunes will dim.
Jaamaasp told Goshtaasp about this secret
And about this eradicated path."

Kesra turns pale from Bozorgmehr's words.
All day he sits with grief and sorrow and retires
To sleep at night with his mind riddled with thoughts.
After three parts of the night pass,
A loud and frightening sound is heard.
It is as if the world is overturned as someone
Reports the destruction of one of the palaces.
The king is deeply concerned, not understanding
How this event could occur. He calls Bozorgmehr
And asks him about the ruined ceiling.

The learned man says, "O King Anushiravan,
Anything you may have seen in dream is unfolding:
The world has filled with chaos.
Know that the fall of the palace ceiling announces
The birth of the man in your dreams.
A rider will soon arrive with two horses to report
That the fire temple of Aazargoshasp has fallen to ruins.

Just then a rider reaches them to let them know
That the fire in the temple has been extinguished.
The king is deeply aggrieved by these events
And expels cold sighs.

Bozorgmehr says to him, "Why are you troubled?
Why worry about a world you will soon leave behind?"

The king does not remain alive long after this discussion.
He soon dies, leaving the world to mourn for him.

Bozorgmehr maintains his face in the dust
For the duration of one month.

May these words remain as a memory of Anushiravan.
Since the revolving dome of sky was not loyal to him,
Since it did not spare such a man,

PART TWENTY-SEVEN

One may expect from it neither justice nor affection.

Here I complete the tale of Kesra Anushiravan.
Now I shall weave embellished words into verse
To usher the ascent of Hormozd to the royal seat
And to relate the story of his reign.

End of Volume Four

APPENDIX

Glossary of Names

Aabteen: Fereydoon's father; killed and served as a meal to Zahaak's snakes. (Vol. 1)

Aarash: Iranian warrior in the army of Kay Khosrow and father of warrior Manoochehr from Khorasan. (Vol. 3)

Aarash: Seventh Ashkanian king. (Vol. 4)

Aarash: Border guard and warrior under the rule of Yazdegerd. (Vol. 4)

Aarezooy: Daughter of Sarv, king of Yemen, and wife of Salm son of Fereydoon. (Vol. 1)

Aaveh: Son of Samkanan and descendant of Fereydoon; ally of Kay Khosrow in the great battle with Afraasiyaab. (Vol. 3)

Aayaas: Of Chin, warrior ally of King Arjaasp. (Vol. 3)

Aazaad Sarv: Lives during Ferdowsi's time in Marv, owns the *Khodaay Nameh,* one of the sources for *The Shahnameh,* and is a man who can trace his origins to Saam, son of Nariman. (Vol. 3)

Aazaad Sarv: A nobleman in the service of King Kesra Anushiravan. (Vol. 4)

Aazaadeh: Lute player and one of the wives of Bahraam (son of Yazdegerd). Killed by her husband, Bahraam. (Vol. 4)

Aazarafrooz: Son of Esfandiar, whose brothers are Bahman, Mehrnoosh, and Nooshaazar. (Vol. 3)

Abbas: Taazian commander leading a host against King Hormoz, son of Kesra Anushiravan. (Vol. 4)

Abol-Fazl: Also Abul-Fazl al-Bal'ami; the vizier of Amir Nasr, died in 940. (Vol. 4)

Afraasiyaab: King of Tooran-Zamin and son of Pashang (son of Zaad-sham). Father of Karookhan, Sorkheh, Jahn, Shiddeh, Gurch, Afraasi-yaab, Faranguis, and Manijeh. Killed by Kay Khosrow. (Vols. 1-3)

Afraasiyaab: Son of Afraasiyaab; Tooranian warrior. (Vol. 3)

Aghriras: Brother of Afraasiyaab and Garsivaz, and son of Pashang. Killed by Afraasiyaab. (Vol. 1)

Aghriras: Tooranian leader who fights in the great war (not to be confused with Afraasiyaab's brother). (Vol. 3)

Ahran: Rumi nobleman who weds the third daughter of the Caesar. (Vol. 3)

Ahriman: Dark spirit whose goal is to promote division and chaos.

Ajnaas: Tooranian warrior in Afraasiyaab's army. (Vols. 1-2)

Akhvaast: Tooranian warrior. Killed by Zangueh in the battle of the heroes. (Vols. 2-3)

Akvan Deev: A threatening creature that resembles a deev with a black stripe down its back. Killed by Rostam. (Vols. 2-3)

Alkoos: Tooranian warrior in Afraasiyaab's army. Killed by Rostam. (Vol. 1)

Alvaah: Zaboli warrior in Rostam's retinue. Killed by Kaamoos. (Vols. 1-2)

Amr: Taazian commander leading a host against King Hormoz, son of Kesra Anushiravan. (Vol. 4)

Andariman: Tooranian warrior and brother of Afraasiyaab. Killed by Gorgeen in the battle of the heroes. (Vols. 2-3)

Andariman: Brother of King Arjaasp, Biderafsh, and Kohram. Killed by Esfandiar. (Vol. 3)

Andman: King of Rey under the reign of Bahraam the Hunter. (Vol. 4)

Anushiravan: Or Khosrow I, Kesra Anushiravan, son of Ghobaad; Sassanian king who rules for forty-eight years, from 531 to 579. (Vols. 3-4)

Arastalis: Aristotle, whom Ferdowsi places in the land of Rum; advisor to Eskandar. Historically, Aristotle was Alexander the Great's tutor up to the time he ascended to the throne in 336 BCE. (Vol. 3)

Ardavan: Also called Ardavan the Great. Descendant of Aarash, he was the ninth Ashkanian king. He has four sons. He is wounded in battle and executed at the order of Ardeshir Babakan. (Vol. 4)

Ardeshir: Bijan's son and Giv's grandson; Iranian warrior in the army of Lohraasp. (Vol. 3)

Ardeshir: Prince, with brother Shiddasp, sons of King Goshtaasp. Killed by Arjaasp troops. (Vol. 3)

Ardeshir: Tooranian warrior in the army of Arjaasp. (Vol. 3)

Ardeshir: Name given by King Goshtaasp to Bahman, son of Esfandiar. (Vol. 3)

Ardeshir: The younger brother of King Shahpoor who is regent and rules for ten years. He is referred to as Nikookaar, or the Benevolent. Dies naturally and leaves the throne to his son Shahpoor. (Vol. 4)

Ardeshir: Grand wise master under the rule of Pirooz and his son. (Vol. 4)

Ardeshir Babakan: Descendant of Esfandiar and son of Sassan and Babak's unnamed daughter. First Sassanian king, who reigns for forty years and two months. He weds Golnaar, Ardavan's daughter, who gives him a child named Shahpoor. Dies at the age of seventy-eight. (Vol. 4)

Arezoo: A jeweler's daughter and lute player who marries Bahraam the Hunter. (Vol. 4)

Arjaasp: King of Tooran; his parentage is somewhat unclear but most likely is the son of Garsivaz (son of Pashang). Killed by Esfandiar in the impregnable castle. (Vol. 3)

Arjang: Deev and army commander in Mazandaran. Killed by Rostam. (Vol. 1)

Arjang: Son of Zerreh and brother of Garooy; Tooranian warrior in the army of Tajov. Killed by Tous. (Vol. 2)

Armail: With brother Garmail, saves intended victims of Zahaak's serpents. (Vol. 1)

Arjasp: Tooranian leader in the army of Afraasiyaab. (Vols. 1-2)

Arnavaaz: Daughter or sister of Jamsheed; concubine of Zahaak, then wife of Fereydoon and mother of Iraj. (Vol. 1)

Ashk: First Ashkanian king and a descendant of Ghobaad. (Vol. 4)

Ashkanian: The Ashkanian Empire, also known as the Parthian Empire or Arsacid Empire, was a political and culture power from 247 BCE to 284 CE in what is now northeastern Iran.

Ashkeboos: Ally of Afraasiyaab from Kushan who fights Rohaam and Rostam. Killed by Rostam. (Vol. 2)

Ashkesh: Of the family of Ghobaad and leader in the Iranian army under the rules of Kay Kaavoos and Kay Khosrow. (Vols. 1-3)

Aspanooy: Slave under the command of Tajov, Afraasiyaab's son-in-law. (Vol. 2)

Baanoogoshasp: Rostam's daughter and Giv's wife. (Vol. 2)

Baarmaan: Tooranian warrior, son of Viseh (son of Zaadsham). (Vols. 1-3) Killed by Ghaaran. (Vol. 1)

Baarman: Tooranian warrior; killed by Rohaam in the battle of the heroes. (Vols. 2-3)

Baazoor: Tooranian sorcerer. (Vol. 2)

Babak: Governor of Estakhr appointed by Ashkanian king Ardavan and father-in-law of Sassan (son of Dara and father of Ardeshir Babakan). (Vol. 4)

Babak: Wise man in service to the Sassanian King Kesra Anushiravan. (Vol. 4)

Babak's daughter: Unnamed wife of Sassan and mother of Ardeshir Babakan. (Vol. 4)

Bahman/Ardeshir: Esfandiar's son and King of Iran; his grandfather Goshtaasp also calls him Ardeshir (some Persian editions of *The Shahnameh* refer to him as Ardeshir); marries his daughter Homay/Chehrzaad. (Vol. 3)

Bahman: Son of Ardavan, the ninth Ashkanian king. Killed in battle. (Vol. 4)

Bahman: Wise man at the court of Kesra Anushiravan. (Vol. 4)

Bahraam: Son of Goodarz and Iranian warrior under the rules of Kay Kaavoos, Kay Khosrow, and King Lohraasp. (Vols. 1-3)

Bahraam: Eighth Ashkanian king. (Vol. 4)

Bahraam: Son of Ormazd (son of King Shahpoor) who rules as Sassanian king for three years and three months. Father of Bahraam. (Vol. 4)

Bahraam: Son of Bahraam (son of King Ormazd) who rules as Sassanian king for nineteen years. Father of Bahraam Bahraamian. (Vol. 4)

Bahraam: Only son of Shahpoor (son of Shahpoor); he rules as a Sassanian king for fourteen years. He has a brother named Yazdegerd and daughter. (Vol. 4)

Bahraam Bahraamian: Son of Bahraam (son of King Bahraam); Sassanian king for four months. Recognized as the King of Kerman. Father of Nersi. (Vol. 4)

Bahraam of Pirooz: Son of Bahraamian; leader under the reign of Bahraam the Hunter. (Vol. 4)

Bahraam the Hunter: Son of Yazdegerd; Sassanian king who rules for sixty-three years. (Vol. 4)

Balaash: Youngest son of King Pirooz and brother of Ghobaad and Jaamaasp; rules as Sassanian king for five years and two months. (Vol. 4)

Bandooy: A wise man and hero during the rule of the Sassanian King

Ghobaad. He and his brother Gostaham rebel against King Hormozd and blind him. (Vol. 4)

Barteh: Iranian warrior and leader of the family of Tavaabeh under the rule of Kay Khosrow. (Vols. 1-3)

Barzeen: Wealthy landowner with three daughters: a lute player, a singer, and a dancer. The three marry Bahraam the Hunter. (Vol. 4)

Baateroon: Rumi army commander. (Vol. 4)

Beed: Deev in the army of Mazandaran. Killed by Rostam. (Vol. 1)

Behaafarid: Daughter of King Goshtaasp; sister of Homay and Esfandiar. (Vol. 3)

Behrooz: Son of Hoor, horseman in the company of Bahraam the Hunter. (Vol. 4)

Behzaad: Siaavosh's horse, then mastered by Kay Khosrow. (Vol. 2)

Behzaad: King Goshtaasp's stallion. (Vol. 3)

Behzaad: Son of Barzeen; warrior from the lineage of Rostam during the reign of Yazdegerd. (Vol. 4)

Bendah: Sindhi leader. (Vol. 3)

Beraham: A tightfisted, wealthy man who lives under the rule of Bahraam the Hunter. (Vol. 4)

Bezanoosh: Rumi leader and descendant of the Caesars; he drives his army against King Shahpoor and later ascends to the Rumi throne. (Vol. 4)

Biderafsh: Powerful Chini/Tooranian leader in the army of King Arjaasp and his brother. Killed by Esfandiar, son of Goshtaasp. (Vol. 3)

Bijan: Son of Giv and Baanoogoshasp, Rostam's daughter; Iranian warrior under the rule of Kay Khosrow. Loses his life in the blizzard after Kay Khosrow disappears. (Vols. 1-3)

Bijan: Fourth Ashkanian king. (Vol. 4)

Bitghoon: Eskandar's vizier who disguises himself as the Caesar. (Vol. 3)

Bivard: Ruler of Kaat and ally of Afraasiyaab. (Vol. 2)

Bivard: Warrior under the rule of Yazdegerd. (Vol. 4)

Booraab: A Rumi blacksmith. (Vol. 3)

Boossepaas: Father of Kooh; Hoomaan pretends to be him when he meets Rostam. (Vol. 2)

Borzeen: Iranian warrior and son of Garshaasp. (Vols. 1-2)

Borzmehr: Iranian wise man and emissary under the rule of Bahraam the Hunter. (Vol. 4)

Borzooy: Name adopted by Bahraam the Hunter to hide his identity from King Shangal of India. (Vol. 4)

Borzooy: Eloquent physician at Kesra Anushiravan's court. (Vol. 4)

Borzvila: Ally of Afraasiyaab in the last great battle during the reign of Kay Khosrow. (Vol. 3)

Bozorgmehr: Learned and wise youth who serves at the court of Kesra Anushiravan. (Vol. 4)

Brahmin: Guide and teacher of the Hindu caste. (Vol. 3)

Caesar of Rum: Title assigned to various Rumi rulers who are often allies of Tooran and Chin. (Vols. 1-4)

Changgesh: Ally of Afraasiyaab who fights Rostam and is killed by him. (Vol. 2)

Chegel: Name of a Turkish tribe famous for the beauty of its people.

Chin: China; generally refers to lands to the east of Iran, as Rum represents the lands to the west.

Daad Barzeen: Warrior under the reign of Bahraam the Hunter. (Vol. 4)

Daaraab: Son of Homay and Bahman who is raised by the laundryman and his wife; husband of Nahid of Rum and father of Eskandar and Dara. (Vol. 3)

Damoor: Tooranian warrior who lends a hand in the slaying of Siaavosh. (Vols. 2-3)

Dara: Son of Daaraab and half-brother of Eskandar. (Vol. 3)

Deev: Child of Ahriman, also referred to as Eblis; represents the material or physical embodiment of Ahriman; a fragment of the dark spirit.

Delafrooz: Descendant of Kay Ghobaad and Iranian warrior in the army of Kay Khosrow. (Vol. 3)

Delafrooz: Lumberjack in a village who helps Bahraam the Hunter. (Vol. 4)

Delafroozeh Farrokhpay: Rumi maiden who rescues King Shahpoor and frees him of the donkey skin. (Vol. 4)

Delarai: Wife of King Dara and mother of Roshanak, Eskandar's wife. (Vol. 3)

Eblis: Name synonymous with Ahriman and deev. Eblis is one of the many physical manifestations of Ahriman.

Elias: Son of Mehraas, King of Khazaria. Defeated by Goshtaasp, son of Lohraasp. (Vol. 3)

Emir: A nobleman who attempts to deceive Haftvaad and is met with death. (Vol. 4)

Emperor of Chin: Or Faghfoor of Chin, title given to the rulers of Chin or China, allies of Afraasiyaab or Tooran-Zamin and, later, descendants of Arjaasp and Afraasiyaab. (Vols. 2-4)

Esfandiar: Son of Goshtaasp and Katayoon, and brother of Pashootan, Behaafarid, Shiroo, Nivezaar, Shiddasp, and Farshidvard; his sons are Bahman, Mehrnoosh, Aazarafrooz, and Nooshaazar. Calls himself Khorraad at the impregnable castle. Killed by Rostam. (Vol. 3)

Eskandar: Persian equivalent to Alexander; son of King Daaraab and Nahid of Rum, and half-brother of Dara; marries Roshanak, daughter of Dara. (Vol. 3)

Faghanish: King of Chaghan and relative of Bahraam the Hunter. (Vol. 4)

Faghfoor: Title assigned to the Emperor of Chin, or China, who governs under the authority of Tooran-Zamin. (Vols. 1-4)

Fanj: Commander of the host of the Emperor of Chin. (Vol. 4)

Faraaeen: A wise man, follower of Kesra during the rule of Sassanian King Ghobaad. (Vol. 4)

Faraamarz: Rostam's son and Iranian warrior under the rules of Kay Kaavoos, Kay Khosrow, King Lohraasp, and King Goshtaasp. Killed in vengeance by King Bahman. (Vols. 1-3)

Faraanak: Fereydoon's mother and Aabteen's wife. (Vol. 1)

Faraanak: Second daughter of the wealthy Barzeen; sister of Maah-Aafareed and Shambeleed; skilled lute player. The three sisters wed Bahraam the Hunter. (Vol. 4)

Faranguis: Afraasiyaab's daughter, wife of Siaavosh, and mother of Kay Khosrow who later marries Fariborz, son of Kaavoos. (Vol. 2)

Farfoorius: Leader of the Caesar's host in the war against Kesra Anushiravan. (Vol. 4)

Farghaar: Skillful warrior who defends Afraasiyaab. (Vol. 2)

Farhaad: Grandson of Goodarz; Iranian warrior under the rules of Kay Kaavoos and Kay Khosrow. (Vols. 1-3)

Farhaad: Leads the left wing of Kesra Anushiravan's host in the war against Rum. (Vol. 4)

Fariborz: Son of Kaavoos and brother of Siaavosh. Loses his life in the blizzard after Kay Khosrow disappears. (Vols. 1-3)

Farrokhzaad: Adoptive name of Goshtaasp, son of Lohraasp, during his stay in Rum. (Vol. 3)

Farrokhzaad: Son of Azar Mahan; illustrious lord and head of King Hormozd's stables (son of Kesra Anushiravan); warrior in the Iranian army of Khosrow Parviz. (Vols. 4-5)

Farshidvard: Tooranian warrior and leader in Afraasiyaab's army; son of Viseh (son of Zaadsham). He and his brother Lahaak are killed by Gostaham, son of Gojdaham. (Vols. 1-3)

Farshidvard: Son of King Goshtaasp and Esfandiar's brother. Killed by Kohram. (Vol. 3)

Farshidvard: A wealthy villager, owner of sheep and cattle, who refuses to offer Bahraam the Hunter shelter for the night because of his extreme parsimony. (Vol. 4)

Fartoos: Ruler of Chaghan and ally of Afraasiyaab. Killed by Fariborz, son of Kaavoos, in the great war. (Vols. 2-3)

Fazl: Son of Ahmad, or Abbas Fazl bin Ahmad; minister of Sultan Mahmoud during the time of Ferdowsi. (Vol. 3)

Fereydoon: Sixth king and son of Aabteen and Faraanak; father of Salm, Toor, and Iraj; great-grandfather of Manoochehr. Dies of old age. (Vol. 1)

Filghoos: Caesar of Rum and father of Nahid, who weds King Daaraab. (Vol. 3)

Five Chambermaids: Rudaabeh's servants. (Vol. 1)

Foor: Leader of the Indian army of Sindh. (Vol. 3)

Foorood: Son of Siaavosh and Jarireh (Piran's daughter). Killed by Bijan. (Vol. 2)

Fooroohal: Iranian warrior in Kay Khosrow's army. (Vol. 3)

Gao: Son of the Indian ruler Jemhoor. (Vol. 4)

Gargooy: Iranian warrior in King Goshtaasp's army. (Vol. 3)

Garmail: With brother Armail, a cook in Zahaak's kitchen. (Vol. 1)

Garooy: Son of Zerreh, descendant of Toor, and Tooranian warrior responsible for Siaavosh's death. Killed at the order of Kay Khosrow. (Vols. 2-3)

Garshaasp: Son of Zu and tenth King of Iran who rules for nine years.

(Vol. 1)

Garshaasp: Son of Nariman and father of Saam and Borzeen; warrior in Manoochehr's army. (Vol. 2)

Garshaasp: Warrior in King Shahpoor's army. (Vol. 4)

Garsivan: Tooranian warrior. (Vol. 3)

Garsivaz: Pashang's son and Afraasiyaab's brother, responsible for Siaavosh's death; father of Andariman, Arjaasp, Biderafsh, and Kohram. Killed at the order of Kay Khosrow. (Vols. 1-3)

Garukhan: A family that supports Kay Khosrow in his great battle against Afraasiyaab. (Vol. 3)

Garzam: Tooranian warrior in Afraasiyaab's army. Killed by Giv. (Vol. 1)

Ghaaloos: Rumi emissary and advisor of the Caesar. (Vol. 3)

Ghaaran: Son of Kaaveh; brother of Kashvaad; Iranian warrior and chief. (Vols. 1-3)

Ghaaran: Ruler of eastern lands and ally of Kay Khosrow in the great battle against Afraasiyaab. (Vol. 3)

Ghaaran: Son of Goshasp, warrior under the rule of Yazdegerd. (Vol. 4)

Ghaaran: Son of Borzmehr warrior under the reign of Bahraam the Hunter. (Vol. 4)

Ghabtoon: King of Egypt during the time of Eskandar. (Vol. 3)

Gharakhan: Tooranian warrior who serves Afraasiyaab. (Vol. 3)

Gharakhan: Army commander under the rule of Kesra Anushiravan. (Vol. 4)

Ghatfar: Hephthalite king. (Vol. 4)

Gheyssian: Or Ghassanids; Arab tribe that resided in Yemen. (Vol. 4)

Ghobaad: Son of Kashvaad (son of Kaaveh); Iranian warrior in Manoochehr's army; not to be confused with Kay Ghobaad. Killed by Baarmaan. (Vol. 1)

Ghobaad: Son of King Pirooz and brother of Balaash and Jaamaasp; he rules for forty years after his brother Balaash is cast aside by Soof-raay. (Vol. 4)

Gholoon: Tooranian warrior in the army of Afraasiyaab. Killed by Rostam. (Vol. 1)

Ghool: Name meaning giant; witch defeated by Esfandiar in the fourth stage of his quest. (Vol. 3)

Ghorcheh: Tooranian warrior in the army of Afraasiyaab. (Vol. 2)

Giv: Son of Goodarz, grandson of Kashvaad, husband of Baanoogo-shasp, and father of Bijan and Goraazeh; Iranian leader and warrior who serves under Kay Kaavoos and Kay Khosrow. Loses his life in the blizzard after Kay Khosrow disappears. (Vols. 1-3)

Gojdaham: Iranian warrior, defender of the White Castle, and father of
Gostaham, Gordaafareed, and Hojir's wife. (Vols. 1-3)

Golbaad: Tooranian warrior killed by Zaal. (Vol. 1)

Golbaad: Tooranian warrior and leader in the army of Afraasiyaab. (Vol. 2-3)

Golgoon: Goodarz's horse. (Vol. 2)

Golgoon: Lohraasp's horse. (Vol. 3)

Golgoon: Bahraam the Hunter's horse. (Vol. 4)

Golnaar: Advisor and treasurer of King Ardavan who falls in love with Ardeshir Babakan. (Vol. 4)

Golrang: Fereydoon's horse. (Vol. 1)

Golrang: Fariborz's horse. (Vol. 2)

Golshahr: Piran's wife and mother of Jarireh. (Vol. 2)

Goodarz: Iranian leader who serves under Kay Kaavoos, Kay Khosrow, and Lohraasp; son of Kashvaad (son of Kaaveh); has 78 sons and grandsons. (Vols. 1-3)

Goodarz: Third Ashkanian king. (Vol. 4)

Gooshbastar: Strange and hairy man Eskandar encounters on his way to Babel. (Vol. 3)

Goraazeh: Son of Giv (son of Goodarz); Iranian warrior under the rules of Kay Kaavoos and Kay Khosrow. (Vols. 1-3)

Gorazm: Iranian warrior of Kianian lineage in the army of Goshtaasp. Killed by King Arjaasp's troops. (Vol. 3)

Gordaafareed: Iranian female warrior who fights with Sohraab; daughter of Gojdaham (of the family of Goodarz). (Vol. 1)

Gorgeen: Son of Milaad and Iranian warrior in the armies of Kay Kaavoos and Kay Khosrow. (Vols. 1-3)

Gorgsaar: Commander of King Arjaasp's host. Captured and later killed by Esfandiar. (Vol. 3)

Goshasp: Warrior in Kesra Anushiravan's host. (Vol. 4)

Goshasp: Wise man and scribe under the rule of Yazdegerd and Bahraam the Hunter; father of Ghaaran. (Vol. 4)

Goshtaasp: Son of Lohraasp, King of Iran; marries Katayoon, daughter of the Rumi Caesar; father of Esfandiar, Shiroo, Nivezaar, Shiddasp, Farshidvard, and Behaafarid; conceals his identity behind the name Farrokhzaad in Rum. (Vol. 3)

Gostaham: Son of Nozar; brother of Tous (different from Gostaham, son of Gojdaham). (Vols. 1-3)

Gostaham: Young son of Gojdaham and brother of Gordaafareed (different from the son of Nozar). (Vols. 1-3)

Gostaham: Iranian warrior under the reigns of Yazdegerd and Khosrow and vizier to Bahraam the Hunter. (Vol. 4)

Gostaham: A wise man and hero during the rule of King Hormozd who is imprisoned with Bandooy by the king. He and Bandooy rebel against the crown and blind King Hormozd.(Vol. 4)

Gueraami: Son of Jaamaasp, Goshtaasp's minister. Killed by Arjaasp's troops. (Vol. 3)

Gurch: Afraasiyaab's fifth son and Tooranian leader. (Vol. 3)

Haaroot: Angel who along with the fairy Maaroot comes to earth to teach spells. They lose access to heaven because of their sins and are imprisoned in Babel. (Vol. 2)

Haftvaad: A resident of Kojaran who has seven sons and one daughter. Killed by Ardeshir. (Vol. 4)

Haftvaad's daughter: Discovers the worm that helps her spin more threads. (Vol. 4)

Haftvaad's worm: Magical worm. Killed by Ardeshir. (Vol. 4)

Hephthalites: Residents of a region in central Asia during the fifth to the eighth centuries CE. (Vol. 4)

Heshoo: Rumi guardian of the shores. (Vol. 3)

Hirbad: Sudaabeh's servant. (Vol. 2)

Hojir: Son of Goodarz; Iranian warrior and Gojdaham's son-in-law. (Vols. 1-3)

Homa: Large and powerful bird in Persian mythology, symbol of happiness; similar to the griffin or the phoenix. (Vols. 1-3)

Homay: King Bahman's daughter, sister of Ardeshir/Sassan, also called Chehrzaad; marries her father, Bahman, and they have a son, Daaraab; upon Bahman's death, she rules as queen for thirty-two years. (Vol. 3)

Homay: A wise emissary who takes a letter to the Tarkhan of Chin under the rule of Bahraam the Hunter. (Vol. 4)

Hoom: A devout descendant of Fereydoon who lives humbly as a hermit in a mountainous cave. (Vol. 3)

Hoomaan: Tooranian leader, son of Viseh (son of Zaadsham). Killed by Bijan. (Vols. 1-3)

Hooshang: Second King of Iran and son of Siaamak who rules for forty years. (Vol. 1)

Hooshdeev: Malicious Tooranian warrior under the command of King Arjaasp. (Vol. 3)

Hormoz: Son of Yazdegerd (son of Bahraam the Hunter) and brother of Pirooz; Sassanian king who rules for one year. Falls into a ditch and dies. (Vol. 4)

Hormozd: Son of Khorraad and warrior in the army of Kesra Anushiravan. (Vol. 4)

Hormozd: Son of King Kesra Anushiravan. (Vol. 4)

Hoshyar: Wise man from Pars and astrologer at the court of Yazdegerd. (Vol. 4)

Illa: Unclear whether he is Afraasiyaab's son or grandson; Tooranian warrior. (Vol. 3)

Iraj: Youngest son of Fereydoon and Arnavaaz; brother of Salm and Toor; grandfather of Manoochehr. Killed by his brothers. (Vol. 1)

Iraj: Ruler of Kabol and ally of Kay Khosrow in the great battle against Afraasiyaab. (Vol. 3)

Israfil: One of the four angels equivalent to Raphael of Uriel; angel of music. (Vol. 3)

Jaamaasp: Astrologer and guide to Goshtaasp. (Vol. 3)

Jaamaasp: Younger brother of Sassanian King Ghobaad. (Vol. 4)

Jahn: Tooranian warrior and Afraasiyaab's son and advisor. Overthrown by Rostam in Gang but survives and is offered the rulership of Tooran-Zamin by Kay Khosrow, who forgives him. (Vols. 2-3)

Jamsheed: Son of Tahmures and fourth King of Iran who rules for 700 years. Killed by Zahaak. (Vol. 1)

Jandal: A wise envoy sent by Fereydoon to find three sisters to marry Toor, Salm, and Iraj. (Vol. 1)

Janoosyar: Vizier and treasurer of King Dara who conspires with Maahiar to kill the king. Killed by Eskandar. (Vol. 3)

Janus: Brother of the Caesar during King Shahpoor's rule. Defeated in war by Shahpoor. (Vol. 4)

Jaranjas: Tooranian leader who fights for Afraasiyaab in the great war. (Vol. 3)

Jarireh: Siaavosh's wife and Foorood's mother; eldest daughter of Piran. (Vol. 2)

Javanooy: Persian emissary and Bahraam the Hunter's treasurer. (Vol. 4)

Jemhoor: Indian ruler under the reign of Kesra Anushiravan and father of Gao. (Vol. 4)

Jooyaa: A warrior leader in the army of the King of Mazandaran. Killed by Rostam. (Vol. 1)

Kaafoor: "Man-eater" Tooranian who dwells in the city of Bidaad. Killed by Rostam. (Vol. 2)

Kaakooleh: Descendant of Toor and Tooranian warrior. (Vol. 3)

Kaakooy: Descendant of Zahaak who battles Manoochehr. Killed by Manoochehr. (Vol. 1)

Kaaloo: Tooranian warrior in the army of Afraasiyaab. (Vol. 2)

Kaamoos: Ruler of Kushan and Afraasiyaab's ally in war. Killed by Rostam. (Vol. 2)

Kaaveh: Father of Kashvaad and Ghaaran; blacksmith who leads the rebellion against Zahaak. (Vol. 1)

Kaboodeh: Servant of Tajov, ruler of Gorooguerd. Killed by Bahraam. (Vol. 2)

Kahaar: From Kahan, an ally of Afraasiyaab. Killed by Rostam. (Vol. 2)

Kahtan: Conqueror of the land of Yemen. (Vol. 3)

Kalaahoor: Warrior rider in the army of the King of Mazandaran. (Vol. 1)

Karkoo: Warrior and ally of Afraasiyaab. (Vol. 2)

Karkooy: Salm's grandson and a relative of Zahaak on his mother's side. Killed by Saam. (Vol. 1)

Karookhan: Tooranian warrior in Afraasiyaab's army and relative of Viseh; Afraasiyaab's minister. (Vol. 1)

Karookhan: Afraasiyaab's eldest son and Tooranian leader. (Vol. 3)

Kashvaad: Son of Kaaveh and brother of Ghaaran; father of Ghobaad, Garshaasp, and Goodarz; Iranian warrior and leader. (Vols. 1-2)

Katayoon: Daughter of the Rumi Caesar; marries Goshtaasp, future King of Iran, and gives birth to their son, Esfandiar. (Vol. 3)

Katib: Father of Nasr, ruler of Mecca at the time of Eskandar's visit. (Vol. 3)

Kay Aarash: Son of Kay Ghobaad. (Vols. 1-2)

Kay Aarmin: Son of Kay Ghobaad. (Vol. 1)

Kay Ghobaad: Descendant of Fereydoon and eleventh King of Iran who rules for one hundred years; father to four sons: Kay Kaavoos, Kay Aarash, Kay Pashin, and Kay Aarmin. (Vol. 1)

Kay Kaavoos: Son of Kay Ghobaad and twelfth King of Iran who rules for 150 years. (Vols. 1-3)

Kay Khosrow: Son of Siaavosh and Faranguis, and grandson of Kay Kaavoos and Afraasiyaab; thirteenth King of Iran. (Vols. 1-3)

Kay Pashin: Son of Kay Ghobaad. (Vols. 1-2)

Kayvan: A learned man in charge of the accounts under the rule of Bahraam the Hunter. (Vol. 4)

Kebord: Tooranian warrior. (Vol. 3)

Kebrooy: A heavy drinker of wine under the rule of Bahraam the Hunter. Killed by a crow. (Vol. 4)

Kehila: Tooranian warrior. Killed by Manoochehr in the great war. (Vol. 3)

Keid: Indian King of Ghennooj. (Vols. 3-4)

Kesra Anushiravan: Son of Sassanian King Ghobaad and the daughter of a landowner, descendant of Fereydoon. He is named Anushiravan upon his ascent to the throne and rules for forty-eight years. (Vol. 4)

Ketmaareh: Iranian warrior and son of Ghaaran. (Vol. 3)

Keydafeh: Queen of Andalusia. (Vol. 3)

Keydroosh: Son of Keydafeh and son-in-law of King Faryan; brother of Teynoosh. (Vol. 3)

Khashaash: Important warrior in King Arjaasp's army. (Vol. 3)

Khazar: Semi-nomadic person from the land of Khazaria. (Vol. 3)

Khazarvan: Tooranian warrior in the army of Afraasiyaab. Killed by Zaal. (Vol. 1)

Khazarvan: Leader under the reign of Bahraam the Hunter. (Vol. 4)

Khezr: Believed to have been a messenger and prophet, guardian of the sea. (Vol. 3)

Khojabr: Tooranian warrior in the army of Afraasiyaab. (Vol. 1)

Khonjast: From Oman, supporter of Khosrow Parviz. (Vol. 4)

Khorraad: Iranian warrior in the army of Kay Kaavoos. (Vols. 1-3)

Khoshnavaz: Son of the Tarkhan under the rule of King Pirooz. (Vol. 4)

Khosrow: Descendant of Kay Pashin; placed on the Sassanian throne as king after the death of Yazdegerd. (Vol. 4)

Khosrow Parviz: Son of Hormozd (son of Kesra Anushiravan) and

Sassanian king who rules for thirty-eight years. (Vol. 4)

Khozaa: Descendant of Abraham and leader of Mecca; Eskandar executes him and his entire family. (Vol. 3)

Khuzan: Ruler of the land of Pars and Iranian warrior leader who fights alongside Kay Khosrow. (Vol. 3)

Kiaanoosh: Fereydoon's brother. (Vol. 1)

King Faryan: Ruler of a fortified city on some border between Egypt and Spain, and father-in-law of Keydroosh, Keydafeh's son. (Vol. 3)

King Firooz: Descendant of Kay Ghobaad and ruler of Gharchehgan; ally of Kay Khosrow in the great battle against Afraasiyaab. (Vol. 3)

King of Alaanan: Ruler of a region in northwestern Iran. (Vol. 4)

King of Cashmere: Ally of Shangal, King of India. (Vol. 4)

King of Chaghan: Refers to the King of Hephthalites. (Vol. 4)

King of Chegel: Warrior leader in King Arjaasp's army. (Vol. 3)

King of Egypt: Ally of the King of Haamaavaran. Killed by Zavaareh in the battle with the three nations. (Vol. 1)

King of Guran: Ally of Kay Khosrow in the great battle against Afraasiyaab. (Vol. 3)

King of Haamaavaran: Father of Sudaabeh, wife of Kay Kaavoos. Killed by Rostam to save Kay Kaavoos. (Vol. 2)

King of Jandal: Ally of Shangal, King of India. (Vol. 4)

King of Kabol: Father-in-law of Shaghaad, Zaal's son. Killed by Faraamarz, Rostam's son. (Vol. 3)

King of Kabol: Ally of Shangal, King of India. (Vol. 4)

King of Kerman: Ally of Kay Khosrow in the great battle against Afraasiyaab. (Vol. 3)

King of Khotan: Afraasiyaab's ally in war. (Vol. 3)

King of Khuzan: Ally of Kay Khosrow in the great battle against Afraasiyaab. (Vol. 3)

King of Mazandaran: Ruler of a kingdom of deevs who captures Kay Kaavoos and is then killed in Rostam's epic seven-stage quest. (Vol. 1)

King of Mokran: Afraasiyaab's ally in the great war. Killed by Tokhaar and Tous. (Vol. 3)

King of Moultan: Ally of Shangal, King of India. (Vol. 4)

King of Rus: King of Russia. (Vol. 3)

King of Sandal: Ally of Shangal, King of India. (Vol. 4)

King of Shaam: King of Syria and ally of the King of Haamaavaran. Captured by Rostam in the battle with three nations (Vol. 1)

King of Sindh: Ally of Afraasiyaab. (Vol. 2)

King of Sindh: Ally of Shangal, King of India. (Vol. 4)

Kiumars: First King of Iran, who rules from a mountaintop for fifty years. (Vol. 1)

Kohram: Tooranian warrior. Killed by Barteh in the battle of the heroes. (Vols. 2-3)

Kohram: Brother of King Arjaasp, Andariman, and Biderafsh. Killed by Shiddasp, son of Goshtaasp. (Vol. 3)

Kohram: King Arjaasp's eldest son. Killed by Esfandiar. (Vol. 3)

Kolbaad: Son of Viseh; Tooranian warrior. Killed by Fariborz, son of Kaavoos, in the battle of the heroes. (Vol. 3)

Konaarang Deev: Guardian of a rocky, desolate place on the way to the White Deev's dwelling. (Vol. 1)

Kondor: From the land of Saghlaab and an ally of Afraasiyaab in war; warrior in the army of King Arjaasp. (Vols. 2-3)

Kooh: Assumed name used by Hoomaan to trick Rostam; son of Boossepaas. (Vol. 2)

Kundrow: Zahaak's minister. (Vol. 1)

Lahaak: Son of Viseh (son of Zaadsham); Tooranian warrior and leader in the army of Afraasiyaab. He and his brother Farshidvard are killed by Gostaham. (Vols. 2-3)

Lambak: Water carrier and kind man who lives under the rule of Bahraam the Hunter. (Vol. 4)

Laundryman: Finds Daaraab, son of Homay and Bahman, floating in a box on the river and raises him with his wife. (Vol. 3)

Lohraasp: Iranian warrior in Kay Khosrow's army who is named King of Iran by Kay Khosrow; son of Arvand Shah (descendant of Kay Pashin, descendant of Kay Ghobaad), and father of Goshtaasp and Zarir. Killed by Arjaasp's troops. (Vol. 3)

Maah Aafareed: One of Iraj's wives and Manoochehr's grandmother. (Vol. 1)

Maah Aafareed: First daughter of the wealthy Barzeen; sister of Faraanak and Shambeleed; skilled singer. The three sisters wed Bahraam the Hunter. (Vol. 4)

Maah-e Aazaadeh Khooy: Daughter of Sarv, King of Yemen, and wife of Toor, son of Fereydoon. (Vol. 1)

Maahiar: Vizier and advisor of King Dara who conspires with Janoosyar to kill the king. Killed by Eskandar. (Vol. 3)

Maahiar: An older nobleman at the court of Bahraam the Hunter. (Vol. 4)

Maahiar: A jeweler whose daughter, Arezoo, marries Bahraam the Hunter. (Vol. 4)

Maakh: A border guard living in Herat during the time of Fereydoon with knowledge of the reign of Hormozd, son of Kesra Anushiravan. (Vol. 4)

Maay: Brother of the Indian ruler Jemhoor who resides in Dambar. He succeeds his late brother on the throne and marries Jemhoor's widow. They have a son named Talhand. (Vol. 4)

Mahbood: Kesra Anushiravan's vizier; father of two sons. His wife and two sons are responsible for the king's meals. His entire family is killed after they are falsely accused of attempting to poison the king. (Vol. 4)

Malekeh: Daughter of Nooshah, Nersi's daughter, and the Arab Taaer. (Vol. 4)

Mamoon: Or al-Mamun (786-833), the seventh Abbasid caliph. (Vol. 4)

Mani: Iranian prophet who wrote the holy book of Manichaeism, *Arjang,* also known as *The Book of Pictures.* He preached throughout the land of Persia in the third century BCE. He appears at King Shahpoor's court. Historical accounts vary on the timeline of his life and on the circumstances of his death, but in *The Shahnameh,* he is skinned and killed at the order of King Shahpoor. (Vols. 3-4)

Manijeh: Afraasiyaab's daughter and Bijan's wife. (Vol. 1)

Manoochehr: Seventh King of Iran and grandson of Iraj, who rules for 120 years; son of Pashang and *Nameless.* (Vol. 1)

Manoochehr: Son of Aarash and warrior from Khorasan; ally of Kay Khosrow. (Vol. 3)

Manooshan: Ruler of the land of Pars and Iranian warrior leader who fights alongside Kay Khosrow. (Vol. 3)

Manshoor: Ruler of Chin and ally of Afraasiyaab. (Vol. 2)

Mardaas: Zahaak's father, ruler in Mesopotamia. Killed by Eblis. (Vol. 1)

Mardooy: Tooranian warrior in the army of Tajov. (Vol. 2)

Mardooy: The treasurer of Kesra Anushiravan. (Vol. 4)

Mazdak: Physician under the rule of Sassanian King Ghobaad who becomes the royal vizier and imposes his own beliefs on the king and his subjects. Hanged by Kesra, son of Ghobaad, along with all his followers. (Vol. 4)

Mehraab: Ruler of Kabol and father of Rudaabeh; descendant of Zahaak. (Vols. 1-2)

Mehraas: King of Khazaria. (Vol. 3)

Mehraas: Envoy serving the Rumi Caesar and intermediary with Kesra Anushiravan. (Vol. 4)

Mehrak: Son of Nooshzaad. Killed by Ardeshir. (Vol. 4)

Mehrak's daughter: Marries Shahpoor, son of Ardeshir. They have a son named Ormazd. (Vol. 4)

Mehran: Wise man with deep foresight who advises the Indian Keid. (Vol. 3)

Mehran: The treasurer of King Yazdegerd, father of Bahraam. (Vol. 4)

Mehran: Warrior in the army of Kesra Anushiravan. (Vol. 4)

Mehran: Scribe in the service of King Hormozd who accompanies Bahraam Choobineh to war against King Saaveh. (Vol. 4)

Mehrbandad: A farmer under the rule of Bahraam the Hunter. (Vol. 4)

Mehr Aazar: Resident of Pars and supporter of Kesra under the rule of Sassanian King Ghobaad. (Vol. 4)

Mehr Barzeen: Son of Khorraad; leader under the reign of Bahraam the Hunter. (Vol. 4)

Mehrnoosh: Son of Esfandiar and brother of Bahman, Aazarafrooz, and Nooshaazar. Killed by Faraamarz. (Vol. 3)

Mehr Pirooz: Son of Behzaad; leader under the reign of Bahraam the Hunter. (Vol. 4)

Milaad: Father of Gorgeen and Iranian hero in the army of Kay Kaavoos and Kay Khosrow. (Vols. 1-2)

Milaad: Warrior under the rule of Yazdegerd. (Vol. 4)

Mirin: Wealthy Rumi descendant of Salm who marries the second daughter of the Caesar. (Vol. 3)

Monzer: King of Yemen and father of Noman; comes from the land of Arabia to teach King Yazdegerd's son, Bahraam. (Vol. 4)

Moolookeh Tavayef: Meaning "King of Tribes"; name assigned to any minor ruler. They held power for a period of two hundred years after the death of Eskandar. (Vols. 3-4)

Moshkenek: One of the four miller's daughters who are wedded to Bahraam the Hunter; name meaning partridge. (Vol. 4)

Moshknaz: One of the four miller's daughters who are wedded to Bahraam the Hunter; name meaning pure musk. (Vol. 4)

Mother of Siaavosh: Descendant of Fereydoon and granddaughter of Garsivaz. (Vol. 2)

Nahel: Tooranian warrior. (Vol. 2)

Nahid: Daughter of Filghoos, Caesar of Rum; wife of King Daaraab and mother of Eskandar. (Vol. 3)

Nameless: Daughter of Maah Aafareed and Iraj; granddaughter of Fereydoon; wife of Pashang, mother of Manoochehr. Ferdowsi does not assign her a name. (Vol. 1)

Namkhaast: Evil sorcerer at the court of King Arjaasp. (Vol. 3)

Nariman: Great Iranian warrior in the army of Manoochehr; Saam's father and Zaal's grandfather. (Vols. 1-2)

Nasr: Son of Katib; ruler of Mecca at the time of Eskandar's visit; he is a descendant of Abraham. (Vol. 3)

Nasr, Amir: Samanid King who ruled from 865 to 892. (Vol. 4)

Nastaar: Guardian of the Rumi Caesar's stables. (Vol. 3)

Nastihan: Tooranian warrior; son of Viseh (son of Zaadsham) and brother of Piran, Pilsam, Hoomaan, Baarmaan, and Kolbaad. Killed by Bijan. (Vols. 2-3)

Nastooh: Son of Goodarz; an Iranian warrior. (Vols. 2-3)

Nastooh: Tooranian commander who fights for Afraasiyaab in the great war. (Vol. 3)

Nastoor: Son of Zarir, son of Lohraasp; King Goshtaasp grants him his daughter's hand. (Vol. 3)

Nazyab: One of the four miller's daughters who are wedded to Bahraam the Hunter; name meaning flirtatious. (Vol. 4)

Nersi: Son of Bahraam Bahraamian; and Sassanian king who rules for seventy years, then dies, surrendering the throne to his son Ormazd. (Vol. 4)

Nersi: Bahraam the Hunter's brother; Bahraam offers him the land of Khorasan to rule. (Vol. 4)

Nivezaar: Son of King Goshtaasp. Killed by Arjaasp's troops. (Vol. 3)

Nooshaazar: Esfandiar's son; his brothers are Bahman, Mehrnoosh, and Aazarafrooz. Killed by Zavaareh. (Vol. 3)

Nooshah: The daughter of Nersi who is abducted by Taaer. They have a daughter he names Malekeh. (Vol. 4)

Nooshzaad: Of Kianian lineage and father of Mehrak. (Vol. 4)

Nooshzaad: Son of Kesra Anushiravan and his Christian wife. Killed in a battle to usurp his father's throne. (Vol. 4)

Nozar: Son of Manoochehr and eighth King of Iran who rules for seven years; father of Tous and Gostaham. Beheaded by Afraasiyaab. (Vol. 1)

Noman: Son of Monzer, King of Yemen; comes from the land of Arabia with his father to teach King Yazdegerd's son, Bahraam. (Vol. 4)

Ormazd: Or Hormozd, *Avesta* name for Ahura Mazda, meaning creator. In the ancient Persian solar calendar, each day had the name of a deity instead of a number. Ormazd represented the first day of the month. Each name evoked a concept. The division then was not based on a seven-day week but on a thirty-day month.

Ormazd: Sixth Ashkanian king. (Vol. 4)

Ormazd: Son of Shahpoor and Mehrak's daughter; third Sassanian king. (Vol. 4)

Ormazd: Son of Nersi (son of Bahraam Bahraamian); Sassanian king who rules for nine years. Father of Shahpoor. (Vol. 4)

Ormazd: Bahraam the Hunter's vizier and counselor. (Vol. 4)

Ostaad: Son of Barzeen and leader of Kesra Anushiravan's right wing. (Vol. 4)

Ostaay: From Gorgan, supporter of Khosrow Parviz. (Vol. 4)

Ostaghila: Ally of Afraasiyaab in the great battle. (Vol. 3)

Palaashan: Tooranian warrior and Afraasiyaab's army leader. Killed by Bijan. (Vol. 2)

Pashang: Iranian warrior from the seed of Jamsheed; Fereydoon's nephew (his brother's son), selected by Fereydoon to marry Fereydoon's *Nameless* granddaughter; father of Manoochehr. (Vol. 1)

Pashang: Son of Zaadsham and father of Aghriras, Afraasiyaab, Garsivaz, Andariman, Sepahram, and Kohram. (Vols. 1-3)

Pashootan: Son of Goshtaasp and Katayoon, and brother and advisor of Esfandiar. King Bahman's vizier. (Vol. 3)

Philosopher: One of the wonders of the Indian Keid who is given to Eskandar as a tribute. (Vol. 3)

Physician: One of the wonders of the Indian Keid who is given to Eskandar. (Vol. 3)

Pilsam: Son of Viseh (son of Zaadsham) and brother of Piran; Tooranian army leader. Killed by Rostam. (Vols. 1-2)

Piran: Son of Viseh (son of Zaadsham) and brother of Pilsam, Hoomaan, Nastihan, Baarmaan, and Kolbaad; Tooranian army leader. Killed by Goodarz in the battle of the heroes. (Vols. 1-3)

Pirooz: Rider from Gorzban and warrior under the rule of Yazdegerd. (Vol. 4)

Pirooz: Son of Yazdegerd (son of Bahraam the Hunter) and brother of Hormoz; father of Balaash, Ghobaad, and Jaamaasp; Sassanian king for eleven years. Falls into a ditch and dies in the battle with Khoshnavaz. (Vol. 4)

Pirooz: From Kerman, supporter of Khosrow Parviz. (Vol. 4)

Poolaad: Of Ghondi; ruler deev in the army of Mazandaran with hooves as feet. Killed by Rostam. (Vol. 1)

Poolaad: Tooranian warrior. (Vols. 2)

Poolaadvand: Fierce Tooranian warrior who dwells in the mountains of Chin. Killed by Rostam. (Vol. 2)

Pormaye: Cow that nurses Fereydoon. (Vol. 1)

Pormaye: Fereydoon's brother; same name as the cow that nursed Fereydoon. (Vol. 1)

Raam Barzeen: Governor of Zabolestan under the reign of Bahraam the Hunter, and governor of Mada'in under the rule of Kesra Anushiravan. (Vol. 4)

Rajah: Title for an Indian king, prince, or local ruler. (Vol. 4)

Rakhsh: Rostam's horse. Killed by Shaghaad, Rostam's brother. (Vols. 1-3)

Rashnavaad: Warrior leader in the army of Queen Homay. (Vol. 3)

Rezvan: Keeper of paradise. (Vol. 2)

Rivniz: Tous's son-in-law and brother-in-law to Zarasp; Iranian warrior who has forty beautiful sisters. Killed by Foorood. (Vol. 2)

Rivniz: Son of Fariborz and grandson of Kaavoos. Killed by the Tooranians under Kaavoos's reign. (Vol. 2)

Rivniz: Son of Zarasp and Iranian warrior, "worshipper of Aazargoshasp." (Vols. 2-3)

Rohaam: Son of Goodarz and brother of Giv, Bahraam, Hojir, and Shiddush; Iranian warrior under the rule of Kay Kaavoos and Kay Khosrow. (Vols. 1-3)

Rohaam: King of Gilan under the reign of Bahraam the Hunter. (Vol. 4)

Rooeen: Son of Piran (son of Viseh) and Tooranian warrior. Killed by

Bijan in the battle of the heroes. (Vols. 1-3)

Roozbeh: King Bahraam the Hunter's grand wise master. (Vol. 4)

Roshanak: Daughter of King Dara and Delarai, and wife of Eskandar; name of Eskandar's wife in Ferdowsi's legend; historically one of Alexander's wives was Roxana, a Bactrian princess, while his Persian wives were Stateira II, daughter of Stateira I and Darius III of Persia, and Parysatis II, daughter of Artaxerxes III of Persia. (Vol. 3)

Rostam: Iranian world hero and son of Zaal and Rudaabeh; marries Shahrbaanoo; father of Faraamarz and Baanoogoshasp. Killed by his brother Shaghaad. (Vols. 1-3)

Rudaabeh: Daughter of Mehraab and Sindokht; wife of Zaal and mother of Rostam. (Vols. 1-3)

Rudaki: Abu Abd Allah Ja'far ibn Muhammad Rudaki (859-940), the first great poet of the Persian language. (Vol. 4)

Saam: Iranian warrior and head of Manoochehr's army; Nariman's son and Zaal's father. (Vol. 1)

Saam: Nobleman and warrior after the death of Yazdegerd; a descendant of Kay Ghobaad. (Vol. 4)

Saam: From Shiraz, supporter of Khosrow Parviz. (Vol. 4)

Saaveh: Relative of Kaamoos and warrior ally of Afraasiyaab. Killed by Rostam. (Vol. 2)

Saaveh: Warrior in Esfandiar's army. (Vol. 3)

Saaveh, King: Turk ruler who challenges Sassanian King Hormozd and his host led by Bahraam Choobineh; father of the Emperor of Chin. Killed by Bahraam Choobineh. (Vol. 4)

Saabeh: Wise man at the court of Kesra Anushiravan. (Vol. 4)

Sabbaah: King of Yemen and ally of Kay Khosrow in the great battle against Afraasiyaab. (Vol. 3)

Saghil: Son of the Rumi Caesar, and brother of Katayoon. (Vol. 3)

Sahi: Daughter of Sarv, King of Yemen, and wife of Iraj, son of Fereydoon. (Vol. 1)

Salm: Son of Fereydoon and Shahrnaaz; brother of Toor and Iraj. (Vol. 1)

Samanid Dynasty: Ruled Iran from 819 to 999. (Vol. 3)

Samkanan: Warrior in the army of Kay Khosrow in the great battle; father of Aaveh. (Vol. 3)

Sanjeh: One of the deevs in the service of Mazandaran; guard of the mountain on the path to the White Deev. (Vol. 1)

Sarv: King of Yemen and father of the three maidens who marry Fereydoon's sons Toor, Salm, and Iraj. (Vol. 1)

Sassan: Named Ardeshir, son of King Bahman and brother of Homay / Chehrzaad; father of Sassan. (Vol. 3)

Sassan: Son of Sassan (son of Bahman). (Vol. 3)

Sassan: Son of Dara, flees Iran and goes to India, where he dies. He leaves behind a son named Sassan. (Vols. 3-4)

Sassan: Son of Sassan and descendant of Bahman / Ardeshir; becomes one of Babak's shepherds and marries Babak's daughter. They have a son named Ardeshir Babakan. (Vol. 4)

Sassanian Dynasty: Ruled Iran from 224 to 651. (Vols. 3-4)

Sepahram: Brother of Afraasiyaab and Tooranian leader. Killed by Hojir. (Vols. 2-3)

Sepinood: Daughter of Shangal, King of India, who weds Bahraam the Hunter when he travels disguised as an emissary. (Vol. 4)

Sevorg: Indian leader assigned to rule by Eskandar. (Vol. 3)

Shaavaran: Father of Zangueh. (Vols. 1-3)

Shabaahang: Farhaad's white horse. (Vol. 2)

Shabaahang: Bijan's horse. (Vol. 3)

Shabdeez: Mehraab's horse (Vol. 1)

Shabdeez: Ghobaad's horse (Vol. 1); Giv's horse (Vols. 1-2).

Shabdeez: Bahraam the Hunter's horse. (Vol. 4)

Shabrang: Bijan's horse. (Vol. 2)

Shadan: Son of Barzeen. (Vol. 4)

Shaghaad: Rostam's brother, born from Zaal and a musically inclined slave. Killed by Rostam. (Vol. 3)

Shahooy: Haftvaad's eldest son. Killed in the battle with Ardeshir. (Vol. 4)

Shahpoor: Iranian warrior who serves the kings from Fereydoon to Lohraasp. (Vols. 1-3)

Shahpoor: Second Ashkanian king. (Vol. 4)

Shahpoor: The son of Ardeshir and Ardavan's daughter; second Sassanian king; weds Mehrak's daughter with whom he has a son named Ormazd. (Vol. 4)

Shahpoor: Son of Ormazd, son of Nersi, and Sassanian king who rules for seventy years. The Arabs call him Zolaktaaf because he pierces his captives' shoulder blades. He marries his cousin, Malekeh, the daughter of Taaer the Arab, and his aunt Nooshah. (Vol. 4)

Shahpoor: Son of King Shahpoor who is too young to rule so his uncle Ardeshir is made regent of the Sassanian Dynasty. Once he matures, he rules for five years and four months. Killed by a canopy pole during a windstorm. (Vol. 4)

Shahpoor: Descendant of Mehrak and enemy of Soofraay under the rule of Ghobaad (son of Pirooz). (Vol. 4)

Shahrbaanoo: Giv's sister and Rostam's wife; mother of Faraamarz. (Vol. 2)

Shahrguir: Warrior who takes Keydroosh and his wife captive near Spain. (Vol. 3)

Shahrguir: Commander of Ardeshir's army. (Vol. 4)

Shahrnaaz: Daughter or sister of Jamsheed; concubine of Zahaak before she weds Fereydoon and gives birth to Salm and Toor. (Vol. 1)

Shahrooy: Wise man and servant of the crown who governs the world while Shahpoor, son of Ormazd, matures. (Vol. 4)

Shaknan: Iranian nobleman and warrior under the rule of Yazdegerd. (Vol. 4)

Shamaasaas: Tooranian warrior in the army of Afraasiyaab. Killed in battle by Ghaaran. (Vol. 1)

Shambeleed: Third daughter of the wealthy Barzeen; sister of Maah-Aafareed and Faraanak; skilled dancer. The three sisters wed Bahraam the Hunter. (Vol. 4)

Shammaakh: Ruler of Syria and ally of Kay Khosrow in the great battle against Afraasiyaab. (Vol. 3)

Shamiran: From Shakni, an ally of Afraasiyaab. (Vol. 2)

Shammas: Commander of the army of Nooshzaad, son of Kesra Anushiravan. (Vol. 4)

Shangal: From India, an ally of Afraasiyaab. Killed by Rostam. (Vol. 2)

Shangal: King of India and enemy of Bahraam the Hunter. (Vol. 4)

Shayban: An Arab tribe that resided in Iraq and the Persian Gulf region in pre-Islamic times. (Vol. 4)

Shemiran Shah: Ancestor of the Sassanians and of Bahraam the Hunter. (Vol. 4)

Shiddasp: Minister under the rule of Tahmures. (Vol. 1)

Shiddasp: Son of King Goshtaasp and brother of Ardeshir. Killed by Arjaasp's warrior. (Vol. 3)

Shiddeh: Also referred to as Pashang. Afraasiyaab's son and Tooranian leader who fights in the great war. Killed by Kay Khosrow. (Vols. 2-3)

Shiddush: Son of Goodarz (son of Kashvaad) and an Iranian warrior serving the kings from Manoochehr to Kay Khosrow. (Vols. 1-3)

Shirkhoon: Guide of Zabolestan in Zaal's retinue. (Vol. 3)

Shiroo: Son of King Goshtaasp. Killed by Arjaasp's troops. (Vol. 3)

Shirooy: Son of Bahraam and commander in the army of Kesra Anushiravan. (Vol. 4)

Shirui: Warrior in Toor's army. (Vol. 1)

Shiruye: Iranian warrior and general in Manoochehr's army. (Vol. 1)

Shiruye: Iranian warrior in Lohraasp's army and grandson of Giv. (Vol. 3)

Shirzad: Herald who serves Kesra Anushiravan. (Vol. 4)

Shitarakh: Tooranian warrior. (Vol. 2)

Shoaib: Taazian leader from the Arabian Peninsula from the lineage of Ghotaib. Killed by Daaraab's troops. (Vol. 3)

Shohreh: Warrior in Bahraam the Hunter's army who is appointed King of Tooran. (Vol. 4)

Siaamak: Son of Kiumars; father of Hooshang. (Vol. 1)

Siaamak: Tooranian warrior. Killed by Goraazeh in the battle of the heroes. (Vol. 3)

Siaavosh: Son of Iranian Kay Kaavoos and descendant of Tooranian Garsivaz. (Vol. 2)

Simah Borzeen: Friend of Bahraam Azarmahan who is deceived by him at the king's command. (Vol. 4)

Simorgh: Bird of knowledge that rescues and raises Zaal. (Vol. 2)

Sindokht: Mother of Rudaabeh and wife of Mehraab. (Vol. 1)

Sohraab: Son of Rostam and Tahmineh. Killed by Rostam. (Vol. 1)

Soofraay: Descendant of Ghaaran, from Shiraz; governor of Kabolestan, Bost, Ghaznein, and Zabolestan, who becomes the vizier of Balaash (youngest son of King Pirooz); father of Zarmehr. Executed at the order of King Ghobaad. (Vol. 4)

Sooroosh: Archangel able to hear and relay divine messages. (Vols. 1-3)

Sooroosh: Indian mystic and astrologer at the court of Yazdegerd. (Vol. 4)

Soossanek: One of the four miller's daughters who are wedded to Bahraam the Hunter; name meaning small lily. (Vol. 4)

Sootooh: Sorcerer in the service of King Arjaasp. (Vol. 3)

Sorkheh: Afraasiyaab's son and Tooranian leader. Killed at the order of Zavaareh. (Vol. 2)

Sudaabeh: Daughter of the King of Haamaavaran; wife of Kay Kaavoos. (Vols. 1-2)

Sultan Mahmoud, Abul Ghassem: Ghaznavid ruler of Iran (999-1030) during Ferdowsi's later years.

Taaer: Ghassanian king and Arab warrior from Syria who invades Iran and abducts Nooshah, Nersi's daughter. They have a daughter he names Malekeh. Killed by Shahpoor. (Vol. 4)

Taazi/Taazian: Bedouins or tribes living in the land of Arabia or Mesopotamia (between the Tigris and the Euphrates), also "field of warriors" or "field of spear-riders"; worshippers of the Black Stone or Kaaba, as given by the Prophet Muhammad; symbolic rather than cultural, national, or geographical.

Tabah: Tooranian warrior in King Arjaasp's host. (Vol. 3)

Tabaak: Ruler of the city of Jahrom and ally of Ardeshir; father to seven sons. (Vol. 4)

Tahmineh: Wife of Rostam and mother of Sohraab; daughter of the king of Samangan. (Vol. 1)

Tahmures: Son of Hooshang and third King of Iran; deev-binder who rules for thirty years. (Vol. 1)

Tajov: Ruler of Gorooguerd, a province of Tooran-Zamin; of Iranian lineage but also Afraasiyaab's son-in-law. (Vol. 2)

Talhand: Son of Maay, Indian ruler, and half-brother of Gao. (Vol. 4)

Taliman: Iranian warrior in Nozar's army (Vol. 1); ally of Kay Khosrow (Vol. 3).

Tarkhan of Chin: Title assigned to rulers of Chin, allies of Tooran-Zamin. (Vols. 2-4)

Tavaabeh: Name of a family of warriors loyal to Kay Khosrow, led by Barteh. (Vol. 2)

Teynoosh: The Rumi, was the Caesar's ambassador during the reign of Yazdegerd. (Vol. 4)

Tevorg: Sentinel who watches over Afraasiyaab's city. (Vol. 2)

Teynoosh: Son of Keydafeh and brother of Keydroosh. (Vol. 3)

Toghrol: A black bird offered to King Bahraam by the Emperor of Chin to assist in the hunt. (Vol. 4)

Tokhaar: Warrior in Foorood's army and Foorood's advisor. (Vol. 2)

Tokhaar: Ruler of Dahestan and leader in Kay Khosrow's army from the noble race of Vashmeh. (Vol. 3)

Toor: Son of Fereydoon and Shahrnaaz; brother of Salm and Iraj. Killed by Manoochehr. (Vol. 1)

Tous: Son of Nozar, brother of Gostaham, and commander of troops under Kay Khosrow; bearer of the Kaaviani banner and the golden boots. Loses his life in the blizzard. (Vols. 1-3)

Turks: The Turks of *The Shahnameh* are nomadic tribes moving through the lands east of Iran with no relation to today's Turkey, which sits west of Iran and which was established in the eleventh century upon the conquest of the Turks by the Byzantines. (Vols. 1-3)

Turkish boy: Servant of Zaal during his courtship with Rudaabeh. (Vol. 1)

Tuvarg: Tooranian warrior. (Vol. 3)

Ulaad: Landowner in the fifth stage of Rostam's epic quest. Ultimately, Rostam makes him ruler of Mazandaran. (Vol. 1)
Ulaad's guardian: Unnamed guardian of the field owned by Ulaad. (Vol. 1)

Varaazaad: King of Sepijaab and warrior who fights for Afraasiyaab. Killed by Faraamarz. (Vol. 2)

Vashmeh: Name of a family, led by Tokhaar, ruler of Dahestan, ally of Kay Khosrow in the great battle. (Vol. 3)

Viseh: Father of Piran, Pilsam, Nastihan, Kolbaad, Baarmaan, and Hoomaan; Tooranian army leader and Afraasiyaab's minister. (Vols. 1-2)

White Deev: Leader in Mazandaran. Killed by Rostam. (Vol. 1)

Wife of the laundryman: Raises Daaraab, son of Homay and Bahman, with her husband. (Vol. 3)

Witch: Woman who conspires with Sudaabeh to avow her innocence. (Vol. 2)

Yajooj and Majooj: Two tribes residing in Manchuria and causing mayhem across the neighboring lands.

Yazdan: Plural of Yzad (divine), encompasses all of divinity, Creator of all that is manifested, unmanifested, and all that is yet to come into existence.

Yazdegerd: Brother of Sassanian King Bahraam who rises to kingship and rules for thirty years; is referred to as Yazdegerd the Wicked. Killed by the white hippopotamus. (Vol. 4)

Yazdegerd: Son of Bahraam the Hunter, who reigns for eighteen years; father of Hormoz and Pirooz. (Vol. 4)

Yazdegerd: A scribe under the rule of Kesra Anushiravan. (Vol. 4)

Yzad: Singular of Yazdan, Divine Creator.

Zaadfarrokh: Illustrious lord and head of King Hormoz's stables (son of Kesra Anushiravan). (Vol. 4)

Zaadsham: Afraasiyaab's grandfather and Pashang's father. (Vols. 1-3)

Zaal: Saam's son; Rudaabeh's husband and Rostam's father; also called Dastan-e Zand by Simorgh and Zaal-e Zar by Saam; father of Shaghaad. (Vols. 1-3)

Zahaak: Son of Mardaas and fifth King of Iran, who rules for one thousand years. Captured by Fereydoon. (Vol. 1)

Zangaleh: Tooranian warrior. Killed by Fooroohal. (Vol. 3)

Zangueh: Son of Shaavaran; Iranian warrior under the rules of Kay Kaavoos and Kay Khosrow. (Vols. 1-3)

Zarasp: Son of King Manoochehr and brother of Nozar; Kay Khosrow's treasurer. (Vols. 1-3)

Zarasp: Son of Tous (son of Nozar) and brother-in-law of Rivniz. A warrior under the rule of Kay Khosrow. Killed at the hands of Foorood. (Vol. 2)

Zarir: Son of Lohraasp; brother of Goshtaasp. Killed by Biderafsh, Arjaasp's brother. (Vol. 3)

Zarmehr: Son of Soofraay who forgives Ghobaad for having killed his father. (Vol. 4)

Zartosht: Zoroaster or Zarathustra, Iranian prophet who lived in the sixth century BCE. (Vol. 3)

Zarvan: King Kesra Anushiravan's chamberlain and enemy of Mahbood. Killed after the king discovers that he conspired against Mahbood. (Vol. 4)

Zavaareh: Rostam's brother. Killed by Shaghaad. (Vols. 1-3)

Zerreh: Father of Garooy and Arjang; Tooranian warrior. (Vol. 2)

Zhendehrazm: Son of the King of Samangan and brother of Tahmineh; uncle of Sohraab. Killed by Rostam. (Vol. 1)

Zirak: A wise interpreter of Zahaak's dream of Fereydoon. (Vol. 1)

Zohir: Iranian warrior in the army of Kay Khosrow. (Vol. 3)

Zu: Son of Tahmaasp, descendant of Fereydoon; and ninth King of Iran, who rules for five years and dies at the age of 86. (Vol. 1)

THE KIANIAN KINGS: LINE OF SUCCESSION
From Kiumars to Kay Kaavoos

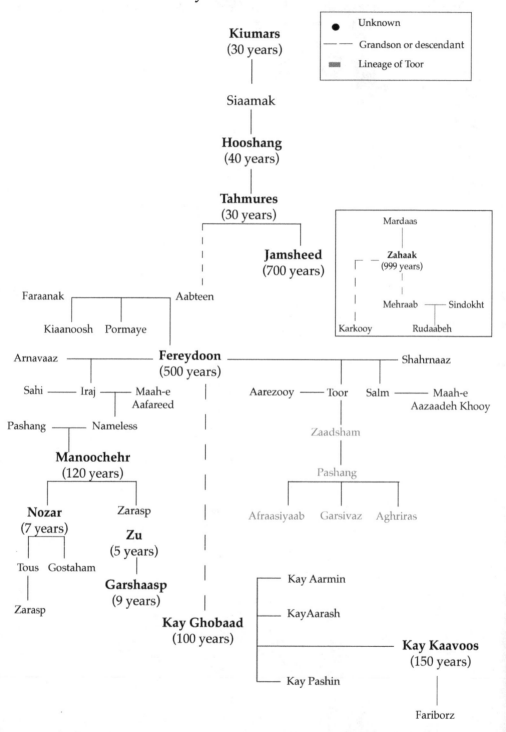

THE KIANIAN KINGS: LINE OF SUCCESSION
From Kay Khosrow to Eskandar

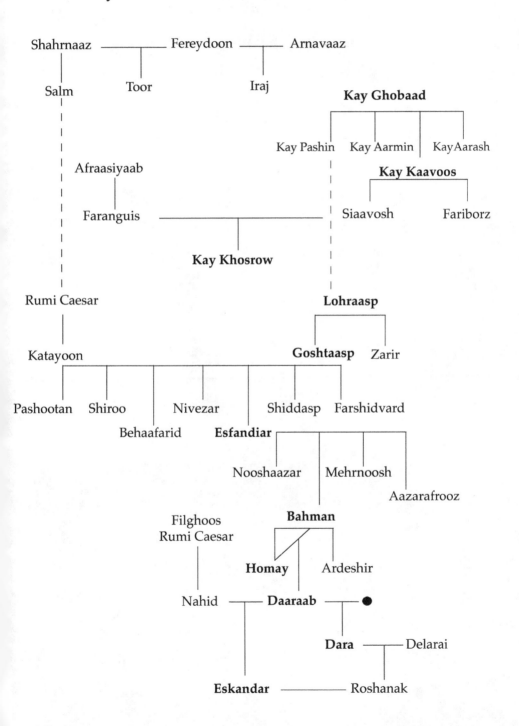

THE ASHKANIAN KINGS: LINE OF SUCCESSION
According to Ferdowsi

Moolookeh Tavayef

Ghobaad
|
|
|
|

Ashk

Shahpoor

Goodarz

Bijan

Nersi

Ormazd

Aarash

Bahraam

Ardavan
|
Bahman

THE SASSANIAN KINGS: LINE OF SUCCESSION
From Ardeshir Babakan to Yazdegerd the Wicked

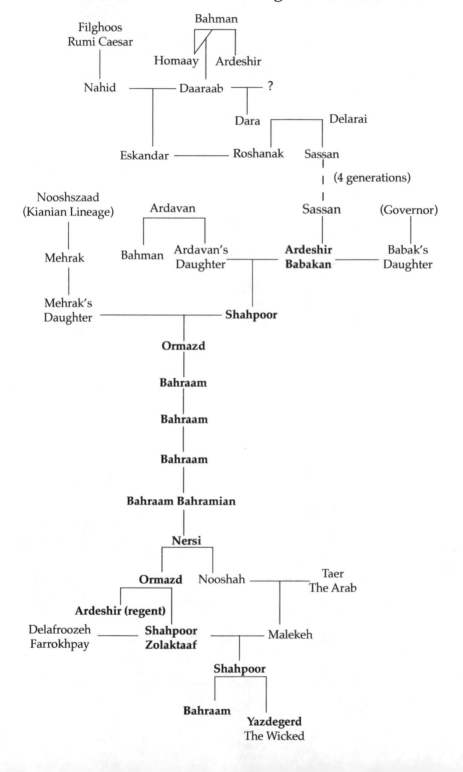

THE SASSANIAN KINGS: LINE OF SUCCESSION
From Yazdegerd the Wicked to Yazdegerd

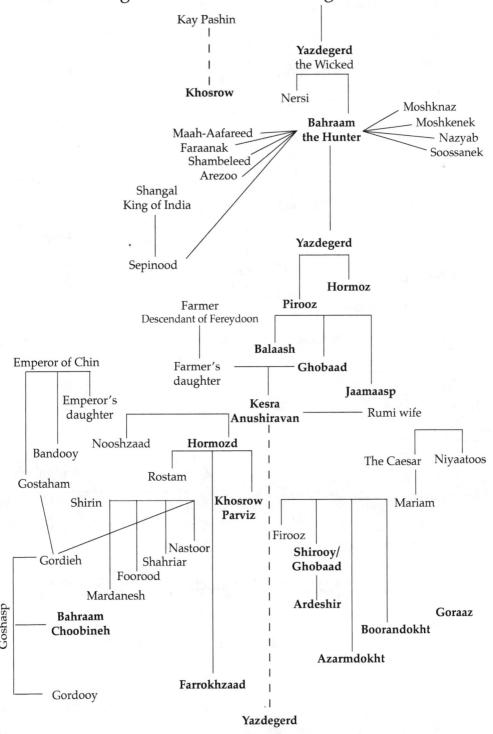

THE IRANIAN HEROES: LINE OF SUCCESSION
Kianian Period

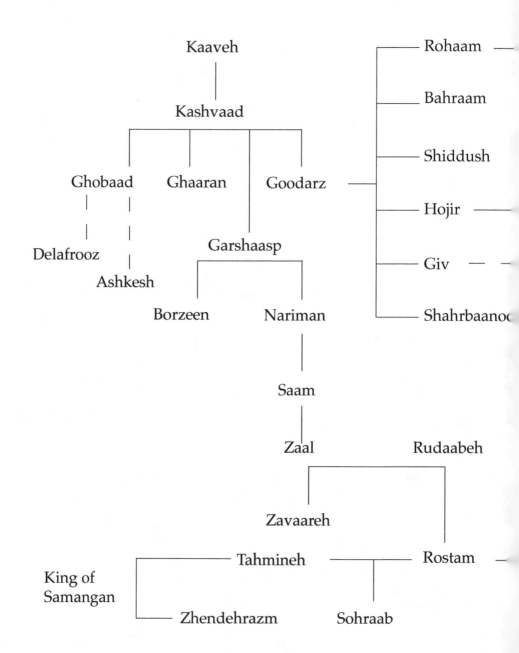

 Farhaad

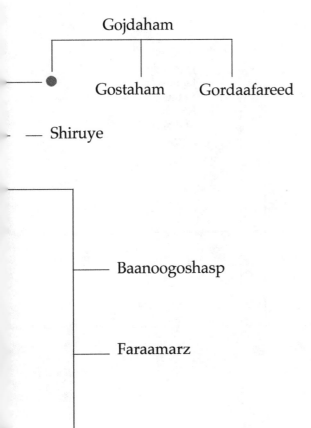

Gojdaham

Gostaham   Gordaafareed

Shiruye

Baanoogoshasp

Faraamarz

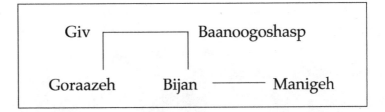

Giv ⌐——————⌐ Baanoogoshasp

Goraazeh   Bijan ———— Manigeh

The Iranian Warriors
Manoochehr-Kay Khosrow

Aarash
Aaveh
Borzeen
Delafrooz
Farhaad
Fooroohal
Gargooy
Goraazeh
Gorazm
Gorgeen
Ketmareh
Khorraad
Manooshan
Milaad
Rashnavaad
Rohaam
Saaveh
Samkanan
Shaavaran
Shahpoor
Shiddush
Taliman
Tokhaar
Zangueh
Zohir

The Iranian Warriors
Lohraasp-Esfandiar

Aarash
Ardeshir
Bitghoon
Delafrooz
Esfandiar
Gargooy
Garukhan
Ghaaran
Gorazm
Gueraami
Iraj
Jaamaasp
Janoosyar
Ketmaareh
Khuzan
Maahiar
Rashnavaad

The Iranian Warriors and Wise Men
Sassanian Period

Aarash
Aazaad Sarv
Andian
Andman
Armani
Azar Goshasp
Aazargoshasp
Baabooy
Babak
Bahraam
Bahraam
Bahraam Choobineh
Bahraam of Pirooz
Balooy
Bandooy
Barsam
Behzaad
Behzaad of Barzeen
Bijan Bivard
Bozorgmehr
Daad Barzeen
Dara Panah
Faraaeen
Farhaad
Farrokhzaad
Farrokhzaad
Garshaasp
Garsioon
Ghaaran
Ghaaran, son of Borzmehr
Gharakhan
Golbooy
Gord
Gordooy
Gostaham
Goshasp
Hamdam Goshasp
Hormozd Shahran
Hormozd son of Khorraad
Izad Goshasp
Janfoorooz
Khazarvan
Khonjast
Khorraad

Khorraad
Khorraad Borzeen
Khorsheed
Khosrow Khazarvan
King of Alaan Mahbood
Konda Goshasp
Koot
Maahooy Soori
Mehr Barzeen, son of Khorraad
Mehr Pirooz, son of Behzaad
Mehran
Mehran Setaad
MilaadOstaad (son of Barzeen)
Nastooh
Ormazd
Oshtaa, son of Pirooz
Ostaay
Pirooz
Pirooz
Pirooz son of Shahpoor
Raadman
Raam Barzeen
Randooy
Rohaam
Rostam son of Hormozd Saam
Saam, son of Esfandiar
Sarguis
Sepansaar
Shahpoor
Shahpoor
Shaknan
Shammaas
Shirezil
Shirooy
Sombaaz
Soofraay
Shohreh
Tokhaar
Tokhaareh
Yalan Sineh
Yazdegerd
Zangooy
Zarmehr

THE TOORANIAN KINGS AND WARRIORS
LINE OF SUCCESSION From Afraasiyaab to Shohreh

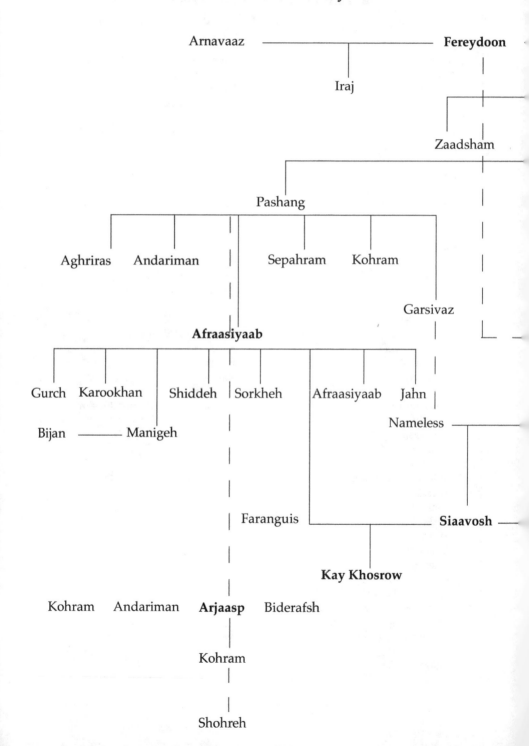

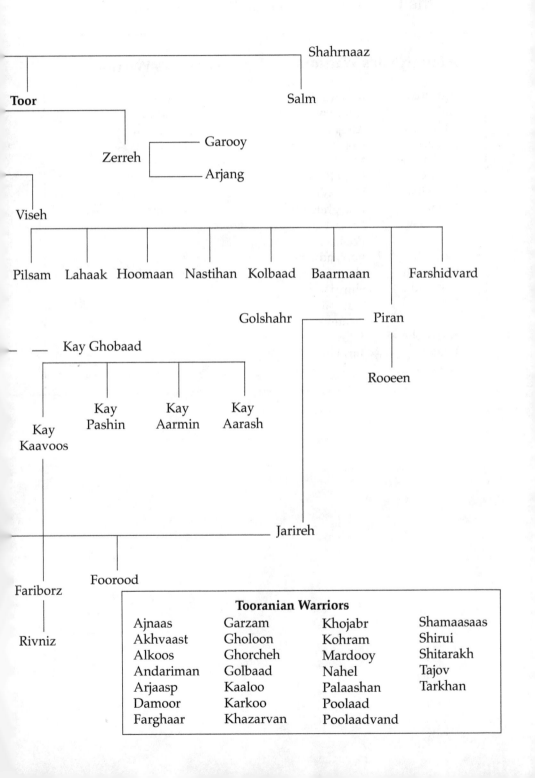

Shahrnaaz

Toor   Salm

                        Zerreh   ┌─── Garooy
                                         └─── Arjang

Viseh

Pilsam   Lahaak   Hoomaan   Nastihan   Kolbaad   Baarmaan   Farshidvard

                                    Golshahr ──────── Piran

─ ─ Kay Ghobaad

                                                          Rooeen

          Kay   Kay   Kay
          Pashin   Aarmin   Aarash
Kay
Kaavoos

                                              Jarireh

Fariborz   Foorood

Rivniz

Tooranian Warriors			
Ajnaas	Garzam	Khojabr	Shamaasaas
Akhvaast	Gholoon	Kohram	Shirui
Alkoos	Ghorcheh	Mardooy	Shitarakh
Andariman	Golbaad	Nahel	Tajov
Arjaasp	Kaaloo	Palaashan	Tarkhan
Damoor	Karkoo	Poolaad	
Farghaar	Khazarvan	Poolaadvand	

THE TOORANIAN HEROES:
Under the Reigns of Afraasiyaab and Arjaasp

Afraasiyaab's Warriors

Aghriras	Kebord
Ajnaas	Khazarvan
Akhvaast	Khojabr
Alkoos	Kohram
Andariman	Mardooy
Arjaasp	Nahel
Borzvilla	Nastooh
Damoor	Ostaghilaa
Farghaar	Palaashan
Garzam	Poolaad
Gholoon	Poolaadvand
Ghorcheh	Shamaasaas
Golbaad	Shirui
Illa	Shitarakh
Jaranjas	Siaamak
Kaakooleh	Tajov
Kaaloo	Tarkhan
Karkoo	

Arjaasp's Warriors

Ayaas
Ardeshir
Biderafsh
Garsivan
Gorgsaar
Hooshdeev
Khashaash
Kohram
Sootooh
Tabah
Tuvarg
Zangaleh

Glossary of Geographical Markers

Aarayesheh Rum: Rumi fort captured by Kesra Anushiravan; name meaning the ornament of Rum.

Aarman-Zamin: On the border of Tooran-Zamin and Iran-Zamin.

Aavaazeh, Castle of: Property of Parmoodeh, Emperor of Chin and son of King Saaveh.

Aazar Abadegan: Refers to today's Azerbaijan.

Aden: An ancient port city in Yemen that is today the temporary capital.

Ahvaz: A city in southwest Iran; capital of the province of Khuzestan.

Alaanan: Region in northwest Iran, north of the Aras River; a part of the Caucasus.

Alborz, Mount: Regarded as a holy mountain in myths and legends. In geographical terms, it stands in northern Iran.

Almas River: Perhaps beyond the borders of Tooran-Zamin.

Amol: A city in Iran where Fereydoon resides before taking residence in his capital city of Tammisheh. Situated in the Mazandaran Province, near the Alborz mountains.

Amoorieh: A Rumi city that no longer exists but would be in present-day Turkey.

Amoy: A city that appears to be somewhere in Chin.

Amu: A city near Amu Darya (Jayhoon River).

Andalusia: Southern region of Spain.

Andaraab: A city in present-day Afghanistan.

Antioch: An ancient Greek city that would be in today's Turkey, near the city of Antakya.

Ardabil: An ancient city in northwestern Iran; it was founded by Sassanian King Pirooz and previously named Baadan-Pirooz.

Arman or Arman-Zamin: On the border of Tooran-Zamin and Iran-Zamin.

Armenia: Armenia.

Aroos: Name for the treasure Kay Khosrow collects in the city of Tous; Persian word that means bride.

Arvand: A river also known as the Shatt al-Arab River. It begins at the confluence of the Tigris and Euphrates rivers.

Asprooz, Mount: Perhaps a mythical mountain on the way to Mazandaran where Kaavoos is blinded by the deevs.

Assyria: Mesopotamia.

Azerbaijan: A region in northwestern Iran.

Baadan-Pirooz: A city founded by Pirooz, Sassanian king, along with the city of Pirooz-Ram; its name was later changed to Ardebil.

Baamian: A city in present-day Afghanistan.

Babel: Or Babylon, ancient city in Babylonia that is situated in today's Iraq.

Badakhshan: In today's northeast Afghanistan and southeast Tajikistan.

Baghdad: Capital of Iraq.

Bahraam, Mount: The name for the heap of heads severed in the battle between Bahraam Choobineh and the Emperor of Chin, Parmoodeh.

Bahrain: A country on the Persian Gulf, once part of the Persian Empire.

Baikand: Must be a fictional region on the border of Iran.

Bait-Al Moghaddas: Jerusalem; meaning pure city.

Balkh: A city in Iran-Zamin, situated in today's Afghanistan.

Balkh Bami: Bami is the old name for Balkh, a city in ancient Iran, today situated in Afghanistan, south of the Jayhoon River (Amu Darya).

Baluchistan: A province in today's Iran bordering Pakistan and Afghanistan.

Barda: A city in present-day Azerbaijan that once was the capital of Caucasian Albania.

Barein: A city in Iran-Zamin.

Barghoveh: With Jaz, perhaps a village under the rule of Bahraam the Hunter.

Barkeh-yeh Ardeshir: A city founded by King Ardeshir.

Bastam: A city in the province of Semnan, in north-central Iran.

Bidaad: Meaning unjust, also referred to as "city of battle"; a city built by Toor with spells and magic in Tooran-Zamin and populated by man-eaters.

Bost: A city and river east of Sistan; situated in today's Afghanistan and now named Lashkargah.

Borz: Another name for Mount Alborz.

Bozgoosh: Area on the way to the dwelling of the White Deev.

Bukhara: A town in Tooran-Zamin; ancient city situated in today's Uzbekistan.

Chaadj: A city near in Tooran-Zamin; near today's Tashkent in Uzbekistan.

Chagal: A city in Tooran-Zamin, in today's Turkestan region.

Chaghan: Or Chaghaniyan, land independent of Iran-Zamin or Tooran-Zamin; a region in Afghanistan north of the Jayhoon River; ruled by an ally of Afraasiyaab.

Chaghvan: A city in the Far East, perhaps Changwon in South Korea.

Chalus: A seaside town on the Caspian Sea; may refer to Mount Koos or Caucasus.

Chin: China; generally refers to lands to the east of Iran, as Rum represents the lands to the west. In later stories, Chin is part of Tooran-Zamin.

Coshmaihan: A region around the city of Marv, near the Jayhoon River.

Ctesiphon: An ancient city near the Tigris River and southeast of Baghdad; the royal capital of the Persian Empire during Parthian and Sassanian times over a period of eight hundred years.

Daaraab-Guerd: A city founded by King Daaraab.

Daghooy: Hunting plains near the border of Tooran-Zamin.

Dahestan: Presently located in Turkmenistan and Iran.

Dahr: Land outside the borders of Iran-Zamin or Tooran-Zamin.

Dajleh: Arabic for Tigris River.

Damavand, Mount: The highest peak on the Alborz mountain range.

Dambar: A place in today's eastern Afghanistan.

Damghan: A city east of Tehran.

Deylam: A city in the Gilan Province of Iran, near the Caspian Sea.

Eram: A Persian garden in Shiraz, Iran; also a heavenly garden in the desert; it is said to appear to the traveler like a mirage.

Eskandarieh: Or Alexandria, an ancient Egyptian city founded in 331 BCE by Eskandar (Alexander the Great). .

Estakhr: An ancient city in southern Iran in the Pars Province, north of Persepolis; seat of Kashvaad's palace.

Faariaab: A city in present-day Afghanistan.

Faarghin: An ancient Rumi city situated in today's Turkey.

Farab: An ancient city on the Silk Road in present-day Kazakhstan.

Fasghoon, Forest of: A forest in Rum (perhaps fictional) where a fierce wolf "with the body of a dragon and the strength of a whale" dwells.

Fort Bahman: A fortress on the border of Iran-Zamin and Tooran-Zamin.

Gang: May be an ancient city on the edge of the Sayhoon River (Syr Darya); seat of Afraasiyaab for some time.

Gang-Behesht: Same as Gang-Dej, the city built by Siaavosh.

Gang-Dej: A fort city built by Siaavosh past the Sea of Chin.

Ghaaf, Mount: A mythical mountain often depicted in images as encircling the world.

Ghaaran, Mount: Perhaps a fictional mountain somewhere in Iran.

Ghabchaagh: A region in Tooran-Zamin.

Ghajghaarbaashi: A town in Tooran-Zamin, situated in today's Turkey.

Ghalinus, Fort: Rumi castle captured by Kesra Anushiravan.

Gharcheh: A city in Iran-Zamin.

Gharchehgan: Land around Gharcheh in Iran-Zamin.

Ghatan: A city located in present-day Afghanistan.

Ghaznein: A city in Iran-Zamin, in present-day Afghanistan.

Ghennooj: A city near or in India.

Ghobaad: A city built by King Ghobaad between Ahvaz and Pars that the Arabs called Awan, situated in present-day western Iran.

Gholoo, Mountain of: Unclear of the location but in Tooran-Zamin.

Gholzom, Sea of: The Red Sea, between Egypt, Saudi Arabia, Sudan, and Yemen.

Ghom: Or Qom, a city between Tehran and Isfahan.

Ghoor: A province in Afghanistan.

Ghoz: A city in Iran-Zamin.

Gilan: A province in today's northwestern Iran bordering the Caspian Sea; Iranian warrior shields often come from this region.

Gilan, Sea of: Caspian Sea.

Golzarioon: A fictional river in Tooran-Zamin.

Gombadan, Fortress of: A castle in Iran where Esfandiar is locked up for some time at his father's order.

Goor: Or Khorreh-yeh Ardeshir; the city of Firozabad in the Pars province of Iran.

Goozganan: A city in present-day Afghanistan.

Gorgan: A city in northern Iran; capital of the Golestan Province.

Gorganj: Land in the region of Khaarazm.

Gorgsaaran: Meaning "land of the wolf," marks the border separating Iran-Zamin from Mazandaran.

Gorooguerd: A province of Tooran-Zamin.

Green Sea: Probably a sea in the Far East, perhaps the Sea of Japan.

Gundeh Shahpoor: Or Gundeh Shahpur, is a city built by King Ardeshir for his son Shahpoor; it is situated in southwestern Iran and is the literary center of the Sassanian Dynasty in the province of Khuzestan.

Guraabeh: Burial site of Saam, the hero.

Guran: In today's Lorestan Province of Iran.

Haamaavaran: Perhaps a fictional land; perhaps a reference to Yemen.

Habash: Or al-Habash, an ancient part of eastern Africa situated in present-day Ethiopia.

Halab: Equivalent to the city of Aleppo in today's Syria; once part of the Persian Empire during the Achaemenid period.

Hamaavan, Mount: A site of retreat for Iranian warriors in Tooran-Zamin.

Hamedan: A city and a province in western Iran.

Haraah: A region ruled by an ally of Afraasiyaab; perhaps al-Harrah in today's western Saudi Arabia, near Jordan.

Haroom: A fictional city of women where each resident has a male breast and a female breast.

Hejaz: A western region on the Arabian Peninsula including the cities of Mecca and Medina.

Hendia: An ancient Rumi city that is Diyarbakir in present-day Turkey.

Herat: Or Hari, a city in Iran-Zamin, situated in today's Afghanistan.

Hirmand: On the border of Iran and Afghanistan.

Hirmand River: Flowing through Sistan and through today's Afghanistan.

House of Goshtaasp: A fire temple founded by King Goshtaasp.

Impregnable castle: The residence of Arjaasp in the land of Chin.

Iran-Zamin: Land of Iran.

Isfahan: A city in Iran, south of Tehran; seat of the hero Giv, where he receives Kay Khosrow upon his arrival in Iran-Zamin.

Jahrom: A city in the Iranian province of Fars.

Jaram: A city situated in today's Afghanistan.

Jayhoon River: Also known as the Oxus River and Amu Darya; located in present-day Afghanistan.

Jaz: With Barghoveh, perhaps a village or hunting plains under the rule of Bahraam the Hunter.

Jeddah: A port city on the Arabian Peninsula by the Red Sea.

Kaaba: Meaning "cube" in Arabic, in pre-Islamic times, it was a holy site of pilgrimage for Taazian Bedouin tribes and idol worshippers in Mecca, an important city and a center for trade. After Islam, it became a shrine at the center of the Great Mosque. Muslims everywhere face its direction at the time of their prayers; some believe that it was built by Abraham and his son Ismail.

Kaasseh Rood: Perhaps a fictional river in Tooran-Zamin.

Kaat: Capital of Khaarazm, or Chorasmia, in ancient times, situated in west-central Asia, south of the Aral Sea.

Kabol: A city in today's Afghanistan.

Kadesia: A region on the Arabian Peninsula.

Kahan: Land independent of Iran or Tooran; its ruler is Kahaar, ally of Afraasiyaab.

Kalaat: A city in present-day Afghanistan.

Kandahar: A city in today's southern Afghanistan.

Karkh: Name for the ancient western section of Baghdad.

Kashaf: A city in northeastern Iran.

Keemaak, Sea of: Most likely refers to the Caspian Sea.

Kerman: A city southeast of Tehran.

Khaarazm: Or Chorasmia; in present-day Tajikistan and Afghanistan, south of the Aral Sea.

Khalkh: Region in present-day Mongolia.

Khalokh: A town in the land of Tooran.

Khargaah: A border town or area near the Jayhoon River and part of Tooran-Zamin.

Khataah: A city near Chin.

Khatl: Unknown location; perhaps in southern Iran.

Khazar Sea: Caspian Sea.

Khazaria: Land northeast of the Caspian Sea occupying today's Uzbekistan.

Khoonehye Asiran: A city in the district of Ahvaz built by King Shahpoor to house Rumi prisoners; meaning "the dwelling of prisoners."

Khorasan: Region in today's northeastern Iran.

Khorm: Perhaps refers to Khorma, a village in today's northern Iran.

Khorraad: Iranian fire temple.

Khorram Abad: A city built by King Shahpoor in Khuzestan, northwestern Iran.

Khorreh-yeh Ardeshir: A city founded by King Ardeshir in the province of Pars after his victory over Ardavan. It is also referred to as Goor or Firuzabad.

Khotan: A town on the southern side of the Silk Road between China and the west; situated in Tooran-Zamin and ruled for some time by Piran.

Khotlan: A city in Maavaronhar.

Khuzan: A small village in today's Alborz Province of Iran.

Kimaak, Sea of: Kimaak was the name of a Turkic tribe; may refer to the Ural River, which discharges into the Caspian Sea.

Kohan-Dej: A castle in Nishapur built by King Shahpoor that houses the royal administrative offices for some time.

Kojaran: A city on the Persian Gulf.

Konaabad: A city in Tooran-Zamin.

Konaabad, Mount: A mountain in Tooran-Zamin

Kondaz: Pahlavi name for the city of Paykand near today's Bukhara.

Kooch and Baluch: Kooch is a village in today's Iran; Kooch and Baluch are two tribes near Baluchistan, Iran.

Koos: Caucasus.

Kufah: A city in Iran-Zamin on the banks of the Euphrates River.

Kushan: A mountainous region in today's China.

Laadan: In present-day Ukraine; site of a battle where the Iranians lost heavily to the Tooranians under Kay Khosrow.

Maachin: Comprises greater China.

Maavaranhar: An area near the Jayhoon River and part of Tooran-Zamin.

Mada'in: An ancient city on the Tigris River between Ctesiphon and Seleucia.

Mai: An area in today's eastern Afghanistan or Indian subcontinent.

Maimargh: A village in the region of Bukhara.

Margh: A city in today's south Khorasan Province of Iran.

Marv: A city in Iran, situated in today's Afghanistan.

Mayam: A fictional river or sea.

Mazandaran: Residence of the deevs and the White Deev in *The Shahnameh* including Gorgsaaran; a non-geographical realm that in no way references the present-day province in northern Iran bordering the Caspian Sea.

Mehr Borzeen: Iranian fire temple established by Goshtaasp Shah.

Milad: Also Malad; appears to be a region in India, north of today's Mumbai.

Milad Castle: Residence of the Indian Keid.

Mokran: In Iran-Zamin and in the coastal region of today's Baluchistan, in southern Iran.

Naarvan: An area in northern Iran, perhaps in present-day Mazandaran.

Nahravan: Village in northwestern Iran.

Nassibin: A city in northern Iraq.

Navand: A village in northwestern Iran where shines the flame of Barzeen.

Nessa: A city in ancient Khorasan Province.

Nile River: A river in northeastern Africa.

Nimrooz: Capital of Zabolestan or Sistan; served as the prime meridian until Europe gained strength and made the switch to Greenwich, England.

Nishabur: A city in Iran-Zamin, situated in today's Afghanistan.

Nohbahaar: Buddhist temple in Balkh.

Ormazd-Ardeshir: A city founded by King Ardeshir in Khuzestan.

Paloyeneh: Unclear location, but in the land of Rum.

Pars: A province in southern Iran with Persepolis as its capital.

Pashan: Perhaps in present-day India; site of a battle where the Iranians heavily lost to the Tooranians under the reign of Kay Khosrow.

Paykand: Or Baykand; a city in Tooran-Zamin, near today's Bukhara (Uzbekistan).

Pirooz-Shahpoor: A city in Syria built by King Shahpoor.

Pirooz-Ram: City founded by Pirooz, Sassanian king.

Raibad: A city in Tooran-Zamin

Raam: An Iranian fire temple.

Raameh-Ardeshir: A city founded by King Ardeshir on the way to Pars.

Rey: The oldest city in the province of Tehran; today it is part of the capital city.

Rum: Name of regions west of Iran; Byzantium, eastern Roman Empire.

Rumi: Adjective meaning from Byzantium.

Rus: Ancient name for Russia.

Saghilaa, Mount: Appears to be a fictional mountain in Rum.

Saghilaa, Fort: A castle in Rum.

Saghlaab: Land outside of Iran-Zamin and Tooran-Zamin; land of the Slavic people; ruled by Kondor, ally of Afraasiyaab.

Sagsaar: East of Afghanistan.

Sagsaaran: Or Sistan, is in today's eastern Iran and southern Afghanistan, near Baluchistan; also named Sakastan.

Samangan: Land in ancient times and a province in present-day Afghanistan.

Samarkand: A city in Tooran-Zamin, a destination on the Silk Road, and in present-day Uzbekistan.

Sari: A town in present-day Mazandaran; once the capital of Iran.

Saroj, Desert of: Region in Iran; unclear of the location.

Sea of Chin: Reference to a body of water in the Far East.

Sea of Sindh: May refer to the Gulf of Oman, south of the Sindh Province, or perhaps the Sindhu (Indus) River.

Sendal: A village in northwestern India.

Sepad, Mount: Appears to be a fictional mountain in Kalaat.

Sepand, Mount: Meaning sacred, holy.

Sepijaab: Area in Tooran-Zamin close to the Jayhoon River.

Shaam: Syria.

Shahd, Mount: Unclear location, perhaps in India.

Shahd River: May be a reference to the Arvand River, also known as the Shatt al-Arab; in today's southern Iraq.

Shaheh: A city in today's Khuzestan Province of Iran.

Shahpoor: A city built by King Shahpoor.

Shahrzoor: Region in today's Iraq.

Shakni: Land outside of Iran and Tooran ruled by Shamira.

Shangan: A city around the border between Iran-Zamin and Tooran-Zamin.

Shirkhan: An area in Damavand in western Iran.

Shooraab: A city in northwestern Iran.

Shushtar: An ancient fortress city in the province of Khuzestan where King Shahpoor has a bridge built by the Rumi Bezanoosh.

Siaavosh-Guerd: A city built by Siaavosh in Tooran-Zamin on land given to him by Afraasiyaab.

Sindh: A province in the southeastern part of India.

Sindhu River: Indus River in India.

Sistan: A province in today's eastern Iran and southern Afghanistan, part of Baluchistan; same as Zabolestan.

Soghdi: A region in Tooran-Zamin.

Sorsan: Or Shorsan, a village in central India.

Sughd: A town in Tooran-Zamin; perhaps in northern Mongolia, near the Chinese border.

Sursan: A city founded by Kesra Anushiravan on the way to Rum; no longer in existence.

Taleghan: A city in the Alborz mountain range.

Tammisheh: Fereydoon's capital in northern Iran; in Mount Koos (meaning Caucasus).

Taraaz: Or Taraz, a city in Turkestan famous for its beautiful women; also a river in today's Kazakhstan.

Tarmaz: A town on the edge of the Jayhoon River, on the border between Iran-Zamin and Tooran-Zamin; ancient city in northern Afghanistan.

Tartar: Situated in Tooran-Zamin, in today's Azerbaijan.

Tehran: Present-day capital of Iran since 1786.

Terek River: A major river north of Iran that flows into the Caspian Sea.

Tooran-Zamin: Land of Toor and his descendants Pashang and Afraasiyaab; also referred to as Turkestan.

Tous: An ancient city in the province of Khorasan in Iran; also the city where Ferdowsi lived and worked.

Transoxiana: Also referred to as Maavaran-nahr (Arabic). It is in the land of Tooran beyond the Jayhoon (Oxus) River and covers the region in today's Uzbekistan and Tajikistan, and parts of Kyrgyzstan and Kazakhstan.

Turkestan: Land of Turks east of Iran; also referred to as Tooran-Zamin.

Urmia, Lake of: A saltwater lake in the northwestern part of Iran.

Viseh-Guerd: A city in Tooran-Zamin named after Piran's father, Viseh; ancient city in northern Afghanistan.

White Castle: A castle defended by Gojdaham and his children in Iran-Zamin, near Tooran's border.

Zaabeh, Mount: Perhaps a mythical mountain in the Alborz mountain range.

Zabol: Capital of Sistan, or Zabolestan; a province in today's eastern Iran, part of Baluchistan.

Zabolestan: Also Sistan; land ruled by the hero Nariman and his descendants Saam, Zaal, and Rostam; in today's southern Afghanistan.

Zam: A city on the border between Iran-Zamin and Tooran-Zamin.

Zarnoosh: A city built by King Dara in the region of Ahvaz, in southwestern Iran.

Zerreh, Sea of: Situated in southwestern Afghanistan.

Zibeh Khosrow: A city founded by Kesra Anushiravan to house the Rumi prisoners, built after the ancient city of Antioch.

The World
of
Ferdowsi's *Shahnameh*

Ural River

KHAZARIA

Terek River

Caucasus Mountains

Black Sea

Koos

Dahestan

Tartar

Caspian Sea
Sea of Gilan

Konaabad

Gorganj

RUM
Byzantium/
Constantinople

Yerevan
ARMENIA

AZERBAIJAN

Barda

Amoorieh

Nassibin

Nahravan

Tammisheh

Khorm

Naarvan

GILAN

Navand

Bastam

Nishabu

Halab

Ghebchaagh

Shooraab

Deylam

Ardabil

Gorgan

GOLESTAN
GORGSAARA

HAMEDAN

Mount Zaabeh

Chalus

Tigris River/ Dajleh

Mount Alborz

Khuzan

Amol

Sari

Euphrates River

LORESTAN

Rey

MAZANDARAN

Mount Damavand

Damghan

Bozgoosh

Jerusalem

Guran

Taleghan

Tehran

Shemiran

Mount Asprooz

Karkh

Baghdad

Khorram Abad

Shirkhan

Kufah

Ctesiphon

Ghom

Margh

Babylon

Mada'in

Arvand River/ Shatt al-Arab

IRAN-ZAMIN

MESOPOTAMIA
ASSYRIA

Shushtar

Ahvaz

Isfahan

Zargh

Ghobaad/Awan

Estakhr

Land of Taazian
Haamaavaran
Egypt
Nile River

Kerman

Shiraz

KAARZI

Mokran

PARS

Bahrein

Jahrom

Zarnoosh

YEMEN

Kojaran

Persian Gulf

The markings on this map are mere reference points to the story and may not be historically accurate

RUS/RUSSIA

Dambar

Mazandaran
Residence of the deevs and the White Deev
in *The Shahnameh* including Gorgsaaran;
a non-geographical realm which in no way
references the present-day province in northern Iran
bordering the Caspian Sea.

Syr Darya/
Sayhoon River

Khalkh

Aral Sea

Khotlan

Farab

MAAVARANHAR

SOGHDI

Kaat   Paykand   Samarkand

Soghd

Bukhara

Mai

Khargaah

Taraaz

Kushan Mountains

Amu Darya
Jayhoon/Oxus

Chaadj   Chagal

TOORAN-ZAMIN

Maimargh

Khataah

ARMAN-ZAMIN
COSHMAIHAN

Ghabchaagh

CHIN/CHINA

Amoy

Bukhara   Samangan

Marv

Tarmaz

Andaraab

Khotan

Tous

Balkh

Kashaf

Baamian   Badakhshan

Dambar

Faariaab

GHOOR

Kabol

KHORASAN

Ghatan

Ghaznein

Herat/Hari

Jaram

Hirmand

Chaghan

Zam

Nimrooz

Zabol

Bost

ZABOLESTAN   Kalat

Kandahar

SISTAN

River Hirmand

Firozabad

Sorsan

BALUCHISTAN

Sindhu River/
Indus River

INDIA

Ghennooj

SINDH

Sendal

Milad

Sea of Sindh

Glossary of Persian Words

Aab: From *aaberoo*, meaning honor, nobility, and integrity; code of honor.

Aaban: Eighth month of the solar year.

Aazar: Ninth month of the year and ninth day of the month.

Aazar Borzeen: Fire temple founded by Lohraasp.

Aazargoshasp: Divine, holy, eternal flame of the Zoroastrians; a revered fire temple for kings and warriors during the Sassanian times in Azerbaijan.

Andisheh: Thought.

Ard: The twenty-ninth day of any month is the day of Ard in ancient Iran.

Arrash: Unit of measurement corresponding to the length of the forearm, from fingertip to elbow.

Aroos: Or bride, name for the treasure Kay Khosrow collects in the city of Tous.

Ayeen: Divine principle or code of human life; path and purpose that reflects all that encompasses the divine, free of barriers set by culture, geography, dogma, or religion.

Babreh Bayan: Armor that is worn only by Rostam. Uncertain about its meaning. Literally refers to leopard skin. Other interpretations refer to beaver skin or dragon skin. It is meant to be waterproof and impenetrable.

Bahman: Name of the second day of the month and the eleventh month of the solar year.

Bahraam: Mars.

Barsom: Sacred twigs from the pomegranate tree used in ancient Zoroastrian prayers and ceremonies.

Barzeen: Zoroastrian fire temple with an ever-burning flame situated in Khorasan, in northeastern Iran.

Bidaad: Meaning unjust.

Daad: Infinite justice; justice that is non-judgmental and unchangeable for it is divine, constant, eternal; different from human justice that is encompassed by a strict set of laws.

Dehghan: Farmer; keeper of land and crops, of rain and sun, and all that grows; keeper of ancient wisdom, poet, and bard.

Dinar: Gold coin.

Dirham: Silver coin.

Esfand: Twelfth month of the Persian solar calendar; begins in February and ends in March; also the name of the plant and herb rue; also meaning sacred or holy, as in *Sepand.*

Esfand: Rue; meaning sacred or holy, as in *Sepand;* also twelfth month of the Persian solar calendar; begins in February and ends in March.

Farr: Divine grace; state of consciousness holding infinite grace of light and life.
Farsang: Ancient unit of measure equivalent to 6.24 kilometers or 3.88 miles.

Gohar: Essence.

Jaan: Life force, soul, spirit.

Kaavian: Belonging to Kaaveh, the blacksmith, who leads the opposition against Zahaak. The Kaaviani banner is made of the cloth of blacksmiths with the colors red, yellow, and purple representing the two ends of the color spectrum as well as the center color.

Kalileh and Demneh: An ancient collection of animal stories originally written in Sanskrit but subsequently translated into Arabic and Persian.

Kamand: Ancient unit of measure.

Kay: King.

Kharvaar: A unit of measure equivalent to about 300 kilograms.

Kherrad: Wisdom; Eternal Wisdom; absolute, pure consciousness.

Khodaay Nameh: Translates as *The Book of Kings.* It is one of the sources, written in prose and in the language of Pahlavi, used by Ferdowsi for his work.

Kianian: Royal; from *kian,* meaning royalty.

Kushti: A sacred belt or girdle worn by Zoroastrians around their waists; it has 72 interwoven white strands of sheep's wool representing seventy-two chapters of a part of *The Avesta.*

Mahn: Reference to a form of weight measurement in the ancient Middle East, around 3 kilograms or 6.6 pounds; so 600 mahns is equivalent to 1,800 kilograms or 3,968 pounds.

Mehr: Complex word that includes deep eternal love, affection, compassion, mercy; also the seventh month of the Iranian calendar.

Mehregan: A festival and memorial to Fereydoon, still celebrated today on the Mehr day of the Mehr month of the year. Iranian fall festival during the month of October.

Mithqal: Unit of measuring weight equivalent to 4.25 grams; often used to weigh precious metal.

Naam: Divine essence, what is contained in space; also defined as "name."

Nowruz: New Day, the Persian New Year, still observed by Iranians of all religions during the spring equinox on or around March 21.

Pahlavan: Noble hero, paladin, warrior, fighter for the cause of *mehr;* guardian of crown and throne, soldier of light.

Pahlavi: Or middle Persian; literary language during the Sassanian rule until the advent of the modern Persian language.

Pandavsi: A Pahlavi currency, each coin equivalent to five dinars.

Pishdaadian: Meaning the era prior to the rule of law. The dynasty comprises the first Persian kings: Kiumars, Hooshang, and Tahmures.

Quintal: An historical unit of mass; 0.01 quintal is equivalent to 1 kilogram or around 2 pounds.

Raai: Will or thought (*andisheh*); intellect or knowing that works in favor of universal time, not human or chronological time.

Ratal: A measure of weight equivalent to 12 to 16 ounces.

Saddeh: Festival to celebrate Hooshang's discovery of fire in *The Shahnameh*; meaning one hundred, it marks one hundred days before the start of spring, or Nowruz; it is a celebration of overcoming darkness. Also referred to as the Feast of Bahman.

Sepand: Same as *esfand,* meaning sacred or holy.

Sitir: Form of measure equivalent to 75 grams.

Shavaal: Tenth month of the Islamic calendar.

Sokhan: Divine Word, ultimate truth.

Tammuz: Tenth month of the Hebrew calendar and the modern Assyrian calendar; corresponds to July on the Gregorian calendar.

Teer: Mercury.

Yazdan: Creator of all that is manifested, unmanifested, and all that is yet to come into existence. Plural of Yzad (divine) encompasses all of divinity.

Zamin: Land of; for instance, Iran-Zamin means land of Iran.

Zand Avesta: *The Avesta* is the Zoroastrian holy scripture; *Zand* is the interpretation

Glossary of Persian Words

Aab: From aaberoo, meaning honor, nobility, and integrity; code of honor.

Aaban: Eighth month of the solar year.

Aazar: Ninth month of the solar year and ninth day of the month.

Aazar Borzeen: Fire temple founded by Lohraasp.

Aazargoshasp: Divine, holy, eternal flame of the Zoroastrians; a revered fire temple for kings and warriors during the Sassanian times in Azerbaijan.

Andisheh: Thought.

Ard: The twenty-ninth day of any month is the day of Ard in ancient Iran.

Arrash: Unit of measurement corresponding to the length of the forearm, from fingertip to elbow.

Aroos: Meaning bride, is the name for the treasure Kay Khosrow collects in the city of Tous.

Aroos: Meaning bride, is the name for the treasure Khosrow Parviz forms from tributes collected from Chin, Bulgaria, Rum, and Russia.

Ayeen: Divine principle or code of human life; path and purpose that reflects all that encompasses the divine, free of barriers set by culture, geography, dogma, or religion.

Baad: Meaning wind; name of the eight treasure Khosrow Parviz forms.

Baadaavar: Meaning windblown, is the name of the second treasure

Khosrow Parviz forms.

Babreh Bayan: Armor that is worn only by Rostam. Uncertain about its meaning. Literally refers to leopard skin. Other interpretations refer to beaver skin or dragon skin. It is meant to be waterproof and impenetrable.

Bahman: Name of the second day of the month and the eleventh month of the solar year.

Bahraam: Mars.

Barsom: Sacred twigs from the pomegranate tree used in ancient Zoroastrian prayers and ceremonies.

Barzeen: Zoroastrian fire temple with an ever-burning flame situated in Khorasan, in northeastern Iran.

Bidaad: Meaning unjust.

Daad: Infinite justice; justice that is non-judgmental and unchangeable for it is divine, constant, eternal; different from human justice that is encompassed by a strict set of laws.

Dehghan: Farmer; keeper of land and crops, of rain and sun, and all that grows; keeper of ancient wisdom, poet, and bard.

Dibah Khosravi: Meaning royal silk; name of the third treasure Khosrow Parviz forms.

Dinar: Gold coin.

Dirham: Silver coin.

Dong: Six parts of a piece of real estate that can be divided and apportioned.

Esfand: Twelfth month of the Persian solar calendar; begins in February and ends in March; also the name of the plant and herb rue; also meaning sacred or holy, as in Sepand.

Esfand: Rue; meaning sacred or holy, as in Sepand; also twelfth month of the Persian solar calendar; begins in February and ends in March.

Farr: Divine grace; state of consciousness holding infinite grace of light and life.

Farsang: Ancient unit of measure equivalent to 6.24 kilometers or 3.88 miles.

Gohar: Essence.

Haft Cheshmeh: Meaning Seven Sources; a jewel given by Fereydoon to his son Iraj.

Hejrat: Or solar Hijri, refers to the calendar adopted in Iran after the Muslim invasion; it dates to the time the Prophet Muhammad traveled from Mecca to Medina in the Gregorian year 622. The calendar year begins on the first day of spring, on Nowruz, at the time of the spring equinox. It is somewhat different from the Hijri Islamic lunar calendar: though journey from Mecca to Medina also mars the starting date, the new year falls in the month of July.

Hoor, day of: The eleventh day of every month, the day of the Sun.

Jaan: Life force, soul, spirit.

Kaavian: Belonging to Kaaveh, the blacksmith, who leads the opposition against Zahaak. The Kaaviani banner is made of the cloth of blacksmiths with the colors red, yellow, and purple representing the two ends of the color spectrum as well as the center color.

Kalileh and Demneh: An ancient collection of animal stories originally written in Sanskrit but subsequently translated into Arabic and Persian.

Kamand: Ancient unit of measure.

Kay: King.

Kharvaar: A unit of measure equivalent to about 300 kilograms.

Khazraa: Meaning green; name of the sixth treasure formed by Khosrow Parviz out of freshwater pearls.

Kherrad: Wisdom; Eternal Wisdom; absolute, pure consciousness.

Khodaay Nameh: Translates as The Book of Kings. It is one of the sources, written in prose and in the language of Pahlavi, used by Ferdowsi for his work.

Kianian: Royal; from kian, meaning royalty.

Kiblah: Or Qiblah, is the direction of the Sacred Mosque in Mecca and the direction of prayer.

Kushti: A sacred belt or girdle worn by Zoroastrians around their waists; it has 72 interwoven white strands of sheep's wool representing seventy-two chapters of a part of The Avesta.

Laajevard: Lapis lazuli; name of the middle seat on the throne of Taakhdis.

Mahn: Reference to a form of weight measurement in the ancient Middle East, around 3 kilograms or 6.6 pounds; so 600 mahns is equivalent to 1,800 kilograms or 3,968 pounds.

Mehr: Complex word that includes deep eternal love, affection, compassion, mercy; also the seventh month of the Iranian calendar.

Mehregan: A festival and memorial to Fereydoon, still celebrated today on the Mehr day of the Mehr month of the year. Iranian fall festival during the month of October.

Mishsar: Ram's head; name of the lower seat on the throne of Taakhdis.

Mithqal: Unit of measuring weight equivalent to 4.25 grams; often used to weigh precious metal.

Naam: Divine essence, what is contained in space; also defined as "name."

Nowruz: New Day, the Persian New Year, still observed by Iranians of all religions during the spring equinox on or around March 21.

Pahlavan: Noble hero, paladin, warrior, fighter for the cause of mehr; guardian of crown and throne, soldier of light.

Pahlavi: Or middle Persian; literary language during the Sassanian rule until the advent of the modern Persian language.

APPENDIX

Pandavsi: A Pahlavi currency, each coin equivalent to five dinars.

Pishdaadian: Meaning the era prior to the rule of law. The dynasty comprises the first Persian kings: Kiumars, Hooshang, and Tahmures.

Quintal: An historical unit of mass; 0.01 quintal is equivalent to 1 kilogram or around 2 pounds.

Raai: Will or thought (andisheh); intellect or knowing that works in favor of universal time, not human or chronological time.

Ratal: A measure of weight equivalent to 12 to 16 ounces.

Saddeh: Festival to celebrate Hooshang's discovery of fire in The Shahnameh; meaning one hundred, it marks one hundred days before the start of spring, or Nowruz; it is a celebration of overcoming darkness. Also referred to as the Feast of Bahman.

Sepand: Same as esfand, meaning sacred or holy.

Sepandarmaz: The fifth day of any month on the solar calendar.

Sitir: Form of measure equivalent to 75 grams.

Shaadvard: Meaning giver of joy; name of the seventh treasure formed by Khosrow Parviz.

Shavaal: Tenth month of the Islamic calendar.

Sokhan: Divine Word, ultimate truth.

Sookhteh: Meaning burnt; name of the fifth treasure formed by Khosrow Parviz.

Tammuz: Tenth month of the Hebrew calendar and the modern Assyrian calendar; corresponds to July in the Gregorian calendar.

Teer: Mercury.

Yazdan: Creator of all that is manifested, unmanifested, and all that is yet to come into existence. Plural of Yzad (divine) encompasses all of divinity.

Zamin: Land of; for instance, Iran-Zamin means land of Iran.

Zand Avesta: Avesta is the Zoroastrian holy scripture; Zand is the interpretation of it.

The Persian Calendar

Based on the solar calendar, the months are named after twelve divinities and correspond to nature's cycles and the signs of the zodiac:

Spring:
Farvardin – Aries; the first month of the year begins with Nowruz, the first day of spring and the spring equinox.
Ordibehesht – Taurus; spans the months of April and May.
Khordaad – Gemini; third month of the year.

Summer:
Teer – Cancer; Mercury; the fourth month begins with the summer solstice.
Mordaad – Leo; fifth month of the year.
Shahrivar – Virgo; sixth month of the solar year.

Fall:
Mehr – Libra; the seventh month begins with the fall equinox or Mehregan.
Aaban – Scorpio; eighth month of the year.
Aazar – Sagittarius; ninth month of the year, ends with the winter solstice or Yalda.

Winter:
Dey – Capricorn; tenth month of the year.
Bahman – Aquarius; eleventh month of the solar year.
Esfand – Pisces; twelfth month of the year.

This translation would not have been possible without the selfless and unwavering dedication of Soudabeh Araghi who spent countless hours with me revising the entire final manuscript. I am immensely grateful for her truly heroic contribution, which played an instrumental role in completing this significant work.

Printed in the USA
CPSIA information can be obtained
at www.ICGtesting.com
LVHW041624041123
762611LV00007B/4